THE OFFICIAL BLACKBOOK PRICE GUIDE TO WORLD COINS

THIRTEENTH EDITION

Tom Hudgeons, Jr. and
Tom Hudgeons, Sr.

HOUSE OF COLLECTIBLES

RANDOM HOUSE REFERENCE • NEW YORK

Important Notice: All the information, including valuations, in this book has been compiled from reliable sources, and efforts have been made to eliminate errors and questionable data. Nevertheless, the possibility of error, in a work of such immense scope, always exists. The publisher will not be responsible for any losses that may occur in the purchase, sale, or other transaction of items because of information contained herein. Readers who feel they have discovered errors are invited to write and inform us, so they may be corrected in subsequent editions.

Please address inquiries about electronic licensing of any products for use on a network, in software, or on CD-ROM to the Subsidiary Rights Department, Random House Information Group, fax 212-572-6003.

This book is available for special discounts for bulk purchases for sales promotions or premiums. Special editions, including personalized covers, excerpts of existing books, and corporate imprints, can be created in large quantities for special needs. For more information, write to Random House, Inc., Special Markets/Premium Sales, 1745 Broadway, MD 6-2, New York, NY 10019 or e-mail specialmarkets@randomhouse.com

Visit the House of Collectibles Web site:
www.houseofcollectibles.com

ISBN: 978-0-375-72315-5

ISSN: 1094-1207

Printed in the United States of America

10 9 8 7 6 5 4 3 2 1

Thirteenth Edition: June 2009

CONTENTS

BOARD OF CONTRIBUTORS

The authors would like to express a special thank you to:

- **Q. David Bowers and Chris Karstedt,** Wolfboro, NH, for the article on "Coin Auction Sales," and information and photographs from the Norweb Collection auction catalog and sale for the section titled "Canadian Numismatic Chronology,"
- **Edd and Johanne Smith,** Sacramento, CA, for their pricing and listing information,
- **Tom Culhane of the Elusive Spondulix,** Union, NJ, for his pricing information on Irish coinage,
- **Michael White at the Department of the Treasury,** United States Mint, Washington, D.C. 20001, for the section "World Coins Minted by U.S. Mints, 1876–1980,"
- **Gold/Silver Institute,** Washington, D.C., for the information on the International World Mints,
- **Arnoldo Efron at the Monetary Research Institute,** Houston, TX, for the International Rates of Exchange Table from their "MRI Bankers' Guide to Foreign Currency,"
- **Tom Bilotta of Carlisle Development,** Carlisle, MA, for his coin listing information from his "Collector's Assistant" software,
- **Phil Taylor of the Royal Canadian Mint,** Ottawa, Ontario, Canada, for the information and photographs on the Royal Canadian Mint and New Canadian Coin Releases,
- **Bill McDonald, president of Numismatic Network Canada,** for information from their Web site for the sections "Numismatic Network Canada—Coin Clubs, Canadian Coin Organizations, Publication—Canadian Coin News,"
- **Bret Evans, editor, *Canadian Coin News,*** St. Catharines, Ontario, Canada, for information for the section on Canadian Coin News.

SHARE YOUR KNOWLEDGE

I would be interested in your questions and comments regarding buying and selling one piece or an entire collection.

OR

You may have information that would be of interest to your fellow collector. In either case please write to:

Tom Hudgeons, P.O. Box 551237,
Orlando, FL 32855-1237

Please send a SASE for a reply.

Are you interested in becoming a . . .

CONTRIBUTOR?

If you would like to join our Board of Contributors and have your name printed in the next edition, please let me hear from you.

Please send a SASE for more information to:
Tom Hudgeons, P.O. Box 551237,
Orlando, FL 32855-1237

THE EURO IS HERE

By Edd & Johanne Smith

On January 1, 2002, twelve of the fifteen countries in the European Community gathered in their old money in exchange for the new European Community euro. No more will we see the German mark, the French, Belgian, and Luxembourg franc, the Italian lira, the Spanish peseta, the Portuguese escudo, the Netherlands gulden, the Greek drachma, the Finnish markka, the Austrian schilling, or the Irish pound. In their place will be the eight coins and seven bills of the European Community, all of which will ignore the national boundaries of the twelve countries using them. In addition, the non–European Community countries of Vatican City, San Marino, and Monaco have also changed to the new currency and coinage, as their monetary systems are tied to those countries that surround them. Also, Andorra, which used the currencies of France and Spain, will change to the euro. Three countries of the European Community, Denmark, Great Britain, and Sweden chose not to participate at this time. In coming years, eleven former Eastern Block countries will be added to the European Community. All these countries will be issuing euro coinage by 2008.

The new coins are the 1 cent, 2 cents, 5 cents, 10 cents, 20 cents, 50 cents, 1 euro, and the 2 euro. The euro is equal to 100 cents. The 1, 2, and 5 cents are comprised of copper coated steel. The 10, 20, and 50 cent coins are comprised of brass. And the 1 and 2 euros are bi-metallic of copper-nickel and brass. Each country can have their own design on the reverse of the coin. The obverse of the coin is standard for all countries.

The following are the subjects on the reverse of the coins by country:

Austria:

1 Cent: The gentian

2 Cents: The edelweiss

5 Cents: Alpine primroses

10 Cents: Stephen's Cathedral

20 Cents: The Belvedere's Palace

50 Cents: Building in Vienna

1 Euro: Wolfgang Amadeus Mozart

2 Euro: Bertha Von Suttner

Belgium:

All coins depict King Albert II

Finland:

1 Cent through 50 Cents: A heraldic lion

1 Euro: Two swans

2 Euro: Cloudberry and cloudberry flowers

France:

1, 2, and 5 Cents: A young Marianne

10, 20, and 50 Cents: A sower
1 and 2 Euro: A tree

Germany:
1, 2, and 5 Cents: An oak twig
10, 20, and 50 Cents: The Brandenburg Gate
1 and 2 Euros: An eagle and stars

Greece:
1 Cent: An Athenian warship
2 Cents: A corvette warship
5 Cents: A modern tanker
10 Cents: Rigas-Fereos Velesttinlis (1757–98)
20 Cents: Joannis Capodistrias (1776–1831)
50 Cents: Eleftherios Venizelos (1864–1936)
1 Euro: An owl
2 Euros: A Spartan mosaic

Ireland:
All coins depict the Celtic harp

Italy:
1 Cent: The Castle del Monte
2 Cents: The Mole Atonelliana Tower
5 Cents: The Flavius amphitheater
10 Cents: The Birth of Venus
20 Cents: A sculpture by Umberto Boccioni
50 Cents: Emperor Marcus Aurelius
1 Euro: Drawing by Leonardo da Vinci
2 Euro: Dante Alighieri

Luxembourg:
All coins depict Grand Duke Henri

Netherlands:
All coins depict Queen Beatrix

Portugal:
1 Cent to 5 Cents: Royal Seal from 1134
10 Cents to 50 Cents: Royal Seal from 1142
1 and 2 Euro: Castles, Coats of Arms, and the Royal Seal from 1144

Spain:
1 Cent to 5 Cents: The cathedral of Santiago de Compostel
10 Cents to 50 Cents: Don Quixote
1 and 2 Euro: King Juan Carlos

Several countries began minting the new coins from 1999 through 2002, so the first year mint sets are multi-year in make up. In the future, official government-packaged sets will most likely be worth more than those put together by private mints and dealers. The private mints and dealers have put together the last year of the old coin sets and the new coin sets from each of the European Community countries. They are sold by a variety of speculators.

For the foreign coin collector, changes will affect the foreign coin market. Not only are the old coins being gobbled up, so are the new euro coins. There is also some concern caused by France and the Netherlands, where voters recently rejected the constitution for the European Community. All members of the EC must vote to approve the constitution before the EC can continue.

It will be exciting to see how the EC adapts to the changes and grows over the coming years. No matter what happens, it will be exciting for the hobby.

COLLECTING WORLD COINS

By Edd & Johanne Smith

The possibilities in collecting World coins are as vast as the world itself, both in modern times and historical times. "World coins" are circulating legal tender—coins and Commemorative coins issued by governments other than the United States. Over the years, hundreds of countries have formed and gone away, many leaving only artifacts of their existence. Among the artifacts are coins. This is especially true for artifacts found before the Christian calendar. In modern times there are countries that formed from city-states. These city-states may no longer be on maps, but their coins are still in demand by world coin collectors.

For countries still on world maps there is a rich history in coins. There are countries like Great Britain that have rulers on their coins or those that, for other reasons, do not. There are countries that use coins to commemorate historical events, people, and objects. Some countries issue coins to commemorate people and events of countries other than their own, such as Liberia and Samoa. There are countries that, because of coin shortages, allowed banks or businesses to issue coinage, such as Canada and Great Britain.

The European Community has established a common exchange of Coins and Currency called the Euro. Twelve countries now accept the Euro. Three other countries, Monaco, San Marino, and Vatican City that tie their currency and monetary system to countries using the Euro, have also changed to the Euro. In addition, several Eastern European countries have applied to join the European Community.

There are also countries that used unusually shaped coins from early time to present day. Early versions of these monies are sometimes referred to as "traditional monies." The earliest forms of these coins come from China, such as knife money and spade money. There are also Kissi pennies, Katanga Cross from 1700 to the late 1800s of West Africa. Modern coins such as animal-, country-, and guitar-shaped are also available. In addition, there are very large and very small coins.

Collectors today may decide to specialize in their collecting. Subjects may include all coins from every country by date and mint to shapes, size, insects, rulers, ships, or a single denomination from all countries, or any other variety of coins. There are countries that issue noncirculating legal coins of gold, silver, and platinum. These coins are in denominations lower than the value of the metal. These are referred to as Bullion coinage.

There is also another area for collecting, and that is Tokens and Medals. This area includes Telephone, Transportation, and "Good For" tokens. These are not too difficult to find, but we do not have any information about this area.

During World War I and after, there was a need for coinage of all kind. Cities, states, and European countries issued both paper and metal money to ease the currency shortage. This money was called Notgeld. Although the coins were very ordinary in appearance, the paper money is considered some of the most beautiful ever printed. The paper currency is somewhat easy to come by, but the coins are somewhat more difficult to come by.

As you read the book, let the beauty and variety of collecting world coins envelop you. Enjoy your hobby.

BUYING AND SELLING WORLD COINS

Intelligent coin buying is the key to building a good collection at a reasonable cost. Today, with the added confusion of grading and the questionable practices of some coin sellers, it is more necessary than ever to be a skilled buyer.

In the interest of supplementing the coin pricing and identification in this book with practical advice on astute buying, the editors present the following article. It reviews major pitfalls to which an uninformed buyer might succumb and gives specific suggestions on getting the most for your money when buying coins.

The editors wish to state clearly that the exposure of questionable practices by some coin sellers, as detailed below, is not intended as a general indictment of the coin trade. The vast majority of professional coin dealers are ethical and try to please. Moreover, it can be safely stated that if the hobbyist restricts his buying exclusively to well-established coin dealers, he runs very little risk.

QUESTIONABLE SOURCES FOR BUYING COINS

Unsatisfactory sources of coins—those entailing a higher than necessary degree of risk—include flea markets, antique shops, garage sales, private parties who are unknown to you, auction sales in which coins are offered along with non-numismatic merchandise, and advertisements in magazines and newspapers published for a general readership rather than for coin collectors. This advice is given to benefit the non-expert buyer and especially the beginner. Advanced collectors with full confidence in their coin-buying skills will sometimes shop these sources to find possible bargains.

Mail-Order Ads in National Magazines

The sharp rise in coin values during 1979 and 1980 encouraged many promoters to deal in coins. (Promoters are persons who aren't coin dealers in the accepted sense of the term, but who utilize coins for large-scale mail-order promotions.) The objective, nearly always, is to sell coins to buyers of limited knowledge and thereby succeed in promising more, and charging more, than would a legitimate professional coin dealer. Undoubtedly such promotions are extremely successful, to judge from the number of such ads that appear regularly.

The ads look and sound impressive. They show enlargement of the merchandise. They quote facts and figures, often with historical data. They present a variety of guarantees about the coins, and there is no misrepresentation in those guarantees. But the price you pay is twice to three times as much as it would be if you bought from a *real* coin dealer. In the legitimate coin trade, the coins sold via these ads are looked upon as "junk coins." They command a very small premium over their bullion value. They are not only the most common dates but are usually in undesirable condition.

To lend credibility, the promoters will normally use a company name, which gives the appearance of being that of a full-time coin dealer. There is nothing illegal in doing this, but it does contribute to the misleading nature of such ads.

Let's examine some of the specific methods used in today's ever-increasing deceptive coin ads. You will soon see why coins, especially silver coins, have become a favorite of mail-order promoters: they can be "hyped" in a most convincing manner, without making statements that are patently false. Thus, the advertisers skirt around—though narrowly—allegations of mail fraud. (Fraud cannot be alleged on the basis of price, as a merchant is free to charge what he pleases for whatever he sells.)

1. Creating the impression that the coins offered originate from a hidden sequestered cache not previously available to the public. This is accomplished by use of such phrases as "just found 2,367 specimens," "now released to the public. . . ." The assertion that they were "just found" is not wholly inaccurate, however. The advertiser has more than likely located a dealer who could supply wholesale quantities of junk coins. The coins themselves were never lost or hidden. "Now released to the public" has nothing to do with official release. It simply means the advertiser is selling them now.

2. Leading the potential customer to believe the coins are scarcer or more valuable than they really are. This is done via numerous techniques. Among the favorites is to compare the advertiser's selling price against prices for other coins of the same series. They are rare, desirable dates in UNC condition, not the common, circulated coins you receive from the advertiser.

When coins are offered, it will be said that "you just can't find them in circulation any longer." It's entirely true that they cannot be found in day-to-day circulation. But coin dealers have them and sell them for less than you will pay through such an ad. The fact that these coins are not found in circulation is not an indication of rarity.

Many coins carrying very little premium value over their face value cannot be found in day-to-day circulation.

3. Emphatic guarantee that the coins are genuine. On this point the advertiser can speak with no fear of legal repercussion. His coins are genuine and nobody can say otherwise. But, even where absolute truth is involved, it can be—and is—presented in such a manner as to give a false impression. By strongly stressing the coins' authenticity, the message is conveyed that many non-authentic specimens exist and that you run a risk in buying from someone else. Such is far from the case. Any large coin dealer can sell you quantities of perfectly genuine coins.

4. Implication that the coins offered are "special," as opposed to specimens of the same coins available at coin shops. This presents an obvious difficulty for the advertiser, as his coins are just the opposite of special; usually heavily circulated, often with actual damage such as nicks, gouges, etc. This problem is not, however, insurmountable. The advertiser can keep silent about the condition of his coins and present them as some sort of special government issue. Usually this is done by selling them in quantities of four or five and referring to them as "Sets," "Government Mint Sets," or something similar. The uninformed reader believes he is ordering a set assembled and packaged by various mints. Mints do assemble and package sets, as everyone knows. But they had no part in these! Assembling and packaging was done by the advertiser. Regardless of how attractive the box or case may be, it is not of official nature and lends absolutely nothing to the value.

5. Failure to state actual silver content. This falls under the heading of deception by silence. The potential customer is left to draw his own conclusions and the advertiser knows full well that those conclusions will be wrong; provided, of course, the ad is worded in such a way that it lends itself to incorrect conclusions. When silver coins are advertised collectors automatically think in terms of 90% silver. Yet the advertiser is legally within his rights in referring to 40% silver coins as silver. As the 40% silver coins look just like their 90% silver predecessors, few purchasers will suspect they've overpaid. Until they have them appraised.

6. Creation of gimmicked names for coins. By calling a coin something different than its traditional numismatic name, it is made to seem more unusual or special.

7. False references. Advertisements of this type are sometimes accompanied by doubtful or fairly obvious fake references on the advertiser's behalf. Taking his cue from legitimate coin dealers, whose ads nearly always refer to their membership in coin organizations and often carry other easily verifiable references as well, he feels he must present similar assurances of his background and reliability. Since he has nothing too convincing to offer in the way of genuine references, he manufactures them. He invents the name of a mythical coin organization, of which he is either a member in good standing, an officer, or perhaps even president. If he chooses not to go quite that far, since he might be caught in the deception, he can take a less volatile course and claim membership in "leading coin collector and dealer organizations" without, of course, naming them.

MAIL ORDER COINS

As stated previously, purchasing world coins through mail order will provide you with the greatest opportunity of finding exactly the coins that you are looking for to add to your collection. While working on this book, we have had the opportunity of coming in contact with many dealers as well as collectors. One mail-order dealer that would be of particular interest to the beginning or novice collector would be Edd and Johanne Smith of Mail Order Coins.

Edd and Johanne Smith have been selling foreign coins for about seventeen years. Like most hobby-oriented businesses, theirs started as a coin collection that got out of control. When they first started collecting coins, they found in reading price lists and advertisements that there were very few dealers that sold *only* foreign coins, particularly the lower-end coins, those coins commonly desired by the new or novice collector. By lower-end coins, I am referring to coins in less than Very Fine grades, priced under $2.50. They decided to target their new business to this collector audience. Although they key their inventory to collector coins, they carry all price ranges of coins.

Their price lists are printed in four sections, grouping the countries alphabetically. The lists contain 7,000 to 8,000 different coins. One section is published every other month. Price lists are sent free upon request.

Both novice and experienced collectors find their price lists easy to read and well organized. They use large type and a maximum of five columns per page to avoid confusion. Their price lists also have brightly colored covers for easy identification and comb bindings so the lists will lie flat on a table.

Edd and Johanne's philosophy for selling coins is simple—a happy coin collector is their product. They grade very conservatively. Often they under-price a coin or two because the grading of a supplier may be higher than what they feel the grade really should be. Customers prefer their grading over many of the other dealers. Edd and Johanne have customers that send change-of-address cards when they move. Customers even call them when their list is late or not received. They are very proud of their customers' loyalty. They do not question when a coin is returned, and they refund immediately. Their policy when refunding an order is to issue a credit memo for amounts under $5 and to refund by check anything over $5.

Edd and Johanne Smith offer more coins priced under $1 and in grades lower than Very Fine than most other dealers. For many collectors on fixed incomes or young collectors who use their allowances to finance their hobby, these coins are quite affordable. Believe it or not, it is difficult to find these types of coins and, as a result, there are many one-of-a-kind coins in their price list.

To better serve their customers, Edd and Johanne Smith have a toll-free phone number (1-800-862-6514), a FAX number (1-916-381-2341) and an e-mail address (*eddcoins@pacbell.net*). They hope to have a web site up and running soon. To save on business costs, they send their price lists by bulk-rate mail. Edd and Johanne both believe their customers deserve the type of service they would expect to get from any business. Please write Edd and Johanne Smith Mail Order Coins at P.O. Box 160083, Sacramento, CA 95816-0083, or call them at their toll-free phone number to be put on their mailing list for a free price list.

RECOMMENDED SOURCES FOR BUYING COINS

As a general rule, coin purchasing should be confined to the following sources:

1. Professional coin dealers who sell coins at a shop and/or by mail order.
2. Auction sales conducted by professional coin dealers or auction houses making a specialty of coins.
3. Shows and conventions for coin collectors.

Another acceptable source, though unavailable to many coin hobbyists, is the fellow collector with duplicate or surplus specimens to sell or trade. This source is acceptable only if the individual is known to you, as transactions with strangers can result in problems.

If a coin shop is located in your area, this is the best place to begin buying. By examining the many coins offered in a shop you will become familiar with grading standards. Later you may wish to try buying at auction. When buying from dealers, be sure to do business only with reputable parties. Be wary of rare coins offered at bargain prices, as they could be counterfeit or improperly graded. Some bargain coins are specimens that have been amateurishly cleaned and are not considered desirable by collectors. The best "bargains" are popular coins in good condition, offered at fair prices.

The dangers of buying from sources other than these are overgraded and consequently overpriced coins; non-graded and likewise overpriced coins; and coins that have been doctored, "whizzed," chemically treated, artificially toned, or otherwise altered. Buying from legitimate, recommended sources greatly reduces but does not absolutely eliminate these risks. The buyer himself is the ultimate safeguard, if he has a reasonably thorough working knowledge of coins and the coin market. In this respect experience is the best teacher, but it can sometimes be costly to learn from bad coin-buying experiences.

COIN-BUYING GUIDELINES

Smart coin buyers follow certain basic strategies or rules. They will not buy a rare coin that they know little or nothing about. They will do some checking first. Has the coin been frequently counterfeited? Are counterfeits recorded of that particular date and mint mark? What are the specific grading standards? What key portions of the design should be examined under magnification to detect evidence of circulation wear?

The smart coin buyer may be either a hobbyist collecting mainly for the sport of it or an investor. In either case he learns not just about coins but the workings of the coin trade: its dealers and auctioneers and their methods of doing business. It's essential to always keep up to date, as the coin market is a continual hotbed of activity.

When buying from the recommended sources there is relatively little danger of fakes, doctored coins, or other obviously unwanted material. If such a coin does slip through and escape the vigilance of an ethical professional dealer, you are protected by his guarantee of authenticity. It is highly unlikely that you will ever be "stuck" with a counterfeit, doctored, or otherwise misrepresented coin bought from a well-established professional.

Merely avoiding fakes is, however, not the sole object of intelligent coin buying. It is, in fact, a rather minor element in the overall picture. Getting the absolute most for your money in terms of properly graded coins at fair prices is the prime consideration. Here the responsibility shifts from seller to buyer. It is the dealer's responsibility not to sell fakes or misidentified coins. But it is the buyer's responsibility to make certain of getting the best deal by comparing prices and condition grades of coins offered by different dealers. Quite often you can save by comparison shopping, even after your incidental expenses are tabulated. The very unique nature of the coin market makes this possible.

Prices do vary from one dealer to another on many coins. That is precisely the reason—or at least one of the primary reasons—for the *Blackbook*. If you could determine a coin's value merely by checking one dealer's price, or even a few dealers' prices, there would be minimal need for a published price guide. The editors review prices charged by hundreds of dealers to arrive at the median or average market prices that are listed in the *Blackbook*. Prices are matched condition grade by condition grade, from UNC down the line. The results are often little short of astounding. One dealer may be asking $50 for a coin priced at $30 by another. And there are sure to be numerous other offerings of the coin at $35, $40, $45, and various midpoint sums.

It is important to understand why prices vary and how you can utilize this situation to your advantage.

Some readers will remark, at this juncture, that prices vary because of inaccurate grading.

It is unquestionably true that personal applications of the grading standards do contribute to price differences. It is one reason for non-uniform prices. *It is not the only one.*

Obviously the lower-priced specimens are not always those to buy. Smart numismatic buying calls for knowing when to take a bargain and when to pass. A low price could result from something directly concerning the coins. Or it may be tied to matters having nothing to do with the coin or coins. A dealer could be oversupplied, or he may be offering coins in which he does not normally deal and wants to move them quickly. He may have a cash flow imbalance and need to raise funds, in which case he has probably reduced most of his prices. He may be pricing a coin low because he made a fortunate purchase in which the coin cost him very little. In all of these cases—and examples of all can be found regularly in the coin trade—the lower than normal price is not a reflection upon the coin's quality or desirability. These coins, if properly graded, are well worth buying. They do save you some money and cause no problems.

Personal circumstances of the dealer are, to one degree or another, reflected in the prices of most of his coins. If the dealer has substantial operating costs to meet, such as shop rent and employee salaries, his overall pricing structure will reflect this. Yet his prices are not likely to be too much higher than the average, as this class of dealer is intent on quick turnover. Also, there is a certain degree of competitiveness between dealers, particularly those whose advertisements run in the same periodicals. Unfortunately, this competitiveness is sometimes carried to extremes by some dealers, resulting in "bargains" that are sometimes overgraded.

Condition has always played a major role in U.S. coin prices. As of this writing there are no accepted international grading standards for foreign coins.

PUTTING YOUR COIN-BUYING KNOWLEDGE TO WORK

1. Deal with someone in whom you can have confidence. The fact that a dealer has been in the business a long period of time may not be an absolute guarantee of his reliability, but it is definitely a point in his favor. Is he a member of coin collector or coin dealer organizations? You do not have to ask about this to find out. If he does hold membership in good standing in any of the more prestigious organizations, that fact will be prominently displayed in his ads, his sales literature, and on the walls of his shop. The leading organization for coin dealers is the PNG, or Professional Numismatists' Guild. Its members are carefully screened and must, after gaining admittance, comply with its code of ethics. Complaints against PNG members are investigated. Those that cannot be easily resolved are brought before an arbitration panel. You are on the safest possible ground when dealing with a PNG member. As the PNG is rather a select group, however, your local dealer may not be a member. This in itself should not make him suspect. One of the requirements of PNG membership is to carry at least $100,000 retail value in coins, and many dealers simply do not maintain that large an inventory. Is your dealer an American Numismatic Association member? A member of the local Chamber of Commerce?

2. Don't expect the impossible, either in a dealer or his coins. The dealers are in business to make a profit and they could not do this by offering bargains on every coin they sell. Treat the dealers fairly. Look at things from their point of view. For example, a long "layaway" on an expensive coin may not be in the dealer's best interest. Dealers will go out of their way for established customers but, even then, they cannot be expected to place themselves at a disadvantage.

BUYING IN PERSON AT A COIN SHOP

1. Plan your visits in advance. Don't shop in a rush or on the spur of the moment. Give yourself time to look, think, examine, and decide.

2. Before entering the shop have a clear idea of the specific coins, or at least the type of coins, you want to see. If more than a few dates and mint marks are involved, do not trust it all to memory. Write a list.

3. Look at everything that interests you before deciding to buy anything.

4. When shopping for rarities, bring along your own magnifier. A small one with attached flashlight is the most serviceable. You may not be able to conduct really in-depth examinations in a shop, but you'll learn more with a magnifier than without one. Don't be reticent about using it. The dealers will not be insulted.

5. If the shop has more than one specimen of the coin that interests you, ask to see them all. Even if all are graded identically and priced identically, you may discover that one seems a shade nicer than the rest.

6. If this is your first visit to the shop, you will want to give some attention to whether or not the shop inspires confidence. An experienced collector tends to get different vibrations from each shop, to the point where he can form an opinion—almost immediately—sometimes before entering. Some coin shops give the distinct impression of being more professional than others. And that impression is usually correct! There are various points on which this can be judged. Do all coins, with the exception of bullion items, have their prices marked on the holder? Is the price accompanied by a statement of condition? Are the holders, and the style of notations on them, fairly uniform from coin to coin? If the coins are housed in various different kinds of holders, with notations that seem to have been made by a dozen different people, they are most likely remnants from the stocks of other dealers or so-called "odd lots." Their condition grades should have been verified and they should have been transferred to uniform holders before being placed for sale. Since the shopkeeper failed to do this, he probably knows very little about their actual condition grades. He merely took the previous owners' word for it. Does the shopkeeper impress you as a person with intimate knowledge of coins? He need not love coins, as his business is selling and not collecting them. But he should appear to regard them a little higher than "just merchandise." He ought to be appreciative of and perhaps even enthusiastic over the finer aspects of a rare coin. Under no circumstances should he treat coins as if he cares nothing about them, such as by handling them roughly or sloppily or touching their surfaces with his fingers.

7. Buying in person gives you an opportunity to converse with the dealer and this can have its advantages. Upon expressing interest in a coin you may discover that the dealer offers a verbal discount from the market price—even without asking for one. If this does not occur, you do, of course, have the right to at least hint at the matter. Just a modest savings can often turn a borderline item into a sound purchase. Don't get the reputation of asking for a discount on every coin you buy. Let the circumstances guide you, and be diplomatic. You are always in a better position to receive a discount when purchasing a number of coins at the same time. Dealers like volume buyers. Never say, "Will you take $300 for this?" or anything that could be construed as making the dealer an offer. The dealers make offers when they buy from the public, and the right to make an offer is something they like to reserve for themselves. You can broach the subject in a more subtle fashion. Instead of mentioning what you would be willing to give for the coins, ask if there is a savings (savings is a much better word than discount) on large purchases. If you pay in cash, you have a better bargaining position as you're saving the dealer the time required in collecting the funds. That is the essence of reasonable discounts; playing fair, not becoming a nuisance, and being willing to accept a small consideration, even if just 5%. At least with the small discounts you are, or should be, getting good coins. If anyone is willing to discount a coin by 50% you can be virtually certain it is a problem item.

BUYING COINS BY MAIL ORDER

There is no reason to shun mail orders. Most coin dealing is done by mail. There are at least a dozen mail-order coin dealers for every one who operates a shop. Your local shop may not specialize in your type of coins, but in dealing by mail you can reach any coin dealer in the country and obtain virtually any coin you may want.

Consider the following before doing any mail-order buying:

1. Compare ads and prices, compare descriptions, compare everything from one ad to another running in the same publication. Look for evidence of the advertiser's professional standing, such as PNG membership. Read his terms of sale. There should be unqualified guarantee of authenticity plus a guarantee of satisfaction. If you are not satisfied with your purchase for any reason, you should have the option of returning it within a specific time period. This time period should be stated in the dealer's terms of sale. (It will usually be ten days or two weeks.) It should likewise be clearly stated that if you do choose to return the coins, you can receive a full refund or credit as you prefer (not as the dealer prefers). Full refund means the sum paid for the coins, with postage and registration fees deducted. Few dealers will refund postage charges. Consequently, when you return a shipment you are paying the postage both ways.

2. Send a small trial order if you haven't previously done business with the advertiser. This will give you the opportunity to judge what sort of coins he supplies. You will also discover how prompt and attentive he is. The results of this trial order should give you a fairly good idea of what you can expect from that dealer when placing large orders.

3. Do not photocopy an ad and circle numbers. Write out your order, simply and plainly. Mention the publication and issue date. The dealer probably has different ads running in different publications.

4. Give second choices only if this is necessary to qualify for a discount. Otherwise don't. Most dealers will send you your first choice if it's available. Some will send the second choice, even if they do still have your first choice. This is called "stock balancing." If they have two remaining specimens of your first choice, and twenty of your second choice, they would much prefer sending you the second choice. Only a relatively small proportion of dealers will ignore your wishes in this manner, but our suggestion still applies: no second choices if you can avoid them. To speed things up, make payment by money order or credit card. A personal check may delay shipment by as much as three weeks.

5. Examine the coins as soon as possible upon receiving them. If a return is necessary, this must be done promptly to be fair to the dealer. Most likely you will not be permitted to remove a coin from its protective holder to examine it. The coins will be in clear mylar (an inert plastic) holders known as "flips" or "flipettes," with a staple at the top. The staple must be in place for return to be honored. While this may seem harsh, it is necessary as a way for the dealer to protect himself against unscrupulous collectors who would switch coins on him. These individuals would replace a high-grade coin with one of lower grade from their collection, and return the lower-grade specimen, asking for a refund. In the unlikely event you receive a coin in a holder which does not permit satisfactory examination, the best course is to simply return it. In making your examination be fair to yourself and to the dealer. Should you have the least doubt about its authenticity, submit the coin to the American Numismatic Association for its opinion and inform the dealer of your action. If the ANA finds the coin to be fake or doctored, you can return it even if the grace period for returns has expired. Under these circumstances many dealers will reimburse you for the ANA's evaluation cost. Chances are, however, that you will never receive a suspect coin.

6. Do not file a complaint against the dealer unless he is clearly in violation of his printed "terms of sale." When it is absolutely necessary to do so, a report of the transaction may be forwarded to the organizations in which he maintains membership, as well as the publications in which he advertises. But even if you place hundreds of mail orders, it is unlikely that the need will ever arise to register a formal complaint against a dealer.

BUYING COINS AT AUCTION SALES

The volume of collector coins sold at auction is enormous. Auction buying is preferred by many collectors, as the opportunity exists to buy coins at somewhat less than their book values. Auctions are covered in detail later in this book.

SELLING COINS TO A DEALER

All coin dealers buy from the public. They must replenish their stock and the public is a much more economical source of supply than buying from other dealers. Damaged, very worn, or common coins are worthless to a dealer. So, too, usually, are sets in which the "key" coins are missing. If you have a large collection or several valuable coins to sell, it might be wise to check the pages of coin publications for addresses of dealers handling major properties, rather than selling to a local shop.

Visit a coin show or convention. There you will find many dealers at one time and place, and you will experience the thrill of an active trading market in coins. You will find schedules of conventions and meetings of regional coin clubs listed in the various trade publications.

To find your local coin dealer, check the Yellow Pages under "Coin Dealers."

Coin collecting offers infinite possibilities as an enjoyable hobby or profitable investment. It need not be complex or problem-laden. But anyone who buys and sells coins—even for the most modest sums—owes it to himself to learn how to buy and sell wisely.

COIN AND PAPER MONEY COLLECTING TECHNOLOGY

By Tom Bilotta
Carlisle Development Corporation

Computers and the Internet have revolutionized coin and paper money collecting. The use of technology to enhance collecting is now widespread and has greatly impacted the hobby.

Exploiting technology requires some basic understanding of the Internet and also of computing. This article is intended to provide you with some basic information, make you aware of the possiblities, and to present, in detail, software which can be used to manage your collection inventory.

THE INTERNET

Many collectors now regularly use the Internet for a variety of purposes. Some of the primary uses are buying and selling, communicating with other collectibles, and educating collectors.

Communication with Other Collectors

Prior to the widespread use of the Internet, contact with other collectors was very limited. For most collectors, such contact was limited to participation in a local coin club and occasional attendance at a coin show. Now with almost universal access to the Internet, a wide array of opportunities for interactions with other collectors is possible. Chat rooms, bulletin boards, e-mail, and instant messaging all have greatly expanded communication among collectors.

Whereas, before the Internet, you might be the only collector in your local area with a particular specialty, it is now possible to locate and engage collectors in any specialty around the country or the globe.

Internet communications also enable effective communication across time zones. An e-mail can be composed and sent at a convenient time for the sender and read and responded to at a convenient time for the receiver. In this way, communications can occur among collectors all over the world without regard to time of day or availability.

Purchase & Sales of Collectibles

A wide array of venues for buying and selling collectibles have sprung up throughout the Internet, ranging from the web stores of traditional retail or mail order dealers to auctions and collector-to-collector transactions. These new venues enable the user to search for desired items, locate people interested in buying a specific collectible, and search for the best price. There is no question that these new venues offer the collector much greater opportunity to locate hard to find items as well as pay the best price. Collectors looking to sell or trade collectibles can directly connect with potential buyers and cut out the middleman, securing a greater profit.

Internet auctions allow collectors who cannot afford the time and expense of attending a real auction to participate in an interactive bidding situation. Not only do they allow participation in auctions all across the country, but technology also allows the collector to view high quality images of the items on which they are bidding.

Internet auctions are now widespread and at any moment there are likely to be several active collectibles' auctions underway. The increased frequency of auctions gives the collector an opportunity to observe market action so that they can participate in an informed way.

Collector Education & Resources

A wide array of informational resources is now only a click away.

Most major collectible manufacturers have substantial Web sites describing their product line and organizational history. Many sites have links to other groups involved with the manufacturers' products.

Many institutions, such as official collectibles associations, museums and libraries have substantial virtual collections accessible on the Internet at no charge. Though it is nice to see the actual collectible in person, virtual collections allow a collector to see objects very quickly no matter their physical location. Objects can be rapidly found in extensive collections using electronic searches. The collector can view an item unhampered by physical security measures.

Special interest groups exist for every collectible imaginable. These groups typically arise from a few interested people and over time word spreads and they grow based on the quality of information that they provide and the size of the collector community. Typically, bulletin boards are used as a communication vehicle allowing collectors to post questions to be answered by other users. These boards are also used to let other collectors know of interesting information.

One caution is that Internet content is largely unregulated and not well reviewed, so there is much misinformation to be found among the useful content.

COIN AND PAPER MONEY INVENTORY SOFTWARE

Most collectors gradually accumulate a large number of items. As a collection grows, keeping track of it becomes increasingly burdensome. Keeping track of your collection is important both to facilitate the process of acquiring items and to insure them from loss.

Collectors typically start with a hardcopy list. Though this works well for small collections, it rapidly becomes too difficult to keep up to date and very cumbersome to change.

Next, some collectors turn to a standard spreadsheet and set up their collections in electronic lists. Though this technique is more adaptable then written lists, it quickly becomes nearly impossible for most collectors to organize and work with their collections as they wish to do.

At that point, collectibles inventory software comes into use, providing a wide array of functionality intended to make the process of collection inventory more enjoyable. They also enable the collector to see their collections in many different ways, making them better collectors.

For many collectors, collectibles inventory software has become an essential tool for managing their collections.

Benefits

Many collectors accumulate hundreds or thousands of items as a part of their collection. Inventory software can signicantly ease the burden of tracking a collection. The benefits of using collection inventory software include:

- Accurate information on the items you have, including their condition and value
- Detailed reporting for insurance purposes
- Generation of want lists
- Understanding of where the value in a collecton is centered

- Tracking of the location of collectibles
- Viewing your collection in different ways
- Generating picture catalogs
- Setting collection objectives that are consistent with your budget
- Tracking change in valuation
- Aid in identifying an item
- Sharing your collection with others

Features

Collectibles inventory software has been available for more than 10 years and has evolved to incorporate a robust set of features. There are many programs available that have only a small number of the features in the list, but the best commercial quality programs should contain most of the features listed below.

- Flexible grouping of your collectible—ability to group your items in a manner which is consistent with how you collect. You do not want to be locked in to a predefined standard grouping. This is one of the most important features separating simplistic programs that mimic hardcopy check lists from modern collectibles inventory programs.
- Unlimited number of items stored—collections often number in the 1000s are sometimes 10,000s of items.
- Flexible handling of duplicates—most collectors have the same item a number of times in different conditions. Inventory software should allow you to define and redefine the grouping of duplications without reentering data.
- Preloaded databases for common collectibles such as coins and paper money—a preloaded database can greatly minimize the time needed to catalog a collecton as well as provide much useful information.
- Data entry screens that are optimized for the collectible—the data entry screens should include an optimally designed set of information fields for the collectible. This will provide greater operational productivity.
- Report Formats that are optimized for the collectible.
- User customization of data entry screens and report formats—many users will have unique needs benefiting from the ability to add a few customized information fields. The availability of customizations as-

sures that simple field omissions will not prevent you from obtaining the information you want.

- Sorting and Filtering of reports as they are viewed or printed—sorting and filtering logic are very important with respect to viewing and reporting on your collection.
- Export of collection data to other applications—there will be times when you want to share some of your listings with others. In those instances, exporting selected data to word processors and spreadsheets will be of great value.
- User modifiable choice lists to facilitate data entry—for applications where full preloaded databases are not available, the availability of user modifiable choice lists is an alternate means of reducing the time and effort required to enter data.
- Tracking of location and insurance information—keeping track of where things are stored and recording detailed lists for insurance purposes are key functions in protecting your collection.
- Automatic valuation with a change in condition—if available, current market values in electronic form can aid in valuation.
- Password protection—other users may have access to your computer who you do not want to access your collection data.
- Specialized reports for generating labels, collectible tags, picture catalogs, etc.—once your data is catalogued you will want to use the catalog to assist in identifying, managing, and sharing information about your collection.
- Search functionality—collection listings can become quite large and ability to quickly locate an item is very important.
- Picture support—most users will want to incorporate pictures of their own items. A variety of common image formats should be supported.
- Sufficient set of information fields for both beginner and expert needs.

Evaluating Inventory Software

There are many programs available to assist you in managing your collectibles. How do you find the right one for you?

The goal of all collectible inventory software is to allow you to catalog your collectibles inventory taking advantage of the advantages a computer can provide.

Once your data is in a computer, it can be viewed and manipulated much more flexibly and easily than a hardcopy listing.

It is important, however, that the computer inventory software have the flexibility to allow you to catalog and work with a collection in a manner consistent with the way you wish to organize your collections. You should select software that allows you to organize your collection your way. If you find that you have to "trick" the software into working as you want or cannot organize your collection easily, it is time to select alternate software.

FLEXIBILITY IN ORGANIZING YOUR COLLECTIBLES

Probably one of the most important features of collectibles inventory software is the ability to define your own groupings of your items. Most collectors have a large number of items to catalog, organized in different ways. A coin collector, for example, might have a Mercury Dime album containing best specimens of each Mercury dime and some empty holes for coins yet to be acquired. In addition, however, the same collector may have hundreds of other Mercury dimes at various grades as well as many other coins.

A traditional hardcopy checklist does not meet this very common collector's need due to its fixed structure and the ability to move one item from one list to another.

For the example given, a coin collector might like to define several groupings:

Mercury dime containing–cataloguing the Mercury dime album
Duplicates collection—all other Mercury dimes

Many collectible inventory software programs have the same structural limitations as the paper inventory checklists. It is important to be sure that the one you choose will allow you to group the items in the way you desire without being forced to follow conventional listings.

Features to look for are:

- Unlimited number of groups/collections
- Ability to include any item of the collectible type in any grouping
- Easy ability to move items between groups
- Robust sorting and filtering capability to assist you in locating items in large groupings with mixed content
- Ability to report on selected subsets of your collection data

VIEWING AND REPORTING

Another feature which can be used to differentiate collectibles inventory programs is the viewing and reporting functionality.

Once you have taken the time to catalog your collection, you will want to exploit the capability of your computer by viewing and reporting on your collection in many different ways.

There are three basic capabilities that should be present in your collectibles inventory program; sorting, filtering, and user customizable formatting.

Sorting—depending on your purpose you will want to sort your collections in many different ways:

- Comprehensive listing sorted by type, major attributes
- Listing for analysis of value sorted by descending value
- Listing sorted by location to assist in locating items
- Listing sorted by condition to assist in identifying items for which better speciments are desired.
- And many others . . .

In order to support this variety of uses, the user should be able to sort on any of the information fields. A multiple level sort of at least 3–4 levels is needed in order to be sure that all desired orderings can be achieved.

Support algorithms also need to be collectibles aware. For example, when sorting by condition, the terms used to define condition should be sorted intelligently, based on the order of condition. For example, very good is higher than good but lower than fine, so an alphabetic sort will not produce the desired listing.

Alphabetic sort of descending grades	**Intelligent sort**
Very good	New
Poor	Almost new
New	Extra Fine
Good	Fine
Fine	Very Good
Extra Fine	Good
Almost New	Poor

As can be seen from this example, a system with only alphabetic sorting capability cannot provide even a simple sort by condition.

Other examples would be sorting of catalog numbers containing numbers and letters or the use of calender dates which mix AD and BC dates.

Filtering—provides the ability to view a selected portion of your collection, meeting user determined criteria. Some sample filters would be:

- All items worth more than $50
- All items manufactured between 1930 and 1950
- All items worth more than $100 made by a particular manufacturer

- All items purchased in the last 3 years
- All items located in box 1
- All items whose values exceed its cost

As in the case of sorting, the user should be able to filter on any of the stored information fields. Intelligence in filtering is also required. Continuing on with the example of condition, if a user seeks to see a list of all items that have a condition of fine or better, the filtering logic may not rely on alphabetic ordering in order to determine if an item is better than fine.

Filtering should be specified in a straightforward manner, supported by choice lists of available information fields, tests, and values. Additionally, simple logical constructions such as "and," and "or" should be provided to allow the use of multiple tests.

User customizable formatting—Every user has a preferred format for viewing information. It is very frustrating if you take the time to enter your data and are not able to view it in the way that you like.

There are two basic types of views and reports, both of which should be available in your collectibles inventory software.

Listings—columnar listings are the most frequently used reports intended to provide a desired set of information fields, sorted and filtered as needed in a very compact manner. The user should be able to define what fields appear in each column, and control column width. Listing formats should support both Portrait and Landscape orientation of the paper as well as different fonts and font sizes so that the user can fit all of the information that they want. Additional features of value include column headings, grid lines and subtotal options.

Dimensional report formats—these specialized formats allow the user to generate picture catalogs, labels, and tags, and formatted mutliline listings. They should incorporate pictures as well as text elements.

QUALITY AND TECHNICAL SUPPORT

Once you have taken the time to catalog your collection, you will want to be sure that your data is protected and will not be lost or become inacccessible.

In evaluating collectibles inventory software you want to be sure that your vendor is providing quality software and that technical support is available. Examine vendor Web sites for technical support functions, including Frequently Asked Questions, Downloadable Service Packages, and contact information.

Look for a 30-day unconditional return privilege to assure that you can return the product if you find it lacking.

AVAILABILITY OF UPDATES

Collectibles change over time and your software will need to keep pace. This is especially true for preloaded databases. For example, collectors of U.S. Coins or U.S. Stamps will want annual database updates with new issues.

Market values for all collectibles change with time and the availability of up-to-date market values enhances the value you will receive from collectibles software.

Enhancements of software functionality should be available on a regular basis to assure comptability with new versions of operating systems as well as to exploit new functionality that becomes available. Frequent updates also provide a steady improvement in product quality.

ABOUT CARLISLE DEVELOPMENT CORPORATION

Carlisle Development Corporation is a leading publisher of Coin and Paper Money Collecting software. It offers a full line of products including the Collector's Assistant inventory program along with various database of U.S. Coins, U.S. Paper Money, World Coins, World Banknotes, Casino Chips and Ancient Coins. It also offers a line of educational software including the Coin Grading Assistant and Coin Collector's Survival Manual.

For more information on Carlisle products, visit our Web site at www.carlisledevelopment.com or contact us at 800-219-0257. You can also reach us by e-mail: *support@carlisledevelopment.com.*

INTERNATIONAL RATES OF EXCHANGE TABLE

Courtesy of The Monetary Research Institute, "MRI Bankers' Guide to Foreign Currency"

The following is a list of the international exchange fixed rates as of January 2007. The right-hand column indicates the number of units (in that country's currency) that equal $1 USA. Please use these rates as only a guide. Rates may vary, so please check with your local bank before making a transaction.

ISO Code	Country / Currency Rates against USD (31 Dec 2006)	Official rate(1)	Parallel Market
AFA	Afghanistan/ New Afghani	49.50	(*)
ALL	Albania/Lek	83.10	(*)
DZD	Algeria/Dinar	67.00	75.00
EUR	Andorra → Euro		
AOA	Angola/(new) kwanza(2)	75.00	(*)
XCD	Anguilla → East Carib dollar	2.67	(*)
XCD	Antigua & Barbuda → E.C.$	2.61	(*)
ARS	Argentina/Peso	3.12	(*)
AMD	Armenia/Dram	304.20	(*)
AWG	Aruba/Florin	1.77	(*)
AUD	Australia/Dollar	1.1460	(*)
EUR	Austria → Euro		
AZM	Azerbaijan/(new) manat	0.8480	(*)
BSD	Bahamas/Dollar	1.00	(*)
BHD	Bahrain/Dinar	.3765	(*)
BDT	Bangladesh/Taka	68.50	(*)
BBD	Barbados/Dollar	1.98	(*)
BYB	Belarus/(new) rubel(2)	2,150	(*)
EUR	Belgium → Euro		
BZD	Belize/Dollar	1.98	(*)
XOF	Benin → CFA franc West	445.50	(*)
BMD	Bermuda/Dollar	1.00	(*)
BTN	Bhutan/Ngultrum	39.32	(*)
BOB	Bolivia/Boliviano	7.64	(*)
BAM	Bosnia-Herzegovina/ K.Marka	1.5010	(*)

ISO Code	Country / Currency Rates against USD (31 Dec 2006)	Official rate(1)	Parallel Market
BWP	Botswana/Pula	6.04	(*)
BRL	Brazil/Real	1.80	2.20(*)
USD	British Virgin Isl → U.S. dollar	1.00	(*)
BND	Brunei/Ringgit	1.4430	(*)
BGN	Bulgaria/(New) lev	1.3282	(*)
XOF	Burkina Faso → CFA franc West	445.50	(*)
BIF	Burundi/Franc	1,120	
KHR	Cambodia/Riel	3,990	(*)
XAF	Cameroon → CFA franc Central	445.50	(*)
CAD	Canada/Dollar	1.0020	(*)
CVE	Cape Verde/Escudo	74.80	(*)
KYD	Cayman Islands/Dollar	1.2345(M)	(*)
XAF	Ctrl.African Rep. → CFA fr Ctrl	445.50	(*)
XAF	CFA franc-Central	445.50	(*)
XOF	CFA franc-West	445.50	(*)
XPF	CFP franc	80.83	(*)
XAF	Chad → CFA franc Central	445.50	(*)
CLP	Chile/Peso	495.8	(*)
CNY	China Peoples Rep/ Yuan	7.27	(*)
COP	Colombia/Peso	2,010	1,900
KMF	Comoros/Franc	334.90	(*)
ZRN	Congo, D.R./Franc Congolaise	538.50	(*)
XAF	Congo, Rep. → CFA Central	120.6	(*)

ISO Code	Country / Currency Rates against USD (31 Dec 2006)	Official rate[1]	Parallel Market
NZD	Cook Islands/Dollar	1.3040	(*)
CRC	Costa Rica/Colón	498.00	(*)
HRK	Croatia/Kuna	4.98	(*)
CUP	Cuba/Peso	22.20	(*)
	Cuba/Peso convertible	1.11[M]	
CYP	Cyprus/Pound	.3622	(*)
CZK	Czech Republic/Koruna	17.70	(*)
DKK	Denmark/Krona	5.052	(*)
DJF	Djibouti/Franc	177.72	(*)
XCD	Dominica → East Carib dollar	2.67	(*)
DOP	Dominican Republic/ Peso	33.30	(*)
XCD	Eastern Caribbean/ Dollar	2.67	(*)
USD	Ecuador → U.S. dollar		(*)
EGP	Egypt/Pound	5.51	7.50
SVC	El Salvador/Colón[3]	8.75	(*)
GBP	England → Sterling pound	1.9740[M]	(*)
XAF	Equat Guinea → CFA franc Ctrl	445.50	(*)
ERN	Eritrea/Nakfa	15.00	17.00
EEK	Estonia/Kroon	10.72	(*)
ETB	Ethiopia/Birr	8.89	10.00
EUR	European Union/Euro	1.4725[M]	(*)
FKP	Falklands-Malvinas/ Pound	1.740[M]	(*)
DKK	Faroes/Krona	5.0520	(*)
FJD	Fiji Is/Dollar	1.5510	(*)
EUR	Finland → Euro		
EUR	France → Euro		
XPF	French Polynesia → CFP franc	80.83	(*)
XAF	Gabon → CFA franc Central	445.50	(*)
GMD	Gambia/Dalasi	22.80	(*)
GEL	Georgia/Lari	1.5930	(*)
EUR	Germany → Euro		
GHC	Ghana/Cedi	9,240	(*)
GIP	Gibraltar/Pound	1.9740[M]	(*)
EUR	Greece → Euro		
DKK	Greenland → Denmark	5.0520	(*)
XCD	Grenada → East Carib dollar	2.67	(*)
GTQ	Guatemala/Quetzal	7.64	(*)
GBP	Guernsey → Sterling pound	1.3282[M]	(*)
XOF	Guinea-Bissau/CFA franc West	445.50	(*)
GNF	Guinea Conakry/Franc	4,300	6,000
GYD	Guyana/Dollar	204.00	(*)
HTG	Haïti/Gourde	36.90	(*)
HNL	Honduras/Lempira	18.89	(*)
HKD	Hong Kong/Dollar	7.77	(*)
HUF	Hungary/Forint	172.80	(*)
ISK	Iceland/Krona	71.00	(*)
INR	India/Rupee	39.32	(*)
IDR	Indonesia/Rupiah	9,460	(*)
IRR	Iran/Rial	9,330	(*)
IQD	Iraq/Dinar	1,214	(*)
EUR	Ireland → Euro		
GBP	Isle of Man → Sterling pound	1.9740[M]	(*)
ILS	Israel/New sheqel	3.81	(*)
EUR	Italy → Euro		
XOF	Ivory Coast → CFA franc West	445.50	(*)
JMD	Jamaica/Dollar	70.80	(*)
JPY	Japan/Yen	108.60	(*)
GBP	Jersey → Sterling pound	1.9740[M]	(*)
JOD	Jordan/Dinar	.7090	(*)
KZT	Kazakhstan/Tenge	127.60	(*)
KES	Kenya/Shilling	66.00	(*)
AUD	Kiribati → Australian dollar		
KPW	Korea PDR/Won	142.00	985
KRW	Korea Republic/Won	941	(*)
KWD	Kuwait/Dinar	.2729	(*)
KGS	Kyrgyzstan/Som	35.00	(*)
LAK	Lao PDR/Kip	9,330	10,500
LVL	Latvia/Lat	.4731	(*)
LBP	Lebanon/Pound	1,512	(*)
LSL	Lesotho/Maloti	6.86	(*)
LRD	Liberia/Dollar	62.50	(*)
LYD	Libya/Dinar	1.22	(*)
CHF	Liechtenstein → Swiss franc		
LTL	Lithuania/Litas	2.3420	(*)
EUR	Luxembourg → Euro		
MOP	Macao/Pataca	8.03	(*)
MKD	Macedonia/New denar	41.80	(*)
MGF	Madagascar/Ariary	1.790	(*)
MWK	Malawi/Kwacha	140.30	(*)
MYR	Malaysia/Ringgit	3.5290	(*)
MVR	Maldives/Rufiya	12.80	(*)
XOF	Mali → CFA franc West	445.50	(*)
MTL	Malta/Lira	.2928	(*)
USD	Marshall Isl → U.S. dollar		
MRO	Mauritania/Ougiya	251.60	(*)
MUR	Mauritius/Rupee	28.50	(*)
MXN	Mexico/(New) Peso	10.90	(*)
MDL	Moldova/Leu	12.85	(*)
EUR	Monaco → Euro		
MNT	Mongolia/Tugrik	1,170	(*)
YUM	Montenegro → Serbia + Mtenegro		
XCD	Montserrat → East Carib dollar	2.67	(*)
MAD	Morocco/Dirham	7.69	9.00
MZM	Mozambique/ Metical	23.60	(*)

ISO Code	Country / Currency Rates against USD (31 Dec 2006)	Official rate[1]	Parallel Market
MMK	Myanmar/Kyat	6.42	1,260
NAD	Namibia/Dollar	6.86	(*)
AUD	Nauru → Australian dollar		
NPR	Nepal/Rupee	62.90	(*)
EUR	Netherlands → Euro		
ANG	Neth Antilles/Gulden	1.77	(*)
XPF	New Caledonia → CFP franc	80.83	(*)
NZD	New Zealand/Dollar	1.3040	(*)
NIO	Nicaragua/Córdoba	18.05	(*)
XOF	Niger → CFA franc West	445.50	(*)
NGN	Nigeria/Naira	118.00	(*)
GBP	Northern Ireland → Strlng pound	1.9740(M)	(*)
NOK	Norway/Krone	5.3450	(*)
OMR	Oman/Rial	.3845	(*)
PKR	Pakistan/Rupee	61.90	64.00
USD	Palau → U.S. dollar		
PAB	Panama/Balboa → U.S. dollar		
PGK	Papua New Guinea/ Kina	2.7670	(*)
PYG	Paraguay/Guaraní	4,805	(*)
PEN	Peru/Nuevo sol	2.9660	(*)
PHP	Philippines/Piso	40.85	(*)
PLN	Poland/New złoty	2.4490	(*)
EUR	Portugal → Euro		
QAR	Qatar/Riyal	3.638	(*)
ROL	Romania/New leu	2.4330	(*)
RUB	Russia/(New) ruble	24.40	(*)
RWF	Rwanda/Franc	544	(*)
SHP	St Helena/Pound	1.9740(M)	(*)
XCD	St Kitts & Nevis → E.Carib $	2.67	(*)
XCD	St Lucia → East Caribbean $	2.61	(*)
XCD	St Vincent → East Caribbean $	2.67	(*)
WST	Samoa/Tala	2.69	(*)
EUR	San Marino → Euro		
STD	São Tome e Principe/ Dobra	6,790	12,700
SAR	Saudi Arabia/Riyal	3.75	(*)
GBP	Scotland → Sterling pound	1.9589(M)	(*)
XOF	Senegal → CFA franc West	445.50	(*)
YUM	Serbia and Montenegro/ Dinar	55.80	(*)
SCR	Seychelles/Rupee	5.86	11.00
SLL	Sierra Leone/Leone	2,975	(*)
SGD	Singapore/Dollar	1.4330	(*)
SKK	Slovakia/Koruna	25.00	(*)
SIT	Slovenia/Tolar	181.60	(*)

ISO Code	Country / Currency Rates against USD (31 Dec 2006)	Official rate[1]	Parallel Market
SBD	Solomon Is/Dollar	7.37	(*)
SOS	Somalia/Shillin	14,400	(*)
	Somaliland/Shilin	2,000	4,000
ZAR	South Africa/Rand	7.01	(*)
EUR	Spain → Euro		
LKR	Sri Lanka/Rupee	108.50	(*)
SDD	Sudan/Dinar	202.00	(*)
SRG	Surinam/Dollar	2.75	(*)
SZL	Swaziland/Lilangeni	6.86	(*)
SEK	Sweden/Krona	6.359	(*)
CHF	Switzerland/Franc	1.1075	(*)
SYP	Syria/Pound	51.10	52.50
TWD	Taiwan/NT Dollar	32.40	(*)
TJR	Tajikistan/Somoni	3.46	(*)
TZS	Tanzania/Shilling	1,175	(*)
THB	Thailand/Baht	35.80	(*)
XOF	Togo → CFA franc West	445.50	(*)
TOP	Tonga/Pa'anga	1.8780	(*)
	Transdniester/ Ruble(2001)	8.3460	(*)
TTD	Trinidad & Tobago/ Dollar	6.31	(*)
TND	Tunisia/Dinar	1.21	1.26
TRL	Turkey/New lira	1.1710	(*)
TMM	Turkmenistan/ Manat	5,200	20,000
USD	Turks & Caicos → U.S. dollar		
AUD	Tuvalu → Australian dollar		
UGX	Uganda/Shilling	1,700	(*)
UAH	Ukraine/Hryvnia	5.05	(*)
AED	United Arab Emirates/ Dirham	3.67	(*)
USD	U.S.A./Dollar	1.00	(*)
UYU	Uruguay/Peso uruguayo	21.50	(*)
UZS	Uzbekistan/Som- Currency	1,230	1,500
VUV	Vanuatu/Vatu	100.60	(*)
EUR	Vatican City → Euro		
VEB	Venezuela/Bolivar	2,147	5,200
VND	Vietnam/Đông	16,080	(*)
YER	Yemen (North)/Rial	198.00	(*)
YUM	Yugoslavia—Serbia & Montenegro		
ZMK	Zambia/Kwacha	3,865	(*)
ZWD	Zimbabwe/dollar	30,000	1,600,000

(1) Fixed or free market rate.
(2) U.S. Dollars co-circulate.
(*) Free, parallel market not needed, or parallel market very close to official rate.
(M) Multiplication rate

GOLD, SILVER, AND PLATINUM BULLION VALUE CHARTS

The following charts can be used to approximate the bullion or "melt" value of any coin that is made of gold, silver, or platinum. When determining the melt or bullion value of a coin, you will need to take into consideration not only the weight of the coin, but also the purity level of the gold, silver, or platinum, i.e., 18K gold (.921), 14K gold (.771), pure silver (.999), sterling silver (.925), etc. These variables make it difficult for an inexperienced dealer to calculate the bullion value of a coin. We recommend contacting dealers that have experience in dealing in bullion coinage.

SILVER (.999% FINE) BULLION CHART

Oz. Weight(Troy)	$4.00	$4.50	$5.00	$5.50	$6.00	$6.50	$7.00	$7.50	$8.00	$8.50
.1	.40	.45	.50	.55	.60	.65	.70	.75	.80	.85
.2	.80	.90	1.00	1.10	1.20	1.30	1.40	1.50	1.60	1.70
.3	1.20	1.35	1.50	1.65	1.80	1.95	2.10	2.25	2.40	2.55
.4	1.60	1.80	2.00	2.20	2.40	2.60	2.80	3.00	3.20	3.40
.5	2.00	2.25	2.50	2.75	3.00	3.25	3.50	3.75	4.00	4.25
.6	2.40	2.70	3.00	3.30	3.60	3.90	4.20	4.50	4.80	5.10
.7	2.80	3.15	3.50	3.85	4.20	4.55	4.90	5.25	5.60	5.95
.8	3.20	3.60	4.00	4.40	4.80	5.20	5.60	6.00	6.40	6.80
.9	3.60	4.05	4.50	4.95	5.40	5.85	6.30	6.75	7.20	7.65
1.0	4.00	4.50	5.00	5.50	6.00	6.50	7.00	7.50	8.00	8.50

GOLD AND PLATINUM (.999%) BULLION CHART

Oz. Weight (Troy)	$340.00	$345.00	$350.00	$355.00	$360.00	$365.00	$ 370.00	$375.00	$380.00	$385.00	$390.00
.1	34.00	34.50	35.00	35.50	36.00	36.50	37.00	37.50	38.00	38.50	39.00
.2	68.00	69.00	70.00	71.00	72.00	73.00	74.00	75.00	76.00	77.00	78.00
.3	102.00	103.50	105.00	106.50	108.00	109.50	111.00	112.50	114.00	115.00	117.00
.4	136.00	138.00	140.00	142.00	144.00	146.00	148.00	150.00	152.00	154.00	156.00
.5	170.00	172.50	175.00	177.50	180.00	182.50	185.00	187.50	190.00	192.50	195.00
.6	204.00	207.00	210.00	213.00	216.00	219.00	222.00	225.00	228.00	231.00	234.00
.7	238.00	241.50	245.00	248.50	252.00	255.50	259.00	262.50	266.00	269.50	273.00
.8	272.00	276.00	230.00	284.00	288.00	292.00	296.00	300.00	304.00	308.00	312.00
.9	306.00	310.50	315.00	319.50	324.00	328.50	333.00	337.50	342.00	346.50	351.00
1.0	340.00	345.00	350.00	355.00	360.00	365.00	370.00	375.00	380.00	385.00	390.00

INTERNATIONAL COIN MINTS AND DISTRIBUTORS

Foreign countries sell their current coinage directly through the government of issue and/or through official U.S. distributors. The following is a list of countries and/or distributors from which current coins can be purchased. Ask to be placed on their mailing lists to receive notification of the most current releases.

ANDORRA
Servei D' Emissions Episcopal
C/. Prat de la Creu
96 4t 5a
Andorra La Vella
PRINCIPAT D' ANDORRA
Telephone: 86 72 80 88 92 80
Fax: +376 869009

(silver coins)
Servei d'Emmisions Vegueria Episcopal
Prata de la Creu 42
PRINCIPA T D' ANDORRA

ARMENIA
Schom-Buchversand
Gerhard Schon
Postfach 71 09 08
D-81459 München
GERMANY

AUSTRALIA *(silver & gold coins)*
North American Office:
Downie's, Ltd. (Royal Australian Mint)
Attn. Craig Whitford
P.O. Box 23064
Lansing, MI 48909
Telephone: (517) 394-4443
Fax: (517) 394-0579

Downie's Ltd. is pleased to announce their appointment as exclusive North American agent for the Royal Australian Mint. Craig Whitford is located in Lansing, Michigan, where he manages his own numismatic auction business. He has a long and distinguished history in the American numismatic arena. Craig has been associated with Downie's as their U.S. agent for over 12 years.

Fred Weinberg & Co., Inc.
16311 Ventura Boulevard, Suite 1288
Encino, CA 91436
Telephone: (818) 986-3733
Fax: (818) 986-2153

Gold Corp. (Perth Mint)
30210 Rancho Viejo Road, Suite C
San Juan Capistrano, CA 92675
Telephone: (714) 443-0600
Fax: (714) 443-0901

Universal Coins
(Royal Australian Mint)
47 Clarence Street, Suite 201
Ottawa, Ontario K1N 9K1, Canada
Telephone: (613) 241-1404

Fax: (613) 241-4568

Royal Australian Mint
Denison Street
Canberra, ACT 2600
AUSTRALIA

The Royal Australian Mint in Canberra is the home of Australia's coins and was officially opened by His Royal Highness, The Duke of Edinburgh on Monday, February 22, 1965.

Commissioned to produce Australia's decimal coinage, introduced into circulation on February 14, 1966, the Royal Australian Mint holds a place in history as the first mint in Australia not to be a branch of the Royal Mint in London.

Since its opening in 1965 the Mint has produced over eight billion circulating coins and currently has the capacity to produce over two million coins per day or over six hundred million coins per year, with staff working a single shift only.

Coins are not the only products of the Mint. Medals, medallions, seals, and tokens are produced for a wide range of government, business, sporting, and tourist needs in Australia and overseas. A small selection includes The Order of Australia, Vietnam Medal, New Zealand Commonwealth Games Victory Medals, Third Pacific Conference Games Medallion, Anzac Peace Medallion, Sydney Monorail Token, and Queensland's Jupiters Casino Token.

The Royal Australian Mint strikes coins for a number of South Pacific nations. Export coins were first struck in 1969 for New Zealand, and since then coins have been produced for Papua New Guinea, Tonga, Western Samoa, Cook Islands, Fiji, Malaysia, Thailand, Nepal, Bangladesh, and Tokelau.

Gold Corp.
Perth Mint (Western Australia Mint)
P.O. Box M924
310 Hay Street
East Perth, Western Australia 6004
AUSTRALIA

AUSTRIA *(silver coins)*
North American office:
Universal Coins
47 Clarence Street, Suite 201
Ottawa, Ontario K1N 9K1, Canada
Telephone: (613) 241-1404
Fax: (613) 241-4568

Austrian Mint
Munze Osterreich AG
A-1031 Wien Postfach 181
Am Heumarkt I
AUSTRIA

BANGLADESH *(silver coins)*
MDM, Munzhandelsgesellschaft
Deutsche Munze
Theodor-Heuss-Str 7
38090 Braunschweig
FEDERAL REPUBLIC OF GERMANY

BELGIUM *(silver coins)*
North American office:
Coin & Currency Institute, Inc.
P.O. Box 1057
Clifton, NJ 07014
Telephone: 1 (800) 421-1866
Fax: (201) 471-1062

Back in the 1980s, the Coin & Currency Institute saw that there was a change developing in the way people were collecting their coins. Retail shops were disappearing, coin shows were intimidating for many, and U.S. coins were looked at by many as an expensive investment. There was a general, steady move into the world of foreign coins. This was a world unlike that of U.S. coins. Not only do the first world coins date back to the sixth century B.C., but they come in dozens of metals from hundreds of issuers—some extinct, others just starting out.

It was impossible for all but the wealthiest and most intrepid of collectors to venture into this vast new world on their own so we decided it was best to bring that world to them. Although we always specialized in foreign coins, the ones most attractive and available were those being offered by the world's mints. But for an American, acquiring these coins was a nightmare! The mints did not take credit cards, did not have toll-free phone numbers, and were scattered about in different time zones. They refused U.S. dollars, which meant that everyone who wanted even one coin had to buy a foreign currency bank draft, which they then had to send overseas. It was just as difficult on the receiving end, where the mints could not efficiently process individual orders to America.

We knew that there was a better way. Through our contacts with many world mints, we established a fulfillment and distribution facility for them here in the states. We offer our toll-free number (1-800-421-1866) for anyone wanting to order or who requests information. We have recently added an e-mail address (coincurin@aol.com), and will soon establish an Internet page showing coins of the world's mints. Furthermore, we accept personal checks as well as VISA, MasterCard, and American Express. We handle all importation and customs formalities, and because coins are shipped to us in quantity, we are able to absorb the costs of international freight.

We send information to collectors by mail at least eight times a year and try to have something for every collector's taste and budget: We offer traditional designs by, for example, the Portuguese and Hungarians, as well as the starkly modern new commemoratives of the Netherlands and Finland. Whether gold, silver, or non-precious metal, whether single coins or special proof and mint sets, it is no wonder that legions of collectors are flocking to the world of world coins. We welcome the readers of the Blackbook *to come and join them.*

Royal Belgian Mint
Monnaie Royale de Belgique
Bd. Pacheco laan 32
1000 Bruxelles
BELGIUM

BERMUDA
Bermuda Monetary Authority
26 Burnaby Street
Hamilton, HM 11
BERMUDA

BRAZIL *(silver & gold coins)*
Casa de Moeda do Brasil
Rua Rene Bitten-Court 371
23565 Distrito Industrial de Santa Cruz
Rio de Janeiro
BRAZIL

BULGARIA *(silver coins)*
Bulgarian Mint
6 Boulevard Russky
Sofia
BULGARIA

CANADA *(silver & gold coins)*
North American office:
Fred Weinberg & Co., Inc.
16311 Ventura Boulevard, Suite 1288
Encino, CA 91436
Telephone: (818) 986-3733
Fax: (818) 986-2153

Universal Coins
47 Clarence Street, Suite 201
Ottawa, Ontario K1N 9K1, Canada
Telephone: (613) 241-1404
Fax: (613) 241-4568

Royal Canadian Mint
320 Sussex Drive
Ottawa, Ontario K1A 0G8
CANADA

CUBA *(silver & gold coins)*
Empresa Cubana de Acunaciones
Calle 18 No. 306 e
3ra y 5ta Avenue Miramar
Ciudad de La Habana
CUBA

CYPRESS
Schom-Buchversand
Gerhard Schon
Postfach 71 09 08
D-81459 München
GERMANY

CZECH REPUBLIC *(silver coins)*
Ceska Mincovna
Czech Mint
Jablonec nad Nisou
CZECH REPUBLIC

Czech National Bank
Currency Department
Na prikope 28, 110, 03
Prague 1
CZECH REPUBLIC

Ivo Cerny
POB 19
695 04 Hodonfn
CZECH REPUBLIC
Telephone: 420 68 26489
Fax: 420 631 322023

(gold coins)
Czechoslovia State Bank
Na Prikope 28
CS-100 03 Praha 1
CZECH REPUBLIC

DENMARK *(silver & gold coins)*
Den Kongelige Mont
Solmarksvej 5
2605 Brondy
DENMARK

EGYPT *(silver & gold coins)*
Egyptian Mint House
Abbessia, Cairo
EGYPT

(silver coins)
Egyptian Coin Center
41 Ramses Street
P.O. Box 77
Mohamed Farid
Cairo
EGYPT

FEDERAL REPUBLIC OF GERMANY
(silver & gold coins)
B.H. Mayer Mint
Turnplatz 2
D-75172 Pforzheim
FEDERAL REPUBLIC OF GERMANY

(silver coins)
Bayerisches Hauptmunzamt
Zamdorfer Strabe 92
81677 Munchen
FEDERAL REPUBLIC OF GERMANY

Staatliche Muenze Hamburg
Bei de neuen Muenze 19
2000 Hamburg
FEDERAL REPUBLIC OF GERMANY

Staatliche Munze Stuttgart
70372 Stuttgart
Reichhaller Strasse 58
W-7500 Stuttgart 50
FEDERAL REPUBLIC OF GERMANY

FEDERAL REPUBLIC OF KOREA
(silver coins)
Korea Security Printing and
Minting Corp.
90 Kajong-dong
Taejon 305-350
FEDERAL REPUBLIC OF KOREA

FINLAND *(silver coins)*
North American office:
Coin & Currency Institute, Inc.
P.O. Box 1057
Clifton, NJ 07014
Telephone: 1 (800) 421-1866
Fax: (201) 471-1062

Mint of Finland
PL 13
SF-01671 Vantaa
FINLAND

(gold coins)
Suomen Pankki-Findlands Bank
P.O. Box 160
00101 Helsinki 10
FINLAND

FRANCE
North American office:
Universal Coins
47 Clarence Street, Suite 201
Ottawa, Ontario K1N 9K1, Canada
Telephone: (613) 241-1404
Fax: (613) 241-4568

Monnaie de Paris
11 quai de Conti
75270 Paris Cedex 06
FRANCE

HUNGARY *(silver coins)*
North American office:
Coin & Currency Institute, Inc.
P.O. Box 1057
Clifton, NJ 07014
Telephone: 1 (800) 421-1866
Fax: (201) 471-1062

Hungarian State Mint
H-1450
Budapest
HUNGARY

IRAN *(gold coins)*
Bank Markazi Iran
P.O. Box 3362
Teheran
ISLAMIC REPUBLIC OF IRAN

IRELAND
Central Bank of Ireland
P.O. Box 61
Dublin 16
IRELAND
Telephone: 01 2955666
Fax: 01 2956536

ISRAEL *(gold coins)*
North American office:
Coin & Currency Institute, Inc.
P.O. Box 1057
Clifton, NJ 07014
Telephone: 1 (800) 421-1866
Fax: (201) 471-1062

J.J. Van Grover, LTD.
P.O. Box 123
Oakland Gardens, NY
11364-0123
Telephone: 1 (800) 56-COINS

Israel Coins & Medals Gallery of
New York
7 East 35th Street, Suite 1013
New York, NY 10016

Israel Government Coins &
Metals Corp.
5 Ahad Ha'am Street
P.O. Box 2270
Jerusalem 91022
ISRAEL

ITALY *(silver & gold coins)*
Instituto Poligrafico e
Zecca Dello Stato
Piazza Giuseppe Verdi, 10
00100 Roma
ITALY

(silver coins)
Stabilimento Stefano Johnson SpA
ViaTerraggio, 15
20123 Milan
ITALY

LITHUANIA
Lithuanian Mint
Eiguliu g. 4
2015 Vilnius
REPUBLIC OF LITHUANIA
Telephone: +370 2 26 23 90
Fax: +370 2 26 24 00

MALTA
Emmanuel Said
43/2 Zachery Street

PO Box 345
Vallette VLT 04
MALTA
Telephone: +356 23 68 53
Fax: +356 246960
E-mail: emsaid@dream.vol.net.mt

MEXICO *(silver & gold coins)*
North American office:
Coin & Currency Institute, Inc.
P.O. Box 1057
Clifton, NJ 07014
Telephone: 1 (800) 421-1866
Fax: (201) 471-1062

Casa de Moneda de Mexico
Paseo de la Reforma 295, 5° Piso
Colonia Cuahtemoc
06500 Mexico, D.F.
MEXICO

NAMBIA *(silver coins)*
E.D.J. Van Roekel B.V.
P.O. Box 1400 AA
Bussom
HOLLAND

NETHERLANDS *(silver & gold coins)*
North American office:
Coin & Currency Institute, Inc.
P.O. Box 1057
Clifton, NJ 07014
Telephone: 1 (800) 421-1866
Fax: (201) 471-1062

Rijks Munt
Leidsweg 90, 3531 BG
Postbus 2407
3500 GK Utrecht
THE NETHERLANDS

NEW ZEALAND
Collectors Coin Division, Banking & Currency Dept.
Reserve Bank of New Zealand
P.O. Box 2498
Wellington
NEW ZEALAND

NIUE *(silver coins)*
MDM, Munzhandelsgesellschaft
Deutsche Munze
Theodor-Heuss-Str 7
38090 Braunschweig
FEDERAL REPUBLIC OF GERMANY

NORWAY *(silver & gold coins)*
Royal Mint of Norway
Hyttegt I
N-3600 Kongsberg
NORWAY

OMAN *(silver coins)*
Central Bank of Oman
Attn. Mr. Ali Khamis, Vice President
P.O. Box 1161
Ruwi, OM 112
SULTANATE OF OMAN

PALAU *(silver & gold coins)*
E.D.J. Van Roekel B.V.
P.O. Box 1400 AA
Bussom
HOLLAND

PEOPLE'S REPUBLIC OF CHINA *(silver & gold coins)*
North American office:
Fred Weinberg & Co., Inc.
16311 Ventura Boulevard, Suite 1288
Encino, CA 91436
Telephone: (818) 986-3733
Fax: (818) 986-2153

Universal Coins
47 Clarence Street, Suite 201
Ottawa, Ontario K1N 9K1, Canada
Telephone: (613) 241-1404
Fax: (613) 241-4568

China Gold Coin, Inc.
Information Division
Room 1103, ACFTU Hotel
No. 1 Zhen Wu Miao Road
XI Cheng District
PEOPLE'S REPUBLIC OF CHINA

PERU *(silver & gold coins)*
Banco Central de Reserva del Peru
Apartado 1958, Correo Central
Lima 1
PERU

POLAND *(silver & gold coins)*
Mint of Poland
MINT-POL S.A.
Pereca Street, 21
00 958 Warsaw
POLAND

(gold coins)
Narodow Bank Polski
Swietokrzyska Street 11/21
00 950 Warszawa
POLAND

PORTUGAL *(silver coins)*
North American office:
Coin & Currency Institute, Inc.
P.O. Box 1057
Clifton, NJ 07014
Telephone: 1 (800) 421-1866
Fax: (201) 471-1062

Portugal State Mint
Impresa Nacional—Casa da Moeda
Av. Dr. Antonio Jose de Almeida
P-1092 Lisboa, Codex
PORTUGAL

(gold coins)
Portugal State Mint
Tua de D. Francisco Manuel de
Menlo 5
P-1092 Lisboa, Codex
PORTUGAL

ROMANIA *(silver coins)*
Romania State Mint
The National Bank of Romania
25 Lipscani Street
Bucharest
ROMANIA

SALOMON ISLANDS *(silver coins)*
MDM, Munzhandelsgesellschaft
Deutsche Munze
Theodor-Heuss-Str 7
38090 Braunschweig
FEDERAL REPUBLIC OF GERMANY

SINGAPORE *(silver coins)*
North American office:
Universal Coins
47 Clarence Street, Suite 201
Ottawa, Ontario K1N 9K1, Canada
Telephone: (613) 241-1404
Fax: (613) 241-4568

BCCS Depot Singapore
10 Depot Walk
SINGAPORE 04 10

(gold coins)
Singapore Mint Pte. Ltd.
249 Jalan Boon Lay
SINGAPORE 2261

SLOVENIJE
Bank of Slovenia
Slovenska 35
1505 Ljubjana
SLOVENIJA
Telephone: +386 61 17 19 000
Fax: +386 61 215 516

Ivo Cerny
POB 19
695 04 Hodonfn
CZECH REPUBLIC
Telephone: 420 68 26489
Fax: 420 631 322023

SOUTH AFRICA
(silver & gold coins)
North American office:
Coin & Currency Institute, Inc.
P.O. Box 1057
Clifton, NJ 07014
Telephone: 1 (800) 421-1866
Fax: (201) 471-1062

South African Mint
P.O. Box 464
Pretoria 000 1
SOUTH AFRICA

(silver coins)
Numismatic Sales
P.O. Box 5580
Hennopsmeer 0046
SOUTH AFRICA

SPAIN *(silver & gold coins)*
Fabrica Nacional de Moneda y Timbre
Jorge Juan, 106
28009 Madrid
SPAIN

SWEDEN *(silver & gold coins)*
AB Tumba Bruk Myntverket
Swedish Mint
Box 401
S-63 1 06 Eskilstuna
SWEDEN

SWITZERLAND *(silver & gold coins)*
Huguenin Medailleurs, S.A.
rue Henry-Grandjean, 5
2400 Le Locle
SWITZERLAND

(silver coins)
Valcambi S.A.
Via Passeggiata
CH-6828 Balerna
SWITZERLAND

THAILAND *(silver coins)*
Royal Thai Mint
The Treasury Department
Rama VI Road
Bankok 10400
THAILAND

TURKEY *(silver & gold coins)*
Turkish State Mint
Darphane Mudurlugu
Yildiz-Istanbul
TURKEY

UNITED KINGDOM
(silver & gold coins)
North American office:
British Royal Mint
RR2, Box 59A South Road
Millbrook, NY 12545
Telephone: 1 (800) 822-2748

Fred Weinberg & Co., Inc.
16311 Ventura Boulevard, Suite 1288
Encino, CA 91436
Telephone: (818) 986-3733
Fax: (818) 986-2153

Universal Coins
47 Clarence Street, Suite 201
Ottawa, Ontario K1N 9K1, Canada
Telephone: (613) 241-1404
Fax: (613) 241-4568

Royal Mint
Llantrisant, Pontyclun
Mid-Glamorgan CF7 8YT
UNITED KINGDOM

UNITED STATES OF AMERICA
(silver & gold coins)
United States Mint
633 Third Street, N.W.
Washington, D.C. 20220
USA

(silver coins)
Sunshine Mint
7405 N. Government Way
Coeur d' Alene, ID 83814
USA

(gold coins)
Franklin Mint
Franklin Center, PA 19091
USA

Liberty Mint
651 Columbia Lane
Provo, UT 84604
USA

VATICAN CITY
North American office:
Universal Coins
47 Clarence Street, Suite 201
Ottawa, Ontario K1N 9K1, Canada
Telephone: 1 (613) 241-1404
Fax: (613) 241-4568

INTERNATIONAL ASSOCIATION OF PROFESSIONAL NUMISMATISTS

OBJECT OF THE ASSOCIATION

The I.A.P.N. was constituted at a meeting held in Geneva in 1951 to which the leading international numismatic firms had been invited. There were 28 foundation members. The objects of the Association are the development of a healthy and prosperous numismatic trade conducted according to the highest standards of business ethics and commercial practice, the encouragement of scientific research and the propagation of numismatics, and the creation of lasting and friendly relations amongst professional numismatists throughout the world.

Membership is vested in numismatic firms, or in numismatic departments of other commercial institutions, and *not* in individuals. Today there are 100 numismatic firms in membership, situated in five continents and twenty-one countries. The General Assembly is the supreme organ of the Association, and this is convened annually, normally in a different country.

The Executive Committee is composed of twelve to fifteen persons from at least six different countries and includes the President, two Vice-Presidents (one from each Hemisphere), the General Secretary, and the Treasurer. There are subcommittees dealing with membership, discipline, publications, and anti-forgery work.

In pursuit of the objective to encourage numismatic research the Association has published or assisted in the publication of a number of important numismatic works. In particular it maintains a close liaison with the International Numismatic Commission, and individual members take an active interest in the work of their national numismatic organizations.

In 1965 the I.A.P.N. held an international congress in Paris to consider the study of and defense against counterfeit coins, and in 1975 the Association established the International Bureau for the Suppression of Counterfeit Coins (I.B.S.C.C.) in London. This Bureau maintains close links with mints, police forces, museums, collectors, and dealers, publishing both a half-yearly Bulletin on Counterfeits and specialized reports on counterfeits. It will give an opinion as to authenticity and further details may be had on application to the Bureau.

International Bureau for the Suppression of Counterfeit Coins.

Mr. Arne Kirsch
P.O. Box 1804
79508 Lörrach
GERMANY
Telephone: ++49 (07621) 48560
Fax: ++49 (07621) 48529
E-mail: ibscckirsch@stepnet.de

The members of the I.A.P.N. guarantee the authenticity of all the coins and medals which they sell—this is a condition of membership—so collectors may purchase numismatic material from any of the firms listed in the following pages in the full knowledge that if any item does prove to be counterfeit or not as described the piece can be returned and the purchase price will be refunded, without regard to date of purchase.

Membership in the Association is not lightly acquired as applicants have to be sponsored by three members, and the vetting of applications involves a rigorous and sometimes protracted procedure. In order to be admitted the applicants must have been established in business as numismatists for at least four years and must be known to a number of members, and the Committee need to be satisfied that they have carried on their business in an honorable manner and that they have a good general knowledge of numismatics as well as expertise in whatever field is their speciality.

The Medal of Honour of the Association was established in 1963 in memory of its first president, Leonard S. Forrer, and is awarded by the President to persons of distinction whom the Association wishes to honor or for distinguished services to the Association.

The Association is a non-profit-making organization established within the terms of paras. 60 *et seq* of the Swiss Civil Code. Its registered office is at P.O. Box 3647, CH-4002 Basle (Switzerland). Further inquiries about the Association may be made to the General Secretary.

Secretary:
Jean-Luc Van der Schueren
14, Rue de la Bourse, B-1000 Bruxelles
Tel.: +32-2-513 3400 — Fax: +32-2-512 2528
e-Mail: *iapnsecret@compuserve.com*

AUSTRALIA

NOBLE NUMISMATICS Pty Ltd
229 Macquarie Street,
SYDNEY NSW 2000
PH: (61) (02) 9223 4578
FX: (61) (02) 9223 6009
Auctions
Specialties: Australian and world coins, banknotes, commemorative and war medals, tokens.

AUSTRIA

HERINEK, G.
Josefstädterstrasse 27,
A-1082 WIEN VIII
PH: (43) (01) 40 64 396
FX: (43) (01) 40 64 396
Publications
Specialties: Antike Münzen, Römisch Deutsches Reich

MOZELT, Erich
(Erich und Christine Mozelt)
Vienna Marriott Hotel,
Parkring 12a, A-1010 WIEN
PH: (43) (01) 512 9807
FX: (43) (01) 512 9783
List
Specialties: Münzen des Römisch Deutschen Reiches, Weltmünzen und Antike

BELGIUM

ELSEN SA, Jean
(Jean Elsen, Olivier Elsen,
Roselyne Dus, Philippe Elsen)
Avenue de Tervuren 65,
B-1040 BRUXELLES
PH: (32) (02) 734 6356; 736 0712
FX: (32) (02) 735 7778
E-mail:numismatique@elsen.be
Specialties: Ancient, Oriental and medieval coins, Low Countries, world coins, medals and books

FRANCESCHI & Fils, B.
10, Rue Croix-de-Fer,
B-1000 BRUXELLES
PH: (32) (02) 217 9395
List Publications Auctions

VAN DER SCHUEREN, Jean-Luc
14, Rue de la Bourse,
B-1000 BRUXELLES
PH: (32) (02) 513 3400
FX: (32) (02) 512 2528
List
Specialties: Ancient and medieval coins, Low Countries, world coins and tokens

CANADA

WEIR NUMISMATICS LTD., Randy
PO Box 64577, UNIONVILLE,
Ont. L3R 0M9
PH: (905) 830 1588
FX: (905) 830 1129
List Mail Bid Sales
Specialties: British Colonial coins, Canadian tokens

EGYPT

BAJOCCHI JEWELLERS
(Cav. Pietro Bajocchi)
45 Abdel Khalek Sarwat Street,
11111 CAIRO
PH: (20) (02) 391 9160 / 390 0030
FX: (20) (02) 393 1696
Specialties: Ptolemaiques, Greco, Romaines d'Alexandrie

FRANCE

ANTIKA 1 (Marcel Pesce)
33, Rue Sainte-Hélène,
F-69002 Lyon
PH: (33) (04) 78 37 23 90+
FX: (33) (04) 78 42 28 10
List Auctions
Specialties: Monnaies antiques, françaises, médailles, jetons, décorations et papier monnaie

BOURGEY, Sabine
7, Rue Drouot, F-75009 PARIS
PH: (33) (01) 47 70 88 67 / 47 70 35 18
FX: (33) (01) 42 46 58 48
List Publications Auctions
Specialties: Monnaies, médailles, jetons, éditions numismatiques

BURGAN, Claude - Maison Florange
(Claude et Isabelle Burgan)
68, Rue de Richelieu, F-75002 PARIS
PH: (33) (01) 42 96 95 57
FX: (33) (01) 42 86 92 43
List Publications Mail Bid Sales
Specialties: Monnaies royales françaises, monnaies antiques, librairie numismatique

MAISON PLATT SA (Gérard Barré, Daniel Renaud Sandrine Barré)
49, Rue de Richelieu, F-75001 PARIS
Postal address: PB 2612,
F-75026 Paris Cedex 01
PH: (33) (01) 42 96 50 48
FX: (33) (01) 42 61 13 99
List Publications Auctions
Specialties: Monnaies antiques, françaises, médailles, jetons, papier-monnaie. Ordres et décorations, librairie numismatique

NUMISMATIQUE et CHANGE DE PARIS
(Annette Vinchon)
3, Rue de la Bourse, F-75002 PARIS
PH: (33) (01) 42 97 53 53 / 42 97 46 85
FX: (33) (01) 42 97 44 56
Publications Mail Bid Sales Auctions
Specialties: Monnaies modernes. Monnaies d'or cotées en bourse. Lingots. Billets, assignats. Ourvages de Référence

O.G.N.
(Pierre Crinon, François Mervy)
64, Rue de Richelieu, F-75002 Paris
PH: (33) (01) 42 97 47 50
FX: (33) (01) 42 60 01 37
List Publications Auctions
Specialties: Monnaies antiques, françaises, étrangères, médailles, jetons

A. POINSIGNON-NUMISMATIQUE
4, Rue des Francs Bourgeois,
F-67000 STRASBOURG
PH: (33) (03) 88 32 10 50
FX: (33) (03) 88 75 01 14
List Auctions
Specialties: Monnaies antiques, françaises, alsaciennes et islamiques, librairie numismatique

SILBERSTEIN, Claude
39, Rue Vivienne, F-75002 PARIS
PH: (33) (01) 42 33 19 55
FX: (33) (01) 42 33 16 15
Specialties: Monnaies, médailles, jetons

VINCHON-NUMISMATIQUE, Jean
(Jean Vinchon et Françoise Berthelot-Vinchon)
77, Rue de Richelieu, F-75002 PARIS
PH: (33) (01) 42 97 50 00
FX: (33) (01) 42 86 06 03
List Publications Auctions
Specialties: Monnaies, médailles, décorations, pierres gravées, cylindres, bijoux anciens, antiquités

WEIL, Alain-SPES NUMISMATIQUE
54, Rue de Richelieu, F-75001 PARIS
PH: (33) (01) 47 03 32 12
FX: (33) (01) 42 60 14 18
List Auctions
Specialties: *Monnaies antiques et françaises, jetons et médailles, documents sur la numismatique, billets de banque*

GERMANY

DILLER, Johannes
(Ohlstadter Str. 21)
PO Box 700429,
D-81304 MÜNCHEN
PH: (49) (089) 760 3550
FX: (49) (089) 769 8939
Specialties: *Münzen (900-1800), Medaillen (1500-1933), Kelten von Süddeutschland, Numism. Antiquariat*

GARLICH, Kurt B.
Albert Schweitzer Str. 24a,
D-63303 DREIEICH-GÖTZENHAIN
PH: (49) (06103) 8 59 70
FX: (49) (06103) 83 01 85
Specialties: *Deutsche Gold-und Silbermünzen ab 1800.*

GIESSENER MÜNZHANDLUNG
DIETER GORNY GmbH
Maximiliansplatz 20,
D-80333 MÜNCHEN
PH: (49) (089) 226876
FX: (49) (089) 2285513
Specialties: *Münzen und Medaillen der Antike und der Neuzeit*

HIRSCH, NACHF., Gerhard
(Dr. Francisca Bernheimer)
Promenadeplatz 10/II,
D-80333 MÜNCHEN
PH: (49) (089) 29 21 50 and 290 7390
FX: (49) (089) 228 36 75
E-mail: coinhirsch@compuserve.com
Specialties: *Münzen und Medaillen der Antike, Mittel-alter und Neuzeit, Kunstwerke der Antike*

JACQUIER, Paul-Francis
Honsellstrasse 8, D-77694 KEHL
PH: (49) (07851) 12 17
FX: (49) (07851) 73 074
Specialties: *Celtic, Greek, Roman, Byzantine coins. Classical art.*

KAISER, Rüdiger,
Münzfachgeschäft
Mittelweg 54, D-60318 FRANKFURT
PH: (49) (069) 597 11 09
FX: (49) (069) 55 38 16
Specialties: *Antike, Europäische Münzen und Medaillen bis 1900*

KRICHELDORF Nachf., H.H.
(Volker Kricheldorf)
Günterstalstrasse 16,
D-79102 FREIBURG i.Br.
PH: (49) (0761) 739 13
FX: (49) (0761) 70 96 70

KÜNKER, Fritz Rudolf,
Münzenhandlung
(F.R. Künker, H.-R. Künker,
P.N. Schulten, Oliver Köpp,
U. Helmig, Gisela Thomas)
Gutenbergstrasse 23,
D-49076 OSNABRÜCK
PH: (49) (0541) 96 20 20
FX: (49) (0541) 96 20 222
E-mail: fritz-rudolf.Kuenker@
T-online.de
Specialties: *Antike, Mittelalter und Neuzeit, Goldmünzen*

KURPFÄLZISCHE
MÜNZENHANDLUNG-KPM
(H. Gehrig, G. Rupertus)
Augusta-Anlage 52, D-68165
MANNHEIM
PH: (49) (0621) 44 88 99 / 44 95 66
FX: (49) (0621) 40 37 52

Specialties: The antiquity, Germany, France, Benelux, paper money

Numismatik LANZ (Dr. Hubert Lanz, Ingrid Franke, Walter Schantl, Florian Eggers)
Luitpoldblock-Maximiliansplatz 10, D-80333 MÜNCHEN
PH: (49) (089) 29 90 70
FX: (49) (089) 22 07 62
Auctions
Specialties: Antike, Mittelalter, Neuzeit, Literatur, Münzen und Medaillen

MENZEL, Niels
Beckerstrasse 6A, D-12157 BERLIN
PH: (49) (030) 855 52 96
FX: (49) (030) 855 04 90
List Auctions

MÜNZEN- UND MEDAILLENHANDLUNG STUTTGART
(Dr. Michael Brandt, Stefan Sonntag)
Charlottenstrasse 4, D-070182 STUTTGART
PH: (49) (0711) 24 44 57
FX: (49) (0711) 23 39 36
List Publications

OLDENBURG, H.G.
Holstenstrasse 22, Postfach 3546, D-24034 KIEL
PH: (49) (0431) 9 46 76
FX: (49) (0431) 9 66 56
List Auctions
Specialties: Antike, Mittelalter und Neuzeit

Bankhaus PARTIN & Co. KG (Eberhard Funk, Klaus Müller)
Numismatische Abt., Bahnhofplatz 1, D-97980 BAD MERGENTHEIM
PH: (49) (07931) 59 25 00 / 501
FX: (49) (07931) 59 24 45
Specialties: Neuzeit und Goldmünzen

PEUS NACHF., Dr. Busso (Dieter Raab, Wilhelm Müseler, Christian Stoess)
Bornwiesenweg 34, D-60322 FRANKFURT/M.
PH: (49) (069) 959 6620
FX: (49) (069) 55 59 95

Münzhandlung RITTER GmbH
(E. & J. Ritter und Klaus Fleissner)
Immermannstr. 19, D-40210 DÜSSELDORF
Postal address: Postfach 24 01 26, D-40090 Düsseldorf
PH: (49) (0211) 367 80-0
FX: (49) (0211) 367 80-25
List
Specialties: Münzen der Antike und Deutschlands. Grosshandel/ Wholesale

SCHRAMM GmbH, H.J.
Scheinerstrasse 9, D-81679 MÜNCHEN
PH: (49) (089) 98 12 43
FX: (49) (089) 98 12 43
Auctions

TIETJEN + CO.
Spitalerstrasse 30, D-20095 HAMBURG
PH: (49) (040) 33 03 68
FX: (49) (040) 32 30 35
Publications Auctions
Specialties: Coins, medals, paper money and books

IRELAND

COINS & MEDALS (Redg.)
(Emil Szauer)
10 Cathedral Street, DUBLIN 1
PH: (353) (01) 874 4033
VAT: (353) IE 9Y50349S
Specialties: Ancient, medieval, modern coins of the world

ISRAEL

EIDELSTEIN, Adolfo
61 Herzl St., HAIFA
Postal address: POB 5135, 31051 Haifa
PH: (972) (04) 8645 035
FX: (972) (04) 831 4074

Specialties: Ancient and modern coins, Judaica

QEDAR, Shraga
3, Granot Street, Entrance 6, JERUSALEM
Postal address: PO Box 520, 91004 Jerusalem
PH: (972) (02) 679 1273
FX: (972) (02) 679 0912
Specialties: Numismatic consulting: Ancient and Islamic coins, ancient weights

ITALY

BERNARDI, Giulio
(G. Bernardi, G. Paoletti)
Via Roma 3 & 22c, PO Box 560, I-34121 TRIESTE
PH: (39) (040) 639 086
FX: (39) (040) 630 430
List Publications
Specialties: Greek, Roman, medieval, Islam, medallions, numismatic books

CARLO CRIPPA s.n.c.
(Carlo e Paolo Crippa)
Via degli Omenoni 2 (angolo Piazza Belgioioso), I-20121 MILANO
PH: (39) (02) 878 680
FX: (39) (02) 878 680
List Publications
Specialties: Grecques et romaines. Italiennes médiévales et modernes, surtout de l'atelier de Milan

DE FALCO (Alberto de Falco)
Corso Umberto 24, I-80138 NAPOLI
PH: (39) (081) 55 28 245
FX: (39) (081) 55 17 645
List
Specialties: Monete dell'Italia meridionale e della Sicilia

FALLANI (Dr. Carlo-Maria Fallani)
Via del Babuino 58a, I-00187 ROMA
PH: (39) (06) 320 7982
FX: (39) (06) 320 7645
Specialties: Grecques, romaines et byzantines. Archéologie

MARCHESI GINO & Figlio
(Giuseppe Marchesi)
V. le Pietramellara 35, I-40121 BOLOGNA
PH: (39) (051) 255 014
FX: (39) (051) 255 014
List (Trimestrale) Publications
Specialties: Greek, Roman and medieval Italian coins

PAOLUCCI, Raffaele
Via San Francesco 154, I-35121 PADOVA
PH: (39) (049) 651 997
FX: (39) (049) 651 552
Specialties: Medieval Italian coins, especially Venetian

RATTO, Mario
Via A. Manzoni 14 (Palazzo Trivulzio), I-20121 MILANO
PH: (39) (02) 79 93 80
FX: (39) (02) 79 64 93
List Publications Auctions
Specialties: Grecques, romaines, italiennes, médiévales et modernes

RINALDI O. & Figlio,
(Alfio e Marco Rinaldi)
Via Cappello 23 (Casa di Giulietta), I-37121 VERONA
PH: (39) (045) 803 40 32
FX: (39) (045) 803 40 32
List Publications
Specialties: Greche, romane, italiane, estere e medaglie

JAPAN

DARUMA INTERNATIONAL GALLERIES
(Yuji Otani)
2-16-32-301, Takanawa, Minato-ku, JP-TOKYO 108
PH: (81) (03) 3447 5567
FX: (81) (03) 3449 3344

List Publications Auctions
Specialties: World gold and silver coins, Japanese coins and banknotes, Chinese coins

LUXEMBOURG

LUX NUMIS (Romain Probst)
Galerie Mercure, 41, Av. de la Gare,
L-1611 LUXEMBOURG
PH: (352) 48 78 77 / 34 04 87
FX: (352) 40 55 17
List Publications Auctions
Specialties: Luxembourg, Monnaies du monde, Monnaies de nécessité, gauloises

MONACO

LE LOUIS D'OR
(Romolo et Claude Vescovi)
9, Ave. des Papalins,
MC-98000 MONACO
PH: (377) 92 05 35 81
FX: (377) 92 05 35 82
List Publications
Specialties: Monnaies Italiennes, Antiques, Médiévales et Françaises

NETHERLANDS

MEVIUS NUMISBOOKS INTERNATIONAL BV
(Johan Mevius, Gabriel Munoz)
Oosteinde 97,
NL-7671 AT VRIEZENVEEN
PH: (31) (0546) 561 322
FX: (31) (0546) 561 352
List Publications
Specialties: Numismatic books, coins & medals of the Netherlands

SCHULMAN BV, Laurens
(Laurens and Carla Schulman)
Brinklaan 84a, NL-1404 GM BUSSUM
PH: (31) (035) 691 6632
FX: (31) (035) 691 0878
List Publications Auctions
Specialties: Coins of the Netherlands, Europe, historical medals, numismatic books and paper money

VAN DER DUSSEN BV, A.G.
(Pauline van der Dussen)
Postbus 728, NL-6200 AS
MAASTRICHT
PH: (31) (043) 321 51 19
FX: (31) (043) 321 60 14
Publications Auctions
Specialties: Coins of the world, medals, numismatic books

WESTERHOF, Jille Binne
Trekpad 38-40,
NL-8742 KP BURGWERD
PH: (31) (0515) 573 364
FX: (31) (0515) 573 364
Auctions
Specialties: Coins of the Netherlands, Europe, historical medals

NORWAY

OSLO MYNTHANDEL AS
(Jan Olav Aamlid, Gunnar Thesen)
Kongens gate 31, Sentrum,
N-0101OSLO1
PO Box 355,
Sentrum, N-0101 Oslo 1
PH: (47) 22 41 60 78
FX: (47) 22 33 32 36
List Publications Auctions
Specialties: Scandinavian coins, Thailand, Ancient coins

SINGAPORE

TAISEI STAMPS & COINS (S) PTE LTD.
(B.H. Lim, S.L. Ang, T.W. Ma,
Lim Ming Lim)
12 Aljunied Rd, #06-02 SCN-Centre,
SINGAPORE 389801
PH: (65) 841 2355
FX: (65) 841 7680

Auctions
Specialties: *Chinese coins, coins of Asia, banknotes, world gold and silver coins*

SPAIN

CALICO, X. & F. (Xavier Jr. Calicó)
Plaza del Angel 2,
E-08002 BARCELONA
PH: (34) (3) 310 55 12 / 310 55 16
FX: (34) (3) 310 27 56
Publications Auctions
Specialties: *Espagne, possessions espagnoles en Europe, Amérique latine, Editeurs de médailles*

CAYON, Juan R., JANO S.L.
Alcala 35, E-28014 MADRID
PH: (34) (1) 522 8030 / 523 3585
FX: (34) (1) 522 0967
List Publications
Specialties: *Spanish world, ancient coins, crowns and numismatic books*

VICO SA, Jesus
(Jesus Vico and Julio Chico)
Lope de Rueda 7, E-28009 MADRID
PH: (34) (1) 431 88 07
FX: (34) (1) 431 01 04
Publications Auctions
Specialties: *Spain, Latin America, Roman, banknotes*

SWEDEN

AHLSTRÖM MYNTHANDEL AB
(Bjarne Ahlström)
Norrmalmstorg 1, I, PO Box 7662,
S-103 94 STOCKHOLM
PH: (46) (08) 10 10 10
FX: (46) (08) 678 77 77
List Publications Auctions
Specialties: *Scandinavian coins*

NORDLINDS MYNTHANDEL AB, ULF
(Hans Hirsch, Ulf Nordlind)
Karlavägen 46, PO Box 5132,
S-102 43 STOCKHOLM
PH: (46) (08) 662 62 61
FX: (46) (08) 661 62 13
List
Specialties: *Scandinavian coins, medals, numismatic literature*

SWITZERLAND

HESS-DIVO AG (J.P. Divo)
Löwenstrasse 55, CH-8001 ZÜRICH
Postal address: Postfach,
CH-8023 Zürich
PH: (41) (01) 225 4090
FX: (41) (01) 225 4099
List Auctions Publications
Specialties: *Swiss coins, coins of the world, medals, ancient coins*

LEU NUMISMATIK AG
(S. Hurter, H. Stotz, Dr. A.S. Walker, D. Hölscher)
In Gassen 20, CH-8001 ZÜRICH
Postal address: Postfach 4738,
CH-8022 Zürich
PH: (41) (01) 211 47 72
FX: (41) (01) 211 46 86
List Publications Auctions
Specialties: *Münzen, Medaillen; Antike, Mittelalter und Neuzeit, Schweiz*

MÜNZEN UND MEDAILLEN AG
(Dr. H. Voegtli,
Dr. U. Kampmann, A. Kirsch,
Dr. B. Schulte)
Malzgasse 25, BASEL
Postal address: Postfach 3647,
CH-4002 Basel
PH: (41) (061) 272 7544
FX: (41) (061) 272 7514
List (monatlich) Publications Auctions
Specialties: *Antike, mittelalterliche und neuzeitliche Münzen*

NUMISMATICA ARS CLASSICA AG
(Paolo del Bello, Roberto Russo,
Arturo Russo)
Niederdorfstrasse 43, Postfach 745,
CH-8025 ZÜRICH
PH: (41) (01) 261 1703
FX: (41) (01) 261 5324

List Publications Mail Bid Sales Auctions
Specialties: Greek, Roman, Byzantine and medieval coins

STERNBERG AG, Frank
(Claudia Sternberg, Paul Rabin, Jürg Richter)
Schanzengasse 10
(Bhf. Stadelhofen), CH-8001 ZÜRICH
PH: (41) (01) 252 30 88
FX: (41) (01) 252 40 67
List Auctions
Specialties: Münzen und Medaillen aller Zeiten und Länder Banknoten, Numismatische Literatur, Antike Gemmen, Kameen und Kunstobjekte

UNITED KINGDOM

BALDWIN & SONS LTD., A.H.
(P.D. Mitchell, A.H.E. Baldwin, B.T. Curtis)
11 Adelphi Terrace,
GB-LONDON WC2N 6BJ
PH: (44) (0171) 930 6879
FX: (44) (0171) 930 9450
Publications Auctions

FORMAT OF BIRMINGHAM LTD.
(Garry Charman, David Vice)
18, Bennetts Hill,
GB-BIRMINGHAM B2 5QJ
PH: (44) (0121) 643 2058
FX: (44) (0121) 643 2210
List
Specialties: World coins and medals 1500-1960

KNIGHTSBRIDGE COINS
(Stephen C. Fenton)
43, Duke Street, St. James's,
GB-LONDON SW1.Y.6DD
PH: (44) (0171) 930 7597 / 930 8215
FX: (44) (0171) 930 8214
Specialties: English coins, coins from USA, Australia and Thailand

LUBBOCK & SON LTD.
(Richard M. Lubbock)
315 Regent Street,
GB-LONDON W1R 7YB
PH: (44) (0171) 580 9922 / 323 0676 / 637 7922
FX: (44) (0171) 637 7602
List
Specialties: Gold coins of the world and rare banknotes

SPINK & SON LTD.
(M. Rasmussen, J. Pett),
D. Saville, B. Fåull, May Sinclair)
69-Southampton Row. Bloomsbury,
GB-LONDON ZIP CODE
PH: 020. 7563-4000
FX: 020. 4563-4066
Auctions List (10 a year) Publications
Specialtics: Ancient, British, and world coins

UNITED STATES OF AMERICA

BERK, LTD., Harlan J.
31 North Clark Street,
CHICAGO, IL 60602
PH: (001) (312) 609 0016
FX: (001) (312) 609 1309
List (bimonthly)
Specialties: All coins 700 BC to 1990's; classical antiquities

BOWERS AND MERENA GALLERIES, INC.
(Q. David Bowers, Raymond N. Merena)
PO Box 1224, WOLFEBORO, NH 03894
PH: (001) (603) 569 5095
FX: (001) (603) 569 5319
List Publications Auctions
Specialties: US coins and currency, foreign

coins, ancient coins, publishers of numismatic books

BULLOWA, C.E. (Mrs. Earl E. Moore).
COINHUNTER
1616 Walnut Street,
PHILADELPHIA, PA 19103
PH: (001) (215) 735 5517 / 5518
FX: (001) (215) 735 5517
List Auctions
Specialties: US, ancient and foreign coins and books.

COIN AND CURRENCY INSTITUTE INC.
(Arthur and Ira Friedberg)
PO Box 1057, CLIFTON, NJ 07014
PH: (001) (973) 471 1441
FX: (001) (973) 471 1062
Publications

COIN GALLERIES
(Robert Archer, Jan Eric Blamberg)
123 West 57 Street, NEW YORK, NY 10019
PH: (001) (212) 582 5955
FX: (001) (212) 582 1945 / 245 5018
List Mail Bid Sales Auctions
Specialties: European, ancient, medieval

CRAIG, Freeman
(Freeman and Marney Craig)
PO Box 4176, SAN RAFAEL, CA 94913
PH: (001) (415) 883 5336
FX: (001) (415) 382 1008
E-mail: raccoonnet@earthlink.net
Specialties: Latin American coinage in gold, silver and minor metals from 1536–1950, including medals

DAVISSON'S LTD.
(Allan Davisson, Ph.D., Marnie Davisson)
COLD SPRING, MN 56320
PH: (001) (320) 685 3835
FX: (001) (320) 685 8636
List (bimonthly) Publications
Mail Bid Sales
Specialties: British, ancient and classical European coins, books

FORD JR., John J.
PO Box 10317,
PHOENIX, AZ 85064
PH: (001) (602) 957 6443
FX: (001) (602) 957 1861
Specialties: US colonial coins, US silver, gold medals

FREEMAN + SEAR (David R. Sear, Robert D. Freeman, Tory Fleming Freeman)
PO Box 641352, LOS ANGELES, CA 90064-6352
PH: (001) (310) 202 0641 and (001) (818) 993 7607
FX: (001) (310) 202 0641 and (001) (818) 993 6119
List Mail Bid Sales Auctions
Specialties: Ancient Greek, Roman and Byzantine coins

FROSETH INC., K.M. (Kent Froseth)
PO Box 23116,
MINNEAPOLIS, MN 55423
PH: (001) (612) 831 9550
FX: (001) (612) 835 3903
E-mail: Kmfcoi19@mail.idt.net
Specialties: US, foreign gold and silver coins

GILLIO INC., Ronald J. (Ronald Gillio)
Goldmünzen International
1103 State Street, SANTA BARBARA, CA 93101
PH: (001) (805) 963 1345
FX: (001) (805) 962 6659
List Publications Auctions
Specialties: US Gold, especially rare dates and proofs, US type coins. All Oriental and Asian numismatics, especially Japan, Korea and Taiwan

HINDERLING, Wade
PO Box 606, MANHASSET, NY 11030
PH: (001) (516) 365 3729
Specialties: Coins of the U.S. and France

KOLBE, George Frederick
Fine Numismatic Books
PO Drawer 3100, CRESTLINE, CA 92325-3100
PH: (001) (909) 338 6527
FX: (001) (909) 338 6980
List Publications Auctions
Specialties: Numismatic literature

KOVACS, Frank L.
PO Box 25300, SAN MATEO, CA 94402
(suburb of San Francisco)
PH: (001) (415) 574 2028
FX: (001) (415) 574 1995
Specialties: Ancient and Byzantine coins and antiquities

KREINDLER, B. & H.
15 White Birch Drive, DIX HILLS, NY 11746
PH: (001) (516) 423-0176
FX: (001) (516) 547-0758
Specialties: Ancient numismatics

MALTER & CO. INC., Joel L.
(Joel and Michael Malter)
17005 Ventura Blvd., ENCINO, CA 91316
PH: (001) (818) 784 7772 / 784 2181
FX: (001) (818) 784 4726
List (quarterly) Publications Auctions
Specialties: Ancient and medieval coins, classical antiquities, numismatic books and literature

MARGOLIS, Richard
(Richard and Sara Margolis)
PO Box 2054, TEANECK, NJ 07666
PH: (001) (201) 848 9379
FX: (001) (201) 847 0134
Publications
Specialties: Foreign coins, medals, tokens, patterns

PONTERIO & ASSOCIATES, Inc.
(Richard Ponterio, Stewart Westdal, M. Fletcher, Kent Ponterio, Carola Ponterio, Kris Ponterio, Cynthia Ponterio)
1818 Robinson Ave., SAN DIEGO, CA 92103
PH: (001) (619) 299 0400
FX: (001) (619) 299 6952
Auctions
Specialties: Coins, medals and banknotes of Mexico and Latin America, world paper money, gold coins and crowns, ancient coins

RARE COIN COMPANY OF AMERICA, Inc.
(E. Milas, J. Bernberg)
6262 South Route 83, WILLOWBROOK, IL 60514
PH: (001) (630) 654 2580
FX: (001) (630) 654 3556
Auctions
Specialties: US, foreign type coins and paper money

ROSS, John G.
55 West Monroe Street, Suite 1070, CHICAGO, IL 60603
PH: (001) (312) 236 4088
Specialties: US coins, coins of the world

RYNEARSON, Dr. Paul
PO Box 4009, MALIBU, CA 90264
PH: (001) (310) 457 7713
FX: (001) (310) 457 6863
List Publications Mail Bid
Specialties: Ancient and world coinage

STACK'S
(Harvey and Lawrence Stack)
123 West 57 Street, NEW YORK, NY 10019

PH: (001) (212) 582 2580
FX: (001) (212) 245 5018
List Publications Auctions
Specialties: United States, European, ancient, medieval

STEPHENS Inc., Karl (Karl Stephens)
PO Box 458, TEMPLE CITY, CA 91780
PH: (001) (818) 445 8154
FX: (001) (818) 447 6591
List
Specialties: Foreign coins, medals, tokens, Eastern Europe, US type and copper coins

SUBAK Inc.
(Carl and Jon Subak, Peter Klem)
22 West Monroe Street,
Room 1506, CHICAGO, IL 60603
PH: (001) (312) 346 0609 / 346 0673
FX: (001) (312) 346 0150
Specialties: Roman, Byzantine, medieval

TELLER NUMISMATIC ENTERPRISES
(M. Louis Teller, Ph.D., A. Wing)
16027 Ventura Blvd., Suite 606,
ENCINO, CA 91436
PH: (001) (818) 783 8454
FX: (001) (818) 783 9083
Specialties: Gold and silver coins of the world. Specialist in Russia, China, 19th century Oriental coins and choice foreign paper money

WADDELL, Ltd., Edward J.
(Edward J. Waddell Jr.)
Suite 316, 444 N. Frederick Ave.,
GAITHERSBURG, MD 20877
(Suburb of Washington, D.C.)
PH: (001) (301) 990 7446
FX: (001) (301) 990 3712
List
Specialties: Greek, Roman, Byzantine and medieval coins; numismatic literature

WORLD-WIDE COINS OF CALIFORNIA
(James F. Elmen)
PO Box 3684,
SANTA ROSA, CA 95402
PH: (001) (707) 527 1007
FX: (001) (707) 527 1204
List Auctions
Specialties: World coins and medals 1500 to date

INTERNATIONAL NUMISMATIC ORGANIZATIONS

The following is a list of international numismatic organizations. This information is current as of the publication date. It is suggested that you write, call, or fax for more up-to-date membership information. If your organization is not listed, please send information to the author for inclusion in subsequent editions.

AUSTRALIA

• NUMISMATIC ASSOCIATION OF AUSTRALIA, P.O. Box 1920 R, GPO Melbourne, Victoria 3001 AUSTRALIA

• TASMANIAN NUMISMATIC SOCIETY, INC., 1 Fern Court, Clarmont, Tasmania 7011 AUSTRALIA. PH: 2-278825

BELGIUM

• SOCIETE ROYALE DE NUMISMATIQUE DE BELGIQUE, Musee de la Banque Natl.e, 14, Blvd. de Berlaymont, B-1000 Brussels, BELGIUM. Contact: Luc Smolderen

CANADA

• CANADIAN NUMISMATIC ASSOCIATION, P.O. Box 226, Barrie, ONTARIO L4M 4T2. Contact: Kenneth B. Prophet, PH: 705-737-0845, FX: 705-737-0293

The CNA is a non-profit educational and social body incorporated by Dominion Charter in 1963. It has grown by leaps and bounds from an idea of dedicated numismatists to form the world's second largest numismatic association.

Their present membership is basically located in Canada and the United States but they do have additional members around the world. They all have one common interest and that is Canadian numismatics.

As a member of the Association you will be eligible to receive the CNA/NESA Numismatic Correspondence Course at a reduced cost. You will receive the Journal *which carries articles, advertisements by dealers/members, and information about other CNA activities.*

The Journal *has been published since 1966 and has carried many of the most important papers relating to Canadian numismatics.*

CHINA

• CHINA NUMISMATIC SOCIETY, 32 Chengfang Street, Xicheng District, Beijing 100800, PEOPLE'S REPUBLIC OF CHINA. Contact: Zhi qiang Dai, Sec. Gen., PH: 86-1-6069935, FX: 86-1-6016414

• ORIENTAL NUMISMATIC SOCIETY (ONS), 30 Warren Road, Woodley, Reading, Berks RG5 3AR, England. Contact: Michael R. Broome, Sec. Gen., PH: 44-1734-693528 *American Region, P.O. Box 356, New Hope, PA. Contact: W.B. Warden, Sec.

The aims of the Society are to promote the systematic study of the coins, medals, and currency, both ancient and modern, of India, the Far East, the Islamic countries and their non-Western predecessors. It was founded in 1970 and its membership of some 650 people is spread over 40 countries.

CROATIA

• CROATIAN NUMISMATIC SOCIETY, RR1, P.O. Box 729-F, Rockville, IN 47872.

A current price list for Bosnian, Croatian, Macedonian, Serbian, Slovenian, and Yugoslavian bank notes and coins is available from the society. This list is free to all interested collectors when accompanied by a stamped, self-addressed envelope from the U.S.A., or cost of postage from other countries. Also available from the society is a limited number of large geographic maps of the Independent State of Croatia, 1941–45, in color.

DENMARK

• DANISH TOKEN CLUB, Støden 3, DK- 4000 Roskilde, DENMARK. Contact: Viktor Søndergaard, PH: 0045-46-35-88-63

• FUNEN NUMISMATIC SOCIETY, Odense Söhusvej, DK- 5270 Odense N., DENMARK. Contact: Ole Halkjaer Nielsen, FX: 45-65978628, E-Mail: ohn@post6.tele.dk

• NORDIC NUMISMATIC UNION, Royal Collection of Coins & Medals, National Museet, DK-1220 Copenhagen K DENMARK. Contact: Jorgen Steen Jensen, Exec. Officer, PH: 45-33134411, FX: 45-33155521

FRANCE

• LA SOCIETE AMERICAINE POUR L' ETUDE DE LA NUMISMATIQUE FRANCAISE, 5140 East Boulevard N.W., Canton, OH 44718

GERMANY

• DEUTSCHE NUMISMATISCHE GESELLSCHAFT, Dr. R. Albert H. Ehrend, Leharstr. 17,6720 Speyer GERMANY

• VERBAND DER DEUTSCHEN MUNZVEREINE, Assoc. of German Numismatic Societies, Reisenbergstr 58A, 8000 Munich 60 GERMANY

GREECE

• HELLENIC NUMISMATIC SOCIETY, Elleniki Nomismatiki Etaireia, Didotou 45, 106 8 Athens, GREECE. PH: 30-1-3615-585, FX: 30-1-3934-296

ISRAEL

• AMERICAN ISRAEL NUMISMATIC ASSOCIATION, P.O. Box 940277, Rockaway Park, NY 11694-0277. Contact: Edward Schuman, PH: 718-634-9266, FX: 718-318-1455

• ISRAEL NUMISMATIC SOCIETY, P.O. Box 750, Jerusalem, ISRAEL. TELEX: 26598, FX: 972-2-249779

• I.N.S.L.A./I.C.C.L.A. ISRAEL NUMISMATIC SOCIETY/ISRAEL COIN CLUB OF LOS ANGELES, 432 South Curson Avenue, Los Angeles, CA 90036. Contact: Murray Singer

The INSLA has been active in the Israel numismatic field over 28 years. Activities are devoted to the study and collection of numismatic items (both ancient and modern) related to Israel in particular and the Holy Land area in general.

Meetings feature educational programs covering coins, medals, paper money, and exonumia, as well as the material of the Palestine Mandata era.

Each meeting of INSLA/ICCLA is affilliated with the ANA, AINA, NASC, and CSNA.

INDIA

• NUMISMATIC SOCIETY OF INDIA, P.O. Box Banaras Hindu University, Varanasi, 221-005 INDIA

LITHUANIA

• LITHUANIAN NUMISMATIC ASSOCIATION—The Knight, P.O. Box 612, Columbia, MD 21045

MALAYSIA

• MALAYSIA NUMISMATIC SOCIETY, P.O. Box 12367, Kuala Lumpur, 50776 MALAYSIA

MEXICO

• SOCIEDAD NUMISMATICA DE MEXICO A. C., Eugene No. 13-301, Col. Nápoles, C. P. 03810, MEXICO. PH: 536-4440, FX: 543-1791

The society publishes a trimestral bi-lingual journal. The society periodically organizes auctions. Members receive catalogs and prices realized of these auctions and may also place numismatic items of their own for auction sale.

• SOCIEDAD NUMISMATICA DE MONTERREY C. A., Apartado Postal No. 422, Monterrey, N. L. MEXICO, C. P. 64000. Contact: Ing. Carlos Olivares Guzmá, PH: 8-331-1331, FX: 8-351-3444, E-Mail: fscagonz@vto.com

The society is a scientific and cultural institution, founded on 10/15/70, for promotion, increasing and divulgation of numismatic concerns for the numismatic and mainly for the Mexican numismatic, through research and knowledge of coins, medals, tokens and bills.

NEW ZEALAND

• ROYAL NUMISMATIC SOCIETY OF NEW ZEALAND, G.P.O., Box 2023, Wellington, NEW ZEALAND

PORTUGAL

• CLUBE NUMISMATIC DE PORTUGAL, Rua Angelina Vidal 40, 1100 Lisbon, PORTUGAL

• SOCIEDADE PORTUGUESA DE NUMISMATICA, Rua De Costa Cabral, 664, 4200 Porto PORTUGAL

RUSSIA

• RUSSIAN NUMISMATIC SOCIETY, P.O. Box 3013, Alexandria, VA 22302. Contact: Sec. Treas., PH: 703-920-2043, FX: 703-920-9345.

The Society was established in 1979. Since 1981 the Society's journal, the JRNS, *is published three times a year and is the principle element holding the Society to its course. In support of its editorial work, the Society maintains a very comprehensive library of standard and specialized works on Russian numismatics, many of which are available on loan to the members. The Society provides advice and support on research resources.*

SOUTH AFRICA

• SOUTH AFRICAN NUMISMATIC SOCIETY, P.O. Box 1689, Cape Town, 8000 SOUTH AFRICA

SPAIN

• ASOCIACION NUMISMATICA ESPAÑOLA, Gran via de las Corts Catalanes 627, 08010 Barcelona, SPAIN. FX: 34-3-3189062

SWITZERLAND

• COMMISSION INTERNATIONAL NUMISMATIQUE (CIN), Rutimeyer Strasse 12, CH-4054, Basel SWITZERLAND

• INTERNATIONAL ASSOCIATION OF PROFESSIONAL NUMISMATISTS (INAP), Loewenstrasse 65, CH-8001 Zurich, SWITZERLAND. Contact: Mr. Jean-Paul Divo, Gen. Sec., PH: 41-1-2211885, FX: 41-1-2112976

• NUMISMATISCHER VEREIN ZURICH, Postfach 4584, 8022, Zurich SWITZERLAND

• SOCIETE SUISSE de NUMISMATIQUE, Schweizerische Numismatische Gesellschaft, c/o Regie de Fribourg, 24 rue de Romong, CH-3701 Fribourg SWITZERLAND

THAILAND

• NUMISMATIC ASSOCIATION OF THAILAND, Royal Mint, 11017 Pradipat Road, Bangkok THAILAND

TURKEY

• TURKISH NUMISMATIC SOCIETY, P.K. 258, Osmanbey, Istanbul TURKEY

UKRAINE

• UKRAINIAN PHILATELIC & NUMISMATIC SOCIETY, P.O. Box 303, Southfields, NY 10975-0303

The Society was founded in 1952 and concentrates on collectibles (coins, banknotes, stamps, etc.) of Ukrainian themes. The Society publishes a bi-monthly newsletter and quarterly journal.

UNITED KINGDOM

• BRITISH ASSOCIATION OF NUMISMATIC SOCIETIES, c/o Bush Boake Allen, LTD., Blackhorse Lane, London E17 5QP, ENGLAND. Contact: P.H. Mernick, PH: 44-181-5236531, FX: 44-181-5318162

• BRITISH NUMISMATIC SOCIETY, c/o Hunterian Museum, Glasgow University, Glasgow G12 8QQ, SCOTLAND. Contact: J.D. Bateson, PH: 44-141-3304221, FX: 44-141-3078059

The British Numismatic Society was founded in 1903. The Society's terms of reference extend to cover all coins struck or used in Great Britain and Ireland from the introduction of coinage into Britain in the first century B.C. down to modern times. It also concerns itself with medals, tokens, etc., and with coinage of present or former British overseas territories and dependencies.

The British Numismatic Journal, *published annually by the Society and distributed to all paid-up members, provides the results of the most recent scholarly research into the history of the coinage, and records significant new numismatic discoveries. It is issued cloth-bound.*

Applications for membership from individuals or corporate bodies should be addressed to the Hon. Sec., Dr. J.D. Bateson, at the Hunterian Museum, University of Glasgow, University Avenue, Glasgow G128QQ.

• BRITISH SOCIETY, c/o Hunterian Museum, Glasgow University, Glasgow G12 8QQ SCOTLAND

• INTERNATIONAL NUMISMATIC COMMISSION, Dept. of Coins and Medals, British Museum, London WC1B 3DG, ENGLAND. Contact: Dr. A.M. Burnett, Sec., PH: 44-171-3238227, FX: 44-171-3238171

• ROYAL NUMISMATIC SOCIETY, Dept. Coins/Medals, British Museum, Great Russell Street, London WC1B 3DG, ENGLAND. Contact: V. Hewitt, PH: 44-171-3238173

The Society was founded in 1836 as the Numismatic Society of London and received the title of the Royal Numismatic Society by Royal Charter in 1904. The Society is an academic body of charitable status concerned with research into all branches of numismatics. Its lectures and publications deal with classical, oriental, medieval, and modern coins, as well as paper money, tokens, and medals.

• THE IPSWICH NUMISMATIC SOCIETY, PO BOX 104, Ipswitch, IP5, 7QL, UNITED KINGDOM. Contact: S. E. Sewell, PH: 01473-626950, FX: Same

U.S.A.

• AMERICAN NUMISMATIC ASSOCIATION, 818 North Cascade Avenue, Colorado Springs, CO 80903-3279. Contact: Robert Leuver, Exec. Dir., PH: 719-632-2646, FX: 719-634-4085, e-mail: ana@money.org

• AMERICAN NUMISMATIC SOCIETY, Broadway at 155th Street, New York, NY 10032, PH: 212-234-3130, FX: 212-234-3381

• ANCIENT COIN CLUB OF LOS ANGELES, P.O. Box 227, Canoga Park, CA 91305. Contact: Ralph J. Marx.

This club was established in 1966 and features highly informative and enjoyable programs on ancient Greek or Roman numismatics and cultures, as well as afternoons of coin trading exhibits and door prizes. Visitors are cordially invited to attend their meetings and meet others who share the same numismatic interests.

The club publishes a monthly newsletter and is a member of COIN and NASC.

• CALIFORNIA EXONUMIST SOCIETY, P.O. Box 6909, San Diego, CA 92166-0909. Contact: Kay Lenker, Sec.

Established in 1960, the California Exonumist Society (CES) encourages the study and collecting of exonumia—medals, tokens, script, orders and decorations, and all non-governmental items used for barter or trade.

CES meets and conducts educational forums in conjunction with the major conventions of GSCS and CSNA (Northern Calif.). CES sponsors an All-Day Collectibles Show with bourse dealers specializing in exonumia items and invitational.

CES's current president is Dorothy Baker. CES publishes a quarterly newsletter, The Medallion.

• COUNCIL OF INTERNATIONAL NUMISMATICS, P.O. Box 3637, Thousand Oaks, CA 91359. Contact: Sally Marx, President, PH: 805-495-1930

The Council of International Numismatics (COIN) was founded in 1963. Their goal is to promote interest in the collecting of foreign and ancient coins, foreign currency, medals, tokens, and other means of exchange.

At the present time there are seven clubs making up the council membership; there is no individual membership in COIN.

• INTERNATIONAL NUMISMATIC SOCIETY AUTHENTICATION BUREAU, P.O. Box 33134, Philadelphia, PA 19142. Contact: Charles R. Hoskins, Treas., PH: 215-365-0752, FX: 215-365-0752

• INTERNATIONAL NUMISMATIC SOCIETY OF SAN DIEGO, P.O. Box 6909, San Diego, CA 92166. Contact: Kay Lenker, Sec.

The International Numismatic Society of San Diego pursues the interest of foreign numismatics.

The club is affilliated with the American Numismatic Association (ANA) and California State Numismatic Association (CSNA).

• NUMISMATICS INTERNATIONAL, P.O. Box 670013, Dallas, TX 75367-0013. Contact: Jack Lewis, Membership Chair., PH: 214-361-7543

Numismatics International was formed in Dallas, Texas, in July 1964 and now has well over 800 members worldwide.

Their objectives are to encourage and promote the science of numismatics by specializing in areas and nations other than the United States; to cultivate fraternal relations among collectors and numismatic students; to encourage and assist new collectors; to foster the interest of youth in numismatics; to stimulate and advance affiliations among collectors and kindred organizations; and to acquire, share, and disseminate numismatic knowledge.

• SOCIETY FOR ANCIENT NUMISMATICS (SAN), P.O. Box 4085, Panarama City, CA 91412-4095. Contact: Dr. Lawrence A. Adams.

The Journal *of the Society for Ancient Numismatics (SAN) is published twice yearly. The SAN* Journal *supports the field of ancient numismatics with its wide range of articles and illustrations by scholars, professional numismatists, collectors, and amateurs with special perspectives. The* Journal *may be found in many of the world's foremost university and museum libraries.*

• SOCIETY FOR INTERNATIONAL NUMISMATICS, P.O. Box 943, Santa Monica, CA 90406. Contact: Barry Lapes, PH: 310-399-1085

The Society for International Numismatics is an international organization dedicated to the promotion of serious numismatic studies, endeavoring to bring to the collecting fraternity special items of interest and fundamental information. They hope their work will stimulate the individual study of numismatics from a practical as well as historical and economic viewpoint.

The Society's publications are: SINformation, *the Society's news journal;* COIN *(Compendium of International Numismatics), composed of original articles by Society members; and* NUMOGRAM, *a "Reader's Digest" of numismatic articles.*

The Society also publishes papers from its various bureaus on a periodic basis and presents educational forums and lecture programs for the collecting fraternity.

• WORLD PROOF NUMISMATIC ASSOCIATION, P.O. Box 4094, Pittsburgh, PA 15201. Contact: Gail P. Gray, PH: 412-782-4477, FX: 412-782-0227

INTERNATIONAL NUMISMATIC PUBLICATIONS

AUSTRALIA

• TASMANIAN NUMISMATIST, Tasmanian Numismatic Society, Inc., 1 Fern Court, Claremont, Tasmania 7011, AUSTRALIA. PH: 2-278825.

AUSTRIA

• NUMISMATIK SPEZIAL, Zeitungsverlag Kuhn und Co.GmbH, Kutschkergasse 42, A-1180 Vienna, AUSTRIA. PH: 01-47686, FX: 01-4768621. **Document type:** Consumer publication.

BELGIUM

• REVUE BELGE DE NUMISMATIQUE ET DE SIGILLOGRAPHIE, Royale de Numismatique de Belgique, c/o J.A. Schoonheit, Treas., 1 av. G. van Nerom, 1160 Brussels, BELGIUM. PH: 32-2-6728904. **Document type:** Academic/scholarly publication.

CANADA

• CANADIAN NUMISMATIC JOURNAL, Canadian Numismatic Association, P.O. Box 226, Barrie, Ontario L4M 4T2, CANADA. PH: 705-737-0845, FX: 705-737-0293. **Summary of content:** Aims to encourage and promote the science of numismatics by the study of coins, paper money, medals, tokens, and all other numismatic items, with special emphasis on material pertaining to Canada.

• CANADIAN COIN NEWS, Trajan Publishing Corp., 202–103 Lakeshore Road, Saint Catherines, Ontario L2N 2T6, CANADA. PH: 905-646-7744, FX: 905-646-0995. **Summary of content:** Whether numismatist or novice, it brings the collector the most complete, most authoritative, and most timely news available, with features on tokens and paper money to the finest coverage of Canadian decimal coinage.

CHINA

• ZHONGGUO QIANBI/CHINA NUMISMATICS (Zhongguo Qianbi Xuehui), Zhongguo Qianbi Bianjibu, 32 Chengfang Jie, Xicheng, Bejing 100800, PEOPLE'S REPUBLIC OF CHINA. PH: 86-10-6015522, FX: 86-10-6016414. **Document type:** Academic/scholarly publication. **Summary of content:** Publishes research on numismatics or the history of coins, news of excavations, and interesting anecdotes about coins; introduces historic coins, presents the experiences of coin collectors, and reports on related events in China and the world. Text in Chinese.

CZECH REPUBLIC

• NUMISMATICKE LISTY, Narodni Muzeum, Vaclavske nan.68, 115 79 Prague 1, CZECH REPUBLIC. Text in Czech; summaries in English, French, German, and Russian.

DENMARK

• NORDISK NUMISMATISK UNION MEDLEMSBLAD, Nordisk Numismatisk Union, c/o Royal Collection of Coins and Medals, National Museum, DK-1220 Copenhagen K, DENMARK. FX: 45-33-15-55-21.

ENGLAND

• COINS MARKET VALUES, Link House Magazines, Ltd, Link Hse, Dingwall Avenue, Croydon, Surrey, CR9 2TA ENGLAND. PH: 0180-686-2599, FX: 0181-760-0973. **Summary of Content:** Numismatics, all British coinage: medieval and modern.

• COIN NEWS, Token Publishing, Ltd., P.O. Box 20, Axminister, Devon, EX13 7YT ENGLAND. PH: 01404-831878, or 01404-831895. **Summary of content:** General magazine for collectors covering coins, medals, and banknotes.

• COIN NEWS COIN YEARBOOK, Token Publishing, Ltd, P.O. Box 20, Axminister, Devon, EX13 7YT ENGLAND. PH: 01401-831878, FX: 01401-831895. **Summary of content:** Yearbook covering all aspects of coin collecting, and price guide to coins, banknotes, and medallions.

• NUMISMATIC CIRCULAR, Spink and Son, Ltd., 5 King Street, St. James's, London, ENGLAND. PH: 44-171-930-7888, FX: 44-171-839-4853. **Document type:** Catalog.

FINLAND

• NUMISMAATIKKO, Suomen Numismaatikkoliitto, P.O. Box 895, FIN-00101 Helsinki, FINLAND. PH: 358-31-631-480, FX: 358-31-631-480.

FRANCE

• NUMISMATIQUE & CHANGE, SEPS, 12 rue Poincare, 55800 Revigny, FRANCE. PH: 29-70-56-33, FX 29-70-57-44.

• REVUE NUMISMATIQUE (Societe Francaise de Numismatique), Societe d'Edition les Belles Lettres, 95 Boulevard Raspail, 75006 Paris, FRANCE. PH: 1-45485826, FX: 1-45485860. **Document type:** Academic/scholarly publication.

GERMANY

• DER GELDSCHEINSAMMLER, H. Gietl Verlag and Publikations Service GmbH, Postfach 166, 93122 Regenstauf, GERMANY. PH: 49-9402-5856, FX: 49-9402-6635. **Document type:** Newsletter.

• NUMISMATISCHES NACHRICHTENBLATT, Deutsche Numismatische Gesellchaft, Hans-Purrmann-Allee 26, 67346 Speyer, GERMANY PH: 49-6232 35752. **Document type:** Newsletter.

GREECE

• NOMISMATIKA KHRONIKA, Hellenic Numismatic Society-Elleniki Nomismatiki Etalreia, Didotou 106 80 Athens, GREECE. PH: 30-1-3615-585, FX: 30-1-3634-296. **Document type:** Academic/scholarly publication, monographic series. **Summary of content:** Covers Greek and related numismatics of all periods. Translations or summaries in English.

INDIA

• JOURNAL NUMISMATIC SOCIETY OF INDIA, Numismatic Society of India, Banaras Hindu University, Varanasi 221005, INDIA. PH: 311074. Text in English.

IRAQ

• AL-MASKUKAT, Ministry of Culture and Information, State Organization of Antiquities and Heritage, Jamal Abdul Nasr Street Baghdad, IRAQ. PH: 4158355.

ISRAEL

• ISRAEL NUMISMATIC JOURNAL, Israel Numismatic Society, P.O. Box 750, Jerusalem, ISRAEL. PH: 26598, FX: 972-2-249779. **Document type:** Academic/scholarly publication. Text in English.

ITALY

• ISTITUTO ITALIANO DI NUMISMATICA, Istituto Italiano di Numismatica, Palazzo Barberini, Via Quattro Fontane 13, 00195 Rome, ITALY. PH: 39-6-4743603, FX: 39-6-4743603. **Document type:** Academic/scholarly publication. **Summary of content:** Presents research on numismatic subjects.

• NUMISMATICA, Gino Manfredini, Ed. & Pub., Via Ferramola 1-A, 25121 Brescia, ITALY. PH: 030-3756211. **Document type:** Newsletter.

• PANORAMA NUMISMATICO, 75000, Via Grimau 6-A, 46029 Suzzara (MN), ITALY. PH: 39-376-532063, FX: 39-376-521304. **Document type:** Academic/scholarly publication. **Summary of content:** Covers ancient and Italian numismatics for collectors and scholars.

• WORLD COLLECTIONS NEWS, World Wide Collections S.r.l., Corso Buenos Aires, 20-4, 16129 Genoa, ITALY. PH: 39-10-581463, FX: 39-10-561855. **Document type:** Newspaper.

NETHERLANDS

• EUROPEAN NUMISMATICS, Uitgeverij Numismatica Nederland N.V., Darwinplantsoen 26, Amsterdam 6, NETHERLANDS. Text in Dutch and English.

• JAARBOEK VOOR MUNT-EN PENNINGKUNDE, Koninklijk Nederlands Genootschap voor Munt-en Penningkunde-Royal Dutch Society of Numismatics, c/o The Netherlands Bank, Postbus 98, 1000 AB Amsterdam, NETHERLANDS. **Document type:** Academic/scholarly publication. Text in Dutch, occasionally in English, French, German; summaries in English.

POLAND

• LODZKI NUMIZMATYK, Polskie Towarzystwo Archeologiczne i Numizmatyczne, Oddzial w Lodzi, Plac Wolnosci 14, Lodz, POLAND.

• WIADOMOSCI NUMIZMATYCZNE/NUMISMATIC NEWS, Ossolineum Publishing House, Foreign Trade Department, Rynek 9, 50-106 Wroclaw, POLAND.

SLOVAKIA

• SLOVENSKA NUMIZMATIKA (Slovenska Akademia Vied) Veda, Publishing House of the Slovak Academy of Sciences, Klemensova 19, 814, 30 Bratislava, SLOVAKIA. Text in Slovak.

SPAIN

• GACETA NUMISMATICA, Asociacion Numismatica Espanola, Gran Via de les Corts Catalanes, 627, 08010 Barcelona, SPAIN. FX: 34-3-3189062. **Document type:** Academic/scholarly publication.

SWEDEN

• NUMISMATISKA MEDDELANDEN NUMISMATIC COMMUNICATIONS, Svenska Numismatiska Foereningen, Banergatan 17 nb, S-115 22 Stockholm, SWEDEN. PH: 46-8-667-55-98, FX: 46-8-6670771. **Document type:** Academic/scholarly publication.

SWITZERLAND

• GAZETTE NUMISMATIQUE SUISSE/SCHWEIZER MUENZBLAETTER, Alexander Wild, Rathausgasse 30, CH-3011 Bern, SWITZERLAND. **Document type:** Newsletter.

• HAUTES ETUDES NUMISMATIQUES (Ecole Pratique des Hautes Etudes, Centre de Recherches d'Histoire et de Philologie, FR), Librairie Droz S.A., 11, rue Massot, CH-1211 Geneva 12, SWITZERLAND. PH: 41-22-3466666, FX: 41-22-3472391, E-mail: drozsa@dial.eunet.ch;. URL:http://www.eunet.ch/customers/droz. circ.500. **Document type:** Monographic series. **Summary of content:** Examines ancient coins.

• MUENZEN-REVUE, International Coin Trend Journal, Verlag Muenzen-Revue AG, Blotzheimerstr.40, CH-4055 Basel, SWITZERLAND. PH: 41-61-3825504, FX: 41-61-3825542. **Document type:** Trade publication. **Summary of content:** Feature news, history, values, new coins, trade, as well as reports of events and auctions for coin hobbyists.

• NUMISMATICA E ANTICHITA CLASSICHE, Amici dei Quaderni Ticinesi di Numismatica e Antichita Classiche, Secretariat, C.P.3157, CH-6901 Lugano, SWITZERLAND. PH: 41-91-6061606. **Document type:** Academic/scholarly publication. Text in English, French, German, and Italian.

• REVUE SUISSE DE NUMISMATIQUE/SCHWEIZERISCHE NUMISMATISCHE RUNDSCHAU, Societe Suisse de Numismatique-

Schweizerische Numismatische Gesellschaft, Niederdorfstr. 43, CH-8001 Zurich, SWITZERLAND. **Document type:** Newsletter.

USA

• AMERICAN JOURNAL OF NUMISMATICS, SERIES 2, American Numismatic Society, Broadway at 155th Street, New York, NY 10032. PH: 212-345-3130, FX: 212-234-3381. **Summary of content:** Academic analysis of numismatic objects contributing to the understanding and interpretation of history, political science, archaeology, and art history.

• CLASSICAL NUMISMATIC REVIEW, Classical Numismatic Group, Inc., P.O. Box 479, Lancaster, PA 17608-0479. PH: 717-390-9194, FX: 717-390-9978.

• COIN WORLD, P.O. Box 4315, Sidney, OH 45365, PH: 1-800-253-4555. **Document type:** Weekly newspaper. **Summary:** Editorials on U.S. and world coinage, price listing, and dealer advertisements.

• PROOF COLLECTORS CORNER, World Proof Numismatic Association, Box 4094, Pittsburgh, PA 15201. PH: 412-782-4477, FX: 412-782-0227. **Document type:** Trade publication. **Summary of content:** Provides current coverage of numismatic issues, with information on the history and background of coins.

• SHEKEL, American Israel Numismatic Association, P.O. Box 940277, Rockaway Park, NY 11694-0277. PH: 718-634-9266, FX: 718-318-1455. **Document type:** Academic/scholarly publication. **Summary of content:** Presents collection of Israel and Judaic coins, medals, and currency from antiquity to the present.

• SINFORMATION, Society for International Numismatics, Box 943, Santa Monica, CA 90406. PH: 213-396-4662. **Document type:** Newsletter.

• THE CELATOR, Journal of Ancient and Medieval Art and Artifacts, Celator, Inc., P.O. Box 123, Lodi, WI 53555. PH: 608-592-4684, FX: 608-592-4684, E-mail: celator@aol.com. **Document type:** Consumer publication. **Summary of content:** Articles and features about ancient coins and artifacts, connoisseurship, and market news.

VIRGIN ISLANDS

• MONETA INTERNATIONAL, Coins and Treasures Monthly, Vernon W. Pickering, P.O. Box 704, Road Town—Tortola, BRITISH VIRGIN ISLANDS, W.I. PH: 809-49-43510, FX: 809-494-4540. **Summary of content:** Covers coin collecting and numismatic research from ancient to modern coins.

COIN AUCTION SALES

$99,000 for an 1825 Russian Ruble of Constantine! $143,000 for an 1862 British Columbia $20! $18,150 for an 1839 British gold 5-pound piece!

by Q. David Bowers

Auctions are a vital part of the coin hobby. Indeed, from the standpoint of news value, auction action captures more headlines than any other field of commercial activity. Just recently Bowers and Merena Galleries (which advertises as America's most successful rare coin auctioneer) sold at auction the finest collection of Canadian coins ever to cross the block—the fabulous Norweb cabinet. The total realization exceeded $2,000,000 (U.S. funds) and many records were set in the meantime. Highlighting the event was a beautiful gold $20 piece struck in British Columbia in 1862, which crossed the block at a record-breaking $143,000.

Representative of the field of world coins in general, the collection formed over a long period of years by Ambassador and Mrs. R. Henry Norweb was echoed in headlines around the United States, indeed all over the world. Records are made to be broken, and this sale had its share. Focusing for a moment on Canadian pieces, the Norweb Collection included the following, giving the highest price in each of various denominations in the Canadian series:

NORWEB COLLECTION CANADIAN COIN HIGHLIGHTS

1. 1925 one-cent piece with special Proof finish	$3,630
2. 1885 five-cent piece. Gem Uncirculated	27,500
3. 1921 five-cent piece. Known as the "Prince of Canadian Coins"	24,200
4. 1875 ten-cent piece with H mintmark, gem Proof	17,600
5. 1886 twenty-five-cent piece, Proof	34,100
6. 1921 fifty-cent piece, Gem Uncirculated "King of Canadian Coins"	82,000
7. 1935 silver dollar, Gem Proof	12,100
8. 1916 sovereign struck at the Ottawa Mint, Gem Uncirculated	16,500

WORLDWIDE ACTIVITY

In America, while Bowers and Merena Galleries was busy selling the Norweb Collection, other firms such as Superior Galleries, Stack's, Ponterio & Wyatt, Sotheby's, Christie's, Heritage, and others were preparing catalogues or scheduling events which often showcased coins of the world, in addition to United States issues. Also important in the program of most auctioneers are ancient coins of Greece and Rome, some of which have exquisite beauty and extraordinary values.

In Canada, Australia, England, Germany, Switzerland, France, and elsewhere, several dozen other auctioneers were and are active. Scarcely a week goes by on the calendar without an important auction of world coins being held somewhere or other on the globe.

A TRUE TEST OF VALUE

Auctions are perhaps the truest test of coin values worldwide. One can talk about "bid" and "ask" prices in various numismatic publications, and general market guides, but do actual transactions occur at these figures? The bottom line is that a coin is worth what someone will pay for it. An auction price, assuming that the sale is conducted in a professional manner, that "reserves" are disclosed, that the catalogue is widely distributed, and that the sale is publicized, represents what a given coin, token, medal, or piece of paper money is worth in a given moment of time. For example, if I were to state to you that a certain coin in Very Fine grade fetched $1,200 at a recent sale, you would be hard pressed to argue that it was only worth $500 or, conversely, it was worth $3,000. Rather, $1,200 represents the current market value at the moment.

However, sometimes in the case of "name" sales, coins will bring more than their normal prices at auctions. Let me explain:

AUCTION "FEVER"

There are a lot of interesting stories that can be told with regard to auction sales. One of my favorites treats the incredible collection of Stanislaw Herstal, which was catalogued by Karl Stephens of our staff, and showcased at auction in February 1974. Herstal, a citizen of Poland, was born in 1908. He grew up in a very artistic family; his mother was a poetess, his sister a pianist, and his brother an actor and producer. This artistic background fostered an early interest in numismatics. During the great European conflict, a great part of his collection—some 11,000 coins in all—disappeared, never to be returned to him. Still his enthusiasm continued, and new areas of study and collecting were explored. The collection grew again. Years later, we were given the privilege of handling his estate. This came on the heels of a major United States collection. For the first event, the United States coins, the gallery was filled to capacity, excitement prevailed, and records were broken. Then the scene shifted to the specialized offering of Polish pieces. At that time, February 7–9, 1974, Poland was solidly behind the Iron Curtain, and few people in that country had the means or opportunity to bid on their own coins. I mention this as often if there is an active coin-collecting community within a country, this strengthens prices. United States citizens mainly want to buy United States coins, Canadian citizens mainly want to buy Canadian coins, British citizens mainly want to buy British coins and so on. However, in the present instance, while Polish citizens may have wanted to buy Polish coins, they were not able to do so. Thus, the market was left to those in other countries. As the last United States coin was sold, the chairs emptied one by one. Finally, just a handful of people remained. Panic! What will happen? These thoughts ran through my mind. Not to worry. It takes only two bidders to run up the price of a coin at auction, or even to set record prices. It turned out that a small group of bidders, while not impressive in numbers, had very well-endowed bank accounts and were determined to buy these coins. A bidding war ensued, and when the dust settled, many pieces sold for five to ten times their previously estimated market values! I will never forget this occurrence.

In another time a beautiful proof silver ruble of Constantine of Russia, 1825, was consigned to one of our sales. This issue is especially desirable as only a few pieces are known with the portrait of this ruler. Even major collections are apt to lack an example, and many specialists have never *seen* a Constantine ruble, let alone have had the opportunity to buy one.

What was the coin worth? When it was catalogued for sale by us in 1994 as an additional consignment to the collection of the Massachusetts Historical Society, no one was sure. $20,000? That figure seemed too low, but certainly a bid at that level would have been competitive. $40,000? Certainly a strong bid, but again there were no answers. The sale day came, and the audience rippled with excitement as the chance of a lifetime was about to occur. Many hands went in the air as the auctioneer called the opening of the lot, and as the bidding progressed a thousand dollars at a time, then in larger jumps, competition narrowed. Finally, amidst applause, the coin was sold for a record $99,000—the buyer being a representative of a financial institution in Russia (which by this time had secured a degree of financial freedom).

The foregoing also illustrates the appeal of world coins. In today's market, American collectors are more active than are those of any other country. Accordingly, United States coins are bid to much higher levels than coins of comparable rarity from other countries. The 1825 Constantine ruble of Russia is rarer than a United States silver dollar of 1804 (15 pieces being known of the latter). The 1804 dollar has sold in the hundreds of thousands of dollars on several occasions, and is valued at about the $1 million mark for a really outstanding specimen. This is about ten times the price of a Constantine ruble! Similarly, gold coins of the United States sell for many multiples than comparable rarities among gold coins of France, England, Australia, or other areas. While Americans will probably always have preference for United States coins, there are certainly interesting purchase opportunities in the price levels of other numismatic specialties.

HOW TO BE A SMART BIDDER

How should one participate in an auction? In my opinion, it is best to plan in advance. I recommend contacting different auction firms requesting sample copies of their catalogues, but please bear in mind that often a charge must be paid as catalogues can be very expensive to publish. Review the catalogues, paying particular attention to the Terms of Sale as they fluctuate from firm to firm. Issues to be concerned with are buyer's fees, return privileges, bidding options, etc. You are legally bound to those terms, and they are put into the catalogue for a specific purpose—not just for entertaining reading. Do not take them lightly or fail to read them! Please bear in mind that certain countries may have different regulations from those in effect in the United States. There are such things as export taxes to be considered, customs, duties, overseas postage, insurance or lack thereof, and so on. If you are bidding in an auction held in the United States, and are a United States citizen, the situation is fairly straightforward. However, if you are bidding elsewhere, be sure to seek specific advice as to the items just discussed. Some procedures are exceedingly complicated!

As a collector of world coins, you have many purchase possibilities. There are dozens of auction houses all over the globe, some of whom conduct major sales on a fairly regular basis, and others who have only occasional offerings. It probably is not practical to subscribe to every auction catalogue published. A good alternative is to sign up as a subscriber to a periodical on the subject, for example *World Coin News* (Krause Publications, Iola, WI 54945). Such a publication contains information as to forthcoming auctions, catalogue ordering information, etc. In this way you can specifically order the catalogues that interest you most.

Beyond this, certain firms have specialties. As an example, in London there are a number of auction houses specializing in British coins. If such are your forte, you may wish to become acquainted with these houses, whereas an auctioneer in Germany, for example, would be apt to have only minor offerings of British coins.

When bidding in a sale, it is also important to learn a bit about exchange rates. While some overseas firms may accept bids in American dollars, usually bids are wanted in the currency of the country in which the sale occurs. Conversion rates change from time to time, and while changes during a period of a few weeks—while your bids are on the way to the sale—will probably not be significant, still there might be a few percentage points. Be careful, and take this into consideration if you are watching your bids closely.

A typical auction firm will issue a catalogue describing each lot in detail. If you have a question about a piece, that question can often be answered on the telephone—assuming you wish to pay international telephone rates and you can find an operator in English. More practical may be the use of a fax. In that way time can be given for the other party to reply. Be sure to include instructions as to your fax number so that they can return the information. Of course, you need to have a personal or office fax address to do this (using a commercial fax service in a public facility may be unsatisfactory, as you may not receive the reply for a few days).

Terms in catalogues issued outside the United States may have different meanings. The numerical system of grading so common here in America has no counterparts elsewhere. Instead, adjectives are typically used, sometimes with descriptions that can mean different things to different buyers. For example, in France *flurde coin,* abbreviated fdc, is the equivalent of "gem." However, gem quality is often in the eye of the beholder. As is true anywhere, grading interpretations can vary.

If you plan to spend a large amount of money in a sale held outside the borders of the United States, you may wish to contact an American foreign coin specialist and commission him or her to exercise your bids. A fee will be charged for this service, but you will have a pair of expert eyes representing you, and this may answer some of your questions about grades, price levels, and so on. The investment would seem to be well worth it. Of course, arrangements have to be made in advance, and you will have to establish your credit with the agent. If an agent spends, say, $10,000 on your behalf at a London auction or one in Paris, he or she will expect you to immediately pay for these coins upon notification. If you don't like the grade of the coins, or have changed your mind about buying them, that is too bad, as the coins are yours and you are obligated to pay for them. This is a responsibility, and it should be carefully considered in advance. Your agent is representing you, not bidding on his or her own account.

Price estimates are sometimes given in auction catalogues, but actual results are apt to vary. While printed estimates can be used as a general guide, it is better to do your homework and see what comparable coins have sold for at other auctions, or ask some friends or dealer acquaintances for suggestions. It is sometimes the policy of auction houses to low-ball the estimates. For example, a coin that a dealer might readily pay $5,000 for in order to buy for stock, might be estimated in a catalogue at the equivalent of $3,000–$4,000. When the auction takes place, such a piece would naturally sell for more than $5,000. Those who are not "in the know" and who observe the prices realized would think that a record price was being set, for the $3,000–$4,000 estimate has been far exceeded. However, the facts of life are that the estimate was too low to begin with. This is a particularly popular practice with art auction houses and general auctioneers, less so with advanced coin specialists. After this particular sale takes place, order a copy of the "prices realized." Bear in mind that it is a practice of some houses not to state whether or not a coin has been sold, and the price might be listed, but may represent a buy-in by the owner. Nevertheless, a listing of prices will have some general value and will certainly guide you to your bids the next time around.

Many firms will gladly accommodate your request for a phone description. Furthermore, if you are an established collector with a history of successful coin buying, and are known to the auctioneer, an arrangement may be made whereby the coin can be sent to you for inspection, providing that the coin is returned the same day and that you pay postage and insurance both ways. This courtesy is commonly referred to as "mail inspection."

Participation in an auction sale can be by mail or in person. Before each auction, there is a lot viewing period during which each lot can be personally inspected. Most auctioneers firmly state that anyone who has had a chance to view lots beforehand, or anyone who is a floor bidder, cannot return a coin for any reason whatsoever, with the exception of authenticity. So do your homework earlier, not later!

BIDDING BY MAIL

If you plan to bid by mail, send in your bid sheet as early as you can. Remember that overseas delivery can be very erratic, and it is not unusual for mail to take a week or more to reach many places on the globe, even large cities. Fax is a better option. Request a return fax verifying the receipt of your bids. In that way you will be secure in the knowledge that the information has been received on a timely basis. If you are unknown to the auction house, start at an early date to establish credit, contacting the auction house as to the amount you wish to spend, and how credit should be arranged. Quite probably, a deposit will be required or an excellent bank reference will be needed. If you employ an agent in America to bid for you, this point becomes moot, as the agent will establish his or her own credit.

As a general bidding strategy, while compiling your bids, first determine the lots you are interested in and the amount which you are willing to pay for each. Be aware of current price levels. If a certain variety of Morgan silver dollar generally brings $500 on the retail market, the chances aren't very good that a bid of $300 will make you the owner. Conversely, there is no particular point in bidding $800 for it if you can buy one somewhere else for $500, unless you like the pedigree, toning, or some other aspect which differentiates the piece.

Many auction houses offer a reduction in the top bid if competition permits, but not all companies follow this practice. In any event, it is best not to count on this for if you bid $1,000, you may very well be charged $1,000. I reiterate that bids may need to be submitted in another currency, and it would be devastating to bid a figure in American dollars if the auction is to be conducted in British pounds—your dollar bids might be mistaken for pound bids, and you'll pay far too much! Conversely, if you are bidding in an auction in Belgium, where the franc is worth very little, a bid inadvertently submitted in dollars would have virtually no chance of success.

Once your bids are compiled, you can determine whether to utilize some of the special bidding options offered by the auction house. These special options help the mail bidder place as many potentially winning bids as possible.

Extreme care must be taken when bidding in overseas auctions, and again I suggest that employing an agent may be the most practical method, at least until you gain auction experience.

FLOOR BIDDING

At the sale itself, coins awarded to floor bidders are usually final. If a coin is overgraded, damaged, or even counterfeit, often that is simply too bad for the buyer—there is no recourse. (In the United States, rare-coin auctioneers generally guarantee the authenticity of what they sell, but this is not always the case in foreign countries.) It is important to study each piece carefully during lot-viewing time permitted before the sale, or have your agent do so. If you attend in person, I suggest viewing some coins that are not in the mainstream. And so forth. For example, if you are bidding on British coins, there is nothing more frustrating than to specialize in silver crown-size coins and look only at these, only to find at the sale itself that there are some wonderful bargains in, say, half crowns or copper pennies. If your numismatic appetite is versatile, be sure to check a few other series as well.

Bidding strategy at the sale itself has furnished the topic for endless discussions. Should I sit in the front? Or, will I better know what is going on if I sit in the back? Or, perhaps on the side would be best. There are no rules. Pick your favorite. In the case of foreign auctions, it's probably best not to decide until the sale itself begins. Watch what is going on, then determine what would be a position advantageous to your best interest.

Most auction houses furnish bidders with paddles or cards with printed numbers. Some bidders flick their paddles almost unnoticeably while others hold them up in the air like a banner. Personal preference is the key, but be sure the auctioneer knows what you are doing. If the auctioneer misses your bid, call out right at the time the lot is being sold. Generally the auctioneer at his discretion may reopen a lot if he feels that a legitimate mistake has been made on the auction floor, but he will not do this on a consistent basis for the same bidder who isn't paying attention.

After the sale, you will be required to make payment, probably on a draft from your bank to the bank of the auctioneer. Relatively few foreign auction firms want to take personal checks from the United States, except perhaps from dealers or other long-established accounts. If your purchases are nominal, you may take the coins with you, but be sure to have appropriate documents for customs. Alternatively, you may wish to have the auctioneer ship the coins to your United States address. Again, some forms will probably need to be filled out and regulations followed.

YOUR ROLE AS A SELLER—FINDING THE RIGHT AUCTIONEER

If you have a group of scarce and rare foreign (non-American) coins to sell, and the coins are valued at several thousand dollars or more in total, auction may be the route for you. By exposing your coins in an auction catalogue, thousands of potential bidders can become acquainted with them. On the other hand, if you have miscellaneous coins of low value, or bullion-type coins, a dealer with an over-the-counter business may offer a better price to buy such items for store stock.

If you live in the United States you can, of course, consign your coins to an auctioneer in a foreign country. However, it is far more practical to pick someone here in America. In that way the seller will talk your language, carefully answer any questions you may have and so on.

As a caveat at this point, I suggest that the vast majority of "miscellaneous foreign coins" owned by American citizens have very low values. In general, coins brought back as souvenirs from an overseas war or a grand tour of Europe, or a cruise to the orient have very little value in the United States. Time and again I have seen little value. For starters, before spending a great amount of emotional energy, if you feel you have coins of value, either have them appraised by a local coin shop (which may involve paying a fee), or secure a copy by purchase or loan of the Krause-Mischler reference, *The Standard Catalog of World Coins*. This immense volume, larger than most metropolitan phone books, lists just about everything.

If you find you have coins that are worth several thousand dollars or more, and the group consists of scarce and rare pieces (rather than bulk), then give some thought to choosing an auctioneer. Here are some questions you should ask:

What is the commission rate? What is the buyer's fee? Some auction houses will offer a reduced commission rate but an increased buyer's fee.

What do I get for this rate? Are there any extra charges? Are catalogue illustrations extra? What about photography? What about advertising? It is a practice for some auction houses to give a "minimum price" or cut-rate fee, and then charge extra to bring the service up to "normal." Find this out in advance.

Once the auction takes place, when will the settlement date be? How will I receive payment? Can I receive a portion of the expected realization in advance? If so, what interest rates are charged? What is the financial reputation of the company? Does the company have adequate insurance? How can I be sure that my valued coins and other numismatic items are in truly safe hands?

Does the auction house allow reserves? Can I bid on my own coins? What is the anticipated market for my consignment? What happens if someone bidding on my coins fails to pay his auction bill?

What type of coins has the firm handled in the past? Does the company specialize only in certain areas or does it offer many different services? How large is the staff and what are the qualifications of the individual staff members?

What is the reputation of the firm? What do past consignors think of the performance of the auction house? Is the company familiar with die varieties, great rarities, and obscure coins in addition to ones normally seen? Does the firm have a specialty such as Mexican coins, British coins, Oriental coins, or any other niche that might correspond to the coins you have?

What do the firm's catalogues look like? Are the descriptions appealing? Are the descriptions authoritative? What is the quality of the mailing list? Does it contain proven bidders? What type of advertising will be done for the catalogue featuring my coins?

In what town or city will the event be held? What are the facilities like?

I suggest that each of the preceding questions be answered with care and you may well think of other questions in addition.

IT'S THE BOTTOM LINE THAT COUNTS

Several years ago, I and another member of the Auctions by Bowers and Merena staff traveled to visit with the heirs to a very large collection of United States and world coins. Our firm offered a 10% commission rate to sell the pieces, stating that they would be presented in a Grand Format™ color-illustrated catalogue with no expense spared when it came to advertising, publicity, and the like.

While the owners of the coins seemed to be very impressed with our track record, the appearance of our past catalogues, our reputation, and other factors, there was one problem: a competitor had offered to do it for no commission rate at all! It was stated that the competitor's profit would be determined only by the buyer's fee.

To make a long story short, the coins were awarded to a company whose main expertise was not in coins but rather, in art and furniture. The sale came and went, and instead of realizing the approximately $1.5 million that the heirs hoped for, (and which I felt could be achieved with proper presentation), only about half that amount was obtained! Dealers at the sale had a field day, for few collectors had received a copy of the catalogue. I later reviewed a copy of the prices realized and noted that many issues sold for fractions of what I felt they could be sold for by my firm or, for that matter, by other leading rare-coins auctioneers. Virtually no advertising was placed by the other auction firm. And, apparently many of the catalogues went to people who were not proven buyers of the type of coins being offered.

To expand upon this further, if an auctioneer sells a coin for a $1,000 hammer price and charges you 10%, thus netting you $900, it might be a much better deal than if another auctioneer sells your coin for $600 and charges you no fee at all—netting you $600. If you were considering having surgery done, or having an architect design your house, or having your portrait painted, I cannot envision you saying "I am looking for the cheapest rate." Rather such considerations as past performance would be more important. So it should be with coins as well. As I believe John Ruskin said, "the bitterness of poor quality lasts much longer than the sweetness of low price."

A LASTING TRIBUTE

There are some aesthetic considerations to selling at auction. A finely prepared catalogue can be a memorial to you and your collecting activities. Although the coins once owned by you are in new hands, the catalogue will remain a lasting tribute to your collection for you to enjoy. In addition, most people who have spent many years collecting coins enjoy the pride and satisfaction that comes with the recognition a beautiful catalogue provides when their collections are sold.

If you form a collection over a long period of years, and if you enjoy numismatics to its fullest extent, selling your collection by auction can be the high point of your accomplishments.

Meanwhile, as you build your collection, auctions provide an interesting and exciting way to acquire pieces that you need.

Have fun!

AUCTIONS BY BOWERS AND MERENA

Auctions by Bowers and Merena, Inc., has had the good fortune of being in the forefront of numismatics for many years. Not only have we been market leaders in United States coins, we have handled many important world and ancient properties as well. Along the way we have received more "Catalogue of the Year" honors awarded by the Numismatic Literary Guild than all of our competitors combined. Of the top three most valuable U.S. coin collections ever to be sold at auction, we have catalogued and sold all three—the $46,000,000 Eliasburg collection, the $25,000,000 Garrett collection, and the $20,000,000 Norweb collection.

Values of world coins are less than United States coins, due to market demand as mentioned earlier. That is, a given Canadian rarity will sell for less than a United States rarity, ditto for a British rarity. Even so, many incredible realizations have been accomplished, including the landmark Guia collection of world gold coins auctioned by us in 1988 on behalf of an overseas client. Many records from this sale still echo today. Sample realizations include:

Spain: Charles III Gold 8 Escudos, 1762 JV. Seville. About Uncirculated. $77,000.

Spain: Ferdinand II (V of Spain). 10 Ducats (quadruple ducado), n.d. Choice Very Fine. $58,300.

Sweden: John III (1568–1592). 2 Rosenobles, or 5 Ducats, n.d. About Uncirculated. $57,200.

Italian States: John Galeazzo Maria Sforza, under the Regency of Lodovico il Moro (1481–1494). 2 Ducats, n.d. About Uncirculated. $55,000.

Italian States: Philip IV. 20 Zecchini, 1643. Extremely Fine. $82,500.

Italian States: Charles Emanuel II. 10 Scudi d'Oro, 1663. Very Fine. $61,600.

Italian States: Republic of Italy. Pattern Doppia, an II (=1803). Milan. Uncirculated, prooflike. $77,000.

If you would like a "World Coin Auction Kit" which includes a current auction catalogue and a full-color brochure on consigning your coins to auction, please send a certified check or money order in the amount of $10 to World Auction Kit, Auctions by Bowers and Merena, Inc., PO Box 1224, Wolfeboro, NH 03894.

We regret that we cannot engage in correspondence or appraisals of miscellaneous world coins, except for a fee of $5 or more per coin, payable in advance. An easy alternative is to acquire a copy of the aforementioned Krause-Mischler catalogue, and develop estimates on your own, or have a coin store in your own area offer information.

Note: There is no appraisal fee for established numismatists who have carefully formed numismatic collections with rarities, proofs, and other delicacies. The fee applies only to common issues without numismatic importance.

If you'd like immediate information on the most profitable way to sell your coins call John Pack, our Auction Manager, at 603-569-5095 ext. 53. Contacting us today may be the most financially rewarding decision you have ever made.

HOW TO USE THIS BOOK

This book was written as a guide to the world's most popular coins. To list every coin that was ever minted by every country in the world would fill a book many times this size. We, therefore, have chosen to list the coins that are readily available to the average collector, with prices that would accommodate the largest number of collectors. Considerable effort was expended to consolidate and verify the information listed. Should you have any questions or corrections, the authors would be grateful to hear your comments. Please write to: *Blackbooks,* P.O. Box 690312, Orlando, FL 32869.

The prices listed in this book represent the current collector values at the time of printing. Since some of the types and varieties of coinage fluctuate in price more than others, it would be wise to consult several sources, i.e. coin dealers and trade publications, before any transaction.

Apart from the chapter immediately following titled "Ancient Coins," each coin listing in this guide contains the following information:

DATE or DATE RANGE—Date ranges were used to conserve space. Likewise, listings for coins later than 1980 were generally omitted because of their minimal collector value.

COIN TYPE—This is the unit of measure on the face value of the coin.

VARIETY—This information usually describes the images that appear on either the obverse (front) or the reverse (back) of the coin. Please note that some varieties of the same denomination may command a higher price than others of the same denomination.

METAL—When known, the metallic content of the coin is listed.

ABP—This is the average buy price that coin dealers are buying from the public. Readers should understand that the actual prices paid by any given dealer will vary based on the dealer's inventory and the market demand in the dealer's specific area. Remember that this book is presented merely as a guide.

There are two reasons for not listing an ABP price for a particular coin. The first concerns *coins that* are not *made from a precious metal* (gold, silver, or platinum). If there is no price listed for this kind of coin, it means that the price that a dealer would pay would be minimal.

ABP prices are also not listed for *coins that* are *made of gold, silver, or platinum.* The reason for this is that the dealers usually buy this kind of coin based on its bullion value. In most cases they will pay you for the amount of gold, silver, or platinum that the coin contains plus a premium, i.e. the bullion "spot" price plus a percentage. When determining the melt or bullion value of the coin, the dealer not only will have to consider the weight of the coin, but he will also have to determine the purity level of the gold, silver, or platinum, i.e. pure silver (.999), sterling silver (.925), etc. These variables make it difficult for an inexperienced dealer to calculate the bullion value of a coin. We recommend contacting dealers that have experience in dealing in bullion coinage. We have included a bullion value chart in this book which you can use to approximate the bullion value, assuming the coin is made from gold, silver, or platinum. Don't forget that the purity level of the gold, silver, or platinum will affect the bullion value.

CURRENT RETAIL VALUES—These prices are listed in either average fine or average UNC (uncirculated) condition. It is of utmost importance that a coin be accurately graded before a value can be determined. Although *there is no universally accepted grading standards for world coinage,* we have adopted the two U.S. grading conditions of AVERAGE FINE and AVERAGE UNC for the purposes of this book.

AVERAGE FINE condition would be represented by a coin that exhibited a moderate amount of wear, but still had visible signs of all of the detail that could be found on a coin of UNC condition. Usually the higher relief areas on the coin show the most wear.

AVERAGE UNC condition or uncirculated condition would be a coin that was never in general circulation. Current issues of uncirculated coins can be purchased directly from the mints where they are made, or from dealers or other collectors. Usually the finish of an uncirculated coin is much brighter, with very few surface scratches. When building a collection with the more current issues, you should try to collect UNC specimens when possible.

PRICES—The prices that are listed are average prices for coins that were minted in that particular date range. The price for a coin of a specific date in that particular date range will vary slightly from the price indicated. This variation in price is based on several variables. Some of the factors that affect the price of a coin are: 1) the amount of coins that were minted, 2) the amount of coins in circulation, 3) the demand for that coin in your geographic area, and 4) the condition in which the coin is generally found.

INVENTORY CHECKLIST—For the purposes of record keeping, we have included a ☐ at the beginning of each listing. Write a check mark or darken the ☐ in front of each coin in your collection. By doing this you will have a portable record of your collection to take with you to coin shows and dealers.

We hope that you enjoy using this book and invite you to become familiar with the other books in the *Official Blackbook Price Guide* series.

There is the best-selling *Official Blackbook Price Guide of U.S. Coins* which lists more than 16,000 prices for every U.S. coin minted, including colonial tokens, farthings, halfpennies, and gold pieces, plus sections on varieties and errors. It is fully illustrated.

There is also the *Official Blackbook Price Guide of U.S. Paper Money* which lists more than 6,000 prices for every national note issued from 1861 to date, including demand notes, national bank notes, silver and gold certificates, treasury notes, federal reserve notes, and confederate currency. It too is fully illustrated.

And finally, there is the *Official Blackbook Price Guide of U.S. Postage Stamps* which lists more than 20,000 prices for general U.S. postage stamps issued from 1847 to date, plus revenue, stock transfer and hunting permit stamps, United Nations issues, mint sheets, and first day covers. It is fully illustrated in color.

These books are available from your local bookstores, coin shops, and from the publisher.

PNG—THE PROFESSIONAL NUMISMATISTS GUILD

The Professional Numismatists Guild, founded in 1955, had its inception in 1950 with Abe Kosoff. At the time, Kosoff was in partnership with Abner Kreisberg in Numismatic Gallery, a firm that was well known for handling major collections and rarities.

Kosoff and several other coin dealers believed that the hobby of coin collecting could be better served if a professional group was organized. After much effort, the Professional Numismatists Guild was established. Its motto, "Knowledge, Integrity, Responsibility" continues to reflect the aims of the not-for-profit organization.

For the first decade, membership in the Professional Numismatists Guild (PNG) was by invitation, and only a small number of dealers were asked to join. As time passed, the PNG achieved stature, experience, and wisdom, and the membership rolls were expanded.

Today, the PNG comprises a membership across the United States and abroad of virtually all leading professional numismatists. The depth and breadth of the membership brings a rich diversity to the group and has made its progress possible.

MEMBERSHIP IN THE GUILD

To join the PNG, a dealer must have experience in the field, must certify that he or she has significant financial worth, and must be elected by a majority of the present members. All the PNG members are subject to the rules and regulations of the Guild, which include an arbitration procedure for resolving disagreements between buyers and sellers of numismatic properties.

The Professional Numismatists Guild looks forward to many more years of enhancing the field of numismatics through adherence to strict ethical and professional standards, cooperative projects with the American Numismatic Association, educational efforts geared to hobbyists, and other programs to benefit what has rightfully been called the world's greatest hobby.

AAMLID, Jan Olav
(PNG #356)
OSLO MYNTHANDEL AS
Ovre Slottsgate 6
0157 OSLO,
(+47) 23 10 00 0
Fax: (+47) 23 10 00 25
Mon. 10-5, Tues.-Fri. 9-5, Sat. 10-2
Fixed price lists, publications, catalogs, auction sales.
eMail: *kontakt@oslomynthandel.no*
web site: *www.oslomynthandel.com*
Specialties: *Scandinavian coins & banknotes. Thai coins & banknotes. Ancient Roman & Greek coins.*

ABBOTT, John T.
(PNG ##203)
ABBOTT'S CORPORATION
33700 Woodward Avenue
Birmingham, MI 48009
(248) 644-8565
Fax: (248) 644-7038
9-6 Mon.–Fri., 9-4 Sat.
eMail: *John@abbottscorp.com*
web site: *www.abbottscorp.com*
Specialties: *Buying & selling collections, appraisals & portfolios.*

ADKINS, Gary
(PNG #352)
MINNEAPOLIS GOLD, SILVER AND NUMISMATIC SERVICES, INC.
5599 West 78th Street
Edina, MN 55439-2701
(952) 946-8877
Fax: (952) 946-8944
By appointment
Fixed price list. PCGS, NGC, ANACS authorized dealer.
Appraisals, liquidations.
eMail: *gary@coindeals.com*
web site: *www.coindeals.com*
Specialties: *Quality U.S. coins—all types for collectors & investors.*

AKERS, David W.
(PNG ##279)
DAVID AKERS NUMISMATICS, INC.
P.O. Box 373
Stuart, FL 34995-0373
(772) 781-4200
Fax: (772) 223-1964
By appointment only
eMail: *DWA38@aol.com*

ALLEVA, Buddy
(PNG #441)
NUMISMATICS UNLIMITED, INC.
504 Hicksville Rd., Suite 2
Massapequa, NY 11758
(516) 798-4170
Fax: (516) 797-8421
eMail: *nuicoins@optonline.net*
Specialties: *Want list specialist. Assistance in building collections & sets of all U.S. coins. Specializing in appraisals, U.S. commemoratives, U.S. currency, U.S. gold coins, patterns, type coins & silver dollars. "Always customer friendly!"*

ANKERMAN, Walt
(PNG #401)
CARLSBAD VILLAGE COINS
P.O. Box 1404
Bonsall, CA 92003
(760) 434-6601
(760) 723-8111
By appointment only
Fixed price lists.
Specialties: *Buying and selling all types of United States & foreign coins; all grading services available.*

AVENA, Daniel J.
(PNG #377)
ARC INC. T/A AVENA RARE COIN
2581 E. Chestnut Ave., Ste. B
Vineland, NJ 08361
(856) 794-1600
Fax: (856) 794-8818
8-5
eMail: *info@avenararecoin.com*
web site: *www.avenararecoin.com*
Specialties: *Buyers and sellers of all U.S. rare coins.*

AVENA, Daniel J. Jr.
(PNG #500)
ARC INC. T/A AVENA RARE COIN
2581 E. Chestnut Ave., Ste. B
Vineland, NJ 08361
(856) 794-1600
Fax: (856) 794-8818
8-5
eMail: *info@avenararecoin.com*
web site: *www.avenararecoin.com*
Specialties: *Buyers and sellers of all U.S. rare coins.*

AVENA, Robert L.
(PNG #377)
ARC INC. T/A AVENA RARE COIN
2581 E. Chestnut Ave., Ste. B
Vineland, NJ 08361
(856) 794-1600
Fax: (856) 794-8818
8-5
eMail: *info@avenararecoin.com*
web site: *www.avenararecoin.com*
Specialties: *Buyers and sellers of all U.S. rare coins.*

BAGG, Richard A.
(PNG #A586)
Q. DAVID BOWERS
P.O. Box 1224
Wolfeboro, NH 03894
Tel: (800) 458-4646
Fax: (603) 569-5319
Hours: 8:30-5 Mon.–Fri.
eMail: *rick@bowersandmerena.com*
web site: *www.bowersandmerena.com*
Specialties: *U.S. Coins, Auctions, Appraisals, Numismatic Literature. "Auction associate to Q. David Bowers in Bowers and Merena Galleries for more than 20 years, Rick Bagg brings to professional numismatics and to his company, a degree of expertise and consummate knowledge of numismatics with few parallels in numismatics including the showcasing of the Garrett Collection for The John Hopkins University, the Eliasberg Collection, the Norweb Collection and many other important auction properties."*
—Q. David Bowers.

BARNETT, Loren D.
(PNG #427)
BARNETT RARITIES CORP.
P.O. Box 2277
Birmingham, MI 48012
(248) 644-1124
Fax: (248) 644-3739
By appointment only
eMail: *BarnettRarities@aol.com*
Specialties: *U.S. gold coins, to the trade.*

BARR, Wallace
(PNG #AF534)
CERTIFIED COIN EXCHANGE (CCE)
10681 Haddington, #130

Houston, TX 77043
(713) 973-1616
Fax: (713) 973-8321
8 a.m. to 5 p.m.
eMail: *wbarr@atchou.com*
web site:
www.certifiedcoinexchange.com
Specialties: *Trading Networks.*

BART, Frederick J.
(PNG #585)
BART, INC.
P.O. Box 2
Roseville, MI 48066
(586) 979-3400
Fax: (586) 979-7976
eMail: *BartIncCor@aol.com*
web site:
www.ERRORNOTES.com
Specialties: *United States paper money.*

BATTAGLIA, Joseph C.
(PNG #A-517)
GOLDLINE INTERNATIONAL
100 Wilshire Blvd., 3rd floor
Santa Monica, CA 90401
(310) 319-0205
Fax: (310) 319-0265
Monday-Friday: 7:00 a.m. to 5:00 p.m. PST
eMail: *clientservices@goldlinecoins.com*
web site: *www.goldline.com*
Specialties: *U.S. gold and silver coins, Saint Gaudens, Morgan Dollars, Peace Dollars, and French and Swiss Francs.*

BENEDETTI, Phillip E.
(PNG #59)
P.O. Box 2007
Westport, CT 06880
(203) 847-5527
By appointment only

BERG , David
(PNG #258)
DAVE BERG, LTD.
P.O. Box 348
Portersville, PA 16051
(724) 452-4586
Fax: (724) 452-0276
eMail: *davbergltd@aol.com*

BERGELT, Jeffrey P.
(PNG #403)
BERGELT INTERNATIONAL, INC.
P.O. Box 1627
Ft. Lee, NJ 07024
(201) 592-8599
(201) 592-8587
Fax: (201) 592-9219
9:30-4:00 Mon.–Fri.
eMail: *jbergelt@msn.com*
Specialties: *U.S. gold coins, World gold coins, U.S. silver dollars.*

BERK, Harlan J.
(PNG #178)
HARLAN J BERK, LTD.
31 North Clark Street
Chicago, IL 60602
(312) 609-0016
Fax: (312) 609-1309
Hours: 9-5
Bimonthly buy or bid sales.
eMail: *info@harlanjberk.com*
web site: *www.harlanjberk.com*
Specialties: *Ancient Greek, Roman and Byzantine coinage of the finest quality. U.S. coins & bullion, antiquities, stamps & autographs.*

BERNBERG, Jeffrey F.
(PNG #297)
RARE COIN COMPANY OF AMERICA, INC., RARCOA, INC.
6262 So. Route 83, Ste. 200
Willowbrook, IL 60527
(630) 654-2580
Fax: (630) 654-3556
8-4 by appointment
eMail: *jbernberg@rarcoa.com*
web site: *www.rarcoa.com*

Specialties: *HESS-DIVO LTD. Zurich, Switzerland All U.S. coins in gold, silver & copper. Ancient & foreign coins in gold, silver & copper; auctions, major market maker & importer of U.S. gold coins. Contact us for a free copy of the Rarcoa Gold Sheet.*

BEYMER, Jack H.
(PNG #259)
JACK BEYMER, INC.
737 Coddingtown Center
Santa Rosa, CA 95401
(707) 544-1621
Fax: (707) 575-5304
Hours: 10-6
Fixed price lists.
Specialties: *Early U.S. Copper coins, Barber series, seated coins, type coins.*

BIANCO, Mike
(PNG #535)
MIKE BIANCO RARE COIN
P.O. Box 231878
Encinitas, CA 92023
(760) 436-3637
Fax: (760) 436-3784
9-4 Mon.-Fri.
eMail: *instone@pacbell.net*
web site: *www.instoneinc.com*
Specialties: *Highgrade gold, type, gold & silver commemoratives. Pre-1930 cigar box labels.*

BOHNERT, Brad
(PNG #442)
THE NUMISMATIC EMPORIUM, INC.
21300 Victory Blvd., Suite 220
Woodland Hills, CA 91367
(818) 887-2723
(800) 530-3050
Fax: (818) 887-0301
Specialties: *U.S. gold coins.*

BOWERS, Q. David
(PNG #58)
P.O. Box 539
Wolfeboro Falls, NH 03896-0539
Hours: 8:30-5 Mon.-Fri.
eMail:
qdbarchive@metrocast.net
Specialties: *Celebrating 50 years in professional numismatics 1953-2003. Past president PNG (1977-1979), past president American Numismatic Association (1983-1985).*

Executive Director
BRUEGGEMAN, Robert
(PNG #AF526)
POSITIVE PROTECTION, INC.
425 E. Alvarado St., Ste. E
Fallbrook, CA 92028
(760) 728-1300
Fax: (760) 728-8507
eMail: *posproin@aol.com*
Specialties: *Security.*

BULLOWA, Mrs. C.E
(PNG #3)
COINHUNTER
1616 Walnut Street, Suite 2112
Philadelphia, PA 19103-5364
(215) 735-5517
Fax: (215) 735-5722
Mon.-Fri. 9:00-4:00, or by appointment
*Appointment preferred for Public auction, mail bid sales.
Specialties: *U.S., foreign, ancients, numismatic books, appraisals. Established 1952.*

BURD, William A.
(PNG #539)
CHICAGO COIN CO., INC
6455 W. Archer Avenue
Chicago, IL 60638
(773) 586-7666
(800) 895-2246
Fax: (773) 586-7754

Mon.-Fri. 8-5, Sat. 8-1
eMail: *chicagocoin@ worldnet.att.net*
web site: *www.chicagocoin.com*
Specialties: *U.S. coins, foreign coins, gold coins, currency. Wholesale bullion to the trade.*

CAMPBELL, H. Robert (Bob)
(PNG #537)
ALL ABOUT COINS, INC.
1123 E. 2100 South
Salt Lake City, UT 84106
(801) 467-8636
Fax: (801) 467-4471
Tues.-Fri. 10-6, Sat. 10-5, MST
Closed Sun. Mon.
We are an old fashioned type of coin shop. We also sell metal detectors.
eMail: *aacbob@aros.net*
Specialties: *Rainbow toning on coins, western trade tokens and medals. Mormon gold coins, tokens & medals. 200+ different books and a complete line of supplies for sale.*

CARTER, Jason L
(PNG #554)
CARTER NUMISMATICS, INC.
2021 S. Lewis, Ste. 350
Tulsa, OK 74104
(918) 583-2646
(800) 817-2646
Fax: (918) 583-9533
Hours: 9:00 a.m.–5:30 p.m. CT
High-end certified U.S. coins, rare bust and seated material.
eMail: *jason@carternumismatics.com*
web site: *www.carternumismatics.com*
Specialties: *Liberty seated rarities, early type coins, gold rarities.*

CASPER, Michael I.
(PNG #576)
MICHAEL I. CASPER, RARE COINS, INC.
P.O. Box 40
Ithaca, NY 14851
Tel. (607) 257-5349
Fax: (607) 266-7904
Hours: 24/7
eMail: *michael@caspercoin.com*
web site: *www.caspercoin.com*
Specialties: *Morgan Silver Dollars.*

CAWLEY, John
(PNG #544)
DILLON GAGE, INC. OF DALLAS
15301 Dallas Pkwy., #200
Addison, TX 75001
(800) 811-6850
Cell: (214) 213-5084
Fax: (972) 490-3218
Mon.-Fri. 8:30-5:30 CT
web site: *www.dillongage.com*
Specialties: *Primarily U.S. gold—circs, slabs, large lots—including rarities & branch mint coins in all grades, damaged to proof.*

CAYON FERNANDEZ, Juan Ramon (PNG #306)
JANO S.L.
Alcala 35,
Madrid 28014, Spain
(00341) 5228030
(00341) 5210832
Fax: (00341) 5233585
Publications, catalogs, auctions and lists.
eMail: *cayon@cayon.com*
web site: *www.cayon.com*
Specialties: *Spanish world & ancient world.*

CHOU, Peter (PNG #546)
CHAMPION GALLERY

CLARK, I. Nelson
(PNG #477)
I. NELSON CLARK BANK-NOTES
P.O. Box 883
Los Alamitos, CA 90720
Tel. (714) 761-3683
Cell: (714) 809-5120
Fax: (714) 761-3683
By appointment only o Fixed price lists
eMail: *inellclark@mediaone.net*
Specialties: *All U.S. type currency-large & small & national currency (all states).*

COOK, Howard C., JR
(PNG #563)
HCC, INC.
3242 Executive Parkway, #203A
Toledo, OH 43606
(419) 537-0080
Fax: (419) 537-9131
By appointment only
eMail: *howard@hcc-coin.com*
web site: *www.hcc-coin.com*
Specialties: *Investment grade rare coins. Banking coin program services.*

CRANE, MARC
(PNG #565)
MARC ONE NUMISMATICS, INC
P.O. Box 8048
Newport Beach, CA 92658
(800) 346-2721
(714) 258-0954
Fax: (714) 258-0965
9-5 by appt. M-F
eMail: *marconeinc@aol.com*
web site: *www.marcone.net*
Specialties: *U.S. gold and all U.S. coins including patterns. Instant payment for all coins, paper money, collections & estates, etc. Portfolio management including acquisitions & liquidations. Numerous references upon request.*

CROSS, William K.
(PNG #181)
CHARLTON PRESS
P.O. Box 820, Station Willowdale B
North York, ONT M2K 2R1
(800) 442-6042
(416) 488-1418
Fax: (800) 442-1542
Call for appointment.
eMail: *chpress@charltonpress.com*
web site: *www.charltonpress.com*

DANNREUTHER, John West
(PNG #299)
Box 1840
Cordova, TN 38088-1840
Tel. (901) 756-2400
Fax: (901) 756-1404
Hours: By appointment only
Fixed price lists, publications.
eMail: *jdrc@mindspring.com*
web site: *www.jdrarecoins.com*
Specialties: *PCGS graded rare & choice U.S. coins.*

DARAY, Dennis A.
(PNG #584)
SOUTHERN COINS & PRECIOUS METALS
474 Metairie Rd.
Metairie, LA 70005
(504) 837-1711
(800) 535-9704
Fax: (504) 833-4549
9:00AM-5:30PM CDT
eMail: *Dennis@scpm.com*
web site: *www.scpm.com*
Specialties: *U.S. Rarities, Morgan & peace dollars. PCGS & NGC certified U.S. gold, silver & type coins.*

DAVISSON, Allan
(PNG #531)
DAVISSONS, LTD
Cold Spring, MN 56320
(320) 685-3835
Fax: (320) 685-8636
Mail auction catalogs. Fixed price lists with relevant articles.
eMail: *coins@cloudnet.com*
web site: *www.britishcoins.com*
Specialties: *British coins, tokens, medals and related literature. Ancient Greek & Roman coins.*

DEGLER, Klaus J.
(PNG #463)
ROCKY MOUNTAIN COIN EXCHANGE, INC.
538 S. Broadway
Denver, CO 80209
(303) 777-GOLD
CoinNet CO-01
Fax: (303) 733-4946
9:30-5:00 M-F
eMail: *RMCoin@earthlink.net*
web site: *www.RMcoin.com*
Specialties: *U.S. gold, gem & rare foreign crowns, national currency, U.S. type coins, medals & tokens.*

DENLY, Thomas M.
(PNG #358)
DENLY'S COINS OF BOSTON
P.O. Box 1010
75 Federal Street, Room 620
Boston, MA
(617) 482-8477
(800) HI-DENLY
Fax: (617) 357-8163
9-5 Mon.-Fri. Call by phone; not open to public
Fixed price lists as published in Bank Note Reporter.
eMail: *denlys@aol.com*
web site: *www.denlys.com*
Specialties: *U.S. paper money both large & small, obsolete currency, colonial currency, Confederate currency, fractional currency, national currency, books on paper money, mylar D currency holders, U.S. coins, Canadian currency, foreign currency. Currency auction representation.*

DERZON, David
(PNG #116)
DAVID DERZON CO., INC.
2069 So. 108th Street
West Allis, WI 53227
(414) 543-8833
Fax: (414) 543-2014
10-5 Mon.-Fri.
Specialties: *U.S. gold coins, type coins, PCGS coins, proofs. Buyers of estates & complete collections.*

DI GENOVA, Silvano A.
(PNG #378)
SUPERIOR GALLERIES
9478 Olympic Blvd.
Beverly Hills, CA 90212-4246
(800) 421-0754
(800) 545-1001
Fax: (310) 203-0496
web site: *www.SGBH.com*
Specialties: *Appraisals, Auctions, Cash Buyers, U.S. Coins, Foreign Coins, All Bullion, Jewelry, Art & Antiques.*

DOMINICK, William
(PNG #479)
WESTWOOD RARE COIN GALLERY, INC
P.O. Box 31
Tappan, NY 10983
(201) 768-4433
Fax: (201) 768-8496
By appointment only
Personalized portfolio management for individuals, financial planners, pension plans,

monthly acquisition plans, free appraisals, want list service and personal consultations.
Specialties: *U.S. gold, key date coins, double die cents, 1856 Eagles, 1895 Morgans.*

DONNELLY, John M.
(PNG #582)
JOHN DONNELLY COINS
2684 N. Reading Rd.
Reinholds, PA 17569
(717) 484-2463
Fax: (717) 484-2299
By appointment
Specialties: *General Line.*

DOWNEY, Sheridan
(PNG #502)
SHERIDAN DOWNEY, NUMISMATIST
4100-10 Redwood Rd., Suite 410
Oakland, CA 94619
(510) 639-7283
(800) 597-9403
Fax: (510) 568-1969
9:00 a.m.–6:00 p.m. Pacific Time
eMail: *sdowney3@aol.com*
web site:
www.sheridanscoins.com
Specialties: *Early U.S. coinage, 1794-1836, with emphasis on U.S. bust half-dollars. Consignments accepted for regular auction sales of bust half dollars.*

DRAGONI, Augusto
(PNG #287)
AUGUSTO DRAGONI
Via Faentina Sud 12
Russi (Ravenna), 48026
39-0544-582163
Fax: 39-0544-580173
By appointment only
Specialties: *Italian, Vatican, San Marino, silver & gold coins.*

DRZEWUCKI, Ronald R., Jr.
(PNG #532)
SILVERTOWNE RARE COINS
P.O. Box 411511
St. Louis, MO 63141
(314) 614-3575
Fax: (314) 205-2650
By appointment only
eMail: *Ronniecoin@aol.com*
Specialties: *U.S. gold.*

DUNCAN, Kathleen
(PNG #518)
PINNACLE RARITIES, INC.
Suite 211
10116 36th Avenue Court SW
Lakewood, WA 98499
(253) 272-7300
(800) 432-6467
Fax: (253) 272-7322
8:00 a.m.-6:00 p.m. (By appt. only)
Fixed price list. Newsletter. On-line inventory. Auction representation, free appraisals.
eMail: *kathleen@ pinnacle-rarities.com*
web site:
www.pinnacle-rarities.com
Specialties: *High grade PCGS & NGC certified U.S. coinage (1793 and 1950). Full service firm servicing collector-investor and dealer community. NGC & PCGS submissions.*

DUNCAN, Richard, Sr.
(PNG #516)
U.S. COINS, INC.
8435 Katy Freeway
Houston, TX 77024
(713) 464-6868
Fax: (713) 464-7548
Fixed price lists, publications.
eMail: *info@buyuscoins.com*
web site: *www.buyuscoins.com*
Specialties: *Investment quality silver & gold certified coins from $50 to $500,00. Type coins,*

proof & mint state, gold, dollars and commemoratives. Free award winning consultations, appraisals & recommendations given with a smile.

EDLER, Joel T.
(PNG #AF574)
KRAUSE PUBLICATIONS
700 E. State St.
Iola, WI 54945
(715) 445-2214
Fax: (715) 445-4087
8:00-5:00
eMail: *edlerj@krause.com*

FEHR, James B.
(PNG #512)
ELLESMERE NUMISMATICS
P.O. Box 727
New Milford, CT 06776
(800) 426-3343
(860) 355-2835
Fax: (860) 355-5408
By appointment only
Publications available.
Publishers of The Winning Edge.
eMail: *ellesmere1@aol.com*
web site:
www.ellesmerecoin.com
Specialties: *PCGS & NGC certified coins.*

FEIGENBAUM, John A.
(PNG #570)
DAVID LAWRENCE RARE COINS
P.O. Box 1061
Virginia Beach, VA 23451
(800) 776-0560
Fax: (757) 491-1064
9-5 p.m. eastern
eMail: *info@davidlawrence.com*
web site:
www.davidlawrence.com
Specialties: *U.S. certified coins.*

FELDMAN, Mark R.
(PNG #294)
A COIN EXCHANGE
18631 Ventura Blvd.
Tarzana, CA 91356
(818) 344-9555
Mon.-Fri. 10-5, Sat. 11-4
eMail:
mark@acoinexchange.com
web site:
www.acoinexchange.com
Specialties: *Retail coin shop. All investor & collector services; buy & sell U.S. coins, foreign coins; gold, silver & platinum bullion; diamonds, jewelry & scrap. Other services include appraisals, estates, pension plans & expert witness testimony. Confidential consultations available at your home, office or bank.*

FENTON, Stephen C.
(PNG #577)
KNIGHTSBRIDGE COINS
43 Duke St., St. James
London, SW1Y6DD
011442079308215
011442079307597
Fax: 011442079308214
Mon-Fri 10:30-5:30
eMail: *stephcf232@aol.com*
Specialties: *Great Britain. USA. Austrailia. South Africa.*

FOLLETT, Mike
(PNG #205)
MIKE FOLLETT RARE COIN CO., INC.
13101 Preston Rd., Suite 300
Dallas, TX 75240
(972) 788-5225
(800) 527-9045
Fax: (972) 788-0161
9-5 Mon.-Fri.
WATTS LINE:(800) 446-0112
Specialties: *U.S. coins & currency.*

FORGUE, Dennis J.
(PNG #239)
HARLAN J. BERK, LTD.
31 North Clark Street
Chicago, IL 60602
(312) 609-0016
Fax: (312) 609-1305
9:00-4:45
Bimonthly buy or bid sales.
web site: *www.harlanjberk.com*
Specialties: *All kinds U.S. coins & currency, autographs. Past president of Prof. Currency Dealers Association.*

FRIEDBERG, Arthur L
(PNG #284)
THE COIN AND CURRENCY INSTITUTE, INC.
P.O. Box 1057
Clifton, NJ 07014
(973) 471-1441
Fax: (973) 471-1062
By appointment only
Fixed price lists, publications, catalogs.
eMail: *coincurin@aol.com*
web site: *www.coin-currency.com*
Specialties: *North American representative for numerous government mints. Publisher of reference books.*

FROSETH, Kent Morris
(PNG #406)
K.M. FROSETH, INC.
P.O. Box 23116
Minneapolis, MN 55423
(952) 831-9550
(800) 648-7662
Fax: (952) 835-3903
By appointment
eMail: *fm26@qwest.net*
web site: *www.kmfroseth.com*
Specialties: *World coins, specializing in Scandinavia. Rare foreign gold.*

FULJENZ, Michael R.
(PNG #519)
MIKE FULJENZ UNIVERSAL COIN & BULLION, LTD.
350 Dowlen, Suite 101
Beaumont, TX 77706
(800) 459-2646
(800) 248-2223
Fax: (409) 866-2022
By appointment only
eMail: *mike@universalcoin.com*
web site: *www.universalcoin.com*
Specialties: *Silver, gold & platinum American Eagles. PCGS & NGC certified Type II & Type III $20 gold Liberties. FREE newsletter, private reports, books & personal consulting for new inquiries.*

GANZ, David L.
(PNG #AF436)
GANZ & HOLLINGER, P.C.
1394 Third Avenue
New York, NY 10021
(212) 517-5500
Fax: (212) 772-2720
eMail: *davidlganz@aol.com*
web site: *www.Ganzhollinger.com*
Specialties: *Lawyer.*

GARRETT, Jeff C.
(PNG #329)
MID-AMERICAN RARE COIN GALLERIES
1707 Nicholasville Road
Lexington, KY 40503
(859) 276-1551
(859) 396-4505-cell
Fax: (859) 278-8640
SARASOTA RARE COIN GALLERIES 640 S. Washington Blvd., # 100, Sarasota, FL 34236 Tel. (941) 366-2191
eMail: *coinman4u@aol.com*
web site: *www.rarecoingallery.com*
Specialties: *Rare U.S. coinage.*

GEHRINGER, Stephen J.
(PNG #480)
KEYSTONE RARE COINS, LLC
1801 Tilghman Street
Allentown, PA 18104
(610) 770-9500
Fax: (610) 770-0248
9:30-5:30 M-F, Sat. 9-1
eMail: *keycoin@aol.com*

GERMANO, Salvatore
(PNG #481)
S.G. RARE COINS, INC.
625 Lafayette Avenue
Hawthorne, NJ 07506
(973) 304-0520
Fax: (973) 304-0914
By appointment only
eMail: *sgrarecoins@aol.com*
Specialties: *Buy, sell PCGS/NGC/ANACS/ICG/SEGS certified coins wholesale. Also GSA dollars, original BU rolls, 1936-54 proof sets, U.S. Patterns, Territorials, and World Gold.*

GILLIO, Dennis M.
(PNG #321)
DENNIS GILLIO RARE COINS
10113 Riverside Drive
Toluca Lake, CA 91602
(818) 985-3900
(805) 563-9234
Fax: (818) 762-6717
Tuesday-Saturday, 10-5
Auction dates: Varies.
eMail: *Gilliocoin@aol.com*

GILLIO, Ronald J.
(PNG #204)
RONALD J. GILLIO, INC.
JOHSON-GILLIO LLC
760 Market St., #501, San Francisco, CA 94102
1103 State Street
Santa Barbara, , CA 93101
(805) 963-1345
Fax: (805) 962-6659
10-5 Mon.-Fri.
Divisions: Gillio Rare Coins & Fine Jewelry, Goldmunzen International, Gillio Coins International, Gillio Coins Hong Kong, R.J. Gillio Auctions, Long Beach Coin, Stamp & Collectibles Expo.Santa Clara Coin, Stamp & Collectibles Expo.
eMail: *rjgillio@gte.net*
web site: *www.gillio.com ; www.exposunlimited.com*
Specialties: *U.S. gold coins, world gold coins, Far East & Asian coins, auctions.*

GOLDBERG, Ira M.
(PNG #153)
IRA & LARRY GOLDBERG COINS & COLLECTIBLES, INC.
350 S. Beverly Drive, #350
Beverly Hills, CA 90212
(310) 551-2646
(800) 978-2646
Fax: (310) 551-2626
9 a.m.-5 p.m. M-F
Antiquities
eMail: *iracoin@aol.com*
web site: *www.goldbergcoins.com*
Specialties: *Ancient Greek, Roman, Judean, Byzantine, U.S. & World coinage.*

GOLDBERG, Lawrence S.
(PNG #154)
IRA & LARRY GOLDBERG COINS & COLLECTIBLES, INC
350 South Beverly Drive, Suite 350
Beverly Hills, CA 90212
(310) 551-2646
(800) 978-2646
Fax: (310) 551-2626
9-5, by appointment only.
Active coin dealer since 1957.

web site:
www.goldbergcoins.com
Specialties: *U.S. gold & silver coins, World gold & silver coins. U.S. paper money. Collectibles & sports items prior to 1955. Sell, appraise & auction. 6 auctions per year.*

GOLDMAN, Kenneth
(PNG #252)
KENNETH GOLDMAN, INC
P.O. Box 920404
Needham, MA 02492
(781) 449-0058
Fax: (781) 326-6758
9-5
We attend all major coin conventions & auctions in the U.S.A. Appraiser for the Federal Trade Commission.
eMail: *KenGoldman@aol.com*
Specialties: *Choice U.S. type coins, gold and silver, pioneer gold, U.S. pattern coins, investment portfolios for qualified clients.*

GORNY, Dieter
(PNG #264)
GORNY & MOSCH
GIESSENER
MUNZHANDLUNG GmbH
Maximiliansplatz 20
D-80333 Munchen,
498924226430
Fax: 49892285513
M-F 10-1, 2:30-6 Mon-Fri; Sat closed
eMail: *info@gmcoinart.de*
web site: *www.gmcoinart.de*
Specialties: *Ancient, foreign & German coins & medals, medieval through modern times, antiquities.*

GRAHAM, Michael A.
(PNG #254)
MT. HIGH COIN &
COLLECTABLES—
185 S.E. 3rd Street
Bend, OR 97702
(541) 385-7113
Fax: (541) 385-7133
10-4:30 p.m.
COINET OR11Fixed price lists, art bar specialist, catalogs.
eMail:
mthighcc@mtnhighcoin.com
web site: *www.mtnhighcoin.com*
Specialties: *Rare U.S. coins, unique collectables, antique jewelry, estates. Silver, Gold, and Bronze mint manufacturing, SPORTS MEMORABILIA.*

GREENBERG, Frank
(PNG #313)
DELAWARE VALLEY RARE
COIN CO., INC
2835 West Chester Pike
Broomall, PA 19008
(610) 356 3555
(800) 345-8188
Fax: (610) 325-0468
Fixed price lists, appraisal services & estate liquidations.
eMail: *contactus@dvrcc.com*
web site: *www.dvrarecoins.com*
Specialties: *Better U.S. coins, especially gold, type coins, dollars.*

GROVICH, Nicholas F.
(PNG #553)
AMERICAN FEDERAL RARE
COIN & BULLION
14602 N. Cave Creek Rd, #C
Phoenix, AZ 85022
(602) 992-6857
(800) 221-7694
Fax: (602) 493-8158
8-5 MST
eMail: *nick@amfedcoins.com*
web site:
www.americanfederal.com

Specialties: *Gold & silver commemoratives, high grade (MS65 & better) U.S. coins. We purchase all types of coins from Indian cents thru proof gold. We will travel to you to inspect collections and pay on the spot or you can take advantage of our Guaranteed Consignment.*

GULLEY, Kent E.
(PNG #455)
SARASOTA RARE COIN GALLERY
640 S. Washington Blvd., # 100
Sarasota, FL 34236
(941) 366-2191
(800) 447-8778
Fax: (941) 954-8833
9-5 Mon.-Fri., 9-4 Sat. o
Catalogs
web site: *www.coingallery.com*
Specialties: *U.S. gold, silver dollars, certified & uncertified bullion.*

HALL, David (PNG #541)
DAVID HALL RARE COINS
P.O. Box 6220
Newport Beach, CA 92658
(800) 759-7575
Fax: (949) 477-5874
7:30-5 PST
Monthly inside view advisory letter.
eMail: *info@davidhall.com*
web site: *www.davidhall.com*
Specialties: *Top quality rare United States coins.*

HALLOCK, George
(PNG #AF485)
HALLOCK COIN, JEWELRY & FINDINGS, INC.
2060 W. Lincoln
Anaheim, CA 92801
(714) 956-2360
(800) 854-3232
Fax: (714) 635-8247

HALPERIN, James L.
(PNG #482)
HERITAGE RARE COIN GALLERIES
HERITAGE AUCTIONS
100 Highland Park Village, Ste. 200
Dallas, TX 75205
(214) 252-4255
(214) 528-3500
Fax: (214) 520-7108
8-6:30
eMail: *jim@heritagecoin.com*
web site:
www.heritagecoin.com

HAMRICK, John B.
(PNG #564)
JOHN B. HAMRICK & CO.
1195 Grimes Bridge Rd., Ste. 5
Roswell, GA 30075
Tel. (770) 552-6679
Fax: (770) 552-6680
Hours: 9-6 Mon.-Fri.
eMail:
jhamrick@mindspring.com
web site: *www.usrarecoins.com*
Specialties: *Certified U.S. coins (PCGS & NGC) 1792–1955. We deal in everything from 1/2 cents to $50 gold coins plus patterns and early commemoratives.*

HANKS, Larry (PNG #241)
HANKS AND ASSOCIATES, INC.
415 North Mesa
El Paso, TX 79901
(915) 544-8188
Fax: (915) 544-8194
10-5 Mon.-Fri.
Fixed price lists, publications, catalogs, auction sales.

eMail: *larry@rare-coins.net*
web site: *www.rare-coins.net*
Specialties: *U.S. & world gold coins, rare paper money purchases, sales, submissions for PCGS & NGC certified coins, syndication of rare coins, pension plan investments.*

HANLON, Terence F.
(PNG #578)
DILLON GAGE
15301 Dallas Parkway
Suite 200
Addison, TX 75001
(972) 788-4765
(972) 489-0684
Fax: (972) 490-3218
8:00 a.m.-6:00 p.m. Central Time
eMail: *thanlon@dillongage.com*
web site: *www.dillongage.com*
Specialties: *Precious Metals Refinery. Jewelry closeouts. Commodities trading. Rare date U.S. gold. Bullion trading*

HANSON, Jon G.
(PNG #87)
P.O. Box 81555
Wellesley, MA 02481
(781) 235-6628
Fax: (781) 235-1142
By appointment only
eMail: *jonontime@aol.com*
Specialties: *Early American coins & medals, U.S. half cents, rare American numismatic books & accumulations, pioneer gold, U.S. assay ingots & horological items.*

HAWN, Reed
(PNG #AF497)
807 Brazas, Ste. 316
Austin, TX 78701-2508
(512) 473-2213
Fax: (512) 473-2461

HENDRICKSON, David J.
(PNG #336)
SILVER TOWNE L.P. COIN SHOP
120 E. Union City Pike
Winchester, IN 47394
(800) 788-7481
Fax: (765) 584-1246
9-5 Mon.-Fri., 9-4 Sat.
eMail: *sales@silvertowne.com*
web site: *www.silvertowne.com*
Specialties: *All U.S. coins. All bullion items. All NGC-PCGS graded coins. Coin & jewelry items.*

HENDRICKSON, Leon E.
(PNG #170)
SILVER TOWNE L.P. COIN SHOP
120 East Union City Pike
P.O. Box 424
Winchester, IN 47394
(765) 584-7481
Fax: (765) 584-1246
9-5 Mon.-Fri., 9-4 Sat.
eMail: *sales@silvertowne.com*
web site: *www.silvertowne.com*
Specialties: *All U.S. coins, all bullion items, all PCGS & NGC graded coin. Gold & silver refining, coin jewelry items.*

HENDRICKSON, Ruhama
(PNG #A-419)
SILVER TOWNE COIN
P.O. Box 424
Winchester, IN 47394
(765) 584-7481
Fax: (765) 584-1246
9-5 Mon.-Fri., 9-4 Sat.
Fixed price lists, catalogs, publications.
Specialties: *PCGS, U.S. gold & silver coins, ANA graded coins, all bullion related items.*

HENRY, Gene L.
(PNG #171)
GENE L. HENRY, INC.
1521 3rd Avenue
Seattle, WA 98101
(206) 624-1458
Fax: (206) 624-4858
Anytime, by appointment only
eMail: *genelhenry@aol.com*
web site: *www.coinsrus.com*
Specialties: *U.S. silver dollars & gold coins, large stock, U.S. coins, raw & slabbed.*

HERTZBERG, Jack Charles
(PNG #445)
JACK HERTZBERG RARE COINS
P.O. Box 807
Wauna, WA 98395
(253) 857-4567
Fax: (732) 701-0458

HOSIER, Donald W., Jr
(PNG #445)
dba D. & E. C.S.
P.O. Box 1346
Point Pleasant, NJ 08742
(732) 701-0454
Fax: (732) 701-0458

HUANG, George
(PNG #568)
LEGEND NUMISMATICS, INC.
P.O. Box 9
Lincroft, NJ 07738
(732) 935-1795
Fax: (732) 935-1807
eMail: *legend@legendcoin.com*
web site: *www.legendcoin.com*
Specialties: *U.S. type coins, Morgan dollars, commems.*

HUMPHREYS, George B.
(PNG #211)
GEORGE B HUMPHREYS RARE COINS
P.O. Box 2006
San Anselmo, CA 94979
Tel. (415) 492-1889
Tel 2. (800) 854-3232
Hours: By appointment only.
eMail: *george@humphreys coins.com*
Specialties: *Estate appraisals and U.S. coins.*

IMHOF, Todd L.
(PNG #525)
PINNACLE RARITIES, INC.
10116 36th Ave Court SW
Ste. 211
Lakewood, WA 98499
(253) 272-7300
Fax: (253) 272-7322
7:00 a.m.-6:00 p.m. (By appointment only)
Free appraisals. NGC & PCGS submissions.
eMail: *todd@pinnacle-rarities.com*
web site: *www.pinnacle-rarities.com*
Specialties: *High quality NGC & PCGS certified U.S. coinage (1793-1950). Full service firm serving the collector & dealer community. Fixed price lists & newsletter. On-line inventory. Auction representation.*

ISKOWITZ, Ronald D.
(PNG #332)
RON ISKOWITZ RARE COINS, INC.
P.O. Box 1606
Palm Harbor, FL 34682
(800) 537-2828
(727) 939-4182
By appointment only
eMail: *rirc@bellatlantic.net*
web site: *www.iskowitzrarecoins.com*
Specialties: *Deep cameo and cameo proof Type coins.*

IVY, Steve (PNG #381)
HERITAGE RARE COIN GALLERIES
HERITAGE NUMISMATIC AUCTIONS
100 Highland Park Village
Dallas, TX 75205
(800) 872-6467
Fax: (214) 448-8409
HERITAGE NUMISMATIC AUCTIONS, Fixed price lists, publications, catalogs, auction sales, wholesale fax list.
eMail: *steve@heritagecoin.com*
web site: *www.heritagecoin.com*
Specialties: *Buying, selling, financing, joint ventures. Coin show and Internet auction sales throughout the year. Advances made on consignment accepted.*

JOHNSON, Robert R.
(PNG #77)
ROBERT R. JOHNSON, INC.
760 Market Street, #501
San Francisco, CA 94102
(415) 421-9701
Fax: (415) 291-8324
By appointment only
Specialties: *Gold coins of the world.*

JONES, Harry E.
(PNG #212)
HARRY E. JONES RARE COINS & CURRENCY
7379 PEARL RD
Cleveland, OH 44130
(440) 234-3330
Fax: (440) 234-3332
Specialties: *National currency, U.S. coins, uncut sheets, error notes.*

KAGIN, A.M. (Art)
(PNG #14)
A.M. KAGIN, NEWCO, INC.
505 Fifth Ave. Ste. 1001
Des Moines, IA 50309-2316
(515) 243-7363
Fax: (515) 288-8681
10-6 by appointment only
Specialties: *U.S. national & regular currency (large stock), pioneer gold, California $1/4, $1/2, $1, U.S. coins, gold tokens & medals.*

KAGIN, Don (PNG #526)
KAGIN'S
98 Main #201
Tiburon, CA 94920
(415) 435-2601
Fax: (415) 435-1627
9-5pm M-F
eMail: *don@kagins.com*
web site: *www.kagins.com*
Specialties: *Pioneer gold, patterns, Calif. Fractional gold, U.S. silver, gold, copper, paper currency.*

KARSTEDT, Christine
(PNG #A587)
Tel. (800) 458-4646
Fax: (603) 569-5319
Hours: 8:30-5 Mon.–Fri.
Specialties: *U.S. Coins, Auctions.*

KERN, Jonathan K.
(PNG #509)
JONATHAN K. KERN CO.
441 S. Ashland Avenue
Lexington, KY 40502
(859) 269-1614
Fax: (859) 266-7900
By appointment only
Sporadic fixed price lists.
eMail: *JKerncoins@aol.com*
web site: *www.JKerncoins.com*
Specialties: *Wholesale ancients, medieval, foreign, U.S., tokens, medals, currency; buying & selling.*

KETTERLING, Don
(PNG #409)
CERTIFIED ASSETS MANAGEMENT, INC.
21300 Victory Blvd. Ste. 220
Woodland Hills, CA 91367
(818) 887-3740
Fax: (818) 887-4043
By appointment only
eMail: *don@certifiedassets.com*
web site:
www.certifiedassets.com
Specialties: *High grade U.S. rare coins and currency. Wholesale service to marketers and dealers. Co-managing the RCA, Ltd. rare coin trading fund. Estate and insurance appraisals along with expert testimony services.*

KLIMAN, Myron M.
(PNG #147)
NUMISMATIC ENTERPRISES
P.O. Box 9365
South Laguna, CA 92652
(949) 496-8589
Fax: (949) 496-8589
9-5 Mon.-Sat., by appointment only
Appraisals and consultations.
Specialties: *U.S. type coins.*

KNIGHT, Lyn F. (PNG #194)
LYN F. KNIGHT
P.O. Box 7364
Overland Park, KS 66207-0364
(913) 338-3779
(800) 243-5211
Fax: (913) 338-4754
By appointment only
Fixed price lists, auction sales, catalogs.
Specialties: *U.S. & Canadian paper money & coins.*

KOPPENHAVER, Paul L.
(PNG #LM5)
THE COIN HAVEN
P.O. Box 34056
Granada Hills, CA 91394-9056
(818) 832-8068
Fax: (818) 832-8987
Former PNG Executive Director 1978-1994. Recipient of Abe Kosoff Founder's Award.
eMail: *plkopp@as.net*
Specialties: *Charlotte, Dahlonega, & Carson City gold, U.S. type coins, tokens, medals, currency & western Americana. Mail order only, token and medal auctions.*

KRAH, Kenneth C.
(PNG #530)
NUMISMATIC GUARANTY CORP.
1500 Independence Blvd., Ste. 220
Sarasota, FL 34234
Tel. (800) 642-2646
Hours: 9-6 EST
eMail: *kkrah@ngccoin.com*
Specialties: *U.S. English colonial, European coins and numismatic literature.*

KRILL, Gregory
(PNG #557)
NORTH BAY RARE COIN & JEWELRY
1241 Adams St. #1002
St. Helena, CA 94574
(707) 287-1919
Fax: (707) 967-1191
Bu> roll deals, all denominations.
eMail: *grkrill@covad.net*
Specialties: *B.U. U.S. gold, dated U.S. gold, B.U. silver dollars.*

KUTCHER, Bruce
(PNG #360)
BRUCE KUTCHER, INC.

P.O. Box 101
Nahant, MA 01908
(781) 581-0631
Fax: (781) 581-9683
By appointment only
Specialties: *U.S. gold & certified coins.*

LAIBSTAIN, Harry
(PNG #536)
HARRY LAIBSTAIN RARE COINS & JEWELRY
240 Main St., Norfolk, VA 23510
11817 Canon Blvd., Suite 202
Newport News, VA 23606
(757) 873-6720
(800) 869-1869
Fax: (757) 873-1977
9-5:30
HLRC mailing list & newsletter; Coin World advertiser.
eMail: *hlaibstain@aol.com*
web site: *www.hlrc.com*
Specialties: *Early type coins, Large cents, Colonials & half cents, key date coins, commemoratives, gold & silver better date U.S. gold, Diamonds.*

LECCE, Robert B.
(PNG #347)
ROBERT B. LECCE, NUMISMATIST, INC.
P.O. Box 480068
Delray Beach, FL 33448
(561) 483-4744
(561) 213-2667
Fax: (561) 483-2660
24 hours.
eMail: *(Business) Rareusgold@aol.com, (Personal) artglass2000@aol.com*
web site: *www.rareusgold.com*

LEE, Larry L. (PNG #350)
COIN AND BULLION RESERVES
2621 East 15th Street
Panama City, FL 32405
(850) 785-9546
Fax: (850) 763-1134
9-6 Mon.-Sat.
eMail: *coinandbullion@knology.net*
web site: *www.coinandbullion.com*
Specialties: *U.S. coins & currency.*

LEIDMAN, Julian M.
(PNG #195)
JULIAN M. LEIDMAN/BONANZA COINS
940 Wayne Avenue
Silver Spring, MD 20910
(301) 585-8467
(301) 585-1480
By appointment
Fixed price lists, occasionally.
eMail: *julian@juliancoin.com*
web site: *www.juliancoin.com*
Specialties: *Choice U.S. rare coins & patterns. Attends most major coin shows & auctions; consultant to quality minded collectors. Available for appraisal & as consultant, any aspect of numismatics; services want lists.*

LEIFER, Bret (PNG #513)
BRET LEIFER NUMISMATICS
Box 5225
Wayland, MA 01778
(508) 655-1125
(800) 331-2646 (COIN)
Fax: (508) 650-1847
By appointment only
eMail: *coins@coinguy.com*
web site: *www.coinguy.com*
Specialties: *Certified gold pieces. High quality type coins. Assistance in building world class collections; will act as a broker for qualified clients; buying and selling. Free consultation and/or appraisal. Grading services provided.*

Always buying coins & accumulations.

LEVENTHAL, Edwin
(PNG #255)
J.J. TEAPARTY, INC.
49 Bromfield Street
Boston, MA 02108-4110
(800) 343-6412
(617) 482-2398
Fax: (617) 542-0023
9-4:30 M-F, 9-2 Sat. (except July & August)
Appointment appreciated. Fixed price lists, monthly.i
eMail: *info@jjteaparty.com*
web site: *www.jjteaparty.com*
Specialties: *U.S. coins. Monthly fixed price list. Portfolio & estate appraisals. Want lists & approval service. Convention & auction attendance.*

LEVINE, Stuart
(PNG #412)
P.O. Box 217
Sudbury, MA 01776
(978) 443-9070
Fax: (978) 443-6539
eMail: *smlevine@ix.netcom.com*
Specialties: *Rare United States regular issue, proof & pattern coinage. U.S. related colonial & territorial issues.*

LEVINSON, Robert A.
(PNG #AF561)
LEVINSON & KAPLAN, A PROFESSIONAL CORPORATION
16027 Ventura Blvd., #600
Encino, CA 91436
(818) 382-3450
Fax: (818) 382-3445
eMail: *Bob@levkaplawyers.com*
web site: *www.levkaplaw.com*
Specialties: *Legal representation for coin dealers, auction houses & parties engaging in numismatic transactions, including issues with interpretation of contracts, auctions, sales, disputes, etc. Attorney is also a collector, and author in several publications regarding numismatic subjects and is general counsel to various numismatic related firms.*

LIPTON, Kevin
(PNG #383)
KEVIN LIPTON RARE COIN, INC.
8601 Wilshire Blvd., Ste. 800
Beverly Hills, CA 90211
(310) 659-8501
Fax: (310) 659-0991
Specialties: *8:00 a.m.–5:30 p.m.*

LOBEL, Richard
(PNG #229)
COINCRAFT
44 & 45 Great Russell Street
London, WC1B 3LU
(0207) 636-1188
(0207) 637-8785
Fax: (0207) 323-2860
9:30-5:00 Mon.-Fri., 10-2:30 Sat.
eMail: *info@coincraft.com*
web site: *www.coincraft.com*
Specialties: *Publishers of "The Phoenix" every 3 weeks, "The Banknote Bulletin," "The Coin Collector," "Bluecard Flyer." Books published: Coincraft's Standard Catalogue of English & U.K. Coins 1066 to Date, Coincraft's Standard Catalogue of the Coins of Scotland, Ireland, Channel Islands & The Isle of Man, Medallions of The Great Exhibition/Choice British coins, banknotes, ancient coins & antiquities.*

LOPRESTO, Samuel L
(PNG #362)
PMB 410

P.O. Box 7000
Redondo Beach, CA
90277-8710
(310) 540-4984
Specialties: *U.S. & foreign coins, tokens, medals, jewelry.*

LOVE, Keith (PNG #575)
ICG—INDEPENDENT COIN GRADING
7901 E. Belleview Ave.
Suite 50
Englewood, CO 80111
(303) 221-4424
Fax: (303) 221-5524
8-5 MST
eMail: *keithlove@icgcoin.com*
web site: *www.icgcoin.com*
Specialties: *Grading.*

MANLEY, Dwight N.
(PNG #522)
DWIGHT MANLEY INC.
620 Newport Center Drive
Newport Beach, CA 92660
(949) 719-1966
Fax: (949) 719-1969

MARKOFF, Steven C.
(PNG #289)
A-MARK PRECIOUS METALS, INC.
100 Wilshire Blvd., 3rd Floor
Santa Monica, CA 90401
(310) 319-0371
Fax: (310) 319-0279
Trading hours: 5:20-5:00 p.m.
Office hours: 8 a.m.-5 p.m.
eMail: *scmarkoff@aol.com*
web site: *www.amark.com*
Specialties: *Wholesaling, trading, marketing & financing of precious metals in coin, bar, plate & grain form, refining of precious metals scrap. Bullion coins.*

MCCAWLEY, Chris Victor
(PNG #397)
CVM
MCCAWLEY, GRELLMAN
P.O. Box 2967
Edmond, OK 73083
(405) 341-2213
Fax: (405) 341-1323
eMail: *cmccawley@aol.com*
web site: *www.uscents.com*
Specialties: *Early American copper coin, half cents, large cents & colonials. Specialty auctions of early copper.*

MCGUIGAN, James R.
(PNG #384)
JIM MCGUIGAN
P.O. Box 133
No. Versailles, PA 15137
(412) 247-4484
Fixed price lists.
Specialties: *Early U.S. copper, silver & gold coins. Attendance at most major shows & auctions. Services offered to collectors, dealers & investors include: auction representation, numismatic counseling, appraisals, solicitation of want lists.*

MEDCALF, Gordon
(PNG #120)
ISLAND COIN EXCHANGE, INC.
658 Front Street, #178
Lahaina, HI 96761
(808) 667-6155
10-8 daily
Fixed price lists occasionally.
Specialties: *U.S., Hawaii & Pacific area coins, tokens & paper money.*

MERCER, Daryl L.
(PNG #314)
TEBO COIN COMPANY, INC.
2863 28th Street
P.O. Box 4900
Boulder, CO 80306

(303) 444-2646
(877) 750-2646
Fax: (303) 449-4653
M-F 9:30-5:30, Sat. 9:30-2:00, Closed Sundays
eMail: *tebocoin@hotmail.com*
web site: *www.tebocoin.com*
Specialties: *U.S. coins & currency, appraisals, foreign & ancient, collector coins & sets. All rare coins/currency.*

MERRILL, Bruce
(PNG #A571)
BRUCE MERRILL, INC.
Box 572
Olathe, KS 66061
(913) 764-8554
Fax: (913) 780-0692

MICHAEL, Alain
(PNG #A572)
P.O. Box 63
Beverly Hills, CA 90213-0063
(310) 278-0712
(877) US-NOTES
Fax: (310) 278-2065
By appt. only
eMail: *uscurrency@earthlink.net*
web site: *www.unitedstatescurrency.com*
Specialties: *Sm. Size Federal Reserve notes: $500-$10,000, Gold Certificates: $10-$1,000.*

MILAS, Edward
(PNG #157)
RARE COIN COMPANY OF AMERICA, INC. RARCOA, INC.
6262 So. Route 83
Willowbrook, IL 60514
(630) 654-2580
Fax: (630) 654-3556
8-4 By Appointment
eMail: *info@rarcoa.com*
web site: *www.rarcoa.com*

MILLER, Wayne
(PNG #547)
WAYNE MILLER COINS
303 Fuller
Helena, MT 59601
(406) 442-0713
Fax: (406) 442-0789
eMail: *waynemiller@waynemillercoins.com*
web site: *www.waynemillercoins.com*
Specialties: *Morgan & Peace dollars, generic certified $20 gold.*

MILLS, Warren T.
(PNG #505)
RARE COINS OF NEW HAMPSHIRE
28 Jones Road, Suite 1
Granite Band Bldg
Milford, NH 03055
(603) 673-9311
(800) 225-7264
Fax: (603) 673-9539
9-7 Mon.-Fri.
eMail: *rcnh@ix.netcom.com*
web site: *www.rare-coins.com*
Specialties: *All United States coins; rarities purchased & sold; auction representation; liquidation services. We specialize in all key & semi key collector coins. Call us regarding coins, currency or tokens. Free appraisals & want list service for raw or certified coins.*

MINSHULL, Lee S.
(PNG #540)
LEE MINSHULL R.C., INC.
P.O. Box 4389
Palos Verdes, CA 90274
(310) 377-1299
Fax: (310) 377-1399
9-6
eMail: *lmrcinc@earthlink.com*

web site:
www.goldcoinbuyer.com
Specialties: *U.S. gold cal gold patterns.*

MONTGOMERY, Paul
(PNG #549)
BOWERS AND MERENA GALLERIES
Box 1224
Wolfeboro, NH 03894
(603) 569-5095
(800) 222-5993
Fax: (603) 569-5319
Hours: 8:30-5 Mon.–Fri.
Rare coin auction firm with frequent auction sales in NYC, Baltimore, Los Angeles and other major metropolitan cities.
eMail:
paul@bowersandmerena.com
web site:
www.bowersandmerena.com
Specialties: *All U.S. coins, world coins, ancient coins, paper money, medals & tokens.*

MUNZNER, Richard T.
(PNG #278)
LAUREL CITY COINS AND ANTIQUES
462 Main Street
P.O. Box 1093
Winsted, CT 06098
(860) 379-0325
Fax: (860) 379-0325
Tue.-Fri. 10-4:30; Sat. 9:30-4:00
Specialties: *Collector coins, Proof & Mint sets, Coin supplies.*

NACHBAR, Richard N.
(PNG #493)
RICHARD NACHBAR RARE COINS
5820 Main Street, Suite 601
Williamsville, NY 14221
(716) 635-9700
(877) 622-4227
Fax: (716) 635-9762
Hours: 9 a.m.-5 p.m. Monday-Friday By Appointment
eMail: *nachbar@coinexpert.com*
web site: *www.coinexpert.com*
Specialties: *Expert appraisals & leading national buyer of coin collections and estates, especially U.S. Gold Coins, Type Coins, Silver Dollars, U.S. Commemoratives, Pioneer Gold, Territorials and U.S. Currency. We travel to purchase collections & have also attended all major national shows for our clients since 1973.*

NAPOLITANO, Chris
(PNG #528)
SUMMIT RARE COINS, INC.
30 E. 7th St., #180
MN World Trade Center
St. Paul, MN 55101
(651) 227-9000
(612) 940-7376
Fax: (651) 225-1634
9-5
eMail: *chrissummitrc@aol.com*
Specialties: *All U.S. coins & currency, from junk to certified gem rarities. PCGS, NGC, ANACS, ICG.*

NOE, Thomas W.
(PNG #310)
VINTAGE COINS & COLLECTIBLES
3509 Briarfield Blvd.
Maumee, OH 43537
(419) 865-2646
(800) 295-2646
Fax: (419) 865-8685
Mon.-Thur. 9-6, Fri. 9-5, Sat. appointment only
eMail: *vcc@vintagecoins.com*
web site:
www.vintagecoins.com

NOXON, Casey
(PNG #431)
TEXAS NUMISMATIC
INVESTMENTS, INC.
P.O. Box 26625
Austin, TX 78755
(512) 343-0343
Fax: (512) 343-6923
eMail: *TNII@flash.net*

NUGGET, Paul (PNG #317)
SPECTRUM EAST
P.O. Box 540
East Meadow, NY 11554
(516) 505-2472
Fax: (516) 505-9193
9-5 by appointment only
Fixed price lists.
Specialties: *United States coins & currency, rare date gold, auction work.*

OAKES, Dean (PNG #127)
DEAN OAKES COINS &
CURRENCY
P.O. Box 1456
Iowa City, IA 52244
(319) 338-1144
Fax: (319) 338-5585

OLMSTEAD, David
(PNG #545)
ALPINE NUMISMATICS, INC.
P.O. Box 532
Franktown, CO 80116
(303) 660-2219
(800) 654-9599
Fax: (303) 660-5872
9-6 Mon.-Fri Mountain time
eMail: *alpinenum@aol.com*
web site:
www.alpinenumismatics.com
Specialties: *U.S. coins 1793-1950. Early type. Rare date seated, barber & 20th century. Early and rare date gold.*

OSWALD, Vernon H., Sr
(PNG #158)
OSSIE'S COIN SHOP
Jan.–June—P.O. Box 810423,
Boca Raton, FL 33498
June–Dec.: 1244 West Jubilee
St., Box 304
Emmaus, PA 18049
Jan.-June: (561) 483-9626
June-Dec. (610) 965-9485
Fax: (610) 967-5852
10-6:00 Mon.-Fri.
eMail: *ossievh@msn.com*
Specialties: *Gold coins. Proof coins, U.S. patterns, all U.S. coins. NGC & PCGS graded coins US type notes (large to sm.) Nat'l currency (Large & sm.) No. 1 type Notes & Nat'l bank notes & rare currency documents, appraisals & estates coins or paper money.*

PAPPACODA, Andrew
(PNG #551)
FLORIDA COIN & JEWELRY,
INC.
P.O. Box15835
Clearwater, FL 33766-5835
Tel. (727) 669-2646
(888) 891-6834
Fax: (727) 723-1956
9-6 Mon.-Fri; or call for
appointment.
eMail: *floridacoin@aol.com*
web site: *www.floridacoin.com*
Specialties: *U.S. gold coins, key dates in all series. Ebay Power Seller: Florida Coin.*

PEARLMAN, Donn
(PNG #AF498)
DONN PEARLMAN
PRODUCTIONS
P.O. Box 750
Skokie, IL 60076
(847) 677-3666
eMail: *donnpr@aol.com*

Specialties: *Public relations & communications counsel to the profession.*

PERLIN, Joel D.
(PNG #391)
H.S. PERLIN CO., INC.
1110 Silverado
La Jolla, CA 92037-4524
(858) 459-4409
Fax: (858) 459-7804
10-6 by appointment only
eMail: *hsperlinco@aol.com*
Specialties: *U.S. rare coins, gold coins of the world, high quality ancient coins; rare coin estates & collections appraised & purchased. 28th year in rare coin business in La Jolla, California.*

PIENTA, Peter
(PNG #283)
NORTHSHORE NUMISMATICS, INC.
358 Main Street
Wakefield, MA 01880
(781) 246-4500
Mon.-Fri. 9-4, Sat. 9-1
eMail: *png283@aol.com*
web site: *www.nscoins.com*
Specialties: *New England's largest display of collector coins.*

PIRET, Diane Augusty
(PNG #A-424)
I.C.T.A
P.O. Box 316
Belle Chasse, LA 70037
(504) 392-0023
Fax: (504) 392-0305
eMail: *dapiret@aol.com*
Specialties: *Government Relations.*

PONTERIO, Richard H.
(PNG #308)
PONTERIO & ASSOCIATES, INC.
1818 Robinson Avenue
San Diego, CA 92103
Tel. (619) 299-0400
Tel. (800) 854-2888
Fax: (619) 299-6952
By appointment only
Mexican coins, medals & paper money.
eMail: *coins@ponterio.com*
web site: *www.ponterio.com*
Specialties: *Ancients, Appraisals, Auctions, World coins and World Currency.*

RATNER, Daniel N.
(PNG #496)
RATNER RARE COIN INVESTMENTS, INC.
P.O. Box 3156
Reston, VA 20195
(703) 620-5366
Fax: (703) 620-5722
By appointment only
eMail:
danratner1@home.com
Specialties: *U.S. Gold, dollar rolls, original commems, all high grade U.S. coins.*

RETTEW, Joel D., Sr.
(PNG #163)
COINS, JEWELRY & COLLECTIBLES, INC.
23685 Moulton Pkwy., B1,
Laguna Hills, CA 92653
(949) 609-0110
Fax: (949) 609-0120
M-F 10-5, Sat., 10-2
Fixed price lists, catalogs, publications, auction sales, newsletters.
eMail: *fastpay@fastcoin.com*
web site: *www.fastcoin.com*
Specialties: *Collector coins, investment grade certified U.S.*

rare coins, PCGS & NGC dealer; appraiser for the Federal Trade Commission.

RHUE, Bob (PNG #559)
ROBERT RHUE ENTERPRISES, INC.
P.O. Box 371437
Denver, CO 80237
(303) 671-0650
Fax: (303) 671-0691
9-5
eMail: *rrhue@qwest.net*
Specialties: *Territorial gold, colonials, C & D gold, early gold, high grade U.S. type gold.*

ROBERTS, Greg
(PNG #414)
SPECTRUM NUMISMATICS
P.O. Box 18523
Irvine, CA 92623
Tel. (949) 955-1250
Fax: (949) 955-1824
Hours: 8:00-5:00

ROBINS, Douglas
(PNG #261)
DOUGLAS ROBINS, INC
(541) 757-1177
Specialties: *Canada: coins & tokens. World coins.*

RODGERS, Brad
(PNG #448)
THE NUMISMATIC EMPORIUM, INC.
21300 Victory Blvd., Suite 220
Woodland Hills, CA 91367
(818) 887-2723
(800) 530-3050
Fax: (818) 887-0301
Specialties: *U.S. gold coins*

ROHAN, Gregory J.
(PNG #449)
HERITAGE RARE COIN GALLERIES
100 Highland Park Village
2nd Floor
Dallas, TX 75205-2788
(214) 528-3500
(800) 872-6467
Fax: (214) 528-2596
8-5
Auction sales, collections purchased.
eMail: *rohan@heritagecoin.com*
web site:
www.heritagecoin.com
Specialties: *Buying, selling, financing, joint ventures, coin show and Internet auction sales throughout the year. Consignments accepted.*

ROSEN, Maurice
(PNG #523)
NUMISMATIC COUNSELING, INC.
P.O. Box 38
Plainview, NY 11803
(516) 433-5800
Fax: (516) 433-5801
9-5
eMail: *MauriceRosen@aol.com*
Specialties: *U.S. coins. Investment counseling & portfolio management; publisher & editor of The Rosen Numismatic Advisory.*

ROSSA, Richard
(PNG #459)
TOKENS AND MEDALS
P.O. Box 297133
Kingsway Station
Brooklyn, NY 11229-7133
(718) 627-6188
Fixed price lists.
Specialties: *Tokens & medals, U.S. colonials, political items, paper/metal notgeld, appraisals.*

ROSSMAN, Will
(PNG #A-533)
PEAK NUMISMATICS
453 Wonderview #150
Estes Park, CO 80517
(970) 577-1740
Fax: (970) 577-1741
By Appointment Only
eMail: *will@peakcoins.com*
web site: *www.peakcoins.com*
Specialties: *Estates, trusts and collections purchased/appraised. Auction Services available. Want lists serviced. Will travel to consult.*

ROWE, John N. III
(PNG #65)
SOUTHWEST NUMISMATIC CORP.
6301 Gaston Avenue, Suite 650
Dallas, TX 75214
(214) 823-9202
(214) 826-3036
Fax: (214) 823-1923
By appointment only
Specialties: *Appraisals, U.S. coins, U.S. and obsolete paper money, Texas currency.*

RUBENSTEIN, M.H.
(PNG #186)
MARTIN RUBENSTEIN COMPANY
1750 Sunrise Highway
Bay Shore, NY 11706
(631) 665-8924
Fax: (631) 665-8945
9-5:30 Mon.-Sat.
Fixed price lists, monthly, FREE for the asking; catalogs; United States, world and wholesale price list.
Specialties: *Coins & currency of U.S., Canada; ancients & world bought & sold; same day jet service since 1961.*

SCHELL, Thomas F.
(PNG #506)
SECURITY RARE COINS
1513 Lititz Pike
Lancaster, PA 17601
(717) 291-9621
Fax: (717) 291-9685
10-6 Mon.-Fri., 10-2 Sat.
Specialties: *All U.S. coins & bullion items. Authorized PCGS, NGC dealer.*

SCHINKE, Glenn
(PNG #520)
GLENN SCHINKE
P.O. Box 3371
Rosemead, CA Rosemead
Tel. (626) 446-6775
Fax: (626) 446-8536
Fixed price lists
Specialties: *Ancient, medieval & foreign coins; tokens & medals; broken banknotes.*

SCHMIDT, Dean
(PNG #451)
DEAN SCHMIDT RARE COIN
P.O. Box 25325
Shawnee Mission, KS 66225
(913) 681-5025
(800) 543-6720
Fax: (913) 681-6090
By appointment
eMail: *dsrc@aol.com*
Specialties: *Collections & estates appraised & purchased. All major U.S. rarities especially wanted.*

SCHMIDT, Gerald A.
(PNG #566)
IMPERIAL COINS
8801 Patterson Ave
Richmond, VA 23229
(804) 740-6481
9:30AM-1:00PM Tues.–Sat.
Specialties: *U.S. & World General.*

SCHUCH, John L.
(PNG #560)
JOHN L. SCHUCH R.C
631-A North Market Blvd
Sacramento, CA 95834
(916) 924-9871
(916) 799-8058
Fax: (916) 924-9140
9:00 a.m.-5:00 p.m. Mon.-Thur., 9:00 a.m.-2:00 p.m. Fri.
Specialties: *Franklin halves Full bell lines. Jefferson Nickels Full Steps.*

SCHWARY, Richard Joseph
(PNG #365)
CALIFORNIA NUMISMATIC INVESTMENTS, INC.
525 West Manchester Blvd.
Inglewood, CA 90301
Tel. (310) 674-3330,
Tel. (800) 225-7531
Fax: (310) 330-3766
Free 24 Hour Quote Line: (888) 443-GOLD Free info. package, authorized PCGS/NGC dealer.
web site: *www.golddealer.com*
Specialties: *All gold, silver & platinum bullion; investment quality, certified rare coins. Buy & sell collections, large or small, & guarantee the best prices in the nation.*

SCIRPO, Anthony Michael
(PNG #494)
FARMINGTON VALLEY RARE COIN & INVESTMENT COMPANY, INC.
P.O. Box 263
New Hartford, CT 06057
Tel. (860) 379-3435
Fax: (860) 738-9243
Hours: 9 a.m.-10 p.m. Mon.-Sat.
We serve the financial planning community & are broker-dealer approved (10 years). Also, the exclusive publisher of The Contrarian View (newsletter), & provide special reports, bulletins & other rare coin educational data. SERIOUS INQUIRIES ONLY, PLEASE.
eMail: *fvrccoin@mindspring.com*
Specialties: *Top quality, select, gold & silver NGC certified investment portfolios, NGC coin certification/PHOTO PROOF submissions, estate planning (tax reduction), rare coin estate/collection sales, auction sales & evaluations. Bullion, U.S. commemoratives and gold coins, patterns, type coins and silver dollars. We also serve the medical, legal & executive profession. Confidentiality & advisorial integrity are foremost considerations at all times for all clientele.*

SHAFER, Leonard W.
(PNG #434)
3202 W. Magnolia Blvd.
Burbank, CA 91505
(818) 846-5655
Specialties: *Coins, medals, tokens, banknotes of the world.*

SIMEK, James A.
(PNG #319)
NUMISGRAPHIC ENTERPRISES
P.O. Box 7157
Westchester, IL 60154-7157
(708) 345-8207
Fax: (708) 345-8207
By appointment only
Specialties: *Quality U.S. coins, U.S. large & small size currency, Nationals, Hawaiiana, black & white & color numismatic photography, catalog production.*

SIMMONS, Van
(PNG #542)

DAVID HALL'S RARE COINS
P.O. Box 6220
Newport Beach, CA 92658
(800) 759-7575
Fax: (949) 477-5874
Hours: 7-5 PST
eMail: *van@davidhall.com*
web site: *www.davidhall.com*
Specialties: *High quality U.S. rare coins.*

SKRABALAK, Andrew William (PNG #591)
ANGEL DEE'S
P.O. Box 5234
Woodbridge, VA 22194
Tel. (703) 491-0336
Fax: (703) 491-0336
Hours: 10 a.m.-10 p.m. EST
7 days a week.
Specialties: *Small cents and nickels, primarily mint state and proof.*

SMITH, Thomas J.
(PNG #527)
THE NUMISMATIC EMPORIUM, INC.
496 Forest Ave.
Glen Ellyn, IL 60137
(630) 790-1564
Fax: (630) 790-0486
Specialties: *Importer and marketmaker in all U.S. gold coins.*

SPANIER, Kurt
(PNG #366)
P.O. Box 37
Las Rozas
Madrid, 28230
011-3491-6302690
By appointment only
Specialties: *Expertise, counseling & estimation on Roman coins, Spanish & colonial coins, Portuguese coins.*

SPENCE, Larry Gerald
(PNG #301)
LARRY SPENCE RARE COINS
1600 West 38th Street
Suite 140
Austin, TX 78731
(512) 454-3003
Fax: (512) 452-4770
9-5

STACK, Harvey G.
(PNG #291)
STACK'S
123 West 57th Street
New York, NY 10019
(212) 582-2580
Fax: (212) 245-5018
10-5 Mon.-Fri
66 years of selling at public auction—1935 to present. Fixed price lists, catalogs, publications, auction sales.
eMail: *info@stacks.com*
web site: *www.stacks.com*
Specialties: *United States gold, silver & copper coins; ancient & foreign gold, silver & copper coins; Coin Galleries—Stack's foreign department.*

STACK, Lawrence R.
(PNG #355)
STACK'S
123 West 57th Street
New York, NY 10019
(212) 582-2580
Fax: (212) 245-5018
10-5 Mon.–Fri.
65 years of selling at public auction—1935 to present. Fixed price lists, catalogs, publications, auction sales.
eMail: *info@stacks.com*
web site: *www.stacks.com*
Specialties: *United States gold, silver & copper coins; ancient & foreign gold, silver & copper coins. English hammered coins.*

Coin galleries—Stack's foreign department.

STAGG, David C., III
(PNG #392)
DAVID C. STAGG III, INC
P.O. Box 640
Santa Rosa, CA 95402
(707) 938-4901
Fax: (707) 591-0902
By appointment only
Specialties: *Quality U.S. material.*

STEINBERG, Robert L.
(PNG #285)
STEINBERG'S
P.O. Box 1565
Boca Raton, FL 33429-1565
tEL. (954) 781-3455
Fax: (954) 781-5865
HOURS: By appointment only
Fixed price lists.
eMail: *info@steinbergs.com*
web site: *www.steinbergs.com*
Specialties: *Gold coins of the world. Request a free copy of our price list or visit our website.*

STEINBERG, Eric
(PNG #590)
BROWARD COUNTY COINS & COLLECTIBLES, INC.
P.O. Box 16237
Plantation, FL 33318
Tel. (954) 474-5002
Fax: (954) 474-8863
Hours: M-F 10 a.m.-4 p.m. By Appointment
eMail: *Browardcc@aol.com*
web site:
www.browardcountycoins.com

STEINMETZ, Dennis E.
(PNG #302)
STEINMETZ COINS & CURRENCY
350 Centerville Road
Lancaster, PA 17601
(717) 299-1211
(800) 334-3903
Fax: (717) 299-0289
9:30-5:30 M/T/Th/F, 9-12 Sat., Closed Wed.
Facts Teletype D-13, Other hours by appointment.
eMail: *dsteinco@aol.com*
web site:
www.steinmetzcoins.com
Specialties: *Numismatic collecting, U.S. coins & currency.*

STOREIM, Michael R.
(PNG #580)
NUMISMATIC PROFESSIONALS, LLC
2922 Evergreen Pkwy., Ste. 203
Evergreen, CO 80439
(303) 670-3212
Fax: (303) 670-3216
By appointment only
eMail: *mike@numispro.com*

STUPPLER, Barry S
(PNG #334)
BARRY STUPPLER & COMPANY, INC.
5855 Topanga Canyon Blvd. #330
Woodland Hills, CA Woodland H
(818) 592-2800
Fax: (818) 594-8599
9:00-5:00 Mon.-Fri
eMail: *barry@coinmag.com*
web site: *www.coinmag.com*
Specialties: *High grade U.S. gold & silver singles, gold, platinum & silver bullion & coins.*

SUNDERLAND, James
(PNG #548)
JAMES & SONS, LTD.
239 Gold Coast Lane
Calumet City, IL 60409
(708) 862-3800
Fax: (708) 862-3800
10-6

web site:
www.jamesandsons.com
Specialties: *U.S. gold & type coins, PCGS dealer.*

SUNDMAN, David M
(PNG #510)
LITTLETON COIN COMPANY, INC.
1309 Mt. Eustis Rd.
Littleton, NH 03561
Tel. (603) 444-3524
(800) 581-2646
Fax: (603) 444-3512
Hours: 7:30-4:00 M-F
Catalogs and fixed price lists sent on request.
eMail:
coinbuy@littletoncoin.com
web site: *www.littletoncoin.com*
Specialties: *All U.S. coins & paper money. Littleton Coin is a family-owned firm offering friendly service to collectors for over 55 years. Extensive color catalogs available FREE. U.S. coins and currency sent on approval to qualified applicants. With over 100,000 customers, we always need to buy U.S. coins and paper money!*

SWIATEK, Anthony
(PNG #511)
MINERVA C & J, LTD.
P.O. Box 218
Manhasset, NY 11030
Tel. (516) 365-4120
Fax: (516) 365-4121
Hours: 9:00 a.m.–7:00 p.m. EST
Free coin grading service.
eMail: *uscoinguru@aol.com*
web site:
www.anthonyswiatek.com
Specialties: *U.S. commemoratives, U.S. type, U.S. gold, U.S. currency.*

TELLER, M. Louis
(PNG #415)
M. LOUIS TELLER NUMISMATIC COMPANY
16055 Ventura Blvd., Ste. 635
Encino, CA 91436
Tel. (818) 783-8454
Fax: (818) 783-9083
Hours: By appointment only
eMail: *mlt@tellercoins.com*
web site: *www.tellercoins.com*
Specialties: *Rare world gold & silver coins, fine quality world banknotes.*

TERRANOVA, Anthony
(PNG #327)
ANTHONY TERRANOVA, INC.
P.O. Box 985, FDR Station
New York, NY 10150
Tel. (212) 787-5682
Specialties: *U.S colonial, state coinage issues, early U.S. mint issues & rare gold. Historical American medals. TO THE TRADE ONLY.*

TOMASKA, Rick J.
(PNG #589)
R & I COINS
P.O. Box 230009
Encinitas, CA 92023
(858) 792-1219
(800) 753-2646
Fax: (858) 792-8758
Hours: 9-5 p.m. Mon.-Fri, 10-3 p.m. Sat.
web site: *www.ricoins.com*
Specialties: *Cameo coinage, mint state Franklin halves. U.S. Proof Coins.*

TRAVERS, Scott A.
(PNG #555)
SCOTT TRAVERS RARE COIN GALLERIES, INC.
P.O. Box 1711, FDR Station

New York, NY 10150-1711
(212) 535-9135
Fax: (212) 535-9138
Mon-Fri 9-5:30 by appointment only
Award-winning author of best selling coin books, including The Coin Collector's Survival Manual, One-Minute Coin Expert, How to Make Money in Coins Right Now, and The Insider's Guide to U.S. Coin Values.
eMail: *travers@inch.com*
web site:
www.inch.com/~travers
Specialties: *All U.S. coins, with a specialty of high-grade rarities, appraisals, consulting to law firms & government agencies, licensed auctioneer & certification service submission center.*

TREGLIA, Jerry
(PNG #A-588)
JERRY TREGLIA RARE COINS
P.O. Box 295
Ridgewood, NJ 07451
(201) 825-9737
(201) 665-8111-CELL
Fax: (201) 825-4055
Hours: 9-5
Specialties: *U.S. gold coins & Pioneer gold.*

VAN BEBBER, Robert
(PNG #556)
RARE COIN GALLERIES OF GLENDALE
228 S. Brand Blvd
Glendale, CA 91204
Tel. (818) 243-2900
Tel. (818) 243-1169
Hours: Mon.-Sat. 9:00-5:30
Specialties: *U.S. coins, world coins, banknotes, medals, antiques & jewelry. World gold & silver coin specialists.*

VAN GROVER, Jacob Jay
(PNG #166)
J.J. VAN GROVER, LTD.
P.O. Box 123
Oakland Gardens, NY 11364
(718) 224-9578
Fax: (718) 224-9393
B Appointment & 9-5 Mon.-Thurs.
Auction "Ark Auction Company"
eMail: *jjvangrover@juno.com*
Specialties: *Modern commemoratives, U.S. & Israel silver dollars—especially GSA CC 1.00.*

VARNER, Mal (PNG #270)
ALHAMBRA COIN CENTER, INC.
254 East Main Street
Alhambra, CA 91801
(626) 282-1151
(800) 932-COIN
Fax: (626) 282-4694
9-5:30 Mon.-Thur., 9-6 Fri., 10-3 Sat.
eMail: *enchantables@aol.com*
Specialties: *Rare U.S. & foreign gold & silver coins; PCGS & NGC certified coins; estate jewelry, diamonds, watches.*

VARTIAN, Armen R.
(PNG #AF515)
ATTORNEY AT LAW
805 Duncan Pl.
Manhattan Beach, CA 90266
(310) 372-1355
Fax: (310) 372-1555
eMail:
armenvartian@justice.com

VYZAS, Evangelos
(PNG ##581)
P.O. Box 450
Pully, 1009

01141796580909
011306944148080
Fax: 01141244957280
Office Hours
eMail: *e.vyzas@bluewin.ch*
Specialties: *Ancient Greek, Byzantine, Modern Greek coins and medals. Greek currency. All Greek world.*

WADDELL, Edward J., Jr
(PNG #275)
EDWARD J. WADDELL, LTD.
P.O. Box 3759
Frederick, MD 21705
(301) 473-8600
(800) 381-6396
Fax: (301) 473-8716
By appointment only
eMail: *ed@coin.com*
web site: *www.coin.com*
Specialties: *Ancient Greek, Roman & Byzantine coins. Coin cases. Numismatic Literature.*

WEINBERG, Fred C.
(PNG #257)
FRED WEINBERG & CO.
16311 Ventura Blvd.
Ste. #1298
Encino, CA 91436
(818) 986-3733
(818) 986-3800
Fax: (818) 986-2153
8-4 with appointment
Fixed price lists.
eMail: *fred@fredweinberg.com*
web site:
www.fredweinberg.com
Specialties: *Major Mint Errors Coins & Currency, PCGS Certified coins, & U.S. Gold. Marketing experience & Consulting.*

WEISS, Martin (PNG #579)
PANDA AMERICA
3460 Torrance Blvd. #100
Torrance, CA 90503
(310) 373-9647
(800) 472-6327
Fax: (310) 378-6024
9:00 a.m.-5:00 p.m.
Winner of the 2002 Sol Kaplan Award for "helping in cleansing our profession of theivery and for upholding the ethics that the PNG stands for."
eMail:
marty@pandaamerica.com
web site:
www.pandaamerica.com
Specialties: *Major market maker of modern world coins, official distributor for leading world mints. Wholesale and retail for gold & silver foreign coins, United States gold commemoratives, etc. Custom minting coins & medals.*

WEITZ, Harold B.
(PNG #375)
HAROLD B. WEITZ, INC
6315 Forbes Avenue, Suite 208
Pittsburgh, PA 15217
(412) 521-1879
(800) 245-4807
Fax: (412) 521-1750
8:30-4:30
Fixed price lists, catalogs.
eMail: *davidwww@aol.com*
web site: *www.weitzcoins.com*

WEITZ, Saul (PNG #393)
HAROLD B. WEITZ, INC.
6315 Forbes Avenue, Suite 208
Pittsburgh, PA 15217
(412) 521-1879
(800) 245-4807
Fax: (412) 521-1750
8:30-4:30
Fixed price lists, catalogs.
eMail: *davidwww@aol.com*
web site: *www.weitzcoins.com*

WHITE, Harlan
(PNG #132)
2425 El Cajon Blvd
San Diego, CA 92104
(619) 298-0137
Fax: (619) 298-7966
9-4:30, Sat 9-12
Specialties: *$5,000, $10,000, $500, $1,000 notes. Territorial & pioneer gold, U.S. coins, Hawaiian coins.*

WHITLOW, Larry
(PNG #169)
17W 695 BUTTERFIELD ROAD
Suite G
OakbrookTerrace, IL 60181
(630) 792-1900
Fax: (630) 792-1929
Hours: 8:00-4:45 Mon.-Fri-Sat. by appointment only
Fixed price lists.
eMail: *mprintz@whitlowltd.com*
web site: *www.whitlowltd.com*
Specialties: *Choice condition rare U.S. coins, particularly all dated series. PCGS specialists for the advanced collector.*

WHITNAH, Paul R.
(PNG #AF440)
M&M WORLD TRAVEL SERVICE
5801 West I-20, Suite 325
Arlington, TX 76017-1078
(817) 561-1252
Fax: (800) 426-8326
eMail: *pwhitnah@mmworldtravel.com*
web site: *www.mmworldtravel.com*

WILKISON, John
(PNG #351)
WILKISON INTERNATIONAL

WILLIAMS, Dale L.
(PNG #432)
WILLIAMS GALLERY, INC.
29 South Tracy
Bozeman, MT 59715
(406) 586-4343
(800) 422-0787
Fax: (406) 586-3921
8:30-5
eMail: *coins@collectorusa.com*
web site: *www.collectorusa.com*
Specialties: *Buying coin collections & estates, selling high quality U.S. rare coins.*

WILLIS, Donald W.
(PNG #A-235)
DONALD WILLIS RARE COINS
1129 Kiowa Drive East
Kiowa, TX 76240
(940) 668-6567
By Appointment
Specialties: *U.S. coins & currency.*

WING, Augusto
(PNG #A-423)
M. LOUIS TELLER NUMISMATIC CO.
16055 Ventura Blvd., Ste. 635
Encino, CA 91436
(818) 783-8454
Fax: (818) 783-9083
By appointment only
eMail: *gus@tellercoins.com*
web site: *www.tellercoins.com*
Specialties: *Chinese, South American crowns & patterns, world gold.*

WINTER, Douglas A.
(PNG #399)
DOUGLAS WINTER NUMISMATICS
P.O. Box 7827
Dallas, TX 75209
(214) 654-9905
Fax: (214) 654-9906

By appointment only
Fixed price lists, appraisals, consulting, writing projects.
eMail: *DWN@ont.com*
web site:
www.raregoldcoins.com
Specialties: *18th & 19th century U.S. gold with an emphasis on choice & rare branch mint issues; pre-1850 proof silver coinage.*

WINTERSTEIN, Christian
(PNG #315)
UBS AG
CH-4002 Basel,
Aeschenvorstadt,
(061) 288-2703
Fax: (061) 288-6673
8:15-4:30 Mon.-Fri.
Fixed price lists, publications, catalogs, auction sales.

WOODSIDE, John J.
(PNG #543)
SCOTSMAN COIN & JEWELRY
11262 Olive Blvd.
St. Louis, MO 63141
(800) 642-4305
Fax: (314) 692-0410
Mon.-Sat. 8-5
Buying guide, selling catalog.
eMail: *mark@scoins.com*
web site: *www.scoins.com*
Specialties: *Coins, currency, jewelry.*

WRUBEL, Gordon J.
(PNG #316)
BOWERS AND MERENA GALLERIES
P.O. Box 1224
Wolfeboro, NH 03894
Tel: (800) 458-4646
Fax: (603) 569-5319
Hours: 8:30-5 Mon.–Fri.
eMail: *gordon@bowersandmerena.com*
web site:
www.bowersandmerena.com
Specialties: *U.S. and Canadian coins, specializing in early copper, high quality U.S. gold and type coins. Rare phonograph records.*

YAFFE, Mark S.
(PNG #387)
NATIONAL GOLD EXCHANGE, INC.
14309 N. Dale Mabry
Tampa, FL 33618
(813) 969-4111
Fax: (813) 969-4003
9-6 Mon-Fri—Catalogs
eMail: *nge@ngegold.com*
web site: *www.ngegold.com*
Specialties: *Circ. & certified, U.S. gold, Foreign gold, proof gold; better date dollars.*

YOUNGERMAN, William J.
(PNG #236)
WILLIAM YOUNGERMAN, INC.
95 S. Federal Highway
Suite 203
Boca Raton, FL 33432
Tel. (561) 368-7707
Tel. (800) 327-5010
Fax: Fax: (561) 394-6084
Hours: 9:30-5:00 M-F
eMail: *wymoney@aol.com*
web site:
www.williamyoungerman.com

ZARIT, Jeffrey S.
(PNG #388)
4455 LBJ Freeway, Suite 807
Dallas, TX 75244
(972) 980-4621
(800) 654-7527
Fax: (972) 980-0041
By appointment only

Fixed price lists (3-5 per year).
eMail: *jeff@klippes.com*
web site: *www.klippes.com*
Specialties: *Foreign silver & copper coins, 1500-date. Ebay Internet Auctions. Ebay Name: "Jeffone."*

ZURAWSKI, Jr., Stanley M.
(PNG #AF237)
NEVADA COIN MART, INC.
P.O. Box 46110
Las Vegas, NV 89114
(702) 369-0500
(800) 634-6732

ANCIENT COINS: COLLECTING HISTORICAL COINS

Courtesy of Victor England, Jr., Senior Director of Classical Numismatic Group, Inc.

Coins are the most important form of money. For over 2,000 years these small pieces of metal have represented units of intrinsic value.

Today we take coins for granted; but since coinage emerged in the late 7th century B.C. it has played an important role in the economics of many cultures. Today we are fortunate to have coins as records of past history.

Through the collecting of coins you can acquire significant historical artifacts that can lead you down many paths of research and exploration. If only these small objects could talk—I am sure they would tell many interesting tales.

The collecting of historical coins from the Greek, Roman, and Byzantine periods is an affordable pastime that can provide many hours of enjoyment. The collecting of ancient coins is perhaps the oldest part of numismatics. Once only the hobby of kings, it is now a rewarding field readily open to all.

A recently published book series, *Ancient Coin Collecting* by Wayne G. Sayles, is a must for anyone wanting to look over this fascinating area of numismatics. These books are available from your favorite bookstore or numismatic bookseller.

Over the next few pages I will introduce you to 32 ancient coins that might form the beginnings of your collection. Condition, strike, and style play important roles in the price of ancient coins. I have provided price ranges you might expect to pay for some of these coins. The price categories in the order they appear on the following pages are as follows:

Fine–Very Fine   Very Fine–Good   Very Fine—Extremely Fine

Over 2,600 years ago in Lydia (Western Turkey), small lumps of metal were stamped with a simple design. These lumps of metal, made from a natural alloy of silver and gold, were called electrum. They represent one of the earliest coins.

1. Uncertain Kings of Lydia. Before 561 B.C. Electrum Third Stater. Obverse: Head of a roaring lion, knob on forehead. Reverse: Double incuse punch. Average weight 4.70 grams.

500–700 1000–1400 1500–2400

Croesus, the last King of the Lydians, lived from 560–546 B.C. He was an extremely powerful ruler who subjected many lands in the area. From the spoils of successful war and a rich supply of bullion in his native land, he became fabulously wealthy. The expression "rich as Croesus" still has meaning today. Croesus introduced us to coins made of refined metals of gold and silver.

2. LYDIA, King Croesus. 560–546 B.C. Silver Siglos. Obverse: Confronted foreparts of lion and bull. Reverse: Double incuse punch. Average weight 5.30 grams.

250–400 500–700 750–1200

Over the next hundred years that followed, coinage became the accepted medium of exchange. People in Greece and other nearby countries soon started making use of coins. The designs on the coins reflected the heritage of the many diverse cities that surrounded the Mediterranean. As a result of commerce and war the coinage of the greatest cities of the ancient world became the trade coins of the day. Many Greek coins were very skillfully made and extremely beautiful. Designs often incorporated the patron deity of the city or the badge of the city itself.

Tarentum was the most important city in Southern Italy in the 5th and 4th centuries before Christ. The foundation myth of the city relates the story of a dolphin saving Taras from a shipwreck at sea. In the place where he came ashore, the city of Tarentum was founded.

3. TARENTUM in Calabria. Circa 334–330 B.C. Silver Nomos. Obverse: Naked horseman on horse left. Taras astride of dolphin right. Average weight 7.80 grams.

150–200 250–400 700–1200

On the island of Sicily, Syracuse became the dominant city. Coinage developed on the island in the 6th century B.C. and reached its height in the 5th century. Some of the finest examples of the engravers' art are found on the coins of Syracuse.

4. SYRACUSE on the island of Sicily. Circa 480–475 B.C. Silver Tetradrachm. Obverse: Charioteer driving slow quadriga to the right, Nike above placing a wreath on the horse's head. Diademed head of Arethusa right, four dolphins swimming around. Average weight 17.00 grams.

400–600 600–800 1500–3000

Throughout most of the 5th century B.C. after the defeat of the Persians, Athens was mistress of the Aegean. She became the cultural and political center of the Greek world.

5. ATHENS in Attica. After 449 B.C. Silver Tetradrachm. Obverse: Helmeted head of Athena. Reverse: Owl standing right in shallow incuse, olive spray behind. Average weight 17.00 grams.

200–300 400–700 900–1500

Aegina was an island off the coast of Athens. The Aeginetans were exceptional maritime merchants. Aegina was the central staging depot for Black Sea grain on its way to the Peloponnisos. These early trade coins circulated throughout the Mediterranean.

6. AEGINA. Circa 525–480 B.C. AR Stater. Obverse sea turtle, with T-back dots, seen from above. Reverse. Skew incuse. Average weight 12.25 grams.

100–250 300–500 800–1500

7. AEGINA. Circa 457–431 B.C. AR Tater. Land tortoise, with segmented shell, seen from above. Reverse: Skew pattern incuse. Average weight 12.25 gm.

200–300 500–650 900–1200

Corinth, situated in central Greece, was one of the great commercial centers in her day. Coins of Corinth were widely imitated by other cities. The flying Pegasus is seen on the coins of many of her trading partners.

8. CORINTH in Corinthia. Circa 345–307 B.C. Silver Stater. Obverse: Pegasus flying left. Reverse: Helmeted head of Athena left. Average weight 8.50 grams.

150–200 300–400 500–1000

In Asia Minor we find the important port and naval base of Aspendos. Her coins depict two naked wrestlers grappling in contest. Sporting events were an integral part of life in ancient Greece. The modern day Olympics trace their origins to Greece and her culture.

9. ASPENDOS in Pamphylia. Circa 370–330 B.C. Silver Stater. Obverse: Two wrestlers grappling. Reverse: Slinger standing right in throwing pose, triskeles in the field. Average weight 10.50 grams.

150–250 250–400 600–1200

Along the north coast of Africa we find the important maritime trading city of Carthage. Due to the great natural harbor and favorable geographical location, Carthage became one of the great powers of the Greek world.

10. CARTHAGE in Zeugitania. Circa 350–260 B.C. Gold/Electrum Stater. Obverse: Wreathed head of Tanit left. Reverse: Horse standing right. Average weight 7.50 grams.

500–600	750–900	1400–2000

In the late 4th century a ruler came to power who would change the shape of the world as it was known at the time. At the age of 20, in 336 B.C., Alexander III (the Great) became ruler of the small kingdom of Macedonia. By the time he died 13 years later at the age of 33, he had conquered an empire that stretched from Greece to India. Alexander's coinage played an important role in his eastern conquests. Local coinages were replaced with his tetradrachms. Over 200 mints produced coins in his name.

11. Alexander III, King of Macedon. 336–323 B.C. Silver Tetradrachm. Obverse: Head of Herakles right, wearing a lion skin. Reverse: Zeus enthroned left, holding an eagle in his outstretched hand. Average weight 17.00 grams.

150–200	250–425	500–800

Alexander was one of the most successful generals who ever lived. Upon his death his kingdom was divided amongst several of his generals. Many of the kings who came after Alexander put his picture on their coins. They believed he was a god.

12. Lysimachos, King of Thrace. 323–281 B.C. Silver Tetradrachm. Obverse: Head of deified Alexander the Great right. Reverse: Athena seated left holding Nike in her outstretched hand. Average weight 17.00 grams.

200–250 300–450 900–1500

As the successors of Alexander established power in their own rights, several powerful kingdoms formed. One of the most powerful of the new kingdoms was the Ptolemaic kingdom in Egypt. Under Ptolemy and his successors, this kingdom would survive until the death of Cleopatra VII, lover of Julius Caesar and Mark Antony. The coins of Ptolemaic Egypt provide us with portraits of important historical rulers.

13. Ptolemy I, King of Egypt. 323–283 B.C. Silver Tetradrachm. Obverse: Diademed bust of Ptolemy right. Reverse: Egyptian eagle standing left on thunderbolt. Average weight 14.50 grams.

100–250 250–350 500–800

14. Cleopatra VII, Queen of Egypt. 51–30 B.C. Bronze 80 Drachmae. Obverse: Diademed bust of Cleopatra right. Reverse: Eagle standing left on thunderbolt. Average weight 18.00 grams.

100–200 300–600 1200–1600

To the east of Egypt was the province of Judaea. The area was under the rule first of the Persians, then Alexander the Great, and later the Ptolemaic kings followed by the Seleucids. During the late 2nd century B.C., Judaea achieved a measure of independence under the Hasmoneans and finally under Alexander Jannaeus, 103–76 B.C., full autonomy. This impoverished area gave birth to two of the world's greatest religions—Judaism and later Christianity.

15. Alexander Jannaeus, Hasmonean King of Judaea. 103–76 B.C. Bronze Prutah. Obverse: Anchor, legend around. Reverse: Wheel with eight spokes. Average weight 1.00 gram.

20–30 40–75 200–400

Late in the 2nd century B.C., the port city of Tyre regained her autonomy in the waning days of Ptolemaic and Seleucid influence. A remarkable silver coinage was struck at Tyre from about 126 B.C. until well into Roman times. The famous tetradrachms (shekels) of this series have achieved some notoriety as the most likely coinage with which Judas was paid his "30 pieces of silver" for the betrayal of Christ.

16. TYRE in Phoenicia. After 126 B.C. Silver Tetradrachm (shekel). Obverse: Laureate bust of Melkart. Reverse: Eagle standing left on prow. Average weight 14.00 grams, declining later to 13.00 grams.

250–400 500–600 750–1200

"And when they had bound him, they led him away, and delivered him to Pontius Pilate the governor." Matthew 27:2

This coin speaks for itself.

17. Pontius Pilate, Roman Prefect of Judaea under Tiberius, Emperor of Rome. 26–29 A.D. Bronze Prutah. Obverse: Lituus with inscription around. Reverse: Date within wreath. Average weight 1.00 gram.

30–50 75–125 400–600

While the Hellenistic kingdoms were vying for control in the east, another power was slowly emerging in the west. On the banks of the river Tiber in Italy in a small village called Rome, a new empire was taking shape. According to legend, twins called Romulus and Remus founded Rome in the middle of the 8th century B.C. By the 3rd century B.C. this small agricultural community had grown and began building one of the greatest empires the world has ever seen.

At first the Romans used coins that were struck on the Greek system that was already in place in Italy.

18. ROMAN REPUBLIC. Circa 225–212 B.C. Silver Didrachm (Quadrigatus). Obverse: Laureate head of Janus. Reverse: Jupiter in a quadriga moving to the right being driven by Victory. Average weight 6.50 grams.

100–200 300–400 700–1200

One of the main reasons the Romans struck coins was to pay the soldiers. As the Roman army expanded the boundaries of the

Empire, a new denomination emerged that would become the standard for many centuries. The Roman silver denarius was struck from the 2nd century B.C. until the 3rd century A.D. In the latter days of the Republic and early days of the Empire a Roman soldier received an annual salary of 225 denarii.

19. ROMAN REPUBLIC. After 200 B.C. Issued by various moneyers. Silver Denarius. Obverse: Helmeted head of Roma right, X below chin. Reverse: The Dioscuri riding right. Average weight 3.85 grams.

50–75 100–150 3500–4500

As the Empire expanded, the political system in Rome suffered. Rome was no longer able to govern itself under rules of just a Senate, and influential people began to try and take control of the reins of power. In 59 B.C., Caius Julius Caesar was elected to be a governing consul. He spent the next eight years campaigning in Britain and Gaul. A power struggle ensued amongst other ruling members of the ruling Roman triumvirate, and, after defeating Pompeii in 48 B.C. Caesar marched into Rome as her undisputed master. After only a short period of supreme power he was assassinated on the Ides (15th) of March in 44 B.C.

20. Julius Caesar. Struck 49 B.C. Silver Denarius. Obverse: Elephant right trampling a serpent, CAESAR below. Reverse: Priestly implements. Average weight 4.00 grams.

150–200 300–400 600–1000

After the assassination of Caesar, another triumvirate was formed to try and govern Rome. Two of the members of this group, Mark Antony and Octavian (Augustus), were to play important roles in the advancement of the Roman empire. Antony was given command of the province of Asia. It was here that he met and was captivated by the last of the Ptolemaic dynasty, Cleopatra VII. Antony then quarrelled with Octavian in a struggle for ultimate power. He was defeated at the battle of Actium and fled with Cleopatra to Egypt where he committed suicide in 30 B.C. During this struggle with Octavian he struck a series of denarii for each of the legions under his command.

21. Mark Antony. 32–31 B.C. Silver Legionary Denarius. Obverse: Manned galley right. Reverse: Aquila surmounted by an eagle and flanked by two standards, the legend LEG followed by a Roman numeral representing the legion. Average weight 3.50 grams.

75–100 150–200 500–700

Having achieved undisputed mastery of the Roman world in 30 B.C., Octavian returned stability to the Roman state. In 27 B.C. the Senate acknowledged his mastery and bestowed upon him the title of Augustus, by which he is best known. Augustus ruled long and prosperously, dying at the age of 77. He left behind the foundations for one of the world's greatest empires.

22. Augustus. 27 B.C.–14 A.D. Silver Denarius. Obverse: Laureate head of Augustus right. Reverse: Caius and Lucius Caesars standing facing, shields and spears between them. Average weight 3.60 grams.

75–100 150–200 400–600

Augustus' long life and treachery within his household resulted in his stepson Tiberius succeeding him. Tiberius proved himself an able administrator. The ministry and crucifixion of Jesus Christ occurred during his reign.

The Tribute Penny. *"Is it lawful to give tribute to Caesar, or not? Shall we give or shall we not give? But he knowing their hypocrisy, said unto them, Why tempt ye me? Bring me a penny, that I may see it. And they brought it. And He said unto them, Whose is this image and superscription? And they said unto Him, Caesar's. And Jesus, answering, said unto them, Render to Caesar the things that are Caesar's, and to God the things that are God's."* Mark 12:14–17

23. Tiberius. 14–37 A.D. Silver "Tribute" Denarius. Obverse: Laureate head right, inscription around. Reverse: Livia as pax seated right on throne. Average weight 3.60 grams.

125–200 250–300 600–750

When no clear line of succession to an emperor was apparent, it was often the Praetorian guard who helped choose a successor. Upon the death of the infamous Caligula, the guard raised Claudius to the purple giving him the title of Augustus. The story of these turbulent times has been re-created on video under the title of *I, Claudius.*

24. Claudius. 41–54 A.D. Bronze As. Obverse: Bare head of Claudius left. Reverse: Minerva standing right hurling javelin. Average weight 11.00 grams.

100–175 250–350 600–800

Nero, the adopted son of Claudius, was one of Rome's most colorful emperors. His unbridled enthusiasm, love of the finer things in life, passion for sporting events, and rumored love of fire, led him to commit suicide.

25. Nero. 54–68 A.D. Bronze As. Obverse: Laureate head of Nero right. Reverse: View of the front of the Temple of Janus. Average weight 11.00 grams.

100–175 250–350 700–1200

By the 2nd century A.D. the Roman Empire had reached gargantuan proportions. One of Rome's best administrators was the emperor Hadrian. He spent much of his career travelling the vast empire. His most lasting legacy is Hadrian's Wall in northern England.

26. Hadrian. 117–138 A.D. Silver Denarius. Obverse: Laureate head of Hadrian right. Reverse: Concordia seated left. Average weight 3.35 grams.

50–75 100–200 400–600

In 248 A.D. Rome celebrated the 1000th anniversary of its foundation. Philip I, emperor of Rome, celebrated this anniversary with magnificent games featuring many wild beasts collected especially for this celebration. By the middle of the 3rd century, the denarius had lost much of its value. A larger silver piece was introduced called the antoninianus.

27. Philip I. 244–249 A.D. Silver Antoninianus. Obverse: Radiate bust of Philip right. Reverse: SAECVLARES AVG around various different animals used in the celebration of the 1000th anniversary. Average weight 3.65 grams.

30–50 75–100 125–225

Christianity was a persecuted religion for much of its first 300 years. The first Roman emperor to embrace Christianity was Constantine I, the Great. It is said that he converted on his deathbed.

28. Constantine I, the Great. 307–337 A.D. Bronze Follis. Obverse: Helmeted and cuirassed bust right. Reverse: Roma seated right holding shield. (Many obverse and reverse variations). Average weight 3.00–4.00 grams.

20–30 40–60 150–250

Christianity did not gain immediate acceptance after the death of Constantine. The "Philosopher" Julian II outlawed Christianity 30 years after the death of Constantine, preferring the old pagan religions.

29. Julian II, the Philosopher. 360–363 A.D. Bronze (uncertain denomination). Obverse: Diademed, draped, and cuirassed bust right. Reverse: Apis bull standing right, two stars above. Average weight 8.50 grams.

150–200 300–500 800–1200

By the 5th century A.D., the Roman empire had split into two empires. The empire in the west was tangled in political upheaval. The center of the empire had moved from Rome to Constantinople. In contrast to the problems in the West, the Eastern division of the Empire enjoyed comparative peace under the leadership of Theodosius II. His most notable achievement was the compilation of the legal code known as the Codex Theodosianus. By the 5th century, silver and bronze coins had been replaced by the gold solidus as the coin of the realm.

30. Theodosius II. 402–450 A.D. Gold Solidus. Obverse: Helmeted and cuirassed three-quarter facing bust, spear over far shoulder. Reverse: Constantinopolis enthroned right, holding globus cruciger and sceptre. Average weight 4.45 grams.

200–300 350–500 700–1200

By the 6th century the last vestiges of the Roman Empire had faded into obscurity. While the west was still in turmoil the east found leadership under the religious successors to the Romans. The Byzantine Empire would last until the fall of Constantinople in 1453.

The Byzantine Empire found solid leadership under Justinian I. He ruled for almost four decades. He consolidated the empire, regaining territory lost to the Goths and Vandals. At home in Constantinople, he built the great church of St. Sophia. This is still standing as one of the great architectural achievements of its time in modern day Istanbul. Justinian is also remembered for his final codification of Roman law. He consolidated the best of Roman law for generations to come.

31. Justinian I. 527–565 A.D. Bronze Follis. Obverse: Helmeted facing bust of Justinian holding globus cruciger. Reverse: Large M, flanked by ANNO on the left, numbers on the right indicating the year of his reign and a mint mark below. Average weight 22.00 grams declining to 15.00 grams.

20–30 75–100 400–600

By the 7th century, new nations were emerging in the west and the Byzantine Empire was locked in perpetual struggle with the Arab world. Justinian II showed his devotion to God by placing the image of Christ on his coinage. He was the first emperor to do this. However, his attempts at introducing his doctrines into the policies of the Church were rejected. In the old city of Rome, the papacy was in its infancy. But once again a gradual shift of power was beginning to occur.

32. Justinian II. 685–695 A.D. Gold Solidus. Obverse: Facing bust of bearded Christ imposed over a cross, hand raised in benediction. Reverse: Justinian standing crowned, wearing loros and holding cross potent on steps. Average weight 4.30 grams.

600–800 900–1200 1800–2200

This is only an abbreviated list of the many thousands of different coins one can purchase. Hopefully this list will start you on the road to discovery and collecting in this fascinating field.

The following is a list of six suggested titles for further reading:

Foss, Clive. *Roman Historical Coins.* 1990
Howgego, Christopher. *Ancient History from Coins.* 1995
Jenkins, G. K. *Coins in History—Ancient Greek Coins.* 1990
Lorber, Cathy. *Treasures of Ancient Coinage: From the Private Collections of American Numismatic Society Members.* 1996
Sayles, Wayne G. *Ancient Coin Collecting.* 1996.
Sear, David. *Byzantine Coins and Their Values.* 1987

One of the best general publications on ancient coins is *The Celator,* ed. Kerry Wetterstrom, published monthly. Contact the publication at P.O. Box 859, Lancaster, PA 17608.

Two organizations that are active in the field of ancient numismatics are the American Numismatic Society (ANS) (contact at Broadway at 155th

St., New York, NY 10032), and the Society for Ancient Numismatics (SAN) (contact at P.O. Box 4095, Panorama City, CA 91412).

I am one of the Directors of the Classical Numismatic Group, Inc. (CNG). For the past 22 years we have been quietly building a full-service numismatic firm dedicated to serving the needs of our customers in the fields of ancient, world, and British numismatics. Each year we conduct three auctions, publish three fixed-price lists, attend numerous shows around the world, and even occasionally publish a book. If you would like to know more about us or the field of ancient numismatics, please get in touch. We would like to be of service. Write, call, or e-mail us at Classical Numismatic Group, Inc., P.O. Box 479, Lancaster, PA 17608–0479. Phone (717) 390-9194, fax (717) 390-9978, e-mail: cng@cngcoins.com. We invite you to learn more about ancient coins at www.cngcoins.com.

ANTILLES (NETHERLANDS)

Key to Grading: Lion

DATE	COIN TYPE/VARIETY/METAL	ABP FINE	AVERAGE FINE
☐ 1952–1970	1 Cent, Lion, Bronze	—	$ .60

Key to Grading: Shield

DATE	COIN TYPE/VARIETY/METAL	ABP FINE	AVERAGE FINE
☐ 1970–1978	1 Cent, Bronze	—	.30

Key to Grading: Lion

DATE	COIN TYPE/VARIETY/METAL	ABP FINE	AVERAGE FINE
☐ 1956–1965	$2^1/_2$ Cents, Lion, Bronze	—	$ .45
Key to Grading: Shield			
☐ 1970–1978	$2^1/_2$ Cents Bronze	—	.35
Key to Grading: Scallop			
☐ 1957–1970	5 Cents, Juliana, Cupro-Nickel	—	.40
Key to Grading: Shield			
☐ 1971–1985	5 Cents Copper Nickel	—	.25
Key to Grading: Bust of Queen			
☐ 1954–1970	$^1/_{10}$ Gulden, Juliana, Silver	—	1.00
Key to Grading: Shield			
☐ 1970–1985	10 Cents Nickel	—	.35
Key to Grading: Bust of Queen			
☐ 1954–1970	$^1/_4$ Gulden, Juliana, Silver	—	.65
Key to Grading: Shield			
☐ 1970–1985	25 Cents Nickel	—	.35
Key to Grading: Flower			
☐ 1989–2000	50 Cents Steel	—	.50
Key to Grading: Shield			
☐ 1952–1970	1 Gulden, Juliana, Silver	—	1.50
Key to Grading: Shield			
☐ 1970–1980	1 Gulden Nickel	—	.70

DATE	COIN TYPE/VARIETY/METAL	ABP FINE	AVERAGE FINE
Key to Grading: Shield			
☐ 1964	2 1/2 Gulden, Juliana, Silver	$2.00	$5.00
Key to Grading: Shield			
☐ 1978–1980	2 1/2 Gulden		2.00
☐ 1981–1988	2 1/2 Gulden		2.00
☐ 1989–2000	2 1/2 Gulden		1.50

ARGENTINA

The first coins were used in 1813, followed by silver reales in 1815, and the copper centavos and gold pesos in the mid-1800s. Cupronickel pesos and aluminum-bronze pesos were used in the 1900s. Decimal coins were used in 1881. The currency today is the peso.

Argentina—Type Coinage

Key to Grading: Shield

DATE	COIN TYPE/VARIETY/METAL	ABP FINE	AVERAGE FINE
☐ 1882–1896	1 Centavo, Bronze	—	$ 1.00
☐ 1939–1944	1 Centavo, Bronze	—	.25
☐ 1945–1948	1 Centavo, Copper	—	.40

Key to Grading: Shield

DATE	COIN TYPE/VARIETY/METAL	ABP FINE	AVERAGE FINE
□ 1882–1896	2 Centavos, Bronze	—	$ .85
□ 1939–1947	2 Centavos, Bronze	—	.35
□ 1947–1950	2 Centavos, Copper	—	.45

Key to Grading: Bust

DATE	COIN TYPE/VARIETY/METAL	ABP FINE	AVERAGE FINE
□ 1896–1942	5 Centavos, Cupro-Nickel	—	.45

DATE	COIN TYPE/VARIETY/METAL	ABP FINE	AVERAGE FINE
□ 1942–1950	5 Centavos, Aluminum-Bronze	—	.25
□ 1950	5 Centavos, Death of San Martin Centennial, Cupro-Nickel	—	.38
□ 1951–1953	5 Centavos, Cupro-Nickel	—	.38
□ 1953–1956	5 Centavos, Copper-Nickel Clad Steel	—	.38
□ 1957–1959	5 Centavos, Nickel Clad Steel	—	.38

Key to Grading: Bust

DATE	COIN TYPE/VARIETY/METAL	ABP FINE	AVERAGE FINE
□ 1881–1883	10 Centavos, Silver	—	7.00

DATE	COIN TYPE/VARIETY/METAL	ABP FINE	AVERAGE FINE
□ 1896–1942	10 Centavos, Cupro-Nickel	—	.45
□ 1942–1950	10 Centavos, Aluminum-Bronze	—	.38
□ 1950	10 Centavos, Death of San Martin Centennial, Cupro-Nickel	—	.30
□ 1951–1953	10 Centavos, Cupro-Nickel	—	.30

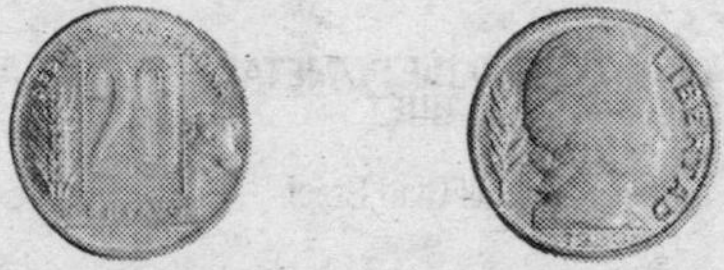

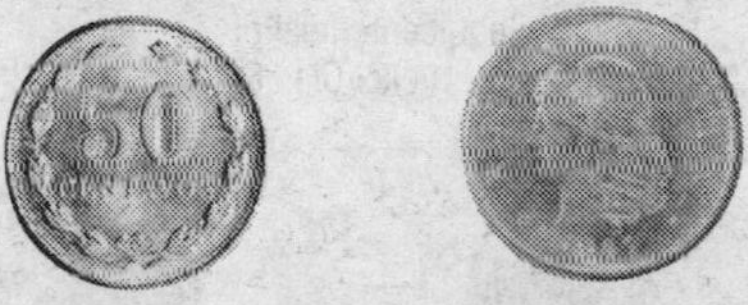

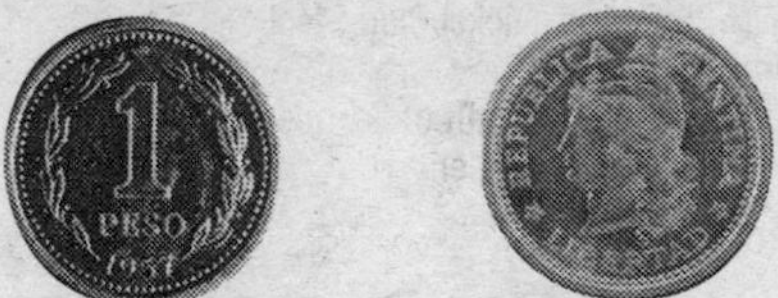

DATE	COIN TYPE/VARIETY/METAL	ABP FINE	AVERAGE FINE
☐ 1952–1956	10 Centavos, Copper-Nickel Clad Steel	—	$ .35
☐ 1957–1959	10 Centavos, Nickel Clad Steel	—	.35
Key to Grading: Bust			
☐ 1881–1883	20 Centavos, Silver	—	15.00
☐ 1896–1942	20 Centavos, Cupro-Nickel	—	.40
☐ 1942–1950	20 Centavos, Aluminum-Bronze	—	.38
☐ 1950	20 Centavos, Death of San Martin Centennial, Cupro-Nickel	—	.38
☐ 1951–1953	20 Centavos, Cupro-Nickel	—	.38
☐ 1952–1956	20 Centavos, Copper-Nickel Clad Steel	—	.38
☐ 1957–1961	20 Centavos, Nickel Clad Steel	—	.38
Key to Grading: Bust			
☐ 1881–1883	50 Centavos, Silver	—	25.00
☐ 1941	50 Centavos, Nickel	—	.45
☐ 1952–1956	50 Centavos, Copper-Nickel Clad Steel	—	.35
☐ 1957–1961	50 Centavos, Nickel Clad Steel	—	.20
Key to Grading: Bust			
☐ 1881–1883	1 Peso, Silver	35.00	85.00
☐ 1957–1962	1 Peso, Nickel Clad Steel	—	.40
☐ 1960	1 Peso, Sesquicentennial of Provisional Government, Nickel Clad Steel	—	.40
Key to Grading: Bust			
☐ 1884	1/2 Argentino, Gold	—	600.00
☐ 1881–1896	Argentino, Gold	—	145.00

Key to Grading: Ship

DATE	COIN TYPE/VARIETY/METAL	ABP FINE	AVERAGE FINE
□ 1961–1968	5 Pesos, Nickel Clad Steel	—	$ .35

Key to Grading: Rider

DATE	COIN TYPE/VARIETY/METAL	ABP FINE	AVERAGE FINE
□ 1962–1968	10 Pesos, Nickel Clad Steel	—	.32
□ 1966	10 Pesos, Sequicentennial of Independence, Nickel Clad Steel	—	.32

Key to Grading: Shield

DATE	COIN TYPE/VARIETY/METAL	ABP FINE	AVERAGE FINE
□ 1964–1968	25 Pesos, Nickel Clad Steel	—	.35

Key to Grading: Bust

DATE	COIN TYPE/VARIETY/METAL	ABP FINE	AVERAGE FINE
□ 1968	25 Pesos, Death of Sarmiento, Nickel Clad Steel	—	.35

Argentina—Current Coinage

Key to Grading: Bust

DATE	COIN TYPE/VARIETY/METAL	ABP FINE	AVERAGE FINE
□ 1970–1975	1 Centavo, Aluminum	—	.32
□ 1983	1 Centavo, Aluminum	—	.32
□ 1970–1975	5 Centavos, Aluminum	—	.32
□ 1985–1988	5 Centavos, Brass	—	.32

Key to Grading: Bust

DATE	COIN TYPE/VARIETY/METAL	ABP FINE	AVERAGE FINE
☐ 1970–1976	10 Centavos, Brass	—	$ .38
☐ 1983	10 Centavos, Aluminum	—	.38

Key to Grading: Bust

☐ 1970–1976	20 Centavos, Brass	—	.32
☐ 1970–1976	50 Centavos, Brass	—	.32
☐ 1983–1984	50 Centavos, Aluminum	—	.32

Key to Grading: Sun Burst

☐ 1974–1976	1 Peso, Aluminum Brass	—	.32
☐ 1984	1 Peso, National Congress, Aluminum	—	.32
☐ 1976–1977	5 Pesos, Aluminum-Bronze	—	.32
☐ 1977	5 Pesos, Bicentennial of Admiral Brown, Aluminum-Bronze	—	.32
☐ 1984–1985	5 Pesos, Buenos Aires City Hall, Brass	—	.32
☐ 1976–1978	10 Pesos, Aluminum-Bronze	—	.32
☐ 1977	10 Pesos, Bicentennial of Admiral Brown, Aluminum-Bronze	—	.32
☐ 1984–1985	10 Pesos, Independence Hall, Brass	—	.32
☐ 1978	50 Pesos, Birth of San Martin 200th Anniversary, Aluminum-Bronze	—	.32
☐ 1979	50 Pesos, Jose de San Martin, Aluminum-Bronze	—	.32

Key to Grading: Soccer Ball

DATE	COIN TYPE/VARIETY/METAL	ABP FINE	AVERAGE FINE
☐ 1977–1978	50 Pesos, World Soccer Championship, Aluminum-Bronze	—	$ .32
☐ 1980–1981	50 Pesos, Jose de San Martin, Brass-Steel	—	.32
Key to Grading: Rider & Horse			
☐ 1980–1981	50 Pesos, Conquest of Patagonia Centennial, Aluminum-Bronze	—	.32
☐ 1985	50 Pesos, Central Bank 50th Anniversary, Aluminum-Bronze	—	.25

Key to Grading: Soccer Ball or Bust

DATE	COIN TYPE/VARIETY/METAL	ABP FINE	AVERAGE FINE
☐ 1977–1978	100 Pesos, World Soccer Championship, Aluminum-Bronze	—	.35
☐ 1978	100 Pesos, Death of San Martin 200th Anniversary, Aluminum-Bronze	—	.35
☐ 1979	100 Pesos, Conquest of Patagonia Centennial, Aluminum-Bronze	—	.35
☐ 1979–1981	100 Pesos, San Martin, Aluminum-Bronze	—	.25
☐ 1980–1981	100 Pesos, Brass-Steel	—	.25
☐ 1977	1000 Pesos, World Soccer Championship, Silver	—	4.50
☐ 1978	1000 Pesos, World Soccer Championship, Silver	—	3.50
☐ 1977	2000 Pesos, World Soccer Championship, Silver	—	4.25
☐ 1978	2000 Pesos, World Soccer Championship, Silver	—	4.25
☐ 1977	3000 Pesos, World Soccer Championship, Silver	—	7.50
☐ 1978	3000 Pesos, World Soccer Championship, Silver	—	7.50

Argentina—Latest Coinage

DATE	COIN TYPE/VARIETY/METAL	ABP FINE	AVERAGE FINE
☐ 1985	1/2 Centavo, Brass	—	.32
☐ 1985–1987	1 Centavo, Ostrich, Brass	—	.32
☐ 1992	1 Centavo, Brass	—	.32

Key to Grading: Animals or Sun Burst

DATE	COIN TYPE/VARIETY/METAL	ABP FINE	AVERAGE FINE
☐ 1985–1988	5 Centavos, Wildcat, Brass	—	$ .35
☐ 1992	5 Centavos, Radiant Sun, Brass	—	.25

Key to Grading: Sun Burst or Building

DATE	COIN TYPE/VARIETY/METAL	ABP FINE	AVERAGE FINE
☐ 1985–1988	10 Centavos, Radiant Sun, Brass	—	.32
☐ 1992	10 Centavos, Radiant Sun, Aluminum-Bronze	—	.32
☐ 1992	25 Centavos, Building, Brass	—	.32

Key to Grading: Bust or Building

DATE	COIN TYPE/VARIETY/METAL	ABP FINE	AVERAGE FINE
☐ 1985–1988	50 Centavos, Brass	—	.32
☐ 1992	50 Centavos, Tucuman Capitol Building, Brass	—	.32
☐ 1989	1 Austral, Buenos Aires City Hall, Aluminum	—	.35

Key to Grading: Building

DATE	COIN TYPE/VARIETY/METAL	ABP FINE	AVERAGE FINE
□ 1989	5 Australes, Tucuman Independence Hall, Aluminum	—	$ .35

Key to Grading: Building or Shield

DATE	COIN TYPE/VARIETY/METAL	ABP FINE	AVERAGE FINE
□ 1989	10 Australes, Casa del Acuerdo, Aluminum	—	.32
□ 1990–1991	100 Australes, Aluminum	—	.32
□ 1990–1991	500 Australes, Aluminum	—	.32

Key to Grading: Shield

DATE	COIN TYPE/VARIETY/METAL	ABP FINE	AVERAGE FINE
□ 1990–1991	1000 Australes, Aluminum	—	.30
□ 1991	1000 Australes, Ibero-American Series, Silver	—	55.00

AUSTRALIA

Australia's currency is based on the decimal system: one hundred cents (100c) equals one Australian dollar ($1). Decimal currency was introduced in Australia on 14 February 1966 and replaced the imperial system of pounds, shillings, and pence.

Like most national currencies, Australia's currency consists of both coins and currency notes. At various times Australian coins have been made in San Francisco, London, Birmingham, Bombay, and Calcutta, but, today, all Australian circulating coins are produced at the Royal Australian Mint in Canberra.

All Australian currency notes are produced by Note Printing Australia, an autonomous division of the Reserve Bank of Australia, located at Craigieburn, just outside Melbourne.

BRIEF HISTORY OF AUSTRALIA'S COINS

The early inhabitants of the penal colony of New South Wales brought with them English coins as well as those from ports of call on the long voyage. Many different coins and tokens were traded in the colony for differing values, sometimes based vaguely on the value of the coin's metal content.

As this was an unsatisfactory way of conducting transactions, Governor King, in 1800, issued a proclamation to establish a uniform value for the most common coins. The lowest value of two pence was given to a copper coin of one ounce. Various other coins such as rupees, ducats, guilders, and guineas were assigned higher values.

Front: Portuguese Johanna
Back: Ducat

The chronic shortage of coin bedevilled several of the colony's early governors (namely, Phillip, Hunter, King, and Bligh). Rum was more freely available and became the common medium of exchange, earning for New South Wales the name, "the rum colony."

Governor Lachlan Macquarie recognized the role of rum in the colony's affairs but also realized that something had to be done about the acute shortage of coin. He overcame the problem, at least partially, when His Majesty's Sloop *Samarang* arrived in 1812 carrying 40,000 Spanish dollars. Macquarie had the ingenious idea of cutting the center out of the dollars and overstamping the two separate pieces with "New South Wales 1813" to make coins of two different denominations, the so-called "holey dollar" and its centerpiece, the "dump." These coins remained in circulation until 1829. Silver coins from England were used from about 1824.

Holey dollar

The Gold Rush of the 1850s led to the belief that some of Australia's coins could be locally produced. In 1855 the Sydney Mint opened—its first coin was the Sydney gold sovereign. Mints were also established in Melbourne (1872) and Perth (1899).

The first federally commissioned coins were issued in 1910. In 1916, numbers of threepence, sixpence, one shilling, and two shilling (florin) coins were minted in Melbourne.

The Sydney Mint closed in 1926 and the Melbourne Mint closed in 1968 when its functions were transferred to the newly established Royal Australian Mint in Canberra. The Royal Australian Mint is the first Australian mint not to be a branch of the Royal Mint in London. It has produced more than 10 billion Australian coins. It has also made circulating coins or collector (numismatic) coins for such countries as Bangladesh, the Cook Islands, Tonga, New Zealand, Papua New Guinea, and Thailand.

TYPE OF COINS

Australia produces three categories of coins:

Circulating Coins: Standard day-to-day currency and used in normal commercial transactions.

Adelaide ingot

Collector Coins: Commemorative or other coins not in general circulation. They are, however, legal tender and may be used for commercial transactions. Collector coins are classified as "proof" or "uncirculated" coins.

Bullion Coins: Gold, silver, or platinum coins. The bullion value of the metal used in the manufacture of each coin is greater than its face value. These are classified as "non-circulating legal tender" (NCLT).

Circulating coins

The denominations of the new decimal currency coins introduced in 1966 were: 1c, 2c, 5c, 10c, 20c, and 50c. All were round in shape.

Round 50c coin (reverse)

There were no mintings of the 50c coin in the next two years and, when it next appeared, in 1969, its shape was changed to dodecagonal (12 sided). The round 50c was made in a silver alloy (80%). As the price of silver rose in the late 1960s, the metal value of the coin rose above its face value. It was a loss-maker for the government as well as confusing to consumers because of its size similarity to the 20c coin.

A $1 coin was introduced in 1984 and a $2 coin was introduced in 1988 to replace $1 and $2 currency notes which were gradually withdrawn.

Composition of circulating coins

The 1c and 2c (bronze) coins are made from copper (97%), zinc (2.5%), and tin (0.5%).

The 5c, 10c, 20c, and 50c coins are made of cupro-nickel; that is, 75% copper and 25% nickel.

The $1 and $2 coins are aluminum-bronze: 92% copper, 6% aluminum, and 2% nickel.

Withdrawal of coins

In 1990 the Australian government announced that from 1992 all 1c and 2c coins would be withdrawn. This is because of the changing worth of small denominations generally. These two coins, however, remain legal tender.

The demand for circulating coins has dropped steadily since the 1970s due mainly to the wider availability and acceptance of credit cards. As a result, the Royal Australian Mint has not only stopped making some coins (for instance, 1c and 2c pieces) but also it has reduced production of others. An unexpected side effect of the withdrawal of 1c and 2c coins, as from February 1992, has been the large number of other coins that have been returned to banks, most particularly 5c and 10c coins. This phenomenon has been called the "money box effect"—because of people emptying their money boxes on bank counters and handing in all their "loose change."

Dodecagonal 50c coin (obverse)

Coin designs

Coins have an obverse side and a reverse side. The obverse side of all Australian decimal coins carries an effigy of Her Majesty Queen Elizabeth II, as she is the Queen of Australia. This side of all coins also carries the year the coin was minted. Designs are approved by the Australian Treasurer.

The theme selected in 1966 for Australia's first decimal coins was Australian native fauna (except for the 50c coin which shows the Australian Coat of Arms). Later coins have featured different subjects.

from left to right, 1c coin: the feather-tail glider (a type of possum) also known as the "flying squirrel"

2c coin: the frill-necked lizard

5c coin: the echidna or spiny anteater

10c coin: the lyrebird

(below) 20c coin: the platypus

(above) 50c coin: Australia's Coat of Arms with a kangaroo on the left side of the coin and an emu on the right. The Coat of Arms shows a shield with six parts, each containing the badge of one of Australia's six states. The same design applies to the 1966 round version of this coin and the later 12-sided one.

$1 coin: the kangaroo

The 1993 $1 coin has water quality as its theme. It features a tree sculpted in flowing water to show the link between water and the environment.

$2 coin: a bust of an Aborigine, taken from an engraving by Ainslie Roberts and set against a background of the Southern Cross and Australian flora. The flora is Xanthorrhoea, *commonly known as the grass tree, which is found throughout Australia.*

Collector coins

In addition to proof and uncirculated sets of coins, which are issued each year, the Royal Australian Mint issues commemorative coins on a regular basis.

The $5 coin is aluminium-bronze: 92% copper, 6% aluminum, and 2% nickel. The first $5 coin was issued to commemorate the opening of Australia's new federal Parliament building. Parliament House in Canberra was officially opened on 9 May 1988 by Her Majesty Queen Elizabeth II. Two $5 coins were released in 1990 in a joint program with New Zealand to celebrate the 75th anniversary of the landing at Gallipoli by Australian and New Zealand forces in 1915. In 1992 a $5 commemorative coin was issued to mark the International Year of Space.

The $10 coin is made of sterling silver (that is, 92.5% silver and the balance made up of copper). The first $10 coin was released in 1982 to commemorate the XII Commonwealth Games, held in Brisbane. Subsequent designs have carried the theme of the Coat of Arms of each of Australia's six states and two territories: Victoria (1985); South Australia (1986); New South Wales (1987); First Fleet Bicentennial design (1988); Queensland (1989); Western Australia (1990); Tasmania (1991), and Northern Territory (1992). The Australian Capital Territory is featured on the 1993 coin.

Tasmania's $10 commemorative coin

A "Birds of Australia" series was introduced in 1989 on a double thickness (piedfort) $10 coin and on a standard proof $10 coin. The first bird featured was a kookaburra—others in the series are a sulphur-crested cockatoo (1990), a jabiru (1991), an emperor penguin (1992), and a palm cockatoo for 1993.

The $200 coin is manufactured from 22K gold (that is, 91.66% gold). The first $200 coin showed a koala on the reverse and was minted in 1980. Subsequent $200 coins have depicted the wedding of the Prince of Wales and Lady Diana Spencer in 1981; the Commonwealth Games in Brisbane (1982); the embarkation of the First Fleet to Australia in 1787 (1987); and the landing by Captain Arthur Phillip at Sydney Cove in 1788 (1988).

Australia's first $250 coin

The "Pride of Australia" series, which began in 1989, adopted Australia's unique wildlife as its theme and has so far shown a frilled-neck lizard (1989), platypus (1990), emu (1991), echidna (1992), and feather-tail glider (1993).

Bullion (or investment) coins

The Perth Mint is Australia's specialist precious metals mint and one of the world's oldest mints still operating from its original premises. Established in 1899 as a branch of Britain's Royal Mint, The Perth Mint became a statutory authority of the Western Australian Government in 1970.

Since then, the Mint's bullion coin programs have established a formidable reputation for Australia as a leader in international precious metals markets. In 1997, The Perth Mint, in a joint venture with the Royal Australian Mint, was granted approval to mint the commemorative precious metal coins for the Sydney 2000 Olympic Games, a most prestigious proof coin program.

THE 1999 CENTENARY AUSTRALIAN BULLION COIN COLLECTION

The Perth Mint—A Century of Minting Excellence

The Perth Mint celebrates its centenary on June 20, 1999, representing a significant milestone in the history of Western Australia and in the development of Australia's gold industry.

Originally opened in 1899 as a branch of the British Royal Mint, The Perth Mint was established to turn the gold from the Western Australian gold rush into sovereigns for the British Empire, which it did until Britain came off the gold standard in 1931. Ownership of the Mint was transferred to the Western Australian government in 1970. Since then, through the introduction of the Australian Family of Precious Metal Coins in gold, platinum, silver, and palladium, The Perth Mint has established a formidable reputation for Australia as a leader in international precious metal investment markets.

Renowned for excellence and innovation, The Perth Mint, together with the Royal Australian Mint, was granted approval to mint the commemorative precious metal coins for the Sydney 2000 Olympic Games, a four-year program which commenced in 1997 and ran through the end of 2000.

In its Centenary year, The Perth Mint was proud to recall its achievements and planned a range of activities and coin issues to commemorate this historic milestone.

As part of the celebrations, the 1999 bullion coins bear their own special commemoration with the incorporation in their design, for the first time, of the "P100" mintmark, encompassing the traditional Perth Mint "P" mintmark and the numerals "100."

The Australian Nugget Gold Bullion Coins

Gold Bullion Collector Coins

The Australian Kangaroo Nugget bullion coin is the only major legal tender, pure gold coin to change its design each year and to limit its mintages annually.

As such, it is the only legal tender, gold bullion coin that offers investors the potential for numismatic appreciation over time, in addition to an investment in the precious metal itself.

The 1999 Nugget design captures the innocence of a baby gray kangaroo, commonly known as a "Joey," and is the tenth design in the internationally acclaimed and remarkably successful Kangaroo series.

In 1999, no more than 350,000 1 oz coins, 100,000 ½ oz coins, 150,000 ¼ oz coins, 200,000 1/10 oz coins, and 200,000 1/20 oz coins were produced.

Gold Bullion Investor Coins

The Australian Nugget Large Bullion Coins (LBCs) are universally recognized as being the most affordable means of purchasing gold bullion in the secure form of official, legal tender coins. The Nugget LBCs feature the Australian Red Kangaroo design, which remains constant from year to year. Only the year of mintage changes.

Technical Specifications of the Australian Nugget

SIZE		KILO	10 OZ	2 OZ	1 OZ	½ OZ	¼ OZ	1/10 OZ	1/20 OZ
Gold Content	Troy oz	32.151	10	2	1	½	¼	1/10	1/20
Denomination	A$	3000	1000	200	100	50	25	15	5
Fineness	% purity	99.99	99.99	99.99	99.99	99.99	99.99	99.99	99.99
Standard Weight	gms	1000.35	311.317	62.265	31.162	15.594	7.807	3.133	1.571
Remedy Allowance	gms	0.25	0.25	0.05	0.055	0.040	0.030	0.022	0.015
Maximum Diameter	mm	75.30	60.30	40.60	32.10	25.10	20.10	16.10	14.10
Maximum Thickness	mm	13.90	7.90	4.00	2.80	2.40	2.00	1.50	1.40
Milled Edge Serrations	no.	320	283	250	180	150	130	120	108

The Australian Koala Platinum Bullion Coins

Platinum Bullion Collector Coins

The Australian Koala is the only legal tender, pure platinum bullion coin to carry a different design each year.

It is also the only platinum bullion coin with a preannounced, limited mintage.

In 1999, no more than 100,000 1 oz coins, 5,000 ½ oz coins, 20,000 ¼ oz coins, 20,000 $\frac{1}{10}$ oz coins, and 20,000 $\frac{1}{20}$ oz coins were produced.

The 1999 design features a young koala clinging to a fallen log, chewing a favored eucalyptus leaf. It is the twelfth design in the series.

Platinum Bullion Investor Coins

The Australian Koala Large Bullion Coins (LBCs) are the most affordable means of buying platinum in the secure form of official, legal tender coins. They feature an unchanging design, depicting a koala sitting in a tree. Only the year of mintage changes annually.

Platinum's critical role in pollution control sees its importance to everyday life increasing each year, yet only about 140 tonnes of newly mined platinum reach Western markets in a typical year, which makes it 17 times rarer than gold and 120 times rarer than silver.

Technical Specifications of the Australian Koala

SIZE		KILO	10 OZ	2 OZ	1 OZ	½ OZ	¼ OZ	1/10 OZ	1/20 OZ
Platinum									
Content	Troy oz	32.151	10	2	1	½	¼	1/10	1/20
Denomination	A$	3000	1000	200	100	50	25	15	5
Fineness	% purity	99.95	99.95	99.95	99.95	99.95	99.95	99.95	99.95
Standard									
Weight	gms	1001.00	311.691	62.313	31.185	15.605	7.815	3.137	1.571
Remedy									
Allowance	gms	0.50	0.50	0.075	0.065	0.045	0.035	0.025	0.015
Maximum									
Diameter	mm	75.30	60.30	40.60	32.10	25.10	20.10	16.10	14.10
Maximum									
Thickness	mm	13.90	7.90	3.80	2.70	2.30	1.90	1.32	1.40
Milled Edge									
Serrations	no.	320	283	250	180	150	130	120	108

The Australian Kookaburra Silver Bullion Coins

Silver Bullion Collector Coins

The Australian Kookaburra is the only major legal tender, pure silver coin to change its design yearly.

The 1999 design features a pair of kookaburras, an adult and a juvenile, perched in their most favored habitat, the branch of a eucalyptus tree, and is the tenth design in the series.

Only 300,000 of these coins are produced annually for sale worldwide compared with the millions of its competitors.

Silver Bullion Investor Coins

The Australian Kookaburra Large Bullion Coins (LBCs) are unique. They are the world's largest bullion coins. They are also more affordable per ounce than any other silver bullion coins and provide investors with the security only official, legal tender coins can provide. The distinctive kookaburra design changes every year.

Technical Specifications of the Australian Kookaburra

SIZE		KILO	10OZ	2OZ	1OZ
Silver Content	Troy oz	32.151	10	2	1
Denomination	A$	30	10	2	1
Fineness	% purity	99.9	99.9	99.9	99.9
Standard Weight	gms	1002.502	312.347	62.77	31.635
Remedy Allowance	gms	1.50	1.00	0.50	0.50
Maximum Diameter	mm	101.00	75.50	50.30	40.60
Maximum Thickness	mm	14.60	8.70	4.50	4.00
Milled Edge Serrations	no.	160*	120*	80*	250

*Interrupted

THE 1998 PROOF SETS

The Australian Family of Precious Metals 1998 Proof Sets

The Perth Mint's three-metal proof sets have always been a popular annual release, with back issues now scarce. Their popularity is partly due to the unique opportunity they offer to secure examples of the Mint's world-renowned proof coins in gold, silver, and platinum. Minted to the highest proof standards and beautifully presented in solid jarrah cases with numbered certificates of authenticity, the 1998 Proof Sets are offered in three handsome formats with very limited mintages.

Endearing Designs

The 1998 Proof Nugget coin, individually struck from 99.99% pure gold, captures the innocence of a baby gray kangaroo, or "Joey." The 1998 Proof Kookaburra features a pair of kookaburras, an adult and juvenile perched in the branch of a eucalyptus tree, and is struck from the finest 99.9% silver. Minted in the rarest of all precious metals, 99.95% pure platinum, the 1998 Proof Koala features a young koala clinging to a fallen log, chewing a favored eucalyptus leaf.

Each coin is an outstanding example of the coin maker's art, minted with painstaking attention to detail at every stage.

As with all Perth Mint proof issues, the "P" mint mark is incorporated into the design, denoting a proud tradition of quality and innovation.

Mintage Limits

PROOF SET	FORMAT	MINTAGE
Mini Three-Metal	1 oz silver Kookaburra, 1/20 oz gold Nugget 1/20 oz platinum Koala	700
Midi Three-Metal	1 oz silver Kookaburra, ½ oz gold Nugget ½ oz platinum Koala	250
1 oz Three-Metal	1 oz silver Kookaburra, 1 oz gold Nugget 1 oz platinum Koala	150

Coins shown actual size

Technical Specifications

		NUGGET			KOALA			KOOKABURRA
Metal Content	Troy oz	1	½	1/20	1	½	1/20	1
Denomination	A$	100	50	5	100	50	5	1
Fineness	%	99.99	99.99	99.99	99.95	99.95	99.95	99.9
Standard Weight	gms	31.162	15.594	1.571	31.185	15.605	1.571	31.635
Remedy Allowance	gms	0.055	0.040	0.015	0.065	0.045	0.015	0.50
Max Diameter	mm	32.10	25.10	14.10	32.10	25.10	14.10	40.60
Max Thickness	mm	2.80	2.40	1.40	2.70	2.30	1.40	4.00
Milled Edge Serrations	no.	180	150	108	180	150	108	250

Australia—Type Coinage

Key to Grading: Busts

DATE	COIN TYPE/VARIETY/METAL	ABP FINE	AVERAGE FINE
☐ 1911–1936	1/2 Penny, George V, Bronze	—	$ 1.00
☐ 1938–1939	1/2 Penny, George VI, Bronze	—	.35
☐ 1939–1948	1/2 Penny, George VI, Bronze	—	.45
☐ 1949–1952	1/2 Penny, George VI, Bronze	—	.45
☐ 1953–1956	1/2 Penny, Elizabeth II, Bronze	—	.45
☐ 1959–1964	1/2 Penny, Elizabeth II, Bronze	—	.30

Key to Grading: Busts

DATE	COIN TYPE/VARIETY/METAL	ABP FINE	AVERAGE FINE
☐ 1911–1936	1 Penny, George V, Bronze	—	.60
☐ 1938–1948	1 Penny, George VI, Bronze	—	.45
☐ 1949–1952	1 Penny, George VI, Bronze	—	.32
☐ 1953	1 Penny, Elizabeth II, Bronze	—	.32
☐ 1955–1964	1 Penny, Elizabeth II, Bronze	—	.32
☐ 1910	3 Pence, Edward VII, Silver	—	5.00
☐ 1911–1936	3 Pence, George V, Silver	—	3.00

Key to Grading: Busts

DATE	COIN TYPE/VARIETY/METAL	ABP FINE	AVERAGE FINE
☐ 1938–1944	3 Pence, George VI, Silver	—	.85
☐ 1947–1948	3 Pence, George VI, Silver	—	.85
☐ 1949–1952	3 Pence, George VI, Silver	—	.85

DATE	COIN TYPE/VARIETY/METAL	ABP FINE	AVERAGE FINE
☐ 1953–1954	3 Pence, Elizabeth II, Silver	—	$3.00
☐ 1955–1964	3 Pence, Elizabeth II, Silver	—	2.00

Key to Grading: Busts

DATE	COIN TYPE/VARIETY/METAL	ABP FINE	AVERAGE FINE
☐ 1910	6 Pence, Edward VII, Silver	—	10.00
☐ 1911–1936	6 Pence, George V, Silver	—	4.00
☐ 1938–1945	6 Pence, George VI, Silver	—	2.40
☐ 1946–1948	6 Pence, George VI, Silver	—	2.40
☐ 1950–1952	6 Pence, George VI, Silver	—	2.40
☐ 1953–1954	6 Pence, Elizabeth II, Silver	—	2.40
☐ 1955–1963	6 Pence, Elizabeth II, Silver	—	2.40
☐ 1910	1 Shilling, Edward VII, Silver	—	6.00
☐ 1911–1936	1 Shilling, George V, Silver	—	8.00

Key to Grading: Busts

DATE	COIN TYPE/VARIETY/METAL	ABP FINE	AVERAGE FINE
☐ 1938–1944	1 Shilling, George VI, Silver	—	5.00
☐ 1946–1948	1 Shilling, George VI, Silver	—	4.15
☐ 1950–1952	1 Shilling, George VI, Silver	—	4.15
☐ 1953–1954	1 Shilling, Elizabeth II, Silver	—	4.15
☐ 1955–1963	1 Shilling, Elizabeth II, Silver	—	4.15
☐ 1910	1 Florin, Edward VII, Silver	15.00	35.00
☐ 1911–1936	1 Florin, George V, Silver	—	20.00

Key to Grading: Busts

DATE	COIN TYPE/VARIETY/METAL	ABP FINE	AVERAGE FINE
☐ 1938–1945	1 Florin, George VI, Silver	—	$5.00
☐ 1946–1947	1 Florin, George VI, Silver	—	4.25
☐ 1951–1952	1 Florin, George VI, Silver	—	2.00
☐ 1953–1954	1 Florin, Elizabeth II, Silver	—	4.25
☐ 1956–1963	1 Florin, Elizabeth II, Silver	—	4.25

Key to Grading: Busts

☐ 1937–1938	1 Crown, George VI, Silver	—	12.00
☐ 1871–1887	1/2 Sovereign, Victoria, Young Head, Gold	—	125.00
☐ 1887–1893	1/2 Sovereign, Victoria, Jubilee Head, Gold	—	125.00
☐ 1893–1901	1/2 Sovereign, Victoria, Old Head, Gold	—	100.00
☐ 1902–1910	1/2 Sovereign, Edward VII, Gold	—	75.00
☐ 1911–1918	1/2 Sovereign, George V, Gold	—	75.00
☐ 1871–1887	1 Sovereign, Victoria, Young Head, Rev: Shield, Gold	—	—
☐ 1871–1887	1 Sovereign, Victoria, Young Head, Rev: St. George, Gold	—	145.00
☐ 1887–1893	1 Sovereign, Victoria, Jubilee Head, Gold	—	115.00
☐ 1893–1901	1 Sovereign, Victoria, Old Head, Gold	—	115.00
☐ 1902–1910	1 Sovereign, Edward VII, Gold	—	125.00
☐ 1911–1931	1 Sovereign, George V, Gold	—	225.00

Australia—Commemorative Coinage

Key to Grading: Busts

☐ 1927	Commemorative Florin, Establishment of Parliament at Canberra, Silver	—	5.00
☐ 1934	Commemorative Florin, Victoria & Melbourne Centennial, Dated 1934–35, Silver	$65.00	125.00
☐ 1951	Commemorative Florin, Fifty-year Jubilee, Silver	—	4.50
☐ 1954	Commemorative Florin, Royal Visit, Silver	—	4.50

Australia—Decimal Coinage

Key to Grading: Bust

DATE	COIN TYPE/VARIETY/METAL	ABP FINE	AVERAGE FINE
☐ 1966 to Date	1 Cent, Elizabeth II, Ring-tailed Opossum, Bronze	—	$ .32
☐ 1966 to Date	2 Cents, Elizabeth II, Frilled Lizard, Bronze	—	.32

Key to Grading: Bust

DATE	COIN TYPE/VARIETY/METAL	ABP FINE	AVERAGE FINE
☐ 1966 to Date	5 Cents, Elizabeth II, Spiny Anteater, Cupro-Nickel	—	.32

Key to Grading: Bust

DATE	COIN TYPE/VARIETY/METAL	ABP FINE	AVERAGE FINE
☐ 1966 to Date	10 Cents, Elizabeth II, Lyre Bird, Cupro-Nickel	—	.32

Key to Grading: Bust

DATE	COIN TYPE/VARIETY/METAL	ABP FINE	AVERAGE FINE
☐ 1966 to Date	20 Cents, Elizabeth II, Duckbill Platypus, Cupro-Nickel	—	.32

Key to Grading: Bust

DATE	COIN TYPE/VARIETY/METAL	ABP FINE	AVERAGE FINE
☐ 1966	50 Cents, Elizabeth II, Silver	—	$4.00
☐ 1969–1984	50 Cents, Elizabeth II, Cupro-Nickel	—	.70
☐ 1970	50 Cents, Elizabeth II, Cook's Voyage—200th Anniversary, Cupro-Nickel	—	.70
☐ 1977	50 Cents, Elizabeth II, Queen's Silver Jubilee, Cupro-Nickel	—	.60
☐ 1981	50 Cents, Elizabeth II, Wedding of Prince Charles and Lady Diana, Cupro-Nickel	—	.50
☐ 1982	50 Cents, Elizabeth II, 12th Commonwealth Games, Cupro-Nickel	—	.75
☐ 1985 to Date	50 Cents, Elizabeth II, Cupro-Nickel	—	.55
☐ 1988	50 Cents, Elizabeth II, Australian Bicentennial, Cupro Nickel	—	.55
☐ 1988	50 Cents, Elizabeth II, Australian Bicentennial, Silver	—	40.00
☐ 1989	50 Cents, Elizabeth II, 12th Commonwealth Games, Silver	—	40.00
☐ 1989	50 Cents, Elizabeth II, Cook's Voyage—200th Anniversary, Silver	—	40.00
☐ 1989	50 Cents, Elizabeth II, Wedding of Prince Charles & Lady Diana, Silver	—	40.00
☐ 1989	50 Cents, Elizabeth II, Queen's Silver Jubilee, Silver	—	40.00
☐ 1991	50 Cents, Elizabeth II, Decimal Currency—25th Anniversary, Cupro-Nickel	—	.80

Key to Grading: Bust

DATE	COIN TYPE/VARIETY/METAL	ABP FINE	AVERAGE FINE
☐ 1984 to Date	1 Dollar, Elizabeth II, Kangaroos, Nickel-Aluminum-Copper	—	1.50

DATE	COIN TYPE/VARIETY/METAL	ABP FINE	AVERAGE FINE
☐ 1986	1 Dollar, Elizabeth II, International Year of Peace, Aluminum-Bronze	—	$1.50
☐ 1988	1 Dollar, Elizabeth II, Aboriginal Art, Aluminum-Bronze	—	2.00
☐ 1988–1990	1 Dollar, Elizabeth II, Masterpieces in Silver—Aboriginal Art, Silver	$18.00	55.00
☐ 1990	1 Dollar, Elizabeth II, Masterpieces in Silver—International Year of Peace, Silver	18.00	55.00
☐ 1990	1 Dollar, Elizabeth II, Masterpieces in Silver—Kangaroos, Silver	18.00	55.00
☐ 1992	1 Dollar, Elizabeth II, Olympics—Javelin Thrower, Aluminum-Bronze	—	2.00

Key to Grading: Bust

DATE	COIN TYPE/VARIETY/METAL	ABP FINE	AVERAGE FINE
☐ 1988–1991	2 Dollars, Elizabeth II, Male Aborigine, Aluminum-Bronze	—	4.00
☐ 1988	5 Dollars, Elizabeth II, House of Parliament, Aluminum-Bronze	—	8.00
☐ 1988	5 Dollars, Elizabeth II, House of Parliament, Silver	—	25.00
☐ 1990	5 Dollars, Elizabeth II, ANZAC Memorial, Aluminum-Bronze	—	14.00
☐ 1992	5 Dollars, Elizabeth II, Australian Space Industry, Aluminum-Bronze	—	14.00
☐ 1982	10 Dollars, Elizabeth II, 12th Commonwealth Games, Silver	—	18.00
☐ 1985	10 Dollars, Elizabeth II, State of Victoria—150th Anniversary, Silver	—	18.00
☐ 1986	10 Dollars, Elizabeth II, South Australia—150th Anniversary, Silver	—	18.00
☐ 1987	10 Dollars, Elizabeth II, New South Wales, Silver	—	18.00
☐ 1988	10 Dollars, Elizabeth II, Governor Philip Landing, Silver	—	18.00
☐ 1989	10 Dollars, Elizabeth II, Queensland, Silver	—	15.00
☐ 1989	10 Dollars, Elizabeth II, Kookaburra, Silver	—	25.00
☐ 1990	10 Dollars, Elizabeth II, Cockatoo, Silver	—	20.00
☐ 1990	10 Dollars, Elizabeth II, Western Australia, Silver	—	16.00

DATE	COIN TYPE/VARIETY/METAL	ABP FINE	AVERAGE FINE
☐ 1991	10 Dollars, Elizabeth II, Birds of Australia—Jabiru Stork, Silver	—	$30.00
☐ 1991	10 Dollars, Elizabeth II, Tasmania, Silver	—	28.00
☐ 1992	10 Dollars, Elizabeth II, Northern Territory, Silver	—	20.00
☐ 1992	10 Dollars, Elizabeth II, Emperor Penguin, Silver	—	30.00
☐ 1992	25 Dollars, Elizabeth II, Queen's 40th Anniversary of Reign—Princess Diana, Silver	—	40.00
☐ 1992	25 Dollars, Elizabeth II, Queen's 40th Anniversary of Reign—Queen Mother, Silver	—	40.00
☐ 1992	25 Dollars, Elizabeth II, Queen's 40th Anniversary of Reign—Princess Margaret, Silver	—	35.00
☐ 1980	200 Dollars, Elizabeth II, Koala, Gold	—	175.00
☐ 1981	200 Dollars, Elizabeth II, Wedding of Prince Charles & Lady Diana, Gold	—	175.00
☐ 1982	200 Dollars, Elizabeth II, 12th Commonwealth Games, Gold	—	175.00
☐ 1985	200 Dollars, Elizabeth II, Koala, Gold	—	175.00
☐ 1986	200 Dollars, Elizabeth II, Koala, Gold	—	180.00
☐ 1987	200 Dollars, Elizabeth II, Arthur Philip, Gold	—	185.00
☐ 1988	200 Dollars, Elizabeth II, Australia Bicentennial, Gold	—	185.00
☐ 1989	200 Dollars, Elizabeth II, Pride of Australia—Frilled-neck Lizard, Gold	—	200.00
☐ 1990	200 Dollars, Elizabeth II, Pride of Australia—Platypus, Gold	—	210.00
☐ 1991	200 Dollars, Elizabeth II, Pride of Australia—Emu, Gold	—	225.00
☐ 1992	250 Dollars, Elizabeth II, Queen's 40th Anniversary of Reign—Princess Diana, Gold	—	425.00
☐ 1992	250 Dollars, Elizabeth II, Queen's 40th Anniversary of Reign—Princess Anne, Gold	—	465.00
☐ 1992	250 Dollars, Elizabeth II, Queen's 40th Anniversary of Reign—Queen Mother, Gold	—	465.00
☐ 1992	250 Dollars, Elizabeth II, Queen's 40th Anniversary of Reign—Princess Margaret, Gold	—	465.00

BELGIUM

The first coins appeared in the 2nd century. The silver denier was popular through the 12th century. During the 1400s, most of the coins produced were gold. In the 1500s, large copper coins were introduced. A new coin system was established in 1612. Most of the coins then included liards, patards, schellings, patagons, ducatons, and sovereigns. The currency used today is based on the franc.

Belgium—Type Coinage

Key to Grading: Lion

DATE	COIN TYPE/VARIETY/METAL	ABP FINE	AVERAGE FINE
☐ 1869–1907	1 Centime, Leopold II—1st Coinage, Copper	—	$2.00
☐ 1912–1914	1 Centime, Albert I, Copper	—	.80
☐ 1869–1909	2 Centimes, Leopold II—1st Coinage, Copper	—	1.75
☐ 1910–1919	2 Centimes, Albert I, Copper	—	1.00
☐ 1894–1901	5 Centimes, Leopold II—1st Coinage, Cupro-Nickel	—	1.50

Key to Grading: Crown

DATE	COIN TYPE/VARIETY/METAL	ABP FINE	AVERAGE FINE
□ 1901–1907	5 Centimes, Leopold II—2nd Coinage, Cupro-Nickel	—	$ .35
□ 1910–1932	5 Centimes, Albert I, Cupro-Nickel	—	.32
□ 1915–1916	5 Centimes, German Occupation, Zinc	—	.32
□ 1930–1932	5 Centimes, Albert I, Nickel-Brass	—	.32
□ 1938–1940	5 Centimes, Leopold III—Belgie-Belgigue, Nickel-Brass	—	.35
□ 1941–1943	5 Centimes, German Occupation, Zinc	—	.35
□ 1894–1901	10 Centimes, Leopold II—1st Coinage, Cupro-Nickel	—	2.00

Key to Grading: Crown

DATE	COIN TYPE/VARIETY/METAL	ABP FINE	AVERAGE FINE
□ 1901–1906	10 Centimes, Leopold II—2nd Coinage, Cupro-Nickel	—	.25
□ 1915–1917	10 Centimes, German Occupation, Zinc	—	.45
□ 1920–1929	10 Centimes, Albert I, Cupro-Nickel	—	.45
□ 1930–1932	10 Centimes, Albert I, Nickel-Brass	$2.00	4.00
□ 1938–1939	10 Centimes, Leopold III—Belgie-Belgigue, Nickel-Brass	—	.50
□ 1941–1946	10 Centimes, German Occupation, Zinc	—	.40

Key to Grading: Crown

DATE	COIN TYPE/VARIETY/METAL	ABP FINE	AVERAGE FINE
☐ 1953–1963	20 Centimes, Baudouin I, Bronze	—	$ .32
☐ 1908–1909	25 Centimes, Leopold II— 2nd Coinage, Cupro-Nickel	—	1.00
☐ 1910–1929	25 Centimes, Albert I, Cupro-Nickel	—	.32
☐ 1915–1918	25 Centimes, German Occupation, Zinc	—	.65
☐ 1938–1939	25 Centimes, Leopold III— Belgie-Belgigue, Nickel-Brass	—	.40
☐ 1942–1947	25 Centimes, German Occupation, Zinc	—	.40

Key to Grading: Crown

DATE	COIN TYPE/VARIETY/METAL	ABP FINE	AVERAGE FINE
☐ 1964–1976	25 Centimes, Cupro-Nickel	—	.25
☐ 1866–1899	50 Centimes, Leopold II— 1st Coinage, Silver	—	5.00
☐ 1901	50 Centimes, Leopold II— 2nd Coinage, Silver	—	2.20
☐ 1907–1909	50 Centimes, Leopold II— 2nd Coinage, Silver	—	2.20
☐ 1910–1914	50 Centimes, Albert I, Silver	—	2.20
☐ 1918	50 Centimes, German Occupation, Zinc	—	2.20
☐ 1922–1934	50 Centimes, Albert I, Nickel	—	.50

Key to Grading: Crown

DATE	COIN TYPE/VARIETY/METAL	ABP FINE	AVERAGE FINE
☐ 1952–1980	50 Centimes, Baudouin I, Bronze	—	.40
☐ 1866–1887	1 Franc, Leopold II—1st Coinage, Silver	—	5.00
☐ 1880	1 Franc, Leopold II—50th Anniversary of Independence, Silver	$7.00	12.00
☐ 1904–1909	1 Franc, Leopold II—2nd Coinage, Silver	—	4.00
☐ 1910–1918	1 Franc, Albert I, Silver	—	1.25

Key to Grading: Figure

DATE	COIN TYPE/VARIETY/METAL	ABP FINE	AVERAGE FINE
☐ 1922–1935	1 Franc, Albert I, Nickel	—	$ .25
☐ 1939–1940	1 Franc, Leopold III—Belgie-Belgigue, Nickel	—	.38
☐ 1941–1947	1 Franc, German Occupation, Zinc	—	.38
☐ 1950–1988	1 Franc, Postwar Issue, Cupro-Nickel	—	.20
☐ 1991–1993	1 Franc, Leopold III	—	.38
☐ 1994	1 Franc, Alber II	—	.38
☐ 1866–1887	2 Francs, Leopold II—1st Coinage, Silver	—	20.00
☐ 1880	2 Francs, Leopold II—50th Anniversary of Independence, Silver	—	45.00
☐ 1904–1909	2 Francs, Leopold II—2nd Coinage, Silver	—	12.00
☐ 1910–1912	2 Francs, Albert I, Silver	—	5.00
☐ 1923–1930	2 Francs, Albert I, Nickel	—	8.00

Key to Grading: Leaf

☐ 1944	2 Francs, Allied Issue, Steel	—	.40

Key to Grading: Bust

☐ 1865–1876	5 Francs, Leopold II—1st Coinage, Silver	—	10.00
☐ 1930–1934	5 Francs, 1 Belga, Albert I, Nickel	—	4.15
☐ 1938–1939	5 Francs, Leopold III—Belgie-Belgigue, Nickel	—	4.15

DATE	COIN TYPE/VARIETY/METAL	ABP FINE	AVERAGE FINE
☐ 1941–1947	5 Francs, German Occupation, Zinc	—	$5.00
☐ 1948–1981	5 Francs, Postwar Issue, Cupro-Nickel	$ .25	.38
☐ 1986–1993	5 Francs, Leopold III	—	.38
☐ 1994–1997	5 Francs, Albert II	—	.38
☐ 1930	10 Francs, 2 Belgás, Albert I: Independence Centennial, Nickel	11.00	28.00
☐ 1969–1979	10 Francs, Leopold III	—	.30
☐ 1867–1882	20 Francs, Leopold II—1st Coinage, Gold	—	210.00
☐ 1914	20 Francs, Albert I, Gold	—	140.00
☐ 1931–1932	20 Francs, 4 Belgas, Albert I, Nickel	20.00	45.00
☐ 1933–1934	20 Francs, Albert I, Silver	20.00	42.00
☐ 1934–1935	20 Francs, Leopold III, Silver	—	4.00
☐ 1949–1955	20 Francs, Postwar Issue, Silver	—	5.00

Key to Grading: Bust

DATE	COIN TYPE/VARIETY/METAL	ABP FINE	AVERAGE FINE
☐ 1980–1992	20 Francs, Bronze	—	2.00
☐ 1984–1997	20 Francs, Bronze Albert II	—	1.25
☐ 1987–1988	5 ECU, European Currency Units, Silver	—	30.00
☐ 1935	50 Francs, Brussels Exposition/ Railway Centennial, Silver	—	60.00

Key to Grading: Bust

DATE	COIN TYPE/VARIETY/METAL	ABP FINE	AVERAGE FINE
☐ 1939–1940	50 Francs, Leopold III, Silver	—	15.00
☐ 1948–1954	50 Francs, Postwar Issue, Silver	—	4.00
☐ 1958	50 Francs, Brussels Fair, Silver	—	4.25
☐ 1960	50 Francs, Marriage Commemorative, Silver	—	6.00
☐ 1987–1993	50 Francs, Leopold III, Nickel	—	4.15
☐ 1994–1997	50 Francs, Albert II	—	4.15
☐ 1989–1990	10 ECU, European Currency Units, Gold	—	175.00
☐ 1948–1954	100 Francs, Postwar Issue, Silver	—	4.00
☐ 1990–1991	20 ECU, European Currency Units, Gold	—	325.00
☐ 1989	25 ECU, European Currency Units, Gold	—	225.00

DATE	COIN TYPE/VARIETY/METAL	ABP FINE	AVERAGE FINE
□ 1976	250 Francs, Jubilee of King Baudouin, Silver	—	$8.00
□ 1987–1988	50 ECU, European Currency Units, Gold	—	185.00
□ 1980	500 Francs, Independence—150th Anniversary, Silver Clad	—	6.15
□ 1989	100 ECU, European Currency Units—Maria Theresa, Gold	—	600.00
□ 1990	500 Francs, King Baudouin—60th Birthday, Silver	—	34.00

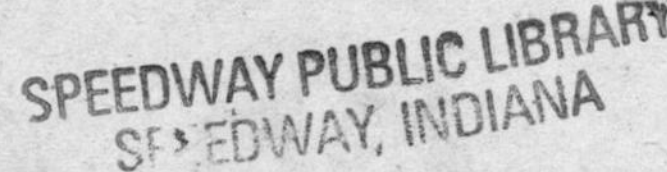

BERMUDA

The first coins were used in 1616. The copper sixpence was followed by the copper penny in the 1700s and the silver crown and bronze cent in the 1900s. The first decimal coins were used in 1970. Today's currency is the dollar.

Bermuda—Bullion/Bermuda*

Key to Grading: Bust

DATE	COIN TYPE/VARIETY/METAL	ABP FINE	AVERAGE FINE
□ 1987	5 Dollars, Sailing Ship—Sea Venture Wreck, Silver	—	140.00
□ 1988	5 Dollars, Sailing Ship—San Antonio, Silver	—	140.00
□ 1992	5 Dollars, Olympic Rings, Silver	—	145.00

*Since these coins were manufactured and sold primarily for their bullion value, their current value is determined by the current spot price of gold.

DATE	COIN TYPE/VARIETY/METAL	ABP FINE	AVERAGE FINE
□ 1987	25 Dollars, Ship—Sea Venture, Palladium	—	$275.00
□ 1988	25 Dollars, Ship—San Antonio Wreck, Palladium	—	300.00

Bermuda—Type Coinage

Key to Grading: Bust

□ 1970–1985	1 Cent, Wild Boar, Bronze	—	.32
□ 1986–1991	1 Cent, Wild Boar, Bronze	—	.32

Key to Grading: Bust

□ 1991–1997	1 Cent, Wild Boar, Zinc	—	.30

Key to Grading: Bust

□ 1970–1985	10 Cents, Bermuda Lily, Cupro-Nickel	—	.38
□ 1986–1997	10 Cents, Bermuda Lily, Cupro-Nickel	—	.38

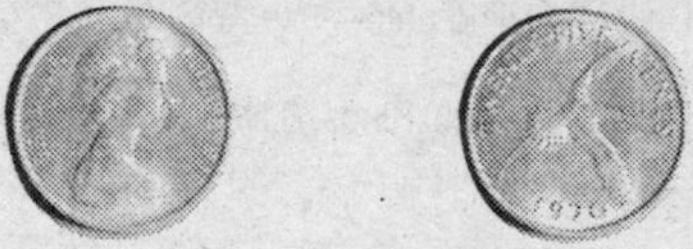

Key to Grading: Bust

□ 1970–1985	25 Cents, Tropical Bird, Cupro-Nickel	—	.32
□ 1984	25 Cents, 375th Anniversary, Cupro-Nickel	—	.50
□ 1959	1 Crown, 350th Anniversary, Silver	—	7.00
□ 1964	1 Crown, Silver	—	6.00

Key to Grading: Bust

DATE	COIN TYPE/VARIETY/METAL	ABP FINE	AVERAGE FINE
□ 1970–1985	50 Cents, Arms of the Bermudas, Cupro-Nickel	—	$ .60
□ 1970	1 Dollar, Elizabeth II, Silver	—	18.00

Key to Grading: Bust

DATE	COIN TYPE/VARIETY/METAL	ABP FINE	AVERAGE FINE
□ 1972	1 Dollar, Silver Wedding Anniversary, Silver	—	7.25
□ 1981	1 Dollar, Royal Wedding, Cupro-Nickel	$2.00	7.25
□ 1981	1 Dollar, Royal Wedding, Silver	—	16.25
□ 1983	1 Dollar, Cahow Over Bermuda, Brass	.75	4.00
□ 1985	1 Dollar, Cruise Ship Tourism, Silver	—	20.00
□ 1985	1 Dollar, Cruise Ship Tourism, Copper-Nickel	1.00	5.00
□ 1986	1 Dollar, World Wildlife Fund—Sea Turtle, Cupro-Nickel	4.00	7.25
□ 1986	1 Dollar, World Wildlife Fund—Sea Turtle, Silver	—	25.00
□ 1986	1 Dollar, World Wildlife Fund—Sea Turtle, Brass	7.00	14.00
□ 1987	1 Dollar, Commercial Aviation—50th Anniversary, Cupro-Nickel	4.00	7.25
□ 1987	1 Dollar, Commercial Aviation—50th Anniversary, Silver	—	25.00
□ 1988	1 Dollar, Railroad, Silver	—	30.00
□ 1988	1 Dollar, Sailboat, Brass	—	2.50
□ 1988	1 Dollar, Railroad, Cupro-Nickel	4.00	6.00
□ 1989	1 Dollar, Monarch Conservation Project, Silver	—	25.00

DATE	COIN TYPE/VARIETY/METAL	ABP FINE	AVERAGE FINE
☐ 1989	1 Dollar, Monarch Conservation Project, Cupro-Nickel	$2.00	$7.00
☐ 1990	1 Dollar, 90th Birthday of Queen Mother, Silver	—	45.00
☐ 1990	1 Dollar, 90th Birthday of Queen Mother, Cupro-Nickel	2.00	4.00
☐ 1992	1 Dollar, Olympic Rings, Bronze	10.00	30.00
☐ 1990	2 Dollars, Cicada Insects, Silver	—	35.00
☐ 1990	2 Dollars, Tree Frog, Silver	—	40.00
☐ 1991	2 Dollars, Yellow-crowned Night Heron, Silver	—	32.00
☐ 1991	2 Dollars, Spiny Lobster, Silver	—	32.00
☐ 1992	2 Dollars, Cedar Tree, Silver	—	32.00
☐ 1992	2 Dollars, Bluebird, Silver	—	35.00
☐ 1983–1986	5 Dollars, Onion Over Map of Bermuda, Brass	—	5.00
☐ 1983–1986	10 Dollars, Hogge Money—Ship, Gold	—	60.00
☐ 1983–1986	10 Dollars, Wildlife—Tree Frog, Gold	—	55.00
☐ 1983–1986	10 Dollars, Hogge Money—Wild Pig, Gold	—	80.00
☐ 1970	20 Dollars, Seagull in Flight, Gold	—	250.00
☐ 1975	25 Dollars, Royal Visit, Cupro-Nickel	25.00	65.00
☐ 1977	25 Dollars, Queen's Silver Jubilee, Silver	—	35.00
☐ 1989	25 Dollars, Hogge Money—Ship, Gold	—	110.00
☐ 1990	25 Dollars, Hogge Money—Wild Pig, Gold	—	125.00
☐ 1977	50 Dollars, Queen's Silver Jubilee, Gold	—	100.00
☐ 1989	50 Dollars, Hogge Money—Wild Pig, Gold	—	275.00
☐ 1990	50 Dollars, Hogge Money—Ship, Gold	—	300.00
☐ 1975	100 Dollars, Royal Visit, Gold	—	75.00
☐ 1977	100 Dollars, Queen's Silver Jubilee, Gold	—	80.00
☐ 1989	100 Dollars, Hogge Money—Ship, Gold	—	725.00
☐ 1990	100 Dollars, Hogge Money—Wild Pig, Gold	—	725.00
☐ 1981	250 Dollars, Wedding of Prince Charles & Lady Diana, Gold	—	465.00

BOLIVIA

The first coins were used in 1574, and nearly all were silver for the following 250 years. The silver "cob" Spanish reales were in use in the 1700s, followed by the silver melgarejo. The cupro-nickel centavos were in evidence in the 1800s, and the cupro-nickel pesos bolivianos in the 1970s. Decimal coins were used in 1864. The currency today is the peso boliviano.

Boliva—Type Coinage

Key to Grading: Coat of Arms

DATE	COIN TYPE/VARIETY/METAL	ABP FINE	AVERAGE FINE
☐ 1864	1 Centecimo, 1st Coinage, Copper	—	$85.00
☐ 1878	1 Centavo, 3rd Coinage, Obv: Date, Rev: Wreath Containing 1, Copper	$65.00	140.00
☐ 1878	1 Centavo, 3rd Coinage, Obv: Value, Rev: Wreath Containing Legend, Copper	100.00	225.00
☐ 1883	1 Centavo, 3rd Coinage, Obv: Value, Rev: Wreath Containing Legend, Bronze	—	5.00

Key to Grading: Coat of Arms

DATE	COIN TYPE/VARIETY/METAL	ABP FINE	AVERAGE FINE
☐ 1864	2 Centecimos, 1st Coinage, Copper	50.00	150.00
☐ 1878	2 Centavos, 3rd Coinage, Obv: Value, Rev: Wreath Containing Legend, Copper	—	80.00
☐ 1878	2 Centavos, 3rd Coinage, Obv: Date, Rev: 2 cent Value Under Condor	—	325.00

DATE	COIN TYPE/VARIETY/METAL	ABP FINE	AVERAGE FINE
☐ 1883	2 Centavos, 3rd Coinage, Obv: Value, Rev: Wreath Containing Legend, Bronze	$4.00	$12.00
☐ 1864–1865	1/20 Boliviano, 1st Coinage, Silver	—	16.00

Key to Grading: Coat of Arms

DATE	COIN TYPE/VARIETY/METAL	ABP FINE	AVERAGE FINE
☐ 1871–1872	5 Centavos, 2nd Coinage, Obv: 11 Stars at Bottom, Rev: Without Weight, Silver	8.00	18.00
☐ 1871	5 Centavos, 2nd Coinage, Obv: 11 Stars at Bottom, Rev: With Weight, Silver	8.00	18.00
☐ 1872–1884	5 Centavos, 3rd Coinage, La Union Es La Fuerza, Silver	—	4.00
☐ 1872	5 Centavos, 2nd Coinage, Obv: 9 Stars at Bottom, Rev: Without Weight, Silver	—	10.00
☐ 1883	5 Centavos, 3rd Coinage, Center Hole; Obv: Value, Rev: Wreath Containing Legend, Cupro-Nickel	4.00	12.00
☐ 1883	5 Centavos, 3rd Coinage, Obv: Value, Rev: Wreath Containing Legend, With Hole, Cupro-Nickel	2.00	4.25
☐ 1885–1900	5 Centavos, 3rd Coinage, La Union Es La Fuerza, Silver	—	5.00
☐ 1892	5 Centavos, 3rd Coinage, Obv: Value, Rev: Wreath Containing Legend, Cupro-Nickel	2.00	4.00
☐ 1893–1919	5 Centavos, 3rd Coinage, Cupro-Nickel	.75	4.00

Key to Grading: Coat of Arms

DATE	COIN TYPE/VARIETY/METAL	ABP FINE	AVERAGE FINE
☐ 1864–1866	1/5 Boliviano, 1st Coinage, Silver	—	$12.00
☐ 1864–1867	1/10 Boliviano, 1st Coinage, Silver	—	12.00
☐ 1870–1871	10 Centavos, 2nd Coinage, Obv: 11 Stars at Bottom, Rev: With Weight, Silver	—	4.25
☐ 1871	10 Centavos, 2nd Coinage, Obv: 11 Stars at Bottom, Rev: Without Weight, Silver	—	6.00
☐ 1872	10 Centavos, 2nd Coinage, Obv: 9 Stars at Bottom, Rev: Without Weight, Silver	—	4.25
☐ 1872–1884	10 Centavos, 3rd Coinage, La Union Es La Fuerza, Silver	—	4.25
☐ 1883	10 Centavos, 3rd Coinage, Obv: Value, Rev: Wreath Containing Legend, Cupro-Nickel	$5.00	15.00
☐ 1883	10 Centavos, 3rd Coinage, Center Hole; Obv: Value, Rev: Wreath Containing Legend, Cupro-Nickel	1.00	5.15
☐ 1885–1900	10 Centavos, 3rd Coinage, La Union Es La Fuerza, Silver	—	5.15

Key to Grading: Coat of Arms

DATE	COIN TYPE/VARIETY/METAL	ABP FINE	AVERAGE FINE
☐ 1892	10 Centavos, 3rd Coinage, Obv: Value, Rev: Wreath Containing Legend, Cupro-Nickel	.50	4.15
☐ 1893–1919	10 Centavos, 3rd Coinage, Cupro-Nickel	.50	4.15
☐ 1870–1871	20 Centavos, 2nd Coinage, Obv: 11 Stars at Bottom, Rev: With Weight, Silver	—	34.00
☐ 1871	20 Centavos, 2nd Coinage, Obv: 11 Stars at Bottom, Rev: Without Weight, Silver	—	34.00
☐ 1871–1872	20 Centavos, 2nd Coinage, Obv: 9 Stars at Bottom, Rev: Without Weight, Silver	—	9.00

DATE	COIN TYPE/VARIETY/METAL	ABP FINE	AVERAGE FINE
☐ 1872–1885	20 Centavos, 3rd Coinage, La Union Es La Fuerza, Silver	—	$4.00
☐ 1879	20 Centavos, Daza, President 1876–1880, Silver	—	18.00

Key to Grading: Coat of Arms

DATE	COIN TYPE/VARIETY/METAL	ABP FINE	AVERAGE FINE
☐ 1885–1907	20 Centavos, 3rd Coinage, La Union Es La Fuerza, Silver	—	6.50
☐ 1870–1871	Boliviano-2nd Coinage obv: 11 stars at bottom, rev: with weight, Silver	—	25.00
☐ 1871–1872	Boliviano, 2nd Coinage, obv: 9 stars at bottom, rev: without weight, Silver	—	18.00
☐ 1872–1893	Boliviano, 3rd Coinage, La Union Es La Fuerza, Silver	—	20.00

BRAZIL

The first coins were used in 1645 and included the gold guilders, followed by the gold "Johannes," gold reis, silver reis, and the copper reis. The stainless-steel centavos were issued in 1975. The decimal system was established in 1942. Today's currency is the cruzeiro.

Brazil—Type Coinage

Key to Grading: Bust

DATE	COIN TYPE/VARIETY/METAL	ABP FINE	AVERAGE FINE
☐ 1868–1870	10 Reis, Pedro II, Bronze	—	.85

Key to Grading: Bust

DATE	COIN TYPE/VARIETY/METAL	ABP FINE	AVERAGE FINE
☐ 1868–1870	20 Reis, Pedro II, Bronze	—	$2.25
☐ 1889–1912	20 Reis, Republic, Bronze	—	2.25
☐ 1918–1935	20 Reis, Republic, Cupro-Nickel	—	1.00

Key to Grading: Bust

DATE	COIN TYPE/VARIETY/METAL	ABP FINE	AVERAGE FINE
☐ 1873–1880	40 Reis, Pedro II, Bronze	—	2.00
☐ 1889–1912	40 Reis, Republic, Bronze	—	4.00

Key to Grading:

DATE	COIN TYPE/VARIETY/METAL	ABP FINE	AVERAGE FINE
☐ 1886–1888	50 Reis, Pedro II, Cupro-Nickel	—	2.25
☐ 1918–1935	50 Reis, Republic, Cupro-Nickel	—	.40
☐ 1871–1875	100 Reis, Pedro II, Cupro-Nickel	—	2.25

DATE	COIN TYPE/VARIETY/METAL	ABP FINE	AVERAGE FINE
☐ 1886–1889	100 Reis, Pedro II, Cupro-Nickel	—	$ .75
☐ 1889–1900	100 Reis, Republic, Cupro-Nickel	—	1.50
☐ 1901	100 Reis, Republic, Cupro-Nickel	—	.50
☐ 1918–1935	100 Reis, Republic, Cupro-Nickel	—	.32
☐ 1932	100 Reis, Republic, Colonization 400th Anniversary, Cupro-Nickel	—	.55
☐ 1936–1938	100 Reis, Republic, National Heroes Series—Tamandare, Cupro-Nickel	—	.38
☐ 1938–1942	100 Reis, Republic, Vargas, Cupro-Nickel	—	.38
☐ 1942–1943	10 Centavos, Republic, Cupro-Nickel	—	.38

Key to Grading: Bust

DATE	COIN TYPE/VARIETY/METAL	ABP FINE	AVERAGE FINE
☐ 1947–1955	10 Centavos, Republic, Obv: Bonifacio, Aluminum-Bronze	—	.38
☐ 1956–1962	10 Centavos, Republic, Aluminum	—	.38
☐ 1854–1867	200 Reis, Pedro II, Silver	—	4.25
☐ 1867–1869	200 Reis, Pedro II, Silver	—	5.00
☐ 1871–1874	200 Reis, Pedro II, Cupro-Nickel	—	2.25
☐ 1886–1889	200 Reis, Pedro II, Cupro-Nickel	—	2.25
☐ 1889–1900	200 Reis, Republic, Cupro-Nickel	$1.25	4.00
☐ 1901	200 Reis, Republic, Cupro-Nickel	—	.75

Key to Grading: Bust

DATE	COIN TYPE/VARIETY/METAL	ABP FINE	AVERAGE FINE
☐ 1918–1935	200 Reis, Republic, Cupro-Nickel	—	.45
☐ 1932	200 Reis, Republic, Colonization 400th Anniversary, Silver	—	1.00
☐ 1936–1938	200 Reis, Republic, National Heroes Series—Maua, Cupro-Nickel	—	.38
☐ 1938–1942	200 Reis, Republic, Vargas, Cupro-Nickel	—	.38
☐ 1942–1943	20 Centavos, Republic, Cupro-Nickel	—	.38

DATE	COIN TYPE/VARIETY/METAL	ABP FINE	AVERAGE FINE
☐ 1948–1956	20 Centavos, Republic, Obv: Barbosa, Aluminum-Bronze	—	$ .32
☐ 1948–1956	20 Centavos, Republic, Obv: Dutra, Aluminum-Bronze	—	.32

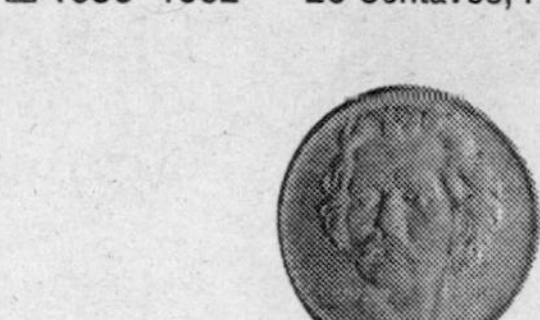

Key to Grading: Coat of Arms

☐ 1956–1962	20 Centavos, Republic, Aluminum	—	.32

Key to Grading: Bust

☐ 1936–1938	300 Reis, Republic, National Heroes Series—Carlos Gomes, Cupro-Nickel	—	.25
☐ 1938–1942	300 Reis, Republic, Vargas, Cupro-Nickel	—	.40
☐ 1900	400 Reis, Republic, Discovery 400th Anniversary, Silver	—	16.00
☐ 1901	400 Reis, Republic, Cupro-Nickel	—	2.00
☐ 1918–1935	400 Reis, Republic, Cupro-Nickel	—	.55
☐ 1932	400 Reis, Republic, Colonization 400th Anniversary, Cupro-Nickel	—	2.20

Key to Grading: Bust

☐ 1936–1938	400 Reis, Republic, National Heroes Series—Oswaldo Cruz, Cupro-Nickel	—	2.20

DATE	COIN TYPE/VARIETY/METAL	ABP FINE	AVERAGE FINE
☐ 1938–1942	400 Reis, Republic, Vargas, Cupro-Nickel	—	$ .50
☐ 1922	500 Reis, Republic, Independence Centennial, Aluminum-Bronze	—	.50
☐ 1932	500 Reis, Republic, First Settler, Aluminum-Bronze	—	2.00
☐ 1939	500 Reis, Republic, Famous Men Series—de Assis, Aluminum-Bronze	—	.75
☐ 1849–1852	500 Reis, Pedro II, Silver	—	10.00
☐ 1853–1867	500 Reis, Pedro II, Silver	—	10.00
☐ 1867–1868	500 Reis, Pedro II, Silver	—	6.00
☐ 1876–1889	500 Reis, Republic, Silver	—	7.00

Key to Grading: Bust

DATE	COIN TYPE/VARIETY/METAL	ABP FINE	AVERAGE FINE
☐ 1906–1913	500 Reis, Republic, Silver	—	4.00
☐ 1924–1930	500 Reis, Republic, Aluminum-Bronze	—	.40
☐ 1935	500 Reis, Republic, National Heroes Series—Diego Feijo, Aluminum-Bronze	$1.50	2.25
☐ 1942–1943	50 Centavos, Republic, Cupro-Nickel	—	.40

Key to Grading: Bust

DATE	COIN TYPE/VARIETY/METAL	ABP FINE	AVERAGE FINE
☐ 1956	50 Centavos, Republic, Aluminum-Bronze	—	.25
☐ 1849–1852	1000 Reis, Pedro II, Silver	—	7.00
☐ 1853–1866	1000 Reis, Pedro II, Silver	—	8.00
☐ 1869	1000 Reis, Pedro II, Silver	—	20.00
☐ 1876–1889	1000 Reis, Pedro II, Silver	—	15.00
☐ 1889	1000 Reis, Republic, Silver	—	15.00
☐ 1900	1000 Reis, Republic, Discovery 400th Anniversary, Silver	—	52.00

DATE	COIN TYPE/VARIETY/METAL	ABP FINE	AVERAGE FINE
☐ 1922	1000 Reis, Republic, Independence Centennial, Aluminum-Bronze	—	$2.00

Key to Grading: Bust

DATE	COIN TYPE/VARIETY/METAL	ABP FINE	AVERAGE FINE
☐ 1906–1913	1000 Reis, Republic, Silver	—	4.00
☐ 1924–1930	1000 Reis, Republic, Aluminum-Bronze	—	1.00
☐ 1932	1000 Reis, Republic, First Governor, Aluminum-Bronze	—	4.00
☐ 1935	1000 Reis, Republic, National Heroes Series—Jose de Anchieta, Aluminum-Bronze	—	1.00
☐ 1939	1000 Reis, Republic, Famous Men Series—Barreto, Aluminum-Bronze	—	.50

Key to Grading: Map & Bust

DATE	COIN TYPE/VARIETY/METAL	ABP FINE	AVERAGE FINE
☐ 1942–1956	Cruzeiro, Republic, Aluminum-Bronze	—	.38
☐ 1956	Cruzeiro, Republic, Aluminum-Bronze	—	.38
☐ 1957–1961	Cruzeiro, Republic, Aluminum	—	.38
☐ 1851–1852	2000 Reis, Pedro II, Silver	—	14.00
☐ 1853–1867	2000 Reis, Pedro II, Silver	—	15.00
☐ 1868–1869	2000 Reis, Pedro II, Silver	—	22.00
☐ 1886–1889	2000 Reis, Pedro II, Silver	—	14.00
☐ 1891–1897	2000 Reis, Republic, Silver	$225.00	475.00
☐ 1900	2000 Reis, Republic, Discovery 400th Anniversary, Silver	—	80.00

Key to Grading: Bust

DATE	COIN TYPE/VARIETY/METAL	ABP FINE	AVERAGE FINE
☐ 1906–1913	2000 Reis, Republic, Silver	—	$6.00
☐ 1924–1934	2000 Reis, Republic, Silver	—	4.00
☐ 1932	2000 Reis, Republic, King John III, Aluminum-Bronze	—	4.00
☐ 1935	2000 Reis, Republic, National Heroes Series—Caxias, Aluminum-Bronze	—	1.00
☐ 1936–1938	2000 Reis, Republic, National Heroes Series—Duke of Caxias, Aluminum-Bronze	—	.75
☐ 1939	2000 Reis, Republic, Famous Men Series—Peixoto, Aluminum-Bronze	—	.75

Key to Grading: Maps or Bust

DATE	COIN TYPE/VARIETY/METAL	ABP FINE	AVERAGE FINE
☐ 1942–1956	2 Cruzeiros, Republic, Aluminum-Bronze	—	.40
☐ 1956	2 Cruzeiros, Republic, Aluminum-Bronze	—	.40
☐ 1957–1961	2 Cruzeiros, Republic, Aluminum	—	.40
☐ 1900	4000 Reis, Republic, Discovery 400th Anniversary, Silver	—	140.00
☐ 1854–1869	5000 Reis, Pedro II, Gold	—	100.00

Key to Grading: Bust

DATE	COIN TYPE/VARIETY/METAL	ABP FINE	AVERAGE FINE
☐ 1936–1938	5000 Reis, Republic, National Heroes Series—Santos Dumont, Silver	—	$ .50
☐ 1942–1943	5 Cruzeiros, Republic, Aluminum-Bronze	—	.75
☐ 1849–1851	10000 Reis, Pedro II, Gold	—	180.00
☐ 1853–1889	10000 Reis, Pedro II, Gold	—	175.00
☐ 1889–1922	10000 Reis, Republic, Gold	—	145.00
☐ 1965	10 Cruzeiros, Republic, Aluminum	—	.40
☐ 1849–1851	20000 Reis, Pedro II, Gold	—	345.00
☐ 1851–1852	20000 Reis, Pedro II, Gold	—	345.00
☐ 1853–1889	20000 Reis, Pedro II, Gold	—	345.00
☐ 1889–1922	20000 Reis, Republic, Gold	—	325.00
☐ 1965	20 Cruzeiros, Republic, Aluminum	—	.40
☐ 1965	50 Cruzeiros, Republic, Cupro-Nickel	—	.40

CANADA

The first coins, sols, and deniers in silver, bullion, and copper were used in 1670. In the 1800s the bronze penny token was in use. The first decimal coins were used in 1858. The currency today is the dollar.

THE ROYAL CANADIAN MINT

Courtesy of the Royal Canadian Mint

In many ways, the history of the Royal Canadian Mint mirrors that of Canada itself.

As Canada struggled toward independence, its first settlers used a rich and sometimes confusing mix of French, American, Spanish, and British currency to support its rapid development and growth. But to a young and vigorous country, national pride demanded that it be able to produce its own coins. At the same time, gold mining in British Columbia and the Yukon had reached unprecedented levels with much of this precious metal exported to the United States. Promoters believed a Canadian Mint would stabilize the price of gold and that a policy of keeping government and banking reserves in domestic coinage should be encouraged. At this time, reserves were held in foreign gold coins or bullion.

Following demands for a Canadian Mint as early as 1880, the new Mint's location on Sussex Drive in Ottawa was purchased from a private land owner for $21,000 and construction began in 1905. Arthur H.W. Cleave, having served at the Royal Mint in London, was appointed Superintendent of the Canadian branch of the Royal Mint. Dr. James Bonar, who had been on the Board of Civil Examiners in London since 1876, became the first Deputy Master of the Mint.

January 2, 1908, marked the historic date of the official opening of the Ottawa Branch of Britain's Royal Mint with the striking of a fifty-cent piece. This historic site on Sussex Drive is still in use today.

The early years saw the Mint efficiently producing gold sovereigns, Canadian coins, and millions of ounces of refined gold. The Mint even produced gun parts for Britain during World War I.

The Royal Canadian Mint was officially placed in Canadian hands on December 1, 1931, reporting to the Department of Finance. After many years of establishing new coinage and refining records, the Canadian government gave the Mint the authority needed to respond more quickly to the changing conditions of a modern world by making it a Crown corporation on April 1, 1969.

Other Important historic dates:

April 30, 1976: A branch of the Mint, dedicated to the high-speed production of domestic and foreign circulation coins, is inaugurated in Winnipeg.

December 17, 1987: The Royal Canadian Mint is financially restructured, allowing it to apply its net earnings to meet operational requirements, replace capital assets, ensure its overall financial stability, and pay a reasonable dividend to the shareholder, the Canadian government.

The Refinery

Fashioned after its British counterpart, the Canadian Branch faced an unusual dilemma in its early history. In Britain there was any number of local, privately owned refineries to choose from so it was not necessary for a refinery to be built as part of the Royal Mint's operations. This was not the case in Canada. The problem came to light in late 1906. Canada must have a refinery. After much debate, construction began in 1909. Until the completion of the refinery in 1911, the Ottawa Mint's Assay Department was given the task of purifying incoming gold, a job that kept the Chief Assayer working long into the night to keep up with demand.

The Mint Today

Today's modern Mint, with its unsurpassed standards of craftsmanship in minting circulation and commemorative collector coins and its reputation as a premier refiner of gold, is known and respected around the globe. As a profit-making Crown corporation, the Mint is run much like any other company, with a mandate to produce a fair return on investment for its sole shareholder, the Canadian government. The President and Master of the Mint is the senior executive officer of the organization, reporting to a Board of Directors appointed by the Minister of Public Works and Government Services. All Royal Canadian Mint stocks are owned by the government, and they are not traded on the stock market.

With its headquarters in Ottawa and a state-of-the-art production facility in Winnipeg, the Royal Canadian Mint today employs some 500 highly skilled and dedicated individuals involved in all aspects of coin design, production, and marketing in one of the largest and most complex minting facilities in operation today.

Refinery and Assay

Since 1908, the Royal Canadian Mint has been assaying and refining gold for mining companies, foreign governments, and private interests. The Mint runs one of the largest gold refineries in the Western Hemisphere, refining an average of 2 million Troy ounces per year.

The Royal Canadian Mint hallmark is recognized worldwide as a guarantee of honest weight and purity. That guarantee is on every gold product produced, including:

- 400 oz. London Good Delivery bars
- 100 oz. Comex bars
- Kilo bars
- Granular gold

Like the Gold Maple Leaf, all Royal Canadian Mint gold products can be traded anywhere gold is bought and sold.

Custom Products

The Royal Canadian Mint produces custom medals, tokens, and trade dollars for a wide number of uses. The Mint is also able to customize some existing numismatic products by transferring an organization's logo or any other print specification onto the coin packaging (available in Canada only).

Bullion Coins

Bullion coins are struck in the purest of precious metals (gold, platinum, or silver), and are not only an attractive coin, but also a means for the general public to buy, own, and invest in precious metals.

Because the Royal Canadian Mint is so well known and respected, the Maple Leaf bullion coins are bought and sold around the world.

Circulation Coins

All circulation coins supplied by the Royal Canadian Mint are manufactured at a high-speed production facility in Winnipeg, Manitoba. This highly automated facility covers 160,000 square feet and has a total production capacity of up to 150 coins per second.

NUMISMATIC COINS

Numismatic coins, produced by the Royal Canadian Mint for collecting or gift giving, are miniature works of fine art that reflect the Canadian identity. Original works by famous Canadian artists are painstakingly reproduced by the Mint's master engravers in the minute detail you see portrayed on each coin. Every coin tells a story of discovery, adventure, and natural beauty unique to Canada, and reflects the Royal Canadian Mint's pride in their great heritage.

2001 Releases

2001 CHINESE LUNAR SERIES— THE YEAR OF THE SNAKE

The centre of the Year (2001) of the Snake coin features an octagonal 24-karat gold covered cameo depicting the Snake. In each year of the series, the design on the gold cameo will change to depict the animal for the year of issue. The twelve animals of the Chinese lunar calendar appear around the circumference of the reverse of the sterling silver coin. Canadian artist Harvey Chan created the design of the Chinese symbols. The obverse of the coin portrays an effigy of her Majesty Queen Elizabeth II by Dora de Pédery-HUNT, surrounded by the inscription 15 DOLLARS, CANADA, 2001.

The Chinese lunar calendar follows a twelve-year cycle and each year is associated with an animal. The twelve animals of the Chinese lunar calendar are the rat, ox, tiger, rabbit, dragon, snake, horse, sheep, monkey, rooster, dog and pig. According to the Chinese astrology, those born in the year of the Snake are regarded as wise and contemplative, but inwardly naïve. They are prudent.

The mint produced 68,888 of the Year of the Snake coins. The coins come in an embossed red velvet box with gold moiré sides.

Coin Specifications:

Composition:	*Coin:* 92.5% silver, 7.5% copper.	
	Cameo: 24 karat gold covered	
Weight:	34 grams	
Diameter:	*Coin:* 40 mm	*Cameo:* 17.5 mm
Edge:	Reeded	
Face Value:	$15.00	
Finish:	Proof: frosted relief on brilliant background	
Mintage:	68,888	
Collector Value:	$115.00	

2001 CHINESE LUNAR SERIES— THE YEAR OF THE SNAKE HOLOGRAM COIN

To celebrate the arrival of the Year of the Snake in the Chinese lunar calendar, the Royal Canadian Mint has introduced the Year of the Snake Hologram Gold Coin. This is the second hologram coin commemorating the Chinese Lunar calendar produced by the Royal Canadian Mint.

Designed by Canadian artist Harvey Chan, the 2001—$150 18-karat Gold Coin features a snake entwined around a bamboo stalk. The 18-karat gold (75% gold and 25% silver) coin has a diameter of 28 mm and weighs 13.61 grams. The coin has a serrated edge and is 1.81 mm thick. The face value is $150 and the mintage is limited to 6,888 coins worldwide.

Collector Value: $340.00

2001 THE FIRST TRANSATLANTIC WIRELESS TRANSMISSION—100th ANNIVERSARY Marconi Sterling Silver Two Coin Set

Produced in partnership with the British Royal Mint, this set commemorates the 100th Anniversary of the first transatlantic wireless transmission. Marconi's achievement marked the beginning of wireless communication era and sparked a technological revolution that continues to transform the world. Canada received the first transmission at Signal Hill in St. Johns, Newfoundland, and is today one of the world leaders in the wireless telecommunications industry.

This set features coins by the Royal Canadian Mint and the Royal British Mint. The reverse of the $5 Royal Canadian Mint coin depicts sound waves travelling from Poldhu near Cornwall in England to St. John's, Newfoundland in Canada. This bi-metallic coin is sterling silver with a 24-karat gold-plated cameo of Guglielmo Marconi. The reverse of the £2 British Royal Mint coin features an elegant symbolic rendition of radio waves emanating from a sundial bearing the year 2001. This coin is presented as a bi-metallic coin in sparkling sterling silver—with the golden outer ring coated in 22 carat gold. The Canadian coin was designed by artist Cosme Saffloti, while the British Coin was designed by Robert Evans.

Collector Value: $48.00 set of 2

2001 The Gold Maple Leaf Five-Coin Hologram Set

The 2001 GML Five-Coin Set represents only the second time such a set has been issued by the Royal Canadian Mint. The first was issued as a 20th anniversary set in 1999. In this set, the distinctive maple leaf appears as a high-resolution dot matrix hologram, which has been struck directly onto each of the five coins. The maple leaf hologram design features hues of red, green, blue, and yellow. Each set includes a 1, 1/2, 1/4, 1/10 and 1/20 troy ounce gold coin.

As with the 1/4 ounce Gold Maple Leaf, each coin is characterized by two finishes. The reverse features the hologram Maple Leaf design on a brilliant background. The obverse maintains the traditional bullion coin finish (brilliant relief on matte field) with the effigy of Her Majesty Queen Elizabeth II by artist Dora de Pédery-Hunt.

Each coin is 99.99% pure gold and mintage has been limited to 600 sets worldwide. The set comes in a mahogany box with a brass plaque featuring the Royal Canadian Mint logo and a numbered certificate of authenticity.

Coin Specifications:

SIZE (TROY OZ.)	GOLD PURITY	TOTAL WEIGHT	DIAMETER	THICKNESS	LEGAL TENDER VALUE
1	99.99%	31.150 g	30 mm	2.87 mm	$50
1/2	99.99%	15.584 g	25 mm	2.23 mm	$20
1/4	99.99%	7.797 g	20 mm	1.78 mm	$10
1/10	99.99%	3.131 g	16 mm	1.13 mm	$5
1/20	99.99%	1.581 g	14.1 mm	0.92 mm	$1

Edge: Reeded
Finish: Traditional bullion coin finish (brilliant relief on a matte field)
Mintage: 600 sets
Collector Value: $2500.00 set

2001 The Gold Maple Leaf 1/4 Ounce Hologram Coin

Guaranteed by the Government of Canada to contain 99.99% pure gold, the 2001 1/4 ounce Gold Maple Leaf Hologram joins the existing family of Royal Canadian Mint's Gold Maple Leaf products unsurpassed for their purity throughout the world.

In this 1/4 ounce GML coin, the high-resolution dot matrix hologram which has been struck directly on the coin, depicts three maple leaves on a branch imbued with hues of red, green, blue, and yellow.

Two finishes characterize each coin. The reverse features the hologram Maple Leaf design on a brilliant background. The obverse maintains the traditional bullion coin finish (brilliant relief on matte field) with the effigy of Her Majesty Queen Elizabeth II by artist Dora de Pédery-Hunt.

Mintage has been limited to 150,000 coins worldwide.

Since Canada's Maple Leaf Bullion Coins were first introduced in 1979, they have become the standard for superior quality as the purest gold coin in the world. The Mint was the first to produce 99.99% pure gold coins in 1982, and has diversified its bullion line with the creation of a guaranteed value gold bullion coin in 1997 as well as a gold bullion wafer and a 99.999% pure gold coin, which set a new standard of purity for Canada and the world.

Collector Value: $200.00

2001 The "Harlequin Duck" Platinum Four Coin Set

The Harlequin Duck (Histrionicus histrionicus) featured on the 2001 Platinum Coin Set of the Royal Canadian Mint is one of the most unique ducks in the world. Designed by Royal Canadian Mint engravers, the four platinum Harlequin Duck coins are the twelfth addition to the platinum wildlife series begun in 1990.

The platinum set consists of a 1/10 ounce $30 coin that features the profile of a Harlequin Duck head, a 1/4 ounce $75 coin that features the duck in flight, a 1/2 ounce $150 coin that features a female duck with chick and a one ounce $300 coin that features a group of ducks. The 2001 platinum coins are available only as a four coin set.

Collector Value: $2400.00 set of 4

2001 LAND SEA AND RAIL SERIES—
The Russell 'Light Four' Model L Touring Car

The Russell 'Light Four' Model L Touring Car was built by the Canadian Cycle & Motor Company Ltd. The Russell was the first mass-produced Canadian car with a Canadian-built engine and chassis. Specially engineered for Canadian driving conditions, the Russell quickly became Canada's first successful selling automobile.

The Model L of 1908 was an affordable car with a hand horn, brass side and tail lamps, acetylene headlamps and a 4-cylinder, 24-hp engine. Its extra 56.5-inch wheel tread prevented it from slipping into carriage ruts in the roads.

After 1910, the Russell became a luxury car. The Canada Cycle & Motor Company Ltd., along with McLaughlin and Ford, became one of the three tycoons of the Canadian automobile industry due to the success of The Russell Model L.

Coin Specifications:

Composition:	92.5% silver, 7.5% copper
Weight:	31.103 grams
Diameter:	38 mm
Thickness:	3.5 mm
Edge:	Interrupted serration
Face Value:	$20
Finish:	Proof (frosted relief on a brilliant background)
Mintage:	15,000 each coin
Collector Value:	$90.00

2001 LAND SEA AND RAIL SERIES— The Marco Polo 150th Anniversary

Built in Saint John, New Brunswick in 1851 by James Smith, the Marco Polo for a time was considered to be the fastest ship in the world and named the "Queen of the Seas." The Marco Polo beat the world record run from England to Australia by a full week and reached England from Canada in 15 days on her record breaking maiden voyage. Furthermore, the Marco Polo was the first ship to circumnavigate the world in less than 6 months.

The ship was designed to carry a crew of 60 and 960 passengers. The 1625-ton vessel with three complete decks carried emigrants and timber across the oceans. In 1883, while transporting a load of pine to England, the Marco Polo encountered a storm in the Gulf of the St. Lawrence and the ship ran ashore.

Coin Specifications:

Composition:	92.5% silver, 7.5% copper
Weight:	31.103 grams

Diameter: 38 mm
Thickness: 3.5 mm
Edge: Interrupted serration
Face Value: $20
Finish: Proof (frosted relief on a brilliant background)
Mintage: 15,000 each coin
Collector Value: $100.00

2001 LAND SEA AND RAIL SERIES—The Scotia

Built in Hamilton, Ontario in 1861, The Scotia was the first locomotive in Canada to be built with a steel boiler in order to reduce heat loss and generate more power.

Coin Specifications:

Composition: 92.5% silver, 7.5% copper
Weight: 31.103 grams
Diameter: 38 mm
Thickness: 3.5 mm
Edge: Interrupted serration
Face Value: $20
Finish: Proof (frosted relief on a brilliant background)
Mintage: 15,000 each coin
Collector Value: $90.00

2001 The Library of Parliament—125th Anniversary

With a commanding presence on the shores of the Ottawa River, it is difficult to imagine that the Library of Parliament was once a transient collection of books traveling between Canada's early political centers. This was precisely the case until Queen Victoria selected Ottawa as Canada's capital and prompted the establishment of a permanent library there.

Construction began in December 1859 and continued for 17 years before the library was completed in 1876, opening with a grand ball on February 28th of that year.

From its inception, the library incorporated the very best that architecture had to offer. Inspiration was found in London and Paris, and the innovative design was immensely popular. Its elaborate iron doors and roof proved their worth when fire threatened the library in 1916 and 1952.

Despite the ravages of history and time, many of the library's original features remain, evoking the grandeur of another age for everyone who visits there.

DESIGN

Reverse: The reverse of the coin features an inside view of the Library of Parliament. The focal point of the coin depicts the statue of Her Majesty Queen Victoria.

Obverse: The obverse features a contemporary effigy of Her Majesty Queen Elizabeth II by artist Dora de Pédery-HUNT.

ARTIST

Robert-Ralph Carmichael was born in Sault Ste. Marie, Ontario. Mr. Carmichael is a graduate of both The Ontario College of Art in Toronto and Carleton University in Ottawa.

Coin Specifications:

Composition:	14 karat gold: 58.33% gold - 41.67% silver
Weight:	13.338 grams
Diameter:	27 mm
Thickness:	2.15 mm
Edge:	Reeded
Face Value:	$100
Mintage:	10,000
Collector Value:	$265.00

2001 The "Mayflower" 99.999% Gold Coin

The Royal Canadian Mint issues its fourth floral coin from the 99.999% Gold Coin Series, with the 2001 $350 gold coin depicting *the Trailing Arbutus (Epigaea repens),* more commonly known as the Mayflower. So profound was this flower's springtime appearance that Nova Scotia's early residents quickly adopted it as a celebrated patriotic symbol. The Mayflower was praised by songwriters and poets. It was showcased on the province's early stamps and coins, as well as the decorative brass of its militia. The Mayflower became the floral emblem of Nova Scotia after an act of legislature in 1901.

The design was created by Canadian artist Bonnie Ross. The obverse of the coin depicts and effigy of Her Majesty Queen Elizabeth II by Dora de Pédery-HUNT surrounded by the inscription "Elizabeth II Canada D.G. Regina Fine Gold 350 Dollars Or Pure," with the year of issue to the left of the Queen and .99999 to the right. The mintage of this new 99.999 percent gold coin is limited to 2,001.

Collector Value: $800.00

2001 NATIONAL BALLET OF CANADA 50th ANNIVERSARY

The National Ballet of Canada, a company with more than 50 dancers and its own full symphony orchestra, Is Canada's premier dance company which ranks as one of the world's top international companies. Founded in 1951 by English dancer Celia Franca, the company was established as a classical company and it is the only Canadian company to present a full range of traditional full evening ballet classics. The company also embraces contemporary works and encourages the creation of new ballets from Canadian choreographers.

The first performance of the company was performed on November 12, 1951 at the Eaton Auditorium in Toronto. The program included Les Sylphides and the Polovtsian Dances from Prince Igor. The principal dancers with the company were Celia Franca, Irene Alpine, Lois Smith, David Adams, and Jury Gotshalks.

The National Ballet of Canada earned its international reputation in 1970 when it was the only classical ballet company to be invited to perform at the Expo '70 in Osaka, Japan. In 1972, the company undertook its first European Tour to Britain, France, Belgium, Monaco, Switzerland, and Germany. Also in 1972, Rudolf Nureyev performed the production of Sleeping Beauty with the company. With this ballet, the National Ballet of Canada made a debut at the New York Metropolitan Opera House in 1973. Since then, the company has made numerous appearances at the New York Opera House.

In 1983, the legendary Erik Bruhn, considered one of the greatest male classical dancers of this century, took over the position of Artistic Director. Bruhn added many new famous ballets to the company's repertoire including The Merry Widow, and The Blue Snake. After having traditionally natured Artistic Directors, James Kudelka was appointed the National Ballet of Canada's Artistic Director in 1996. A world-renowned choreographer, Mr. Kudelka transformed the company to the forefront on the international dance scene as a first-class creative organization.

DESIGN

Reverse: The reverse of the coin depicts a scene from the company's debut performance of the classical ballet Les Sylphides, designed by Canadian artist Scott McKowen. The ballerina is being held in an arabesque pose by her partner in the foreground with the corps de ballet in the background.

Obverse: The obverse of the coin features an effigy of Her Majesty, Queen Elizabeth II, by artist Dora de Pédery-HUNT.

ARTIST

Scott McKowen received a Bachelor of Fine Arts from the University of Michigan School of Art in 1978. McKowen has combined his skills as a graphic designer and his longtime theater background to establish a career specializing in theater posters and graphics for the performing arts. Residing in Stratford, Ontario, Mr. McKowen is an active participant of the Stratford Festival designing their promotional material.

The 2001 Silver Dollar Coin is the 38th in a series celebrating Canadian Historical Events, People and Places begun in 1935. The 2001 coin is available in proof finish or brilliant uncirculated finish. For 2001, the silver dollar will have a limited mintage: 125,000 for the proof coin, and 65,000 for the brilliant uncirculated coin. The proof finish coin is encapsulated and presented in a green display case lined with green flock. The protective sleeve features graphics representative of the theme. The proof finish includes a numbered certificate of authenticity. The brilliant uncirculated coin is presented in a plastic capsule and protected with matchbox style packaging

Coin Specifications:

Composition:	Sterling Silver 92.5% silver, 7.5% copper
Weight:	25.175 grams
Diameter:	36.07 mm
Thickness:	3.02 mm
Edge:	Reeded
Face Value:	$1.00
Collector Value:	$28.00 brilliant uncirculated $60.00 cased proof

2001 THE ROYAL MILITARY COLLEGE OF CANADA—125th ANNIVERSARY

Located in Kingston, Ontario, the Royal Military College is Canada's only national military university. Steeped in tradition, it boasts an impressive alumni of Canada's military leaders, political figures and captains of industry that have served Canada well. Mr. Gerald T. Locklin of the Royal Military College was the artist of record for the coin's design.

The proof finish coin is encapsulated and presented in a blue display case lined with blue flock. The protective sleeve features graphics representative of the theme. The proof finish includes a numbered certificate of authenticity. The brilliant uncirculated coin is presented in a plastic capsule and protected with matchbox style packaging.

Coin Specifications:

Composition:	92.5% silver 07.5% copper
Finish:	Proof
Weight:	5.35 grams
Diameter:	21.20 mm
Thickness:	1.93 mm
Certificate:	included
Mintage:	40,000 coins
Face Value:	5 cents
Artist:	Gerald T. Locklin
Price:	16.95 CAD / 11.95 USD
Collector Value:	$25.00

The Spirit of Canada
25-cent Silver Maple Leaf Coloured Coin

Since Canada's Maple Leaf Bullion Coins were first introduced in 1979, they have become the standard for superior quality as the purest silver coin in the world. In 2001, the coin is available in a beautiful new design of three leaves in brilliant fall colours. The design was created by Canadian artist Debbie Adams, which suggests a palette of muted earth neutrals and stunning arboreal reds and yellows. Designed by artist Silke Ware of Kitchener, Ontario, this coin is only one of three colorised coins ever issued by the Royal Canadian Mint. At the centre is a red maple leaf, Canada's distinctive emblem.

"This new *Spirit of Canada* coin is a powerful symbol of the values that have made Canada strong," said the Honourable Alfonso Gagliano, Minister of Public Works and Government Services Canada and Minister responsible for the Royal Canadian Mint. "It supports our constant desire to promote tradition and pride among Canadians."

Collector Value: $24.00

2000 Releases

2000 Millennium Sterling Silver Proof 25-cent Coins

The monthly coins issued in the 2000 Millennium coin series are available individually in sterling silver, presented in a deluxe display case. Designed by individual Canadians from all walks of life, these coins celebrate a future full of promise.

January 2000

Canada's first coin of the year 2000 showcases the artistic talents of Winnipeg freelance graphic designer Donald F. Warkentin, whose passion for his country and optimism about its future shines through his inspiring design "Pride."

Mr. Warkentin's design honors our country's vibrant character and expresses Canadians' celebration of life, of our people, of peace, stability, and a flourishing bounty. It sends a signal, from east to west, that Canada is a nation looking forward to a future filled with promise.

Collector Value: $20.00

February 2000

The February 2000 coin, Ingenuity, features the work of John Jaciw of Windsor, Ontario. The coin celebrates Canadian ingenuity, representing a model society—prosperous farms, innovative cities, rapid safe transportation, and an eye toward space.

John immigrated to Canada in 1949. After studies at the Creative School of Art in Edmonton, and the Meizinger Art School in Detroit,

Michigan, John worked as a graphic designer for Hiram Walker and Sons Limited for thirty years.

The Ingenuity coin was launched on February 4, 2000, at an event at DaimlerChrysler Canada's Windsor Assembly Plant. DaimlerChrysler Canada is responsible for the creation of the minivan, considered one of the past century's most innovative and commercially successful vehicles.

Collector Value: $18.00

March 2000

Collector Value: $18.00

April 2000

Collector Value: $18.00

May 2000

Collector Value: $18.00

June 2000

Collector Value: $18.00

July 2000

Collector Value: $18.00

August 2000

Collector Value: $18.00

September 2000

Collector Value: $18.00

October 2000

Collector Value: $18.00

November 2000

Collector Value: $18.00

December 2000

Collector Value: $18.00

Commemorative Set

2000 Sterling Silver 25-cent Coins

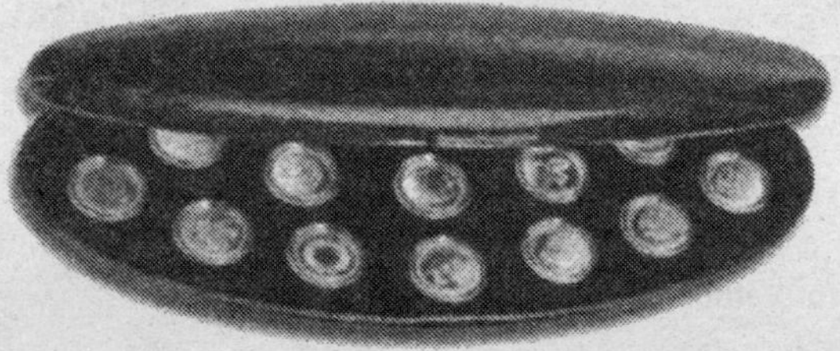

Designed by individual Canadians from all walks of life, these Millennium 25-cent coins celebrate a future full of promise. This exclusive set brings together all twelve 25-cent coins issued in 2000 to celebrate this nation's future. The coins feature the initials of their designer. This deluxe collector set of twelve sterling-silver 25-cent coins comes in a flawless proof finish and is presented in a sleek display case.

Collector Value: $160.00

Proof Set

2000 Uncirculated Gift Set

This prestigious set features Canada's circulation coins struck in a proof finish. All coins except the one-cent and one-dollar circulation coin are sterling silver. The Proof Set includes the 2000 Proof Silver Dollar: the Voyage of Discovery. The coins are displayed in specially designed acrylic lenses that allow two-sided viewing, all housed in a dark green Nabuka case.

Collector Value: $110.00

Souvenir Set

2000 Nickel 25-cent Coins

Designed by individual Canadians from all walks of life, these Millennium 25-cent coins celebrate a future full of promise. The Millennium souvenir set features all twelve coins in nickel with brilliant relief on brilliant background. The coins are displayed in a map of Canada seen from space. Also included in this set is the exclusive Millennium medallion—available only in this Royal Canadian Mint Millennium souvenir set.

Collector Value: $42.00

Specimen Set

2000 Uncirculated Gift Set

The Specimen set features a superb collection of Canada's circulation coins, struck with new dies and hand-selected to guarantee the highest quality finish with brilliant relief on a lined matte background. The two-dollar coin features frosted relief on a brilliant background. The alloys are the same as found in circulation coins.

Collector Value: $38.00

Uncirculated Set

2000 Uncirculated Gift Set

Coins are individually sealed in plastic and presented in a keepsake envelope. The uncirculated set features the two-dollar coin with the polar bear and an envelope with a striking image of a polar bear in the Canadian arctic.

Colloctor Value: $28.00

Tiny Treasures

2000 Uncirculated Gift Set

Uncirculated Tiny Treasures coin set features a finish with a brilliant field on a brilliant relief. The two-dollar coins offered in these sets feature the brilliant field and maintain the frósted polar bear relief. The alloys are the same as found in circulation coins.

Ideal for young children, this set comes in a display case illustrated with cute and cuddly teddy bears and includes a special card that children can mail back to receive a special surprise gift from the Royal Canadian Mint on their next birthday.

Collector Value: $30.00

The Adventures of Zachary and Penny Money

Based on the 1999 Millennium Coins

Have fun reading, playing, and discovering our heritage with Zachary and Penny Money!

Zachary and Penny are first cousins who love to explore. On their journey of discovery, they meet wonderful heroes and memorable characters who help them discover Canada's rich and remarkable history.

The Adventures of Zachary and Penny Money come to you in twelve beautifully illustrated stories based on each of Canada's 25-cent 1999 Millennium coins.

The Adventures of Zachary and Penny Money includes:

- Twelve stories and games in six superb booklets, representing all twelve Millennium coins.
- A nifty display card to collect your twelve 1999 25-cent Millennium coins.

Collector Value: $15.00

First Recorded Modern Hockey Game—125th Anniversary (1875)

2000 50¢ Sterling Silver Proof Coin

The first recorded hockey game that was played with regulations similar to those that rule the ice today was played on March 3, 1875, at the Victoria Skating Rink in Montreal.

This design evokes the speed and skill of the sport as a modern hockey player maneuvers a puck across the ice.

The coins for the 2000 issue in this series were designed by Canadian artist Brian Hughes.

Coin Specifications:

Composition:	Sterling silver (.925 silver, .075 copper)
Edge:	Reeded
Weight:	9.30 grams
Diameter:	27.13 mm
Face Value:	50 cents
Collector Value:	$22.00

Introduction of Curling to North America—240th Anniversary (1760)

2000 50¢ Sterling Silver Proof Coin

Although there are no official records, the winter of 1759–60 is often cited as curling's North American debut. History recalls how Scottish soldiers stationed in Quebec City during the Seven-Year War transformed a French cannon into curling irons.

This design captures the precision and technique modern curlers must exercise to propel a curling stone toward its target.

The coins for the 2000 issue in this series were designed by Canadian artist Brian Hughes.

Coin Specifications:

Composition:	Sterling silver (.925 silver, .075 copper)
Edge:	Reeded
Weight:	9.30 grams
Diameter:	27.13 mm
Face Value:	50 cents
Collector Value:	$22.00

Mother and Child

2000 $200 22-Karat Gold Coin

It is a mother's love and devotion that enable the Inuit to thrive in one of the world's harshest environments. Here, mothers are an endless source of security, warmth, and beauty in an unforgiving land.

The gaze between an Inuit woman and her child speaks the universal language of a mother's love. Her hand-crafted parka and boots reveal the care that is taken to transform life's necessities into works of art.

Designed by celebrated Inuit artist Germaine Arnaktauyok, whose work also appears on the 1999 $2 Canadian Coin, entitled Drum Dance.

This coin is the final issue in the four-coin "Native Cultures and Traditions" series (1997–2000).

Coin Specifications:

Purity:	22-karat or 91.67% gold, 8.33% silver
Edge:	Reeded
Weight:	17.135 grams
Gold Content:	15.552 grams (minimum ½ Troy ounces)
Diameter:	29 mm
Face Value:	$200.00
Mintage:	10,000
Collector Value:	$340.00

Northwest Passage

2000 $100 14-Karat Gold Coin

Sir John Franklin's disappearance in the Arctic prompted dozens of search-and-rescue expeditions. While the 1850 rescue attempt by Robert McClure failed to locate Franklin, it did succeed in unlocking the final link to the coveted Northwest Passage.

McClure's crew struggles against harsh frozen terrain while their ship, the *HMS Investigator,* remains locked in ice.

John Mardon was born in Welland, Ontario, and has received international acclaim for his work.

Coin Specifications:

Content:	58.33% gold, 41.67% silver
Edge:	Reeded
Weight:	13.338 grams
Diameter:	27 mm
Face Value:	$100.00
Mintage:	15,000
Collector Value:	$240.00

Voyage of Discovery

2000 Proof Silver Dollar

The next millennium promises to be an era of profound exploration as the boundaries of science, medicine, technology, and space continue to be challenged.

Highlights the newest frontier unlocked during the last millennium—

space. Internationally recognized symbols including the space shuttle, solar panels, the earth's atmosphere, and a robotic arm are brought together to create a stylized maple leaf to celebrate Canada's continued contribution to the space program.

Designed by artist and designer Donald F. Warkentin of Winnipeg, Manitoba.

Coin Specifications:

Composition:	Sterling silver, 92.5% silver, 7.5% copper
Edge:	Reeded
Weight:	25.175 grams
Diameter:	36.07 mm
Face Value:	$1.00
Collector Value:	$42.00
Also available:	Brilliant uncirculated sterling-silver dollar

1999 Releases

1999 225th Anniversary of the Voyage of Juan Pérez and the Sighting of the Queen Charlotte Islands

The Royal Canadian Mint salutes the spirit of explorers by commemorating the discovery of the Queen Charlotte Islands by Juan Pérez on a sterling-silver dollar coin.

"The Queen Charlotte Islands are a beautiful part of Canada's natural and cultural heritage," said Danielle Wetherup, President of the Royal Canadian Mint. "The 1999 Silver Dollar celebrates their discovery and the historic meeting of Europeans and Native Canadians."

The reverse of the silver dollar coin, designed by Canadian artist David Craig, portrays Haida canoes approaching the *Santiago,* a 225-ton Spanish frigate. Captain Juan Pérez and his crew of 86 sailed from Monterrey to explore the northern coast of North America and discovered Queen Charlotte Islands. The obverse of the coin features an effigy of Her Majesty Queen Elizabeth II by Canadian artist Dora de Pedery-Hunt.

The 1999 silver dollar coin is the 35th in a series celebrating Canadian Historical Events, People, and Places begun in 1935. They are available proof finish or brilliant uncirculated finish. The proof finish coin is encapsulated and presented in a green display case lined with green flock. The protective sleeve features Queen Charlotte Islands and the *Santiago.* The proof finish includes a numbered certificate of authenticity. The brilliant uncirculated coin is presented in a plastic capsule and protected with matchbox-style packaging that doubles to display the coin.

Coin Specifications:

Composition:	Sterling silver, 92.5% silver, 7.5% copper
Weight:	17.135 grams
Diameter:	36.07 mm
Thickness:	2 mm
Edge:	Reeded
Face Value:	$1.00
Collector Value:	Proof $34.00
Brilliant UNC:	$38.00

1999 Aviation Series—Part II

The de Havilland DHC-8 Dash 8

In the early 1980s, the rapidly expanding market for small, 30- to 40-seat airliners for the commuter trade gave rise to this elegant turboprop aircraft. Designed to operate economically at crowded airports with short runways, the DHC-8 Dash 8 is a fast, quiet high-wing, multipurpose regional transport aircraft. The sleek airframe enables the aircraft to reach cruising speeds rapidly and to climb fast and steep to flying altitude. The Dash 8 made its first official flight on June 20, 1983.

With the development of the Dash 8's older cousins—the Twin Otter and the Dash 7, smaller and larger respectively than the Dash 8—de Havilland had already established a stronghold in the area of STOL; with the Dash 8, de Havilland entered the fast-growing regional transport field. During the design phase, the manufacturers sent teams far and wide to collect information on the requirements of small airlines so that the Dash 8 could be tailor-made to satisfy the market. The resulting aircraft has sold briskly both to regional airlines and corporate clients.

The cameo portrays Robert H. Fowler, OC. Mr. Fowler, who joined de Havilland in 1952 as a test pilot, contributed to the development of flight control and propeller systems which helped de Havilland to become a world leader in the STOL concept. Later, he performed the first flights of the Dash 8.

Coin Specifications:

Composition:	92.5% sterling silver, with a 24-karat gold-covered cameo
Edge:	Interrupted serrations
Diameter:	38 mm
Reverse:	The de Havilland DHC-6 Twin Otter
Obverse:	Effigy of Her Majesty Queen Elizabeth II
Designed By:	Neil Aird
Face Value:	$20.00
Finish:	Proof (frosted relief on brilliant background)
Mintage:	50,000
Packaging:	*Single coin:* Aluminum case modeled after the wing of an aircraft with a propeller embossed on the cover. Comes with a numbered certificate of authenticity. *Complete series:* a ten-coin case is available for the entire series of ten coins.
Collector Value:	$65.00

The de Havilland DHC-6 Twin Otter

The appearance of a new power plant in the late 1950s (a propeller turbine that gave more power for a much lower installed weight than any equivalent piston engine) cleared the way for the design of a new, twin-prop aircraft that would equal the STOL performance of its predecessor and exceed its speed and capacity. De Havilland also worked closely with the military in the late 1950s to refine its STOL technology. The DHC-6 Twin Otter, the result of these efforts, made its first test flight on May 20, 1965.

Though developed mainly for the bush plane market, the Twin Otter has become one of the most lauded commuter aircraft in the world today, and it is also used for military operations. Able to land and take off from short runways, water, and snow, the aircraft is suerbly versatile. A total of 844 Twin Otters were built between 1965 and 1988 and sold all over the world. As of 1990, more than 600 of these planes were still in service, reaching out to previously inaccessible areas.

The cameo portrays George Neal, Chief Test Pilot and Flight Operations Director with de Havilland. Mr. Neal participated in the testing of the Twin Otter and its predecessor, the Otter. In 1989 he received the McKee trophy and in 1995 was elected to the aviation Hall of Fame.

Coin Specifications:

Composition:	92.5% sterling silver, with a 24-karat gold-covered cameo
Edge:	Interrupted serrations
Diameter:	38 mm
Reverse:	The de Havilland DHC-6 Twin Otter
Obverse:	Effigy of Her Majesty Queen Elizabeth II
Designed By:	Neil Aird
Face Value:	$20.00
Finish:	Proof (frosted relief on brilliant background)
Mintage:	50,000
Packaging:	*Single coin:* Aluminium case modeled after the wing of an aircraft with a propeller embossed on the cover. Comes with a numbered certificate of authenticity. *Complete series:* A ten-coin case is available for the entire series of ten coins
Collector Value:	$65.00

1999 "The Butterfly" $200 22-Karat Gold Coin

The Royal Canadian Mint has introduced a $200 22-karat gold coin featuring Mi'kmaq art. The coin depicts a butterfly in a design incorporating the traditional Mi'kmaq double curve symbol of the balance between the physical and spiritual worlds.

"Our Native Cultures and Traditions gold coin series features beautiful original works by Canada's finest artists," said Danielle Wetherup, president of the Royal Canadian Mint. "The Butterfly coin reflects the richness of Mi'kmaq traditions and the fine talent the Mi'kmaq bring to Canada's artistic heritage."

Mi'kmaq artist Alan Syliboy of Nova Scotia drew his inspiration for the design on the reverse of the coin from the rock drawings or petroglyphs of Kejimkujik Park, Nova Scotia. The double curve butterfly design is surrounded by other ancient petroglyph symbols such as the five-pointed star symbolizing eternity, and the fir branch representing prosperity. The obverse depicts an effigy of Her Majesty Queen Elizabeth II by Canadian artist Dora de Pédery-Hunt, surrounded by the inscription 200 Dollars, Canada, 1998, Elizabeth II.

The 1999 Butterfly $200 gold coin is the third in a series of four coins celebrating Canada's Native Cultures and Traditions. The Mint will produce 25,000 of the Butterfly coins which are available encapsulated, in a no-frills shipper, or encapsulated and presented in an elegant metal-trimmed case and protective box. Both packaging options for the coins include a numbered certificate of authenticity from the Mint. The Royal Canadian Mint also commissioned a collector box created by native artist Mary Anne Barkhouse to house all four coins and their accompanying certificates. The coins are available directly from the Mint by calling 1-800-267-1871 in Canada, 1-800-268-6468 in the United States, for $414.95 ($274.95 U.S.) with the case, $409.95 ($271.95 U.S.) without the case. The four-coin case is available for $79.95 ($52.95 U.S.). The coins are also available from the Royal Canadian Mint's global network of dealers and distributors.

The Royal Canadian Mint is the Crown Corporation responsible for the minting and distribution of Canada's circulation coins. The Royal Canadian Mint is recognized as one of the largest and most versatile mints in the world, offering a wide range of specialized, high-quality coinage products and related services on an international scale.

Coin Specifications:

Purity:	22-karat or 91.67% gold, 8.33% silver
Weight:	17.135 grams
Gold Content:	15.552 grams (minimum Troy ounce of fine gold)
Diameter:	29 mm
Thickness:	2 mm
Edge:	Reeded
Face Value:	$200
Mintage:	25,000
Collector Value:	$340.00

1999 Millennium Sterling Silver Proof 25-Cent Coins

Each of the Millennium Sterling Silver Proof 25-Cent Coins is available separately and has its own mark of distinction, especially since it features the month it was issued.

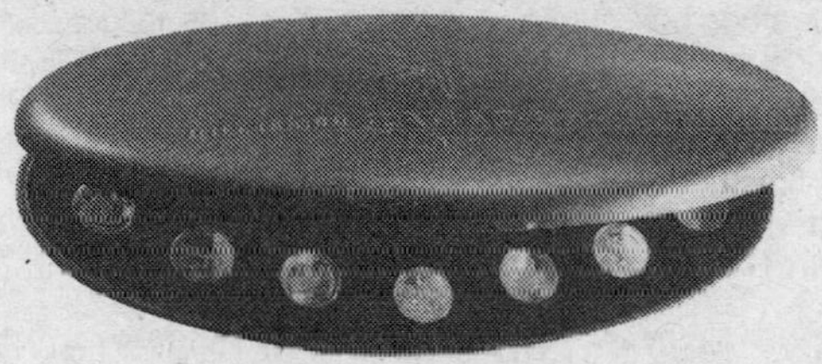

The individual coins are presented in a deluxe display case accompanied by a Certificate of Authenticity. Whatever the occasion, celebrate it with a 1999 Millennium Sterling Silver Coin.

Coin Specifications:

Composition: Sterling silver (92.5% Ag; 7.5% Cu)
Finish: Frosted relief on brilliant background
Edge: Reeded
Weight: 5.9 grams
Diameter: 23.88
Thickness: 1.66 mm
Obverse: Contemporary effigy of Her Majesty Queen Elizabeth II, by artist Dora de Pédery-Hunt.
Face Value: 25 cents
Collector Value: $35.00

1999 90th Anniversary Coin Set

Struck to commemorate the opening of the Mint on January 2, 1908, the specimen sets were the first numismatic products to be offered by the Royal Mint, Ottawa. They were presented in a handsome red leather box stamped with these words in gold lettering: "First Coinage in Canada/1908/Royal Mint Ottawa." In 1998, to commemorate the ninetieth anniversary of the Royal Canadian Mint, the Mint's master engravers reproduced the original 1908 designs with an antique finish. The obverse of each coin bears the effigy of her Majesty Queen Elizabeth II by artist Dora de Pédery-Hunt.

Coin Specifications:

Denomination:	50 cents	25 cents	10 cents	5 cents	1 cent
Reverse:	Maple Leaves with Imperial State Crown	Maple Leaves with Imperial State Crown	Maple Leaves with Imperial State Crown	Maple Leaves with Imperial State Crown	Circle of Maple Leaves
Composition:	.925 silver .075 copper	.925 silver .075 copper	.925 silver .075 copper	.925 silver .075 copper	Copper-plated on .925 silver .075 copper
Weight (g):	11.62	5.81	2.32	1.167	5.67
Diameter (mm):	29.72	23.62	18.034	15.494	25.4
Edge:	Reeded	Reeded	Reeded	Reeded	Plain
Collector Value:	$140.00				

1999 Royal Canadian Mint One-Ounce Gold Wafers

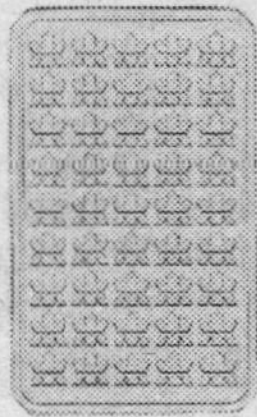

The Royal Canadian Mint launched a new gold investment product in the form of a 24-karat One-Ounce Gold Wafer.

"The Royal Canadian Mint strives to serve the needs of its customers with a variety of innovative products. Our gold wafer provides investors with a new investment vehicle made of the same high purity gold as our world-famous Gold Maple Leaf bullion investment coins," said Danielle Wetherup, president of the Royal Canadian Mint.

The One-Ounce Gold Wafer is rectangular (40.20 mm long by 24.20 mm wide) with a thickness of 1.717 mm and weighs 31.160 gm. The obverse of the wafer features a brilliant raised Hallmark of the Royal Canadian Mint and the inscription **1 oz .9999** and **FINE GOLD OR PUR** on a parallel finish field with a frosted edge. The reverse design is comprised of a repetitive series of frosted Mint logos with a brilliant logo in the center of the wafer.

As with other Royal Canadian Mint investment products, the One-Ounce Gold Wafer is available through the Royal Canadian Mint North American network of bullion dealers and distributors at a cost based on the price of gold on the open market, plus a small premium. The gold wafers are offered individually in a blister pack.

Over the years, the Royal Canadian has built a reputation for its innovative approach in the world of investment. The Mint was the first to introduce a bullion coin of 24-karat-gold purity in 1982 and in 1997, it was the first to introduce a guaranteed value gold investment coin. In 1998, the Mint also introduced a limited edition .99999 pure gold coin.

The Royal Canadian Mint is the Crown Corporation responsible for the minting and distribution of Canada's circulation coins. The Royal Canadian Mint is recognized as one of the largest and most versatile mints in the world. It has successfully diversified its operations and extended the scope of its marketing activities beyond Canada's borders and now offers a wide range of specialized, high-quality coinage products and related services on an international scale.

Wafer Specifications:

Composition:	.9999 gold
Weight:	1 ounce 31.160 grams
Width:	24.20 mm
Length:	40.20 mm
Thickness:	1.717 mm
Shape:	Rectangular
Finish:	Field: Parallel lines Lettering and hallmark: Brilliant relief Design and edge: Frosted
Packaging:	Blister pack

1999 Sporting Firsts

Basketball

Springfield, Massachusetts, USA: The YMCA Training School was exceptionally clean that day—not a box to be found anywhere. Nothing to toss balls into as a stay-in-shape winter exercise. However, the janitor did find some peach baskets, which Canadian James Naismith (1861–1939) promptly mounted to the gymnasium balconies.

No rackets nor bats, just skill and aim to sink the ball into the basket, just like his childhood game of "duck on a rock." Remove the original target from above. Technique, not force.

In December 1891, eighteen students grabbed a soccer ball and sampled Naismith's game according to his set of thirteen rules. It was the indoor exercise that drew a crowd. A student suggested the name "Naismith ball" but the inventor preferred "basket ball." Within a year of its creation, two of Naismith's students were teaching the game at the YMCA in Montreal and St. Stephen, New Brunswick. Eight years later, the peach basket was replaced by a bottomless net.

Coin Specifications:

Composition:	Sterling silver (92.5% silver, 7.5% copper)
Weight:	9.30 grams
Diameter:	27.13 mm
Edge:	Reeded
Obverse:	Effigy of Her Majesty Queen Elizabeth II

Face Value: 50 cents
Designed By: Donald Curley
Finish: Proof (frosted relief on a brilliant background)
Packaging: *Single coin:* Encapsulated coin housed in an innovative metal box
Twelve-coin set: Individual metal boxes are displayed within a collectible metal box
Collector Value: $20.00

Football

Who would have guessed that a move to promote sports in Canada would emerge as an icon in Canadian and North American football? It was June 1, 1909, when the Governor General of Canada, Lord Earl Grey, donated the Grey Cup for the amateur Rugby Football Championship of Canada.

The trophy was originally produced by Birks Jewellers at a cost of $48.00. The first Grey Cup game was played on December 4, 1909. On June 19, 1963, Lord Earl Grey was inducted into the Canadian Football Hall of Fame for his contribution to Canadian sports.

Coin Specifications:

Composition: Sterling silver (92.5% silver, 7.5% copper)
Weight: 9.30 grams
Diameter: 27.13 mm
Edge: Reeded
Obverse: Effigy of Her Majesty Queen Elizabeth II
Face Value: 50 cents
Designed By: Donald Curley
Finish: Proof (frosted relief on a brilliant background)
Packaging: *Single coin:* Encapsulated coin housed in an innovative metal box
Twelve-coin set: Individual metal boxes are displayed within a collectible metal box
Collector Value: $20.00

Golf

The coin shows golfers at play in period costume and commemorates the first Canadian Open Golf Championship, held during Dominion Day weekend, July 1, 1904. Hosted by North America's oldest golf organization, the Royal Montreal Golf Club, twelve contenders teed up for this premiere. It is believed to be the third oldest professional golf tournament in the world after the British Open (1860) and the U.S. Open (1895).

The one-day, 36-hole tournament was sponsored by the Royal Canadian Golf Association. J. H. Oke of the Royal Ottawa Golf Club, who claimed the $60 purse, played the winning score of 156. Donald H. Curley, a fine artist of Nova Scotia, created this unique design.

Coin Specifications:

Composition:	Sterling silver (.925 silver, .075 copper)
Weight:	9.30 grams
Diameter:	27.13 mm
Edge:	Reeded
Reverse:	Commemorates the first Canadian Open Golf Championship (1904)
Obverse:	Effigy of Her Majesty Queen Elizabeth II
Face Value:	50 cents
Designed By:	Donald H. Curley
Finish:	Proof: Frosted relief on a brilliant background
Packaging:	*Single coin:* Encapsulated coin housed in an innovative metal box *Twelve-coin set:* Single boxed coins housed within a collectible metal case
Collector Value:	$20.00

Yachting

The coin features a racing yacht at full sail. The first international yacht race held between Canada and the United States took place over a 30-mile course on Lake St. Clair: racers were required to finish the course within seven hours. With a twenty-six-minute lead in the third race and her captain and designer Alexander Cuthbert at the helm, Ontario's *Annie Cuthbert* sailed past the finish line on Monday, August 10, 1874, beating her American challenger, the *Cora* of Chicago.

Captain Cuthbert then proudly accepted the Fisher Cup—known as the Goodwin Cup until 1882—believed to be the oldest trophy in international freshwater yachting. Donald H. Curley, a fine artist of Nova Scotia, created this unique design.

Composition:	Sterling silver (.925 silver, .075 copper)
Weight:	9.30 grams
Diameter:	27.13 mm
Edge:	Reeded
Reverse:	Commemorates the first international yacht race between Canada and the United States (1874)
Obverse:	Effigy of Her Majesty Queen Elizabeth II
Face Value:	50 cents
Designed By:	Donald H. Curley
Finish:	Proof: Frosted relief on a brilliant background
Packaging:	*Single coin:* Encapsulated coin housed in an innovative metal box *Twelve-coin set:* Single boxed coins housed within a collectible metal case
Collector Value:	$20.00

Nunavut

1999 Millennium Two-Dollar Coin

In June 1999, the Royal Canadian Mint introduced the Nunavut 1999 Millennium $2 coin to celebrate the birth of Canada's youngest territory on April 1, 1999. The coin features an Inuit man completely absorbed in his spiritual, almost hypnotic drum dance—an age-old ritual that remains highly visible throughout *Nunavut* today. The new design will temporarily replace the polar bear that has graced the $2 coin since 1996. The Nunavut 1999 Millennium $2 coin was designed by the Inuit artist Germaine Arnaktauyok and is available in 22-karat gold (shown above), sterling silver, and as part of a complete, uncirculated set or specimen set.

Composition: Gold: 22-karat-gold inner core with 4.1-karat-gold outer ring
Sterling silver: 92.5% sterling silver (inner core 22-karat gold plated)
Finish: Proof (frosted relief on brilliant background)
Designed By: Inuit artist Germaine Arnaktauyok
Mintage: Gold: 10,000 worldwide
Sterling silver: 40,000 worldwide
Includes numbered certificate of authenticity
Collector Value: Gold: $575.00, Proof Silver: $40.00

Cameo for Macau

1999 Sterling Silver Coin with Gold Cameo

This extraordinary sterling-silver coin with its gold cameo inset was produced for the Autoridade Monetaria e Cambial de Macau (AMCM—the Macau minting authority). It celebrates the establishment of the Macau Special Administrative Region of China on December 20, 1999.

The design features a Portuguese ship and a Chinese barque, portraying Macau as a city where cultures of the East and West become one. The oval-shaped 24-karat-gold cameo depicts a historic temple in Macau. The reverse of the coin bears the Coat of Arms of the city of Macau. It is presented in a deluxe red velvet case with gold moiré sides inside a red presentation box with gold lining. A numbered Certificate of Authenticity is included.

Collector Value: $80.00

The Path of Life

1999 Sterling Silver Dollar

This is the first Canadian coin design to be inspired by a commemorative postage stamp. The design features a couple in their golden years travelling the road of life. The trees symbolize the passage of time as they progress from spring blossoms to fall foliage. A collaborative effort by illustrator Shelagh Armstrong-Hodgson and designer Paul Hodgson, the design evokes a sense of movement—the new vitality of this colorful period of life.

The United Nations declared 1999 the International Year of Older Persons to increase awareness of the world's aging population and a shift in perceptions and policies. Signed October 1, 1998, the resolution calls for solidarity, respect, and mutual exchange between generations. As a founding UN member-state, Canada has generated a domestic initiative to create a society for all ages.

Collector Value: $70.00

1998 RELEASES

$200 22-Karat-Gold Coin Featuring the Legend of the White Buffalo

The design depicts the white buffalo coming alive and leaping into action. The legend of the white buffalo tells of the healing and regeneration of the Chipewyan people of Western Canada. It states that when a white buffalo calf is born, people will awaken to the light and

Mother Earth will be healed. This powerful message for the people of the First nations is captured in a striking gold issue, designed by Canadian native artist Alex Janvier.

The 1999 $200 gold coin featuring the Harmony design is one of a series celebrating Canadian native cultures and traditions. This series was developed in collaboration with the Canadian Museum of Civilization.

Coin Specifications:

Purity:	22-karat or 91.67% gold, 8.33% silver
Weight:	17.135 grams
Gold Content:	15.552 grams (minimum Troy ounce of fine gold)
Diameter:	29 mm
Thickness:	2 mm
Edge:	Reeded
Face Value:	$200
Mintage:	25,000
Collector Value:	$500.00

1998 Canada's Ocean Giants

With Killer whales leaping in the background, the Royal Canadian Mint launched the "Canada's Ocean Giants" series of four fifty-cent sterling-silver coins featuring the Killer, Humpback, Beluga, and Blue whales at the Vancouver Aquarium. A contest with a grand prize of a family whale-watching adventure in Victoria, British Columbia, was also announced during the show.

The whales found in Canada's oceans are fascinating creatures and visitors from around the world come to Canada for whale-watching. "Our coins show the grace and beauty of these majestic animals," said Mint president Danielle Wetherup. "We are proud to offer Canadians and visitors to Canada a chance to win an exciting whale-watching adventure."

The 1998 "Canada's Ocean Giants" coins are available individually or as a four-coin set, and continue the Discovering Nature series featuring Canadian wildlife began in 1995. The coins are encapsulated and come in a presentation box with a protective sleeve. The four-coin set comes with an illustrative booklet featuring a photo and profile of the artist as well as information on the four whales featured on the coins. All designs were created by Québec wildlife artist Pierre Leduc. The obverse of each coin features an effigy of Her Majesty Queen Elizabeth II by artist Dora de Pédery-Hunt.

The coins are available worldwide through the Royal Canadian Mint's network of dealers and distributors or directly from the Mint in North America by calling 1-800-267-1871 (Canada), 1-800-268-6468 (U.S.). Individual coins cost $19.95 in Canadian funds ($14.65 U.S.). The four-coin set is available for the price of three individual coins at $59.95 Canadian ($44.45 U.S.).

The Royal Canadian Mint is the Crown Corporation responsible for the minting and distribution of Canada's circulation coins. The Royal Canadian Mint is recognized as one of the largest and most versatile mints in the world. Over the years, the Mint has successfully diversified its operations and extended the scope of its marketing activities beyond Canada's borders and now offers a wide range of specialized, high-quality coinage products and related services on an international scale.

Killer Whale

Although the black-and-white Killer whale is off all Canadian ice-free coasts, it is most common on Canada's west coast. On the east coast and in the eastern Arctic, it is an unpredictable visitor in most localities. Killer-whale schools have been studied in the coastal waters around Vancouver Island and their short-term and seasonal movements are well known. Adult males (8–10 m and 7–8 tons) are easily identified by the tall, upright dorsal fin. The species is highly social and nearly always seen in schools comprised of long-lasting kinship groups. Despite years of scientific observation, the Killer whale retains some of its secrets, and the length and timing of the reproductive cycle is not completely understood. Killer whales feed on fish, including salmon, and are also partial to seals.

Humpback

Humpback whales are common off eastern Canada during summer, particularly in the coastal waters off southwestern Nova Scotia and southeastern Newfoundland. They have little fear of ships and will often come to whale-watching boats, rolling on their backs or lying on their sides, with long flippers waving in the air and arching the tail flukes out of the water. Humpbacks are not large by baleen whale standards; the calves are born in the tropics and are about 4.5 m in length. Adult males may reach 15–16 m and weigh 15–25 tons and migrate for thousands of kilometers between the warm-water breeding areas and the rich feeding zones of the temperate and sub-Arctic North Atlantic and North Pacific. Humpback whales eat primarily oceanic shrimp and small fish, capturing the food in their huge mouths and straining out the water through the two rows of their baleen plates.

Beluga or White Whale

The Beluga is relatively abundant in several regions of the Arctic and thousands of animals move inshore after the ice-break in Hudson's Bay. Many can be seen near Churchill, Manitoba. The Belugas of the small population (approximately 600) in the estuary of the St. Lawrence are often easily viewed from tour boats or sometimes from the lighthouse at the mouth of the Saguenay River in Quebec. There is concern about the future status of this isolated population, so regulations for viewing Belugas are strict. The species is relatively small; adults reach only 4–4.5 meters in length, but Belugas are easily seen when they surface and some can be quite curious, making close approaches to boats if not alarmed. Beluga calves are harder to see because they are bluish gray or brownish for the first two years of life.

Blue Whale

The Blue whale is much rarer than the Humpback in Canadian waters. Occasionally seen off the west coast and the Atlantic Provinces, this gigantic, mottled blue-gray whale is best viewed in the waters off the Sept-Iles region of Quebec where up to 300 mammals are known to range in the summer months, feeding on large shoals of pelagic shrimp called "krill." This species is the largest mammal that the earth has ever known, dwarfing most dinosaurs. Adult Blue whales attain lengths of more than 30 m and may weigh over 150 tons, especially in Antarctic months. The female gives birth to a single calf, about 6–8 meters in length, every two or three years. The Blue whale is a highly migratory species but, because most of its movements are offshore, they are not as well understood as other species.

Coin Specifications:

Composition: Sterling silver (.925 silver, .075 copper)
Weight: 9.3 grams
Diameter: 27.13 mm
Edge: Reeded
Face Value: 50 cents
Collector Value: $20.00 each

1998 Fine Silver Two-coin Set
Norman Bethune Commemorative Coin Set

This set of two silver coins, jointly issued by the Royal Canadian Mint and the China Gold Coin Incorporation, honors an extraordinary Canadian—Dr. Norman Bethune. Bethune, who was born in Gravenhurst, Ontario, in 1890, served humanity during three wars—the First World War, the Spanish Civil War, and the Sino-Japanese War. In 1938, Bethune went to China to become chief surgeon for the Eighth Route Army during the Sino-Japanese War. As well as designing a Model Hospital, writing text books, and training young Chinese doctors, Bethune served on the battlefield, invented a collapsible operating table, and organized medical supply units that could be transported on mule back. The 49-year-old doctor died in 1939, while still in China.

Coin Specifications:

Composition: .9999 Fine silver
Finish: Proof (frosted relief on brilliant background)
Edge: Reeded
Weight: 31.39 grams
Diameter: 38 mm
Thickness: 3.3 mm
Reverse: Depicts Norman Bethune travelling with the mobile surgery unit (Canadian coin)
Designed By: Harvey Chan (Canadian coin)
Obverse: Effigy of Her Majesty Queen Elizabeth II
Face Value: $5.00
Mintage: Maximum of 80,000 sets worldwide
Collector Value: $85.00

1998 Proof Silver Dollar
125th Anniversary of the Creation of the North-West Mounted Police

In 1873, the NWMP was created as part of Prime Minister Sir John A. MacDonald's National Policy. It was to replace the militia in Manitoba and to maintain law and order in Canada's unruly and unpatrolled northwestern frontier. The NWMP force was conceived and established to administer Canadian law, to end the whiskey trade and the lawlessness that accompanied it, and to establish peaceful relations with natives before CPR workers and settlers arrived.

The "pill-box" hat was the first forage cap approved for use by the North-West Mounted Police. Its design reflects the British military style of the era. In 1902, the now familiar wide-brimmed Stetson was officially introduced.

The scarlet tunic and red serge jacket that are part of the uniform worn today by the Royal Canadian Mounted Police are identical to those worn by the North-West Mounted Police 125 years ago.

1998 Proof Silver Dollar Specifications:

Composition:	92.5% sterling silver
Finish:	Proof (frosted relief on brilliant background)
Edge:	Reeded
Weight:	25.175 grams
Diameter:	36.07 mm
Thickness:	2.95 mm
Reverse:	125th anniversary of the creation of the North-West Mounted Police
Designed By:	Adeline Halvorson
Obverse:	Effigy of Her Majesty Queen Elizabeth II
Face Value:	$1.00
Collector Value:	$115.00

1998 Fifty-cent Sterling-Silver Coins
Canadian Sports' Firsts

These coins are the first issued in a three-year program. The series commemorates important Canadian sporting events. Four sports per year will be honored. The first two chosen themes for this year are as follows:

The First Canadian to Win the Grand Prix of Canada for F1 Auto Racing (1978)

This coin commemorates that thrilling moment on October 8, 1978, in Montreal, when a red Ferrari, driven by Gilles Villeneuve, roared into the lead and over the finish line. It was the first time that a Canadian had won a Formula One Grand Prix race, and the crowd exploded in wild national pride. Since then, many young Canadians have been inspired by Villeneuve's victory to participate in this demanding sport.

The First Overseas Canadian Soccer Tour (in Ireland, England, and Scotland) in 1888

This coin commemorates Canada's first overseas soccer tour in 1888. The final match of the 23-game rout of Britain was played at the Kennington Oval, London. Ten thousand spectators watched skeptically to see how the colonials played Britain's national game. Though the British scored a narrow victory, the cliff-hanger left them surprised and respectful, calling the Canadians "truly formidable opponents." In Canada today, soccer is second only to hockey in popularity.

The First Official Amateur Figure-Skating Championships Held by The Amateur Skating Association of Canada (1888)

This coin, designed by Friedrich Peter, commemorates Canada's first national figure-skating championships, held in Toronto in 1888. It was a time when the so-called "fancy skating" was beginning to take off, with amateur skaters thronging the rinks of skating clubs all over Canada. Organized competition, however, was in its infancy. Though the national championships lapsed in the years immediately after 1888, it was nevertheless the beginning of a competitive tradition that has since taken Canadians to the highest levels worldwide.

The First Canadian Ski-Running and Ski-Jumping Championships (1898)

This coin, designed by Friedrich Peter, commemorates the first Canadian Ski Racing and Ski Jumping Championships, held in Rossland, B.C. in 1898. Imagine being there in the crowd and watching, breathless, as pioneer ski racers zoomed down the icy slopes. Ski racing—or "running"—was new to Canada in the 19th century. Brought here by Scandinavian immigrants, skiing quickly became part of life in Canada. Today, more than five million Canadians ski.

Coin Specifications:

Composition:	Sterling silver (92.5%)
Finish:	Proof (frosted relief on brilliant background)
Edge:	Reeded
Weight:	9.30 grams
Thickness:	2.11 mm
Diameter:	27.13 mm
Reverse:	Four designs depicting Canadian Sports Firsts

Designed By:	Friedrich G. Peter
Obverse:	Effigy of Her Majesty Queen Elizabeth II
Face Value:	50 cents
Collector Value:	$22.00 each

1998 Twelve-Year Lunar Series
Year of the Tiger

Centuries ago, the Chinese invented a calendar based on the lunar—rather than the solar—cycle. These symbols roughly approximate the signs of the zodiac in Western culture; however, they denote years instead of months. In 1998, the Royal Canadian Mint began production of the twelve-year annual series with a coin commemorating the Year of the Tiger. All twelve of the Lunar animals—the Rat, the Ox, the Tiger, the Rabbit, the Dragon, the Snake, the Horse, the Sheep, the Monkey, the Rooster, the Dog, and the Pig—appear in a circular arrangement around the rim of each coin, with a different animal highlighted each year in a central cameo. The coin's obverse bears the effigy of Her Majesty Queen Elizabeth II by artist Dora de Pédery-Hunt.

Coin Specifications:

Composition:	92.5% silver, 7.5% copper
Finish:	Proof (frosted relief on brilliant background)
Edge:	Reeded
Weight:	34 grams
Diameter:	Coin: 40 mm; Cameo: 17.5 mm
Reverse:	Year of the Tiger
Designed By:	Harvey Chan
Obverse:	Effigy of Her Majesty Queen Elizabeth II
Face Value:	$15.00
Mintage:	68,888
Collector Value:	$425.00

1998 Platinum Proof Coin Set
The Gray Wolf

The gray wolves are the largest wild members of the dog family. Because of vigorous efforts to eliminate them in other parts of the world, Canada is their last and most important stronghold; however, even here they are in retreat. Yet the gray wolf has a vital role to play in preserving the Canadian wilderness. As the country's largest predator, the wolf helps to maintain an ecological balance between the animal populations and habitat capacity. Most of Canada's wolves—some 58,000 strong—live in the far north.

Coin Specifications:

	1 oz.	½ oz.	¼ oz.	1/10 oz.
Purity (%)	99.95	99.95	99.95	99.95
Weight (g)	31.16	15.59	7.80	3.132
Diameter (mm)	30	25	20	16
Face Value	$300.00	$150.00	$75.00	$30.00

Finish: Proof (frosted relief on brilliant background)
Edge: Reeded
Designed By: Kerri Burnett
Obverse: Effigy of Her Majesty Queen Elizabeth II
Collector Value: $3200.00

1998 Aviation Series—Part II
The Canadair (Bombardier) CP-107 Argus

Coin 7—The Canadair CP-107 Argus

Built for antisubmarine maritime reconnaissance, the Canadair CP-107 Argus navigated and fought more effectively than any other aircraft in its class. Powered by huge piston engines, the airframe was strengthened for the rigors of low-level flying over the open sea. The heart of the Argus was the Air Navigation and Tactical Control System (ANTAC). It became the world's most advanced ASW aircraft. The Argus entered squadron service with the RCAF in 1958 and flew its last mission in 1981.

The Argus was flown by a unique team: the pilot and the flight engineer. It was the flight engineer's responsibility to control all power settings from his position behind the copilot. The pilot determined the power setting and the flight engineer set the exact amount of power requested.

Coin Specifications:

Composition:	92.5% sterling silver, with a 24-karat-gold-covered cameo
Finish:	Proof (frosted relief on brilliant background)
Edge:	Interrupted serrations
Weight:	31.103 grams
Diameter:	38 mm
Thickness:	3.50 mm
Reverse:	The Canadair (Bombardier) CP-107 Argus
Designed By:	Peter Mossman
Obverse:	Effigy of Her Majesty Queen Elizabeth II
Face Value:	$20.00
Mintage:	50,000
Price:	$57.95 per coin
Packaging:	Aluminum case modeled after the wing of an aircraft with a propeller embossed on the cover
Collector Value:	$90.00

1998 Aviation Series—Part II
The Canadair (Bombardier) CL-215 Waterbomber

Coin 8—The Canadair CL-215 Waterbomber

Designed primarily for forest protection and fire control, the Canadair CL-215 can spray chemical retardants and water while still in flight. In just 10 seconds, this twin-engined amphibian aircraft will scoop enough water to spray an area of 12 by 100 meters. Probes scoop up the water as the aircraft skims across the surface of a suitable body of water. In June of 1978, a CL-215 in Manitoba made 160 drops in one day, spraying nearly 1,000 tons of water. This aircraft can spray and reload as many as 30 times an hour.

Forest fires could be fought with CL-215s in three ways. One method involves the spraying of pre-mixed long-term chemical fire retardants pumped into the tanks at the base. The second involves the use of short-term retardants that are mixed with water during scooping. The third is the use of plain water scooped up from any ¾-mile stretch of lake or ocean.

Coin Specifications:

Composition:	92.5% sterling silver, with a 24-karat-gold-covered cameo
Finish:	Proof (frosted relief on brilliant background)
Edge:	Interrupted serrations
Weight:	31.103 grams
Diameter:	38 mm
Thickness:	3.50 mm
Reverse:	The Canadair (Bombardier) CL-215 Waterbomber
Designed By:	Peter Mossman
Obverse:	Effigy of Her Majesty Queen Elizabeth II
Face Value:	$20.00
Mintage:	50,000
Price:	$57.95 per coin
Packaging:	Aluminum case modeled after the wing of an aircraft with a propeller embossed on the cover.
Collector Value:	$85.00

1998 Pure Gold Coin
.99999 Gold Coin

The Royal Arms of Canada were established by proclamation of the King in 1921. They signify national sovereignty and are used by Canada on federal government possessions (such as buildings, official seals, money, passports, proclamations, etc.) as well as rank badges of some members of the Canadian Forces. The current version of the Arms of Canada was drawn by Mrs. Cathy Bursey-Sabourin and approved in 1994.

At the base of the Coat of Arms are the four floral emblems: the English Rose, the Scottish Thistle, the Irish Shamrock, and the French Fleur-de-lis. Of particular interest is the fact that the English Rose is not a cultivated flower. Rather, it is a combination of the white Tudor rose of the House of York and the red rose of the House of Lancaster. The Scottish Thistle is *Onopordum acanthium,* the traditional bull thistle. The Irish Shamrock has three petals, as does the French Fleur-de-lis (*Lilium candidum* or Lily).

Coin Specifications:

Composition:	.99999 pure gold
Finish:	Proof (frosted relief on brilliant background)
Edge:	Reeded
Weight:	38.05 grams
Diameter:	34 mm
Thickness:	2.7 mm
Reverse:	Depicts an arrangement of the floral emblems found on the Canadian Coat of Arms
Designed By:	Pierre Leduc
Obverse:	Effigy of Her Majesty Queen Elizabeth II
Face Value:	$350.00
Mintage:	Maximum of 1,998 coins worldwide
Collector Value:	$1175.00

1998 Proof Set

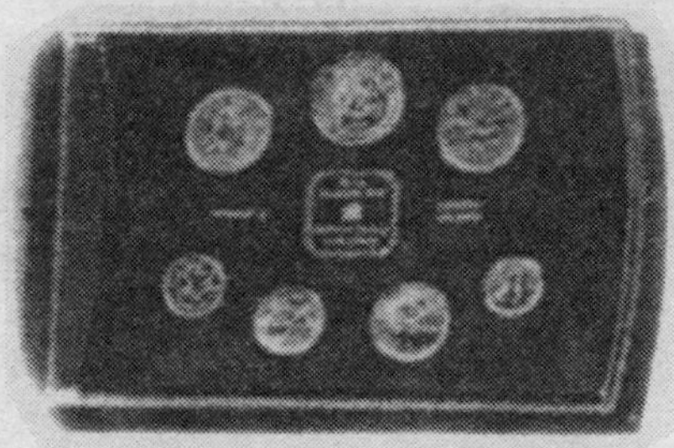

A proof finish means the relief (raised part of the design) is given a frosted texture, while the background remains brilliant (shiny).

The Royal Canadian Mint Proof Set is the premium collector set for people interested in Canada's circulation coin designs. In addition to the current silver dollar, each year the set features the proof numismatic variety of the current selection of circulation coins, most of these struck in precious metals exclusively for this set.

Coin Specifications:

Denomination:	Proof Dollar	2 dollars	1 dollar	50 cents	25 cents	10 cents	5 cents	1 cent
Reverse:	125th Anniversary of the founding of the North-West Mounted Police	Polar Bear	Common Loon	Coat of Arms of Canada	Caribou	Fishing Schooner	Beaver	Maple Leaf
Alloy:	92.5% sterling silver	92.5% sterling silver 24 kt. gold-plated inner core	Nickel electro-plated with bronze	92.5% sterling silver	92.5% sterling silver	92.5% sterling silver	92.5% sterling silver	Bronze
Weight (g):	25.175	8.83	7.00	9.30	5.90	2.40	5.35	2.50
Diameter (mm):	36.07	28.07	26.50 11-sided	27.13	23.88	18.03	21.20	19.10
Edge:	Reeded	Interrupted serrations	Plain	Reeded	Reeded	Reeded	Plain	Plain

Collector Value: $35.00

1998 Specimen Set

The Specimen Set is a collection including one example of each Canadian circulation coin, struck with numismatic dies onto specially prepared coin blanks. The finish is a threefold combination of brilliant and frosted relief on a line finish background. The alloys are the same as found in circulation coins, except for the one-cent coin, which is solid bronze instead of reflecting the plated composition of the circulating one-cent coin.

Coin Specifications:

Denomination:	2 dollars	1 dollar	50 cents	25 cents	10 cents	5 cents	1 cent
Reverse:	Polar Bear	Common Loon	Coat of Arms of Canada	Caribou	Fishing Schooner	Beaver	Maple Leaf
Alloy:	Outer ring: 99+% Nickel Inner core: 92% Copper	Nickel electroplated with bronze	Nickel	Nickel	Nickel	Cupronickel	Bronze
Weight (g):	7.30	7.00	8.10	5.05	2.07	4.60	2.50
Diameter (mm):	28 26.50	27.13 11-sided	23.88	18.03	21.20	19.10	
Edge:	Interrupted serrations	Plain	Reeded	Reeded	Reeded	Plain	Plain
Collector Value:	$30.00						

1998 Uncirculated Sets

The finish of the 1998 coins offered in the Uncirculated, O Canada!, and Tiny Treasures coin sets is a brilliant field on a brilliant relief. The two-dollar coins offered in these sets feature the brilliant field but maintain the frosted polar bear relief introduced in the 1997 Uncirculated Set. The alloys are the same as found in circulation coins.

As of 1998, all Uncirculated Sets are produced at the Royal Canadian Mint's Winnipeg plant, using numismatic dies and specially prepared blanks. All Uncirculated Sets include a mint mark on the obverse of each coin to indicate from which plant they originate.

People wishing to collect an uncirculated version of Canadian circulation coins will usually purchase the Uncirculated Set, while the "O Canada!" Gift Set and Tiny Treasures Gift Set are attractively presented for use as gifts.

Coin Specifications:

Denomination	2 dollars	1 dollar	50 cents	25 cents	10 cents	5 cents	1 cent
Reverse:	Polar Bear	Common Loon	Coat of Arms of Canada	Caribou	Fishing Schooner	Beaver	Maple Leaf

Alloy:	Outer ring: 99+% Nickel Inner core: 92% Copper	Nickel electro-plated with bronze	Nickel	Nickel	Nickel	Cupro-nickel zinc	Copper-plated-
Weight (g):	7.30	7.00	8.10	5.05	2.07	4.60	2.25
Diameter (mm):	28	26.50	27.13 11-sided	23.88	18.03	21.20	19.05
Edge:	Interrupted serrations	Plain	Reeded	Reeded	Reeded	Plain	Plain
Collector Value:	$42.00						

1997 RELEASES

1997 500th Anniversary Proof Silver Ten-Cent Coin

The theme of the 1997 proof silver ten-cent coin commemorates the momentous voyage from Bristol, England, to the east coast of Canada, made in 1497 by John Cabot (Giovanni Caboto). Caboto was an Italian but he sailed under the English flag, sanctioned by the King of England.

On May 2, 1497, navigator and cartographer John Cabot departed from Bristol, England, aboard the *Matthew,* a small ship with a crew of 18 men, in search of westward routes to the Far East.

On June 24, 1497, they made landfall somewhere on what is today the coast of Newfoundland, naming it "Buena Vista." Cabot sailed briefly along the coast exploring what he called "the country of the Great Khan," believing it to be Asia. Upon his return to England in August 1497, Cabot reported waters rich with fish and a land of plenty.

Coin Specifications:

Composition:	Sterling silver (92.5% silver, 7.5% copper)
Finish:	Proof (frosted relief on brilliant background)
Edge:	Reeded
Weight:	2.4 grams
Diameter:	18.03 mm

Thickness: 1.2 mm
Reverse: Depicts the historic voyage of John Cabot's boat, the *Matthew,* approaching land
Designed By: Donald H. Curley
Obverse: Contemporary effigy of Her Majesty Queen Elizabeth II, by artist Dora de Pédery-Hunt
Face Value: 10 cents
Mintage: 50,000 worldwide
Collector Value: $28.00

1997 Fifty-Cent Sterling-Silver Proof Coins, Canada's Best Friends

Nova Scotia Duck Tolling Retriever

"Tolling" is a hunting expression, meaning "to lure game by appealing to their curiosity." In nature, it is the fox who entices ducks to shore by playing and gambolling on the waterfront: the canine equivalent is a dog developed in the 1860s in Yarmouth, Nova Scotia. Hunters, observing the behavior of the fox, developed a new breed by crossing several retrievers, including the Irish Setter which gives the Duck Tolling Retriever its characteristic red or orange color. This alert and lively animal works with a concealed hunter, fetching sticks and luring the curious ducks shoreward with its playful antics. Originally limited to Nova Scotia, the breed is now known across Canada and internationally.

Coin Specifications:

Composition: Sterling silver (92.5% silver, 7.5% copper)
Finish: Proof (frosted relief on brilliant background)
Edge: Reeded
Weight: 9.30 grams
Diameter: 27.13 mm
Reverse: Nova Scotia Duck Tolling Retriever

Designed By: Arnold A. Nogy
Obverse: Effigy of Her Majesty Queen Elizabeth II
Face Value: 50 cents
Collector Value: $22.00

Canadian Eskimo Dog

This strong northern breed goes back some 2,000 years in Canada. Brought here by Mongolian migrants from Asia, for centuries the Eskimo Dog served northern peoples as a sled dog in winter and as a pack animal in summer. This breed is known for its toughness and endurance. Its thick coat protects it in even the coldest of temperatures. It can pull weights of up to 80 kilos and, even when food is scarce, it can travel as much as 100 kilometers a day. In recent years, the Eskimo Dog has been largely replaced by the snowmobile in northern life. From a population of 20,000 animals in the 1920s, its numbers fell to a low of some 200 in the 1970s. Since then, efforts to reestablish the breed have begun to find success.

Coin Specifications:

Composition: Sterling silver (92.5% silver, 7.5% copper)
Finish: Proof (frosted relief on brilliant background)
Edge: Reeded
Weight: 9.30 grams
Diameter: 27.13 mm
Reverse: Canadian Eskimo Dog
Designed By: Arnold A. Nogy
Obverse: Effigy of Her Majesty Queen Elizabeth II
Face Value: 50 cents
Collector Value: $22.00

Labrador Retriever

The Labrador, whose ancestors were discovered in Newfoundland and Labrador by 18th-century colonists, is probably descended from dogs abandoned there by European fishermen almost two centuries earlier. Left on their own, the dogs developed into skillful hunters. In the early 1800s a few specimens were taken back to Britain where they soon proved their worth as retrievers of fish and game. The British further developed the breed by crossing it with a number of existing retrievers. Soon, the Labrador had become the most valued game dog in Britain. Recognized by the Kennel Club of Britain in 1903 and a few years later by Canada, the black, yellow, and chocolate-colored Labradors are known for their intelligence and for their gentle, affectionate natures.

Coin Specifications:

Composition: Sterling silver (92.5% silver, 7.5% copper)
Finish: Proof (frosted relief on brilliant background)

Edge: Reeded
Weight: 9.30 grams
Diameter: 27.13 mm
Reverse: Labrador Retriever
Designed By: Arnold A. Nogy
Obverse: Effigy of Her Majesty Queen Elizabeth II
Face Value: 50 cents
Collector Value: $24.00

Newfoundland

This massive dog is the "gentle giant" of Canadian breeds. The origins of the Newfoundland are lost in time but may go back nearly a thousand years to the crossing of indigenous breeds with the giant bear dogs of Viking explorers. Literature is full of heroic tales of this brave and affectionate dog. The Newfoundland seems to have a life-saving instinct and is known to have rescued many children, fishermen, and shipwrecked sailors from drowning. The dog's thick, water-repellent coat, rudderlike tail, and webbed feet make it a water dog par excellence, and for centuries it has worked side by side with the Newfoundland fisherman. Its large size and strength have combined with intelligence and character to produce an exceptionally loyal and good-natured dog.

Coin Specifications:

Composition: Sterling silver (92.5% silver, 7.5% copper)
Finish: Proof (frosted relief on brilliant background)
Edge: Reeded
Weight: 9.30 grams
Diameter: 27.13 mm
Reverse: Newfoundland
Designed By: Arnold A. Nogy
Obverse: Effigy of Her Majesty Queen Elizabeth II
Face Value: 50 cents
Collector Value: $24.00

1997 Commemorative Proof Silver Dollar, 1972 Canada/Russia Hockey Series

The theme of the 1997 commemorative silver dollar celebrates more than the 25th anniversary of the 1972 Canada/USSR Hockey Series. It also celebrates the qualities of sportsmanship, teamwork, and self-discipline athletic sports such as hockey teaches to young athletes around the world. Such qualities were clearly recognizable in the athletes of both teams throughout the dramatic eight-game series. In Canada, through the dedication of volunteer coaches, the support of businesses, and Canadian Hockey, thousands of young people learn to be the best they can be. The 1997 silver dollar is a tribute to their tireless efforts.

The 1972 Canada/USSR Series began September 2 and concluded September 28, 1972. This special exhibition series was arranged by Hockey Canada, the Canadian Amateur Hockey Association, and the Soviet Hockey Federation. Hockey Canada and the Canadian Amateur Hockey Association have since merged to become Canadian Hockey. The first four games were played in Montreal, Toronto, Winnipeg, and Vancouver. The last four were played in Moscow. When the series was over Canada had four wins, the Soviets three, and one game had been tied. There had been breathtaking displays of athletic excellence, cultural exchanges, and a new adventure in diplomacy

The series was a turning point in the history of hockey. Until 1972 international rules had prevented Canadian players from the National Hockey League from playing in a world hockey championship. Today players from professional teams can now compete in amateur championships and honor those who stood behind them throughout their career.

1997 Commemorative Proof Silver Dollar Specifications:

Composition:	92.5% sterling silver
Finish:	Proof (frosted relief on brilliant background)
Edge:	Reeded
Weight:	25.175 grams
Diameter:	36.07 mm
Thickness:	2.95 mm
Reverse:	Commemorates the climactic goal of the Canada/ Russia series' eighth and final game

Designed By: Roger Hill
Obverse: Effigy of Her Majesty Queen Elizabeth II
Face Value: $1.00
Collector Value: $42.00

1997 14-Karat Gold Coin, The Telephone

The theme for the 1997 $100 gold coin focuses on Alexander Graham Bell. His invention of the telephone revolutionized the manner in which people communicate across the globe. The satellite view of the world encircled by the telephone wire reinforces the impact this invention has had on our lives. In this design, the artist has carefully paid tribute to Alexander Graham Bell's birthplace in Scotland and to his new home in North America. The following are excerpts from *The Telephone Story,* courtesy of the Baddeck Public Library "search for Yesterday," April 1981.

> In July of 1874, Bell hit upon the principle of the telephone. That summer, while visiting his parents in Brantford, Bell worked on a phonautograph, a somewhat macabre device to translate sounds into visible marking with equipment using the actual ear of a dead man. When the words were spoken, the ear membrane vibrated and moved a lever that etched a wave pattern on a piece of smoked glass.

August 3, 1876	Bell completed the first one-way call of five miles from a store in Mount Pleasant, Ontario, to the telegraph office in Brantford.
August 4, 1876	Bell tested the telephone over a line 3 miles long from the telegraph office in Brantford to the Bell homestead, Tutelo Heights, Brantford, Ontario.
August 10, 1876	Bell made what is considered the world's first long-distance telephone call. He was stationed in Robert White's Boot and Shoe Store, Paris, Ontario, and his father and others were stationed in the Dominion Telegraph Company's office in Brantford, Ontario. The distance was eight miles.
October 9, 1876	The first two-way long-distance call was set

up between Boston and Cambridgeport. Bell and Watson used two miles of private wire that belonged to the Walworth Manufacturing Company.

August 29, 1877	The first telephone was leased in Canada.

Coin Specifications:

Composition:	58.33% gold, 41.67% silver
Finish:	Proof (frosted relief on brilliant background)
Edge:	Reeded
Weight:	13.338 grams
Diameter:	27 mm
Thickness:	2.15 mm
Reverse:	Depicts the profile of a mature Alexander Graham Bell, an old-fashioned telephone, and a satellite view of the world
Designed By:	Donald H. Curley
Obverse:	Effigy of Her Majesty Queen Elizabeth II
Face Value:	$100.00
Mintage:	Maximum of 25,000 coins worldwide
Collector Value:	$385.00

1997 22-Karat-Gold Coin, Haida

This coin features the Haida legend of Raven Bringing Light to the World, a beautiful example of Haida totemic art by British Colombia–based Haida artist Robert Davidson. The design is based on Raven, the Haida cultural hero. An ancient Haida narrative tells the story of the time when Raven took the sun back from the Chief of the Sky and returned it to the people of the earth.

The 1997 $200 gold coin featuring the Haida design is the first of a series celebrating Canadian native cultures and traditions. This series was developed in collaboration with the Canadian Museum of Civilization.

Coin Specifications:

Composition:	91.67% pure gold
Finish:	Proof (frosted relief on brilliant background)
Edge:	Reeded
Weight:	17.135 grams

Diameter: 29 mm
Thickness: 2 mm
Reverse: "Raven Bringing Light to the World" (1986–87) is an excellent example of totemic art
Designed By: Robert Davidson
Obverse: Effigy of Her Majesty Queen Elizabeth II
Face Value: $200.00
Mintage: Limited to only 25,000 coins worldwide
Collector Value: $650.00

1997 Silver Aviation Cameo Series—Part II Powered Flight in Canada Beyond World War II

Coin 6—The Canadair CT-114 Tutor: The Snowbirds

Skill, professionalism, and teamwork describe the key characteristics of the pilots who fly the Snowbirds. Audiences worldwide have enjoyed the aerobatics of the Canadair CT-114 Tutor. The Tutor was designed in 1958 as an all-purpose jet training aircraft for the flight instruction of military pilots. This aircraft is an all-metal, side-by-side, two-seat monoplane with a single jet engine. The high maneuverability and relatively slow speed of the Tutor is ideally suited for aerobatics. A well-tuned engine enhances engine response in low-level flying. The basic Tutor was slightly modified for use by the Snowbirds. Required was a smoke-generating system with a unique paint scheme for added crowd appeal.

Coin 6 features a close-up view of a Canadair CT-114 Tutor, the Snowbirds flying in a "Big Diamond" formation, and the Snowbird squadron crest. The cameo portrays the likeness of Edward Higgins, a former Vice-President of Canadair. Mr. Higgins was the driving force behind the design and construction of the Tutor.

Coin Specifications:

Composition: 92.5% sterling silver, with a 24-karat-gold-covered cameo
Finish: Proof (frosted relief on brilliant background)
Edge: Interrupted serrations
Weight: 31.103 grams
Diameter: 38 mm
Thickness: 3.50 mm

Reverse:	Avro Canada CF-105 Arrow with gold cameo of Jim Chamberlin
Designed By:	Ross Buckland (1997 issues)
Obverse:	Effigy of Her Majesty Queen Elizabeth II
Face Value:	$20.00
Mintage:	Maximum of 50,000 of each coin worldwide
Collector Value:	$95.00

1997 Silver Aviation Cameo Series—Part II Powered Flight in Canada Beyond World War II

Coin 5—The Canadair F-86 Sabre: The Golden Hawks

Innovative and talented, the expertise of the Canadian aviation industry continued to excite the imagination. The technology of the Canadair F-86 Sabre was world renowned. The Sabre became one of the top military aircraft in Europe during the 1950s. Chosen to fulfill Canada's fighter aircraft commitment to NATO, a team of Sabres went on to become famous as the Golden Hawks. Painted gold with a red-and-white hawk emblazoned on each side, the Golden Hawks thrilled audiences with their aerobatic maneuvers.

Over the years Canadair built over 1,800 Sabres in six variants. Air forces in several countries, as well as the RCAF and RAF, flew the Sabre. The Canadian-built Mk. 6, powered by an Orenda engine, was the finest variant of the Sabre line.

This aerobatic team was formed in 1959 to commemorate two milestones in Canadian aviation history: the 50th Anniversary of powered flight in Canada, and the 35th Anniversary of the RCAF.

Coin 5 features a close-up view of a Canadair Mk. 6 Sabre, four Golden Hawks in their "Diamond" formation, and the Golden Hawk insignia. The cameo portrays the likeness of Fern Villeneuve, the first leader of the Golden Hawks.

Coin Specifications:

Composition:	92.5% sterling silver, with a 24-karat-gold-covered cameo
Finish:	Proof (frosted relief on brilliant background)
Edge:	Interrupted serrations

Weight:	31.103 grams
Diameter:	38 mm
Thickness:	3.50 mm
Reverse:	Avro Canada CF-105 Arrow with gold cameo of Jim Chamberlin
Designed By:	Ross Buckland (1997 issues)
Obverse:	Effigy of Her Majesty Queen Elizabeth II
Face Value:	$20.00
Mintage:	Maximum of 50,000 of each coin worldwide
Collector Value:	$100.00

1997 Platinum Proof Coins, The Wood Bison

The wood bison is a unique part of Canada's natural history. Wood bison once roamed the meadows of the boreal forests of northwestern Canada by the thousands, providing food, shelter, and clothing for native peoples. Under hunting pressure that accompanied early exploration and the fur trade, the wood bison population was cut down to a mere 250 by 1900. Active protection by the Government of Canada reversed this trend. By the time Wood Buffalo Park was established in 1922, wood bison numbers had recovered to at least 1500.

Unfortunately a release of surplus plains bison—a much smaller animal—from southern Canada into Wood Buffalo National Park in the late 1920s resulted in the mixing of the two subspecies and the introduction of serious cattle diseases. Since then, seven healthy, free-roaming populations most representative of the original wood bison have been established as part of a national recovery program. Thanks to an environmental campaign that began at the turn of the century, the wood bison will likely continue to be part of Canada's natural heritage.

Coin Specifications:

	1 oz.	**1/2 oz.**	**1/4 oz.**	**1/10 oz.**
Purity (%):	99.95	99.95	99.95	99.95
Weight (g):	31.16	15.59	7.80	3.132
Diameter (mm):	30	25	20	16
Face Value:	$375.00	$185.00	$100.00	$45.00

Finish: Proof (frosted relief on brilliant background)
Edge: Reeded
Reverse: Depicts the wood bison in four different scenes: a mother and father guarding their calf; a majestic wood bison in full profile; two calves at play; and a stately portrait of the wood bison.
Designed By: Chris Bacon
Obverse: Effigy of Her Majesty Queen Elizabeth II
Mintage: Maximum of 1,000 sets; 1,000 1/2 oz. coins; 1,000 1/10 oz. coins worldwide
Collector Value: $2750.00 set

1996 Releases

1996 Silver Aviation Cameo Series—Part II Powered Flight in Canada Beyond World War II

Coin 3—Avro Canada CF-105 Arrow

One of the finest achievements in Canadian aviation history, the Avro Canada CF-105 Arrow was never allowed to fulfill its mission. Intended to replace the Avro Canada CF-100 Canuck as a supersonic all-weather interceptor, the Arrow incorporated advanced technical innovations. A source of national pride, this aircraft became a symbol of Canadian excellence.

For various reasons, mostly due to high costs, the Federal Government cancelled the Avro Arrow program on February 20, 1959. Almost everything connected to the program was destroyed. Fortunately, the forward fuselage of the first MK. 2 Arrow was saved and is on display at the National Aviation Museum in Ottawa (Canada).

Coin Specifications:

Composition:	92.5% sterling silver, with a 24-karat-gold-covered cameo
Finish:	Proof (frosted relief on brilliant background)
Edge:	Interrupted serrations
Weight:	31.103 grams
Diameter:	38 mm
Thickness:	3.50 mm
Reverse:	Avro Canada CF-105 Arrow with gold cameo of Jim Chamberlin
Designed By:	Robert Bradford (1995 issues), Jim Bruce (1996 issues)
Obverse:	Effigy of Her Majesty Queen Elizabeth II
Face Value:	$20.00
Mintage:	Maximum of 50,000 of each coin worldwide
Collector Value:	$75.00

Coin 4—Avro Canada CF-100 Canuck

Determined to eliminate reliance on foreign manufactured aircraft, the RCAF commissioned Avro Canada to design and build the Avro Canada CF-100. A fledgling company, Avro attracted experienced Canadian aviation personnel employed during the Second World War. The Avro CF-100 Canuck became a major Canadian aviation success.

Designed to patrol the Canadian frontier, the CF-100 excelled in its mission as a sub-sonic all-weather interceptor. Nicknamed the "Clunk," this aircraft is a twin engine, two-seat fighter. The first of the two CF-100 prototypes was flown in January 1950. Powerful Canadian designed-and-built Orenda engines replaced the British Rolls-Royce Avon engines in 1952. Today, two RCAF CF-100 Mk. 5s are part of the collection at the National Aviation Museum in Ottawa (Canada).

Coin Specifications:

Composition:	92.5% sterling silver, with a 24-karat-gold-covered cameo
Finish:	Proof (frosted relief on brilliant background)
Edge:	Interrupted serrations
Weight:	31.103 g
Diameter:	38 mm
Thickness:	3.50 mm
Reverse:	Avro Canada CF-100 Canuck with gold cameo of Jan Zurakowski
Designed By:	Robert Bradford (1995 issues), Jim Bruce (1996 issues)
Obverse:	Effigy of Her Majesty Queen Elizabeth II
Face Value:	$20.00
Mintage:	Maximum of 50,000 of each coin worldwide
Collector Value:	$75.00

Canadian Art Series—$200 Gold Coin

The first $200 22-karat gold coin in a new Canadian Art Series. The first coin in the series features the famous painting *The Habitant Farm,* by Canadian Artist Cornelius Krieghoff.

The Habitant Farm, one of Cornelius Kreighoff's famous depictions of life in rural Quebec during the 19th century, is featured on the reverse of the coin. The obverse features a contemporary effigy of Her Majesty Queen Elizabeth II by artist Dora de Pédery-HUNT.

The $200 22-karat gold coin series will continue an exploration of the development of Canadian art as it travels through our history. The Royal Canadian Mint first introduced the $200, 22-karat gold coin series in 1990 to commemorate Canadian culture and heritage. From 1997 to 2000, the series featured art from Canada's Native peoples in a series called Native Cultures and Traditions. The development of art in Canada and its journey across the country's history form the subject for this new 4 years series dedicated to Canadian Art. The coins of this new series will feature works of Canadian artists from the permanent exhibition at the National Gallery of Canada.

The coin is available in two different packaging options, the encapsulated coin comes with a numbered Certificate of Authenticity or the encapsulated coin is presented in a slick metal die-cast case with a gold plated logo and a pakka wood interior in a protective box, accompanied by a numbered Certificate of Authenticity.

The reverse design, the Habitant Farm, c. 1856, features a typical farmhouse scene in rural Quebec during the mid-1800s. The obverse of the coin features a contemporary effigy of Her Majesty Queen Elizabeth II by artist Dora de Pédery-HUNT.

Coin Specifications:

Purity:	22-karat or 91.67% gold & 8.33% silver
Weight:	17.135 grams
Gold Content:	15.552 grams (Minimum 1/2 Troy ounce of fine gold)
Diameter:	29 mm
Thickness:	2 mm
Edge:	Reeded
Face Value:	$200
Mintage:	10,000
Collector Value:	$475.00

Canadian Festivals Series

In 2001, the Royal Canadian Mint launched a new series of sterling silver 50-cent coins commemorating Canadian festivals from coast to coast.

Themes of Canadian Festivals

2001

Quebec Winter Carnival (Quebec)
Toonik Tyme (Nunavut)
Newfoundland and Labrador Folk Festival (Newfoundland)
Festival of the Fathers (Prince Edward Island)

2002

Annapolis Valley Blossom Festival (Nova Scotia)
Stratford Festival of Canada (Ontario)
Folklorama (Manitoba)
Calgary Stampede (Alberta)
Squamish Days Logger Sports (British Columbia)

2003

Yukon International Storytelling Festival (Yukon Territory)
Festival acadien de Caraquet (New Brunswick)
Back to Batoche (Saskatchewan)
Great Northern Arts Festival (Northwest Territories)

Canadian Festivals #1—50 cent sterling silver coin—Quebec Winter Carnival Folk Festival

The first in a series of 13 coins celebrating Canadian Festivals

Coin Specifications:

Composition:	Sterling Silver 92.5% silver, 7.5% copper
Weight:	9.30 grams
Diameter:	27.13 mm
Thickness:	2.08 mm
Edge:	Reeded
Face Value:	50 Cents
Mintage:	Singles—unlimited; Full 13 coin set—20,00
Collector Value:	$42.00

Canadian Festivals #2—50 cent sterling silver coin—Toonik Tyme Folk Festival

The second in a series of 13 coins celebrating Canadian Festivals. Nunavut's biggest festival, now in its 37th season, celebrates the coming of Spring and honours special people in the community. The people of Iqaluit come together to enjoy traditional Inuit games, snowmobiling, dog team races, entertainment and a wide variety of traditional dishes.

The reverse of the coin designed by Canadian artist John Mardon depicts events that are characteristic of the Toonik Tyme celebration such as dog sled racing, drum dancing and ski-doo racing. The obverse features the portrait of Her Majesty Queen Elizabeth II by Dora de Pédery-Hunt.

Individual coins in the Canadian Festivals series are encapsulated and housed in folder-style packaging with full colour graphics.

Coin Specifications:

Composition:	Sterling Silver 92.5% silver, 7.5% copper
Weight:	9.30 grams
Diameter:	27.13 mm
Thickness:	2.08 mm
Edge:	Reeded
Face Value:	50 Cents
Mintage:	Singles—unlimited; Full 13 coin set—20,00
Collector Value:	$50.00

Canadian Festivals #3—50 cent sterling silver coin—Newfoundland and Labrador Folk Festival

The third in a series of 13 coins celebrating Canadian Festivals. The design is the work of Saskatchewan born David Craig who has already produced a number of coin designs for the Royal Canadian Mint.

Individual coins in the Canadian Festivals series are encapsulated and housed in folder-style packaging with full colour graphics.

Coin Specifications:

Composition:	Sterling Silver 92.5% silver, 7.5% copper
Weight:	9.30 grams
Diameter:	27.13 mm
Thickness:	2.08 mm
Edge:	Reeded
Face Value:	50 Cents
Mintage:	Singles—unlimited; Full 13 coin set—20,00
Collector Value:	$50.00

Canadian Festivals #4—50 cent sterling silver coin— Prince Edward Island's Festivals of the Fathers

The fourth in a series of 13 coins celebrating Canadian Festivals. The design is the work of Montague born artist Brenda Artist Brenda Whiteway who currently resides in Charlottetown.

Individual coins in the Canadian Festivals series are encapsulated and housed in folder-style packaging with full colour graphics.

Coin Specifications:

Composition:	Sterling Silver 92.5% silver, 7.5% copper
Weight:	9.30 grams
Diameter:	27.13 mm
Thickness:	2.08 mm
Edge:	Reeded
Face Value:	50 Cents
Mintage:	Singles—unlimited; Full 13 coin set—20,00
Collector Value:	$50.00

NUMISMATIC NETWORK CANADA— ASSOCIATED COIN CLUBS AND SOCIETIES

Numismatic Network Canada is the Internet network designed for those interested in coins, tokens, paper money, and related numismatic material. It is sponsored and created by the principal nonprofit organizations in Canada to meet the needs of collectors, historians, researchers, and other people interested in numismatics, wherever their location.

British Columbia

Alberni Valley Coin Club
4689 10th Ave., Port Alberni, British Columbia V9Y 4Y1

Chinese Coin & Stamp Club
c/o: #9-8500 Anderson Rd., Richmond, British Columbia V6Y 1S6

Nelson Area Coin Club
P.O. Box 344, Rossland, British Columbia V0G 1Y0

North Coast Coin & Stamp Club
P.O. Box 1180, Prince Rupert, British Columbia V8J 4H6

North Shore Numismatic Society
P.O. Box 44009, 6518 E. Hastings, Burnaby, British Columbia V5B 4Y2

Vancouver Numismatic Society
4645 West 6th Ave., Vancouver, British Columbia V6R 1V6

U.B.C. Coin and Stamp Club
Box 185-6138 SUB Blvd., Vancouver, British Columbia V6T 1Z1

Victoria Numismatic Society
Gordon Vanden Brock
P.O. Box 46023, Quadra Post Office, Victoria, British Columbia V8T 5Q7
E-mail: *gvdbroek@netzero.net*
Internet: *http://victoria.tc.ca/Recreation/VNS*

Alberta

Calgary Numismatic Society
Buster Hunter, Secretary
P.O. Box 633, Calgary, Alberta T2P 2J3
Internet: *http//www.ucalgary.ca/~cns*
E-mail: *B_R_Hunter@msn.com*

Edmonton Numismatic Society
P.O. Box 75024, Ritchie P.O., Edmonton, Alberta T6E 6K1
E-mail: *dang@compusmart.ab.ca*

Medicine Hat Coin & Stamp Club
P.O. Box 1163, Medicine Hat, Alberta T1A 7H3

Director for Alberta and the Northwest Territories for the CNA
Chris Clifton
E-mail: *clifton@telusplanet.net*

Saskatchewan

Regina Coin Club
P.O. Box 174, Regina, Saskatchewan S7K 1L6
Internet: *http://www.geocities.com/reginacoinclub*
E-mail: *reginacoinclub@hotmail.com*

Saskatoon Coin Club
P.O. Box 2205, Clarence Ave., Saskatoon, Saskatchewan S7K 1L6

Manitoba

Manitoba Coin Club
P.O. Box 321, Winnipeg, Manitoba R3C 2H6

Ontario

Brantford Numismatic Society
P.O. Box 28015, N. Park Plaza, Brantford, Ontario N3R 7K5

Cambridge Coin Club
c/o: Wolfe Derle, 232 Myers Rd., Cambridge, Ontario N1R 7M4
E-mail: *wolfed@sympatico.ca*

Canadian Association of Wooden Money Collectors—Southern Ontario Chapter
c/o: Norm Belsten, 86 Hamilton Dr., New Market, Ontario, L3Y 3E8
E-Mail: *nbelsten@sympatico.ca*

Champlain Coin Club
c/o: Mrs. Linda Huggins, 100 James Street, Orillia, Ontario L3V 1L5

Chedoke Numismatic Society
c/o: Bruce Brace, 654 Hiawatha Blvd., Ancester, Ontario L9G 3A5

Greater Kingston Coin Club
c/o: Raymond Vos, 334 Princess St., Kingston, Ontario K7L 1B6

Hamilton Coin Club
c/o: Ken Lord, 60 Rice Ave., Unit #19, Hamilton, Ontario L9C 7S3

Ingersoll Coin Club
c/o: Hubert Grimminck, 1806 Sunningdale Rd. W., London, Ontario, N6H 5J7

Kent Coin Club
c/o: Lou's Coin & Stationary, 109 King St., West, Chatham, Ontario N7M 1E2

Kirkland Lake District Coin Club
c/o: C. Enair, 34 Grierson Ave. Kirkland Lake, Ontario P2N 1C7

Lake Superior Coin Club
P.O. Box 10245, Thunder Bay, Ontario P7B 6T7

London Numismatic Society
c/o: Ted Leitch, 543 Kininvie Dr., London, Ontario N2G 1P1

Mississauga-Etobicoke Coin, Stamp and Collectibles Club (formerly Mississauga and Thistletown Coin Clubs)
c/o: Robert J. Porter, 46 Bankfield Dr., Rexdale, Ontario M9V 2P8
E-Mail: Paul Petch, *p.petch@rogers.com*

Niagara Falls Coin Club
c/o: Gord Nichols, Lakeport, P. O. Box 28039, 600 Ontario St., St. Catherines, Ontario L2N 7P8

Nickel Belt Coin Club
c/o: Roland Albert, Secretary, 30 Gutcher Dr., Sudbury, Ontario P3C 3H6

Nipissing Coin Club
c/o: W.R. Caesar, 895 Clarence St., North Bay, Ontario P1B 3W1

North York Coin Club
P.O. Box 58508, Sheppard Centre P.O., 4841 Yonge Street, North York, Ontario, M2N 6R7
E-mail: *p.petch@rogers.com*

Oshawa & District Coin Club
P.O. Box 30557, Oshawa Centre, Oshawa, Ontario L1J 8L8
E-mail: *papman@idirect.com*

City of Ottawa Coin Club
P.O. Box 42004, R.P.O. St. Laurent, Ottawa, Ontario K1K 4L8

Paisley Road Coin Club
406 Paisley Rd., Guelph, Ontario N1H 2R3

Pembroke Centennial Coin Club
c/o: R.J. Graham, 395 Fraser St., Pembroke, Ontario K8A 1Y5

Peterborough Numismatic Society
c/o: Don C. Hurl, Box 1318, 1e Chippewa Avenue, Lakefield, Ontario, K0L 2H0

Sarnia Coin Club
c/o: Gerry Sprenger, 920 Toro St., Sarnia, Ontario N7V 3N9

Scarborough Coin Club
P.O. Box 562, Pickering, Ontario L1V 2R7
E-mail: *cpms@idirect.com*

South Wellington Coin Society
Scott Douglas, 273 Mill St. East, Acton, Ontario, L7J 1J7
E-mail: *scott.douglas@sympatico.ca,*

Stratford Coin Club
P.O. Box 21031, Stratford, Ontario N5A 7V4

St. Catharines Coin Club
P.O. Box 511, Thorold, Ontario L2V 4W1

St. Thomas Numismatic Association
c/o: 79 Myrtle St., St. Thomas, Ontario N5R 2E9

Tillsonburg Coin Club
c/o: Ralph Harrison, 36 Kamps Cres., Tillsonburg, Ontario N4G 4Z3

Timmins Coin Club
c/o: Randy Maass, P.O. Box 1434, Timmins, Ontario P4N 7N2

Toronto Coin Club
c/o: Del & Aline Murchison, 1 Pleasant Ave., Stoney Creek, Ontario, L8G 2L1
E-Mail: *cancomic@idirect.com*

Waterloo Coin Society
P.O. Box 40044, Waterloo Square, 75 King St., Waterloo, Ontario N2J 4V1
E-mail: *cholling@uoguelph.ca*
Web site: *http://www.angelfire.com/tx/wcshomepage/index.html*

Watford Coin Club
c/o: Dalton Richardson, 356 St. Clair St., Walford, Ontario N0M 2S0

Windsor Coin Club
c/o: 110 Eugenie St. W., Suite 505, Windsor, Ontario N8X 4Y6

Woodstock Coin Club
c/o: Jim Watson, RR#5, Woodstock, Ontario N4S 7V9

Quebec

Association des Collectioneurs de Monnaies des Laurentides
P.O. Box 252, St-Jerome, Quebec J7Z 5T9

Association des Numismates et des Philatelliste de Boucherville Inc.
C.P. 1111, Boucherville, Quebec J4B 5E6

Association des Numismates de St. Hyacinthe
C.P. 81, St. Hyacinthe, Quebec J2S 7B2

Club Numismatique de la Mauricie
C.P. 141, Grande Mere, Quebec G9T 5R7

Club de Numismates du Bas St-Laurent
C.P. 1475, Rimouski, Quebec G5L 8M3

Club Philatelique et Numismatique de Granby
a/s: Gilles Lamoureux, 149 Laurier, Granby, Quebec, J2G 5K3
Tel: 514-372-8243
E-mail: *gilles@granby.net*

CSRC Collectors Club
c/o: Walter Klus, 600 Maque, Isle Brazzard, Quebec H9C 2T4

Club Timbres et Monnaies de Sorel
c/o: Lucie St-Martin, 120 Barabe, Sorel, Quebec J3P 3E7

La Societe D'Archeologie et de Numismatique de Montreal
280 Est Rue Notre-Dame, Montreal, Quebec H2Y 1C5

Lakeshore Coin Club
P.O. Box 1137, Pointe Claire Postal Stn., Pointe Claire, Quebec, H9S 4H9

Montreal Numismatic Society
MacDonald Steward Foundation, 1195 Sherbrooke St. West, Montreal, Quebec H3A 1H9

Societe Numismatique de Quebec
C.P. 56036, Quebec City, Quebec G1P 2W0

New Brunswick

Atlantic Provinces Numismatic Association
c/o: Geoff Bell, 118 Cameron St., Moncton, New Brunswick E1C 5Y6
E-mail: *coincbnt@nbnet.nb.ca*

Frèdericton Numismatic Society
c/o: Ian Graham, 11 Scenic Dr., Fredericton, New Brunswick E3E 1A1

Miramichi Coin Club
P.O. Box 107, Newcastle, New Brunswick E1V 3M2

Moncton Coin Club
P.O. Box 54, Moncton, New Brunswick E1C 8R9
E-mail: *coincbnt@nbnet.nb.ca*

St. John Coin Collectors Club
c/o: Mrs. Donald Lohnes, 60 Somerset Park, Saint John, New Brunswick E2K 2R8

Nova Scotia

Cape Breton Coin Club
c/o: Harley Isenor, 30 MacRae Ave., Sydney River, Nova Scotia B1S 1M2

Halifax Coin Club
c/o: Dartmouth Seniors' Service Centre, 45 Ochterloney Street, Dartmouth, NS, B2Y 4M7

Sou'West Coin Club
c/o: Douglas B. Shand, P.O. Box 78, Shag Harbour, Nova Scotia B0W 3B0

Prince Edward Island

PEI Numismatic Association
234 Mt. Edward Rd., Charlottetown, PEI, C1A 5T6
Slate of officers: President: Ralph Dickieson, Secretary: Harley Ings, Treasurer: Gloria Houston
E-Mail: *ralph.d@pei.sympatico.ca*

Newfoundland

Central Newfoundland Numismatic Club
c/o: Robert Lodge, 57 Lincoln Road, Grand Falls-Windsor, NFLD, A2A 1N1
Phone: 709-292-4520 (B), Fax: 709-292-4521

CANADIAN COIN ORGANIZATIONS

The following information is printed with the permission of the organizations listed and was obtained from the Numismatic Network of Canada.

Assoc. des Numismates Francophones du Canada
C.P. 9904, Ste. Foy, Quebec G1V 4C5
E-mail: *antc@cam.org*
Internet: *http://www.cam.org/~anfc/anfc.html*

Canadian Association of Token Collectors
c/o: Harry James, 94 Park Ave., St. Thomas, Ontario N5R 4W1

Canadian Association of Wooden Money Collectors
c/o: Norm Belsten, 86 Hamilton Drive, Newmarket, Ontario, L3Y 3E8
E-Mail: *nbelsten@sympatico.ca*

Canadian Numismatic Association
P.O. Box 226, Barrie, Ontario L4M 4T2
E-mail: *cdn.numismatic@on.aibn.com*

Canadian Numismatic Research Society
c/o: Ron Greene, Box 1351, Victoria, British Columbia V8W 2W7
E-mail: *pdgreene@pinc.com*

Canadian Tire Coupon Collectors Club
c/o: Roger Fox, 382 Selby Cres., Newmarket, Ontario L3Y 6E1

Classical & Medieval Numismatic Society
P.O. Box 956, Station "B," Willowdale, Ontario M2K 2T6
E-mail: *billmcdo@idirect.com*

Club de Collectionneurs de Coupons Canadian Tire
C.P. 21, New Glasgow, Quebec J0R 1J0
Tel: 514-432-5040

National Currency Collection Bank of Canada

Curator, Bank of Canada, Ottawa, Ontario K1A 0G9

Ontario Numismatic Association
P.O. Box 40033, Waterloo Square P.O., 75 King St., Waterloo, Ontario N2J 4V1
E-mail: *rmcph@internet.look.ca*

Atlantic Provinces Numismatic Association

The APNA is a nonprofit numismatic organization consisting of members located mainly throughout Canada's Eastern Maritime provinces. Seven coin clubs and organizations also hold membership in the Association. The objectives of APNA are to encourage and promote the collection and study of all numismatic material and dispense numismatic information wherever possible. Its aim is also to cultivate fraternal relations among members at meetings, conventions, and other gatherings.

The Association assists in the formation of new coin clubs and aids those that may be losing ground. It acts as an advisory board, if called upon, to adjudicate unfair practices and generally provides a strong and united voice when needed in the interests of numismatics generally.

APNA publishes a quarterly newsletter in which it offers free advertising to members. It organizes a biannual convention in various locations through the maritimes. Membership is open to anyone of good repute, regardless of their location.

APNA dues are:

$15 Regular membership
$15 Junior membership (first year free)
$15 Corporate membership (clubs, libraries, etc.)
$125 Life membership (after one year of membership)

You may contact the APNA by writing to **Treasurer, Atlantic Provinces Numismatic Association, Attn: Randy Larsen, 131 Stillwater Lake, Nova Scotia, B3Z IG2, CANADA**

E-mail address is *r-larsen@sympatico.ca*

The editor of *The Atlantic Numismatist* is *Rick Chalmers*. Our editor will welcome comments, suggestions, member ads and articles, etc. via e-mail: *g.chalmers@ns.sympatico.ca* or at our mailing address: c/o The Dartmouth Seniors Service Center, 45 Ochterloney Street, Dartmouth, N.S., B2Y 4M7, CANADA

Canadian Numismatic Association

The CNA is a nonprofit educational organization formed in 1950 and incorporated by Canada Charter in 1963. It has grown by leaps and bounds from an idea of a few dedicated numismatists to become one of the world's largest numismatic associations. Present membership is basically located in Canada and the United States of America but we do have additional members around the world. They all have one common interest and that is Canadian numismatics.

CNA Services and Advantages Offered

Being a member of CNA offers a great opportunity to meet other people with similar interests, correspond with them, and cultivate new friendships. As a member of the Association you will be eligible to receive the CNA/NESA Numismatic Correspondence Course at a reduced cost.

You will receive the *CNA Journal* which carries articles and papers on Canadian coins, tokens, and other numismatic subjects, advertisements by dealers and members, and information about other CNA activities. The *Journal* has been published since 1956 and has carried many of the most important papers relating to Canadian numismatics. A number of these articles have been published in French. In the *Journal* you will be able to advertise your coins, and buy from or sell to other members. Advertising rates are published in the *Journal*.

The highlight of the year is the CNA Annual Convention, which has been held in various cities across Canada since 1954. The Convention is Canada's oldest continuing numismatic event where people with a common interest come together. An auction at every Convention helps collectors build their collections and provides a basis for determining values when buying or selling all kinds of numismatic material. Dealers from across Canada and the United States take bourse space at the Convention to offer a great variety of material for sale.

At the CNA Convention, other numismatic organizations hold their annual meetings or conduct educational programs. These include the Canadian Numismatic Research Society, the Canadian Paper Money Society, the Canadian Association of Token Collectors, the Canadian Association of Wooden Money Collectors, the Love Token Society, the Classical and Medieval Numismatic Society, and others. Delegates from coin clubs across Canada meet and exchange views on common problems to help the hobby and the collector. Members of the CNA exhibit items from their collections in competition for display awards, thus sharing their knowledge with everyone. Once you attend a CNA Convention and join in the activities you will come back again and again.

Members have access to the Association's extensive library. A catalogue is available to all members on request. The catalogue is available in either a written version or on a computer disc (Word Perfect 5.0). There is a charge of $5.00 to assist in mailing the catalog or disc. The library has both books and slide programs. Members may borrow books for a period of one month. Slides and films may be borrowed for two weeks. On valuable shipments the borrower is required to pay the postage and registration both ways. Inside Canada a special postage rate is available. For further information, contact the librarian: Geoffrey G. Bell, P.O. Box 5228, Shediac, N.B. E4P 8T9 or E-mail: *gbel@nb.sympatico.ca.*

Note: The CNA does not buy, sell, or evaluate numismatic material, with the exception that it sells its own publications and medals, etc., which are advertised in the *Journal.*

Reduced rates, broad coverage, and numismatic insurance in Canada and the United States are also available to members. Details on request.

CNA Correspondence Course

The Canadian Numismatic Association and Numismatic Educational Services Association have recently launched an exceptional, inexpensive correspondence course for Canadian coin collectors of all ages. Whether you're just beginning to collect coins or have been involved in the hobby for some time, this course is for you! Renowned Canadian coin experts lead you through the stages of coin production and the history of Canadian coins, tokens, medals, and paper money. Through a series of 12 easy-to-read modules and self-paced tests you'll learn the ABC's of coin collecting, including tips on what to collect, how to build a collection, housing and handling your coins, grading coins, the organized hobby, "extinct" Canadian coins, the "coining" process, Canadian commemorative coins, and how to join formal organizations geared toward collectors like yourself. This course is an absolute must for anyone interested in Canadian coins and collecting.

For further information or an application form to sign up for the course, please contact the Executive Secretary of the CNA.

CNA Membership/Subscription

Regarding the cost of membership/subscription in the CNA, the following rules apply:

- Dues are payable in Canadian dollars to Canadian addresses and, because of high postal costs, in U.S. dollars to all other addresses.
- Payment may be made by money order, bank draft, or personal check.
- We regret that we are unable to offer credit card services.

- Postage stamps are not acceptable.
- Currency (U.S. or Canadian only) is acceptable and should be sent by security-registered mail only.
- Membership is not GST taxable.

Various memberships offered are:

REGULAR—Applicants 18 years of age or over **$33.00**
JUNIOR—Applicants under 18 years of age **$16.50**
Must be sponsored by a parent or guardian
FAMILY—Husband, wife, and children at home, under 18 years of age, *One* Journal *only* **$44.00**
CORPORATE—Clubs, societies, libraries, and other nonprofit organizations **$33.00**
LIFE MEMBERSHIP **$595.00**
After one year of regular membership. Details on deferred-payment plan available on request.

First-class mailing of the *Journal* is available on remittance of $9 (Cdn.) to Canadian addresses, $7.50 (U.S.) to USA addresses, and $15 (U.S.) to all other addresses.

For membership/subscription information or a free sample copy of our publication, contact: John Regitko, F.C.N.A., Executive Secretary, Canadian Numismatic Association, 4936 Yonge Street, Suite 601, North York, ON M2N 6S3, Telephone 416-223-5980, Fax: 416-223-6782 E-mail: *cnainfo@look.ca*

Canadian Numismatic Research Society

The Canadian Numismatic Research Society (CNRS) was founded in 1963 by a group of respected Canadian numismatists who wished to stimulate public awareness and understanding of numismatics related to Canada, through the promotion of research and study, and the dissemination of knowledge.

Membership in the CNRS is by invitation only. The main criteria are that a prospective member be actively engaged in numismatic research and has published the results of his/her research in a widely distributed journal or book. Current members have a wide range of interests from ancient coins to Canadian banking history and include coins, tokens, medals, paper money and numismatic literature.

The society does not evaluate or grade material.

The Society publishes a quarterly in conjunction with the Canadian Association of Token Collectors. This quarterly, *Numismatica Canada,* is available to non-members on an annual basis for Can. $15.00 within Canada or U.S. $15.00 elsewhere, postpaid. The content is primarily concerned with Canadian tokens and their histories, but there are numerous articles on medals, modern municipal trade dollars and other numismatic topics. Please contact the editor: Harry

James, P.O. Box 22022, Elmwood Sq. P.O., 2024 First Avenue, St. Thomas, Ontario, Canada N5R 4W1.

Back issues of our former publication, The Transactions, are still available for some years. Please contact the editor.

Ronald Greene, Secretary Canadian Numismatic Research Society, P.O. Box 1351, Victoria, BC, Canada V8W 2W7, Fax: 250-598-5539 E-mail: *ragreene@telus.net*

Edmonton Numismatic Society

The Edmonton Numismatic Society is a not-for-profit organization dedicated to the needs of fellow numismatists in our local area of Edmonton, Alberta, Canada, as well as the northern Alberta area, the rest of Canada, and the world! It was formerly known as The Edmonton Coin Club and was formed in 1953.

All members receive a newsletter as part of their dues. The newsletter supplies information on current events, as well as articles on coins, paper money, tokens, and medals.

MEMBERSHIP *(Canadian funds unless noted otherwise):* Family: $12, Regular: $10 Junior (16 AND UNDER): $3. U.S. addresses in U.S. funds, overseas add $5. Dues apply for one (1) calendar year membership in the Edmonton Numismatic Society (Jan. to Dec.)—(half price if joining from Sept. to Dec.). Subject to approval by the Membership, an official receipt and membership card will be issued.

For more information please phone 403-433-7288. Meets second Wednesday of the month at the Provincial Museum of Alberta, 12845-102 Ave., Edmonton, Alberta, Canada.

Ontario Numismatic Association

In 1962 the idea for this Association originated at a meeting of delegates from various numismatic clubs of Ontario. The meeting took place at the Waterloo Coin Society's annual banquet and from this the ONA was born. The delegates at the first meeting recognized the need for an organization to serve the educational and social needs of the Ontario clubs and hobbyists. The ONA was incorporated in 1962 as a nonprofit educational and social organization dedicated to the collector.

Since that time, the Executive has grown to include 11 Regional Directors, an Editor-Librarian, an Audio-Visual Service Director, and a Speakers Circuit and Convention Coordinator. Appeals were made throughout Ontario clubs for memberships, numismatic books for the library, and for audio-visual programs that the member clubs could use at their meetings. The appeals proved very successful and to date over 50 audio-visual programs and 500 books and pamphlets are in the library. Membership to date stands at over 35 clubs and numismatic organizations, over 65 life members, and varying membership from both Canada and the United States. Appeals for all these mentioned above are still in effect and the donations to the audio-visual service and the library would be gratefully received.

From the first convention held at Prudhommes Garden Hotel near St: Catharines, where over 1,700 attended and 250 were at the banquet, and conventions held in most major cities across Ontario from Windsor to Ottawa and from Sudbury to Niagara Falls, the ONA is active and prosperous. One of the excellent initiatives put into effect was the Award of Merit. Another was the establishment of the Speakers Circuit.

The conventions held annually offer numismatic groups the opportunity to get together and hold annual meetings. Also, the Club Delegates Meeting provides each club representative an opportunity to voice opinions, share ideas, and benefit from the experience and ideas of the other clubs. Displays in many numismatic categories at the convention offer the collectors an opportunity to not only see exceptional and often very rare material, but to gain knowledge from the research done by the exhibitor to create the display.

In the future the ONA will continue to search out new ideas that will improve the hobby for the clubs and the individual collector. The ONA will also continue:

- to encourage clubs and members to participate in all activities of the Association;
- to expand the audio-visual and numismatic library;
- to provide liability insurance coverage in the amount of $2,000,000 for all participating member clubs and individual members;
- to expand the Speakers Circuit;
- to select active clubs in Ontario towns and cities to host successful future conventions.

The ONA motto is *"VIRES ACQUIRIT EUNDO."* It means *"AS IT GROWS, IT GATHERS STRENGTH."* The accomplishments of the ONA over the years since 1962 serve to prove the validity of this motto for our organization. Finally, it is a pleasure to invite all who are not now members of the ONA to join so we can share the many pleasures and benefits of numismatics together in future years.

ONA dues per calendar year are:
$15 Regular membership
$5 Junior membership (up to age 18)
$17 Husband and wife (one journal)
$20 Club or association
$150 Life membership (subject to by-laws)

For further information contact: Ontario Numismatic Association, P.O. Box 40033, Waterloo Sq. P.O., 75 King Street South, Waterloo, ON, N2J 4V1, CANADA. E-mail: *robb4359@hotmail.com.*

Publication—*Canadian Coin News*

Canadian Coin News has been around for more than 30 years and in that time it has become the definitive source for information about coin collecting and numismatics from a Canadian perspective.

Although we cover the entire world of numismatics, the majority of our readers are Canadians, and we concentrate on the unique circumstances surrounding collecting in our native land. Our editorial pages include information on new and old issues, as well as commentary, investment tips, and Canada's most up-to-date listings of prices.

We haven't put the entire magazine online, but we have included an archive of interesting and relevant articles and pictures. We have also included information on how to subscribe or how to reach us. We are eager to hear your comments, suggestions, advice, and even a few flames. Our aim is to give you some of the basic information and contacts you need as a collector. We have also completed the first version of our *Canadian Numismatic FAQ.*

If you offer products or services of interest to Canadian numismatists, the best way to reach them is through *Canadian Coin News,* either online or in print.

For more information, or to receive a sample copy of *Canadian Coin News* along with our media kit and rate card, please contact: Advertising Manager, Canadian Coin News, 202-103 Lakeshore Rd., St. Catharines, ON, L2N 2T6, Canada.

Have *Canadian Coin News* delivered directly to your door every two weeks! Here are our subscription rates, which offer a significant savings off the cover price of $2.50 per issue: Basic rates: 1 year (26 issues) Canada (includes GST): $37.40. United States and possessions: $37.40. Foreign: $67.95.

To order by telephone using a credit card: Call 1-800-408-0352 Ext 236, Monday through Friday, 9:00 A.M. to 5 P.M. Eastern Time.

To order by mail: Send your request to Trajan Publishing Corporation, 202-103 Lakeshore Rd., St. Catharines, ON, L2N 2T6, Canada.

To order by fax: Fax your order 24 hours a day to 1-905-646-0995.

To order by E-mail: Send E-mail to *orders@trajan.com.*

For mail, fax, and E-mail orders please include your name, mailing address, and daytime telephone number. For credit-card orders, please include your card number, type of card, and expiration date.

CAND (Canadian Association of Numismatic Dealers)

What Is CAND?

The Canadian Association of Numismatic Dealers is a nonprofit association of professional numismatists organized in 1975 under letters patented as Canada 70,067 Inc. CAND's function is to ensure a high degree of professionalism by its members. Each CAND member has signed a strict code of ethics, which is enforceable by our by-laws.

CAND members are engaged in the retail numismatic trade, primarily in Canadian numismatics, and may conduct business from anywhere in the world. CAND members include coin dealers, show operators, publishers, supply manufacturers, bullion dealers, foreign exchange dealers, auctioneers, paper money dealers, and foreign coin and paper money dealers.

CAND features a mechanism for redress of grievances against members, and a performance fund for at least partial compensation to wronged collectors should the dealer be unable to fulfill his obligation.

How to Reach CAND

Telephone: (905) 643-4988 (with answering machine)
Facsimile: (905) 643-6329
E-mail: *info@cand.org*
Mail: CAND, Attn: Jo-Anne Simpson, Executive Secretary, Box 10272, Winona PO, Stoney Creek, Ontario L8E 5R1

List of Members

Legend: [a] Canadian Decimal, [b] Gold Coins, [c] Royal Canadian Mint Products, [d] Canadian Paper Money, [e] Canadian Pre-decimal Tokens, [f] Foreign Coins & Foreign Mint Products, [g] Foreign Paper Money, [h] Foreign Exchange, [i] Jewelry, [j] Gold/Silver Bullion, [k] Coin Supplies, [l] Auctions, [m] Promotional Items, [n] Publishing, [o] Show Operator

Abbott, Mr. John
Abbott's Corporation
33700 Woodward Avenue
Birmingham, MI 48009-0912
USA
Tel: (248) 644-8565
Fax: (248) 644-7038
E-mail: *john@abbottscorp.com, www.abbottscorp.com*

Albern Coins and Foreign Exchange Ltd
1511 Centre Street NW
Calgary, AB
CANADA T2E 2S1
Tel: (403) 276-8938
Fax: (403) 276-5415
E-mail: *info@albern.com. www.albern.com*

Armstrong, Mr. Robert
Bob Armstrong Coins
[a, e]
P.O. Box 333
Owen Sound, Ontario
N4K 5P5 Canada
Tel: (519) 371-8021

Bailey, Mr. Ted
Ted's Collectables
281-A Grand River Street North
Paris, ON
CANADA N3L 2N9
Tel: (519) 442-3474
Fax: (519) 442-2969
E-mail: *teds.s.w.o.n.22@sympatico.ca*

Bell, Mr. Geoffrey
Member, Dealer Control Committee
The Coin Cabinet
118 Cameron Street
Moncton, NB E1C 5Y6
Tel: (506) 857-9403
Fax: (506) 857-9403
E-mail: *coincbnt@nbnet.nb.ca*
The Coin Cabinet
154 Waterloo St.
Saint John, NB E2L 3R1
E-mail: *Coins118@hotmail.com*

Bevers, Mr. Cameron or Sandham, Mr. Todd
Colonial Acres Coins
[a, c, d, k]
#7-300 Victoria St. N
Kitchener, Ontario
N2H 6R9 Canada
Tel: (519) 579-9302
Fax: (519) 579-0532
E-mail:
coins@colonialacres.com
http://www.colonialacres.com

Borins, Mr. Paul
PB Numismatic Auctions Inc.

Bromberg, Mr. Steven
Canadian Coin Auctions & Sales [a, d, l, m]
Box 32539, 9665 Bayview Ave.
Richmond Hill, Ontario
L4C 0A2 Canada
Tel: (905) 883-6339
Fax: (905) 883-5929

Burton, Mr. Willard
B & W Coins
CAND President
15-6400 Millcreek Drive
Mississauga, ON
Tel: (416) 254-6569
Fax: (416) 456-9625
E-mail: *bw@globalserve.net*

Calgary Coin Gallery
Box 1608 Station M
Calgary, AB T2P 2L7
Store: 811 M. 1st Street SW
Tel: (403) 266-6527
Fax: (403) 266-6527
E-mail: *robert@calgarycoin.com*
www.calgarycoin.com

Champagne, Mr. Claude
Montreal Timbres et Monnaies [a, d, o]
1878 Ste-Catherine Est
Montreal, Quebec
PQ H2K 2H5 Canada
Tel: (514) 527-1526
Fax: (514) 527-6168

Charlton, Mr. James
Retired, Honorary Member
Tel: (905) 562-5567

Chicoine, Mr. Yvon
Member, Dealer Control Committee
Monnaie de Versailles
[a, b, d, e, f]
7275 Sherbrooke Est, local 2219
Montreal, Quebec
PC H1N 1E9 Canada
Tel: (514) 352-9101
Fax: (514) 352-0057

Cyr, Mr. Pierre [a, b, d, e]
Au Verseau, Inc.
298 Boul. Theriault
Riviere-du-Loup, Quebec
PQ G5R 4C2
Tel: (418) 862-0103
Fax: (418) 862-0103

Davis, Mr. Paul
Arctic Coins (Ottawa)
[a, b, c, d, e, f, g, h, j, k, m]
2573 Carling Ave.
Ottawa, Ontario
K2B 7H7 Canada

Tel: (613) 596-9648
Fax: (613) 596-6908
E-mail: *paul@coinmaster.com*

Doucett, Mr. Rayburn [a, d, e]
P.O. Box 1032
Belledune, New Brunswick
E8G 2X9
Tel: (506) 237-4107
Fax: (506) 237-4105
E-mail: *delray@nbnet.nb.ca*

Dowsett, Mr. Bob
B.C. Enterprises
Stratford, ON
Tel: (519) 271-8884
Fax: (519) 275-2684
E-mail: *bccoins@cyg.net*

Evans, Mr. Brett
Trajan Publishing Corp.
103 Lakeshore Suite No. 202
St. Catharines, ON L2N 2T6
Tel: (905) 646-7744
Fax: (905) 646-0995
E-mail:
Editor, Bret Evans:
bret@trajan.com
Advertising:
lindann@trajan.com

Findlay, Mr. Michael
Certified Coins of Canada
[a, b, d, e, f, g, n]
P.O. Box 2043
Angus, ON L0M 1B0
Tel: (705) 423-1140
Fax: (705) 423-1069
E-mail: *ccdn@bconnex.net*

Garrison, Mr. Harry
Colonial Valley Coins
4343 South Broad Street
Hamilton, NJ 08650 USA
Tel: (609) 585-8104,
585-0254
Fax: (609) 581-1261
E-mail: *HWG2@erols.com*

Graham, Mr. Ian
Royal Canadian Mint [c]
320 Sussex Dr.
Ottawa, Ontario
K1A 0G8 Canada
Tel: (613) 993-0805
Tel: (800) 496-6660
Fax: (613) 998-1330
E-mail: *graham@ibm.net*

Grant-Duff, Mr. Brian
All Nations Coin & Stamp
434 Richards Street
Vancouver, BC V6B 2Z5
Tel: (604) 684-4613
Fax: (604) 684-4618
E-mail: *collect@direct.ca*
http://www.downtownstamps.bc.ca

Grecco, Mr. Andy
Andy Grecco Coins
Tel: (905) 357-4684

Hill, Mr. David
Dave's Numismatics
PO Box 2080
Angus, Ontario
L0M 1B0 Canada
Tel: (705) 424-0005
Fax: (705) 424-0005
E-mail: *daveH@csolve.net*

Hoare, Wendy
Jeffrey Hoare Auctions, Inc.
CAND Secretary/Treasurer
Chairman, Dealer Control Committee
319 Springbank Drive
London, ON N6J 1G6
Tel: (519) 473-7491
Fax: (519) 473-1541
E-mail:
jhoare@jeffreyhoare.on.ca
http://www.jeffreyhoare.on.ca

Hoskins, Mr. Vern
Cameo Coins
PO Box 879

Port Dover, ON N0A 1N0
Tel: (519) 583-2526
E-mail:
cameoshoppe@kwic.com

Iorio, Mr. Joseph
J & M Coin & Jewellery
[a, b, c, d, e, f, i, j, k, l]
106 West Broadway
Vancouver, British Columbia
V5Y 1P3 Canada
Tel: (604) 876-7181
Fax: (604) 876-1518
E-mail: *jandm@jandm.com*
http://www.jandm.com

Isaacs, Sean
Alliance Coin & Banknote
300 Earl Grey Drive, Suite 446
Kanata, ON K2T 1C1
Tel: (613) 592-8842
Fax: (613) 591-9151
E-mail: *sean@alliancecoin.com*
http://www.alliancecoin.com/

Jenner, Mr. Brian
Brian Jenner Inc.
PO Box 2466
Pasco, WA 99302, USA
Tel: (509) 735-2172
Fax: (509) 783-4622

King, Ross [a, e, f]
Box 271
Chesley, Ontario
N0G 1L0 Canada
Tel: (519) 363-3143
Fax: (519) 363-3143
E-mail: *rdking@bmts.com*

Kosowan, Mr. Morris
Classic Cash
5223-48th Avenue
Sylvan Lake, AB
T4S 1G5

Kostyk, Mr. Peter
Niagara Falls, ON
Tel: (905) 356-5006

Kwallek, Mr. Keith J. [a, b, d, e]
P.O. Box 256
Chetek, Wisconsin 54728 USA
Tel: (715) 924-4529
Fax: (715) 924-3288

Laing, Mr. Ian
Gatewest Coin & Stamp
[a, b, c, d, e, f, j, k,]
1711 Corydon Ave.
Winnipeg, Manitoba
R3N 0J9 Canada
Tel: (204) 489-9112
Fax: (204) 489-9118
E-mail: *info@gatewestcoin.com*
http://www.gatewestcoin.com

Laramee, Mr. Serge
North American Numismatics, Inc. [a, b, d, e, l]
CP 131
Boucherville, Quebec
PQ J4B 5E6
Tel: (450) 449-1888
Fax: (450) 449-1797
E-mail: *info@grouptq.qc.ca*

Lawson, Mr. James
The Lawson Gallery [a]
1 Crossing Bridge Ct.
Stittsville, Ontario
K2S 1S2 Canada
Tel: (613) 831-2815
Fax: (613) 831-6106

Leardi, Mr. Frank
Frank Leardi Coins [a, d, e, f]
P.O. Box 361, Station T
Toronto, Ontario
M6B 4A3 Canada
Tel: (416) 781-3170
Fax: (416) 781-3170

Lehman, Mr. Vince
Provincial Coin Company
[a, b, c, d, e, i]
449 King St. East

Hamilton, Ontario
L8N 1C5 Canada
Tel: (905) 525-1649
Fax: (905) 525-6408

Lestrade, Mr. Guy
G.L. Timbres et Monnaires Enr.
[a, b, d]
2152, boul. Lapiniere, #110
Bossard, Quebec
PQ J4W 1L9 Canada
Tel: (450) 656-7756
Fax: (450) 656-7729

Lockwood, Peter
The Coin & Currency Exchange
[a, b, c, d, f, h, j]
1100 Burnhamthorpe
Road W, #14
Mississauga, Ontario
L5C 4G4 Canada
Tel: (905) 949-2646

Ma, Mr. Tony
Vancouver Bullion Exchange
[a, b, d, j]
2576 Granville Street
Vancouver, British Columbia
V6H 3G8 Canada
Tel: (604) 739-3997
Fax: (604) 739-3912

MacHugh, Mr. Terry
Terry's Coins [a, c, d, e, f]
P.O. Box 61538, Fennell PO
Hamilton, Ontario
L8T 5A1 Canada
Tel: (905) 318-6458
Fax: (905) 318-1638

Manz, Mr. George
George Manz Coins
P.O. Box 3626
Regina, SK S4P 3L7
Tel: (306) 352-2337
E-mail: *george@georgemanzcoins.com*

McDonald, Mr. Peter
PO Box 171
Beaconsfield, PQ H9W 5T6
Tel: (514) 231-4106
Fax: (514) 426-0100
E-mail: *pmcoins@total.net*

Merkley, Mr. William
London Coin Centre
[a, b, c, d, e, f, j, k]
345 Talbot St.
London, Ontario
N6A 2R5 Canada
Tel: (519) 663-8099
Fax: (519) 663-8019
E-mail: *coins@coins.on.ca*
http://www.coins.on.ca

Moore, Mr. Charles D.
Charles Moore Numismatics
Inc. [a, d, e, l]
P.O. Box 5233
Walnut Creek, California
94596-5233 USA
Tel: (925) 946-0150
Fax: (925) 930-7710
E-mail: *moorecoins@aol.com*

Olmstead, Mr. Don
Olmstead Currency
PO Box 487
St. Stephen, NB E3L 3A6
Tel: (506) 466-2078
Fax: (506) 466-5726
E-mail: *banknote@nbnet.nb.ca*

Osaduke, Mr. Ron
Fairway Foreign Exchange & Coin Shop
560 Fairway Rd. S
Kitchener, ON N2C 1X3
Tel: (519) 748-1770
Fax: (519) 748-2961
E-mail: *info@fairwaycoins.com*

Paydli, Mr. Loran
Loran's Canadian Coins and Paper
Box 460

Bruno, SK S0K 0S0
Tel: (306) 369-4165
Fax: (306) 369-2369

Popynick, Mr. William
Global Coin X-change
[a, b, d, e, i, j]
P.O. Box 120361
Fort Lauderdale, Florida 33312-0007 U.S.A.
Tel: (954) 587-7529
Fax: (954) 974-2562

Powell, Mr. Hugh
Newcan Coins & Collectables
[a, d, e]
P.O. Box 2991
Kenora, Ontario
P9N 4C8 Canada
Tel: (807) 548-4866
Fax: (807) 548-5540
E-mail: *newcan@voyageur.ca*
http://www.newcancoins.com

Richardson, Mr. Jim
Western Coins & Stamps Ltd.
#2-6380 #3 RD
Richmond, BC V6Y 2B3

Sauro, Mr. Rudy [a, d]
Hamilton, Ontario L9B 2H1
Tel: (905) 388-9066
Fax: (905) 388-9066
E-mail: *rsauro@sympatico.ca*
www.coins-militaria.com

Schaffer, Mr. Dale
Schaffer's Inc. [a, e]
7107 South Yale Ave., No. 199
Tulsa, Oklahoma 74136 U.S.A.
Tel: (918) 496-3008
E-mail:
dale.schaffer@home.com

Schaller, Mr. Paul or
McDonald, Mrs. Ursala
Mintmaster Numismatics Inc.
[a, b, c, d, h, j]
390 St. Jacques Ouest
Montreal, Quebec
H2Y 1S1 Canada
Tel: (514) 844-2549
Fax: (514) 287-1573

Sebag, Mr. Gabriel
Maison de la Monnair (House of Coins)
368 Sherbrooke Ouest
Montreal, PQ H3A 1B2
Tel: (514) 842-6898
Fax: (514) 842-4499
E-mail: *houscoin@dsuper.net*

Sidebotham, Mr. Vince
Bayfield Collector's Gallery
Kozlov Centre - 400 Bayfield St.
Suite 202
Barrie, ON L4M 5A1
Tel: (705) 734-3903
Fax: (705) 734-9380

Simpson, Mr. Richard
CAND Vice President
R & S Coins
[a, b, c, d, m]
P.O. Box 10272, Winona PO
Stoney Creek, Ontario
L8E 5R1 Canada
Tel: (905) 643-4988
Fax: (905) 643-6329
E-mail: *rick@rscoins.ca*

Smith, Mr. Brian
Torex
P.O. Box 267, STN A
Toronto, ON M5W 1B2
Tel: (416) 861-9523
Fax: (416) 861-8466
E-mail: *brian@torex.net*
http://www.torex.net

Smith, Mr. George
Traders GoldCorp
1 Rosscliffe Drive
Hamilton, ON L9A 4E5
Tel: (905) 536-7897
E-mail: *tgoldcorp@attcanada.ca*

Smith, Ingrid K.
Torex [o]
P.O. Box 865, Adelaide St. PO
Toronto, Ontario
M5C 2K1
Tel: (416) 260-9070
Fax: (416) 260-9070
E-mail: *ingrid@torex.net*

Stanley, Mr. William J.
Canadian Wholesale Supply [k]
Box 301, 3 Yeo St.
Paris, Ontario
N3L 3G2 Canada
Tel: (519) 442-4441
Tel: (800) 265-0720
Fax: (519) 442-7761
cws@collectorssupplyhouse.com
www.collectorssupplyhouse.com

Thompson, Mr. Ron
Canada Coin & Paper Money
P.O. Box 425
St. Albert, AB T8N 7A2
Tel: (780) 459-6868
E-mail: *ronscoins@shaw.ca*
www.members.shaw.ca/ronscoins

Walsh, Mr. Michael
The Canadian Coinoisseur, Inc.
[a, b, d, l]
Box 345 101-1001
West Broadway
Vancouver, BC V6H 4E4
Canada
Tel: (604) 737-2044
Fax: (604) 737-7889
E-mail: *mail@coinoisseur.com*
http://www.coinoisseur.com

Whitmore, Mr. Verrol
Member, Dealer Control Committee
Trilogy Collectables
[a, b, c, d, e, f]
2399 Rushbury Court
Burlington, ON L7P 3V8
Tel: (905) 336-4062
Fax: (905) 336-4062

Wiese, Mr. Randall
Randall's Coins [a]
PO Box 55301, RPO Temple
Calgary, AB T1Y 6R6
Tel: (403) 861-0527

CANADIAN NUMISMATIC CHRONOLOGY

Courtesy of Q. David Bowers

Decimal Issues 1857–1967

The following listing comprises some of the many events that played a part in Canadian numismatics, leading to the discipline as we know it today. The study begins with the authorization of decimal coins in 1857 and concludes with the end of production of circulating silver coins in 1967. The study relates to decimal coin issues, with an acknowledgment that many other noteworthy events relating to paper money, tokens, and medals took place before and during the same time period.

1857: Decimal coinage system is adopted, and government records are now required to be kept in dollars and cents. This follows legislative action dating back to 1850 when Canadian coinage was proposed, but British authorities objected. Circulating coinage consists of a rich mixture of private copper tokens, United States coins, English coins, Spanish-American silver, and other issues. Forthcoming Canadian decimal coins are to be on par with United States coins. Although Canadian coins are to be denominated in dollars and fractions thereof, no one-dollar coins will be made for circulation until 1935.

1858: First decimal coins are struck for the Province of Canada: 1¢, 5¢, 10¢, and 20¢. Circulation strikes as well as a few Specimens are made, all at the Royal Mint, London, which will continue to be the main facility for striking Canadian coins until the Ottawa Mint opens in 1908. Coins feature the portrait of Queen Victoria, reigning monarch of England.

1859: Bronze cents are struck in large quantities for the Province of Canada, but no silver coins will be produced in this or any other year. By the time silver coinage is resumed in 1870, the Dominion of Canada will have been formed. So many bronze cents are made in 1859 that there will be a glut of them in the channels of commerce until the mid-1870s. Nova Scotia adopts a decimal system based upon the pound sterling rated at an exact $5.

1860: At the Royal Mint in London, bronze replaces copper for minor coins, and a revised portrait of Queen Victoria is created as is a new border style featuring tiny dots instead of the previous toothed-denticle format. The beaded border causes problems with the rim of the die breaking off, and denticles are reverted to. Meanwhile, both the new portrait of Victoria and the beaded border are used for a time in the early 1860s on certain bronze coins and patterns relating to Canadian maritime provinces. On April 9 New Brunswick approves a decimal coinage. The Heaton Mint begins construction of a new facility on Icknield Street, Birmingham, which will be ready in 1862 at which time 11 screw presses and one lever press will be used.

1861: First decimal coins are struck for Nova Scotia and New Brunswick at the Royal Mint, London, using the British farthing (1/4 penny) and halfpenny dies for the obverses. Bronze half cents and cents will be struck for Nova Scotia through 1864. New Brunswick half cents are struck by mistake and apparently mixed in with Nova Scotia coinage; obverse die of British farthing utilized. Other New Brunswick coins will be struck through 1864. Now as in future years, coinage orders from various entities in British North America placed with the Royal Mint will receive secondary attention in comparison to domestic coinage for England.

1862: In New Westminster, British Columbia, a few $10 and $20 gold coins are struck using gold from the Fraser River district, these being Canada's first gold coinage. Examples of these pieces are sent to London for exhibit in the International Exposition there; one each of the gold $10 and $20 from this showing will be presented to the British Museum in due course. The Numismatic Society of Montreal is founded on December 6 and will publish *The Canadian Antiquarian.* Adélard J. Boucher (born in 1835; secretary beginning in 1854 of the Montreal & Bytown Railway Co.) is named as its first president. In England, George William Wyon, young resident engraver at the Royal Mint since 1860, dies at the age of 26 years, and the Royal Mint strikes a memorial medal utilizing a reverse device that is also found on the New Brunswick 20-cent pieces of this year, creating a curiosity that will delight future generations of collectors. Vancouver adopts a decimal currency system. Ralph Heaton II dies in the same year that his new facility is ready for business. The firm becomes known as Ralph Heaton & Sons.

1863: United States coins are rare in circulation in the United States itself—which is in the middle of its Civil War—but are in oversupply in Canada. Particularly numerous are the old U.S. copper "large" cents dated from about the 1820s through 1857, with some worn earlier issues as well. During the decade Devins & Bolton, Montreal pharmacists, will counterstamp thousands of these American cents with their advertising message. Newfoundland adopts an exchange rate under which a Newfoundland dollar is worth one Spanish silver dollar, the latter being worth four shillings two pence in sterling; thus £1 sterling is worth $4.80 in Newfoundland decimal currency. This rate will be maintained until the banking crisis of 1894; in 1895 Newfoundland money will be at par with Canadian. The Numismatic Society of Montreal appoints a committee to prepare a catalogue of Canadian coin varieties, but the project will lapse.

1864: At the Royal Mint, London, Master Thomas Graham (who served in the post from April 27, 1856, until his death on September 16, 1869) discontinues the practice, considered wasteful, of scrapping dated English coin dies at the end of the calendar year. However, post-date use of *colonial* coin dies until they wore out is already the norm and is continued. This will wreak havoc with the accuracy of certain Royal Mint yearly coinage figures as related to coin dates. The Dominion of Canada is formed by the union of Nova Scotia, Quebec, and Ontario.

1865: Newfoundland bronze half cents are struck for circulation. Coins for Newfoundland will be produced by various mints through 1947. Newfoundland $2 gold coins are inaugurated this year and will be made intermittently through 1888, sometimes using the identical obverse dies employed to strike 10-cent pieces. These $2 pieces will become the only widely circulating Canadian gold coins of the 19th century and will be a delight to numismatists of generations to come. The mainland of British Columbia adopts a decimal system (but does not strike coins); Vancouver has been on the decimal system since 1862.

1866: United States coins remain a glut in the channels of commerce in Canada, but are the standard of trade. Liberty Seated half dimes, dimes, quarter dollars, and half dollars are ubiquitous in Montreal, Quebec, Vancouver, and other cities. They sell at varying discounts from face value, engendering a lively trade for money brokers of which there are dozens in the larger eastern cities, Montreal being a special center of activity. In January the collectors' group there changes its name to the Numismatic and Antiquarian Society of Montreal, reflecting members' interest in history as well as coins. The Boucher Collection, which had been awarded first prize at the Provincial Exhibition in 1863, is the first major numismatic property to be sold by public auction. John J. Arnton conducts the event, and the 726 lots—including many rare Canadian tokens—realize about $400. In November the James Rattray Collection is auctioned.

1867: The British North America Act unites the Confederation (New Brunswick, Nova Scotia, Quebec, and Ontario) as the Dominion of Canada. The government begins to take action to decrease United States coins in circulation. There are abundant Liberty Seated silver coins just about everywhere in Canada—as there have been since the 1850s—while in the United States itself they still are not seen in circulation, and transactions are conducted with paper Fractional Currency notes, bronze Indian cents, and some new issues including two-cent, nickel three-cent, and nickel five-cent pieces. The collections of William V. B. Hall and H. Laggatt (the latter cabinet known as the Bronsdon Collection) cross the auction block.

1868: Charles W. Fremantle becomes deputy director and comptroller of the Royal Mint; his tenure would last through 1894. A numismatist, Fremantle will see to it that Proofs (Specimens) were struck of many dates so that the British Museum and others will have some for display purposes.

1869: A catalogue, *Coins, Tokens and Medals of the Dominion of Canada,* by Alfred Sandham, is published by the Numismatic and Antiquarian Society of Montreal. Thomas Graham passes away on September 16; he had been master of the Royal Mint since April 27, 1856, and had been important in the contract coinage for the Province of Canada, 1858 and 1859. Graham insisted that all British coins struck in a given calendar year be dated correctly, but no such rule applied to colonial coinages (which were nearly always given second shrift at the mint).

1870: Silver coins for the Dominion of Canada are minted for the first time, by the Royal Mint in London. Denominations include the bronze 1¢ and the silver 5¢, 10¢, 25¢ (instead of the 20¢ used in the 1858 Province of Canada coinage), and 50¢. Dies of the decade will be made by hand by entering various elements such as Victoria's portrait, inscription letters, etc., by single punches, yielding a wealth of minor die varieties such as repunched and misaligned letters and numerals. Legislation provides for the revision of value of the millions of copper bank and provincial tokens in circulation, currently passing at 120 to the dollar for the halfpenny size; henceforth they will be worth one cent each, or 100 to the dollar. The fewer large copper tokens such as the copper pennies are to be worth two cents each. Minister of Finance Sir Francis Hincks and William Weir are two important government figures in the campaign to get rid of Liberty Seated silver coinage from the United States. Weir is put in charge and decides to export vast quantities. Meanwhile, as the new 25-cent pieces for Canada have not arrived from England, an issue of 25¢ paper currency is floated. Years later, Weir will write a book about his experiences during this era. In 1880 a consortium of commercial interests will recognize his service and give him a silver tea service in which United States silver coins are embedded. The Royal Mint, London, publishes its first annual report. Beginning in 1884 it will include technical information about Canadian and related foreign coinages.

1871: The Royal Mint in London, too busy to take on outside work, subcontracts certain Dominion of Canada coinage to a private facility, Ralph Heaton & Sons, simply known as the "Heaton Mint." Birmingham, more than any other city in the entire world, has a rich history of private coinage facilities, these being especially active in the previous century and dominated by the famous Soho Mint operated by Boulton and Watt. On an intermittent basis from now until 1903 the Heaton Mint will produce Canadian coins from cents to 50-cent pieces, each bearing an H mintmark. Dies for Dominion coinage are made at the Royal Mint and shipped to Heaton. On December 18 the first Canadian coins are struck by Heaton and consist of 1,000 50-cent pieces made under the watch of personnel from the Royal Mint, with special security precautions. This year the Heaton Mint also produces bronze cents for Prince Edward Island, but the H is inadvertently omitted; this picturesque coin with its arboreal theme will remain as that island's only official decimal coinage. Heaton coinage for Newfoundland ranges from the cent to the 50-cent piece. The Dominion Currency Act is passed and helps standardize exchange values within British North America. British Columbia becomes part of the Dominion of Canada on July 20. The Assay Office in British Columbia is closed.

1872: The *Canadian Antiquarian and Numismatic Journal* makes its debut and will continue to be published through 1933. Canadian coinage is accomplished exclusively at the Heaton Mint, Birmingham, as it will be for the next several years. The Royal Mint, using machinery that was modern 60 years earlier when it was installed, but which is now obsolete, struggles to keep pace with orders for British coins and leans upon Heaton to supply planchets for bronze issues.

1873: Prince Edward Island becomes part of the Dominion of Canada, thus isolating its 1871 cent as the only decimal coinage of that province. Canadian circulating coinage continues to be accomplished exclusively at the Heaton Mint.

1874: Canadian circulating coinage is accomplished exclusively at the Heaton Mint, thus contributing to a cluster of issues of this era with H mintmarks.

1875: Silver coinage this year continues to be concentrated at the Heaton Mint, typically in small quantities—thus delighting numismatists of a later generation who will consider most of the 1875-H issues to be objects of great desire. At the suggestion (it is said) of Charles W. Fremantle the Royal Mint strikes a few mintmarkless coins for cabinet purposes. In due course these will become numismatic rarities.

1876: Bronze cents, not minted since 1859, are again produced, this year at the Heaton Mint plus a few Specimen strikings at the Royal Mint where all dies are produced. Old provincial and private copper tokens, mostly of the one-cent trading value, begin to be gradually withdrawn from circulation. For the numismatists of the era, such copper pieces provide a rich area for collecting, and most emphasis in numismatic circles is on the tokens. There are not enough decimal coin varieties by this time to attract much attention. In this year Canadian circulating coinage production continues exclusively at the Heaton Mint, Birmingham. From time to time the Heaton Mint sets aside samples of the Canadian coinage for possible showing to other world countries and entities that might like to have their coinage made by the same factory. Not all of these will be passed out, and circa 1975 they will be mentioned to an executive of Paramount International Coin Corporation of Dayton, Ohio, U.S.A., who will recognize their importance. In due course over the next 10 years—1975 to the early 1980s—Raymond N. Merena and David W. Akers of Paramount, followed by Spink & Son, Ltd., London, will distribute these pieces in numismatic channels. Joseph LeRoux, M.D. (born April 9, 1849), of Montreal begins to collect coins with great enthusiasm, and in the next decade he will publish several numismatic guides including a catalogue of Canadian coins (1882), the *Numismatic Atlas for Canada* (1883), *The Collectors' Vade Mecum* (1885), the monthly *Collectionneur* magazine (beginning in 1886), and the *Canadian Coin Cabinet* (1888 with a supplement in 1890 and new edition in 1890).

1877: Canadian circulating coinage is once again only made at the Heaton Mint.

1878: The Royal Mint, London, source for all Canadian decimal coin dies, adopts a new steam-hammer method of die forging to replace the former tedious hand forging. New dies will be stronger and last longer, yielding more coins per die. Continuing what is becoming a tradition, Canadian circulating coinage is struck exclusively at the Heaton Mint.

1879: R.W. McLachlan's detailed study of Canadian coins, begun in 1877, first appears in the *American Journal of Numismatics* and will run for several years. A pioneer in the field, McLachlan gives much information that is new to his general audience, including mintage figures. Canadian circulating coinage continues to be made only at the Heaton Mint. Charles W. Fremantle, in charge of the Royal Mint, becomes a member of the Numismatic Society in London. His interest in coins is hardly new, for earlier in the decade he had tapped numismatist William Webster to catalogue the Mint's own collection. Gaps in the holdings were found, and Fremantle obtained permission from the Treasury to produce impressions from old dies (*i.e.,* restrikes) of the past century or so, from King George III through Queen Victoria, along the way creating some "restrikes" of which there were no "originals" (*e.g.,* certain 1870-, 1871-, and 1875-dated silver coins).

1880: Canadian circulating coinage is once again exclusively struck at the Heaton Mint, Birmingham. Gerald E. Hart, Montreal numismatist, sells a collection of Canadian coins, tokens, and medals to the Canadian government for $2,500 and writes a catalogue of it; the government states its intention to publish and distribute the catalogue and pay him an extra $500, but the project eventually lapses.

1881: Canadian circulating coinage is accomplished exclusively at the Heaton Mint. In banking and exchange circles $72.75 in British Columbia money is worth $73 in Canadian money. In April the Canadian government ships $50,000 face value in 1858 20-cent pieces to the Heaton Mint to be converted into other coins (also see note under Lot 279 in the present catalogue).

1882: No surprise: Canadian circulating coinage is again struck only with H mintmarks. The Royal Mint, London, is being renovated and updated, and Heaton produces all Imperial bronze coins and all British colonial issues. Certain presses obtained decades earlier from Matthew Boulton are replaced by new models made in Birmingham by Heaton, capable of striking 90 coins per minute (5,400 per hour), giving the Royal Mint a capacity of about 75,000 coins per hour when all facilities are running. During this era the *American Numismatic Journal,* published by the American Numismatic and Archaeological Society (founded 1858), continues to include important articles by R.W. McLachlan on Canadian coins. The Heaton Mint strikes Newfoundland $2 gold coins this year only, creating the only Canadian-related gold coins to bear an H mintmark. Other Newfoundland $2 coins from 1865 through 1888 are made at the Royal Mint, London.

1883: Canadian circulating coinage is again accomplished exclusively at the Heaton Mint.

1884: The *Fifteenth Annual Report of the Deputy Master of the Mint* includes much technical information about Canadian coinage made under contract. Such detailed information will continue to be a part of the report until 1907. After a lapse of over a decade during which time the

Heaton Mint did all of the coinage, the Royal Mint, now with expanded facilities, begins once again striking coins for Canada, although the Heaton Mint will be called upon from time to time to do work.

1885: Mintage quantities for certain Canadian and Newfoundland coins are low this year, creating varieties that numismatists yet unborn will venerate as rarities, especially if in high grades. The government of Canada redeems $18,000 face value in old 1858 20-cent pieces and causes them to be melted.

1886: In this year at least three significant date-punch variations occur on the 10-cent piece. On the 25-cent piece the 1886/3 overdate is made, one of the relatively few overdates in Canadian coinage of this or any other era.

1887: There is little call for silver 50-cent pieces in the eastern provinces, although they are popular in British Columbia on the West Coast, hardly a new situation and one that will continue into the 1890s.

1888: Joseph LeRoux publishes a reference on Canadian coins and will continue to update it through 1892. At the Royal Mint, London, maker of all dies for Dominion of Canada decimal coins, a new method is adopted whereby dies would be forged to their approximate finished size, rather than being made much larger and then machined to smaller dimensions. This results in greater efficiency. Canadian coins are becoming increasingly stereotyped, with die varieties being minor and mostly limited to date repunching and numeral size variations. In Monroe, Michigan, Dr. George F. Heath launches the *American Numismatist,* name soon changed to *The Numismatist.* In due course it will attract many Canadian subscribers and will publish many articles on Canadian coinage. The government redeems $17,174 worth of 1858 20-cent pieces for the melting pot.

1889: Despite a published high mintage the 1889 10-cent piece will prove to be a major rarity in the Canadian series. A later generation of numismatists will conclude that while many coins were struck in calendar year 1889, most pieces were dated earlier. Twenty-cent pieces continue to be called in, and $16,585 face value goes to the melting pot. The Heaton minting facility changes its name to The Mint, Birmingham, Ltd. Ralph Heaton III retires, and a contract with the newly renamed firm, now a public company, specifies the hiring of Ralph Heaton IV (1864-1930) as general manager.

1890: Pierre Napoleon Breton publishes the *Illustrated Canadian Coin Collector.* Breton, born in Montreal on June 10, 1858, just in time to be on hand for the first Canadian decimal coins, became interested in coins at the age of 15, and in 1889 he opened a store to sell books, numismatic items, and curios (in those days few coin dealers anywhere in North America dealt exclusively in numismatics). His first love was the copper "bouquet sou" token series, many of which were struck by Gibbs in Belleville, New Jersey. Meanwhile, as the father of 15 children, he must have been busy as well with family matters. Breton will live until 1917 and at that time will be widely mourned. In the Canadian Parliament a proposal for a domestic mint is introduced on March 4 as a measure to help gold-mining interests convert metal to coin. However, nothing comes of the idea at the time, which is viewed as being primarily beneficial to interests in the western part of the Dominion. In Newfoundland the dollar is revalued to place it on a par with Canadian and American dollars. It is found that two Royal Mint staff members are shareholders in the Heaton Mint, an uncomfortable situation in view of the Royal Mint giving contracts to the Birmingham coiner; the offending staffers sell their shares. Moreover, Royal Mint superintendent Robert Anderson Hill is connected by marriage to the Heaton family.

1891: In this year several date and leaf variations on the reverse of the bronze cent are created, but are of little notice at the time, but decades later will loom large when two of the several major varieties will be determined as being quite hard to find. The American Numismatic Association is formed in Chicago and will go on to become the world's largest organization of coin collectors, to hold annual conventions including in Canada in 1909 and 1923, and years later in 1941–1942 to have a Canadian, J. Douglas Ferguson, serve as president.

1892: In this year there is no coinage for Nova Scotia, nor had there been in 1891, nor will there be in 1893. In numismatic circles the most popular discipline is the acquisition of early 19th-century tokens, a trend that will continue until well into the 20th century.

1893: Joseph Hooper, of Ontario, is one of the most active writers and researchers of the era and contributes many items to *The Numismatist*. Canadian numismatic activity is intense and is focused almost exclusively on private tokens and related issues.

1894: P.N. Breton's *Illustrated History of Coins and Tokens Related to Canada* is published and in due course becomes the standard reference in the field. Over a period of time "Breton numbers" will be used to identify the multitudinous varieties of early 19th-century tokens as well as later ones. To a much lesser extent information is given on decimal coins. Breton notes that R.W. McLachlan, born in 1845 and who began collecting coins in 1857, has the largest numismatic cabinet in Canada, numbering over 8,000 pieces and ranging from ancient Greek issues to modern coins. Meanwhile, J.W. Scott & Co., New York City, publishes its *Standard Catalogue* series on various coins and treats Canadian tokens extensively, but gives very little detail on Canadian decimal coins. Serious collectors view the widely distributed Scott catalogues to be beneficial for the popularization of the hobby, but to be rather superficial in numismatic content. The Canadian government causes $14,518 worth of 1858 20-cent pieces to be melted. By now, they are becoming elusive in circulation and have long since been replaced by the 25-cent pieces. However, the denomination circulates actively in Newfoundland, with inscriptions pertaining to that island, and will continue to be minted for Newfoundland for years in the future. A major financial crisis occurs in Newfoundland, the island's two banks collapse, and four banks from the Canadian mainland set up facilities to provide financial services. Newfoundland residents hoard "hard" money including the gold $2 coins of the island minted 1865–1888, which soon become virtually nonexistent in circulation. Charles W. Fremantle, now at the age of 60, retires from the Royal Mint, having made many technological improvements during his watch and having encouraged the production of many Proof issues for museum and other cabinet purposes.

1895: Newfoundland money is set at par with Canadian money. Many fishermen and traders under foreign flags stop at Newfoundland, with the result that during this time the circulating coinage of the island is a varied mixture of world denominations, much more so than in the Dominion of Canada. In the United States the most active dealer in tokens and medals of Canada is Lyman H. Low.

1896: Gold is discovered in the Klondike, Yukon Territory. In the next year the "north to Alaska" slogan will draw thousands of fortune hunters through the Chilkoot Pass on their way north. Seattle, Washington, becomes the main jumping-off place for debarkation.

1897: Klondike fever is in full force and is the first gold rush to attract a press corps. Novelist Jack London is among those on the scene. This new find of gold revives interest (see 1890) in establishing a domestic mint, and discussion continues for several years thereafter, but no firm steps will be taken until 1901.

1898: The J.W. Scott & Co. series of *Standard Catalogues,* published in multiple editions during this era, continues to list and illustrate coins and tokens (mainly) of Canada and the provinces, but provides virtually nothing in the way of historical material. Nevertheless, their wide circulation continues to draw collectors to the Canadian series, mostly to the area of tokens, but rarely decimal coinage.

1899: The Canadian government redeems $18,895 face value in obsolete silver coins including 5-, 10-, and 20-cent pieces.

1900: Various proposals are made for the institution of a Canadian gold coinage, including one from a government accountant in Winnipeg who suggests that these be called the "beaver" and to be of "bold and active" appearance and be decorated with seven stars to represent the different provinces. By this time, the last year of the 19th century, the once ubiquitous provincial and private copper tokens have largely disappeared from circulation, even in remote areas. In larger cities they have been scarce for most of the decade. Many private coin collectors, and dealers too, issue their own brass tokens, and many bear Canadian addresses.

1901: The visage of Queen Victoria, familiar on British coins since 1838 and Canadian decimal issues since 1858, appears for the last time. By this time British coinage uses the "Old Head" or "Veiled Head," adopted in 1893, but Canadian coinage portrays her as somewhat younger. On May 21 the Ottawa Mint Act is introduced to provide for a Canadian branch of the Royal Mint, London, following efforts of Hon. W.S. Fielding, minister of finance. It is anticipated that this will provide a facility to coin vast quantities of gold from British Columbia and the Yukon, the latter being the site of the Klondike gold rush. Otherwise, the gold would be shipped to foreign mints. In

July the Department of the Interior opens an assay office in Vancouver. Meanwhile, the Royal Mint, London, is in the midst of a modernization program which in 1907 will result in the replacement of steam power by electricity.

1902: The coinage now depicts the heir to Victoria's throne, King Edward VII. Construction of the new mint is anticipated to begin, but does not.

1903: Only one million 10-cent pieces are coined, which will stand as the low-water mark for mintage of this denomination during the current reign.

1904: The mintage of 400,000 25-cent pieces is the lowest of this denomination during the reign of Edward VII. This and other silver coins of Edward are not well detailed on the obverse and become quickly abraded, creating issues that numismatists decades later will find to be rarities in Mint State, even if large numbers of pieces are made for circulation.

1905: Construction of the Ottawa Mint begins. Only 40,000 50-cent pieces are struck at the Royal Mint, London, which will prove to be the smallest mintage of the reign of Edward VII.

1906: The Canadian government redeems $7,461 face value in obsolete silver coins including 5-, 10-, and 20-cent pieces. By now the 1858 Canadian 20-cent piece is very scarce in circulation, except in Newfoundland where they are mixed in with Newfoundland coins of the same denomination (which continue to be minted). United States silver coins are accumulating in commercial channels, reminiscent of the Liberty Seated coinage nuisance of decades earlier. Canadian banks act as depots to receive United States coins and ship them to the New York City office of the Bank of Montreal. The Finance Department in Canada reimburses the banks for shipping charges and pays a commission of 3/8 of one percent to reimburse the institutions for their handling expenses. From March 1 through August 1 over $500,000 worth of silver coins is exported. However, quantities remain north of the border, and in January 1908 when Deputy Minister of Finance T.C. Boville seeks to determine the situation, he learns that in British Columbia—always a heavy user of larger silver denominations—about 75% of circulating coinage is from the United States.

1907: The Ottawa Mint is completed. The mintage of only 800,000 1907-H cents is at once the only Heaton Mint coin of this denomination, the lowest cent mintage of the Edwardian era, and the last H-mintmarked coinage ever made for the Dominion of Canada.

1908: Ottawa Mint opens on January 2. Governor General Earl Grey strikes the first coin, a silver 50-cent piece, and a few minutes later his wife, Countess Grey, strikes a bronze cent. Production of business strike silver coins commences on February 19. Specimen sets are issued for sale to the public. From this point onward, nearly all Dominion of Canada coins will be minted here, as will some contract coinage for other entities, notably Newfoundland. Dies continue to be made at the Royal Mint, London. Gold sovereigns (worth

£1 sterling) are struck for the first time, bear a C mintmark (the first such use), and will be made continuously through 1919. Few circulate within Canada, however, and they are mainly used in international trade. Unfortunately the gold production of British Columbia and the Yukon, which provided a reason in 1901 to begin steps to establish the mint, has diminished greatly.

1909: The American Numismatic Association holds its annual convention for the first time in Canada. Montreal furnishes the venue for a lot of in-fighting and bickering which had begun in 1908 and will continue through 1910. Numismatic entrepreneur Farran Zerbe is the controversial focal point of much dissension, with not many approving of his recent purchase of *The Numismatist* from the widow of its founder, Dr. George F. Heath of Monroe, Michigan. Just about everyone expected that it would be sold to the ANA, but, apparently, Zerbe sweet-talked Mrs. Heath into a private sale. Enter prominent Canadian collector W.W.C. Wilson, who will soon become the main factor in smoothing things when he purchases *The Numismatist* from Zerbe (who finds that running the magazine is a lot of work and not profitable) and presents it to the American Numismatic Association.

1910: Edward VII dies on May 6. This year is the swan song for his portrait on coins.

1911: The new coinage depicts King George V who is crowned on June 22. Specimen sets are issued for sale to the public, but not many find buyers. Dominion of Canada coins omit mention of the Deity (DEI GRA., for DEI GRATIA, "by the grace of God") on the obverse inscription, causing some public outcry (in 1907 a similar situation had occurred in the United States with the new gold $10 and $20 designs which omitted IN GOD WE TRUST; partway through 1908 President Theodore Roosevelt restored the motto). A separate gold refinery is set up at the Ottawa Mint; earlier refining had been done by the Assay Office at the same institution.

1912: Canadian $5 and $10 gold pieces are struck for the first time. This attractive coinage will continue for two more years, after which the government will have ideas of its own about controlling the gold supply, and this does not include the minting of coins (see 1914). The last 20-cent pieces are struck for Newfoundland; the denomination had been first minted in 1865. Meanwhile, the ephemeral 20-cent coinages for the Province of Canada (1858) and the United States (1875-1878) have been largely forgotten. In 1917 the Newfoundland 20-cent piece will be superseded in its silver series by a 25-cent piece, a value not coined earlier for this island.

1913: Interest in collecting early tokens of Canada, exceedingly popular in the 1890s (especially after the publication of Breton's 1894 book) and continuing past the turn of the century, begins to fade. The same happens on the United States token series as such scholars as Low and Wright are no longer on the scene. Thomas L. Elder will become a minority voice when he states that token collecting is a basic foundation stone of numismatics.

1914: $5 and $10 gold coins are minted for the last time. The Finance Department of the government seeks to control gold, and early in 1915 it decrees that henceforth it will prefer gold bars to coins of these denominations, but gold sovereigns, minted under a different authorization and supplied on demand to depositors of gold bullion, will continue to be made for the next several years. In August the World War commences after an unfortunate incident in Sarajevo. Canadians respond to the call, and volunteers assemble the First Canadian Division and go to France.

1915: Boom times begin in Canada and the United States as factories work overtime to provide material for the war in Europe. The economy expands, and for the next several years mintage quantities will increase.

1916: The Ottawa Mint strikes only 6,111 gold sovereigns, thus creating a coin that decades later will be recognized as a classic rarity. Apparently, most went to the United States Treasury and were melted.

1917: Newfoundland taps the Ottawa Mint to produce coins for it, and the 25-cent piece replaces the old 20-cent denominations; the Ottawa Mint will strike coins for Newfoundland through 1947, but 25-cent pieces are made only once again, in 1919. Coins bear a C mintmark. The Ottawa Mint does its part for the World War effort and makes sights and eyepieces for guns and also helps the Royal Mint (London) by making six million planchets for shillings.

1918: World War I ends in Europe, but over 50,000 Canadian soldiers will never come home. The momentum of the boom economy lingers and good times and high coinage quantities continue through 1920. The Ottawa Mint strikes coins under contract for Jamaica, these being in copper-nickel metal, the first quantity coinage of that alloy made in Ottawa.

1919: The last Canadian gold sovereign drops from the press, ending a series which started in 1908. The government has preferred gold bars for a long time (see 1914), and newly refined gold often goes to government vaults as security for gold-backed paper currency. A slightly modified bronze alloy is adopted for cents partway through the year, this making the planchets somewhat easier to strike and less susceptible to defects.

1920: The old-style "large cent" format, first used in 1858, gives way to the new small cent. Both types of cents are coined. Silver is high-priced on the international market, playing havoc with certain coinages in this metal. To forestall any problems, the fineness of the alloy in Canadian silver coins is reduced from 92.5% silver (sterling standard) to 80%.

1921: It is a tough year for the economy. The boom times engendered by the World War in Europe and the position of Canada as a supplier of material comes to an end. Times are tough, and commerce is slow. Although quite a few coins are minted as a result of the kinetic energy remaining from preceding good years, it turns out that there is an oversupply of coins, and in succeeding years many will be melted, including nearly all of the 1921-dated silver five-cent and

50-cent coins, which in time will become famous rarities. It turns out that this is the last year the silver five-cent piece will be minted.

1922: The format of the five-cent piece is changed to pure nickel and larger diameter, with a new reverse design. This will use up a lot of nickel, a metal with which Canada is well endowed, but which is a bit scarce in the United States. Mintage of the cent will total just 1,243,635, the smallest since the opening of the Ottawa Mint. Production quantities of coins will remain low for the next several years and will be non-existent for silver denomination.

1923: The American Numismatic Association holds its annual convention in Montreal, the second (and final) time a Canadian venue is selected. Years later the ANA Board of Governors will strongly reconsider the idea at the behest of John Jay Pittman, but border-crossing rules will make it virtually impossible for collectors and dealers to take coins back and forth easily. However, in 1962 a joint convention of the ANA and the Canadian Numismatic Association will be held in Detroit.

1924: No silver coinage is produced this year, nor has there been any since 1921, nor will there be any more until 1928. There is not a great deal of demand in the eastern provinces for silver, and British Columbia, where such pieces are widely used, apparently has enough.

1925: It is a good *numismatic* year for cents and nickels, what with their low mintages. Still no new silver coins. In November in New York City at the Anderson Galleries, Wayte Raymond conducts a three-day sale of the W.W.C. Wilson Collection, strong in Canadian Proofs and patterns (but with few circulation strikes and hardly complete by date) and many other important pieces. The catalogue notes: "No such assemblage of numismatic material pertaining to [Canada] has ever before been offered for sale. He bought many collections belonging to Canadian amateurs of his time, perhaps the most important being that of the late Thomas Wilson. . . . Canadian collectors will no doubt be appreciative of the opportunity to acquire rarities seldom offered."

1926: Some nickel five-cent pieces are struck with "Far 6," a minor date position variation. In later years some numismatists will consider it to be highly important, others will dismiss it as trivial.

1927: Supplies of silver coins minted 1921 and earlier are still adequate, and no new issues are produced.

1928: New issues of gold are contemplated. $5 and $10 denominations have not been struck since 1914, and base metal patterns with new designs are made, but no circulating coinage materializes. Silver coinage is resumed as more pieces are needed, especially by the central provinces.

1929: A new commercial demand arises for 50-cent pieces, which have not been minted since 1921. Many undistributed earlier coins are melted and recoined into currently dated pieces, creating a supply of this denomination that will suffice until 1931. Newfoundland silver five-cent and 10-cent pieces are coined for the first time since 1919, but will not be made again until 1938.

1930: Welcome to the first full year of the Depression. Although

50-cent pieces had been needed in 1929, enough were made then to fill all demand, and none are made in 1930.

1931: The Ottawa Mint changes its name to Royal Canadian Mint on December 1 and is put under the management of the Department of Finance of the Canadian government. It now operates independently, rather than as a small branch of the Royal Mint, London.

1932: The record high mintage of one-cent pieces, 21,316,190, will not be exceeded until 1939.

1933: Economic times continue to be difficult, and interest in Canadian numismatics is sluggish.

1934: In October, Prime Minister R.B. Bennett proposes issuing a silver dollar, and plans are made for implementation in the following year. Interest in coin collecting increases somewhat, perhaps reflective of the growing interest in hobbies to occupy one's spare time when jobs are scarce, and also in view of renewed strength in the United States coin market.

1935: Silver dollars are struck for the first time as circulating coinage, the purpose being to observe the 25th year on the throne of King George V. This becomes Canada's first commemorative coin. Like other commemoratives of the next several decades will be, it is made for circulating purposes and not sold at a premium. The new dollar is widely admired and attracts many to Canadian numismatics.

1936: King George V dies, and Edward VIII is expected to assume the throne and does on December 11. However, his complex personal life and intended marriage to an American divorcée preclude his remaining there, and he abdicates. George VI becomes king and in the next year is crowned. Meanwhile, early in 1937 it will be desired to make new Canadian coins featuring George VI, but dies will not be ready. Old dies of George V dated 1936 will be pressed (literally) into service, and to signify that the 1936-dated coins were actually made in calendar year 1937, a tiny dot will be placed on the bottom of the reverse of the cent, 10 cents, and 25 cents. In time these will become known as the "1936 Dot" issues, although no notice or account will be published of them at the time. The Toronto Coin Club is formed. This is the last year of the large-size bronze cent for Newfoundland, to be replaced in 1938 (there being no 1937 coinage for this island) by a small-diameter version.

1937: The year's coinage is the first to depict King George VI. Specimen sets are issued for sale to the public, drawing from an inventory of 1,295 struck. Designs of Canadian coins become distinctive and feature new reverses for the cent (maple leaf), five cents (beaver), 10 cents (fishing schooner), 25 cents (caribou), and 50 cents (arms of Canada). However, the Royal Mint in London is too busy to make the masters, and the work is farmed out to the Paris Mint. The dollar reverse continues the voyageur motif first used in 1935. In early 1937, "1936 Dot" coins (see preceding year) are minted and quietly released by the hundreds of thousands into circulation. For some unexplained reason, "Dot" cents and 10-cent pieces prove to be numismatic rarities, perhaps because the holes drilled into the dies to create the dot filled with debris, rendering the dot invisible. In New York City, Wayte Raymond, who deals in numismatic items and sells popular "National" brand albums, who recently distributed Oregon Trail commemorative half dollars, and who published the *Standard Catalogue of United States Coins,* issues *The Coins and Tokens of Canada.* This little guide will come out in later editions in 1947 and 1952 (and in the 1952 edition the rarity of the 1921 50-cents will be recognized for the first time). Before this time collectors have had no guide as to which decimal coins had been minted and which had not, which were rarities and which were common, and how many were minted. This paves the way for collecting decimal coins on a widespread basis. Raymond's "National" brand coin albums could be adapted for Canadian coins, thus making them easy to collect, and quite a few are sold for this purpose. In coming years it will be discovered that many "common" decimal coins are, in fact, great rarities if in Uncirculated preservation. However, right now no one has a clue that the 1921 five-cent and 1921 50-cent pieces are rarities, for their high mintage figures suggest otherwise. Further on the 1937 coinage of Canada, this is from the *Royal Canadian Mint Report:* "From a numismatic point of view, 1937 will long be remembered for the first important change since Confederation in the general type of Canadian subsidiary coins which now, in addition to the new series of reverse designs . . . have on the obverse the uncrowned Royal effigy, hitherto reserved for the coins of Great Britain, instead of the crowned effigy of former reigns. When in 1935 consideration was being given to the design of the first silver dollar, the legend on the obverse of which included a reference to the 25th anniversary of the accession of His late Majesty King George V, an informal suggestion that the Royal effigy on the new coin should be uncrowned was not favorably received, but I may now be permitted to say that the portrait of His former Majesty, King Edward VIII, approved for the new series of Canadian coins, but never actually used, was uncrowned. The uncrowned portrait now appears on the coinage of Great Britain, Canada, Australia, New Zealand, and South Africa, the crowned effigy [of George VI] being retained for the coinage of British India and of the British colonies and possessions."

1938: The mintage of only 90,304 silver dollars this year is a tiny fraction of the previous two years' quantity. The voyageur reverse is used this year, but will not be seen again until 1945.

1939: The "Royal Visit" by English monarchy in late spring furnishes the occasion to create a new reverse for the silver dollar, representing a view of the main section of the Canadian Parliament. This becomes Canada's second commemorative coin. On September 1 the Nazis invade Poland, and soon thereafter England and other countries including Canada (on September 10) declare war on Germany. The Canadian economy goes into overdrive and with it there is a tremendous additional demand for coins.

1940: Ottawa numismatist James Hector notices that some 1936 25-cent pieces have a strange little "dot" on the reverse. An inquiry is set into motion that eventually leads to the story of the "1936 Dot" coinage. G.R.L. Potter, prominent numismatist, eventually will publish the facts after consulting with Maurice Lafortune, an employee at the Mint when the "Dot" coinage was made. The Royal Mint, London, can no longer handle contract coinage for Newfoundland, and punches and masters for the island's denominations are shipped to the Royal Canadian Mint in Ottawa.

1941: Mintage of the 1941-C Newfoundland 10-cents is 483,630, far and away the highest production figure before or after for this island and denomination. A record is also set for the 1941-C silver five-cent piece with 612,641 made.

1942: Five-cent pieces are struck in tombac alloy, a kind of brass, to conserve nickel needed for war efforts; this alloy will also be used in 1944. To prolong die life the Mint chrome-plates one- and five-cent dies, thus giving the finished coins a mirrorlike appearance in many instances. Some die pairs of this and other years through 1944 are transitional, with one die being chrome-plated and the other not, thus resulting in one side of the coins being frosty and the other mirrorlike. Canadian Bankers Association proposes that a three-cent piece be coined, but the idea does not go beyond the idea stage.

1943: The "Victory" design adopted for the reverse of the five-cent piece bears a Morse Code inscription around the border. WE WIN WHEN WE WORK WILLINGLY. The World War II effort is in full swing. The Victory motif will be used through the last year of the war, 1945.

1944: Five-cent pieces are struck in steel for the first time and will continue in this metal through 1945, after which nickel will be reinstituted.

1945: Silver dollars are coined for the first time since 1939. The voyageur reverse, first used in 1935, is employed, as it will be on most other dollars for the next two decades. *Royal Canadian Mint Report:* "Every effort has been made during the last few years to increase the number of coins struck by each die or pair of dies. After much study and research more satisfactory results in lengthened die life are at last being achieved. Careful selection of the most suitable die steel for Mint work; efficient heat-treatment of the steel die in progress and proper hardening and tempering of the finished die; chromium plating the design of all dies; correct annealing of the silver and copper blanks for coinage; and constant training of the press operators, appears responsible for the increase of over 150% in the number of pieces struck per pair of dies. One pair of one-cent dies struck over 5,000,000 coins before being discarded through the wearing away of the design."

1946: Only 2,041 (estimated, per account of Mint official) 1946-C silver five-cent pieces are struck for Newfoundland, creating a modern day rarity. Actually, these will not be made until January 1947, but from 1946-C dies.

1947: It is déjà vu, and the "1936 Dot" scenario will be replayed, this time early in 1948 using 1947-dated dies marked with a tiny raised maple leaf for identification. The occasion will be the need for a new obverse die omitting mention of India, which is no longer a part of the British Empire. New dies will not be ready for 1948 coinage, so 1947 dies will be pressed (that pun again) into service in early 1948. An instant collectible will be created, and 1947 Maple Leaf coins from the cent to the dollar will become all the rage among what relatively few Canadian collectors there are at the time. This will set the scene for more numismatic excitement in 1948. In the date 1947 on certain coins, varieties are created in the shape and size of the downward tail. In this year the last coinage made specifically for Newfoundland leaves the presses at the Royal Canadian Mint. Fred Bowman's article, "The Decimal Coinage of Canada," appears in the March 1947 issue of *The Numismatist* and is the first detailed treatment of the subject ever to be published.

1948: The low mintage for the silver dollar this year creates a flurry of numismatic and investment interest, and buyers scurry to banks to buy all they can find.

1949: Newfoundland joins the Dominion of Canada, and the year's silver dollar, nearly all of which were made with prooflike surfaces, features on the reverse the ship that Henry Cabot used when he "discovered" Newfoundland in the 18th century. Dr. William H. Sheldon's grading system for United States large cents of the 1793–1814 era is published as part of *Early American Cents* (which will be retitled *Penny Whimsy* when an updated version is published in 1958). Years later, Sheldon's numerical system of numbers 1 to 70 will spread to Canada, and soon such designations as MS-60, MS-62, MS-65, etc., will be used, with most thinking that at long last, grading would be precise. Coin clubs are started in Ottawa, Regina, and Vancouver. This is a great era for coin clubs—the ideal forum to while away an evening discussing numismatics, in an era when television was not yet popular and no one had ever heard of personal computers, both of which will in due course absorb a lot of recreational time, to the detriment of sedentary hobbies.

1950: The Canadian Numismatic Association is formed. Numismatist Leslie C. Hill takes a survey in an effort to determine the relative rarity of certain classic Canadian rarities and finds these coins: 1936 Dot cent (located the whereabouts of 2); 1921 five cents (36) 1946-C Newfoundland five-cent piece (26); 1889 10 cents (16); 1936 Dot 10 cents (2); 1921 50 cents (5). While others would come to light later, this listing does serve to illustrate which varieties were on the "most wanted" lists of collectors at the time.

1951: In addition to the regular five-cent piece of the year, a special commemorative is made to observe the 200th anniversary of the isolation of nickel as a metal. Nickel, found in large quantities in Ontario, is a major factor in the Canadian economy. The Windsor Coin Club is formed.

1952: James E. Charlton, quiet-spoken dealer who operates the Canada Coin Exchange, issues his first guide. The *Catalogue of Canadian Coins, Tokens & Fractional Currency* will become the standard for the hobby and do much to advance it. G.R.L. Potter writes "Variations in Re-Engraved Dates of Canada's Large Cent of 1859" for the Canadian Numismatic Association *Bulletin.* Potter, active in the hobby for many years, is widely viewed as *the* old-timer to consult about technical and historical numismatic matters, and he shares some of his views about rarity with New York City dealer John J. Ford, Jr., among others. From the *Royal Canadian Mint Report,* 1952, relative to the coming year's coinage: "Canada has adopted for its coins the same uncrowned or classical effigy as the United Kingdom, Australia, New Zealand, the Union of South Africa, Southern Rhodesia and Ceylon. Canadian coins, however, will continue to use the form of inscription or royal title adopted some years ago. This inscription will read: 'Elizabeth II Dei Gratia Regina.' Her Majesty's profile on the coins is facing towards the right. It is a tradition in coinage practice that the royal effigy of a new sovereign should face in the direction opposite to that used on coins issued in the reign of the preceding sovereign. . . . Seventeen artists sent in models for the design for the uncrowned effigy of the Queen and that of Mrs. Mary Gillick was finally selected. Mrs. Gillick was accorded the privilege of sittings by Her Majesty. For the first time in the history of Canadian coinage, the master dies are being made at the Royal Canadian Mint, Ottawa. The plaster model of the uncrowned royal effigy was sent to Canada from the Royal Mint, London. The inscription was cut in the plaster model surrounding the effigy and an electrotype made, from which the dies are being reduced to the dimensions of all denominations of Canadian coins."

1953: This is the first year of coinage depicting Queen Elizabeth II. James E. Charlton, who is rapidly becoming recognized as the standard authority on Canadian coin prices, creates the word "prooflike," as the Royal Canadian Mint disavows that it ever made any Proof coins. A coin club is formed in London, Ontario. Many others will be formed in the 1950s and will do much to spur the hobby. On the United States side of the border John Jay Pittman is the most active collector of Canadian coins, having started his cabinet in the 1940s; later he becomes the first American to be president of the Canadian Numismatic Association. In Cleveland, Ohio, Emery May Holden Norweb, one of the leading collectors of American coins, begins in a serious way her specialty in Canadian coins by the acquisition of the remarkable William B. Tennant Collection through the efforts of John J. Ford, Jr. A Teletype service links Canadian and United States dealers. "Specimen" sets are widely sold to collectors for the first time, but some coins seem to be more mirrorlike than others. James E. Charlton will suggest later that only about 10% of the sets are prooflike enough to be equivalent to United States Proof coins.

1954: The Mint solves some of its quality-control problems, and beginning this year all of the sets sold to collectors at a premium are fully prooflike. In Cairo, Egypt, the collections of deposed King Farouk are sold at auctions; the coin holdings include many rarities. Among those attending from the United States are Hon. and Mrs. R. Henry Norweb and John Jay Pittman, who make many purchases including Canadian coins. Other Americans on hand include James P. Randall, Abe Kosoff, Sol Kaplan, Maurice Storck, and Hans M.F. Schulman, the last being on hand to try to collect from the Egyptian military junta some unpaid bills of the exiled king. The Canadian Numismatic Association holds its first convention; this will become an annual event. No Charlton catalogue is issued this year, the only break in the annual series.

1955: A shipment of silver dollars to the Playtex factory in Arnprior, Ontario, is found to contain coins which have the "error" of only two-and-one-half water lines to the right of the canoe, rather than the requisite four, an anomaly due to die preparation, not to any design change. The search is on for "Arnprior dollars," and, eventually, other earlier dates of silver dollars will be examined closely and found to have a shortage of water lines too, giving rise to the strange name, for example, "1950 Arnprior dollar"; Arnprior, although it remains capitalized, becomes an adjective meaning "two-and-one-half water lines," although some suggest that three water lines are okay, and still others yawn at the idea of being concerned at all about the little ripple lines. Interest in die varieties of all kinds increases.

1956: United States Proof sets rise in value to unprecedented heights, to peak in the spring. Meanwhile, Canadian prooflike sets seem ridiculously cheap by comparison, and investors in the United States start buying up some of these Canadian "Proof sets," as most call them. The *Canadian Numismatic Journal* makes its debut as successor to the *Bulletin* published by the Canadian Numismatic Association.

1957: Fred Bowman publishes his study on Canadian pattern coins, superseding R.W. McLachlan's earlier works. Jerome H. Remick is among the relatively few who research and publish about die varieties; his byline will extend over many years.

1958: "Totem Pole dollars" are struck with motifs pertaining to British Columbia. These catch the fancy of United States dealers, and Wilson Pollard (of Indiana) and other professionals buy large quantities of them for sale to collectors and investors.

1959: The Canadian market is very active and prooflike sets are in special demand.

1960: The boom in the Canadian coin market starts in earnest.

1961: Through articles in the *Canadian Numismatic Journal* that will continue to be published over a long period of succeeding years, R.C. Willey describes many technical die varieties of Canadian and provincial coinage and explores Canadian numismatic history.

1962: The investment market for Canadian coins is very active, and many United States collectors review mintage figures and coin availability of Canadian issues and conclude there are many good buys to be found. Bags and other quantities of newly minted Canadian coins are hoarded. Mint errors and oddities become popular, and it is found that significant errors are much rarer than in the United States series—remember all of those rejected coins in the 19th-century Royal Mint reports? In Detroit, Michigan, the 71st annual convention of the American Numismatic Association is held in cooperation with the ninth annual Canadian Numismatic Association convention, the first joint show of the two groups.

1963: The Canadian market for investment coins continues to be extremely active. The Canadian Numismatic Research Society is formed. J. Douglas Ferguson (1901-1982), one of the most prominent figures on the collecting scene, begins the transfer of his vast holdings of coins, currency, and tokens to the Bank of Canada, thus making strong the foundation for the National Currency Collection.

1964: New Netherlands Coin Co.'s 58th Sale, September 22–23, includes many Canadian rarities and other issues and attracts a lot of attention. Cataloguer John J. Ford, Jr., is perhaps the most technically knowledgeable United States dealer in the Canadian field, although many others are active. Canadian silver dollar features Charlottetown motif. The coin market reaches its apex—more dealers, more investors, higher prices than ever before. The Canadian Paper Money Society is formed.

1965: The "investor market" for Canadian coins all but disappears, and eventually many old-time numismatists who were sitting on the sidelines, checkbook in pocket, will reappear and became active buyers.

1966: The softening of the market continues as its hoped-for quick revival (and that of the related United States coin market) fail to materialize.

1967: New products at the Mint this year including a $20 gold coin give the market an upbeat pulse, but the stimulus is brief.

1968: The Royal Canadian Mint is extremely busy, and the work of coining some five-cent pieces is farmed out to the Philadelphia Mint. James A. Haxby publishes articles on Canadian decimal coinage and their history. In 1971 Haxby will join with researcher R.C. Willey to publish the first issue of *Coins of Canada,* a guide to information and prices. The Canadian coin market lapses back into relative desuetude, but in the 1970s it will revive with a new group of collectors.

ONE-CENT COIN

The first one-cent coin produced in Canada was struck by the Countess of Grey at the official opening of the Ottawa Branch of the Royal Mint on January 2, 1908. It weighed 5.67 grams and included 95% copper.

In 1937 the reverse design was changed to the maple leaf still used today. To speed production of Canadian coinage tools, the Royal Mint sent the model for the maple leaf design to the Paris Mint for conversion into master coining tools.

Today's one-cent coin, modified in 1997, is made of copper-plated zinc and costs approximately 0.9 cents to make.

The one-cent coin features two maple leaves on a sprig. Even between 1876 and 1901, before this current design was introduced, the maple leaf appeared on all Canadian coins. The maple tree's contribution of maple sap for food products, wood for building, and its distinctive visibility in the Canadian landscape makes it a valuable contributor to Canada's development. Featured on the Canadian flag and the coat of arms of Canada, the maple leaf has become one of the most prominent Canadian symbols.

	ABP FINE	AVERAGE FINE
Large Cent, Victoria, Copper, 1858–1901		
☐ 1858	$80.00	$200.00
☐ 1859, Bronze	5.00	8.00
☐ 1859, Brass	3000.00	5000.00
☐ 1859, Double Strike 9/8	250.00	400.00
☐ 1859, Double Strike 9/9	125.00	135.00
☐ 1876H	5.00	6.00
☐ 1881H	5.00	8.00
☐ 1882H	2.50	6.00
☐ 1884	4.00	8.00
☐ 1886	12.00	16.00
☐ 1887	4.00	7.00
☐ 1888	3.00	5.00
☐ 1890H	14.00	18.00
☐ 1891, Large Date	14.00	18.00
☐ 1891, Small Date, Large Leaves Reverse	125.00	175.00
☐ 1891, Small Date, Small Leaves Reverse	75.00	130.00
☐ 1892	7.00	14.00
☐ 1893	4.00	6.00
☐ 1894	12.00	20.00
☐ 1895	8.00	15.00
☐ 1896	2.00	6.00
☐ 1897	4.00	7.00
☐ 1898H	7.00	15.00
☐ 1899	5.00	7.00
☐ 1900	7.00	14.00
☐ 1900H	4.00	5.00
☐ 1901	2.00	4.00

Large Cent, Edward VII, Copper, 1902–1910

	ABP FINE	AVERAGE FINE
☐ 1902	$4.15	$7.25
☐ 1903	4.15	7.25
☐ 1904	4.15	7.25
☐ 1905	7.00	8.00
☐ 1906	4.15	7.25
☐ 1907	4.15	7.25
☐ 1907H	20.00	26.00
☐ 1908	4.15	7.25
☐ 1909	4.15	7.25
☐ 1910	4.15	7.25

Large Cent, George V, Copper, 1911–1920

	ABP FINE	AVERAGE FINE
☐ 1911	2.50	4.15
☐ 1912	2.50	4.15
☐ 1913	2.50	4.15
☐ 1914	2.50	4.15
☐ 1915	2.50	4.15
☐ 1916	.80	1.40
☐ 1917	.80	1.40
☐ 1918	.80	1.40
☐ 1919	.80	1.40
☐ 1920	.80	1.40

	ABP FINE	AVERAGE FINE
Small Cent, George V, Copper, 1920–1936		
☐ 1920	$2.25	$3.00
☐ 1921	2.25	3.00
☐ 1922	18.00	25.00
☐ 1923	18.00	32.00
☐ 1924	5.00	8.00
☐ 1925	20.00	32.00
☐ 1926	4.00	6.00
☐ 1927	2.00	4.00
☐ 1928	1.00	2.00
☐ 1929	1.00	2.00
☐ 1930	4.00	5.00
☐ 1931	1.20	2.00
☐ 1932	1.20	2.00
☐ 1933	1.20	2.00
☐ 1934	.75	1.50
☐ 1935	.75	1.50
☐ 1936	.75	1.50

	ABP FINE	AVERAGE FINE
Small Cent, George VI, Copper, 1937–1952		
☐ 1937	.42	.80
☐ 1938	.42	.80
☐ 1939	.42	.80
☐ 1940	.20	.40
☐ 1941	.20	.40
☐ 1942	.20	.40
☐ 1943	.20	.40
☐ 1944	.50	1.00
☐ 1945	.18	.28
☐ 1946	.18	.28
☐ 1947	.20	.35
☐ 1947, Reverse Change	.20	.35
☐ 1948	.50	.80
☐ 1949	.20	.32
☐ 1950	.20	.32
☐ 1951	.20	.32
☐ 1952	.20	.32

	ABP FINE	AVERAGE FINE
Small Cent, Elizabeth II, Copper, 1953 to Date		
☐ 1953	$ 2.00	$3.00
☐ 1953, No Shoulder Mark Obverse	.30	.60
☐ 1954	.35	.60
☐ 1954, No Shoulder Mark Obverse (Proof Only)		$475.00
☐ 1955	.25	.50
☐ 1955, No Shoulder Mark Obverse	125.00	200.00
☐ 1956	.32	.60
☐ 1957	.32	.60
☐ 1958	.32	.60
☐ 1959	.35	.60
☐ 1960	.35	.60
☐ 1961	.20	.30
☐ 1962	.20	.30
☐ 1963	.20	.30
☐ 1964	.20	.30
☐ 1965, Small Dots, Pointed 5 Reverse	1.00	1.25
☐ 1965, Small Dots, Flat 5 Reverse	.15	.30
☐ 1965, Large Dots, Flat 5 Reverse	.50	.80
☐ 1965, Large Dots, Pointed 5 Reverse	.50	.80
☐ 1966–1969	.75	1.75
☐ 1970–1979	.75	1.75
☐ 1980–1985	.40	.80
☐ 1985 Pointed 5	.35	.80
☐ 1986 to 1990	—	.20
☐ 1991 to Date*	—	—

*Face Value

FIVE-CENT COIN

Up until 1922 Canada's five-cent coins were made mostly of silver (92.5%, or sterling silver, until 1920, then 80%, or fine silver). In 1918 and 1919, the five-cent coin required more than one-third the silver allotted for coining.

The composition of the five-cent coin was changed to 100% nickel in 1922, saving the Canadian government about $150,000 per year.

Today's five-cent coin weighs 4.6 grams and is made of 75% copper and 25% nickel.

The five-cent coin shows a beaver on a log on a mound of earth rising out of the water. From the days of the first Canadian explorers, much-sought-after beaver pelts were central to the Canadian economy, given that the European fashion of the day demanded them for fur hats. Canada's largest rodent grew to represent Canada on the shield of the Hudson's Bay Company, on the armorial bearings of Quebec City and the city of Montreal, and even on the first Canadian postage stamp—the "Three Penny Beaver." Today the beaver is recognized as an emblem of Canada.

	ABP FINE	AVERAGE FINE
Five Cents, Victoria, Silver, 1858–1901		
☐ 1858, Small Date	$50.00	$80.00
☐ 1858, Large Date/Small Date	200.00	400.00
☐ 1870	18.00	32.00
☐ 1871	18.00	35.00
☐ 1872H	35.00	75.00
☐ 1874, Small Date	100.00	125.00
☐ 1874, Large Date	45.00	80.00
☐ 1875H, Small Date	265.00	535.00
☐ 1875H, Large Date	350.00	650.00
☐ 1880H	15.00	25.00
☐ 1881H	25.00	42.00
☐ 1882H	22.00	50.00
☐ 1883H	75.00	125.00
☐ 1884	160.00	400.00
☐ 1885, Small 5	30.00	50.00
☐ 1885, Large 5	40.00	75.00
☐ 1886, Small 6	30.00	50.00
☐ 1886, Large 6	18.00	40.00
☐ 1887	60.00	100.00
☐ 1888	20.00	30.00
☐ 1889	55.00	120.00
☐ 1890H	25.00	40.00
☐ 1891	15.00	35.00
☐ 1892	16.00	40.00
☐ 1893	12.00	20.00
☐ 1894	50.00	85.00
☐ 1896	20.00	30.00
☐ 1897	20.00	30.00

	ABP FINE	AVERAGE FINE
☐ 1898	$30.00	$55.00
☐ 1899	12.00	22.00
☐ 1900, Large Date, Round 0 Reverse	12.00	22.00
☐ 1900, Small Date, Condensed 0 Reverse	45.00	80.00
☐ 1901	12.00	22.00

Five Cents, Edward VII, Silver, 1902–1910

	ABP FINE	AVERAGE FINE
☐ 1902	5.00	10.00
☐ 1902H, Small Mint Mark	10.00	20.00
☐ 1902H, Large Mint Mark	4.00	10.00
☐ 1903	10.00	20.00
☐ 1903H Small Mint Mark	4.00	10.00
☐ 1903H Large Mint Mark	32.00	75.00
☐ 1904	6.00	12.00
☐ 1905	6.00	12.00
☐ 1906	4.00	6.00
☐ 1907	4.00	6.00
☐ 1908	14.00	22.00
☐ 1909	8.00	15.00
☐ 1910	4.00	7.00
☐ 1910 Type II	25.00	40.00

Five Cents, George V, Silver, 1911–1921

	ABP FINE	AVERAGE FINE
☐ 1911	4.25	6.15
☐ 1912	4.25	6.15
☐ 1913	4.25	6.15
☐ 1914	4.25	6.15
☐ 1915	15.00	25.00
☐ 1916	4.25	8.00
☐ 1917	4.25	5.00
☐ 1918	4.25	5.00

	ABP FINE	AVERAGE FINE
☐ 1919	$4.00	$6.25
☐ 1920	4.00	6.25
☐ 1921	1500.00	2400.00

Five Cents, George V, Nickel, 1922–1936

☐ 1922	2.00	5.00
☐ 1923	2.10	5.00
☐ 1924	1.60	5.00
☐ 1925	75.00	150.00
☐ 1926, 6 Close To Leaf Reverse	10.00	20.00
☐ 1926, 6 Far From Leaf Reverse	140.00	225.00
☐ 1927	2.40	4.15
☐ 1928	2.40	4.15
☐ 1929	2.40	4.15
☐ 1930	2.40	4.15
☐ 1931	2.40	4.15
☐ 1932	2.40	4.15
☐ 1933	2.40	4.50
☐ 1934	2.15	4.15
☐ 1935	2.15	4.15
☐ 1936	2.15	3.50

Five Cents, George VI, Nickel, 1937–1942

☐ 1937	.80	2.15
☐ 1938	1.50	4.00
☐ 1939	1.50	2.25
☐ 1940	1.15	2.15
☐ 1941	1.15	2.15
☐ 1942	1.15	2.15

	ABP FINE	AVERAGE FINE
☐ 1942, Beaver Reverse, Brass, 12 Sided	$ 1.00	$ 1.75
☐ 1943, Brass, 12 Sided	.30	.50
☐ 1944, Steel, 12 Sided	.60	1.15
☐ 1945, Steel, 12 Sided	.60	1.15
☐ 1946, Resume Nickel, 12 Sided	.60	1.15
☐ 1947	.60	1.15
☐ 1948	1.10	1.65
☐ 1949	.32	.70
☐ 1950	.32	.50
☐ 1951	.32	.50
☐ 1951, Commemorative Reverse	.32	.80
☐ 1952	.32	.80

Five Cents, Elizabeth II, Nickel-Clad Steel, 1953 to Date

☐ 1953	.20	.38
☐ 1954	.30	.50
☐ 1955, Nickel	.28	.38
☐ 1956	.28	.38
☐ 1957	.28	.38
☐ 1958	.28	.38
☐ 1959	.20	.40
☐ 1960	.15	.32
☐ 1961–1969	.15	.32
☐ 1970–1979	.15	.32
☐ 1980 to 1995	.12	.20
☐ 1996 to Date*	—	—

*Face Value

TEN-CENT COIN

With the price of silver rising in 1968, people began hoarding ten-cent coins as their composition still included 50% silver. Production of nickel coins was authorized in August of that year, but the Royal Canadian Mint could not meet the demand created by the combination of hoarding and circulation requirements.

The Canadian government was required, for the first time since the opening of the Mint, to fill part of the demand elsewhere. Eighty-five million ten-cent coins were ordered from the Philadelphia branch of the U.S. mint.

Ten-cent coins today are still made of 100% nickel. Each weighs 2.07 grams.

The ten-cent coin bears the image of a fishing schooner under sail. The fishing industry has traditionally been an important contributor to the Canadian coastal economy, not to mention the role of the great "tall ships" in the discovery of the "new world" and the colonization of Canada.

	ABP FINE	AVERAGE FINE
Ten Cents, Victoria, Silver, 1870–1901		
☐ 1858	$60.00	$125.00
☐ 1870, Condensed 0 Reverse	60.00	125.00
☐ 1870, Round 0 Reverse	125.00	220.00
☐ 1871	125.00	220.00
☐ 1871H	125.00	220.00
☐ 1872H	240.00	400.00
☐ 1874H	38.00	70.00
☐ 1875H	600.00	1000.00
☐ 1880H	55.00	85.00
☐ 1881H	55.00	85.00
☐ 1882H	55.00	85.00
☐ 1883H	150.00	250.00
☐ 1884	525.00	875.00
☐ 1885	150.00	225.00
☐ 1886, Small Date 6	110.00	150.00
☐ 1886, Large Date 6	110.00	150.00
☐ 1887	150.00	225.00
☐ 1888	40.00	80.00
☐ 1889	1400.00	2000.00
☐ 1890H	70.00	120.00
☐ 1891	70.00	120.00
☐ 1892	35.00	60.00
☐ 1893	75.00	140.00
☐ 1894	100.00	140.00
☐ 1896	35.00	65.00
☐ 1898	35.00	65.00

	ABP FINE	AVERAGE FINE
☐ 1899, Small Date 9	$35.00	$50.00
☐ 1899, Large Date 9	40.00	75.00
☐ 1900	40.00	55.00
☐ 1901	40.00	55.00

Ten Cents, Edward VII, Silver, 1902–1910

	ABP FINE	AVERAGE FINE
☐ 1902	20.00	45.00
☐ 1902H	10.00	20.00
☐ 1903	50.00	85.00
☐ 1903H	20.00	50.00
☐ 1904	38.00	60.00
☐ 1905	38.00	65.00
☐ 1906	25.00	42.00
☐ 1907	25.00	42.00
☐ 1908	32.00	60.00
☐ 1909, Victorian Leaf Reverse	32.00	50.00
☐ 1909, Wide Leaf Reverse	26.00	60.00
☐ 1910	10.00	30.00

Ten Cents, George V, Silver, 1911–1936

	ABP FINE	AVERAGE FINE
☐ 1911	12.00	25.00
☐ 1912	6.00	12.00
☐ 1913, Small Leaf Reverse	6.00	12.00
☐ 1913, Large Leaf Reverse	250.00	425.00
☐ 1914	4.00	8.00
☐ 1915	20.00	35.00
☐ 1916	4.00	6.25
☐ 1917	4.00	6.25
☐ 1918	4.00	6.25
☐ 1919	4.00	6.25

	ABP FINE	AVERAGE FINE
☐ 1920	$4.25	$6.50
☐ 1921	4.25	6.50
☐ 1928	4.25	6.50
☐ 1929	4.25	6.50
☐ 1930	4.25	6.50
☐ 1931	4.25	6.50
☐ 1932	6.00	10.00
☐ 1933	6.00	10.00
☐ 1934	15.00	25.00
☐ 1935	12.00	20.00
☐ 1936	4.00	7.00

Ten Cents, George VI, Silver, 1937–1952

	ABP FINE	AVERAGE FINE
☐ 1937	2.25	3.00
☐ 1938	2.25	5.00
☐ 1939	2.25	3.00
☐ 1940	2.25	4.00
☐ 1941	2.75	5.00
☐ 1942	4.00	6.25
☐ 1943	4.00	6.25
☐ 1944	4.00	6.25
☐ 1945	4.00	6.25
☐ 1946	4.00	6.25
☐ 1947	4.00	5.00
☐ 1947, Date Leaf Reverse	.25	2.50
☐ 1948	4.75	8.00
☐ 1949	3.00	4.25
☐ 1950	3.00	4.25
☐ 1951	3.00	4.25
☐ 1952	3.00	4.25

	ABP FINE	AVERAGE FINE
Ten Cents, Elizabeth II, Silver, 1953–1968		
☐ 1953	$2.00	$3.00
☐ 1954	2.00	3.00
☐ 1955	.80	1.40
☐ 1956	.80	1.40
☐ 1957	.80	1.40
☐ 1958	.80	1.40
☐ 1959	.80	1.40
☐ 1960	.42	.80
☐ 1961	.42	.80
☐ 1962	.42	.80
☐ 1963	.42	.80
☐ 1964	.42	.80
☐ 1965	.42	.80
☐ 1966	.42	.80
☐ 1967, 50% Silver	.32	.60
☐ 1968, 50% Silver	.32	.60

Ten Cents, Elizabeth II, Nickel, 1969 to Date		
☐ 1969	1.00	2.00
☐ 1970–1979	.60	.60
☐ 1980–1989	.20	.45
☐ 1990 to Date*	—	—

*Face Value

Twenty Cents, Victoria, Silver, 1858		
☐ 1858	100.00	150.00

TWENTY-FIVE-CENT COIN

In 1968 the twenty-five-cent coin composition was changed from part silver to 100% nickel for the same reason as the ten-cent coin.

To a collector the oldest coins are not always the most valuable. Because so few twenty-five-cent coins were made by the Mint in 1991, one of these in really good condition (showing minimal or no wear) may be worth up to $15 in numismatic circles.

The twenty-five-cent coin features the head of a caribou. The majestic caribou is a familiar sight in northern Canada, travelling in bands of 10 to 50 or herds of up to 100,000 during migration. They are a gregarious, curious animal whose easy adaptation to the changing Canadian seasons make it an ideal representative of Canadian wildlife.

	ABP FINE	AVERAGE FINE
Twenty-five Cents, Victoria, Silver, 1870–1901		
☐ 1870	$40.00	$80.00
☐ 1871	80.00	125.00
☐ 1871H	100.00	175.00
☐ 1872H	35.00	80.00
☐ 1874H	35.00	80.00
☐ 1875H	1200.00	1500.00
☐ 1880H, Condensed 0 Reverse	200.00	350.00
☐ 1880H, Wide 0 Reverse	500.00	635.00
☐ 1881H	60.00	120.00
☐ 1882H	80.00	135.00
☐ 1883H	80.00	135.00
☐ 1885	400.00	600.00
☐ 1886	65.00	125.00
☐ 1887	325.00	600.00
☐ 1888	50.00	120.00
☐ 1889	400.00	600.00
☐ 1890H	80.00	150.00
☐ 1891	180.00	325.00
☐ 1892	75.00	140.00
☐ 1893	240.00	450.00
☐ 1894	100.00	175.00

	ABP FINE	AVERAGE FINE
☐ 1899	$35.00	$55.00
☐ 1900	30.00	55.00
☐ 1901	30.00	55.00

Twenty-five Cents, Edward VII, Silver, 1902–1910

☐ 1902	30.00	55.00
☐ 1902H	30.00	55.00
☐ 1903	30.00	55.00
☐ 1904	100.00	150.00
☐ 1905	80.00	125.00
☐ 1906	35.00	60.00
☐ 1907	22.00	35.00
☐ 1908	60.00	100.00
☐ 1909	30.00	55.00
☐ 1910	25.00	52.00

Twenty-five Cents, George V, Silver, 1911–1936

☐ 1911	25.00	40.00
☐ 1912	20.00	32.00
☐ 1913	20.00	32.00
☐ 1914	20.00	32.00
☐ 1915	100.00	165.00
☐ 1916	12.00	25.00
☐ 1917	12.00	18.00
☐ 1918	12.00	18.00
☐ 1919	12.00	18.00
☐ 1920	12.00	18.00
☐ 1921	40.00	75.00

	ABP FINE	AVERAGE FINE
☐ 1927	$80.00	$125.00
☐ 1928	12.00	22.00
☐ 1929	12.00	22.00
☐ 1930	12.00	22.00
☐ 1931	15.00	30.00
☐ 1932	20.00	38.00
☐ 1933	20.00	38.00
☐ 1934	20.00	38.00
☐ 1935	20.00	32.00
☐ 1936	8.00	15.00

Twenty-five Cents, George VI, Silver, 1937–1952

	ABP FINE	AVERAGE FINE
☐ 1937	2.00	4.15
☐ 1938	2.25	5.00
☐ 1939	2.00	4.15
☐ 1940	2.00	4.15
☐ 1941	2.00	4.15
☐ 1942	2.00	4.15
☐ 1943	2.00	4.15
☐ 1944	2.00	4.15
☐ 1945	2.00	4.15
☐ 1946	2.50	5.00
☐ 1947	2.50	5.00
☐ 1947, Date Leaf Reverse	2.00	4.15
☐ 1948	2.00	4.15
☐ 1949	2.00	4.15
☐ 1950	2.00	4.15
☐ 1951	2.00	4.15
☐ 1952	2.00	4.15

	ABP FINE	AVERAGE FINE
Twenty-five Cents, Elizabeth II, Silver, 1953–1968		
☐ 1953	$2.00	$3.50
☐ 1954	2.60	5.00
☐ 1955	3.00	4.25
☐ 1956	3.00	4.25
☐ 1957	3.00	4.25
☐ 1958	3.00	4.25
☐ 1959	1.20	2.40
☐ 1960	1.20	2.40
☐ 1961	1.20	2.40
☐ 1962	1.20	2.40
☐ 1963	1.20	2.40
☐ 1964	.75	2.00
☐ 1965	.75	2.00
☐ 1966	.75	2.00
☐ 1967	.75	2.00
☐ 1968, 50% Silver	—	2.00

	ABP FINE	AVERAGE FINE
Twenty-five Cents, Elizabeth II, Nickel, 1969 to Date		
☐ 1969	—	.60
☐ 1970–1980	—	.40
☐ 1980 to Date*	—	—

*Face Value

FIFTY-CENT COIN

On January 2, 1908, the official opening of the Ottawa branch of the Royal Canadian Mint was commemorated with the striking of a fifty-cent piece by Governor General Earl Grey.

Today, because there is so little public demand for it, relatively few fifty-cent coins are struck each year. For example, only 629,000 fifty-cent coins dated 1995 were struck, compared with 559,047,000 of the Canadian coin that generates the highest demand, the one-cent coin.

Canada's fifty-cent coin bears the coat of arms of Canada. The design, modified in 1994, honors the four founding nations of Canada (England, Scotland, Ireland, and France). The inscription,

"A Mari usque ad Mare," meaning "from sea to sea," scrolls across the ribbon flowing above the Four Floral Emblems. A second inscription, "Desiderantes meliorem patriam," meaning "they desire a better country," is written on a ribbon placed behind the shield.

	ABP FINE	AVERAGE FINE
Fifty Cents, Victoria, Silver, 1870–1901		
□ 1870	$1500.00	$2400.00
□ 1870, Initial LCW Obverse	225.00	375.00
□ 1871	240.00	400.00
□ 1871H	350.00	500.00
□ 1872H	250.00	400.00
□ 1872H, A/V Obverse	450.00	825.00
□ 1881H	250.00	400.00
□ 1888	400.00	700.00
□ 1890H	1200.00	2000.00
□ 1892	235.00	500.00
□ 1894	1000.00	1500.00
□ 1898	250.00	500.00
□ 1899	325.00	600.00
□ 1900	160.00	300.00
□ 1901	165.00	300.00

	ABP FINE	AVERAGE FINE
Fifty Cents, Edward VII, Silver, 1902–1910		
□ 1902	125.00	150.00
□ 1903H	125.00	150.00
□ 1904	200.00	425.00
□ 1905	700.00	1000.00
□ 1906	75.00	140.00

	ABP FINE	AVERAGE FINE
☐ 1907	$85.00	$125.00
☐ 1908	110.00	235.00
☐ 1909	200.00	275.00
☐ 1910	40.00	90.00

Fifty Cents, George V, Silver, 1911–1936

☐ 1911	175.00	325.00
☐ 1912	80.00	140.00
☐ 1913	80.00	140.00
☐ 1914	115.00	225.00
☐ 1916	32.00	75.00
☐ 1917	35.00	50.00
☐ 1918	28.00	42.00
☐ 1919	28.00	42.00
☐ 1920	28.00	42.00
☐ 1921	25,000.00	30,000.00
☐ 1929	20.00	35.00
☐ 1931	45.00	85.00
☐ 1932	225.00	425.00
☐ 1934	72.00	125.00
☐ 1936	72.00	125.00

Fifty Cents, George VI, Silver, 1937–1952

☐ 1937	6.00	8.00
☐ 1938	8.00	18.00
☐ 1939	8.00	18.00
☐ 1940	4.00	6.15
☐ 1941	4.00	6.15
☐ 1942	4.00	6.15
☐ 1943	4.00	6.15
☐ 1944	4.00	6.15

	ABP FINE	AVERAGE FINE
☐ 1945	$2.00	$5.00
☐ 1946	2.00	5.00
☐ 1947, Straight 7 Reverse	7.00	12.00
☐ 1947, Curved 7 Reverse	7.00	12.00
☐ 1947, Straight 7 With Leaf Reverse	25.00	50.00
☐ 1947, Curved 7 With Leaf Reverse	800.00	1500.00
☐ 1948	45.00	100.00
☐ 1949	4.00	6.00
☐ 1950	4.00	6.00
☐ 1951	4.00	6.00
☐ 1952	4.00	6.00

Fifty Cents, Elizabeth II, Silver, 1953–1967

	ABP FINE	AVERAGE FINE
☐ 1953, Small Date	2.00	4.00
☐ 1953, Large Date	2.25	5.00
☐ 1953, Large Date With Shoulder Line Reverse	2.25	5.00
☐ 1954	2.25	5.00
☐ 1955	3.00	5.00
☐ 1956	1.50	3.50
☐ 1957	2.00	4.00
☐ 1958	2.00	4.00
☐ 1959	2.00	4.00
☐ 1960	2.00	4.00
☐ 1961	2.00	4.00
☐ 1962	2.00	4.00
☐ 1963	2.00	4.00
☐ 1964	2.00	4.00
☐ 1965	2.00	4.00
☐ 1966	2.00	4.00
☐ 1967	2.00	4.00

	ABP FINE	AVERAGE FINE
Fifty Cents, Elizabeth II, Nickel, 1968 to Date		
☐ 1968	—	$ 1.25
☐ 1969	—	1.20
☐ 1970–1979	—	1.20
☐ 1980–1989	—	.60
☐ 1990 to Date*	—	—

*Face Value

ONE-DOLLAR COIN

Canada's first one-dollar coin for circulation was struck in 1935 and featured the classic voyageur design showing an Indian and a voyageur, a traveling agent for a fur company, paddling a canoe. The Royal Canadian Mint had intended to use this same design when reintroducing a circulating one-dollar coin in 1987 but the dies were lost on their way to the Winnipeg manufacturing facility, so another design—the now famous common loon—was chosen to replace it.

The one-dollar coin depicts a loon in water. The haunting call of the loon characterizes wildlife habitats throughout the Canadian wetlands. It is one of Canada's most graceful birds, illustrated for this coin by one of Canada's most well-known wildlife artists, Robert-Ralph Carmichael.

Dollars, George V, Silver, 1935–1936		
☐ 1935	12.00	20.00
☐ 1936	10.00	16.00

	ABP FINE	AVERAGE FINE
Dollars, George VI, Silver, 1937–1952		
☐ 1937	$8.00	$15.00
☐ 1938	20.00	50.00
☐ 1939	4.00	9.00
☐ 1945	75.00	125.00
☐ 1946	12.00	25.00
☐ 1947, 7 Without Tail Reverse	55.00	100.00
☐ 1947, 7 With Tail Reverse	100.00	175.00
☐ 1948	400.00	625.00
☐ 1949, Ship Reverse	10.00	18.00
☐ 1950	10.00	18.00
☐ 1950, Water Line Reverse	10.00	18.00
☐ 1951	4.00	7.00
☐ 1951, Water Line Reverse	16.00	30.00
☐ 1952	8.00	14.00
☐ 1952, Water Line Reverse	8.00	14.00

	ABP FINE	AVERAGE FINE
Dollars, Elizabeth II, Silver, 1953–1967		
☐ 1953	4.00	10.00
☐ 1953, Line On Shoulder Obverse	4.00	10.00
☐ 1954	6.00	10.00
☐ 1955	4.00	10.00
☐ 1955, No Water Lines Reverse	35.00	65.00
☐ 1956	6.00	15.00
☐ 1957	5.00	10.00
☐ 1957, No Water Lines Reverse	4.00	6.00
☐ 1958, Commemorative Reverse	4.50	8.00
☐ 1959	4.00	6.50
☐ 1960	4.00	6.00
☐ 1961	4.00	6.00
☐ 1962	4.00	6.00
☐ 1963	4.00	6.00
☐ 1964, Commemorative Reverse	4.00	6.00
☐ 1965, Small Dot Obverse, 5 With Tail Reverse	4.00	6.00
☐ 1965, Small Dot Obverse, 5 Without Tail Reverse	4.00	6.00

	ABP FINE	AVERAGE FINE
☐ 1965, Large Dot Obverse, 5 With Tail Reverse	$4.00	$6.00
☐ 1965, Large Dot Obverse, 5 Without Tail Reverse	4.00	6.00
☐ 1966, Small Dot Obverse	4.00	6.00
☐ 1966, Large Dot Obverse	4.00	6.00
☐ 1967, Commemorative Reverse	4.00	6.00

Dollars, Elizabeth II, Nickel, 1968–1987

	ABP FINE	AVERAGE FINE
☐ 1968	—	1.75
☐ 1969	—	1.75
☐ 1970, Commemorative Manitoba Reverse	—	1.75
☐ 1971, Commemorative British Columbia Reverse	—	1.75
☐ 1972	—	1.75
☐ 1973, Commemorative Prince Edward Reverse	—	1.75
☐ 1974, Commemorative Winnipeg Reverse	—	1.75
☐ 1975	—	1.75
☐ 1976	—	1.75
☐ 1977, Short Line Reverse	—	2.00
☐ 1977, Long Line Reverse	—	2.00
☐ 1978	—	1.75
☐ 1979	—	1.75
☐ 1980	—	1.75
☐ 1981	—	1.75
☐ 1982	—	1.75
☐ 1983, Commemorative Constitution Reverse	—	1.75
☐ 1984	—	1.75
☐ 1984, Commemorative Jaques Carter Reverse	—	2.50
☐ 1985	—	1.50
☐ 1986	—	4.00
☐ 1987, Commemorative Voyager Reverse—Sets Only	—	4.00

	ABP FINE	AVERAGE FINE
Dollars, Elizabeth II, Nickel-Bronze, 1987 to Date		
☐ 1987, Loon Reverse	—	$1.40
☐ 1988, Loon Reverse	—	1.40
☐ 1989, Loon Reverse	—	1.40
☐ 1990, Loon Reverse	—	1.40
☐ 1991, Loon Reverse	—	1.40
☐ 1992, Loon Reverse	—	1.40
☐ 1992, Commemorative Canada's 125th Birthday Reverse	—	1.25
☐ 1993, Loon Reverse	—	1.25
☐ 1994, Loon Reverse	—	1.25
☐ 1994, Commemorative War Memorial Reverse	—	1.25
☐ 1995, Commemorative Peace Reverse	—	1.25
☐ 1995, Loon Reverse to Date*	—	1.25

*Face Value

TWO-DOLLAR COIN

February 19, 1996, was the birthday of Canada's two-dollar coin. The Canadian government will save an estimated $250 million over the first 20 years of the coin's use because the coins last about 20 times longer than the $2 notes they replaced.

The two-dollar coin is the newest addition to Canadian circulation coinage and introduces a bimetallic coin-locking mechanism patented by the Royal Canadian Mint. The reverse of the coin shows an adult polar bear in early summer on an ice floe. The polar bear, native to northern Canada and the Arctic, is the largest land-based carnivore, with a full-grown male sometimes attaining a total length of 9.5 feet and weighing up to 1,600 pounds.

	ABP FINE	AVERAGE FINE
Two Dollar, Elizabeth II, Nickel-Aluminum-Bronze, 1996		
□ 1996 to 1999	—	$4.00
□ 2000 to Date*	—	—

*Face Value

Gold Coinage of Canada

Courtesy of Q. David Bowers

Gold sovereigns (equivalent to one pound sterling in British funds) were made at the Ottawa Mint from 1908 to 1916. The designs were the same as sovereigns made elsewhere in the British Empire and were identified as being of Canadian origin only by their C mint mark. The Canadian and other British Empire pieces bore no mark of denominations, and were mainly used as international trade coins. Some numismatists have suggested that these are British, not Canadian, coins but as they were struck at the Ottawa Mint and bear C mint marks, virtually every Canadian specialist we have encountered desires examples as part of an advanced cabinet.

In 1908 gold coins of the United States were readily available at Canadian banks in medium- and large-size cities, as they had been for many years. The $2 gold issues of Newfoundland 1865–1888 had been popular at one time, but were mostly withdrawn beginning about 1894, due to a financial crisis on that island. When plans were laid in 1901 for the Ottawa Mint, gold from the Klondike and British Columbia was plentiful, and a generous annual production of Canadian gold coins was anticipated, perhaps up to two million a year. However, by 1908 when the Ottawa Mint opened, newly refined gold supplies had diminished sharply. Thus, given the American gold coins already in circulation and the smaller incoming quantities of raw metal, the need for domestically minted gold coins lessened.

Fewer than a thousand gold sovereigns were struck in Ottawa in 1908, these all being matte Specimens intended for souvenirs and numismatic purposes, after which production quantities increased, but never even remotely challenged the two-million capacity. These gold sovereigns did not replace the United States issues, but were primarily used in export transactions or acquired by travellers desiring to go to other countries in the British Empire, throughout which sovereigns were ubiquitous. Most Canadian sovereigns of the 1908–1919 years thus found their way to foreign banks. The writer recalls that in the late 1960s and early 1970s cloth bags of unsorted British Empire sovereigns were a popular investment with "hard money" advocates. Most such quantities came from Swiss banks.

Among the pieces, which were mostly made in England, would be found a few coins with worldwide mint marks including C for Ottawa. The typical grade of such coins was EF to AU with lustre.

The Coinage Act of 1910 authorized Canadian denominations of $2.50, $5, $10, and $20 in 90% gold and of weights of 64.5, 129, 258, and 516 grains. However, only the $5 and $10 values were ever struck. Under this legislation Canadian $5 gold coins of slightly heavier weight and of different design were made from 1912 through 1914, were denominated as FIVE DOLLARS, and were used within Canada (and also in the export trade). Canadian coins denominated TEN DOLLARS were made from 1912 through 1914 inclusive. The reverse design of the $5 and $10 gold coins, by W. H. J. Blakemore, displays a Canadian coat of arms depicting the four founding provinces (clockwise from upper left): Ontario, Quebec, New Brunswick, and Nova Scotia. Both of these denominations differed from the "generic" gold sovereigns in that the $5 and $10 pieces had inscriptions specifically relating to Canada. An effort was made to call these coins "Georges" and "Double Georges," but the cognomens never took hold.

In 1928 strong consideration was given to the revival of Canadian gold-coin production, and patterns were struck in bronze. However, no circulating coinage materialized. After 1933, when the United States discontinued striking gold coins, the thought of Canadian gold issues became even more distant. In 1967 gold commemoratives were issued and sold at a premium, but by this time no world country had a circulating coinage in this metal. Later, additional gold commemoratives were produced. To cater to demand for bullion gold, Canada has issued "Maple Leaf" gold discs from 1979 to the present.

	ABP UNC	AVERAGE UNC
Five Dollar, George V, 1912–1914		
☐ 1912	$125.00	$195.00
☐ 1913	125.00	195.00
☐ 1914	175.00	300.00

	ABP UNC	AVERAGE UNC
Ten Dollar, George V, Gold, 1912–1914		
☐ 1912	300.00	350.00
☐ 1913	300.00	350.00
☐ 1914	200.00	400.00

	ABP UNC	AVERAGE UNC
Sovereigns, Edward VII, Gold, 1908–1910		
☐ 1908C	1500.00	2500.00
☐ 1909C	175.00	300.00
☐ 1910C	175.00	300.00

	ABP UNC	AVERAGE UNC
Sovereigns, George V, Gold, 1911–1919		
☐ 1911C	85.00	225.00
☐ 1913C	400.00	600.00
☐ 1914C	200.00	325.00
☐ 1916C	6500.00	12000.00
☐ 1917C	175.00	215.00
☐ 1918C	175.00	215.00
☐ 1919C	175.00	215.00

Canada—Coinage of New Brunswick

Courtesy of Q. David Bowers

As is the case with other districts of British North America, coins in circulation in New Brunswick in the early days were a curious admixture of United States, British, and other foreign issues to which were added examples from a New Brunswick halfpenny and penny coinage of 1843 and 1854 struck for the province by private firms in England (Soho Mint and Heaton Mint respectively).

In 1850 and 1851, discussions were held concerning the adoption of a decimal system, culminating in a meeting of various agents of British North America districts held in Toronto on June 1 of the latter year. At the time the American dollar was in the widest use in local trade, but England preferred that its scheme of pounds, shillings, and pence take precedence. The ideas of residents of New Brunswick were often at odds with those of the English authorities to whom they reported. Moreover, what was happening in distant New Brunswick and the needs of that province seemed to be of minor importance in England.

Among proposals made in the 1850s and 1860s was for a gold coin to be smaller than a British gold sovereign, equal to $2 or 100 pence, and to be called a ducat or royal. Another suggestion was for a North American gold "pound" to contain 92.877 grains of pure gold. By mathematics it was determined that as a British gold sovereign had 113 grains of gold and was worth close to $4.87 in United States funds, this North American pound would be worth $4 U.S., and the half pound would be worth $2. The coinage of a gold dollar was also considered, but confreres believed that the United States had found this denomination too small for convenience, and the thought was dropped. Although New Brunswick never had its own gold coins of any denomination, the Newfoundland $2 issue of 1865 was a direct result of these monetary discussions.

In 1858 the Province of Canada placed an order for decimal-based coins with England, prompting New Brunswick to consider similar action. On April 9, 1860, the lieutenant-governor of New Brunswick approved a request that $10,000 worth of bronze cents, $5,000 in silver 5-cent coins, $15,000 in 10-cent pieces, and $30,000 face value of 20-cent pieces be struck in England. The designs were to be similar to the Canadian issues of 1858, except for the marking NEW BRUNSWICK instead of CANADA.

Across the Atlantic Ocean, the British Colonial Office felt that it would be a mistake for New Brunswick to have 10- and 20-cent coins made, as they had heard via Inspector General A.T. Gault that Canada was experiencing difficulty distributing its similarly denominated issues of 1858. The office suggested that values of 12½ cents and 25 cents be coined instead. No matter, the Executive Council in New Brunswick wanted the coins it had originally ordered, and reiterated the request. Meanwhile, there was a coin shortage in New Brunswick, and between October 29, 1860, and October 31, 1861, $8,000 face value of Canadian bronze cents—presumably mostly dated 1859—were brought in. Apparently, others were brought in as well, as a number of Canadian numismatic texts place the number of coins at 100,000 (or $10,000 face).

On November 22, 1861, 12 reverse dies for New Brunswick were made at the Royal Mint, London. Two major errors were made in the process. Instead of following the instructions to adapt Province of Canada designs by changing the wording to NEW BRUNSWICK, someone at the Royal Mint decided to use *Nova Scotia* designs instead, the latter province having ordered copper coins at around the same time. The reverse motif of the Nova Scotia pieces, designed by C. Hill and cut by Leonard Charles Wyon, was of Nova Scotia flavor and depicted a wreath of roses and mayflowers well known in that district, but not relative at all to New Brunswick. Apparently, Wyon thought that one British North America province was about the same as another. On a later occasion in 1862, the Province of Canada maple leaf design was arbitrarily assigned to the reverse of the New Brunswick silver 20-cent piece.

In another misjudgment, 12 reverse dies were made at the Royal Mint for a New Brunswick *half cent,* although that province had placed no such order (but Nova Scotia had). Once again, the coinage interests of New Brunswick were of little importance to the British authorities, and certain of the resulting issues differed from what had been requested.

While Canadian cents of 1858 and 1859 had been struck to the ratio of 100 coins per one pound weight avoirdupois, the cents of New Brunswick and Nova Scotia were made at the weight of 80 to the pound, concurrent with the new British halfpenny standard adopted in 1860. The diameter of one inch was the same as the Canadian cent, however.

The first New Brunswick silver coins were received from the Royal Mint on August 18, 1862. Silver issues with a face value of $50,206.65 cost the province $48,165.62, thus the seignorage was negligible, unlike the bronze issues which yielded a large profit.

As it turned out, coinage for New Brunswick was ephemeral and lasted only through 1864. In that year the province joined with Quebec, Ontario, and Nova Scotia to form the Dominion of Canada, thus ending the need for a local coinage. Further historical details are given under the individual descriptions below.

One of the finest books ever to be published on a Canadian specialty, Richard W. Bird's *Coins of New Brunswick,* is recommended for readers interested in the fascinating historical details and other aspects of the coinage. Certain of the coins illustrated are from our past auction sales.

	ABP FINE	AVERAGE FINE
Half Cent, Victoria, Copper, 1861		
☐ 1861	$150.00	$250.00

	ABP FINE	AVERAGE FINE
Large Cents, Victoria, Copper, 1861–1864		
☐ 1861	12.00	20.00
☐ 1864	12.00	20.00

	ABP FINE	AVERAGE FINE
Five Cents, Victoria, Silver, 1862–1864		
☐ 1862	140.00	225.00
☐ 1864	140.00	225.00

	ABP FINE	AVERAGE FINE
Ten Cents, Victoria, Silver, 1862–1864		
☐ 1862	$115.00	$220.00
☐ 1862, Double 2 Reverse	150.00	250.00
☐ 1864	115.00	220.00

Twenty Cents, Victoria, Gold, 1862–1864		
☐ 1862	65.00	120.00
☐ 1864	65.00	120.00

Canada—Newfoundland

Small Cents, Victoria, Copper, 1865–1896		
☐ 1865	$7.00	12.00
☐ 1872H	7.00	12.00
☐ 1873	12.00	20.00
☐ 1876H, 0 In Date	8.00	15.00
☐ 1880, Condensed 0, Reverse	150.00	275.00
☐ 1880, Wide 0 In Date Reverse	10.00	20.00
☐ 1885	60.00	100.00
☐ 1888	35.00	80.00
☐ 1890	12.00	18.00
☐ 1894	12.00	18.00
☐ 1896	12.00	18.00

	ABP FINE	AVERAGE FINE
Small Cents, Edward VII, Copper, 1904–1909		
☐ 1904H	$20.00	$40.00
☐ 1907	6.00	10.00
☐ 1909	6.00	10.00

	ABP FINE	AVERAGE FINE
Small Cents, George V, Copper, 1913–1936		
☐ 1913	2.60	4.15
☐ 1917C	2.60	4.15
☐ 1919C	2.60	4.15
☐ 1920C	2.60	4.15
☐ 1929	2.60	4.15
☐ 1936	2.60	4.15

	ABP FINE	AVERAGE FINE
Small Cents, George VI, Copper, 1938–1947		
☐ 1938	.85	2.20
☐ 1940	2.25	5.00
☐ 1941C	1.15	2.20
☐ 1942	1.15	2.20
☐ 1943C	1.15	2.20
☐ 1944C	2.00	5.00
☐ 1947C	2.00	4.00

	ABP FINE	AVERAGE FINE
Five Cents, Victoria, Silver, 1865–1896		
☐ 1865	$60.00	$115.00
☐ 1870	75.00	125.00
☐ 1872H	60.00	115.00
☐ 1873	175.00	335.00
☐ 1873H	1400.00	2200.00
☐ 1876H	100.00	200.00
☐ 1880	70.00	125.00
☐ 1881	100.00	175.00
☐ 1882H	40.00	80.00
☐ 1885	200.00	335.00
☐ 1888	80.00	165.00
☐ 1890	50.00	80.00
☐ 1894	50.00	80.00
☐ 1896	12.00	20.00

Five Cents, Edward VII, Silver, 1903–1908		
☐ 1903	22.00	50.00
☐ 1904H	18.00	30.00
☐ 1908	8.00	15.00

	ABP FINE	AVERAGE FINE
Five Cents, George V, Silver, 1912–1929		
☐ 1912	$6.00	$12.00
☐ 1917C	6.00	12.00
☐ 1919C	7.00	14.00
☐ 1929	6.00	8.00

	ABP FINE	AVERAGE FINE
Five Cents, George VI, Silver, 1938–1947		
☐ 1938	2.00	5.00
☐ 1940C	2.00	5.00
☐ 1941C	2.00	4.00
☐ 1942C	2.00	4.00
☐ 1943C	2.00	4.00
☐ 1944C	2.00	4.00
☐ 1945C	2.00	4.00
☐ 1946C	160.00	325.00
☐ 1947C	4.00	7.00

	ABP FINE	AVERAGE FINE
Ten Cents, Victoria, Silver, 1865–1896		
☐ 1865	$75.00	$140.00
☐ 1870	300.00	575.00
☐ 1872H	40.00	75.00
☐ 1873	85.00	185.00
☐ 1876H	70.00	140.00
☐ 1880	90.00	190.00
☐ 1882H	90.00	190.00
☐ 1885	165.00	325.00
☐ 1888	85.00	175.00
☐ 1890	28.00	45.00
☐ 1894	28.00	45.00
☐ 1896	28.00	45.00

Ten Cents, Edward VII, Silver, 1903–1904		
☐ 1903	50.00	80.00
☐ 1904H	20.00	45.00

Ten Cents, George V, Silver, 1912–1919		
☐ 1912	12.00	20.00
☐ 1917C	12.00	20.00
☐ 1919C	12.00	20.00

	ABP FINE	AVERAGE FINE
Ten Cents, George VI, Silver, 1938–1947		
☐ 1938	$1.50	$4.00
☐ 1940	2.00	4.00
☐ 1941C	2.00	4.00
☐ 1942C	2.00	4.00
☐ 1943C	2.00	4.00
☐ 1944C	1.75	4.00
☐ 1945C	1.00	2.00
☐ 1946C	8.00	14.00
☐ 1947C	2.25	6.00

	ABP FINE	AVERAGE FINE
Twenty Cents, Victoria, Silver, 1865–1900		
☐ 1865	30.00	85.00
☐ 1870	70.00	150.00
☐ 1872H	30.00	75.00
☐ 1873	60.00	115.00
☐ 1876H	75.00	140.00
☐ 1880	75.00	140.00
☐ 1881	50.00	100.00
☐ 1882H	45.00	75.00
☐ 1885	50.00	115.00
☐ 1888	70.00	115.00
☐ 1890	70.00	115.00
☐ 1894	30.00	55.00
☐ 1896, Small Date	30.00	55.00
☐ 1896, Large Date	65.00	100.00
☐ 1899, Small Date	65.00	100.00

	ABP FINE	AVERAGE FINE
☐ 1899, Large Date	$45.00	$75.00
☐ 1900	15.00	25.00

Twenty Cents, Edward VII, Silver, 1904

☐ 1904H	45.00	80.00

Twenty Cents, George V, Silver, 1912

☐ 1912	10.00	14.00

Twenty-five Cents, George V, Silver, 1917–1919

☐ 1917C	4.00	8.00
☐ 1919C	4.00	8.00

	ABP FINE	AVERAGE FINE
Fifty Cents, Victoria, Silver, 1870–1900		
□ 1870	$90.00	$175.00
□ 1872H	115.00	140.00
□ 1873	120.00	230.00
□ 1874	65.00	185.00
□ 1876H	80.00	185.00
□ 1880	175.00	235.00
□ 1881	80.00	185.00
□ 1882H	135.00	200.00
□ 1885	80.00	185.00
□ 1888	125.00	275.00
□ 1894	70.00	115.00
□ 1896	70.00	115.00
□ 1898	70.00	115.00
□ 1899, Small Date	25.00	65.00
□ 1899, Large Date	30.00	75.00
□ 1900	25.00	70.00

	ABP FINE	AVERAGE FINE
Fifty Cents, Edward VII, Silver, 1904–1909		
□ 1904H	18.00	32.00
□ 1907	18.00	32.00
□ 1908	18.00	32.00
□ 1909	18.00	32.00

	ABP FINE	AVERAGE FINE
Fifty Cents, George V, Silver, 1911–1919		
□ 1911	6.00	10.00
□ 1917C	6.00	10.00

	ABP FINE	AVERAGE FINE
□ 1918C	$6.00	$10.00
□ 1919C	8.00	15.00

$2 GOLD COINAGE

Courtesy of Q. David Bowers

The Newfoundland $2 gold coins, minted from 1865 to 1888, stand today as one of the most popular specialties within the Canadian series. The expanse of date and mint mark (just one from the Heaton Mint) varieties exceeds that of the Dominion of Canada $5 and $10 pieces combined. In addition, three different obverse varieties lend interest and collecting possibilities. In some instances the same obverse die was used to strike Newfoundland 10¢ pieces and $2 gold coins, both being of like diameter. The study of die characteristics of a significant number of pieces would help identify specific linkages.

The obverse pictures Queen Victoria and, as noted, is similar to that used on the Newfoundland 10-cent piece. On the reverse these coins were denominated three different ways: TWO HUNDRED CENTS, 2 DOLLARS, and TWO HUNDRED PENCE. These were sometimes called "double dollars."

They served excellent duty not only on the Island of Newfoundland, but throughout the eastern section of Canada, where they were readily accepted in commerce. In 1894 the Newfoundland banks "crashed," and the island's monetary system was taken over by outside banks that came in to stabilize the currency. Around this time, the supply of $2 coins virtually disappeared, as they were ideal "hard money" in comparison to paper notes which were widely distrusted. Similarly, large-denomination Newfoundland 25¢ and 50¢ pieces were hoarded.

Today the typically encountered Newfoundland $2 coin is apt to be in EF or AU grade, reflective of their one-time utility. Mint State examples are in all instances rare and for some issues exceedingly rare. A few Specimen strikings are known from polished dies, and the Norweb cabinet is remarkable in its selection of these. Typically, even a single Specimen issue is not found even in an advanced collection.

Two Dollar, Victoria, Gold, 1865–1888

	ABP FINE	AVERAGE FINE
☐ 1865	$215.00	$325.00
☐ 1870	215.00	325.00
☐ 1872	300.00	400.00
☐ 1880	800.00	1000.00
☐ 1881	150.00	250.00
☐ 1882H	265.00	365.00
☐ 1885	265.00	365.00
☐ 1888	125.00	250.00

Canada—Coinage of Nova Scotia

Courtesy of Q. David Bowers

The history of the coinage of Nova Scotia is short, sweet, and interesting.

Nova Scotia adopted a decimal system in 1859 based upon the pound sterling rated at an exact $5. Under this system, British sixpence passed for 12½¢, shillings for 25¢, and florins for 50¢. While plentiful British coins could serve handily for larger denominations, there arose a need for cents and half cents, the latter being needed to make change when sixpence pieces were tendered.

Half cents were struck with the dates 1861 and 1864, the obverse being the die used for regular British farthings (¼ penny) and the reverse showing a wreath enclosing a crown and the date. Cents were similar, were dated 1861, 1862, and 1864, and utilized obverse dies for contemporary British halfpennies. Thus, for the circulating copper coinage of Nova Scotia there is a direct die linkage with British issues.

Nova Scotia could have used British farthings and halfpennies by fiat, but did not, presumably because the inscription on the reverse of the British halfpenny, identifying it as such, might be confused with its Nova Scotia valuation of one cent. As it turned out, the Nova Scotia half cent was not a popular denomination, and commercial circulation was limited. Presumably, they did not fit well into trade outside of Nova Scotia in a milieu in which the popular private issues, Bank of Montreal issues, and the like, passed as cents, and no small half cent coin was needed.

The Nova Scotia coinage is a compact and interesting numismatic series. The half cent has an interesting connection with the 1861 coin of the same denomination made for New Brunswick.

	ABP FINE	AVERAGE FINE
Half Cents, Victoria, Copper, 1861–1864		
☐ 1861	$12.00	$20.00
☐ 1864	12.00	20.00

	ABP FINE	AVERAGE FINE
Large Cents, Victoria, Copper, 1861–1864		
☐ 1861	6.00	12.00
☐ 1862	50.00	80.00
☐ 1864	6.00	12.00

Canada—Coinage of Prince Edward Island

Courtesy of Q. David Bowers

Through the Act of April 17, 1871, the island adopted a decimal coinage with one dollar composed of 100 cents, although legislation in this regard had been introduced in the House of Assembly as early as February 23, 1860. By that time the island, called Saint John (earlier Ile St. Jean) until 1798, was home to numerous varieties of private tokens (the best known being the SHIPS, COLONIES & COMMERCE issues) and used British, United States, and other coins in commerce, but had no government issues.

On September 13, 1871, the Royal Mint sought bids for two million cents for Prince Edward Island, these to be made to the same standard as British bronze issues. On December 25, 1871, Christmas Day, Ralph Heaton & Sons, Birmingham, was given the nod over the other bidder, James Watt & Co. (with some slight historical connections to the old Boulton & Watt firm), which was asserting itself as an up-and-coming rival, but which would cease coining in the 1890s. No other denominations were ever struck. Dies were cut at the Royal Mint, London, as per usual practice for British colonial coins, and shipped to Heaton.

In due course Heaton struck the coins and arranged with the Union Bank of London to receive the funds for them, with the pieces to be picked up by the Birmingham and Midland Bank and shipped in boxes to the Bank of Prince Edward Island, Charlottetown, Prince Edward Island. The newly minted pieces were rolled in paper wrappers of 50 coins each and packed in 200 boxes, each with 10,000 cents. On November 25 they left the Heaton Mint, and in December they arrived at their intended destination across the Atlantic.

The quantity of two million was staggering, to say the least, inasmuch as there were only about 75,000 people in the district at the time. This amounted to about 27 coins per person! No wonder that quantities of these pieces remained in the vaults of the Bank of Prince Edward Island, Charlottetown, undistributed for eight years. Following an authorization dated December 11, 1878, the dregs were parceled out at a 10% discount (shades of the Randall Hoard of American large cents!). This offer was eagerly received, and 10,000 were shipped to Halifax, 70,000 were sold to A. J. Tait of Montreal, and 130,000 went to various towns in New Brunswick. By that time the island was a part of the Dominion of Canada, having joined in 1873, although it did not fully adopt the Dominion Uniform Currency Act until eight years later.

In 1894 P. N. Breton commented: "There was a very large issue of this coin, over 2,000,000. It is thus found plentifully in circulation, and will be considered very common for some time to come." Breton was right, and these cents circulated in the eastern part of Canada until well into the present century.

	ABP FINE	AVERAGE FINE
Large Cent, Victoria, Copper, 1871		
☐ 1871	$10.00	$14.00

CHINA

The first coins, cast in molds, were used in the 6th century B.C. Imitation coins were made of cast bronze. Hoe-shaped coins were produced in the mid-3rd century B.C. Round coins with holes were made at a few mints. The round coins and the tool coins were issued in different denominations, based on the weight of the metal in each coin. The bronze 5-grain coin was introduced in 118 B.C. and was the standard until the early 7th century A.D. Bronze coins with square holes remained through the 13th century. The silver dirhem was in evidence in the 13th century, followed by the brass coin and the silver dollar in the 18th and 19th centuries. Decimal coins appeared in the 1st century A.D. The currency today is the yuan.

China—People's Republic

Key to Grading: Coat of Arms

DATE	COIN TYPE/VARIETY/METAL	ABP FINE	AVERAGE FINE
□ 1955–2000	1 Fen, People's Republic, Aluminum	—	$ .38

Key to Grading: Coat of Arms

DATE	COIN TYPE/VARIETY/METAL	ABP FINE	AVERAGE FINE
☐ 1955–2000	2 Fen, People's Republic, Aluminum	—	$ .38

Key to Grading: Coat of Arms

DATE	COIN TYPE/VARIETY/METAL	ABP FINE	AVERAGE FINE
☐ 1955–2000	5 Fen, People's Republic, Aluminum	—	.25
☐ 1980–2000	Jiao, People's Republic, Copper-Zinc	—	.55
☐ 1987	Jiao, People's Republic, 6th National Games—Soccer, Brass	—	.55
☐ 1987	Jiao, People's Republic, 6th National Games—Volleyball, Brass	—	.40

Key to Grading: Coat of Arms or Figures

DATE	COIN TYPE/VARIETY/METAL	ABP FINE	AVERAGE FINE
☐ 1987	Jiao, People's Republic, 6th National Games—Gymnast, Brass	—	.50
☐ 1980–1986	2 Jiao, People's Republic, Copper-Zinc	—	.65
☐ 1980–1986	5 Jiao, People's Republic, Copper-Zinc	—	.65
☐ 1983	5 Jiao, People's Republic, Marco Polo, Silver	—	80.00
☐ 1991–1996	5 Jiao, People's Republic, Brass	—	.50
☐ 1980	Yuan, People's Republic, 1980 Olympics—Alpine Skiing, Brass	$5.25	8.15
☐ 1980	Yuan, People's Republic, 1980 Olympics—Equestrian, Brass	5.25	8.15
☐ 1980	Yuan, People's Republic, 1980 Olympics—Wrestling, Brass	5.25	8.15
☐ 1980	Yuan, People's Republic, 1980 Olympics—Archery, Brass	5.25	8.15
☐ 1980	Yuan, People's Republic, 1980 Olympics—Biathlon, Brass	5.25	8.15
☐ 1980	Yuan, People's Republic, 1980 Olympics—Figure Skating, Brass	5.25	8.15

DATE	COIN TYPE/VARIETY/METAL	ABP FINE	AVERAGE FINE
☐ 1980	Yuan, People's Republic, 1980 Olympics—Soccer, Brass	—	$8.25
☐ 1980	Yuan, People's Republic, 1980 Olympics—Speed Skating, Brass	—	8.25
☐ 1980–1986	Yuan, People's Republic, Cupro-Nickel	—	.60
☐ 1982	Yuan, People's Republic, World Cup Soccer, Copper	—	7.00
☐ 1983	Yuan, People's Republic, Panda, Brass	$8.00	15.00
☐ 1984	Yuan, People's Republic, Panda, Brass	8.00	15.00
☐ 1984	Yuan, People's Republic, 35th Anniversary, Cupro-Nickel	—	5.00
☐ 1985	Yuan, People's Republic, Tibet 20th Anniversary, Cupro-Nickel	—	4.25

Key to Grading: Figures or Buildings

DATE	COIN TYPE/VARIETY/METAL	ABP FINE	AVERAGE FINE
☐ 1985	Yuan, People's Republic, Sinkiang 30th Anniversary, Cupro-Nickel	—	2.00
☐ 1986	Yuan, People's Republic, Year of Peace, Cupro-Nickel	—	4.15
☐ 1987	Yuan, People's Republic, Mongolian 40th Anniversary, Cupro-Nickel	—	2.00
☐ 1988	Yuan, People's Republic, Ninghsia 30th Anniversary, Cupro-Nickel	—	5.00
☐ 1988	Yuan, People's Republic, People's Bank 40th Anniversary, Cupro-Nickel	—	4.15
☐ 1988	Yuan, People's Republic, Kwangsi 30th Anniversary, Cupro-Nickel	—	4.15
☐ 1989	Yuan, People's Republic, 40th Anniversary, Nickel-clad Steel	—	4.15
☐ 1990	Yuan, People's Republic, XI Asian Games—Female Archer, Nickel-clad Steel	—	4.15
☐ 1990	Yuan, People's Republic, XI Asian Games—Sword Dancer, Nickel-clad Steel	—	4.15
☐ 1991	Yuan, People's Republic, 1978 Party Conference, Nickel-plated Steel	—	4.15

DATE	COIN TYPE/VARIETY/METAL	ABP FINE	AVERAGE FINE
☐ 1991	Yuan, People's Republic, Women's Soccer Championship—Player, Nickel-plated Steel	—	$ .65
☐ 1991	Yuan, People's Republic, Planting Trees Festival—Seedling, Cupro-Nickel	—	.55
☐ 1991	Yuan, People's Republic, Chinese Communist Party 1st Meeting, Nickel-plated Steel	—	.75
☐ 1991	Yuan, People's Republic, Planting Trees Festival—Globe, Cupro-Nickel	—	.80
☐ 1991	Yuan, People's Republic, Women's Soccer Championship—Goalie, Nickel-plated Steel	—	.65
☐ 1991	Yuan, People's Republic, Planting Trees Festival—Portrait, Cupro-Nickel	—	.80
☐ 1991	Yuan, People's Republic, Party Meeting, Nickel-plated Steel	—	.65
☐ 1983	5 Yuan, People's Republic, Marco Polo, Silver	—	60.00
☐ 1984	5 Yuan, People's Republic, Olympics—High Jumper, Silver	—	30.00
☐ 1984	5 Yuan, People's Republic, Soldier Statues, Silver	—	28.00
☐ 1985	5 Yuan, People's Republic, Founders of Chinese Culture—Lao-Tse, Silver	—	28.00
☐ 1985	5 Yuan, People's Republic, Founders of Chinese Culture—Wu Guang, Silver	—	28.00
☐ 1985	5 Yuan, People's Republic, Founders of Chinese Culture—Qu Yuan, Silver	—	28.00
☐ 1985	5 Yuan, People's Republic, Founders of Chinese Culture—Sun Wu, Silver	—	30.00
☐ 1986	5 Yuan, People's Republic, Chinese Culture—Chemist, Silver	—	30.00
☐ 1986	5 Yuan, People's Republic, Chinese Culture—Mathematician, Silver	—	30.00
☐ 1986	5 Yuan, People's Republic, Soccer—2 Players, Silver	—	26.00
☐ 1986	5 Yuan, People's Republic, Chinese Culture—Historian, Silver	—	35.00
☐ 1986	5 Yuan, People's Republic, Great Wall, Silver	—	22.00
☐ 1986	5 Yuan, People's Republic, Wildlife—Giant Panda, Silver	—	28.00
☐ 1986	5 Yuan, People's Republic, Year of Peace, Silver	—	180.00

DATE	COIN TYPE/VARIETY/METAL	ABP FINE	AVERAGE FINE
☐ 1986	5 Yuan, People's Republic, Soccer, Silver	—	$38.00
☐ 1986	5 Yuan, People's Republic, Chinese Culture—Paper Making, Silver	—	38.00
☐ 1987	5 Yuan, People's Republic, Poet Du Fu, Silver	—	50.00
☐ 1987	5 Yuan, People's Republic, Princess Cheng Wen & Song Zuan Gan Bu, Silver	—	50.00
☐ 1987	5 Yuan, People's Republic, Poet Li Bal, Silver	—	50.00
☐ 1987	5 Yuan, People's Republic, Bridge Builder Li Chun, Silver	—	50.00
☐ 1988	5 Yuan, People's Republic, Olympics—Downhill Skier, Silver	—	50.00
☐ 1988	5 Yuan, People's Republic, Olympics—Sailboat Racing, Silver	—	50.00
☐ 1988	5 Yuan, People's Republic, Poetess Li Qing-zhao, Silver	—	50.00
☐ 1988	5 Yuan, People's Republic, Yue Fei—Military Hero, Silver	—	50.00
☐ 1988	5 Yuan, People's Republic, Olympics—Woman Hurdler, Silver	—	50.00
☐ 1988	5 Yuan, People's Republic, Poet Su Shl, Silver	—	50.00
☐ 1988	5 Yuan, People's Republic, Olympics—Fencing, Silver	—	50.00
☐ 1988	5 Yuan, People's Republic, Bi Sheng Inventor of Movable Type Printing, Silver	—	42.50
☐ 1989	5 Yuan, People's Republic, Soccer Players, Silver	—	38.00
☐ 1989	5 Yuan, People's Republic, Playwright Guan Hanging, Silver	—	45.00
☐ 1989	5 Yuan, People's Republic, Kublai Khan, Silver	—	50.00
☐ 1989	5 Yuan, People's Republic, Huang Daopo—Invented Water Wheel, Silver	—	50.00
☐ 1989	5 Yuan, People's Republic, Save the Children Fund, Silver	—	50.00
☐ 1989	5 Yuan, People's Republic, Scientist Guo Shousing, Silver	—	50.00
☐ 1990	5 Yuan, People's Republic, Bronze Archaeological Finds—Elephant Pitcher, Silver	—	50.00
☐ 1990	5 Yuan, People's Republic, Historian Luo Guan Zhong, Silver	—	45.00

DATE	COIN TYPE/VARIETY/METAL	ABP FINE	AVERAGE FINE
□ 1990	5 Yuan, People's Republic, Soccer—Goalie, Silver	—	$38.00
□ 1990	5 Yuan, People's Republic, Seafarer Zeng He, Silver	—	50.00
□ 1990	5 Yuan, People's Republic, Bronze Archaeological Finds—Rhinocerus, Silver	—	40.00
□ 1990	5 Yuan, People's Republic, Soccer Players, Silver	—	35.00
□ 1990	5 Yuan, People's Republic, Revolutionary Li Zicheng, Silver	—	48.00
□ 1990	5 Yuan, People's Republic, Bronze Archaeological Finds—Mythical Creature, Silver	—	48.00
□ 1990	5 Yuan, People's Republic, Bronze Archaeological Finds—Leopard, Silver	—	42.00
□ 1990	5 Yuan, People's Republic, Naturalist Li Shi Zhen, Silver	—	42.00
□ 1991	5 Yuan, People's Republic, Scientist Song Ying Xing, Silver	—	52.00
□ 1991	5 Yuan, People's Republic, Writer Cao Xue Qin, Silver	—	52.00
□ 1991	5 Yuan, People's Republic, Official—Lin Ze Xu, Silver	—	52.00
□ 1991	5 Yuan, People's Republic, Revolutionary Hong Xu Quan, Silver	—	52.00
□ 1992	5 Yuan, People's Republic, Ancient Kite Flying, Silver	—	48.00
□ 1992	5 Yuan, People's Republic, Metal Working Scene, Silver	—	48.00
□ 1992	5 Yuan, People's Republic, First Compass, Silver	—	48.00
□ 1992	5 Yuan, People's Republic, Great Wall, Silver	—	48.00
□ 1992	5 Yuan, People's Republic, First Seismograph, Silver	—	40.00

***BV** = These coins are relatively current so their collector value is minimal. Since these coins were minted and sold primarily for their bullion value, their current value is determined by the current "spot" price of the precious metal indicated. For accurate prices, contact your local coin dealer.

CUBA

Cuba was never provided with its own coinage. Spanish coins were used, with the silver peso in 1915, the gold peso in 1916, the silver centavo in 1920, and the aluminum centavo in 1981. The decimal system was established in 1915. Today's currency is the peso.

Cuba—Type Coinage

Key to Grading: Bust or Coat of Arms

DATE	COIN TYPE/VARIETY/METAL	ABP FINE	AVERAGE FINE
☐ 1953	1 Centavo, Marti Centennial, Brass	—	$ .32
☐ 1915–1938	1 Centavo, Cupro-Nickel	—	.32
☐ 1943	1 Centavo, Brass	—	.28
☐ 1946–1961	1 Centavo, Cupro-Nickel	—	.28

Key to Grading: Bust

☐ 1958	1 Centavo, Cupro-Nickel	—	.38

Key to Grading: Coat of Arms

☐ 1915–1916	2 Centavos, Cupro-Nickel	—	.40

Key to Grading: Coat of Arms

DATE	COIN TYPE/VARIETY/METAL	ABP FINE	AVERAGE FINE
□ 1915–1920	5 Centavos, Cupro-Nickel	—	$ 1.00
□ 1943	5 Centavos, Brass	—	.75
□ 1946–1961	5 Centavos, Cupro-Nickel	—	.70
□ 1952	10 Centavos, Republic 50th Anniversary, Silver	—	.70

Key to Grading: Coat of Arms

DATE	COIN TYPE/VARIETY/METAL	ABP FINE	AVERAGE FINE
□ 1915–1949	10 Centavos, Silver	—	3.85

Key to Grading: Coat of Arms

DATE	COIN TYPE/VARIETY/METAL	ABP FINE	AVERAGE FINE
□ 1952	20 Centavos, Republic 50th Anniversary, Silver	—	2.75
□ 1915–1949	20 Centavos, Silver	—	4.00
□ 1953	25 Centavos, Marti Centennial, Silver	—	2.75

Key to Grading: Coat of Arms

DATE	COIN TYPE/VARIETY/METAL	ABP FINE	AVERAGE FINE
☐ 1952	40 Centavos, Republic 50th Anniversary, Silver	—	$5.00
☐ 1915–1920	40 Centavos, Silver	—	8.00
☐ 1953	50 Centavos, Marti Centennial, Silver	—	5.00
☐ 1898	1 Peso, Silver	—	375.00
☐ 1953	1 Peso, Marti Centennial, Silver	—	7.50

Key to Grading: Coat of Arms

DATE	COIN TYPE/VARIETY/METAL	ABP FINE	AVERAGE FINE
☐ 1915–1934	1 Peso, Silver	—	20.00
☐ 1915–1916	1 Peso, Gold	—	65.00
☐ 1934–1939	1 Peso, Silver	—	30.00
☐ 1915–1916	2 Pesos, Gold	—	80.00
☐ 1915–1916	4 Pesos, Gold	—	115.00
☐ 1915–1916	10 Pesos, Gold	—	275.00
☐ 1915–1916	20 Pesos, Gold	—	325.00

EGYPT

The first coins were used in the 4th century B.C. The earliest coins were silver pieces and gold coins. The silver "owl" drachmas appeared in the 5th century B.C., followed by bronze coins, gold drachmas, and gold solidi. The copper fals was in evidence in the 760s, then the gold dinar, silver ghirsh, the cupro-nickel, gold piastres, and bronze milliemes. The decimal system was established in 1916. Today's currency is the Egyptian pound.

Egypt—Type Coinage

Key to Grading: Bust

DATE	COIN TYPE/VARIETY/METAL	ABP FINE	AVERAGE FINE
☐ 1917	1/2 Millieme, Hussein Kamil, Bronze	—	$2.65
☐ 1924	1/2 Millieme, Fuad I, Bronze	—	2.65
☐ 1929–1932	1/2 Millieme, Fuad I, Bronze	—	6.00
☐ 1938	1/2 Millieme, Farouk I, Bronze	—	3.00
☐ 1917	1 Millieme, Hussein Kamil, Cupro-Nickel	—	2.65
☐ 1924	1 Millieme, Fuad I, Bronze	—	2.65
☐ 1929–1935	1 Millieme, Fuad I, Bronze	—	2.65
☐ 1938–1950	1 Millieme, Farouk I, Bronze	—	2.65

Key to Grading: Sphinx

DATE	COIN TYPE/VARIETY/METAL	ABP FINE	AVERAGE FINE
☐ 1954–1958	1 Millieme, Republic, Aluminum-Bronze	—	.75

Key to Grading: Bust

DATE	COIN TYPE/VARIETY/METAL	ABP FINE	AVERAGE FINE
☐ 1916–1917	2 Milliemes, Hussein Kamil, Cupro-Nickel	—	1.80
☐ 1924	2 Milliemes, Fuad I, Cupro-Nickel	—	1.80

Key to Grading: Bust

DATE	COIN TYPE/VARIETY/METAL	ABP FINE	AVERAGE FINE
☐ 1929	2 Milliemes, Fuad I, Cupro-Nickel	—	1.65
☐ 1938	2 Milliemes, Farouk I, Cupro-Nickel	—	2.50
☐ 1933	2 1/2 Milliemes, Fuad I, Cupro-Nickel	—	2.50

Key to Grading: Bust

DATE	COIN TYPE/VARIETY/METAL	ABP FINE	AVERAGE FINE
☐ 1916–1917	5 Milliemes, Hussein Kamil, Cupro-Nickel	—	$4.15
☐ 1924	5 Milliemes, Fuad I, Cupro-Nickel	—	4.15
☐ 1929–1935	5 Milliemes, Fuad I, Cupro-Nickel	—	4.15

Key to Grading: Bust

DATE	COIN TYPE/VARIETY/METAL	ABP FINE	AVERAGE FINE
☐ 1938–1941	5 Milliemes, Farouk I, Cupro-Nickel	—	2.20
☐ 1938–1943	5 Milliemes, Farouk I, Bronze	—	2.20
☐ 1954–1958	5 Milliemes, Republic, Aluminum-Bronze	—	4.15
☐ 1916–1917	10 Milliemes, Hussein Kamil, Cupro-Nickel	—	4.15
☐ 1924	10 Milliemes, Fuad I, Cupro-Nickel	—	4.15
☐ 1929–1935	10 Milliemes, Fuad I, Cupro-Nickel	—	2.20

Key to Grading: Bust

DATE	COIN TYPE/VARIETY/METAL	ABP FINE	AVERAGE FINE
☐ 1938–1941	10 Milliemes, Farouk I, Cupro-Nickel	—	2.20
☐ 1938–1943	10 Milliemes, Farouk I, Bronze	—	2.20
☐ 1954–1958	10 Milliemes, Republic, Aluminum-Bronze	—	2.20
☐ 1916–1917	2 Piastres, Hussein Kamil, Silver	—	3.50
☐ 1920	2 Piastres, Fuad, Silver	—	4.00

Key to Grading: Lettering

DATE	COIN TYPE/VARIETY/METAL	ABP FINE	AVERAGE FINE
☐ 1885–1910	1/40 Ghirsh, Abdul Hamid II, Minted in Europe, Bronze	—	$2.15
☐ 1910–1914	1/40 Ghirsh, Mohammed V, Bronze	—	1.60
☐ 1885–1910	1/20 Ghirsh, Abdul Hamid II, Minted in Europe, Bronze	—	1.60
☐ 1910–1914	1/20 Ghirsh, Mohammed V, Bronze	—	2.15

Key to Grading: Lettering

DATE	COIN TYPE/VARIETY/METAL	ABP FINE	AVERAGE FINE
☐ 1916–1917	5 Piastres, Hussein Kamil, Silver	—	5.25
☐ 1920	5 Piastres, Fuad, Silver	—	25.00
☐ 1864	4 Para, Abdul Aziz, Minted in Europe, Bronze	—	5.25
☐ 1885–1910	1/10 Ghirsh, Abdul Hamid II, Minted in Europe, Cupro-Nickel	—	2.15
☐ 1910–1914	1/10 Ghirsh, Mohammed V, Cupro-Nickel	—	2.15

Key to Grading: Lettering

DATE	COIN TYPE/VARIETY/METAL	ABP FINE	AVERAGE FINE
☐ 1916–1917	10 Piastres, Hussein Kamil, Silver	—	7.00
☐ 1920	10 Piastres, Fuad, Silver	—	30.00
☐ 1885–1910	2/10 Ghirsh, Abdul Hamid II, Minted in Europe, Cupro-Nickel	—	2.15

DATE	COIN TYPE/VARIETY/METAL	ABP FINE	AVERAGE FINE
☐ 1910–1914	2/10 Ghirsh, Mohammed V, Cupro-Nickel	—	$4.50
☐ 1916–1917	20 Piastres, Hussein Kamil, Silver	—	18.00
☐ 1862–1876	10 Para, Abdul Aziz, Silver	—	22.00
☐ 1864–1870	10 Para, Abdul Aziz, Minted in Europe, Bronze	—	4.00
☐ 1868–1871	10 Para, Abdul Aziz, Copper	—	4.00
☐ 1876–1878	10 Para, Abdul Hamid II, Silver	—	80.00
☐ 1861–1875	20 Para, Abdul Aziz, Silver	—	28.00

Key to Grading: Lettering

DATE	COIN TYPE/VARIETY/METAL	ABP FINE	AVERAGE FINE
☐ 1863–1870	20 Para, Abdul Aziz, Minted in Europe, Bronze	—	5.50
☐ 1868–1871	20 Para, Abdul Aziz, Copper	—	15.00
☐ 1876–1878	20 Para, Abdul Hamid II, Silver	—	80.00

Key to Grading: Lettering

DATE	COIN TYPE/VARIETY/METAL	ABP FINE	AVERAGE FINE
☐ 1885–1910	5/10 Ghirsh, Abdul Hamid II, Minted in Europe, Cupro-Nickel	—	2.15
☐ 1910–1914	5/10 Ghirsh, Mohammed V, Cupro-Nickel	—	2.15
☐ 1868–1871	40 Para, Abdul Aziz, Copper	450.00	750.00
☐ 1870	40 Para, Abdul Aziz, Minted in Europe, Bronze	—	5.00
☐ 1861–1876	1 Ghirsh, Abdul Aziz, Silver	—	10.00
☐ 1876	1 Ghirsh, Mohammed V, Minted in Europe, Silver	—	4.00
☐ 1876–1880	1 Ghirsh, Abdul Hamid II, Silver	—	4.00
☐ 1885–1908	1 Ghirsh, Abdul Hamid II, Minted in Europe, Silver	—	4.00
☐ 1897–1908	1 Ghirsh, Abdul Hamid II, Minted in Europe, Cupro-Nickel	—	2.00

DATE	COIN TYPE/VARIETY/METAL	ABP FINE	AVERAGE FINE
☐ 1910–1911	1 Ghirsh, Mohammed V, Silver	—	$4.00
☐ 1910–1914	1 Ghirsh, Mohammed V, Cupro-Nickel	—	5.25
☐ 1916	100 Piastres, Hussein Kamil, Gold	—	85.00
☐ 1885–1908	2 Ghirsh, Abdul Hamid II, Minted in Europe, Silver	—	5.25
☐ 1910–1911	2 Ghirsh, Mohammed V, Silver	—	6.00
☐ 1864	2½ Ghirsh, Abdul Aziz, Minted in Europe, Silver	—	65.00
☐ 1868–1875	2½ Ghirsh, Abdul Aziz, Silver	—	325.00
☐ 1861–1870	5 Ghirsh, Abdul Aziz, Silver	—	300.00
☐ 1862–1876	5 Ghirsh, Abdul Aziz, Gold	—	45.00
☐ 1864	5 Ghirsh, Abdul Aziz, Minted in Europe, Silver	—	80.00

Key to Grading: Lettering

DATE	COIN TYPE/VARIETY/METAL	ABP FINE	AVERAGE FINE
☐ 1877–1882	5 Ghirsh, Abdul Hamid II, Gold	—	325.00
☐ 1885–1908	5 Ghirsh, Abdul Hamid II, Minted in Europe, Silver	—	10.00
☐ 1891–1909	5 Ghirsh, Abdul Hamid II, Gold	—	70.00
☐ 1910–1914	5 Ghirsh, Mohammed V, Silver	—	12.00
☐ 1862–1871	10 Ghirsh, Abdul Aziz, Silver	—	250.00
☐ 1864	10 Ghirsh, Abdul Aziz, Minted in Europe, Silver	—	85.00
☐ 1870–1874	10 Ghirsh, Abdul Aziz, Gold	—	100.00
☐ 1885–1908	10 Ghirsh, Abdul Hamid II, Minted in Europe, Silver	—	45.00
☐ 1892–1909	10 Ghirsh, Abdul Hamid II, Gold	—	60.00
☐ 1910–1914	10 Ghirsh, Mohammed V, Silver	—	28.00
☐ 1861–1862	20 Ghirsh, Abdul Aziz, Silver	—	425.00
☐ 1876–1880	20 Ghirsh, Abdul Hamid II, Silver	—	1000.00
☐ 1885–1908	20 Ghirsh, Abdul Hamid II, Minted in Europe, Silver	—	22.00
☐ 1910–1914	20 Ghirsh, Mohammed V, Silver	—	22.00
☐ 1868–1875	25 Ghirsh, Abdul Aziz, Gold	—	85.00
☐ 1871–1876	50 Ghirsh, Abdul Aziz, Gold	—	175.00
☐ 1861–1876	100 Ghirsh, Abdul Aziz, Gold	—	175.00
☐ 1864	100 Ghirsh, Abdul Aziz, Minted in Europe, Gold	—	350.00

DATE	COIN TYPE/VARIETY/METAL	ABP FINE	AVERAGE FINE
☐ 1876–1883	100 Ghirsh, Abdul Hamid II, Gold	—	$485.00
☐ 1887	100 Ghirsh, Abdul Hamid II, Minted in Europe, Gold	—	250.00
☐ 1868–1875	500 Ghirsh, Abdul Aziz, Gold	—	3500.00
☐ 1876–1881	500 Ghirsh, Abdul Hamid II, Gold	—	3000.00
☐ 1955	1 Pound, Republic, Revolution 3rd & 5th Anniversaries, Gold	—	165.00
☐ 1955	5 Pounds, Republic, Revolution 3rd & 5th Anniversaries, Gold	—	725.00

Egypt—United Arab Republic

Key to Grading: Eagle

☐ 1960–1966	Millieme, UAR, Aluminum-Bronze	—	.38

Key to Grading: Eagle

☐ 1962–1966	2 Milliemes, UAR, Aluminum-Bronze	—	.38

Key to Grading: Eagle

☐ 1960–1966	5 Milliemes, UAR, Aluminum-Bronze	—	.38

Key to Grading: Eagle

DATE	COIN TYPE/VARIETY/METAL	ABP FINE	AVERAGE FINE
☐ 1958–1966	10 Milliemes, UAR, Aluminum-Bronze	—	$ .80
☐ 1958	20 Milliemes, UAR, Agriculture & Industry Fair, Aluminum-Bronze	—	.80
☐ 1958	1/2 Pound, UAR, Founding of the United Arab Republic, Gold	—	140.00
☐ 1960	Pound, UAR, Aswan Dam, Gold	—	150.00
☐ 1960	5 Pounds, UAR, Aswan Dam, Gold	—	725.00

FINLAND

Evidence of coinage became common late in the Middle Ages. The first coins were used around 1410. Most were silver ortugs, and nearly all bore the king's name. In the 1800s, the ruble was declared Finland's monetary unit, then the penni and the markka. In 1963, the new 1 penni equaled the old 1 markka.

Finland—Type Coinage

Key to Grading: Crown & Lettering

DATE	COIN TYPE/VARIETY/METAL	ABP FINE	AVERAGE FINE
□ 1864–1917	1 Penni, Copper	—	$ .55
□ 1919–1924	1 Penni, Copper	—	.55

Key to Grading: Lettering

DATE	COIN TYPE/VARIETY/METAL	ABP FINE	AVERAGE FINE
□ 1963–1969	1 Penni, Copper	—	.32
□ 1969–1979	1 Penni, Aluminum	—	.32

Key to Grading: Crown & Lettering

DATE	COIN TYPE/VARIETY/METAL	ABP FINE	AVERAGE FINE
□ 1865–1917	5 Pennia, Copper	—	.60
□ 1918–1940	5 Pennia, Copper	—	.50
□ 1941–1943	5 Pennia, Copper	—	.30
□ 1963–1977	5 Pennia, Copper	—	.38
□ 1977–1990	5 Pennia, Aluminum	—	.38

Key to Grading: Crown & Lettering

DATE	COIN TYPE/VARIETY/METAL	ABP FINE	AVERAGE FINE
☐ 1865–1917	10 Pennia, Copper	—	$1.00
☐ 1919–1940	10 Pennia, Copper	—	.38
☐ 1941–1943	10 Pennia, Copper	—	.38
☐ 1943–1945	10 Pennia, Iron	—	.38
☐ 1865–1917	25 Pennia, Silver	—	1.25
☐ 1921–1940	25 Pennia, Cupro-Nickel	—	.50
☐ 1940–1943	25 Pennia, Copper	—	.50
☐ 1943–1945	25 Pennia, Iron	—	.50

Key to Grading: Coat of Arms

DATE	COIN TYPE/VARIETY/METAL	ABP FINE	AVERAGE FINE
☐ 1864–1917	50 Pennia, Silver	—	1.65
☐ 1921–1940	50 Pennia, Cupro-Nickel	—	.35
☐ 1940–1943	50 Pennia, Copper	—	.35
☐ 1943–1948	50 Pennia, Iron	—	.45
☐ 1963–1982	10 Pennia, Aluminum-Bronze	—	.45
☐ 1983–1990	10 Pennia, Aluminum	—	.35
☐ 1990 to Date	10 Pennia, Cupro-Nickel	—	.40
☐ 1864–1915	Markka, Silver	—	4.25
☐ 1921–1924	Markka, Cupro-Nickel	$2.00	4.00
☐ 1928–1940	Markka, Cupro-Nickel	—	.38
☐ 1940–1951	1 Markka, Copper	—	.38
☐ 1943–1952	1 Markka, Iron	—	.38
☐ 1952–1962	1 Markka, Iron	—	.38

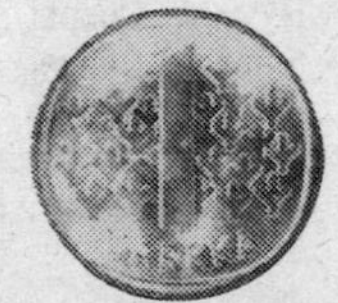

Key to Grading: Coat of Arms

DATE	COIN TYPE/VARIETY/METAL	ABP FINE	AVERAGE FINE
☐ 1964–1968	1 Markka, Silver	—	$1.00
☐ 1969–1993	1 Markka, Cupro-Nickel	—	.45
☐ 1993 to Date	Markka, Aluminum-Bronze	—	.45
☐ 1865–1908	2 Markkaa, Silver	—	8.00
☐ 1928–1946	5 Markkaa, Aluminum-Bronze	—	.80

Key to Grading: Lettering

DATE	COIN TYPE/VARIETY/METAL	ABP FINE	AVERAGE FINE
☐ 1946–1952	5 Markkaa, Brass	—	.40
☐ 1952–1962	5 Markkaa, Iron	—	.40
☐ 1972–1978	5 Markkaa, Aluminum-Bronze	—	1.40
☐ 1979–1993	5 Markkaa, Aluminum-Bronze	—	1.40
☐ 1992–1997	5 Markkaa, Aluminum-Bronze	—	1.40

Key to Grading: Coat of Arms

DATE	COIN TYPE/VARIETY/METAL	ABP FINE	AVERAGE FINE
☐ 1878–1913	10 Markkaa, Gold	—	115.00
☐ 1928–1939	10 Markkaa, Aluminum-Bronze	$1.50	2.00
☐ 1952–1962	10 Markkaa, Aluminum-Bronze	.65	1.25

Key to Grading: Coat of Arms & Bust

DATE	COIN TYPE/VARIETY/METAL	ABP FINE	AVERAGE FINE
☐ 1967–1977	10 Markkaa, Commemorative, Silver	—	5.00
☐ 1963–1990	20 Pennia, Aluminum-Bronze	—	.35

Key to Grading: Coat of Arms

DATE	COIN TYPE/VARIETY/METAL	ABP FINE	AVERAGE FINE
☐ 1878–1913	20 Markkaa, Gold	—	$175.00
☐ 1931–1939	20 Markkaa, Aluminum-Bronze	$2.50	4.00
☐ 1952–1962	20 Markkaa, Aluminum-Bronze	—	.40

Key to Grading: Coat of Arms or Building

☐ 1978–1979	25 Markkaa, Commemorative, Silver	—	6.25
☐ 1963–1990	50 Pennia, Aluminum-Bronze	—	.38
☐ 1990 to Date	50 Pennia, Cupro-Nickel	—	.38

Key to Grading: Coat of Arms

☐ 1952–1962	50 Markkaa, Aluminum-Bronze	—	4.25

Key to Grading: Bust

☐ 1981–1985	50 Markkaa, Commemorative, Silver	—	22.00
☐ 1926	100 Markkaa, Gold	—	435.00

DATE	COIN TYPE/VARIETY/METAL	ABP FINE	AVERAGE FINE
□ 1956–1960	100 Markkaa, Silver	—	$12.00
□ 1989–1992	100 Markkaa, Commemorative, Silver	—	32.00
□ 1926	200 Markkaa, Gold	—	700.00
□ 1956–1959	200 Markkaa, Silver	—	12.00

Key to Grading: Lettering

□ 1951–1952	500 Markkaa, Commemorative Coin Issued on the Occasion of the Olympic Games in Helsinki, Silver	—	28.00
□ 1960	1000 Markkaa, Commemorative Coin Issued on the Occasion of the Centonary of the Finnish Mint, Silver	—	8.00

FRANCE

The earliest coins date from about 500 B.C. The silver drachma was the typical coin from the 4th century B.C., with the gold stater prominent in the 2nd century B.C. The silver denier became popular around 600 A.D. The Middle Ages saw a great amount of feudal coinage, followed by coins influenced by the French Revolution. By the First World War, paper money was substituted for gold. In 1961, the range of coins still used today was introduced.

France—Type Coinage

Key to Grading: Bust

DATE	COIN TYPE/VARIETY/METAL	ABP FINE	AVERAGE FINE
☐ 1848–1852A	Un Centime, Second Republic, Copper	—	$4.25
☐ 1853–1862	Un Centime, Second Empire, Bronze	—	6.00
☐ 1872–1920	Un Centime, Third Republic, Bronze	—	4.25
☐ 1962–1993	Un Centime, Fifth Republic, Chrome-Steel	—	.40
☐ 1853–1862	Deux Centimes, Second Empire, Bronze	—	2.00
☐ 1877–1920	Deux Centimes, Third Republic, Bronze	—	4.25
☐ 1808BB	Cinq Centimes, Copper	$80.00	120.00

Key to Grading: Bust & Eagles

DATE	COIN TYPE/VARIETY/METAL	ABP FINE	AVERAGE FINE
☐ 1853–1865	Cinq Centimes, Second Empire, Bronze	—	5.15
☐ 1871–1921	Cinq Centimes, Third Republic, Bronze	—	5.15
☐ 1914–1938	Cinq Centimes, Third Republic, Copper-Nickel	—	.38
☐ 1938–1939	Cinq Centimes, Third Republic, Nickel-Bronze	—	.38
☐ 1961–1964	Cinq Centimes, Fifth Republic, Chrome-Steel	—	.38
☐ 1966–1993	Cinq Centimes, Fifth Republic, Aluminum-Bronze	—	.38
☐ 1814–1815BB	Decime, Strasbourg Provisional Issue, Bronze	14.00	22.00
☐ 1807–1809	Dix Centimes, Buillon	—	7.00

Key to Grading: Bust

DATE	COIN TYPE/VARIETY/METAL	ABP FINE	AVERAGE FINE
☐ 1852–1864	Dix Centimes, Bronze	—	$4.25
☐ 1870–1921	Dix Centimes, Third Republic, Bronze	—	4.25
☐ 1914	Dix Centimes, Third Republic, Nickel	$200.00	450.00
☐ 1917–1938	Dix Centimes, Third Republic, Copper-Nickel	—	.38
☐ 1938–1939	Dix Centimes, Third Republic, Nickel-Bronze	—	.38
☐ 1941–1945	Dix Centimes, Third Republic, Zinc	—	.38
☐ 1962–1993	Dix Centimes, Fifth Republic, Aluminum-Bronze	—	.38

Key to Grading: Bust

DATE	COIN TYPE/VARIETY/METAL	ABP FINE	AVERAGE FINE
☐ 1849–1850	Vingt Centimes, Second Republic, Silver	—	15.00
☐ 1853–1889	Vingt Centimes, Second Empire, Silver	—	15.00
☐ 1941–1945	Vingt Centimes, Second Empire, Zinc	—	.70
☐ 1962–1993	Vingt Centimes, Fifth Republic, Aluminum-Bronze	—	.45
☐ 1806–1807	Quart Franc, Silver	—	75.00
☐ 1807	Quart Franc, Negro Head, Silver	—	140.00
☐ 1807–1845	Quart Franc, Laureate Head, Silver	—	140.00
☐ 1845–1846	25 Centimes, Silver	—	15.00

Key to Grading: Bust

DATE	COIN TYPE/VARIETY/METAL	ABP FINE	AVERAGE FINE
☐ 1903–1917	25 Centimes, Third Republic, Nickel	—	$ .80
☐ 1917–1937	25 Centimes, Third Republic, Copper-Nickel	—	.45
☐ 1938–1940	25 Centimes, Third Republic, Nickel-Bronze	—	.45
☐ 1807	Demi Franc, Negro Head, Silver	—	162.50
☐ 1807–1845	Demi Franc, Laureate Head, Silver	—	25.00
☐ 1845–1846	50 Centimes, Silver	—	15.00
☐ 1849–1850	50 Centimes, Second Republic, Silver	—	40.00
☐ 1852	50 Centimes, Second Republic, President Louis Napoleon, Silver	—	40.00
☐ 1853–1867	50 Centimes, Second Empire, Silver	—	10.00

Key to Grading: Bust

DATE	COIN TYPE/VARIETY/METAL	ABP FINE	AVERAGE FINE
☐ 1871–1920	50 Centimes, Third Republic, Silver	—	4.00
☐ 1921–1939	50 Centimes, Third Republic, Aluminum-Bronze	—	.38
☐ 1941–1945	50 Centimes, Third Republic, Aluminum	—	.38
☐ 1962–1964	50 Centimes, Third Republic, Aluminum-Bronze	—	.38

Key to Grading: Figure

DATE	COIN TYPE/VARIETY/METAL	ABP FINE	AVERAGE FINE
☐ 1965–1993	1/2 Franc, Nickel	—	.45
☐ 1807	1 Franc, Negro Head, Silver	—	400.00
☐ 1807–1848	1 Franc, Laureate Head, Silver	—	22.00
☐ 1849–1868	1 Franc, Second Republic, Silver	—	45.00

Key to Grading: Figure or Bust

DATE	COIN TYPE/VARIETY/METAL	ABP FINE	AVERAGE FINE
☐ 1871–1920	1 Franc, Third Republic, Silver	—	$4.25
☐ 1920–1941	1 Franc, Third Republic, Chamber of Commerce, Aluminum-Bronze	—	.38
☐ 1941–1959	1 Franc, Third Republic, Aluminum	—	.38
☐ 1943	1 Franc, Third Republic, Zinc	$500.00	825.00
☐ 1960–1999	1 Franc, Fifth Republic, Nickel	—	.38
☐ 1807	2 Francs, Negro Head, Silver	—	650.00
☐ 1807–1846	2 Francs, Laureate Head, Silver	—	85.00
☐ 1849–1850	2 Francs, Second Republic, Silver	—	170.00
☐ 1853–1868	2 Francs, Second Empire, Silver	—	170.00

Key to Grading: Bust or Figure

DATE	COIN TYPE/VARIETY/METAL	ABP FINE	AVERAGE FINE
☐ 1870–1920	2 Francs, Third Republic, Silver	—	9.00
☐ 1920–1941	2 Francs, Third Republic, Chamber of Commerce, Aluminum-Bronze	—	2.00
☐ 1941–1946	2 Francs, Third Republic, Aluminum	—	.38
☐ 1979–1999	2 Francs, 5 Republic	—	.38
☐ 1814–1815	5 Francs, First Restoration, Silver	—	70.00
☐ 1815	5 Francs, The Hundred Days, Silver	—	235.00
☐ 1816–1830	5 Francs, Second Restoration, Silver	—	45.00
☐ 1830–1846	5 Francs, Second Restoration, Louis Phillipe, Silver	—	50.00
☐ 1848–1852	5 Francs, Second Republic, Silver	—	30.00
☐ 1854–1860	5 Francs, Second Empire, Gold	—	55.00
☐ 1861–1870	5 Francs, Second Empire, Silver	—	55.00
☐ 1862–1869	5 Francs, Second Empire, Gold	—	40.00

Key to Grading: Figures or Busts

DATE	COIN TYPE/VARIETY/METAL	ABP FINE	AVERAGE FINE
☐ 1870–1878	5 Francs, Third Republic, Silver	—	$40.00
☐ 1871	5 Francs, Third Republic, Trident, Silver	—	200.00
☐ 1933–1939	5 Francs, Third Republic, Nickel	—	2.00
☐ 1938–1946	5 Francs, Third Republic, Aluminum-Bronze	—	3.00
☐ 1945–1952	5 Francs, Third Republic, Aluminum	—	.40
☐ 1960–1969	5 Francs, Fifth Republic, Silver	—	4.00
☐ 1970–1999	5 Francs, Fifth Republic, Copper-Nickel	—	2.20
☐ 1989	5 Francs, Fifth Republic, Eiffel Tower Centennial, Platinum	—	315.00
☐ 1989	5 Francs, Fifth Republic, Eiffel Tower Centennial, Gold	—	225.00
☐ 1989	5 Francs, Fifth Republic, Eiffel Tower Centennial, Copper-Nickel	—	4.15
☐ 1989	5 Francs, Fifth Republic, Eiffel Tower Centennial, Silver	—	22.00
☐ 1850–1914	10 Francs, Gold	—	25.00
☐ 1929–1939	10 Francs, Silver	—	4.00
☐ 1945–1949	10 Francs, Copper-Nickel	—	.35
☐ 1950–1958	10 Francs, Aluminum-Bronze	—	.35

Key to Grading: Figures

DATE	COIN TYPE/VARIETY/METAL	ABP FINE	AVERAGE FINE
☐ 1965–1973	10 Francs, Fifth Republic, Silver	—	5.00
☐ 1974–1987	10 Francs, Fifth Republic, Nickel-Brass	—	2.15
☐ 1982	10 Francs, Fifth Republic, Leon Gambetta—100th Anniversary, Copper-Nickel	—	2.15

DATE	COIN TYPE/VARIETY/METAL	ABP FINE	AVERAGE FINE
☐ 1983	10 Francs, Fifth Republic, Montgolfier Balloon—200th Anniversary, Nickel-Bronze	—	$2.00
☐ 1983	10 Francs, Fifth Republic, Birth of Stendhal—200th Anniversary, Nickel-Bronze	—	4.25
☐ 1984	10 Francs, Fifth Republic, Birth of Francois Rudei—200th Anniversary, Nickel-Bronze	—	4.25
☐ 1985	10 Francs, Fifth Republic, Victor Hugo Centennial, Silver	—	25.00
☐ 1986	10 Francs, Fifth Republic, Robert Schumann—100th Anniversary, Gold	—	125.00
☐ 1986	10 Francs, Fifth Republic, Robert Schumann—100th Anniversary, Silver	—	24.00
☐ 1986	10 Francs, Fifth Republic, Robert Schumann—100th Anniversary, Nickel-Bronze	—	2.50
☐ 1987	10 Francs, Fifth Republic, French Millennium, Silver	—	25.00
☐ 1987	10 Francs, Fifth Republic, French Millennium, Platinum	—	285.00
☐ 1987	10 Francs, Fifth Republic, French Millennium, Nickel-Bronze	—	5.00
☐ 1987	10 Francs, Fifth Republic, French Millennium, Gold	—	175.00
☐ 1988	10 Francs, Fifth Republic, Rolland Garros—100th Anniversary, Aluminum-Bronze	—	4.25
☐ 1988–1997	10 Francs, Fifth Republic, Bastille, Dual Metal	—	4.25
☐ 1988	10 Francs, Fifth Republic, Rolland Garros—100th Anniversary, Silver	—	12.00
☐ 1988	10 Francs, Fifth Republic, Rolland Garros—100th Anniversary, Gold	—	200.00
☐ 1989	10 Francs, Fifth Republic, Montesquieu—300th Anniversary, Dual Metal	—	4.25
☐ 1990–1990	European Currency Units, Charlemagne, Silver	—	115.00
☐ 1991–1991	European Currency Units, Descartes, Silver	—	65.00
☐ 1992–1992	European Currency Units, Monet, Silver	—	45.00
☐ 1814	20 Francs, Gold	—	50.00

Key to Grading: Bust

DATE	COIN TYPE/VARIETY/METAL	ABP FINE	AVERAGE FINE
☐ 1929–1939	20 Francs, Silver	—	$5.00
☐ 1950–1954	20 Francs, Aluminum-Bronze	—	.38
☐ 1992–1997	20 Francs, Mont St. Michel, Tri Metal	—	4.25

Key to Grading: Rooster

DATE	COIN TYPE/VARIETY/METAL	ABP FINE	AVERAGE FINE
☐ 1855–1904	50 Francs, Gold	—	275.00

Key to Grading: Rooster

DATE	COIN TYPE/VARIETY/METAL	ABP FINE	AVERAGE FINE
☐ 1950–1954	50 Francs, Aluminum-Bronze	—	.65
☐ 1974–1980	50 Francs, Silver	—	7.50
☐ 1990	European Currency Units, Charlemagne, Gold	—	300.00
☐ 1990	European Currency Units, Charlemagne, Platinum	—	485.00
☐ 1991	European Currency Units, Descartes, Gold	—	400.00
☐ 1991	European Currency Units, Descartes, Platinum	—	62.00
☐ 1992	European Currency Units, Monet, Platinum	—	62.00

DATE	COIN TYPE/VARIETY/METAL	ABP FINE	AVERAGE FINE
☐ 1992	European Currency Units, Monet, Gold	—	$700.00
☐ 1855–1936	100 Francs, Gold	—	625.00

Key to Grading: Busts or Figures

DATE	COIN TYPE/VARIETY/METAL	ABP FINE	AVERAGE FINE
☐ 1954–1958	100 Francs, Copper-Nickel	—	4.25
☐ 1982–1993	100 Francs, Pantheon, Silver	—	25.00
☐ 1984	100 Francs, Marie Curie—50th Anniversary, Silver	—	135.00
☐ 1984	100 Francs, Marie Curie—50th Anniversary, Gold	—	525.00
☐ 1985	100 Francs, Germinal Centennial, Gold	—	500.00
☐ 1985	100 Francs, Germinal Centennial, Silver	—	140.00
☐ 1986	100 Francs, Statue of Liberty Centennial, Platinum	—	345.00
☐ 1986	100 Francs, Statue of Liberty Centennial, Gold	—	285.00
☐ 1986	100 Francs, Statue of Liberty Centennial, Silver	—	70.00
☐ 1986	100 Francs, Statue of Liberty Centennial, Palladium	—	230.00
☐ 1987	100 Francs, Lafayette—230th Anniversary, Platinum	—	450.00
☐ 1987	100 Francs, Lafayette—230th Anniversary, Gold	—	375.00
☐ 1987	100 Francs, Lafayette—230th Anniversary, Palladium	—	225.00
☐ 1987	100 Francs, Lafayette—230th Anniversary, Silver	—	45.00
☐ 1988	100 Francs, Fraternity, Gold	—	600.00
☐ 1988	100 Francs, Fraternity, Platinum	—	575.00
☐ 1988	100 Francs, Fraternity, Silver	—	42.00
☐ 1988	100 Francs, Fraternity, Palladium	—	235.00
☐ 1989	100 Francs, Olympics—Ice Skating, Silver	—	42.00
☐ 1989	100 Francs, Olympics—Alpine Skating, Silver	—	42.00
☐ 1989	100 Francs, Human Rights, Palladium	—	285.00
☐ 1989	100 Francs, Human Rights, Gold	—	850.00

DATE	COIN TYPE/VARIETY/METAL	ABP FINE	AVERAGE FINE
☐ 1989	100 Francs, Human Rights, Platinum	—	$875.00
☐ 1990	100 Francs, Olympics—Speed Skating, Silver	—	35.00
☐ 1990	100 Francs, Charlemagne, Silver	—	55.00
☐ 1990	100 Francs, Olympics—Bobsledding, Silver	—	55.00
☐ 1990	100 Francs, Olympic—Slalom Skier, Silver	—	35.00
☐ 1990	100 Francs, Olympic—Freestyle, Silver	—	42.00
☐ 1991	100 Francs, Olympic—Hockey Player, Silver	—	50.00
☐ 1991	100 Francs, Olympic—Ski Jumper, Silver	—	45.00
☐ 1991	100 Francs, Basketball—100th Anniversary, Silver	—	75.00
☐ 1991	100 Francs, Descartes, Silver	—	45.00
☐ 1991	100 Francs, Olympic—Cross Country Skier, Silver	—	50.00
☐ 1992	100 Francs, Paralympics, Silver	—	100.00
☐ 1993	100 Francs, Louvre Bicentennial—Victory, Silver	—	48.00
☐ 1993	100 Francs, Louvre Bicentennial—Mona Lisa, Silver	—	50.00
☐ 1993	100 Francs, Louvre Bicentennial—Victory, Gold	—	475.00
☐ 1993	100 Francs, Louvre Bicentennial—Liberty, Silver	—	45.00
☐ 1993	100 Francs, Louvre Bicentennial—Liberty, Gold	—	525.00
☐ 1989	500 Francs, Olympic—Alpine Skiing, Gold	—	350.00
☐ 1989	500 Francs, Olympic—Ice Skating, Gold	—	350.00
☐ 1990	500 Francs, Olympic—Freestyle Skier, Gold	—	240.00
☐ 1990	500 Francs, Olympic—Bobsledding, Gold	—	365.00
☐ 1990	500 Francs, Olympic—Slalom Skier, Gold	—	365.00
☐ 1990	500 Francs, Olympic—Speed Skating, Gold	—	200.00
☐ 1991	500 Francs, Olympic—Coubertin, Gold	—	420.00
☐ 1991	500 Francs, Olympic—Hockey Player, Gold	—	440.00
☐ 1991	500 Francs, Olympic—Cross Country Skier, Gold	—	440.00
☐ 1991	500 Francs, Basketball—100th Anniversary, Gold	—	375.00

DATE	COIN TYPE/VARIETY/METAL	ABP FINE	AVERAGE FINE
☐ 1991	500 Francs, Olympic—Ski Jumpers, Gold	—	$275.00
☐ 1993	500 Francs, Louvre—Mona Lisa, Gold	—	3000.00

*BV—These coins are relatively current so their collector value is minimal. Since these coins were minted and sold primarily for their bullion value, their current value is determined by the current "spot" price of the precious metal indicated. For accurate prices, contact your local coin dealer.

GERMANY (FED. REP.)

The first coins were used in the 3rd century B.C. as gold staters. In the 1st century B.C., small silver coins were produced. A local gold coin, known as a rainbow-cup, came to an end in the mid-1st century B.C. The silver denar was produced in the 800s. The bracteates became popular in the 1100s, as did pfennigs. A larger silver piece was used in the 14th century, along with other gold coinage. In the 1600s, good coinage had to be restored, with medallic taler being produced. The first decimal coins were used in 1871. Today's currency is the mark.

GERMANY (DEM. REP.)

The first coins were used in 1949 when the German Democratic Republic was formed. Its coinage was based on 100 pfennig to the mark, some in aluminum and some in brass. The mark was cupronickel or silver.

Germany—German Empire Coinage

Key to Grading: Eagle

DATE	COIN TYPE/VARIETY/METAL	ABP FINE	AVERAGE FINE
☐ 1873–1889	1 Pfennig (1st Coinage), Rev: Small Eagle, Copper	—	$5.00
☐ 1890–1916	1 Pfennig (2nd Coinage), Rev: Large Eagle, Copper	—	.55

Key to Grading: Eagle

DATE	COIN TYPE/VARIETY/METAL	ABP FINE	AVERAGE FINE
☐ 1873–1877	2 Pfennig (1st Coinage), Rev: Small Eagle, Copper	—	.80
☐ 1904–1916	2 Pfennig (2nd Coinage), Rev: Large Eagle, Copper	—	.65

Key to Grading: Eagle

DATE	COIN TYPE/VARIETY/METAL	ABP FINE	AVERAGE FINE
☐ 1874–1889	5 Pfennig (1st Coinage), Rev: Small Eagle, Cupro-Nickel	—	1.15
☐ 1890–1915	5 Pfennig (2nd Coinage), Rev: Large Eagle, Cupro-Nickel	—	.70

Key to Grading: Eagle

DATE	COIN TYPE/VARIETY/METAL	ABP FINE	AVERAGE FINE
☐ 1873–1889	10 Pfennig (1st Coinage), Rev: Small Eagle, Cupro-Nickel	—	$1.25
☐ 1890–1915	10 Pfennig (2nd Coinage), Rev: Large Eagle, Cupro-Nickel	—	.65
☐ 1873–1877	20 Pfennig (1st Coinage), Rev: Small Eagle, Silver	—	12.00
☐ 1887–1888	20 Pfennig (1st Coinage), Rev: Small Eagle, Cupro-Nickel	—	15.00
☐ 1890–1892	20 Pfennig (2nd Coinage), Rev: Large Eagle, Cupro-Nickel	—	20.00
☐ 1909–1912	25 Pfennig (2nd Coinage), Rev: Large Eagle, Nickel	—	6.00
☐ 1877–1878	50 Pfennig (1st Coinage), Rev: Small Eagle, Silver	—	25.00
☐ 1875–1877	50 Pfennig (1st Coinage), Rev: Small Eagle, Silver	—	25.00
☐ 1896–1901	50 Pfennig (2nd Coinage), Rev: Large Eagle, Silver	$115.00	140.00

Key to Grading: Eagle

☐ 1905–1919	1/2 Mark (2nd Coinage), Rev: Large Eagle, Silver	—	5.25

Key to Grading: Eagle

DATE	COIN TYPE/VARIETY/METAL	ABP FINE	AVERAGE FINE
☐ 1873–1887	1 Mark (1st Coinage), Rev: Small Eagle, Silver	—	$6.25

Key to Grading: Eagle

DATE	COIN TYPE/VARIETY/METAL	ABP FINE	AVERAGE FINE
☐ 1891–1916	1 Mark (2nd Coinage), Rev: Large Eagle, Silver	—	6.25

Germany—World War I Coinage

Key to Grading: Eagle

DATE	COIN TYPE/VARIETY/METAL	ABP FINE	AVERAGE FINE
☐ 1916–1918	1 Pfennig, WWI, Rev: Large Eagle, Aluminum	—	.75
☐ 1915–1922	5 Pfennig, WWI, Rev: Large Eagle, Iron	—	.38
☐ 1915–1922	10 Pfennig, WWI, Rev: Small Eagle, Iron	—	.38
☐ 1916–1917	10 Pfennig, WWI, Rev: Small Eagle, Zinc	$32.00	80.00
☐ 1916	1 Kopek, WWI, Iron	—	4.15
☐ 1916	2 Kopeks, WWI, Iron	—	4.15
☐ 1916	3 Kopeks, WWI, Iron	—	4.15

Germany—Weimar Republic Coinage

Key to Grading: Wheat Heads

DATE	COIN TYPE/VARIETY/METAL	ABP FINE	AVERAGE FINE
☐ 1923–1929	1 Rentenpfennig, Weimar Republic, Bronze	—	.38
☐ 1924–1936	1 Reichspfennig, Weimar Republic, Bronze	—	.38
☐ 1923–1924	2 Rentenpfennig, Weimar Republic, Bronze	—	.38
☐ 1924–1936	2 Reichspfennig, Weimar Republic, Bronze	—	.38
☐ 1932–1933	4 Reichspfennig, Weimar Republic, Rev: Large Eagle, Bronze	—	4.00

Key to Grading: Wheat Heads

DATE	COIN TYPE/VARIETY/METAL	ABP FINE	AVERAGE FINE
☐ 1923–1925	5 Rentenpfennig, Weimar Republic, Aluminum-Bronze	—	$ .38
☐ 1924–1936	5 Reichspfennig, Weimar Republic, Rev: Large Eagle, Aluminum-Bronze	—	.38

Key to Grading: Wheat Head

DATE	COIN TYPE/VARIETY/METAL	ABP FINE	AVERAGE FINE
☐ 1923–1925	10 Rentenpfennig, Weimar Republic, Aluminum-Bronze	—	.42
☐ 1924–1936	10 Reichspfennig, Weimar Republic, Rev: Large Eagle, Aluminum-Bronze	—	.42

Key to Grading: Wheat Heads

DATE	COIN TYPE/VARIETY/METAL	ABP FINE	AVERAGE FINE
☐ 1919–1922	50 Pfennig, Weimar Republic, Aluminum	—	.42

Key to Grading: Wheat Heads

DATE	COIN TYPE/VARIETY/METAL	ABP FINE	AVERAGE FINE
☐ 1923–1924	50 Rentenpfennig, Weimar Republic, Aluminum-Bronze	—	$14.0
☐ 1924–1925	50 Reichspfennig, Weimar Republic, Aluminum-Bronze	—	800.0
☐ 1924–1925	Mark, Weimar Republic, Rev: Large Eagle, Silver	—	8.0
☐ 1925–1927	1 Reichsmark, Weimar Republic, Rev: Large Eagle, Silver	—	12.0
☐ 1925–1931	2 Reichsmark, Weimar Republic, Rev: Large Eagle, Silver	—	20.0
☐ 1922–1923	3 Mark, Weimar Republic, 3rd Anniversary—Weimar Constitution, Aluminum	—	4.25
☐ 1925	3 Reichsmark, Weimar Republic, Commemorative—Millenium Unification of Rhineland, Silver	—	20.00
☐ 1926	3 Reichsmark, Weimar Republic, Commemorative—700th Anniversary of the Freedom of Lubeck, Silver	—	80.00
☐ 1927	3 Reichsmark, Weimar Republic, Commemorative—Bremhaven Centennial, Silver	—	85.00
☐ 1927	3 Reichsmark, Weimar Republic, Commemorative—University of Marburg 400th Anniversary, Silver	—	80.00
☐ 1927	3 Reichsmark, Weimar Republic, Commemorative—University of Tubingen 450th Anniversary, Silver	—	200.00
☐ 1927	3 Reichsmark, Weimar Republic, Commemorative—Nordhausen Millenium, Silver	—	80.00
☐ 1928	3 Reichsmark, Weimar Republic, Commemorative—City of Naumburg—900th Anniversary, Silver	—	100.00
☐ 1928	3 Reichsmark, Weimar Republic, Commemorative—City of Dinkelsbuhl Millenium, Silver	—	325.00
☐ 1928	3 Reichsmark, Weimar Republic, Commemorative—Death of Durer—400th Anniversary, Silver	—	200.00
☐ 1929	3 Reichsmark, Weimar Republic, Commemorative—Birth of Lessing Bicentennial, Silver	—	40.00
☐ 1929	3 Reichsmark, Weimar Republic, Commemorative—Waldeck-Prussia Union, Silver	—	100.00

DATE	COIN TYPE/VARIETY/METAL	ABP FINE	AVERAGE FINE
☐ 1929	3 Reichsmark, Weimar Republic, Commemorative—City of Meissen Millenium, Silver	—	$45.00
☐ 1929	3 Reichsmark, Weimar Republic, Commemorative—Constitution 10th Anniversary, Silver	—	32.00
☐ 1930	3 Reichsmark, Weimar Republic, Commemorative—End of Rhineland Occupation, Silver	—	38.00
☐ 1930	3 Reichsmark, Weimar Republic, Commemorative—Flight of Graf Zeppelin, Silver	—	65.00
☐ 1930	3 Reichsmark, Weimar Republic, Commemorative—Death of Vogelweide 700th Anniversary, Silver	—	50.00
☐ 1931	3 Reichsmark, Weimar Republic, Commemorative—Death of von Stein Centennial, Silver	—	70.00
☐ 1931	3 Reichsmark, Weimar Republic, Commemorative—Magdeburg Rebuilding 300th Anniversary, Silver	—	150.00
☐ 1931–1933	3 Reichsmark, Weimar Republic, Rev: Large Eagle, Silver	—	160.00
☐ 1932	3 Reichsmark, Weimar Republic, Commemorative—Death of Goethe, Silver	—	48.00

Key to Grading: Eagle

DATE	COIN TYPE/VARIETY/METAL	ABP FINE	AVERAGE FINE
☐ 1922	3 Mark, Weimar Republic, Obv: Large Eagle, Aluminum	—	2.00
☐ 1924–1925	3 Mark, Weimar Republic, Rev: Large Eagle, Silver	—	32.00
☐ 1925	5 Reichsmark, Weimar Republic, Commemorative—Millennium Unification of Rhineland, Silver	—	62.00
☐ 1927–1933	5 Reichsmark, Weimar Republic, Rev: Large Eagle, Silver	—	62.00

DATE	COIN TYPE/VARIETY/METAL	ABP FINE	AVERAGE FINE
☐ 1927	5 Reichsmark, Weimar Republic, Commemorative—University of Tubingen 450th Anniversary, Silver	—	$225.00
☐ 1929	5 Reichsmark, Weimar Republic, Commemorative—Birth of Lessing Bicentennial, Silver	—	75.00
☐ 1929	5 Reichsmark, Weimar Republic, Commemorative—Constitution 10th Anniversary, Silver	—	75.00
☐ 1929	5 Reichsmark, Weimar Republic, Commemorative—City of Meissen Millennium, Silver	—	185.00
☐ 1930	5 Reichsmark, Weimar Republic, Commemorative—End of Rhineland Occupation, Silver	—	90.00
☐ 1930	5 Reichsmark, Weimar Republic, Commemorative—Flight of Graf Zeppelin, Silver	—	90.00
☐ 1932	5 Reichsmark, Weimar Republic, Commemorative—Death of Goethe, Silver	—	725.00

Key to Grading: Eagle

☐ 1923	200 Mark, Weimar Republic, Obv: Large Eagle, Aluminum	—	.80

Key to Grading: Eagle

☐ 1923	500 Mark, Weimar Republic, Obv: Large Eagle, Aluminum	—	.80

Germany—Third Reich Coinage

Key to Grading: Eagle

DATE	COIN TYPE/VARIETY/METAL	ABP FINE	AVERAGE FINE
☐ 1936–1940	1 Reischspfennig, Third Reich, Obv: Hindenburg, Bronze	—	$1.65
☐ 1940–1945	1 Reischspfennig, Third Reich, Zinc	—	1.00

Key to Grading: Eagle

DATE	COIN TYPE/VARIETY/METAL	ABP FINE	AVERAGE FINE
☐ 1936–1940	2 Reischspfennig, Third Reich, Obv: Hindenburg, Bronze	—	1.15

Key to Grading: Eagle

DATE	COIN TYPE/VARIETY/METAL	ABP FINE	AVERAGE FINE
☐ 1936–1939	5 Reischspfennig, Third Reich, Obv: Hindenburg, Aluminum-Bronze	—	1.40
☐ 1940–1941	5 Reischspfennig, Third Reich, German Army, Zinc w/o White Spots	$32.00	45.00
☐ 1940–1944	5 Reischspfennig, Third Reich, Zinc w/o White Spots	—	1.40

Key to Grading: Eagle

DATE	COIN TYPE/VARIETY/METAL	ABP FINE	AVERAGE FINE
☐ 1936–1939	10 Reischspfennig, Third Reich, Obv: Hindenburg, Aluminum-Bronze	—	$2.20
☐ 1940–1941	10 Reischspfennig, Third Reich, German Army, Zinc w/o white spots	—	55.00
☐ 1940–1945	10 Reischspfennig, Third Reich, Zinc w/o White Spots	—	2.20

Key to Grading: Eagle

DATE	COIN TYPE/VARIETY/METAL	ABP FINE	AVERAGE FINE
☐ 1935	50 Reischspfennig, Third Reich, Aluminum	—	2.20
☐ 1938–1939	50 Reischspfennig, Third Reich, Nickel	—	15.00
☐ 1939–1944	50 Reischspfennig, Third Reich, Aluminum	$2.00	6.00
☐ 1933–1939	1 Reischsmark, Third Reich, Nickel	15.00	25.00
☐ 1933	2 Reischsmark, Third Reich, Commemorative—Birth of Martin Luther 450th Anniversary, Silver	5.00	12.00
☐ 1934	2 Reischsmark, Third Reich, Commemorative—Anniversary of Nazi Rule, Silver	5.00	8.50
☐ 1934	2 Reischsmark, Third Reich, Commemorative—Birth of Schiller 175th Anniversary, Silver	20.00	38.00
☐ 1936–1939	2 Reichsmark, Third Reich, Obv: Hindenburg, Silver	5.00	8.50
☐ 1933	5 Reischsmark, Third Reich, Commemorative—Birth of Martin Luther 450th Anniversary, Silver	26.00	85.00

DATE	COIN TYPE/VARIETY/METAL	ABP FINE	AVERAGE FINE
☐ 1934	5 Reischsmark, Third Reich, Commemorative—Anniversary of Nazi Rule, Silver	$8.00	$14.00
☐ 1934	5 Reischsmark, Third Reich, Commemorative—Birth of Schiller 175th Anniversary, Silver	60.00	100.00
☐ 1934–1935	5 Reischsmark, Third Reich, Silver	1.50	6.00
☐ 1935–1936	5 Reischsmark, Third Reich, Obv: Hindenburg, Silver	4.00	8.00
☐ 1936–1939	5 Reichsmark, Third Reich, Obv: Hindenburg, Silver	4.00	8.00

Germany—Allied Occupation Coinage

Key to Grading: Eagle

☐ 1944	1 Reichspfennig, Allied Occ, Zinc	—	2200.00
☐ 1944–1946	1 Reichspfennig, Allied Occ, Zinc	—	48.00

Key to Grading: Leaves

☐ 1948–1949	1 Pfennig, Allied Occ, Bank Deutscher, Lander, Bronze-Steel	—	.35
☐ 1944–1946	5 Reichspfennig, Allied Occ, Zinc	—	15.00

Key to Grading: Leaves

☐ 1949	5 Pfennig, Allied Occ, Bank Deutscher Lander, Brass-Steel	—	.35
☐ 1945–1948	10 Reichspfennig, Allied Occ, Zinc	16.00	25.00

Key to Grading: Leaves

DATE	COIN TYPE/VARIETY/METAL	ABP FINE	AVERAGE FINE
□ 1949	10 Pfennig, Allied Occ, Bank Deutscher Lander, Brass-Steel	—	$ .42

Key to Grading: Figure

□ 1949–1950	50 Pfennig, Allied Occ, Bank Deutscher Lander, Cupro-Nickel	—	.60

Germany—German Federal Republic Coinage

□ 1950 to Date	1 Pfennig, Federal Republic, Bundesrepublik Deutschland, Bronze-Steel	—	.42

DATE	COIN TYPE/VARIETY/METAL	ABP FINE	AVERAGE FINE
☐ 1950–1968	2 Pfennig, Federal Republic, Bundesrepublik Deutschland, Bronze	—	$ .42
☐ 1969 to Date	2 Pfennig, Federal Republic, Bundesrepublik Deutschland, Bronze-Steel	—	.42

Key to Grading: Leaves

☐ 1950 to Date	5 Pfennig, Federal Republic, Bundesrepublik Deutschland, Brass-Steel	—	.38

Key to Grading: Leaves

☐ 1950 to Date	10 Pfennig, Federal Republic, Bundesrepublik Deutschland, Brass-Steel	—	.38

Key to Grading: Leaves

☐ 1950–1971	50 Pfennig, Federal Republic, Bundesrepublik Deutschland, Cupro-Nickel	—	.38
☐ 1972 to Date	50 Pfennig, Federal Republic, Bundesrepublik Deutschland, Cupro-Nickel	—	.38

Key to Grading: Eagle

DATE	COIN TYPE/VARIETY/METAL	ABP FINE	AVERAGE FINE
☐ 1950 to Date	1 Deutsche Mark, Federal Republic, Bundesrepublik Deutschland, Cupro-Nickel	—	$1.20
☐ 1951	2 Deutsche Mark, Federal Republic, Bundesrepublik Deutschland, Cupro-Nickel	$20.00	35.00
☐ 1957–1971	2 Deutsche Mark, Federal Republic, Bundesrepublik Deutschland, Cupro-Nickel	—	2.00
☐ 1957–1971	2 Deutsche Mark, Federal Republic, Bundesrepublik Deutschland, Rev: Max Planck, Cupro-Nickel	—	2.00
☐ 1968–1991	2 Deutsche Mark, Federal Republic, Bundesrepublik Deutschland, Rev: Ludwig Erhard, Cupro-Nickel	—	2.00
☐ 1969–1987	2 Deutsche Mark, Federal Republic, Bundesrepublik Deutschland, Rev: Konrad Adenauer, Cupro-Nickel	—	2.00
☐ 1970–1987	2 Deutsche Mark, Federal Republic, Bundesrepublik Deutschland, Rev: Theodor Heuss, Cupro-Nickel	—	2.15
☐ 1979–1991	2 Deutsche Mark, Federal Republic, Bundesrepublik Deutschland, Rev: Kurt Schumacher, Cupro-Nickel	—	2.15
☐ 1990–1991	2 Deutsche Mark, Federal Republic, Bundesrepublik Deutschland, Rev: Franz Strauss, Cupro-Nickel	—	2.15

Key to Grading: Eagle

DATE	COIN TYPE/VARIETY/METAL	ABP FINE	AVERAGE FINE
☐ 1951–1974	5 Deutsche Mark, Federal Republic, Bundesrepublik Deutschland, Silver	—	$7.15
☐ 1975 to Date	5 Deutsche Mark, Federal Republic, Rev: Large Eagle, Cupro-Nickel	—	7.15
☐ 1952	5 Deutsche Mark, Federal Republic, Commemorative—Nurnberg Museum Centennial, Silver	—	525.00
☐ 1955	5 Deutsche Mark, Federal Republic, Commemorative—von Schiller 150th Anniversary of Death, Silver	—	325.00
☐ 1955	5 Deutsche Mark, Federal Republic, Commemorative—Birth of Ludwig von Baden 300th Anniversary, Silver	—	240.00
☐ 1957	5 Deutsche Mark, Federal Republic, Commemorative—Death of von Eichendorff Centennial, Silver	—	250.00
☐ 1964	5 Deutsche Mark, Federal Republic, Commemorative—Death of Fichte 150th Anniversary, Silver	—	140.00
☐ 1966	5 Deutsche Mark, Federal Republic, Commemorative—Death of Leibniz 250th Anniversary, Silver	—	32.00
☐ 1967	5 Deutsche Mark, Federal Republic, Commemorative—Wilhelm & Alexander von Humboldt, Silver	—	25.00
☐ 1968	5 Deutsche Mark, Federal Republic, Commemorative—Birth of Ralfellsen 150th Anniversary, Silver	—	6.25
☐ 1968	5 Deutsche Mark, Federal Republic, Commemorative—Death of von Pettenkoffer 150th Anniversary, Silver	—	5.15
☐ 1969	5 Deutsche Mark, Federal Republic, Commemorative—Birth of Fontana 150th Anniversary, Silver	—	5.15
☐ 1969	5 Deutsche Mark, Federal Republic, Commemorative—Death of Mercator 375th Anniversary, Silver	—	5.15
☐ 1970	5 Deutsche Mark, Federal Republic, Commemorative—Birth of Beethoven 200th Anniversary, Silver	—	7.00
☐ 1971	5 Deutsche Mark, Federal Republic, Commemorative—Birth of Durer 500th Anniversary, Silver	—	5.15
☐ 1971	5 Deutsche Mark, Federal Republic, Commemorative—German Unification, Silver	—	7.00

DATE	COIN TYPE/VARIETY/METAL	ABP FINE	AVERAGE FINE
☐ 1973	5 Deutsche Mark, Federal Republic, Commemorative—Birth of Copernicus 500th Anniversary, Silver	—	$6.15
☐ 1973	5 Deutsche Mark, Federal Republic, Commemorative—Frankfurt Parliament 125th Anniversary, Silver	—	6.15
☐ 1974	5 Deutsche Mark, Federal Republic, Commemorative—Birth of Kant 250th Anniversary, Silver	—	6.15
☐ 1974	5 Deutsche Mark, Federal Republic, Commemorative—Constitutional Law 25th Anniversary, Silver	—	6.15
☐ 1975	5 Deutsche Mark, Federal Republic, Commemorative—Birth of Schweitzer Centenary, Silver	—	7.00
☐ 1975	5 Deutsche Mark, Federal Republic, Commemorative—Death of Ebert 250th Anniversary, Silver	—	6.15
☐ 1975	5 Deutsche Mark, Federal Republic, Commemorative—European Monument Protection, Silver	—	7.00
☐ 1976	5 Deutsche Mark, Federal Republic, Commemorative—Death of von Grimmelshausen 300th Anniversary, Silver	—	5.65
☐ 1977	5 Deutsche Mark, Federal Republic, Commemorative—Birth of Stresemann 100th Anniversary, Silver	—	5.65
☐ 1977	5 Deutsche Mark, Federal Republic, Commemorative—Birth of von Kleist 200th Anniversary, Silver	—	5.65
☐ 1977	5 Deutsche Mark, Federal Republic, Commemorative—Birth of Gauss 200th Anniversary, Silver	—	5.65
☐ 1978	5 Deutsche Mark, Federal Republic, Commemorative—Death of Neumann 275th Anniversary, Silver	—	5.65
☐ 1979	5 Deutsche Mark, Federal Republic, Commemorative—Birth of Hahn 100th Anniversary, Cupro-Nickel	$4.00	6.00
☐ 1979	5 Deutsche Mark, Federal Republic, Commemorative—Birth of Hahn 100th Anniversary, Silver	—	22,500.00
☐ 1979	5 Deutsche Mark, Federal Republic, Commemorative—German Archaeological Institute Anniversary, Silver	—	6.00

DATE	COIN TYPE/VARIETY/METAL	ABP FINE	AVERAGE FINE
☐ 1980	5 Deutsche Mark, Federal Republic, Commemorative—Cologne Cathedral 100th Anniversary, Cupro-Nickel	$4.00	$6.00
☐ 1980	5 Deutsche Mark, Federal Republic, Commemorative—Death of Vogelwelde 750th Anniversary, Cupro-Nickel	4.00	6.00
☐ 1981	5 Deutsche Mark, Federal Republic, Commemorative, Death of von Stein 150th Anniversary, Cupro-Nickel	4.00	6.00
☐ 1981	5 Deutsche Mark, Federal Republic, Commemorative—Death of Lessing 200th Anniversary, Cupro-Nickel	2.00	4.00
☐ 1982	5 Deutsche Mark, Federal Republic, Commemorative—Death of von Goethe 150th Anniversary, Cupro-Nickel	1.25	4.60
☐ 1982	5 Deutsche Mark, Federal Republic, Commemorative, U.N. Environmental Conference 10th Anniversary, Cupro-Nickel	1.25	4.60
☐ 1983	5 Deutsche Mark, Federal Republic, Commemorative—Death of Karl Marx 100th Anniversary, Cupro-Nickel	1.25	4.60
☐ 1983	5 Deutsche, Mark, Federal Republic, Commemorative—Birth of Martin Luther 500th Anniversary, Cupro-Nickel	1.25	4.60
☐ 1984	5 Deutsche Mark, Federal Republic, Commemorative—Birth of Bartholdy 175th Anniversary, Cupro-Nickel	1.25	4.60
☐ 1984	5 Deutsche Mark, Federal Republic, Commemorative—German Customs Union 150th Anniversary, Cupro-Nickel	1.25	4.60
☐ 1985	5 Deutsche Mark, Federal Republic, Commemorative—German Railroad 150th Anniversary, Cupro-Nickel	1.25	4.60
☐ 1985	5 Deutsche Mark, Federal Republic, Commemorative—European Year of Music, Cupro-Nickel	1.25	4.60
☐ 1986	5 Deutsche Mark, Federal Republic, Commemorative—Death of Frederick the Great 200th Anniversary, Cupro-Nickel	1.25	4.60

DATE	COIN TYPE/VARIETY/METAL	ABP FINE	AVERAGE FINE
☐ 1986	5 Deutsche Mark, Federal Republic, Commemorative—Heidenberg University 600th Anniversary, Cupro-Nickel	$2.00	$4.00
☐ 1972	10 Deutsche Mark, Federal Republic, Commemorative—Munich Olympics—Stadium, Silver	—	8.00
☐ 1972	10 Deutsche Mark, Federal Republic, Commemorative—Munich Olympics—Munchen, Silver	—	9.00
☐ 1972	10 Deutsche Mark, Federal Republic, Commemorative—Munich Olympics—Deutschland, Silver	—	9.00
☐ 1972	10 Deutsche Mark, Federal Republic, Commemorative—Munich Olympics—Athletes, Silver	—	9.00
☐ 1972	10 Deutsche Mark, Federal Republic, Commemorative—Munich Olympics—Flame, Silver	—	9.00
☐ 1972	10 Deutsche Mark, Federal Republic, Commemorative—Munich Olympics—Knot, Silver	—	12.00
☐ 1987	10 Deutsche Mark, Federal Republic, Commemorative—Berlin 750 Anniversary, Silver	—	10.00
☐ 1987	10 Deutsche Mark, Commemorative—European Unity, Silver	—	10.00
☐ 1988	10 Deutsche Mark, Commemorative—Death of Zeiss 100th Anniversary, Silver	—	7.00
☐ 1988	10 Deutsche Mark, Federal Republic, Commemorative—Birth of Schopenhauer, Silver	—	8.25
☐ 1989	10 Deutsche Mark, Federal Republic, Commemorative—Port of Hamburg 800th Anniversary, Silver	—	8.25
☐ 1989	10 Deutsche Mark, Federal Republic, Commemorative—Republic 40th Anniversary, Silver	—	9.50
☐ 1989	10 Deutsche Mark, Federal Republic, Commemorative—City of Bonn 200th Anniversary, Silver	—	9.50
☐ 1990	10 Deutsche Mark, Federal Republic, Commemorative—Teutonic Order 800th Anniversary, Silver	—	9.50

DATE	COIN TYPE/VARIETY/METAL	ABP FINE	AVERAGE FINE
☐ 1989	10 Deutsche Mark, Federal Republic, Commemorative—Port of Hamburg 800th Anniversary, Silver	—	$7.65
☐ 1989	10 Deutsche Mark, Federal Republic, Commemorative—Republic 40th Anniversary, Silver	—	7.65
☐ 1989	10 Deutsche Mark, Federal Republic, Commemorative—City of Bonn 2000th Anniversary, Silver	—	8.15
☐ 1990	10 Deutsche Mark, Federal Republic, Commemorative—Teutonic Order 800th Anniversary, Silver	—	8.15
☐ 1990	10 Deutsche Mark, Federal Republic, Commemorative—Death of Barbarossa, Silver	—	7.75
☐ 1991	10 Deutsche Mark, Federal Republic, Commemorative—Brandenburg Gate, Silver	—	7.75
☐ 1992	10 Deutsche Mark, Federal Republic, Commemorative—Civil Pour le Merite Order, Silver	—	10.00
☐ 1992	10 Deutsche Mark, Federal Republic, Commemorative—Kathe Kollwitz Artist, Silver	—	8.00

Germany—Democratic Republic Coinage

Key to Grading: Wheat Head

DATE	COIN TYPE/VARIETY/METAL	ABP FINE	AVERAGE FINE
☐ 1948–1950	1 Pfennig, Democratic Republic, Aluminum	—	1.00
☐ 1952–1953	1 Pfennig, Democratic Republic, Aluminum	—	.50

Key to Grading: Wheat Head

DATE	COIN TYPE/VARIETY/METAL	ABP FINE	AVERAGE FINE
☐ 1948–1950	5 Pfennig, Democratic Republic, Aluminum	—	1.25
☐ 1952–1953	5 Pfennig, Democratic Republic, Aluminum	—	1.80

Key to Grading: Wheat Head

DATE	COIN TYPE/VARIETY/METAL	ABP FINE	AVERAGE FINE
□ 1948–1950	10 Pfennig, Democratic Republic, Aluminum	—	$.85
□ 1952–1953	10 Pfennig, Democratic Republic, Aluminum	—	.85

Key to Grading: Buildings

DATE	COIN TYPE/VARIETY/METAL	ABP FINE	AVERAGE FINE
□ 1949–1950	50 Pfennig, Democratic Republic, Aluminum-Bronze	—	1.80

GREECE

The first coins were used in mid-6th century B.C. Except for a few white-gold coins, early Greek coins were silver. The first gold coins were produced toward the end of the Peloponnesian War. The first bronze coins appeared in the late 5th century B.C. Roman coins were introduced in Greece around the mid-1st century B.C. Bronze coins became more popular, though all coins varied from period to period. Independent coinage was begun in 1827, and the first Greek coinage was struck in Aegina, including copper and silver coins. All had a phoenix rising from the ashes to symbolize the rebirth of the nation and the date of the Greek Revolt (1821). The first decimal coins were used in 1831. The currency today is the drachma.

Greece—Type and Democratic Republic Coinage

Key to Grading: Bust

DATE	COIN TYPE/VARIETY/METAL	ABP FINE	AVERAGE FINE
□ 1869–1870	1 Lepton, Georgios I, Young Head, Copper	—	$5.20
□ 1878–1879	1 Lepton, Georgios I, Older Head—Second Coinage, Copper	—	5.20
□ 1869	2 Lepta, Georgios I, Young Head, Copper	—	4.00
□ 1878	2 Lepta, Georgios I, Older Head—Second Coinage, Copper	—	4.00
□ 1869–1870	5 Lepta, Georgios I, Young Head, Copper	—	4.00
□ 1878–1882	5 Lepta, Georgios I, Older Head—Second Coinage, Copper	—	7.00
□ 1894–1895	5 Lepta, Georgios I, Third Coinage, Cupro-Nickel	—	4.20
□ 1912	5 Lepta, Georgios I, Third Coinage, Nickel	—	4.20

Key to Grading: Bust or Crown

DATE	COIN TYPE/VARIETY/METAL	ABP FINE	AVERAGE FINE
□ 1954–1971	5 Lepta, Aluminum	—	.45
□ 1869–1870	10 Lepta, Georgios I, Young Head, Copper	—	8.00
□ 1878-1882	10 Lepta, Georgios I, Older Head—Second Coinage, Copper	—	10.00
□ 1894–1895	10 Lepta, Georgios I, Third Coinage, Cupro-Nickel	—	4.00

Key to Grading: Owl, Bust or Crown

DATE	COIN TYPE/VARIETY/METAL	ABP FINE	AVERAGE FINE
□ 1912	10 Lepta, Georgios I, Third Coinage, Nickel	—	$2.20
□ 1922	10 Lepta, Konstantinos I, Second Reign, Aluminum	—	2.20
□ 1954–1971	10 Lepta, Aluminum	—	.42
□ 1973–1978	10 Lepta, Aluminum	—	.42
□ 1869–1883	20 Lepta, Georgios I, Young Head, Silver	—	5.00
□ 1893–1895	20 Lepta, Georgios I, Older Head—Third Coinage, Cupro-Nickel	—	4.00

Key to Grading: Figure or Bust

DATE	COIN TYPE/VARIETY/METAL	ABP FINE	AVERAGE FINE
□ 1912	20 Lepta, Georgios I, Third Coinage, Nickel	—	.60
□ 1926	20 Lepta, Republic, Cupro-Nickel	—	.38
□ 1954–1971	20 Lepta, Aluminum	—	.38
□ 1973–1978	20 Lepta, Aluminum	—	.38
□ 1868–1883	50 Lepta, Georgios I, Young Head, Silver	—	4.00
□ 1921	50 Lepta, Konstantinos I, Second Reign, Cupro-Nickel	—	300.00
□ 1926	50 Lepta, Republic, Cupro-Nickel	—	.65

Key to Grading: Bust

DATE	COIN TYPE/VARIETY/METAL	ABP FINE	AVERAGE FINE
□ 1954–1965	50 Lepta, Paulos I, Cupro-Nickel	—	.38
□ 1973–1986	50 Lepta, Brass	—	.38
□ 1868–1883	1 Drachma, Georgios I, Young Head, Silver	—	25.00
□ 1910–1911	1 Drachma-Georgios I, Third Coinage, Silver	—	6.00
□ 1926	1 Drachma, Republic, Cupro-Nickel	—	.85

Key to Grading: Bust

DATE	COIN TYPE/VARIETY/METAL	ABP FINE	AVERAGE FINE
☐ 1954–1965	1 Drachma, Paulos 1, Cupro-Nickel	—	$ .38
☐ 1973–1986	1 Drachma, Brass	—	.38
☐ 1988–1990	Drachma, Copper	—	.38
☐ 1868–1883	2 Drachmai, Georgios I, Young Head, Silver	—	45.00
☐ 1911	2 Drachmai, Georgios I, Third Coinage, Silver	—	8.00

DATE	COIN TYPE/VARIETY/METAL	ABP FINE	AVERAGE FINE
☐ 1926	2 Drachmai, Republic, Cupro-Nickel	—	.60
☐ 1954–1965	2 Drachmai, Paulos I, Cupro-Nickel	—	.60
☐ 1973–1980	2 Drachmai, Brass	—	.38
☐ 1982–1986	2 Drachmai, Brass	—	.38
☐ 1988–1990	2 Drachmai, Copper	—	.38
☐ 1875–1876	5 Drachmai, Georgios I, Older Head—Second Coinage, Silver	—	38.00
☐ 1876	5 Drachmai, Georgios I, Young Head, Gold	—	285.00

Key to Grading: Eagle, Bust

DATE	COIN TYPE/VARIETY/METAL	ABP FINE	AVERAGE FINE
☐ 1930	5 Drachmai, Republic, Nickel	—	$1.50
☐ 1954–1965	5 Drachmai, Paulos I, Cupro-Nickel	—	.38
☐ 1973–1980	5 Drachmai, Cupro-Nickel	—	.38
☐ 1982–1990	5 Drachmai, Cupro-Nickel	—	.38
☐ 1876	10 Drachmai, Georgios I, Young Head, Gold	—	200.00
☐ 1930	10 Drachmai, Republic, Silver	—	6.00

Key to Grading: Bust

DATE	COIN TYPE/VARIETY/METAL	ABP FINE	AVERAGE FINE
☐ 1959–1965	10 Drachmai, Paulos I, Nickel	—	.38
☐ 1973–1980	10 Drachmai, Cupro-Nickel	—	.38
☐ 1982–1990	10 Drachmai, Cupro-Nickel	—	.38
☐ 1876	20 Drachmai, Georgios I, Young Head, Gold	—	125.00
☐ 1884	20 Drachmai, Georgios I, Older Head—Second Coinage, Gold	—	80.00
☐ 1930	20 Drachmai, Republic, Silver	—	6.25
☐ 1935	20 Drachmai, Georgios II, Restoration Commemorative, Gold	—	3500.00

Key to Grading: Bust

DATE	COIN TYPE/VARIETY/METAL	ABP FINE	AVERAGE FINE
☐ 1960–1965	20 Drachmai, Paulos I, Silver	—	2.50
☐ 1973–1980	20 Drachmai, Cupro-Nickel	—	.38
☐ 1982–1988	20 Drachmai, Cupro-Nickel	—	.38
☐ 1963	30 Drachmai, Paulos I, Centennial of Royal Greek Dynasty, Silver	—	5.00
☐ 1876	50 Drachmai, Georgios I, Older Head—Second Coinage, Gold	—	2200.00
☐ 1980	50 Drachmai, Cupro-Nickel	—	.55
☐ 1982	50 Drachmai, Cupro-Nickel	—	.55
☐ 1986–1990	50 Drachmai, Brass	—	1.00

DATE	COIN TYPE/VARIETY/METAL	ABP FINE	AVERAGE FINE
☐ 1876	100 Drachmai, Georgios I, Older Head—Second Coinage, Gold	—	$5000.00
☐ 1935	100 Drachmai, Georgios II, Restoration Commemorative, Gold	—	7000.00
☐ 1935	100 Drachmai, Georgios II, Restoration Commemorative, Silver	—	1000.00
☐ 1978–1982	100 Drachmai, Silver	—	20.00
☐ 1988	100 Drachmai, 28th Chess Olympics, Cupro-Nickel	—	20.00
☐ 1990–1991	100 Drachmai, Alexander the Great, Brass	—	1.20
☐ 1981–1982	250 Drachmai, Pan-European Games, Silver	—	8.00
☐ 1979	500 Drachmai, Common Market Membership, Silver	—	225.00
☐ 1981–1982	500 Drachmai, Pan-European Games, Silver	—	14.00
☐ 1984	500 Drachmai, Olympics—Torch, Silver	—	80.00
☐ 1988	500 Drachmai, 28th Chess Olympics, Silver	—	125.00
☐ 1991	500 Drachmai, XI Mediterranean Games, Silver	—	58.00
☐ 1985	1000 Drachmai, Decade for Women, Silver	—	75.00
☐ 1990	1000 Drachmai, Italian Invasion of Greece—50th Anniversary, Silver	—	85.00
☐ 1981–1982	2500 Drachmai, Pan-European Games, Gold	—	135.00
☐ 1981–1982	5000 Drachmai, Pan-European Games, Gold	—	240.00
☐ 1984	5000 Drachmai, Olympics—Apollo, Gold	—	450.00
☐ 1979	10,000 Drachmai, Common Market Membership, Gold	—	600.00
☐ 1985	10,000 Drachmai, Decade for Women, Gold	—	340.00
☐ 1991	10,000 Drachmai, XI Mediterranean Games, Gold	—	350.00
☐ 1990	20,000 Drachmai, Italian Invasion of Greece—50th Anniversary, Gold	—	1500.00

HUNGARY

The first coins were used in the 3rd century B.C. and were of silver. In the 2nd century B.C., bronze coins were produced. The silver denar appeared in the 11th century, followed by copper denars, gold ducats, and silver talers. The decimal system was established in 1857. Today's currency is the forint.

Hungary—Type Coinage

Key to Grading: Bust

DATE	COIN TYPE/VARIETY/METAL	ABP FINE	AVERAGE FINE
☐ 1882	5/10 Krajczar, Franz Joseph, Rev: Shield, Copper	$2.25	$5.00
☐ 1868–1892	1 Krakczar, Franz Joseph, Rev: Shield, Copper	2.25	6.15
☐ 1892–1906	1 Filler, Franz Joseph, Rev: Crown, Bronze	2.25	5.00

Key to Grading: Crown

DATE	COIN TYPE/VARIETY/METAL	ABP FINE	AVERAGE FINE
☐ 1926–1938	1 Filler, Horthy Regency, Crown, Bronze	—	.45

Key to Grading: Crown

DATE	COIN TYPE/VARIETY/METAL	ABP FINE	AVERAGE FINE
☐ 1892–1915	2 Filler, Franz Joseph, Rev: Crown, Bronze	—	$ .50
☐ 1926–1938	2 Filler, Horthy Regency, Crown, Bronze	—	.38
☐ 1940–1944	2 Filler, Horthy Regency, Stainless Steel	—	.50
☐ 1946–1947	2 Filler, Republic, Hungarian Arms, Bronze	—	.38
☐ 1950–1989	2 Filler, Republic, Rev: Spray, Aluminum	—	.38
☐ 1948–1951	5 Filler, Republic, Rev: Spray, Aluminum	—	.38

Key to Grading: Bust

DATE	COIN TYPE/VARIETY/METAL	ABP FINE	AVERAGE FINE
☐ 1868–1889	10 Krajczar, Franz Joseph, Rev: Shield, Silver	—	18.00
☐ 1892–1896	10 Filler, Franz Joseph, Rev: Crown, Cupro-Nickel	—	.65
☐ 1906–1916	10 Filler, Franz Joseph, Rev: Crown, Nickel	—	.38
☐ 1926–1938	10 Filler, Horthy Regency, Crown, Cupro-Nickel	—	.80
☐ 1940–1944	10 Filler, Horthy Regency, Stainless Steel	—	.60

Key to Grading: Bust

DATE	COIN TYPE/VARIETY/METAL	ABP FINE	AVERAGE FINE
☐ 1946–1947	10 Filler, Republic, Dove, Copper-Aluminum	—	.38
☐ 1948–1951	10 Filler, Republic, Rev: Spray, Aluminum	—	.38
☐ 1868–1872	20 Krajczar, Franz Joseph, Rev: Shield, Silver	—	14.00
☐ 1892–1894	20 Filler, Franz Joseph, Rev: crown, Cupro-Nickel	—	2.20

DATE	COIN TYPE/VARIETY/METAL	ABP FINE	AVERAGE FINE
☐ 1906–1914	20 Filler, Franz Joseph, Rev: Crown, Nickel	—	$2.20
☐ 1926–1938	20 Filler, Horthy Regency, Crown, Cupro-Nickel	—	4.00
☐ 1940–1944	20 Filler, Horthy Regency, Center Hole, Stainless Steel	—	.75
☐ 1946–1947	20 Filler, Republic, Ears of Wheat, Copper-Aluminum	—	.75
☐ 1948–1950	20 Filler, Republic, Rev: Spray, Aluminum	—	.75
☐ 1926–1938	50 Filler, Horthy Regency, Crown, Cupro-Nickel	—	1.00
☐ 1948–1950	50 Filler, Republic, Rev: Spray, Aluminum	—	1.00

Key to Grading: Bust or Coat of Arms

DATE	COIN TYPE/VARIETY/METAL	ABP FINE	AVERAGE FINE
☐ 1926–1939	1 Pengo, Horthy Regency, Arms, Silver	—	1.50
☐ 1941–1944	1 Pengo, Horthy Regency, Hungarian Arms, Aluminum	—	.45
☐ 1892–1916	1 Korona, Franz Joseph, Rev: Crown, Silver	—	5.00
☐ 1946–1949	1 Forint, Republic, Hungarian Arms, Aluminum	—	4.00
☐ 1929–1938	2 Pengo, Horthy Regency, Madonna, Silver	—	4.00
☐ 1935	2 Pengo, Horthy Regency, Rakoczi, Silver	—	4.00
☐ 1935	2 Pengo, Horthy Regency, University of Budapest, Silver	—	4.00
☐ 1936	2 Pengo, Horthy Regency, Liszt, Silver	—	2.00
☐ 1941	2 Pengo, Horthy Regency, Hungarian Arms, Aluminum	—	.75
☐ 1912–1914	2 Korona, Franz Joseph, Silver	—	4.20
☐ 1946–1947	2 Forint, Republic, Hungarian Arms, Aluminum	—	4.20

Key to Grading: Bust

DATE	COIN TYPE/VARIETY/METAL	ABP FINE	AVERAGE FINE
□ 1950–1952	2 Forint, Republic, Star With Rays, Hammer and Wheat, Rev: Wreath, Cupro-Nickel	$1.00	$2.20
□ 1938	5 Pengo, Horthy Regency, Death of St. Stephen 900th Anniversary, Silver	4.00	7.00
□ 1943	5 Pengo, Horthy Regency, 75th Birthday of Admiral Horthy, Aluminum	—	2.20
□ 1939	5 Pengo, Horthy Regency, Bust of Admiral Horthy, Silver	—	6.00
□ 1945	5 Pengo, Horthy Regency, Parliament Building, Aluminum	—	2.20
□ 1948	5 Forint, Republic, Revolution Commemorative, Silver	—	2.20
□ 1900–1909	5 Korona, Franz Joseph, Rev: Angels Holding Crown, Silver	—	15.00
□ 1907	5 Korona, Franz Joseph, Jubilee Coronation Scene, Silver	—	25.00
□ 1930	5 Pengo, Horthy Regency, Bust, Silver	—	6.15
□ 1946–1947	5 Forint, Republic, Head of Kossuth, Silver	—	4.00
□ 1948	10 Forint, Republic, Revolution Commemorative, Silver	—	5.00
□ 1948	20 Forint, Republic, Revolution Commemorative, Silver	—	6.15

ICELAND

Iceland's coinage was originally that of its neighbors, Norway and Denmark. Although an independent republic, Iceland did not have its own currency, the krona, until 1922. In 1944, new denominations were added. In 1981, a new krona was introduced that was equal to 100 old kronur.

Iceland—Type Coinage

Key to Grading: Crown

DATE	COIN TYPE/VARIETY/METAL	ABP FINE	AVERAGE FINE
□ 1926–1942	1 Eyrir, Kingdom, Bronze	—	$2.00
□ 1946–1966	1 Eyrir, Republic, Bronze	—	.40

Key to Grading: Crown

DATE	COIN TYPE/VARIETY/METAL	ABP FINE	AVERAGE FINE
□ 1926–1942	2 Aurar, Kingdom, Bronze	—	2.20

Key to Grading: Crown

DATE	COIN TYPE/VARIETY/METAL	ABP FINE	AVERAGE FINE
☐ 1926–1942	5 Aurar, Kingdom, Bronze	—	$2.00
☐ 1946–1966	5 Aurar, Republic, Bronze	—	.45
☐ 1981	5 Aurar, Sting Ray, Bronze	—	.45

Key to Grading: Coat of Arms

DATE	COIN TYPE/VARIETY/METAL	ABP FINE	AVERAGE FINE
☐ 1922–1942	10 Aurar, Kingdom, Cupro-Nickel	$1.00	5.00
☐ 1946–1969	10 Aurar, Republic, Cupro-Nickel	—	.38
☐ 1970–1974	10 Aurar, Republic, Aluminum	—	.38
☐ 1981	10 Aurar, Cuttlefish, Bronze	—	.38

Key to Grading: Coat of Arms

DATE	COIN TYPE/VARIETY/METAL	ABP FINE	AVERAGE FINE
☐ 1926–1942	25 Aurar, Kingdom, Cupro-Nickel	—	1.50
☐ 1948–1967	25 Aurar, Republic, Cupro-Nickel	—	.38
☐ 1969–1974	50 Aurar, Republic, Brass	—	.38
☐ 1981	50 Aurar, Lobster, Bronze	—	—

Key to Grading: Coat of Arms

DATE	COIN TYPE/VARIETY/METAL	ABP FINE	AVERAGE FINE
☐ 1926–1942	1 Krona, Kingdom, Cupro-Nickel	—	2.50
☐ 1946	1 Krona, Republic, Aluminum-Bronze	—	.38
☐ 1957–1975	1 Krona, Republic, Brass	—	.38
☐ 1976–1980	1 Krona, Republic, Aluminum	—	.38
☐ 1981–1987	1 Krona, Cod, Cupro-Nickel	—	.38
☐ 1990	1 Krona, Cod, Stainless Steel	—	.38

Key to Grading: Coat of Arms

DATE	COIN TYPE/VARIETY/METAL	ABP FINE	AVERAGE FINE
□ 1925–1940	2 Kronur, Kingdom, Cupro-Nickel	—	$2.00
□ 1946	2 Kronur, Republic, Aluminum-Bronze	—	.38
□ 1958–1966	2 Kronur, Republic, Brass	—	.38
□ 1969–1980	5 Kronur, Republic, Cupro-Nickel	—	.38
□ 1981–1987	5 Kronur, Dolphins, Cupro-Nickel	—	.38
□ 1967–1980	10 Kronur, Republic, Cupro-Nickel	—	.38
□ 1984–1987	10 Kronur, Capelins, Cupro-Nickel	—	.38
□ 1968	50 Kronur, Sovereignty—50th Anniversary, Nickel	—	1.75
□ 1970–1980	50 Kronur, Parliament, Cupro-Nickel	—	.38
□ 1987	50 Kronur, Crab, Brass	—	.38
□ 1961	500 Kronur, Sesquicentennial—Sigurdsson, Gold	—	175.00
□ 1974	500 Kronur, 1st Settlement—1100th Anniversary, Silver	—	14.00
□ 1986	500 Kronur, Icelandic Bank Notes—100th Anniversary, Silver	—	50.00
□ 1974	1000 Kronur, 1st Settlement—1100th Anniversary, Silver	—	22.00
□ 1974	10000 Kronur, 1st Settlement—1100th Anniversary, Gold	—	175.00

INDIA

The first coins were used in the early 4th century B.C., as seen in silver punch-marked coins. Copper-cast coins appeared in 200 B.C., with lead coins in 100 A.D. The silver dramma was in evidence in 190 A.D., and the copper drachmas and gold denara in 350. The gold mohur appeared in the 1500s, and the silver rupees in the 1600s. The copper paisas were in use in the 1800s and the cupro-nickel rupees in 1974. Decimal coins were used in 1957. The currency today is the rupee.

India—Decimal and Non-Decimal Coinage

Key to Grading: Lions

DATE	COIN TYPE/VARIETY/METAL	ABP FINE	AVERAGE FINE
□ 1957–1962	1 Naye Paisa, Bronze	—	$ .38
□ 1962–1963	1 Naye Paisa, Brass	—	.38
□ 1964	1 Paisa, Bronze	—	.38
□ 1964	1 Paisa, Brass	—	.32

Key to Grading: Lions

DATE	COIN TYPE/VARIETY/METAL	ABP FINE	AVERAGE FINE
☐ 1965–1970	1 Paisa, Aluminum	—	$ .38

Key to Grading: Lions

DATE	COIN TYPE/VARIETY/METAL	ABP FINE	AVERAGE FINE
☐ 1950–1955	1 Pice, Bronze	—	.38
☐ 1957–1963	2 Naye Paise, Cupro-Nickel	—	.38
☐ 1964	2 Paise, Cupro-Nickel	—	.38

Key to Grading: Lions

DATE	COIN TYPE/VARIETY/METAL	ABP FINE	AVERAGE FINE
☐ 1965–1981	2 Paise, Aluminum	—	.32

Key to Grading: Lions

DATE	COIN TYPE/VARIETY/METAL	ABP FINE	AVERAGE FINE
☐ 1964–1981	3 Paise, Aluminum	—	.38
☐ 1950–1955	½ Anna, Cupro-Nickel	—	.38

Key to Grading: Lions

DATE	COIN TYPE/VARIETY/METAL	ABP FINE	AVERAGE FINE
☐ 1957–1990	5 Naye Paise, Cupro-Nickel	—	.38
☐ 1964–1966	5 Paise, Cupro-Nickel	—	.38

Key to Grading: Lions

DATE	COIN TYPE/VARIETY/METAL	ABP FINE	AVERAGE FINE
☐ 1967–1984	5 Paise, Aluminum	—	$ .38
☐ 1976	5 Paise, FAO Issues: Food & Work For All, Aluminum	—	.38
☐ 1977	5 Paise, FAO Issues: Save For Development, Aluminum	—	.38
☐ 1978	5 Paise, FAO Issues: Food & Shelter For All, Aluminum	—	.38
☐ 1979	5 Paise, International Year of the Child, Aluminum	—	.38
☐ 1950–1955	1 Anna, Cupro-Nickcl	—	.38

Key to Grading: Lions

DATE	COIN TYPE/VARIETY/METAL	ABP FINE	AVERAGE FINE
☐ 1957–1963	10 Naye Paise, Cupro-Nickel	—	.32
☐ 1964–1967	10 Paise, Cupro-Nickel	—	.32
☐ 1968–1982	10 Paise, Brass	—	.32

Key to Grading: Figures

DATE	COIN TYPE/VARIETY/METAL	ABP FINE	AVERAGE FINE
☐ 1974	10 Paise, FAO Issue, Brass	—	.38
☐ 1975	10 Paise, FAO Issue—Woman's Year, Brass	—	.38
☐ 1976	10 Paise, FAO Issue—Food & Work For All, Brass	—	.38

DATE	COIN TYPE/VARIETY/METAL	ABP FINE	AVERAGE FINE
☐ 1977	10 Paise, FAO Issue—Save For Development, Brass	—	$ .32
☐ 1978	10 Paise, FAO Issue—Food & Shelter For All, Brass	—	.32
☐ 1979	10 Paise, International Year of the Child, Brass	—	.32
☐ 1980	10 Paise, Rural Women's Advancement, Brass	—	.38
☐ 1981	10 Paise, World Food Day, Brass	—	.38
☐ 1982	10 Paise, IX Asian Games, Brass	—	.38
☐ 1983–1990	10 Paise, Aluminum	—	.38
☐ 1950–1955	2 Annas, Cupro-Nickel	—	.38

Key to Grading: Lions

DATE	COIN TYPE/VARIETY/METAL	ABP FINE	AVERAGE FINE
☐ 1968–1971	20 Paise, Brass	—	.32
☐ 1969	20 Paise, Aluminum-Bronze	—	.32
☐ 1970–1971	20 Paise, FAO Issue, Aluminum-Bronze	—	.32
☐ 1982–1991	20 Paise, Aluminum	—	.32
☐ 1982	20 Paise, World Food Day, Aluminum	—	.32
☐ 1983	20 Paise, FAO Issue—Fisheries, Aluminum	—	.32

Key to Grading: Lions

DATE	COIN TYPE/VARIETY/METAL	ABP FINE	AVERAGE FINE
☐ 1950–1956	1/4 Rupee, Nickel	—	.38

Key to Grading: Lions

DATE	COIN TYPE/VARIETY/METAL	ABP FINE	AVERAGE FINE
☐ 1957–1968	25 Paise, Nickel	—	$ .32
☐ 1957–1963	25 Paise, Nickel	—	.32
☐ 1972–1990	25 Paise, Cupro-Nickel	—	.32
☐ 1980	25 Paise, Rural Women's Advancement, Cupro-Nickel	—	.38
☐ 1981	25 Paise, World Food Day, Cupro-Nickel	—	.38
☐ 1982	25 Paise, IX Asian Games, Cupro-Nickel	—	.38
☐ 1985	25 Paise, Forestry, Cupro-Nickel	—	.38
☐ 1988–1991	25 Paise, Rhinoceros, Stainless Steel	—	.38

Key to Grading: Lions

DATE	COIN TYPE/VARIETY/METAL	ABP FINE	AVERAGE FINE
☐ 1950–1956	½ Rupee, Nickel	—	.32
☐ 1964–1983	50 Paise, Nickel	—	.32
☐ 1964	50 Paise, Nehru Death, Nickel	—	.32
☐ 1969	50 Paise, Centennial—Mahatma Gandhi, Nickel	—	.32
☐ 1972–1973	50 Paise, Independence—25th Anniversary, Cupro-Nickel	—	.32

DATE	COIN TYPE/VARIETY/METAL	ABP FINE	AVERAGE FINE
☐ 1973	50 Paise, FAO Issue—Grow More Food, Cupro-Nickel	—	.32
☐ 1982	50 Paise, National Integration, Cupro-Nickel	—	.32
☐ 1984–1990	50 Paise, Cupro-Nickel	—	.32
☐ 1985	50 Paise, Indira Gandhi—Death, Cupro-Nickel	—	.38
☐ 1985	50 Paise, Reserve Bank of India—Golden Jubilee, Cupro-Nickel	—	.38
☐ 1986	50 Paise, FAO—Fisheries, Cupro-Nickel	—	.38

DATE	COIN TYPE/VARIETY/METAL	ABP FINE	AVERAGE FINE
☐ 1988–1997	50 Paise, Parliament Building, Stainless Steel	—	$ .40
☐ 1950–1954	1 Rupee, Nickel	—	1.25
☐ 1962–1974	1 Rupee, Nickel	—	1.00

Key to Grading: Lions

DATE	COIN TYPE/VARIETY/METAL	ABP FINE	AVERAGE FINE
☐ 1964	1 Rupee, Nehru Death, Nickel	—	.55
☐ 1969	1 Rupee, Mahatma Gandhi Centennial, Nickel	—	.55
☐ 1975–1991	1 Rupee, Cupro-Nickel	—	.32
☐ 1985	1 Rupee, Youth Year, Cupro-Nickel	—	.32
☐ 1987	1 Rupee, FAO—Small Farmers, Cupro-Nickel	—	.32
☐ 1989	1 Rupee, FAO—Food & Environment, Cupro-Nickel	—	.32
☐ 1989	1 Rupee, Nehru's Birth—100th Anniversary, Cupro-Nickel	—	.32
☐ 1990	1 Rupee, SAARC Year—Care For the Girl Child, Cupro-Nickel	—	.32
☐ 1990	1 Rupee, ICDS—15th Anniversary, Cupro-Nickel	—	.32
☐ 1990	1 Rupee, FAO Farming Scene, Cupro-Nickel	—	.38
☐ 1990	1 Rupee, Dr. Ambedker, Cupro-Nickel	—	.38
☐ 1991	1 Rupee, Rajiv Gandhi, Cupro-Nickel	—	.38
☐ 1991	1 Rupee, Parliamentary Conference, Cupro-Nickel	—	.38
☐ 1982	2 Rupees, IX Asian Games, Cupro-Nickel	—	.38
☐ 1982–1992	2 Rupees, National Integration, Cupro-Nickel	—	.30
☐ 1985	2 Rupees, Reserve Bank of India—Golden Jubilee, Cupro-Nickel	$20.00	28.00 Proof
☐ 1985	5 Rupees, Indira Gandhi Death, Cupro-Nickel	—	.30
☐ 1989	5 Rupees, Nehru's Birth—100th Anniversary, Cupro-Nickel	—	.70

DATE	COIN TYPE/VARIETY/METAL	ABP FINE	AVERAGE FINE
□ 1969	10 Rupees, Centennial Birth of Mahatma Gandhi, Silver	—	$2.00

Key to Grading: Lions

DATE	COIN TYPE/VARIETY/METAL	ABP FINE	AVERAGE FINE
□ 1970	10 Rupees, FAO Issue, Silver	—	3.25
□ 1972	10 Rupees, Independence—25th Anniversary, Silver	—	2.75
□ 1973	10 Rupees, FAO Issue, Silver	—	4.00
□ 1974	10 Rupees, FAO Issue, Cupro-Nickel	—	2.00
□ 1975	10 Rupees, FAO—Women's Year, Cupro-Nickel	—	1.80
□ 1976	10 Rupees, FAO—Food & Work For All, Cupro-Nickel	—	1.80
□ 1977	10 Rupees, FAO—Save For Development, Cupro-Nickel	—	1.40
□ 1978	10 Rupees, FAO—Food & Shelter For All, Cupro-Nickel	—	1.50
□ 1979	10 Rupees, International Year of the Child, Cupro-Nickel	—	1.40
□ 1980	10 Rupees, Rural Women's Advancement, Cupro-Nickel	—	2.40
□ 1981	10 Rupees, World Food Day, Cupro-Nickel	—	2.40
□ 1982	10 Rupees, IX Asian Games, Cupro-Nickel	—	2.40
□ 1982	10 Rupees, National Integration, Cupro-Nickel	—	1.85
□ 1985	10 Rupees, Youth Year, Cupro-Nickel	—	12.00
□ 1985	10 Rupees, Reserve Bank of India—Golden Jubilee, Cupro-Nickel	—	12.00

DATE	COIN TYPE/VARIETY/METAL	ABP FINE	AVERAGE FINE
☐ 1973	20 Rupees, FAO Issue, Silver	—	$8.00
☐ 1985	20 Rupees, Death of Indira Gandhi, Cupro-Nickel	$12.00	20.00
☐ 1986	20 Rupees, FAO Fisheries, Cupro-Nickel	—	20.00
☐ 1987	20 Rupees, FAO—Small Farmers, Cupro-Nickel	—	20.00
☐ 1989	20 Rupees, Nehru's Birth—100th Anniversary, Cupro-Nickel	—	20.00
☐ 1974	50 Rupees, FAO Issue, Silver	—	7.25
☐ 1975	50 Rupees, FAO—Women's Year, Silver	—	20.00
☐ 1976	50 Rupees, FAO—Food & Work For All, Silver	—	20.00
☐ 1977	50 Rupees, FAO—Save For Development, Silver	—	20.00
☐ 1978	50 Rupees, FAO—Food & Shelter For All, Silver	—	20.00
☐ 1979	50 Rupees, International Year of the Child, Silver	—	20.00
☐ 1980	100 Rupees, Rural Women's Advancement, Silver	—	25.00
☐ 1981	100 Rupees, International Year of the Child, Silver	—	30.00
☐ 1981	100 Rupees, World Food Day, Silver	—	28.00
☐ 1982	100 Rupees, National Integration, Silver	—	35.00
☐ 1982	100 Rupees, IX Asian Games, Silver	—	28.00
☐ 1985	100 Rupees, Youth Year, Silver	—	42.00
☐ 1985	100 Rupees, Death of Indira Gandhi, Silver	—	42.00
☐ 1985	100 Rupees, Reserve Bank of India—Golden Jubilee, Silver	—	50.00
☐ 1986	100 Rupees, FAO—Fisheries, Silver	—	42.00
☐ 1987	100 Rupees, FAO—Small Farmers, Silver	—	42.00
☐ 1989	100 Rupees, Nehru's Birth—100th Anniversary, Silver	—	42.00

IRELAND

The first coins—pennies—appeared in the late 10th century, followed by farthings and halfpennies around 1190. In the mid-1400s, groats were issued, and shillings in the mid-1500s. In the mid-17th century, the Inchiquin was formed. In 1649, half crowns and crowns were issued. Cupro-nickel replaced silver in 1951, and a decimal currency system was set up in 1971.

Ireland—Type Coinage

Key to Grading: Harp

DATE	COIN TYPE/VARIETY/METAL	ABP FINE	AVERAGE FINE
Farthing-Copper			
☐ 1806		$4.00	$7.00
Half Penny-Copper			
☐ 1805		6.00	8.50
☐ 1822		8.00	12.00
☐ 1823		8.00	12.00
Penny-Copper			
☐ 1805		10.00	16.00
☐ 1822		10.00	15.00
☐ 1823		10.00	15.00
Bank of Ireland Tokens			
5 Pence-Silver			
☐ 1805		7.00	10.00
☐ 1806		12.00	20.00
10 Pence-Silver			
☐ 1805		12.00	18.00
☐ 1806		10.00	15.00
☐ 1813		6.00	10.00
30 Pence-Silver			
☐ 1808		18.00	25.00
6 Shilling			
☐ 1804		120.00	175.00

Key to Grading: Harp

DATE	COIN TYPE/VARIETY/METAL	ABP FINE	AVERAGE FINE
Farthing-Bronze			
☐ 1928		—	$ .85
☐ 1930		—	1.00
☐ 1931		—	6.00
☐ 1932		—	7.00
☐ 1933		—	.85
☐ 1935		—	6.75
☐ 1936		—	6.75
☐ 1937		—	.85
☐ 1939		—	.85
☐ 1940		—	2.50
☐ 1941		—	.80
☐ 1943		—	.80
☐ 1944		—	.85
☐ 1946		—	.65
☐ 1949		—	1.00
☐ 1953		—	.50
☐ 1959		—	.50
☐ 1966		—	.50

Key to Grading: Harp

DATE	COIN TYPE/VARIETY/METAL	ABP FINE	AVERAGE FINE
Half Penny Bronze			
☐ 1928		—	1.20
☐ 1933		—	7.00
☐ 1935		—	4.00
☐ 1937		—	1.50
☐ 1939		—	15.00
☐ 1940		—	1.50
☐ 1941		—	.50
☐ 1942		—	.50
☐ 1943		—	.50

DATE	COIN TYPE/VARIETY/METAL	ABP FINE	AVERAGE FINE
☐ 1946		—	$1.50
☐ 1949		—	.65
☐ 1953		—	.65
☐ 1964		—	.28
☐ 1965		—	.42
☐ 1966		—	.28
☐ 1967		—	.42

Key to Grading: Harp

Penny-Bronze

DATE	COIN TYPE/VARIETY/METAL	ABP FINE	AVERAGE FINE
☐ 1928		—	.80
☐ 1931		—	1.00
☐ 1933		—	2.00
☐ 1935		—	.80
☐ 1937		—	.80
☐ 1940		—	4.50
☐ 1941		—	.50
☐ 1942		—	.50
☐ 1943		—	1.00
☐ 1946		—	.50
☐ 1948		—	.50
☐ 1949		—	.50
☐ 1950		—	.50
☐ 1952		—	.50
☐ 1962		—	1.00
☐ 1963		—	.50
☐ 1964		—	.50
☐ 1965		—	.50
☐ 1966		—	.50
☐ 1967		—	.50
☐ 1968		—	.50

Key to Grading: Harp

3 Pence-Nickel

DATE	COIN TYPE/VARIETY/METAL	ABP FINE	AVERAGE FINE
☐ 1928		—	$1.00
☐ 1933		—	4.20
☐ 1934		—	1.50
☐ 1935		—	4.20
☐ 1939		—	14.00
☐ 1940		—	2.00
Copper-Nickel			
☐ 1942		—	.50
☐ 1943		—	.75
☐ 1946		—	1.75
☐ 1948		—	1.75
☐ 1949		—	.50
☐ 1950		—	.50
☐ 1953		—	.50
☐ 1956		—	.50
☐ 1961		—	.50
☐ 1962		—	.50
☐ 1963		—	.50
☐ 1964		—	.35
☐ 1965		—	.50
☐ 1966		—	.50
☐ 1967		—	.50
☐ 1968		—	.30

Key to Grading: Harp

6 Pence-Nickel

DATE	COIN TYPE/VARIETY/METAL	ABP FINE	AVERAGE FINE
☐ 1928		—	.80
☐ 1934		—	1.50
☐ 1935		—	1.25
☐ 1939		—	1.15
☐ 1940		—	1.15
Copper-Nickel			
☐ 1942		—	1.15
☐ 1945		—	2.50
☐ 1946		—	2.25
☐ 1947		—	1.90
☐ 1948		—	1.90
☐ 1949		—	1.90

DATE	COIN TYPE/VARIETY/METAL	ABP FINE	AVERAGE FINE
☐ 1950		—	$1.50
☐ 1952		—	.70
☐ 1953		—	.70
☐ 1955		—	1.75
☐ 1956		—	1.15
☐ 1958		—	1.15
☐ 1959		—	.55
☐ 1960		—	.55
☐ 1961		—	.55
☐ 1962		—	.55
☐ 1963		—	.55
☐ 1964		—	.55
☐ 1966		—	.55
☐ 1967		—	.55
☐ 1968		—	.55
☐ 1969		—	.55

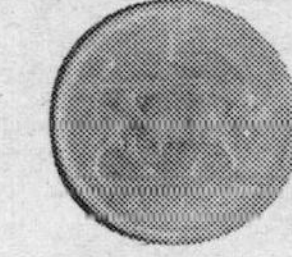

Key to Grading: Harp

Shilling-Silver

DATE	COIN TYPE/VARIETY/METAL	ABP FINE	AVERAGE FINE
☐ 1928		—	4.15
☐ 1930		—	7.00
☐ 1931		—	5.00
☐ 1933		—	8.00
☐ 1935		—	4.15
☐ 1937		—	15.00
☐ 1939		—	4.15
☐ 1940		—	4.15
☐ 1941		—	7.00
☐ 1942		—	5.00
Copper-Nickel			
☐ 1951		—	.80
☐ 1954		—	.85
☐ 1955		—	1.25
☐ 1959		—	.55
☐ 1962		—	.65
☐ 1963		—	.60
☐ 1964		—	.60
☐ 1966		—	.60
☐ 1968		—	.60

Key to Grading: Harp

DATE	COIN TYPE/VARIETY/METAL	ABP FINE	AVERAGE FINE
Florin-Silver			
☐ 1928		—	$5.00
☐ 1930		—	10.00
☐ 1931		—	10.00
☐ 1933		—	5.75
☐ 1934		—	15.00
☐ 1935		—	8.00
☐ 1937		—	15.00
Florin-Silver			
☐ 1939		—	4.00
☐ 1940		—	5.25
☐ 1941		—	5.25
☐ 1942		—	8.50
☐ 1943		$1200.00	1800.00
Copper-Nickel			
☐ 1951		—	1.60
☐ 1954		—	1.25
☐ 1955		—	1.60
☐ 1959		—	.70
☐ 1961		—	1.00
☐ 1962		—	.65
☐ 1963		—	.55
☐ 1964		—	.55
☐ 1965		—	.65
☐ 1966		—	.55
☐ 1968		—	.55
Half Crown-Silver			
☐ 1928		—	6.00
☐ 1930		—	8.00
☐ 1931		—	15.00
☐ 1933		—	8.00
☐ 1934		—	7.00
☐ 1937		—	75.00
☐ 1939		—	6.25
☐ 1940		—	6.25
☐ 1941		—	7.00
☐ 1942		—	8.00
☐ 1943		—	275.00

DATE	COIN TYPE/VARIETY/METAL	ABP FINE	AVERAGE FINE
Copper-Nickel			
□ 1951		—	$4.00
□ 1954		—	2.75
□ 1955		—	2.20
□ 1959		—	2.20
□ 1961		—	1.75
□ 1962		—	.85
□ 1963		—	1.40
□ 1964		—	1.40
□ 1966		—	1.00
□ 1967		—	1.25
10 Shillings-Silver			
□ 1966		—	10.00

Decimal Coinage

DATE	COIN TYPE/VARIETY/METAL	ABP FINE	AVERAGE FINE
½ Penny-Bronze			
□ 1971		—	.38
□ 1975		—	.38
□ 1976		—	.38
□ 1978		—	.38
□ 1980		—	.38
□ 1982		—	.38
□ 1985		—	.38
□ 1986		—	.38
Penny-Bronze			
□ 1971		—	.38
□ 1974		—	.38
□ 1975		—	.38
□ 1976		—	.38
□ 1978		—	.38
□ 1980		—	.38
□ 1982		—	.38
□ 1985		—	.38

DATE	COIN TYPE/VARIETY/METAL	ABP FINE	AVERAGE FINE
□ 1986		—	$ .32
□ 1988		—	.32
□ 1990		—	.32
Copper-Plated Steel			
□ 1990		—	.32
□ 1992		—	.32
□ 1993		—	.32

Key to Grading: Harp

DATE	COIN TYPE/VARIETY/METAL	ABP FINE	AVERAGE FINE
2 Pence-Bronze			
□ 1971		—	.40
□ 1975		—	.50
□ 1976		—	.38
□ 1978		—	.38
□ 1979		—	.38
□ 1980		—	.38
□ 1982		—	.38
□ 1985		—	.38
□ 1986		—	.38
□ 1988		—	.38
□ 1990		—	.38
Copper-Plated Steel			
□ 1988		—	.30
□ 1992		—	.30

Key to Grading: Harp

DATE	COIN TYPE/VARIETY/METAL	ABP FINE	AVERAGE FINE
5 Pence-Copper-Nickel			
□ 1969		—	.55
□ 1970		—	.38
□ 1971		—	.38
□ 1974		—	.38
□ 1975		—	.38
□ 1976		—	.38
□ 1978		—	.38
□ 1980		—	.38

DATE	COIN TYPE/VARIETY/METAL	ABP FINE	AVERAGE FINE
☐ 1982		—	$ .38
☐ 1985		—	.38
☐ 1986		—	.42
☐ 1990		—	.25
☐ 1992		—	.42
Reduced Size			
☐ 1992		—	.35
☐ 1993		—	.60
☐ 1994		—	.30
☐ 1995		—	.40

Key to Grading: Harp

DATE	COIN TYPE/VARIETY/METAL	ABP FINE	AVERAGE FINE
10 Pence-Copper-Nickel			
☐ 1969		—	.75
☐ 1971		—	1.15
☐ 1973		—	.75
☐ 1974		—	1.15
☐ 1975		—	.50
☐ 1976		—	.75
☐ 1978		—	.50
☐ 1980		—	.60
☐ 1982		—	.50
☐ 1985		—	.65
☐ 1986		—	2.00
Reduced Size			
☐ 1993		—	.35
20 Pence-Nickel-Bronze			
☐ 1986		—	2.15
☐ 1988		—	2.15
☐ 1990		—	1.15
☐ 1992		—	1.15
☐ 1993		—	2.20
☐ 1994		—	2.20

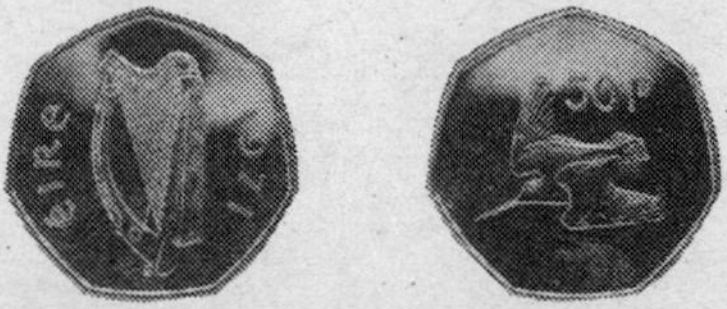

Key to Grading: Harp

DATE	COIN TYPE/VARIETY/METAL	ABP FINE	AVERAGE FINE
50 Pence-Copper-Nickel			
☐ 1970		—	$3.15
☐ 1971		—	3.15
☐ 1974		—	2.75
☐ 1975		—	2.25
☐ 1976		—	1.50
☐ 1977		—	2.00
☐ 1978		—	1.80
☐ 1979		—	1.80
☐ 1981		—	1.15
☐ 1982		—	2.00
☐ 1983		—	1.15
☐ 1986		—	5.00
☐ 1988		—	1.15
50 Pence-Copper-Nickel			
Dublin—Millennium			
☐ 1988		—	4.00
Pound-Copper-Nickel			
☐ 1990		—	5.00
Mint Sets			
☐ 1940 & 1950s Mixed Dates in Green-and-Blue Boxes			
Ireland-Issued Sets with Mixed			
Dates to Represent Types			55.00
		—	
☐ 1966		—	30.00
☐ 1971		—	12.00
☐ 1978		—	8.00
☐ 1982		—	8.00
Proof Sets			
☐ 1928 (8) coins		—	285.00
☐ 1951 (3) coins		2500.00	3250.00
☐ 1966 (2) coins		—	80.00
☐ 1971 (6) coins		—	22.00
☐ 1986 (7) coins		—	75.00
☐ 1928–1938	Sixpence, Saorstat Eireann, Nickel	—	2.20
☐ 1939–1942	Sixpence, Eire, Nickel	—	2.20
☐ 1942–1969	Sixpence, Eire, Cupro-Nickel	—	.80

ISRAEL

The first coins were used in the 5th century B.C. In 300 B.C. silver tetradrachms and gold staters were produced. Bronze coins appeared in 26 A.D. The copper fals was in evidence in the 600s and 700s, followed by the gold bezant and the base-silver denier. Bronze mils, cupro-nickel prutot, and the silver lira became popular in the 20th century. Today's currency is the livre.

Israel—Type Commemorative and Monetary Reform Coinage

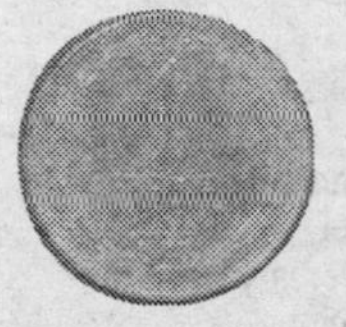

Key to Grading: Wreath

DATE	COIN TYPE/VARIETY/METAL	ABP FINE	AVERAGE FINE
☐ 1948–1949	1 Prutáh, Hebrew Date 5709 Anchor, Aluminum	—	$ .65

Key to Grading: Lire

DATE	COIN TYPE/VARIETY/METAL	ABP FINE	AVERAGE FINE
□ 1949	5 Prutot, Hebrew Date 5709 Harp, Bronze	—	$ .38

Key to Grading: Pitcher

DATE	COIN TYPE/VARIETY/METAL	ABP FINE	AVERAGE FINE
□ 1949	10 Prutot, Hebrew Date 5709 Amphora, Bronze	—	.38
□ 1952	10 Prutot, Hebrew Date 5712, Aluminum	—	.38

Key to Grading: Wheat Heads

DATE	COIN TYPE/VARIETY/METAL	ABP FINE	AVERAGE FINE
□ 1960–1980	1 Agora, Aluminum	—	.38
□ 1973	1 Agora, 25th Anniversary of Bank of Israel, Nickel	—	.38
□ 1973	1 Agora, 25th Anniversary of Independence, Aluminum	—	1.15

Key to Grading: Grapes

DATE	COIN TYPE/VARIETY/METAL	ABP FINE	AVERAGE FINE
□ 1948–1949	25 Mils, Hebrew Date 5708–09 Grape Clusters, Aluminum	—	28.00

Key to Grading: Grapes

DATE	COIN TYPE/VARIETY/METAL	ABP FINE	AVERAGE FINE
☐ 1949	25 Prutot, Hebrew Date 5709 Grape Clusters, Cupro-Nickel	—	$ .32
☐ 1954	25 Prutot, Hebrew Date 5714, Nickel-clad Steel	—	.32

Key to Grading: Leaves

DATE	COIN TYPE/VARIETY/METAL	ABP FINE	AVERAGE FINE
☐ 1949–1954	50 Prutot, Hebrew Date 5709–14 Fig Leaves, Cupro-Nickel	—	1.25
☐ 1954	50 Prutot, Hebrew Date 5714, Nickel-clad Steel	—	.38

Key to Grading: Design

DATE	COIN TYPE/VARIETY/METAL	ABP FINE	AVERAGE FINE
☐ 1960–1975	5 Agorot, Aluminum-Bronze	—	1.65
☐ 1973	5 Agorot, 25th Anniversary of Independence, Cupro-Nickel	—	1.65
☐ 1973	5 Agorot, 25th Anniversary of Bank of Israel, Nickel	—	1.65
☐ 1974–1979	5 Agorot, Cupro-Nickel	—	.75
☐ 1976–1979	5 Agorot, Aluminum	—	.32

Key to Grading: Palm Tree

DATE	COIN TYPE/VARIETY/METAL	ABP FINE	AVERAGE FINE
☐ 1949–1955	100 Prutot, Hebrew Date 5709 Palm Tree, Cupro-Nickel	—	$ .65
☐ 1954	100 Prutot, Hebrew Date 5714, Nickel-clad Steel	—	.55

Key to Grading: Palm Tree

DATE	COIN TYPE/VARIETY/METAL	ABP FINE	AVERAGE FINE
☐ 1960–1977	10 Agorot, Aluminum-Bronze	—	.32
☐ 1973	10 Agorot, 25th Anniversary of Independence, Cupro-Nickel	—	.55
☐ 1973	10 Agorot, 25th Anniversary of Bank of Israel, Nickel	—	1.25
☐ 1974–1979	10 Agorot, Cupro-Nickel	—	.38
☐ 1977–1980	10 Agorot, Aluminum	—	.38

Key to Grading: Wheat Head

DATE	COIN TYPE/VARIETY/METAL	ABP FINE	AVERAGE FINE
☐ 1949	250 Prutot, Hebrew Date 5709 Ears of Wheat, Silver	—	2.20
☐ 1949	250 Prutot, Hebrew Date 5709 Ears of Wheat, Cupro-Nickel	—	1.15

Key to Grading: Lire

DATE	COIN TYPE/VARIETY/METAL	ABP FINE	AVERAGE FINE
☐ 1960–1979	25 Agorot, Aluminum-Bronze	—	$ .30
☐ 1974–1979	25 Agorot, Cupro-Nickel	—	.75
☐ 1974–1979	25 Agorot, 25th Anniversary of Bank of Israel, Nickel	—	1.15

Key to Grading: Pomegranates

DATE	COIN TYPE/VARIETY/METAL	ABP FINE	AVERAGE FINE
☐ 1949	500 Prutot, Hebrew Date 5709 Pomegranates, Silver	—	5.00
☐ 1961–1962	1/2 Lira, Feast of Purim, Cupro-Nickel	—	2.20

Key to Grading: Menorah

DATE	COIN TYPE/VARIETY/METAL	ABP FINE	AVERAGE FINE
☐ 1963	1/2 Lira, 25th Anniversary of Bank of Israel, Nickel	—	1.50
☐ 1963	1/2 Lira, 25th Anniversary of Independence, Cupro-Nickel	—	.55
☐ 1963–1979	1/2 Lira, Cupro-Nickel	—	.38
☐ 1958	1 Lira, Law Is Light, Cupro-Nickel	—	.38
☐ 1960	1 Lira, Henrietta Szold—Hadassa Medical Center, Cupro-Nickel	—	15.00
☐ 1960	1 Lira, Deganya, Cupro-Nickel	—	2.00

DATE	COIN TYPE/VARIETY/METAL	ABP FINE	AVERAGE FINE
□ 1961	1 Lirah, Heroism & Sacrifice, Cupro-Nickel	—	$5.00
□ 1962	1 Lirah, Chanuka—Italian Lamp, Cupro-Nickel	—	8.15
□ 1963	1 Lirah, Chanuka—North African Lamp, Cupro-Nickel	—	8.15

Key to Grading: Menorah

□ 1963–1967	1 Lira, Cupro-Nickel	—	.38

Key to Grading: Design on Coin

□ 1958	5 Lirot, Tenth Anniversary of Republic, Silver	—	7.00
□ 1959	5 Lirot, Ingathering of Exiles, Silver	—	6.00
□ 1960	5 Lirot, Dr. Theodore Herzi, Silver	—	12.00
□ 1961	5 Lirot, Bar Mitzvahr, Silver	—	20.00
□ 1962	50 Lirot, 10th Anniversary—Death of Chaim Weizman, Gold	—	200.00
□ 1962	5 Lirot, Industrialization of the Negev, Silver	—	32.00
□ 1963	5 Lirot, Seafaring, Silver	—	265.00
□ 1964	5 Lirot, Israel Museum, Silver	—	38.00

Key to Grading: Lion's Mane

DATE	COIN TYPE/VARIETY/METAL	ABP FINE	AVERAGE FINE
☐ 1978–1979	5 Lirot, Cupro-Nickel	—	$ .80
☐ 1960	20 Lirot, Dr. Theodore Herzi, Gold	—	125.00
☐ 1964	50 Lirot, 10th Anniversary—Bank of Israel, Gold	—	235.00
☐ 1962	100 Lirot, 10th Anniversary—Death of Chaim Weizman, Gold	—	340.00

ITALY

The first coins were used in the 6th century B.C., with an unusual technique called incuse, involving the use of similar designs on both sides of the coin. The early coins were silver, but from about 440 B.C. bronze coins came into evidence, then gold coins appeared toward the end of the 5th century. Julius Caesar's head appeared on coins in 44 B.C., right before his assassination. Around 31 B.C. the Roman coinage system had denominations in gold, silver, and bronze that survived for the next 200 years. The decimal system was set up in 1804, and today's currency is the lira.

Italy—Type and Republic Coinage

DATE	COIN TYPE/VARIETY/METAL	ABP FINE	AVERAGE FINE
☐ 1861–1867	1 Centesimo, Vittorio Emanuel, Copper	—	$4.25
☐ 1895–1900	1 Centesimo, Umberto I, Copper	—	1.80
☐ 1902–1908	1 Centesimo, Vittorio III, Bronze	—	4.25
☐ 1908–1918	1 Centesimo, Vittorio III, Bronze	—	1.80

Key to Grading: Bust

DATE	COIN TYPE/VARIETY/METAL	ABP FINE	AVERAGE FINE
□ 1861–1867	2 Centesimi, Vittorio Emanuel, Copper	—	$ 1.25
□ 1895–1900	2 Centesimi, Umberto I, Copper	—	1.25
□ 1903–1908	2 Centesimi, Vittorio III, Bronze	—	1.25
□ 1908–1917	2 Centesimi, Vittorio III, Bronze	—	1.80
□ 1861–1867	5 Centesimi, Vittorio Emanuel, Copper	—	1.80
□ 1895–1896	5 Centesimi, Umberto I, Copper	$12.00	18.00
□ 1908–1918	5 Centesimi, Vittorio III, Bronze	—	1.50

Key to Grading: Bust

DATE	COIN TYPE/VARIETY/METAL	ABP FINE	AVERAGE FINE
□ 1919–1937	5 Centesimi, Vittorio III, Bronze	—	.55
□ 1936–1939	5 Centesimi, Vittorio III, Bronze	—	.75
□ 1939–1943	5 Centesimi, Vittorio III, Aluminum-Bronze	—	.55

Key to Grading: Bust

DATE	COIN TYPE/VARIETY/METAL	ABP FINE	AVERAGE FINE
□ 1862–1867	10 Centesimi, Vittorio Emanuel, Copper	—	4.15
□ 1893–1894	10 Centesimi, Umberto I, Copper	—	4.15
□ 1908	10 Centesimi, Vittorio III, Bronze	—	Rare
□ 1911	10 Centesimi, Vittorio III, 50th Anniversary of Kingdom, Bronze	—	4.00
□ 1919–1937	10 Centesimi, Vittorio III, Bronze	—	.80
□ 1939–1943	10 Centesimi, Vittorio III, Aluminum-Bronze	—	.80
□ 1863–1867	20 Centesimi, Vittorio Eman, Silver	—	6.00

Key to Grading: Crown

DATE	COIN TYPE/VARIETY/METAL	ABP FINE	AVERAGE FINE
☐ 1894–1895	20 Centesimi, Umberto I, Cupro-Nickel	—	$ .55
☐ 1908–1935	20 Centesimi, Vittorio III, Nickel	—	.75
☐ 1918–1920	20 Centesimi, Vittorio III, Cupro-Nickel	—	.55
☐ 1936–1938	20 Centesimi, Vittorio III, Nickel	—	20.00
☐ 1939–1943	20 Centesimi, Vittorio III, Stainless Steel	—	.55
☐ 1902–1903	25 Centesimi, Vittorio III, Nickel	—	20.00

Key to Grading: Bust

DATE	COIN TYPE/VARIETY/METAL	ABP FINE	AVERAGE FINE
☐ 1861–1863	50 Centesimi, Vittorio Eman, Silver	—	20.00
☐ 1863–1867	50 Centesimi, Vittorio Eman, Silver	—	6.00
☐ 1889–1892	50 Centesimi, Umberto I, Silver	—	35.00
☐ 1919–1935	50 Centesimi, Vittorio III, Nickel	—	4.00
☐ 1936–1938	50 Centesimi, Vittorio III, Nickel	—	20.00
☐ 1939–1943	50 Centesimi, Vittorio III, Stainless Steel	—	.40
☐ 1861–1867	1 Lira, Vittorio Emanuele II, Silver	—	22.00
☐ 1863	1 Lira, Vittorio Emanuele, Silver	—	22.00
☐ 1883–1900	1 Lira, Umberto I, Silver	—	4.00
☐ 1901–1907	1 Lira, Vittorio III, Silver	—	5.65
☐ 1908–1913	1 Lira, Vittorio III, Silver	—	5.65
☐ 1915–1917	1 Lira, Vittorio III, Silver	—	4.50

Key to Grading: Figure

DATE	COIN TYPE/VARIETY/METAL	ABP FINE	AVERAGE FINE
☐ 1922–1935	1 Lira, Vittorio III, Nickel	—	1.15
☐ 1936–1938	1 Lira, Vittorio III, Nickel	—	18.00
☐ 1939–1943	1 Lira, Vittorio III, Stainless Steel	—	.40
☐ 1946–1950	1 Lira, Republic, Aluminum	—	6.00
☐ 1951–1995	1 Lira, Republic, Aluminum	—	.35
☐ 1861–1863	2 Lire, Vittorio Emanuele I, Silver	—	14.00
☐ 1863	2 Lire, Vittorio Emanuele, Silver	—	14.00

DATE	COIN TYPE/VARIETY/METAL	ABP FINE	AVERAGE FINE
☐ 1881–1899	2 Lire, Umberto I, Silver	—	$6.00
☐ 1901–1907	2 Lire, Vittorio III, Silver	—	15.00
☐ 1908–1912	2 Lire, Vittorio III, Silver	—	8.00
☐ 1911	2 Lire, Vittorio III, 50th Anniversary of Kingdom, Silver	—	20.00
☐ 1914–1917	2 Lire, Vittorio III, Silver	—	6.00

Key to Grading: Bust

DATE	COIN TYPE/VARIETY/METAL	ABP FINE	AVERAGE FINE
☐ 1923–1935	2 Lire, Vittorio III, Nickel	—	4.00
☐ 1936–1938	2 Lire, Vittorio III, Nickel	$12.00	20.00
☐ 1939–1943	2 Lire, Vittorio III, Stainless Steel	—	.55
☐ 1946–1950	2 Lire, Republic, Aluminum	4.00	10.00
☐ 1953–1995	2 Lire, Republic, Aluminum	—	.55
☐ 1861	5 Lire, Vittorio Emanuele I, Italian Unification, Silver	—	435.00
☐ 1861–1878	5 Lire, Vittorio Emanuele I, Silver	—	15.00
☐ 1863–1865	5 Lire, Vittorio Emanuele, Gold	—	85.00
☐ 1878–1879	5 Lire, Umberto I, Silver	—	30.00
☐ 1901	5 Lire, Vittorio III, Silver	—	4500.00
☐ 1911	5 Lire, Vittorio III, 50th Anniversary of Kingdom, Silver	—	200.00
☐ 1914	5 Lire, Vittorio III, Silver	—	615.00

Key to Grading: Bust

DATE	COIN TYPE/VARIETY/METAL	ABP FINE	AVERAGE FINE
☐ 1926–1935	5 Lire, Vittorio III, Silver	—	6.00
☐ 1936–1941	5 Lire, Vittorio III, Silver	—	16.00
☐ 1946–1950	5 Lire, Republic, Aluminum	—	.80
☐ 1951–1995	5 Lire, Republic, Aluminum	—	.80
☐ 1861	10 Lire, Vittorio Emanuele, Gold	—	1200.00
☐ 1863–1865	Vittorio III, Gold	—	115.00
☐ 1910–1927	10 Lire, Vittorio III, Gold	—	600.00
☐ 1926–1934	10 Lire, Vittorio III, Silver	—	42.00

Key to Grading: Bust

DATE	COIN TYPE/VARIETY/METAL	ABP FINE	AVERAGE FINE
☐ 1946–1950	10 Lire, Republic, Aluminum	—	$ .80

Key to Grading: Wings

DATE	COIN TYPE/VARIETY/METAL	ABP FINE	AVERAGE FINE
☐ 1951–1995	10 Lire, Republic, Aluminum	—	.38
☐ 1923	20 Lire, Vittorio III, Anniversary of Fascist Government, Gold	—	250.00
☐ 1928	20 Lire, Vittorio III, End of WWI 10th Anniversary, Gold	—	120.00
☐ 1879–1897	20 Lire, Umberto I, Gold	—	120.00
☐ 1902–1910	20 Lire, Vittorio III, Gold	—	275.00
☐ 1910–1927	20 Lire, Vittorio III, Gold	—	275.00
☐ 1927–1934	20 Lire, Vittorio III, Silver	—	120.00
☐ 1936–1941	20 Lire, Vittorio III, Silver	—	255.00

Key to Grading: Bust

DATE	COIN TYPE/VARIETY/METAL	ABP FINE	AVERAGE FINE
☐ 1957–1959	20 Lire, Republic, Aluminum-Bronze	—	.35
☐ 1864	50 Lire, Vittorio Emanuele, Gold	—	8800.00
☐ 1884–1891	50 Lire, Umberto I, Gold	—	1000.00
☐ 1910–1927	50 Lire, Vittorio III, Gold	—	600.00
☐ 1911	50 Lire, Vittorio III, 50th Anniversary of Kingdom, Gold	—	425.00

DATE	COIN TYPE/VARIETY/METAL	ABP FINE	AVERAGE FINE
☐ 1931–1933	50 Lire, Vittorio III, Gold	—	$200.00
☐ 1936	50 Lire, Vittorio III, Gold	—	800.00

Key to Grading: Bust

DATE	COIN TYPE/VARIETY/METAL	ABP FINE	AVERAGE FINE
☐ 1954 to Date	50 Lire, Republic, Stainless Steel	—	.75
☐ 1864–1878	100 Lire, Vittorio Emanuele, Gold	—	1800.00
☐ 1880–1891	100 Lire, Umberto I, Gold	—	1000.00
☐ 1903–1905	100 Lire, Vittorio III, Gold	—	1500.00
☐ 1910–1927	100 Lire, Vittorio III, Gold	—	1200.00
☐ 1923	100 Lire, Vittorio III, Anniversary of Fascist Government, Gold	—	825.00
☐ 1925	100 Lire, Vittorio III, 25th Anniversary of Reign & 10th Anniversary of WWI, Gold	—	1400.00
☐ 1931–1933	100 Lire, Vittorio III, Gold	—	175.00
☐ 1936	100 Lire, Vittorio III, Gold	—	1400.00
☐ 1937	100 Lire, Vittorio III, Gold	—	4200.00
☐ 1974	100 Lire, Republic, Birth of Marconi 100th Anniversary, Stainless Steel	—	.38
☐ 1979	100 Lire, Republic, F.A.O. Issue, Stainless Steel	—	.38
☐ 1981	100 Lire, Republic, Livorno Naval Academy Centennial, Stainless Steel	—	.38

Key to Grading: Bust

DATE	COIN TYPE/VARIETY/METAL	ABP FINE	AVERAGE FINE
☐ 1955 to Date	100 Lire, Republic, Stainless Steel	—	.38

Key to Grading: Bust

DATE	COIN TYPE/VARIETY/METAL	ABP FINE	AVERAGE FINE
☐ 1980	200 Lire, Republic, World Food Day, Aluminum-Bronze	—	$ .38
☐ 1980	200 Lire, Republic, F.A.O. Issue & International Woman's Year, Aluminum-Bronze	—	.38

Key to Grading: Bust

DATE	COIN TYPE/VARIETY/METAL	ABP FINE	AVERAGE FINE
☐ 1988	200 Lire, Republic, University of Bologna 900th Anniversary, Silver	—	16.00
☐ 1989	200 Lire, Republic, Taranto Naval Yards, Bronzital	—	.30
☐ 1989	200 Lire, Republic, Christopher Columbus, Silver	—	12.00
☐ 1989	200 Lire, Republic, Soccer, Silver	—	12.00
☐ 1990	200 Lire, Republic, State Council Building, Bronzital	—	.35
☐ 1991	200 Lire, Republic, Italian Flora & Fauna, Silver	—	12.00
☐ 1992	200 Lire, Republic, Genoa Stamp Exposition, Aluminum-Bronze	—	.35

Key to Grading: Design of Coin

DATE	COIN TYPE/VARIETY/METAL	ABP FINE	AVERAGE FINE
☐ 1958–1989	500 Lire, Republic, Silver	—	$4.00
☐ 1961	500 Lire, Republic, Italian Unification Centennial, Silver	—	5.00
☐ 1965	500 Lire, Republic, Birth of Alighieri 700th Anniversary, Silver	—	5.00
☐ 1974	500 Lire, Republic, Birth of Marconi 100th Anniversary, Silver	—	14.00
☐ 1975	500 Lire, Republic, Birth of Michelangelo 500th Anniversary, Silver	—	14.00
☐ 1981	500 Lire, Republic, Birth of Virgil 2000th Anniversary, Silver	—	14.00
☐ 1982	500 Lire, Republic, Death of Garibaldi 100th Anniversary, Silver	—	14.00
☐ 1982–1995	500 Lire, Republic, Dual Metal	—	.50
☐ 1982	500 Lire, Republic, Galileo Galilei, Silver	—	14.00
☐ 1984	500 Lire, Republic, Common Market Presidency, Silver	—	22.00
☐ 1984	500 Lire, Republic, Los Angeles Olympics, Silver	—	20.00
☐ 1985	500 Lire, Republic, Etruscan Culture, Silver	—	20.00
☐ 1985	500 Lire, Republic, European Year of Music, Silver	—	22.00
☐ 1985	500 Lire, Republic, Birth of Manzoni 200th Anniversary, Silver	—	25.00
☐ 1985	500 Lire, Republic, Duino College, Silver	—	22.00
☐ 1986	500 Lire, Republic, Birth of Donatello 600th Anniversary, Silver	—	30.00
☐ 1986	500 Lire, Republic, Soccer Championship, Silver	—	28.00
☐ 1986	500 Lire, Republic, Year of Peace, Silver	—	28.00
	Championship, Silver	—	15.00
☐ 1987	500 Lire, Republic, Leopardi, Silver	—	65.00
☐ 1987	500 Lire, Republic, Year of the Family, Silver	—	22.00

DATE	COIN TYPE/VARIETY/METAL	ABP FINE	AVERAGE FINE
☐ 1988	500 Lire, Republic, Constitution 40th Anniversary, Silver	—	$15.00
☐ 1988	500 Lire, Republic, University of Bologna 900th Anniversary, Silver	—	52.00
☐ 1988	500 Lire, Republic, Death of Bosco 100th Anniversary, Silver	—	52.00
☐ 1988	500 Lire, Republic, Summer Olympics—Seoul, Silver	—	35.00
☐ 1989	500 Lire, Republic, Soccer, Silver	—	15.00
☐ 1989	500 Lire, Republic, Christopher Columbus, Silver	—	20.00
☐ 1989	500 Lire, Republic, Fight Against Cancer, Silver	—	42.00
☐ 1990	500 Lire, Republic, Birth of Tizian 500th Anniversary, Silver	—	55.00
☐ 1990	500 Lire, Republic, Columbus—Discovery of America, Silver	—	20.00
☐ 1990	500 Lire, Republic, Ponte Milvio 2100th Anniversary, Silver	—	30.00
☐ 1990	500 Lire, Republic, EEC Council Presidency, Silver	—	25.00
☐ 1991	500 Lire, Republic, Discovery of America, Silver	—	38.00
☐ 1991	500 Lire, Republic, Flora & Fauna, Silver	—	40.00
☐ 1992	500 Lire, Republic, Olympics Building & Track, Silver	—	16.00
☐ 1992	500 Lire, Republic, Christopher Columbus, Silver	—	40.00
☐ 1992	500 Lire, Republic, Rossini, Silver	—	40.00
☐ 1992	500 Lire, Republic, Flora & Fauna, Silver	—	40.00
☐ 1992	500 Lire, Republic, Lorenzo De'Medici, Silver	—	25.00
☐ 1970	1000 Lire, Republic, Centennial of Rome, Silver	—	12.00

JAPAN

The first coins were used in 708 and were silver and copper imitations of Chinese cast-bronze coins. Copper coins were used for the next 250 years. After 958 no copper coins were issued, and by the end of the 10th century they were no longer in use. Imported Chinese bronze coins began circulating in the 13th century. Rectangular-shaped coins were in use in the 17th and 18th centuries. The first decimal coins were produced in 1870. Today's currency is the yen.

Japan—Type Coinage

Key to Grading: Dragon

DATE	COIN TYPE/VARIETY/METAL	ABP FINE	AVERAGE FINE
☐ 1873–1888	1/2 Sen, Obv: Sun With Rays, Rev: Value in Wreath, Bronze	—	$4.00
☐ 1916–1919	5 Rin, Kiri Crest, Bronze	—	.60
☐ 1873–1915	1 Sen, Obv: Sun With Rays, Rev: Value in Wreath, Bronze	—	2.20

Key to Grading: Flowers

DATE	COIN TYPE/VARIETY/METAL	ABP FINE	AVERAGE FINE
□ 1916–1937	1 Sen Kiri Crest, Bronze	—	$ .38
□ 1941–1943	1 Sen, Mt. Fuji, Aluminum	—	.38
□ 1873–1884	2 Sen, Obv: Sun With Rays, Rev: Value in Wreath, Bronze	—	2.20
□ 1870–1871	5 Sen, Obv: Coiled Dragon, Rev: Sun, Silver	—	220.00
□ 1873–1880	5 Sen, Obv: Coiled Dragon, Rev: Value in Wreath, Silver	—	25.00
□ 1897–1905	5 Sen, Obv: Sun With Rays, Rev: Value in Wreath, Cupro-Nickel	—	12.00

Key to Grading: Chrysanthemum

DATE	COIN TYPE/VARIETY/METAL	ABP FINE	AVERAGE FINE
□ 1917–1932	5 Sen, Petaled Flower Around Hole, Cupro-Nickel	—	4.00
□ 1940–1942	5 Sen, Kite, Aluminum	—	2.00
□ 1870–1872	10 Sen, Obv: Coiled Dragon, Rev: Sun, Silver	—	25.00
□ 1873–1906	10 Sen, Obv: Coiled Dragon, Rev: Value in Wreath, Silver	—	8.00
□ 1907–1917	10 Sen, Obv: Sun With Rays, Rev: Value in Wreath, Silver	—	2.20
□ 1920–1932	10 Sen, Petaled Flower Around Hole, Cupro-Nickel	—	.38
□ 1940–1943	10 Sen, Chrysanthemum, Aluminum	—	.38
□ 1946	10 Sen, Phoenix, Rev: Rice Plants, Aluminum	—	.30
□ 1870–1872	20 Sen, Obv: Coiled Dragon, Rev: Sun, Silver	—	25.00
□ 1873–1905	20 Sen, Obv: Coiled Dragon, Rev: Value in Wreath, Silver	—	8.00
□ 1906–1911	20 Sen, Obv: Sun With Rays, Rev: Value in Wreath, Silver	—	6.25
□ 1870–1871	50 Sen, Obv: Coiled Dragon, Rev: Sun, Silver	—	32.00

Key to Grading: Dragon

DATE	COIN TYPE/VARIETY/METAL	ABP FINE	AVERAGE FINE
☐ 1873–1905	50 Sen, Obv: Coiled Dragon, Rev: Value in Wreath, Silver	—	$18.00
☐ 1906–1917	50 Sen, Obv: Sun With Rays, Rev: Value in Wreath, Silver	—	5.00
☐ 1946	50 Sen, Phoenix, Rev: Rice Plants, Bronze	—	.42
☐ 1947–1948	50 Sen, Chrysanthemum & Blossoms, Brass	—	.42
☐ 1870–1872	Yen, Obv: Coiled Dragon, Rev: Sun, Silver	—	175.00

Key to Grading: Dragon

DATE	COIN TYPE/VARIETY/METAL	ABP FINE	AVERAGE FINE
☐ 1874–1915	Yen, Obv: Coiled Dragon, Rev: Value in Wreath, Silver	—	32.00
☐ 1948–1950	Yen, Blossoms, Brass	—	.55
☐ 1875–1878	Trade Dollar, Obv: Dragon, Rev: Wreath, Silver	—	335.00

LUXEMBOURG

The first coins were used in the late 10th century and were silver deniers. In the 1300s, silver sterlings were in evidence, followed by silver double gros and bronze centimes. The silver franc was popular in the mid-1900s, and the cupro-nickel franc in the latter 1900s. Decimal coins were used in 1854. The currency today is the franc.

Luxembourg—Type Coinage

DATE	COIN TYPE/VARIETY/METAL	ABP FINE	AVERAGE FINE
☐ 1854–1908	2½ Centimes, Bronze	—	$4.00
☐ 1854–1860	5 Centimes, Bronze	—	5.00
☐ 1901	5 Centimes, Adolphe, Cupro-Nickel	—	.45

Key to Grading: Bust

DATE	COIN TYPE/VARIETY/METAL	ABP FINE	AVERAGE FINE
☐ 1908	5 Centimes, Guillaume IV, Cupro-Nickel	—	.38
☐ 1915	5 Centimes, "Holed," Zinc	—	1.20
☐ 1918–1922	5 Centimes, Iron	—	1.75
☐ 1924	5 Centimes, Charlotte (1st), Cupro-Nickel	—	.38
☐ 1930	5 Centimes, Charlotte (1st), Bronze	—	.38

Key to Grading: Crown or Bust

DATE	COIN TYPE/VARIETY/METAL	ABP FINE	AVERAGE FINE
☐ 1854–1870	10 Centimes, Bronze	—	$4.00
☐ 1901	10 Centimes, Adolphe, Cupro-Nickel	—	.45
☐ 1915	10 Centimes, "Holed," Zinc	—	1.50
☐ 1918–1923	10 Centimes, Iron	—	4.00
☐ 1924	10 Centimes, Charlotte (1st), Cupro-Nickel	—	.38
☐ 1930	10 Centimes, Charlotte (1st), Bronze	—	.38
☐ 1918–1922	25 Centimes, Iron	—	3.00
☐ 1927	25 Centimes, Charlotte (1st), Cupro-Nickel	—	.50

Key to Grading: Crown or Bust

DATE	COIN TYPE/VARIETY/METAL	ABP FINE	AVERAGE FINE
☐ 1946–1947	25 Centimes, Charlotte (2nd) Letzeburg, Bronze	—	.38
☐ 1954–1972	25 Centimes, Charlotte (2nd) Letzeburg, Aluminum	—	.38
☐ 1980	25 Centimes, Charlotte (2nd), Silver	—	12.00
☐ 1924–1935	1 Franc, Charlotte (1st), Nickel	—	.38

Key to Grading: Crown

DATE	COIN TYPE/VARIETY/METAL	ABP FINE	AVERAGE FINE
☐ 1939	1 Franc, Charlotte (1st), Letzeburg, Bronze	—	$ .45
☐ 1946–1947	1 Franc, Charlotte (2nd), Letzeburg, Cupro-Nickel	—	.25
☐ 1952	1 Franc, Charlotte (2nd), Letzeburg, Cupro-Nickel	—	.32
☐ 1953–1964	1 Franc, Charlotte (2nd), Letzeburg, Cupro-Nickel	—	.32
☐ 1965–1984	1 Franc, Charlotte (2nd), Millennium Commemorative, Cupro-Nickel	—	.35
☐ 1980	1 Franc, Charlotte (2nd), Millennium Commemorative, Silver	—	12.00
☐ 1986–1987	1 Franc, Charlotte (2nd), Cupro-Nickel	—	.45
☐ 1988 to Date	1 Franc, Charlotte (2nd), Nickel-Steel	—	.45
☐ 1924	2 Francs, Charlotte (1st), Nickel	—	1.00
☐ 1929	5 Francs, Charlotte (1st), Silver	—	2.00
☐ 1949	5 Francs, Charlotte (2nd), Letzeburg, Cupro-Nickel	—	.45
☐ 1962	5 Francs, Charlotte (2nd), Cupro-Nickel	—	.45
☐ 1971–1981	5 Francs, Jean (2nd), Cupro-Nickel	—	.45

Key to Grading: Bust

DATE	COIN TYPE/VARIETY/METAL	ABP FINE	AVERAGE FINE
☐ 1986 to Date	5 Francs, Jean (2nd), Brass	—	.42
☐ 1929	10 Francs, Charlotte (1st), Silver	—	4.00
☐ 1971–1980	10 Francs, Jean (2nd), Nickel	—	.42
☐ 1946	20 Francs, Charlotte (2nd), 600th Anniversary Death of John the Blind, Silver	—	4.25
☐ 1980	20 Francs, Jean (2nd), Silver	—	25.00

Key to Grading: Bust

DATE	COIN TYPE/VARIETY/METAL	ABP FINE	AVERAGE FINE
□ 1980–1983	20 Francs, John (2nd), Bronze	—	$ 1.25
□ 1989	20 Francs, John (2nd), 150th Anniversary of Grand Duchy, Gold	—	125.00
□ 1990–1991	20 Francs, John (2nd), Bronze	—	—
□ 1946	50 Francs, Charlotte (2nd), 600th Anniversary Death of John the Blind, Silver	—	8.00
□ 1987 to Date	50 Francs, John (2nd), Nickel	—	1.25
□ 1946	100 Francs, John (2nd), 600th Anniversary Death of John the Blind, Silver	—	12.00
□ 1963	100 Francs, Charlotte (2nd), Silver	—	12.00
□ 1963	250 Francs, Charlotte (2nd), Millennium Commemorative, Silver	—	35.00

MALTA

The first coins, which were bronze, were used in the 3rd century B.C. The silver tari was in evidence in the 1500s, followed by the copper grano. In the early 1700s, the gold zecchini was in use, and the silver tari appeared in the mid-1700s. The bronze 10 cents was in use in the 1970s since decimal coins came into use in 1972. The currency today is the pound.

Malta—Type Coinage

Key to Grading: Bust

DATE	COIN TYPE/VARIETY/METAL	ABP FINE	AVERAGE FINE
☐ 1827	1/3 Farthing, Head of George IV, Copper	—	$12.00
☐ 1835	1/3 Farthing, Head of William IV, Copper	—	8.00
☐ 1844	1/3 Farthing, Head of Victoria, Copper	$20.00	30.00
☐ 1866–1885	1/3 Farthing, Value in Wreath, Bronze	—	5.25
☐ 1902	1/3 Farthing, Head of Edward VII, Bronze	—	5.25
☐ 1913	1/3 Farthing, Head of George V, Bronze	—	5.25

MEXICO

The first coins—the silver Spanish reales—were used in 1536. At first coins were struck in silver, gold, and copper but copper was soon discontinued. The silver reales were popular in the 1800s, followed by the brass quartillas, gold pesos, bronze centavos, and silver pesos in the 1900s. The decimal system was established in 1863 and the currency today is the peso.

Mexico—Type and Republic Coinage

Key to Grading: Eagle

Republic 1863–1905

1 Centavo Copper Seated Liberty			
☐ 1863	Round 3 Reed Edge	8.00	14.00
☐ 1863	Round 3 Plain Edge	10.00	16.00
☐ 1863	Flat Top 3	8.00	14.00
1 Centavo SLP Mint Mark			
☐ 1863		6.00	15.00
1 Centavo Standing Eagle			
☐ 1875	Mint Mark As	—	Rare
☐ 1876	Mint Mark As	75.00	115.00
☐ 1880	Mint Mark As	8.00	20.00
☐ 1874–1897	Mint Mark Cn	—	18.00

DATE		ABP FINE	AVERAGE FINE
☐ 1879–1891	Mint Mark Do	—	$10.00
☐ 1872–1890	Mint Mark Ga	—	8.00
☐ 1875	Mint Mark Ho	$350.00	500.00
☐ 1876	Mint Mark Ho	35.00	60.00
☐ 1880–1881	Mint Mark Ho	—	10.00
☐ 1869–1897	Mint Mark Mo	—	6.00
☐ 1872–1875	Mint Mark Oa	—	400.00
☐ 1871–1891	Mint Mark Pi	—	12.00
☐ 1872–1881	Mint Mark Zs	—	8.00
1 Centavo Copper/Nickel			
☐ 1882		—	8.00
☐ 1883		—	1.25
1 Centavo Copper			
☐ 1898		—	5.00
1 Centavo Copper			
☐ 1899		—	160.00
☐ 1900–1905		—	22.00
Emperor Maximillian 1864–1867			
1 Centavo Copper			
☐ 1864		20.00	35.00
Estados Unidos Mexicanos			
1 Centavo Bronze 20mm			

Key to Grading: Eagle

DATE	ABP FINE	AVERAGE FINE
☐ 1905	—	4.00
☐ 1906 Narrow Date	—	1.15
☐ 1906 Wide Date	—	1.15
☐ 1910	—	1.50
☐ 1911	—	1.15
☐ 1912	—	1.15
☐ 1913	—	1.15
☐ 1914	—	1.15
☐ 1915	8.00	12.00
☐ 1916	25.00	40.00
☐ 1920	8.00	20.00
☐ 1921	—	5.00
☐ 1922	6.00	10.00
☐ 1923	—	1.15

DATE	ABP FINE	AVERAGE FINE
☐ 1924/3	$40.00	$60.00
☐ 1924	—	4.15
☐ 1925	—	4.15
☐ 1926	—	2.00
☐ 1927/6	15.00	25.00
☐ 1927	—	.55
☐ 1928	—	.70
☐ 1929	—	.70
☐ 1930	—	.75
☐ 1933	—	.38
☐ 1934	—	.38
☐ 1935–1942	—	.38
☐ 1943	—	.38
☐ 1944–1949	—	.38
1 Centavo Zapata Issue 16mm		
☐ 1915	12.00	18.00
1 Centavo Brass 16mm		
☐ 1950–1969	—	.38
1 Centavo Brass Reduced Size 13mm		
☐ 1970	—	.38
☐ 1972	—	.38
☐ 1972/2	—	.70
☐ 1973	—	2.15
Republic 1863–1904		
2 Centavos Copper/Nickel		
☐ 1882–1883	—	2.15
Estados Unidos Mexicanos		
2 Centavos Bronze 25mm		

Key to Grading: Eagle

DATE	ABP FINE	AVERAGE FINE
☐ 1905	80.00	125.00
☐ 1906 Inverted 6	20.00	30.00
Wide Date	—	5.00
☐ 1906 Narrow Date	—	7.00
☐ 1920	—	8.00
☐ 1921	—	5.00
☐ 1922	200.00	275.00
☐ 1924	8.00	12.00

DATE		ABP FINE	AVERAGE FINE
☐ 1925		—	$4.00
☐ 1926		—	1.25
☐ 1927		—	.85
☐ 1928		—	.85
☐ 1929		$35.00	55.00
☐ 1935		—	4.50
☐ 1939		—	.70
☐ 1941		—	.70
2 Centavos Bronze Zapata Issue			
☐ 1915		—	7.00
Republic 1863–1904			
5 Centavos Republic Silver			
☐ 1868–1870	Mint Mark Ca	—	32.00
☐ 1863	Mint Mark SLP	18.00	75.00
5 Centavos Republic Silver Cap & Rays			
☐ 1867–1868	Mint Mark Mo	22.00	32.00
☐ 1868	Mint Mark P	22.00	32.00
☐ 1869	Mint Mark P	80.00	220.00
5 Centavos Republic Silver Standing Eagle			
☐ 1874–1895	Mint Mark As	10.00	25.00
☐ 1871–1895	Mint Mark CH, Ca	—	5.00
☐ 1873	M. Crude Date Mint Mark CH, Ca	65.00	100.00
☐ 1871–1897	Mint Mark Cn	—	4.00
☐ 1871P	Mint Mark Cn	100.00	140.00
☐ 1890D	Mint Mark Cn	100.00	140.00
☐ 1874–1881	Mint Mark Do	100.00	140.00
☐ 1887–1894	Mint Mark Do	—	4.00
☐ 1877–1893	Mint Mark Ga	—	5.50
☐ 1877–1893	Mint Mark Go	—	4.00
☐ 1874–1878	Mint Mark Ho	60.00	100.00
☐ 1880–1894	Mint Mark Ho	—	5.50
☐ 1869–1897	Mint Mark Mo	—	4.00
☐ 1873M	Mint Mark Mo	30.00	45.00
☐ 1890E	Mint Mark Oa	—	Rare
☐ 1890N	Mint Mark Oa	60.00	80.00
☐ 1869–1886	Mint Mark Pi	40.00	75.00
☐ 1887–1893	Mint Mark Pi	—	2.00
☐ 1870–1876	Mint Mark Zs	60.00	80.00
☐ 1877–1897	Mint Mark Zs	—	4.00
5 Centavos Republic Copper-Nickel			
☐ 1882		—	.80
☐ 1883		18.00	25.00
5 Centavos Republic Silver			
☐ 1898–1904	Mint Mark Cn	—	4.00
☐ 1898–1900	Mint Mark Go	—	2.20

DATE		ABP FINE	AVERAGE FINE
☐ 1898–1904	Mint Mark Mo	—	$2.20
☐ 1898–1904	Mint Mark Zs	—	4.00
Emperor Maximillian 1864–1867			
5 Centavos Silver			
☐ 1864–1866	Mint Mark G	$30.00	45.00
☐ 1864–1866	Mint Mark M	15.00	25.00
☐ 1864	Mint Mark P	60.00	100.00
☐ 1865	Mint Mark Z	15.00	25.00
Estados Unidos Mexicanos			
5 Centavos Nickel			
☐ 1905		—	5.00
☐ 1906/5		—	10.00
☐ 1906		—	2.20
☐ 1907		—	2.20
☐ 1909		—	4.00
☐ 1910		—	2.20
☐ 1911 Wide Date		—	4.00
☐ 1911 Narrow Date		—	2.20
☐ 1912 Small	Mint Mark	56.00	100.00
☐ 1912 Large	Mint Mark	40.00	75.00
☐ 1913		—	2.20
☐ 1914		—	2.20
5 Centavos Bronze			
☐ 1914		—	—
☐ 1915		—	4.00
☐ 1916		8.00	15.00
☐ 1917		28.00	60.00
☐ 1918		16.00	25.00
☐ 1919		60.00	110.00
☐ 1920		—	6.00
☐ 1921		—	10.00
☐ 1924		35.00	50.00
☐ 1925		—	6.50
☐ 1926		—	6.50
☐ 1927		—	4.00
☐ 1928 Small Date		18.00	25.00
☐ 1928 Large Date		6.00	10.00
☐ 1930 Small Square in O		30.00	50.00
☐ 1930 Oval in O		—	4.00
☐ 1931		335.00	475.00
☐ 1933		—	2.00
☐ 1934		—	2.00
☐ 1935		—	1.25
5 Centavos Copper-Nickel			
☐ 1936		—	.35

DATE		ABP FINE	AVERAGE FINE
☐ 1937		—	$ .38
☐ 1938		—	3.00
☐ 1940		—	.55
☐ 1942		—	.75
5 Centavo Bronze Josefa Dominguez			
☐ 1942		—	12.00
☐ 1943		—	.38
☐ 1944		—	.38
☐ 1945		—	.38
☐ 1946		—	.38
☐ 1951		—	.38
☐ 1952		—	.75
☐ 1953		—	.50
☐ 1954		—	.38
☐ 1955		—	1.00
5 Centavo Copper/Nickel "White Josefa"			
☐ 1950		—	.50
5 Centavo Brass			
☐ 1954 w/Dot		—	5.00
☐ 1954 w/o Dot		—	7.00
☐ 1955		—	.38
☐ 1956–1969		—	.38
5 Centavos Copper-Nickel			
☐ 1960		$125.00	165.00
☐ 1962		125.00	165.00
5 Centavos Brass Reduced Size 18mm			
☐ 1970–1976		—	.32
5 Centavos Stainless Steel			
☐ 1992–1999		—	.32
Republic 1863–1904			
10 Centavos Silver			
☐ 1864–1870	Mint Mark Ca	12.00	28.00
☐ 1863	Mint Mark SLP	40.00	75.00
10 Centavos Silver Cap & Rays			
☐ 1867–1868	Mint Mark Mo	15.00	28.00
☐ 1868–1869	Mint Mark P	30.00	45.00
10 Centavos Silver			
☐ 1874–1893	Mint Mark As	—	10.00
☐ 1871–1895	Mint Mark CH, Ca	—	5.00
☐ 1871–1887	Mint Mark Cn	20.00	35.00
☐ 1888–1896	Mint Mark Cn	4.00	6.00
☐ 1878–1886	Mint Mark Do	50.00	80.00
☐ 1887–1895	Mint Mark Do	—	4.25
☐ 1871–1895	Mint Mark Ga	—	4.25
☐ 1869–1897	Mint Mark Go	—	5.00

DATE		ABP FINE	AVERAGE FINE
☐ 1875S	Mint Mark Go	$200.00	$250.00
☐ 1880S	Mint Mark Go	40.00	100.00
☐ 1874–1893	Mint Mark Ho	—	7.50
☐ 1868–1897	Mint Mark Mo	—	7.50
☐ 1889E	Mint Mark Oa	160.00	200.00
☐ 1890E	Mint Mark Oa	65.00	100.00
☐ 1890N	Mint Mark Oa	—	Rare
☐ 1869–1886	Mint Mark Pi	60.00	100.00
☐ 1886–1893	Mint Mark Pi	—	6.00
☐ 1885C	Mint Mark Pi	—	Rare
☐ 1870–1877	Mint Mark Zs	100.00	125.00
☐ 1878–1897	Mint Mark Zs	—	6.00
10 Centavos Silver Restyled Eagle			
☐ 1898–1904	Mint Mark Cn	—	4.00
☐ 1898M	Mint Mark Cn	35.00	60.00
☐ 1898–1900	Mint Mark Go	—	4.00
☐ 1898–1905	Mint Mark Mo	—	4.00
☐ 1898–1905	Mint Mark Zs	—	4.00
Emperor Maximillian 1864–1867			
10 Centavos Silver			
☐ 1864–1865	Mint Mark G	20.00	32.00
☐ 1864–1866	Mint Mark M	20.00	32.00
☐ 1864	Mint Mark P	35.00	75.00
☐ 1865	Mint Mark Z	20.00	32.00

Estados Unidos Mexicanos

10 Centavos Silver .0643 ASW

Key to Grading: Eagle

DATE		ABP FINE	AVERAGE FINE
☐ 1905		—	4.15
☐ 1906		—	4.15
☐ 1907/6		12.00	25.00
☐ 1907		—	2.00
☐ 1909		—	5.15
☐ 1910/00		—	6.00
☐ 1910		—	5.15
☐ 1911 Wide Date		—	5.15
☐ 1911 Narrow Date		—	6.00
☐ 1912		—	6.00

DATE		ABP FINE	AVERAGE FINE
☐ 1912 Low 2		—	$5.25
☐ 1913/2		—	5.25
☐ 1913		—	5.25
☐ 1914		—	4.00
10 Centavos Silver Reduced Size			
☐ 1919		—	5.25
10 Centavos Bronze			
☐ 1919		—	10.00
☐ 1920		—	5.00
☐ 1921		—	25.00
☐ 1935		—	6.00
10 Centavos Silver .0384 ASW			
☐ 1925/15		—	12.00
☐ 1925/3		—	8.00
☐ 1925		—	4.00
☐ 1926/16		—	12.00
☐ 1926		—	4.25
☐ 1927		—	4.25
☐ 1928		—	2.00
☐ 1930		—	4.25
☐ 1933		—	1.15
☐ 1934		—	1.15
☐ 1935		—	1.15
10 Centavos Copper-Nickel			
☐ 1936–1946		—	.50
☐ 1937		—	2.00
☐ 1938		—	.80
10 Centavos Benito Juarez			
☐ 1955		—	.38
☐ 1956		—	.38
☐ 1957–1967		—	.38
10 Centavos Copper/Nickel 5 Rows of Corn			
☐ 1974–1980		—	.38
☐ 1977		—	.50
☐ 1980/79		—	1.50
☐ 1980		—	.40
10 Centavos 5½ Rows of Corn			
☐ 1974–1980		—	.38
10 Centavos Stainless Steel			
☐ 1992–1996		—	.38
Republic 1863–1904			
20 Centavos Silver			
☐ 1898–1904	Mint Mark Cn	—	7.15
☐ 1898–1900	Mint Mark Go	—	7.15
☐ 1898–1905	Mint Mark Mo	—	4.00
☐ 1898–1905	Mint Mark Zs	—	7.15

DATE	ABP FINE	AVERAGE FINE
Estados Unidos Mexicanos		
20 Centavos Silver		

Key to Grading: Eagle

DATE	ABP FINE	AVERAGE FINE
☐ 1905	—	$7.15
☐ 1906	—	7.15
☐ 1907 Str 7	—	4.25
☐ 1907 crvd 7	—	5.15
☐ 1908	—	45.00
☐ 1910	—	5.15
☐ 1911	—	5.15
☐ 1912	—	20.00
☐ 1913	—	8.00
☐ 1914	—	5.15
20 Centavos Silver Zapata Issue		
☐ 1915	—	16.00
20 Centavos Bronze		
☐ 1920	—	25.00
☐ 1935	—	4.15
20 Centavos Silver		
☐ 1920	—	4.15
☐ 1921	—	4.15
☐ 1925	—	4.15
☐ 1926/25	—	10.00
☐ 1926	—	4.15
☐ 1927	—	4.15
☐ 1928	—	4.15
☐ 1930	—	4.15
☐ 1933–1943	—	4.15
20 Centavos Bronze		
☐ 1943–1946	—	.55
☐ 1951	—	1.50
☐ 1952	—	2.00
☐ 1954	—	.50
☐ 1955	—	1.50
20 Centavos Bronze Restyled Eagle		
☐ 1955	—	.38
☐ 1956	—	.38
☐ 1957	—	.38

DATE		ABP FINE	AVERAGE FINE
☐ 1959		—	$2.00
☐ 1960–1971		—	.38
20 Centavos Bronze Restyled Eagle			
☐ 1971–1973		—	.38
20 Centavos Copper-Nickel			
☐ 1974–1983		—	.25
☐ 1977/9 Dbl Die		—	.60
☐ 1981 clsd 8		—	.32
☐ 1981/82		—	15.00
20 Centavos Bronze			
☐ 1983–1984		—	.32
Republica Mexicanos			
¼ Real Copper			
☐ 1829–1837		$20.00	30.00
¼ Real Silver			
☐ 1834RG	Mint Mark Ca	80.00	120.00
☐ 1855LR	Mint Mark C	—	100.00
☐ 1842LR	Mint Mark Do	25.00	40.00
☐ 1843LR	Mint Mark Do	9.00	25.00
☐ 1842–1862	Mint Mark Ga	—	20.00
☐ 1852LR	Mint Mark Ga	80.00	115.00
☐ 1854/3LR	Mint Mark Ga	80.00	115.00
☐ 1842–1863	Mint Mark Mo	—	15.00
☐ 1854	Mint Mark S.L.P.	175.00	220.00
☐ 1842/1 LR	Mint Mark Zs	—	12.00
☐ 1842 LR	Mint Mark Zs	—	12.00
Republic 1864–1904			
25 Centavos Silver			
☐ 1874–1890	Mint Mark A, As	—	16.00
☐ 1877L	Mint Mark A, As	175.00	235.00
☐ 1881L	Mint Mark A, As	300.00	400.00
☐ 1871M	Mint Mark CA, CH, Ca	—	28.00
☐ 1872	M Crude Date Mint Mark CA, CH, Ca	30.00	50.00
☐ 1883–1889	Mint Mark CA, CH, Ca	—	15.00
☐ 18871–1892	Mint Mark Cn	100.00	125.00
☐ 1877–1890	Mint Mark Do	18.00	35.00
☐ 1873	Mint Mark Do	—	Rare
☐ 1878/7E	Mint Mark Do	200.00	250.00
☐ 1878B	Mint Mark Do	—	Rare
☐ 1880–1889	Mint Mark Ga	20.00	35.00
☐ 1870–1880	Mint Mark GO	—	15.00
☐ 1881–1890	Mint Mark GO	—	10.00
☐ 1874–1890	Mint Mark Ho	—	15.00
☐ 1883M	Mint Mark Ho	80.00	115.00
☐ 1869–1890	Mint Mark Mo	—	20.00

DATE		ABP FINE	AVERAGE FINE
☐ 1869–1990	Mint Mark Pi	—	$12.00
☐ 1870–1890	Mint Mark Zs	—	10.00
Estados Unidos Mexicanos			
25 Centavos Silver			
☐ 1950–1953		—	.38
25 Centavos Copper-Nickel			
☐ 1964		—	.38
☐ 1966 clsd beak		—	.38
☐ 1966 open beak		—	.75
Republica Mexicanos			
½ Real Silver			
☐ 1824JM	Mint Mark Mo	$20.00	45.00
½ Real Silver			
☐ 1862PG	Mint Mark A	—	Rare
☐ 1844RG	Mint Mark Ca	55.00	80.00
☐ 1845RG	Mint Mark Ca	55.00	80.00
☐ 1846–1869	Mint Mark C, Co	—	18.00
☐ 1832–1869	Mint Mark D, Do	—	22.00
☐ 1829LF	Mint Mark EoMo	80.00	165.00
☐ 1825–1862	Mint Mark Ga	—	16.00
☐ 1844–1851	Mint Mark GC	—	30.00
☐ 1826–1868	Mint Mark Go	—	16.00
☐ 1826	MJ Mint Mark Go	30.00	120.00
☐ 1839PP	Mint Mark Ho	—	Unique
☐ 1862FM	Mint Mark Ho	350.00	500.00
☐ 1867PR/FM	inv 6 & 7/7 Mint Mark Ho	80.00	125.00
☐ 1825–1863	Mint Mark Mo	—	14.00
☐ 1831–1863	Mint Mark Pi	—	15.00
☐ 1845AM	Mint Mark Pi	125.00	255.00
☐ 1826–1869	Mint Mark Z, Zs	—	14.00
Republic 1863–1904			
50 Centavos Silver Balance Scales			
☐ 1875–1885	Mint Mark A, As	12.00	18.00
☐ 1888L	Mint Mark A, As	—	Counterfeits
☐ 1883–1887	Mint Mark Ca, Cha	—	20.00
☐ 1871P	Mint Mark Cn	340.00	400.00
☐ 1873P	Mint Mark Cn	340.00	400.00
☐ 1874P	Mint Mark Cn	100.00	210.00
☐ 1875–1881	Mint Mark Cn	—	18.00
☐ 1881G	Mint Mark Cn	100.00	140.00
☐ 1882D	Mint Mark Cn	85.00	175.00
☐ 1882G	Mint Mark Cn	50.00	125.00
☐ 1883–1892	Mint Mark Cn	40.00	80.00
☐ 1888M	Mint Mark Cn	—	Counterfeit
☐ 1871P	Mint Mark Do	—	Rare

DATE		ABP FINE	AVERAGE FINE
☐ 1873P–1873P M	Mint Mark Do	$100.00	$145.00
☐ 1874–1887	Mint Mark Do	20.00	32.00
☐ 1869–1888	Mint Mark Go	—	20.00
☐ 1874–1894	Mint Mark Ho	8.00	16.00
☐ 1888G	Mint Mark Ho	—	Counterfeit
☐ 1895G	Mint Mark Ho	140.00	225.00
☐ 1869–1873	Mint Mark Mo	25.00	50.00
☐ 1874/3M	Mint Mark Mo	80.00	200.00
☐ 1874/2–1887	Mint Mark Mo	18.00	30.00
☐ 1880	Mint Mark Mo	40.00	100.00
☐ 1883/2	Mint Mark Mo	120.00	185.00
☐ 1884M	Mint Mark Mo	120.00	185.00
☐ 1888M	Mint Mark Mo	—	Counterfeit
☐ 1870–1887	Mint Mark Pi	9.75	25.00
☐ 1888R	Mint Mark Pi	—	Counterfeit
☐ 1870–1887	Mint Mark Zs	8.00	25.00
☐ 1876S	Mint Mark Zs	45.00	100.00
☐ 1886Z	Mint Mark Zs	85.00	160.00

Emperor Maximillian 1864–1867

50 Centavos Silver

☐ 1866	Mint Mark Mo	40.00	55.00

Estados Unidos Mexicanos

50 Centavos Silver

Key to Grading: Eagle

☐ 1905	—	8.00
☐ 1906	—	6.25
☐ 1907 str 7	—	6.25
☐ 1907 crvd7	—	6.25
☐ 1908	20.00	30.00
☐ 1912	—	5.25
☐ 1913/07	—	20.00
☐ 1913/2	—	10.00
☐ 1913	—	5.25
☐ 1914	—	5.25
☐ 1916	12.00	22.00
☐ 1917	—	6.00
☐ 1918	18.00	30.00

DATE		ABP FINE	AVERAGE FINE
50 Centavos Reduced Size			
□ 1918/7		—	$250.00
□ 1918		—	8.00
□ 1919		—	8.00
50 Centavos Silver			
□ 1919		—	8.00
□ 1920		—	4.00
□ 1921		—	5.00
□ 1925		—	8.25
□ 1937		—	5.00
□ 1938		—	20.00
□ 1939		—	6.15
□ 1942		—	6.15
□ 1943–1945		—	4.15
50 Centavos Silver			
□ 1935		—	4.15
50 Centavos Silver Cuauhtemoc			
□ 1950		—	2.20
□ 1951		—	2.20
50 Centavos Bronze			
□ 1955		—	1.00
□ 1956		—	.40
□ 1957		—	.60
□ 1958		—	.38
50 Centavos Copper-Nickel			
□ 1964–1969		—	.38
50 Centavos C/N Stylized Eagle			
□ 1970–1983		—	.38
□ 1972		—	.50
□ 1977		—	3.00
50 Centavos Stainless Steel			
□ 1983		—	.38
50 Centavos Aluminum/Bronze			
□ 1992–1996		—	.38
Republica Mexicanos 1824–1864			
1 Real Silver Hooked Neck Eagle			
□ 1824 RL		2200.00	3000.00
1 Real Silver Upright Eagle			
□ 1844–1845	Mint Mark Ca	—	500.00
□ 1855	Mint Mark Ca	—	100.00
□ 1846–1851	Mint Mark C	6.00	12.00
□ 1851–1869	Mint Mark C	—	12.00
□ 1856	Mint Mark C	20.00	30.00
□ 1832–1864	Mint Mark Do	10.00	16.00
□ 1862/1CP	Mint Mark Do	—	275.00

DATE		ABP FINE	AVERAGE FINE
☐ 1828LF	Mint Mark EoMo	$100.00	$225.00
☐ 1826–1862	Mint Mark Ga	8.00	16.00
☐ 1830FS	Mint Mark Ga	—	225.00
☐ 1831LP/FS	Mint Mark Ga	—	325.00
☐ 1839JG	Mint Mark Ga	200.00	250.00
☐ 1848JG		300.00	415.00
☐ 1844–1851	Mint Mark GC	30.00	45.00
☐ 1826–1868	Mint Mark Go	—	10.00
☐ 1867–1968	Mint Mark Ho	40.00	60.00
☐ 1825–1863	Mint Mark Mo	—	12.00
☐ 1831JM	Mint Mark Mo	85.00	120.00
☐ 1852GC	Mint Mark Mo	200.00	275.00
☐ 1831–1862	Mint Mark Pi	10.00	18.00
☐ 1837JS	Mint Mark Pi	600.00	750.00
☐ 1838/7JS	Mint Mark Pi	175.00	240.00
☐ 1826–1869	Mint Mark Zs	—	8.00
Emperor Maximillian 1864–1867			
1 Peso Silver			
☐ 1866	Mint Mark GO	200.00	335.00
☐ 1866–1867	Mint Mark Mo	30.00	45.00
☐ 1868	Mint Mark Pi	30.00	60.00
Republic 1864–1904			
1 Peso Silver Balance Scales			
☐ 1872/1–1873	Mint Mark CH	20.00	32.00
☐ 1872	P/M Mint Mark CH	360.00	750.00
☐ 1872P	Mint Mark CH	200.00	435.00
☐ 1870–1873	Mint Mark Cn	—	26.00
☐ 1870–1873	Mint Mark Do	—	26.00
☐ 1872PT	Mint Mark Do	100.00	125.00
☐ 1870C	Mint Mark Ga	500.00	675.00
☐ 1871–1873	Mint Mark Ga	14.00	45.00
☐ 1871–1873	Mint Mark Go	12.00	25.00
☐ 1869–1873	Mint Mark Mo	10.00	16.00
☐ 1869–1873	Mint Mark Oa	15.00	30.00
☐ 1869C	Mint Mark Oa	—	Pattern
☐ 1870	OA E Lrg A Mint Mark Oa	100.00	120.00
☐ 1870–1873	Mint Mark Zs	—	15.00
1 Peso Silver Cap & Rays			
☐ 1898–1905	Mint Mark Cn	8.00	15.00
☐ 1898–1900	Mint Mark Go	10.00	20.00
☐ 1898–1909	Mint Mark Mo	—	14.00
☐ 1898–1905	Mint Mark Zs	—	14.00
1 Peso Gold			
☐ 1888L	Mint Mark As	—	Rare
☐ 1888	AsL/MoM Mint Mark As	—	Rare

DATE		ABP FINE	AVERAGE FINE
☐ 1888Ca/MoM	Mint Mark Ca	—	Rare
☐ 1873/1888	Mint Mark Cn	$30.00	$120.00
☐ 1889M	Mint Mark Cn	—	Rare
☐ 1891–1905	Mint Mark Cn	70.00	100.00
☐ 1870–1900	Mint Mark Go	70.00	100.00
☐ 1875–1888	Mint Mark Ho	—	Rare
☐ 1870–1905	Mint Mark Mo	40.00	65.00
☐ 1872–1890	Mint Mark Zs	60.00	125.00

Estados Unidos Mexicanos 1905–Present

1 Peso Silver Caballito

Key to Grading: Eagle

DATE	ABP FINE	AVERAGE FINE
☐ 1910	—	32.00
☐ 1911 Long Left Low Ray	—	32.00
☐ 1911 Short Left Low Ray	30.00	50.00
☐ 1912	60.00	100.00
☐ 1913/2	—	25.00
☐ 1914	240.00	320.00
1 Peso Silver Cap & Rays		
☐ 1918	—	20.00
☐ 1919	—	20.00
1 Peso Silver		
☐ 1920–1945	—	6.00
☐ 1920/10	—	35.00
1 Peso Silver		
☐ 1947–1948	—	5.00
☐ 1949	150.00	300.00
1 Peso Silver Jose Morelos y Pavon		
☐ 1950	—	2.20
1 Peso 100th Anniv. of Constitution		
☐ 1957	—	4.00
1 Peso Jose Morelos y Pavon		
☐ 1957–1962	—	.38
☐ 1959	—	.50
☐ 1963–1967	—	.38
1 Peso Copper/Nickel		
☐ 1970–1983	—	.38
☐ 1970 Wide Date	—	.50

DATE		ABP FINE	AVERAGE FINE
☐ 1977 Thin Date		—	$ .60
1 Peso Stainless Steel			
☐ 1984–1988		—	.38

Key to Grading: Eagle

DATE		ABP FINE	AVERAGE FINE
1 New Peso Bimetallic			
☐ 1992–1996		—	.38
Republica Mexicanos 1824–1864			
2 Reales Silver Hooked Neck Eagle			
☐ 1824 DO RL	Mint Mark D, Do	$28.00	50.00
☐ 1824 D RL	Mint Mark D, Do	55.00	125.00
☐ 1824 JM	Mint Mark Mo	—	32.00
2 Reales Sliver Facing Eagle			
☐ 1872	AM Mint Mark A	22.00	45.00
☐ 1863ML	Mint Mark Ce	75.00	125.00
☐ 1832–1855	Mint Mark Ca	10.00	25.00
☐ 1846–1869	Mint Mark C	—	16.00
☐ 1826–1834	Mint Mark Do	—	25.00
☐ 1835/4 RM/RL	Mint Mark Do	175.00	225.00
☐ 1841–1861	Mint Mark Do	—	16.00
☐ 1846/36	Mint Mark Do	60.00	100.00
☐ 1855CP	Mint Mark Do	200.00	260.00
☐ 1856CP	Mint Mark Do	45.00	100.00
☐ 1828 LF	Mint Mark EoMo	250.00	400.00
☐ 1825–1862	Mint Mark Ga	—	15.00
☐ 1851JG	Mint Mark Ga	250.00	325.00
☐ 1854/3JG	Mint Mark Ga	250.00	325.00
☐ 1857JG	Mint Mark Ga	100.00	240.00
☐ 1844–1851	Mint Mark GC	35.00	50.00
☐ 1850MP	Mint Mark GC	58.00	120.00
☐ 1825–1868	Mint Mark Go	—	16.00
☐ 1848PF	Mint Mark Go	40.00	100.00
☐ 1861	Mint Mark Ho	100.00	200.00
☐ 1825–1868	Mint Mark Mo	—	16.00
☐ 1832JM	Mint Mark Mo	40.00	120.00
☐ 1840ML	Mint Mark Mo	100.00	175.00
☐ 1829–1869	Mint Mark Pi	—	20.00
☐ 1863RO	Mint Mark Pi	60.00	100.00
☐ 1825–1870	Mint Mark Zs	—	16.00

DATE		ABP FINE	AVERAGE FINE
Estados Unidos Mexicanos			
2 Pesos Gold			
☐ 1919–1948		$20.00	$32.00
2 Pesos Silver 100th Anniv. of Independence			
☐ 1921		—	25.00

Key to Grading: Eagle

2 New Pesos Bimetallic			
☐ 1992–1995		—	.45
2 Pesos Bimetallic Denom w/o N			
☐ 1996–1999		—	.45
Republic 1864–1905			
2 ½ Peso Restyled Eagle Gold			

Key to Grading: Eagle

☐ 1888 As/MoL	Mint Mark As	—	Rare
☐ 1893M	Mint Mark Cn	1000.00	1500.00
☐ 1888C	Mint Mark Do	—	Rare
☐ 1871S	Mint Mark Go	1000.00	1500.00
☐ 1888	Go/MoR Mint Mark Go	875.00	1500.00
☐ 1874R	Mint Mark Ho	—	Rare
☐ 1888G	Mint Mark Ho	—	Rare
☐ 1870–1892	Mint Mark Mo	200.00	265.00
☐ 1872–1890	Mint Mark Zs	200.00	265.00
Estados Unidos Mexicanos 1905–Present			
2 ½ Pesos Gold			
☐ 1918–1948		—	30.00
☐ 1947		100.00	225.00
Republica Mexicanos 1824–1864			
4 Reales Upright Eagle Silver			
☐ 1863ML	Large C Mint Mark Ce	175.00	235.00

DATE		ABP FINE	AVERAGE FINE
☐ 1863ML	Small C Mint Mark Ce	$250.00	$325.00
☐ 1846CE	Mint Mark C	300.00	400.00
☐ 1850CE	Mint Mark C	55.00	80.00
☐ 1852CE	Mint Mark C	115.00	200.00
☐ 1857CE	Mint Mark C	—	Rare
☐ 1858CE	Mint Mark C	55.00	100.00
☐ 1860PV	Mint Mark C	12.50	25.00
☐ 1843–1850	Mint Mark Ga	25.00	40.00
☐ 1852JG	Mint Mark Ga	—	Rare
☐ 1854JG	Mint Mark Ga	—	Rare
☐ 1856JG	Mint Mark Ga	—	Rare
☐ 1855–1863	Mint Mark Ga	80.00	120.00
☐ 1844–1850	Mint Mark GC	1400.00	1800.00
☐ 1835–1870	Mint Mark Go	—	25.00
☐ 1841/31PJ	Mint Mark Go	80.00	155.00
☐ 1861FM	Mint Mark Ho	185.00	235.00
☐ 1867/1PR/FM	Mint Mark Ho	185.00	235.00
☐ 1827–1855	Mint Mark Mo	185.00	235.00
☐ 1850GC	Mint Mark Mo	—	Rare
☐ 1852GC	Mint Mark Mo	—	Rare
☐ 1854GC	Mint Mark Mo	—	Rare
☐ 1859–1868	Mint Mark Mo	13.00	35.00
☐ 1861FR	Ornamental Edge Mint Mark O	95.00	225.00
☐ 1861FR	Herringbone Edge Mint Mark O	200.00	325.00
☐ 1861FR	Obliquely Reed Edge Mint Mark O	100.00	200.00
☐ 1837–1853	Mint Mark Pi	12.50	30.00
☐ 1854–1860	Mint Mark Pi	200.00	325.00
☐ 1859MC	Mint Mark Pi	—	Scarce
☐ 1861–1869	Mint Mark Pi	25.00	42.00
☐ 1863–1870	Mint Mark ZS	25.00	42.00
Republic 1864–1905			
5 Pesos Restyled Eagle Gold			
☐ 1878L	Mint Mark As	800.00	1200.00
☐ 1888M	Mint Mark Ca	—	Rare
☐ 1873–1903	Mint Mark CN	160.00	300.00
☐ 1873–1879	Mint Mark Do	450.00	750.00
☐ 1871S	Mint Mark Go	400.00	650.00
☐ 1887R	Mint Mark Go	250.00	625.00
☐ 1888R	Mint Mark Go	—	Rare
☐ 1893R	Mint Mark Go	—	Rare
☐ 1874R	Mint Mark Ho	—	Scarce
☐ 1877R	Mint Mark Ho	600.00	775.00
☐ 1887A	Mint Mark Ho	600.00	775.00
☐ 1888G	Mint Mark Ho	—	Rare
☐ 1870–1905	Mint Mark Mo	200.00	250.00

DATE		ABP FINE	AVERAGE FINE
Estados Unidos Mexicanos			
5 Peso Gold			
☐ 1918–1944		—	$45.00
5 Peso Silver Cuauhtemoc			
☐ 1947–1948		—	5.00
5 Pesos Silver Railroad			
☐ 1950		—	16.00
5 Pesos Silver Miguel Costilla			
☐ 1951–1953		—	5.00
☐ 1954		—	20.00
5 Pesos Silver 200th Anniv. Hiadalgo's Birth			
☐ 1953		—	4.15
5 Pesos Silver Costilla Reduced Size			
☐ 1955–1957		—	4.15
5 Pesos Silver 100th Anniv. Constitution			
☐ 1957		—	4.15
5 Pesos Silver 100th Anniv. Carranza's birth			
☐ 1959		—	4.15
5 Pesos C/N Guerrero			
☐ 1971–1978		—	.42
5 Pesos C/N Quetzalcoatl			
☐ 1980–1985		—	.50
5 Pesos Brass			
☐ 1985–1988		—	.35
☐ 1987		—	4.00

Key to Grading: Eagle

DATE		ABP FINE	AVERAGE FINE
5 Pesos Bimetallic			
☐ 1992–1995		—	.80
☐ 1996–1999		—	.80
Republica Mexicanos 1824–1963			
8 Reales Silver Hooked-Neck Eagle			
☐ 1824RL	Mint Mark Do	$150.00	250.00
☐ 1824–1825	Mint Mark Go	400.00	500.00
☐ 1823–1824	Mint Mark Mo	85.00	150.00
Republic 1864–1905			
8 Reales Upright Eagle Silver			

Key to Grading: Eagle

DATE		ABP FINE	AVERAGE FINE
☐ 1864PG	Mint Mark A, As	$500.00	$725.00
☐ 1865PG	Mint Mark A, As	300.00	500.00
☐ 1866PG	Mint Mark A, As	1000.00	1400.00
☐ 1867DL	Mint Mark A, As	800.00	1200.00

Key to Grading: Eagle

☐ 1868–1895	Mint Mark A, As	9.00	25.00
☐ 1863ML	Mint Mark Ce	150.00	375.00
☐ 1864 CeML/PiMc	Mint Mark Ce	325.00	450.00
☐ 1831–1841	Mint Mark Ca	325.00	450.00
☐ 1842–1850	Mint Mark Ca	—	40.00
☐ 1851–1857	Mint Mark Ca	70.00	150.00
☐ 1858–1895	Mint Mark Ca	—	40.00
☐ 1865FP	Mint Mark Ca	800.00	1200.00
☐ 1866JC	Mint Mark Ca	—	Rare
☐ 1866FP	Mint Mark Ca	600.00	1000.00
☐ 1866JG	Mint Mark Ca	400.00	850.00
☐ 1846–1854	Mint Mark C, Cn	90.00	225.00
☐ 1855–1897	Mint Mark C, Cn	—	40.00
☐ 1825–1847	Mint Mark Do	—	40.00
☐ 1848–1853	Mint Mark Do	50.00	100.00
☐ 1854–1895	Mint Mark Do	—	30.00
☐ 1825–1832	Mint Mark Ga	100.00	175.00
☐ 1833–1839	Mint Mark Ga	45.00	70.00
☐ 1840–1865	Mint Mark Ga	30.00	50.00
☐ 1844–1852	Mint Mark GC	150.00	225.00
☐ 1825–1828	Mint Mark Go	150.00	225.00
☐ 1829–1897	Mint Mark Go	—	25.00
☐ 1835PP	Mint Mark Ho	—	Rare

DATE		ABP FINE	AVERAGE FINE
☐ 1836PP	Mint Mark Ho	—	Rare
☐ 1839PR	Mint Mark Ho	—	Unique
☐ 1861FM	Reed Edge Mint Mark Ho	—	Scarce
☐ 1862FM	Plain Edge Mint Mark Ho	—	Rare
☐ 1862FM	Snake Tail Left Mint Mark Ho	—	Scarce
☐ 1862FM	Snake Tail Right Mint Mark Ho	—	Scarce
☐ 1863–1867	Mint Mark Ho	$100.00	$240.00
☐ 1868–1895	Mint Mark Ho	22.00	42.00
☐ 1824–1897	Mint Mark Mo	22.00	42.00
☐ 1833ML	Mint Mark Mo	250.00	500.00
☐ 1847ML	Mint Mark Mo	—	Scarce
☐ 18580 AE	Mint Mark O, Oa	—	Scarce
☐ 18580a AE	Mint Mark O, Oa	—	Unique
☐ 1859–1861	Mint Mark O, Oa	120.00	180.00
☐ 1862–1893	Mint Mark O, Oa	20.00	30.00
☐ 1827JS	Mint Mark Pi	—	Rare
☐ 1828/7JS	Mint Mark Pi	110.00	250.00
☐ 1828JS	Mint Mark Pi	100.00	225.00
☐ 1829–1848	Mint Mark Pi	20.00	30.00
☐ 1849–1861	Mint Mark Pi	—	120.00
☐ 1862–1863	Mint Mark Pi	18.00	25.00
☐ 1863FC	Mint Mark Pi	—	Rare
☐ 1864RO	Mint Mark Pi	—	Rare
☐ 1867CA	Mint Mark Pi	450.00	675.00
☐ 1867RL	Mint Mark Pi	250.00	525.00
☐ 1867PS/CA	Mint Mark Pi	—	Rare
☐ 1868–1893	Mint Mark Pi	20.00	32.00
☐ 1825–1897	Mint Mark Zs	20.00	32.00
☐ 1860VL	Mint Mark Zs	—	Counterfeit
☐ 1867JS	Mint Mark Zs	—	Rare
½ Escudo Gold Upright Eagle			
☐ 1848–1870	Mint Mark C	35.00	65.00
☐ 1833–1864	Mint Mark Do	35.00	65.00
☐ 1825–1861	Mint Mark Ga	35.00	65.00
☐ 1846–1851	Mint Mark GC	35.00	65.00
☐ 1845–1863	Mint Mark Go	35.00	65.00
☐ 1825–1869	Mint Mark Mo	35.00	65.00
☐ 1860–1862	Mint Mark Zs	35.00	65.00
10 Pesos Balance Scale			
☐ 1874–1895	Mint Mark AS	325.00	475.00
☐ 1874DL	Mint Mark AS	—	Rare
☐ 1884L	Mint Mark AS	—	Rare
☐ 1892 L	Mint Mark AS	—	Rare
☐ 1894/3	Mint Mark AS	—	Rare
☐ 1888M	175 Pcs Mint Mark Ca	—	6500.00

DATE		ABP FINE	AVERAGE FINE
☐ 1881–1903	Mint Mark Cn	$300.00	$425.00
☐ 1883D	Mint Mark Cn	—	Rare
☐ 1872–1884	Mint Mark Do	300.00	400.00
☐ 1882P	Mint Mark Do	—	Rare
☐ 1870–1891	Mint Mark Ga		
	Low Mintage for This MM	500.00	700.00
☐ 1872S	Mint Mark Go	1000.00	2000.00
☐ 1887R	Mint Mark Go	—	Rare
☐ 1888R	Mint Mark Go	—	Rare
☐ 1874R	Mint Mark Ho	—	Rare
☐ 1876R	Mint Mark Ho	—	Rare
☐ 1878A	Mint Mark Ho	1200.00	1750.00
☐ 1879A	Mint Mark Ho	1200.00	1750.00
☐ 1880A	Mint Mark Ho	1200.00	1750.00
☐ 1881A	Mint Mark Ho	—	Rare
☐ 1870–1905	Mint Mark Mo	155.00	600.00
☐ 1870–1895	Mint Mark Oa	140.00	500.00
Estados Unidos Mexicanos			
10 Pesos Gold Miguel Hidago			
☐ 1905		70.00	100.00
☐ 1906–1910		40.00	72.50
☐ 1916		120.00	165.00
☐ 1917–1919		120.00	165.00
☐ 1920		80.00	140.00
☐ 1959	Restrikes	40.00	70.00
10 Pesos Silver Hidalgo			
☐ 1956–1956		—	8.00

Key to Grading: Eagle

10 Pesos Silver Anniv. Constitution			
☐ 1957		—	7.00
10 Pesos Silver Anniv. War of Independence			
☐ 1960		—	5.00

DATE		ABP FINE	AVERAGE FINE

Key to Grading: Eagle

DATE		ABP FINE	AVERAGE FINE
10 Pesos C/N Hidalgo			
☐ 1974–1977	Thin Flan	—	$ .80
10 Pesos C/N Hidalgo			
☐ 1978–1985	Thick Flan	—	.80
10 Pesos Stainless Steel			
☐ 1985–1990		—	.80
10 Pesos Bimetallic			
☐ 1992–Present		$2.00	4.00
Republica Mexicanos			
1 Escudo Gold Upright Eagle			
☐ 1846–1870	Mint Mark C	40.00	60.00
☐ 1833–1864	Mint Mark Do	40.00	60.00
☐ 1825–1860	Mint Mark Ga	200.00	400.00
☐ 1844–1851	Mint Mark GC	85.00	120.00
☐ 1845–1862	Mint Mark Go	60.00	100.00
☐ 1825–1869	Mint Mark Mo	45.00	80.00
☐ 1853–1862	Mint Mark Zs	80.00	125.00
Emperor Maximilian 1863–1967			
20 Pesos gold			
☐ 1866		350.00	500.00

Key to Grading: Eagle

DATE		ABP FINE	AVERAGE FINE
Republic 1867–1905			
20 Pesos Gold Restyled Eagle			
☐ 1876–1888	Mint Mark As	—	Rare
☐ 1872–1895	Mint Mark CH, Ca	400.00	525.00
☐ 1870–1905	Mint Mark Cn	400.00	525.00
☐ 1870–1877	Mint Mark Do	400.00	600.00
☐ 1878	Mint Mark Do	—	Rare

DATE		ABP FINE	AVERAGE FINE
☐ 1870–1900	Mint Mark Go	$400.00	$525.00
☐ 1874–1888	Mint Mark Ho	—	Rare
☐ 1870–1905	Mint Mark Mo	400.00	525.00
☐ 1870–1871	Mint Mark Oa	500.00	800.00
☐ 1871–1889	Mint Mark Zs	—	Scarce

Estados Unidos Mexicanos

20 Pesos Gold

☐ 1917–1959		—	375.00

Key to Grading: Eagle

20 Pesos C/N

☐ 1980–1984		—	.45

20 Pesos Brass

☐ 1985–1990		—	.32

20 Pesos Bimetallic

☐ 1993–1995		—	7.00
☐ 1996		—	6.00

Key to Grading: Eagle

25 Pesos Silver Olympics

☐ 1968	Type I	—	8.00
☐ 1968	Type II	—	7.00
☐ 1968	Type III	—	7.00

25 Pesos Silver Benito Juarez

☐ 1972		—	8.00

Key to Grading: Eagle

DATE		ABP FINE	AVERAGE FINE
25 Pesos Silver Soccer Games			
□ 1985 Proof		—	$14.00
Republica Mexicanos 1832–1904			
2 Escudos Gold Upright Eagle			
□ 1846–1857	Mint Mark C	$100.00	150.00
□ 1833–1844	Mint Mark Do	300.00	450.00
□ 1828LF	Mint Mark EoMo	700.00	1000.00
□ 1835–1870	Mint Mark Ga	100.00	175.00
□ 1844–1850	Mint Mark GC	125.00	220.00
□ 1845MP	Mint Mark GC	1200.00	1650.00
□ 1846MP	Mint Mark GC	1200.00	1650.00
□ 1845–1862	Mint Mark Go	100.00	160.00
□ 1861FM	Mint Mark Ho	650.00	1000.00
□ 1825–1869	Mint Mark Mo	60.00	160.00
□ 1860–1964	Mint Mark Zs	300.00	450.00
Estados Unidos Mexicanos 1905–Present			
50 Pesos Gold Centennial of Independence			
□ 1921–1947		—	450.00

Key to Grading: Eagle

50 Pesos C/N Coyolxauhqui			
□ 1982–1984		—	.80
50 Pesos C/N Benito Juarez			
□ 1984–1988		—	.32
□ 1986		—	270.00
□ 1988		—	4.00
50 Pesos Stainless Steel			
□ 1988–1992		—	.38
50 Pesos Silver Soccer			
□ 1985		—	6.00
50 Pesos Silver Oil Industry			
□ ND(1988)		—	12.00
50 Pesos Bimetallic			
□ 1992		—	12.00
Republica Mexicanos 1834–1864			
4 Escudos Gold Upright Eagle			
□ 1846CE	Mint Mark C	1200.00	1600.00
□ 1847CE	Mint Mark C	450.00	650.00
□ 1848CE	Mint Mark C	600.00	800.00
□ 1832–1852	Mint Mark Do	—	Rare

DATE		ABP FINE	AVERAGE FINE
☐ 1844MC	Mint Mark Ga	$600.00	$750.00
☐ 1844JC	Mint Mark Ga	500.00	600.00
☐ 1844–1850	Mint Mark Go	300.00	425.00
☐ 1861FM	Mint Mark Ho	1000.00	1400.00
☐ 1829–1869	Mint Mark Mo	400.00	550.00
☐ 1861FR	Mint Mark O, Oa	1800.00	2200.00
☐ 1862VL	Mint Mark Zs	1000.00	1400.00

Estados Unidos Mexicanos 1905–Present

100 Pesos Silver Jose Pavon

Key to Grading: Eagle

DATE		ABP FINE	AVERAGE FINE
☐ 1977 Low 7's		—	4.15
☐ 1977 High 7's		—	4.15
100 Pesos Silver Jose Pavon			
☐ 1977–1979	Date in Line	—	4.15
100 Pesos Aluminum-Bronze			
☐ 1984–1992		—	.50
☐ 1986		—	1.00
100 Pesos Silver (.72 ASW) Soccer			
☐ 1985		—	16.50
100 Pesos Silver (1.0 ASW) Soccer			
☐ 1985		—	16.50
100 Pesos Silver Monarch Butterflies			
☐ 1987		—	45.00
100 Pesos Silver Oil Industry			
☐ 1988		—	32.00
100 Pesos Silver Save the Children			
☐ 1991		—	55.00
100 Pesos Silver Ibero Pillars			
☐ 1991–1992		—	55.00
100 Pesos Silver Save the Harbor Porpoise			
☐ 1992		—	55.00

Republica Mexicanos 1823–1864

DATE		ABP FINE	AVERAGE FINE
8 Escudos Gold Hooked-Neck Eagle			
☐ 1823JM	Snake Tail Curved Mint Mark Mo	2400.00	3000.00
☐ 1823	JM Snake Tail Looped Mint Mark Mo	2400.00	3000.00
8 Escudos Gold Upright Eagle			
☐ 1864–1872	Mint Mark A	900.00	1200.00
☐ 1841–1871	Mint Mark Ca	250.00	465.00

DATE		ABP FINE	AVERAGE FINE

Key to Grading: Eagle

DATE		ABP FINE	AVERAGE FINE
☐ 1846–1870	Mint Mark C	$250.00	$440.00
☐ 1832–1870	Mint Mark Do	250.00	440.00
☐ 1828–1829	Mint Mark EoMo	2200.00	3200.00
☐ 1825–1866	Mint Mark Ga	465.00	615.00
☐ 1844–1852	Mint Mark Gc	465.00	615.00
☐ 1828–1873	Mint Mark Go	350.00	500.00
☐ 1863–1873	Mint Mark Ho	350.00	500.00
☐ 1824–1869	Mint Mark Mo	175.00	325.00
☐ 1858AE	Mint Mark O	1400.00	2000.00
☐ 1858–1871	Mint Mark Zs	250.00	360.00

Key to Grading: Eagle

Estados Unidos Mexicanos

DATE	ABP FINE	AVERAGE FINE
200 Pesos C/N Anniv. Independence		
☐ 1985	—	.38
200 Pesos C/N Anniv. 1910 Revolution		
☐ 1985	—	.38
200 Pesos C/N Soccer		
☐ 1986	—	.38
200 Pesos Silver Soccer		
☐ 1986	24.00	32.00
250 Pesos Gold Soccer		
☐ 1985–1986	85.00	135.00

Key to Grading: Eagle

DATE	ABP FINE	AVERAGE FINE
500 Pesos Gold Soccer		
□ 1985–1986	$1200.00	$2200.00
500 Pesos Silver Anniv. 1910 Revolution		
□ 1985	—	42.00
500 Pesos C/N Francisco Madero		
□ 1986–1992	—	1.20
500 Peso Gold Oil Industry		
□ 1988	—	2250.00
1000 Pesos Gold Anniv. of Independence		
□ 1985	—	365.00
1000 Pesos Gold Soccer		
□ 1986	—	450.00
1000 Pesos Gold Oil Industry		

Key to Grading: Eagle

□ 1988	—	400.00
1000 Pesos Aluminum-Bronze		
□ 1988–1992	—	.75
2000 Pesos Gold Soccer		
□ 1986	—	1000.00
5000 Pesos C/N Oil Industry		
□ N/D(1988)	—	28.00

MOROCCO

The first coins were used in the 2nd century B.C., with the silver denarius in 50 B.C., bronze coins in the 1st century B.C., and copper fals in 731 A.D. The silver dirham was in evidence in the 700s, followed by the gold dinar, silver square dirham, and gold double dinar in the 12th and 13th centuries. The copper double fals was in use in the 1800s and the cupro-nickel francs in the mid-1900s. Decimal coins were used in 1921. The currency today is the dirham.

Key to Grading: Coin Design

Morocco—Type Coinage

DATE	COIN TYPE/VARIETY/METAL	ABP FINE	AVERAGE FINE
☐ 1310	1/2 Mazuna, Hasan I, Bronze	$100.00	$200.00
☐ 1310	1 Mazuna, Hasan I, Bronze	75.00	185.00
☐ 1320–1321	1 Mazuna, Abd Al-Aziz 2nd Coinage, Bronze	2.00	4.15
☐ 1330	1 Mazuna, Yusuf: 1st Coinage, Bronze	—	4.15
☐ 1320–1321	2 Mazuna, Abd Al-Aziz 2nd Coinage, Bronze	—	4.15
☐ 1330	2 Mazuna, Yusuf: 1st Coinage, Bronze	—	4.15
☐ 1310	2 1/2 Mazuna, Hasan I, Bronze	75.00	140.00
☐ 1310	5 Mazuna, Hasan I, Bronze	40.00	75.00
☐ 1320–1322	5 Mazuna, Abd Al-Aziz 2nd Coinage, Bronze	5.00	8.00
☐ 1330–1340	5 Mazuna, Yusuf: 1st Coinage, Bronze	—	4.15
☐ 1310	10 Mazuna, Hasan I, Bronze	25.00	72.00
☐ 1320–1323	10 Mazuna, Abd Al-Aziz 2nd Coinage, Bronze	—	4.00
☐ 1330–1340	10 Mazuna, Yusuf: 1st Coinage, Bronze	—	2.00
☐ 1974	1 Santim, Monetary Reform, Gold	—	485.00
☐ 1974–1975	1 Santim, Monetary Reform, Aluminum	—	1.20
☐ 1299–1314	1/2 Dirham, Hasan I, Silver	—	4.15
☐ 1313–1319	1/2 Dirham, Abd Al-Aziz 1st Coinage, Silver	—	4.15
☐ 1320–1321	1/20 Rial, Abd Al-Aziz 2nd Coinage, Silver	—	4.15
☐ 1974	5 Santimat, Monetary Reform, Gold	—	550.00
☐ 1974–1978	5 Santimat, Monetary Reform, Brass	—	.32
☐ 1987	5 Santimat, Monetary Reform, Brass	—	.32

Key to Grading: Bust

DATE	COIN TYPE/VARIETY/METAL	ABP FINE	AVERAGE FINE
☐ 1299–1314	1 Dirham, Hasan I, Silver	—	5.00
☐ 1313–1318	1 Dirham, Abd Al-Aziz 1st Coinage, Silver	—	7.15
☐ 1320–1321	1/10 Rial, Abd Al-Aziz 2nd Coinage, Silver	—	7.15
☐ 1331	1/10 Rial, Yusuf: 1st Coinage, Silver	—	35.00

Key to Grading: Coat of Arms

DATE	COIN TYPE/VARIETY/METAL	ABP FINE	AVERAGE FINE
☐ 1974–1978	10 Santimat, Monetary Reform, Brass	—	$ .32
☐ 1974	10 Santimat, Monetary Reform, Gold	—	675.00
☐ 1974	20 Santimat, Monetary Reform, Gold	—	700.00
☐ 1974–1978	20 Santimat, Monetary Reform, Brass	—	.32
☐ 1299–1314	2½ Dirham, Hasan I, Silver	—	6.00
☐ 1313–1318	2½ Dirham, Abd Al-Aziz 1st Coinage, Silver	—	8.25
☐ 1320–1321	¼ Rial, Abd Al-Aziz 2nd Coinage, Silver	—	6.00
☐ 1329	¼ Rial, Hafiz, Silver	—	7.00
☐ 1331	¼ Rial, Yusuf: 1st Coinage, Silver	—	32.00
☐ 1921–1924	25 Centimes, Yusuf: 2nd Coinage, Cupro-Nickel	—	4.15
☐ 1299–1314	5 Dirham, Hasan I, Silver	—	10.00

Key to Grading: Coin Design

DATE	COIN TYPE/VARIETY/METAL	ABP FINE	AVERAGE FINE
☐ 1313–1318	5 Dirham, Abd Al-Aziz 1st Coinage, Silver	—	12.00
☐ 1320–1323	½ Rial, Abd Al-Aziz 2nd Coinage, Silver	—	10.00
☐ 1329	½ Rial, Hafiz, Silver	—	10.00
☐ 1331–1336	½ Rial, Yusuf: 1st Coinage, Silver	—	11.00

Key to Grading: Star Design

DATE	COIN TYPE/VARIETY/METAL	ABP FINE	AVERAGE FINE
☐ 1921–1924	50 Centimes, Yusuf: 2nd Coinage, Cupro-Nickel	—	$ 1.15
☐ 1945	50 Centimes, Muhammad V: 2nd Coinage, Aluminum-Bronze	—	.28
☐ 1974	50 Santimat, Monetary Reform, Gold	—	775.00
☐ 1974–1978	50 Santimat, Monetary Reform, Brass	—	.38
☐ 1987	1/2 Dirham, Monetary Reform, Cupro-Nickel	—	.38
☐ 1299	10 Durham, Hasan I, Silver	—	18.00

Key to Grading: Star

DATE	COIN TYPE/VARIETY/METAL	ABP FINE	AVERAGE FINE
☐ 1313	10 Durham, Abd Al-Aziz 1st Coinage, Silver	—	85.00
☐ 1320–1321	1 Rial, Abd Al-Aziz 2nd Coinage, Silver	—	28.00
☐ 1329	1 Rial, Hafiz, Silver	—	18.00
☐ 1331–1336	1 Rial, Yusuf: 1st Coinage, Silver	—	15.00

Key to Grading: Star

DATE	COIN TYPE/VARIETY/METAL	ABP FINE	AVERAGE FINE
☐ 1921–1924	1 Franc, Yusuf: 2nd Coinage, Cupro-Nickel	—	.75
☐ 1945	1 Franc, Muhammad V: 2nd Coinage, Aluminum-Bronze	—	.38
☐ 1951	1 Franc, Muhammad V: 3rd Coinage, Aluminum	—	.38
☐ 1960	1 Dirham, Hasan II: Monetary Reform, Silver	—	1.00
☐ 1965–1969	Dirham, Al Hasan II: Monetary Reform, Nickel	—	.38
☐ 1974	Dirham, Monetary Reform, Gold	—	825.00

DATE	COIN TYPE/VARIETY/METAL	ABP FINE	AVERAGE FINE
□ 1974–1978	Dirham, Monetary Reform, Cupro-Nickel	—	$ .32
□ 1945	2 Francs, Muhammad V: 2nd Coinage, Aluminum-Bronze	—	.38
□ 1951	2 Francs, Muhammad V: 3rd Coinage, Aluminum	—	.32

Key to Grading: Star

DATE	COIN TYPE/VARIETY/METAL	ABP FINE	AVERAGE FINE
□ 1347–1352	5 Francs, Muhammad V: 1st Coinage, Silver	—	2.00
□ 1951	5 Francs, Muhammad V: 3rd Coinage, Aluminum	—	.45
□ 1965	5 Dirhams, Al Hasan II: Monetary Reform, Silver	—	4.00
□ 1975–1980	5 Dirhams, Monetary Reform, Cupro-Nickel	—	.55
□ 1975	5 Dirhams, Monetary Reform, Silver	—	80.00
□ 1975	5 Dirhams, Monetary Reform, Gold	—	1250.00
□ 1987	5 Dirhams, Monetary Reform, Dual Metal	—	2.20

Key to Grading: Star

DATE	COIN TYPE/VARIETY/METAL	ABP FINE	AVERAGE FINE
□ 1347–1352	10 Francs, Muhammad V: 1st Coinage, Silver	—	4.00
□ 1366	10 Francs, Muhammad V: 2nd Coinage, Cupro-Nickel	—	.75
□ 1371	10 Francs, Muhammad Bin Yusuf: 3rd Coinage, Aluminum-Bronze	—	.32

Key to Grading: Star

DATE	COIN TYPE/VARIETY/METAL	ABP FINE	AVERAGE FINE
□ 1347–1352	20 Francs, Muhammad V: 1st Coinage, Silver	—	$7.00
□ 1366	20 Francs, Muhammad V: 2nd Coinage, Cupro-Nickel	—	.55
□ 1371	20 Francs, Muhammad V: 3rd Coinage, Aluminum-Bronze	—	.38

Key to Grading: Star

DATE	COIN TYPE/VARIETY/METAL	ABP FINE	AVERAGE FINE
□ 1371	50 Francs, Muhammad V: 3rd Coinage, Aluminum-Bronze	—	.80
□ 1975	50 Dirham, Monetary Reform: 20th Anniversary of Independence, Gold	—	1400.00
□ 1975	50 Dirham, Monetary Reform: 20th Anniversary of Independence, Silver	—	32.00
□ 1976–1980	50 Dirham, Monetary Reform: Anniversary of Green March, Gold	—	1800.00
□ 1976–1980	50 Dirham, Monetary Reform: Anniversary of Green March, Silver	—	65.00
□ 1979	50 Dirham, Monetary Reform: King Hassan Birthday, Silver	—	42.00
□ 1979	50 Dirham, Monetary Reform: King Hassan Birthday, Gold	—	1600.00
□ 1979	50 Dirham, Monetary Reform: Year of the Child, Silver	—	42.00
□ 1979	50 Dirham, Monetary Reform: Year of the Child, Gold	—	1500.00

Key to Grading: Star

DATE	COIN TYPE/VARIETY/METAL	ABP FINE	AVERAGE FINE
☐ 1953	100 Francs, Muhammad V: 3rd Coinage, Silver	—	$4.15
☐ 1983	100 Dirham, 9th Mediterranean Games, Silver	—	5.00
☐ 1985	100 Dirham, Olympic Games, Silver	—	32.00
☐ 1985	100 Dirham, 25th Year of King Hassan, Silver	—	35.00
☐ 1986	100 Dirham, Papal Visit, Silver	—	65.00
☐ 1986	100 Dirham, Anniversary of Green March, Silver	—	42.00
☐ 1987	100 Dirham, Rabat Mint Opening, Silver	—	42.00
☐ 1980	150 Dirham, Hejira Calendar Century, Gold	—	1800.00
☐ 1980	150 Dirham, Hejira Calendar Century, Silver	—	55.00
☐ 1981	150 Dirham, King Hassan's Coronation 20th Anniversary, Gold	—	1800.00
☐ 1981	150 Dirham, King Hassan's Coronation 20th Anniversary, Silver	—	50.00
☐ 1953	200 Francs, Muhammad Bin Yusuf: 3rd Coinage, Silver	—	4.25
☐ 1987	200 Dirham, Moroccan American Friendship Treaty, Silver	—	45.00
☐ 1989	200 Dirham, First Francophonie Games, Silver	—	42.00

Key to Grading: Bust

DATE	COIN TYPE/VARIETY/METAL	ABP FINE	AVERAGE FINE
☐ 1956	500 Francs, Mohammed V, Silver	—	7.25
☐ 1979–1985	500 Dirham, King Hassan Birthday, Gold	—	425.00

MOZAMBIQUE

The first coins, crude copper and silver, were used in 1725. The silver onca, a rectangular coin, was in evidence in the 1800s, followed by the silver rupee in the 1860s and the cupro-nickel escudo in the 1930s. Decimal coins appeared in 1935. The currency today is the metical.

Mozambique—Type Coinage

DATE	COIN TYPE/VARIETY/METAL	ABP FINE	AVERAGE FINE
□ 1975	1 Centimo, Peoples Republic, Aluminum	$22.00	$45.00
□ 1975	2 Centimos, Peoples Republic, Copper-Zinc	22.00	32.00
□ 1975	5 Centimos, Peoples Republic, Copper-Zinc	5.00	20.00
□ 1936	10 Centavos, Bronze	—	4.15
□ 1942	10 Centavos, New Reverse Arms, Bronze	—	2.00
□ 1960–1961	10 Centavos, Reduced Size	—	.38
□ 1975	10 Centimos, Peoples Republic, Copper-Zinc	12.00	22.00
□ 1936	20 Centavos, Bronze	—	2.20
□ 1941	20 Centavos, New Reverse Arms, Bronze	—	2.20

Key to Grading: Coat of Arms

DATE	COIN TYPE/VARIETY/METAL	ABP FINE	AVERAGE FINE
□ 1949–1950	20 Centavos, New Reverse Arms, Bronze	—	$ .55
□ 1975	20 Centimos, Peoples Republic, Copper-Zinc	—	45.00
□ 1936	50 Centavos, Cupro-Nickel	—	2.20
□ 1945	50 Centavos, New Reverse Arms, Bronze	—	2.20
□ 1950–1951	50 Centavos, New Reverse Arms, Nickel-Bronze	—	.55

Key to Grading: Coat of Arms

DATE	COIN TYPE/VARIETY/METAL	ABP FINE	AVERAGE FINE
□ 1953–1957	50 Centavos, Decree of January 21, 1952, Bronze	—	.32
□ 1975	50 Centimos, Peoples Republic, Copper-Zinc	$32.00	50.00
□ 1980–1982	50 Centavos, Monetary Reform: Instrument, Aluminum	—	.38

Key to Grading: Coat of Arms

DATE	COIN TYPE/VARIETY/METAL	ABP FINE	AVERAGE FINE
□ 1936	1 Escudo, Cupro-Nickel	—	4.15
□ 1945	1 Escudo, New Reverse Arms, Bronze	—	2.00
□ 1950–1951	1 Escudo, New Reverse Arms, Nickel-Bronze	—	.75
□ 1953–1974	1 Escudo, Decree of January 21, 1952, Bronze	—	.28
□ 1975	1 Metical, Peoples Republic, Cupro-Nickel	18.00	30.00
□ 1980–1982	1 Metical, Monetary Reform: Female Student, Brass	—	4.15
□ 1986	1 Metical, Monetary Reform: Female Student, Aluminum	—	.38

Key to Grading: Coat of Arms

DATE	COIN TYPE/VARIETY/METAL	ABP FINE	AVERAGE FINE
☐ 1935	2½ Escudos, Silver	—	$7.00
☐ 1938–1951	2½ Escudos, New Reverse Arms, Silver	—	4.15
☐ 1952–1973	2½ Escudos, Decree of January 21, 1952, Cupro-Nickel	—	.38
☐ 1975	2½ Meticais, Peoples Republic, Cupro-Nickel	$15.00	40.00
☐ 1980–1986	2½ Meticais, Monetary Reform: Harbor Scene, Aluminium	—	.45
☐ 1935	5 Escudos, Silver	—	8.00
☐ 1938–1949	5 Escudos, New Reverse Arms, Silver	—	4.15
☐ 1960	5 Escudos, Decree of January 21, 1952, Silver	—	2.00
☐ 1980–1986	5 Meticais, Monetary Reform: Tractor, Aluminum	—	.55
☐ 1936	10 Escudos, Silver	—	12.00
☐ 1938	10 Escudos, New Reverse Arms, Silver	—	10.00
☐ 1952–1966	10 Escudos, Decree of January 21, 1952, Silver	—	4.15
☐ 1968–1974	10 Escudos, Copper-Nickel	—	.32
☐ 1980–1981	10 Meticais, Monetary Reform: Industrial Skyline, Cupro-Nickel	—	.45
☐ 1986	10 Meticais, Monetary Reform: Industrial Skyline, Aluminum	—	.38
☐ 1952–1966	20 Escudos, Decree of January 21, 1952, Silver	—	2.00
☐ 1970–1972	20 Escudos, Nickel	—	.45
☐ 1980–1982	20 Meticais, Monetary Reform: Panzer Tank, Cupro-Nickel	—	1.20
☐ 1986	20 Meticais, Monetary Reform: Panzer Tank, Aluminum	—	1.20
☐ 1983	50 Meticais, Monetary Reform: World Fisheries Conference, Cupro-Nickel	—	2.20
☐ 1983	50 Meticais, Monetary Reform: World Fisheries Conference, Gold	—	1400.00
☐ 1983	50 Meticais, Monetary Reform: World Fisheries Conference, Silver	—	55.00
☐ 1986	50 Meticais, Monetary Reform: Woman & Soldier, Aluminum	—	.80

DATE	COIN TYPE/VARIETY/METAL	ABP FINE	AVERAGE FINE
☐ 1985	250 Meticais, Monetary Reform: 10th Anniversary of Independence, Cupro-Nickel	—	$12.00
☐ 1985	250 Meticais, Monetary Reform: 10th Anniversary of Independence, Silver	—	48.00
☐ 1980	500 Meticais, Monetary Reform: 5th Anniversary of Independence, Silver	—	48.00
☐ 1989	500 Meticais, Monetary Reform: Defense of Nature—Moorish Idol Fish, Silver	—	48.00
☐ 1989	500 Meticais, Monetary Reform: Defense of Nature—Lions, Silver	—	48.00
☐ 1989	500 Meticais, Monetary Reform: Defense of Nature—Giraffes, Silver	—	48.00
☐ 1988	1000 Meticais, Monetary Reform: Papal Visit, Silver	—	48.00
☐ 1985	2000 Meticais, Monetary Reform: 10th Anniversary of Independence, Gold	—	800.00
☐ 1980	5000 Meticais, Monetary Reform: 5th Anniversary of Independence, Gold	—	525.00

NEPAL

The first coins, used in the 6th century A.D., were of silver and copper. Small gold, silver, and copper coins were used in the 12th to 16th centuries. The silver mohur was used in the 17th century, followed by the gold presentation coin in the 1700s, the copper paisa in the 1800s, and the aluminum paisa in the 1900s. Decimal coins were used in 1932. The currency today is the rupee.

Nepal—Type Coinage

DATE	COIN TYPE/VARIETY/METAL	ABP FINE	AVERAGE FINE
☐ 1953–1957	5 Paisa, Bronze	$ .30	$ .55
☐ 1953–1955	10 Paisa, Hands Praying, Bronze	—	.20
☐ 1953–1954	20 Paisa, Copper-Nickel	10.00	25.00
☐ 1932–1947	20 Paisa, Trident, Rev: Sword, Silver	—	4.15
☐ 1932–1948	50 Paisa, Trident, Rev: Sword, Silver	—	4.15
☐ 1953–1954	50 Paisa, Head of Tribhubana, Silver	—	.40
☐ 1950	Rupee, Trident, Rev: Sword, Silver	—	4.15
☐ 1932–1948	Rupee, Trident, Rev: Sword, Silver	—	4.15

NETHERLANDS

The first coins were base-gold tremisses, then silver deniers. A revival of gold coinage occurred in the 14th century. In 1606 a new range of coins was established, including the gold ducat and the silver rijksdaalder. In 1680 gulden pieces were added. In 1830 a decimal system, consisting of 100 cents to the gulden, was established and is still in use today.

Netherlands—Type Coinage

☐ 1850–1877	½ Cent, Copper	7.00	11.00

Key to Grading: Lion

DATE	COIN TYPE/VARIETY/METAL	ABP FINE	AVERAGE FINE
☐ 1878–1901	1/2 Cent, Obv: KONINGRIJK, Bronze	—	$6.00
☐ 1903–1906	1/2 Cent, Obv: KONINKRIJK, Bronze	—	.80
☐ 1909–1940	1/2 Cent, Wilhelmina—3rd Coinage, Bronze	—	.80
☐ 1860–1877	1 Cent, Copper	$4.00	6.15

Key to Grading: Lion

DATE	COIN TYPE/VARIETY/METAL	ABP FINE	AVERAGE FINE
☐ 1877–1901	1 Cent, Obv: KONINGRIJK, Bronze	2.00	4.00
☐ 1901	1 Cent, Obv: KONINKRIJK, Bronze	—	2.20
☐ 1902–1907	1 Cent, Obv: KONINKRIJK, Bronze	—	2.20
☐ 1913–1941	1 Cent, Wilhelmina—3rd Coinage, Bronze	—	2.20
☐ 1941–1944	1 Cent, WWII Occupation, Zinc	—	2.20
☐ 1948	1 Cent, Wilhelmina, Bronze	—	.38
☐ 1950–1980	1 Cent, Juliana, Bronze	—	.38

Key to Grading: Lion

DATE	COIN TYPE/VARIETY/METAL	ABP FINE	AVERAGE FINE
☐ 1877–1898	2 1/2 Cents, Obv: KONINGRIJK, Bronze	1.00	5.00
☐ 1903–1906	2 1/2 Cents, Obv: KONINKRIJK, Bronze	—	4.15
☐ 1912–1941	2 1/2 Cents, Wilhelmina—3rd Coinage, Bronze	1.00	4.15
☐ 1941–1942	2 1/2 Cents, WWII Occupation, Zinc	—	.80

DATE	COIN TYPE/VARIETY/METAL	ABP FINE	AVERAGE FINE
☐ 1850–1887	5 Cents, Willem III, Silver	—	$8.15
☐ 1907–1909	5 Cents, Wilhelmina—2nd Coinage, Cupro-Nickel	—	8.15
☐ 1913–1940	5 Cents, Wilhelmina—3rd Coinage, Cupro-Nickel	—	2.00
☐ 1941–1943	5 Cents, WWII Occupation, Zinc	—	4.00
☐ 1948	5 Cents, Wilhelmina, Bronze	—	.38
☐ 1950 to Date	5 Cents, Juliana, Bronze	—	.25
☐ 1849–1890	10 Cents, Willem III, Silver	—	14.00
☐ 1892–1897	10 Cents, Wilhelmina—1st Coinage, Obv: Child Head, Rev: Value in Wreath, Silver	—	5.00
☐ 1898–1901	10 Cents, Wilhelmina—2nd Coinage, Obv: Young Head, Silver	—	8.00
☐ 1903	10 Cents, Wilhelmina—2nd Coinage, Obv: Large Head, Silver	—	4.15
☐ 1904–1906	10 Cents, Wilhelmina—2nd Coinage, Obv: Small Head, Silver	—	7.00

Key to Grading: Bust

DATE	COIN TYPE/VARIETY/METAL	ABP FINE	AVERAGE FINE
☐ 1910–1925	10 Cents, Wilhelmina—3rd Coinage, Obv: Adult Head, Silver	—	2.00
☐ 1926–1945	10 Cents, Wilhelmina—4th Coinage, Obv: Older Head, Silver	—	1.20
☐ 1941–1943	10 Cents, WWII Occupation, Zinc	—	.75
☐ 1948	10 Cents, Wilhelmina, Nickel	—	.38
☐ 1950 to Date	10 Cents, Juliana, Nickel	—	.38
☐ 1849–1890	25 Cents, Willem III, Silver	—	80.00
☐ 1892–1897	25 Cents, Wilhelmina—1st Coinage, Obv: Child Head, Rev: Value in Wreath, Silver	—	10.00
☐ 1898–1906	25 Cents, Wilhelmina—2nd Coinage, Silver	—	7.50
☐ 1910–1925	25 Cents, Wilhelmina—3rd Coinage, Obv: Adult Head, Silver	—	5.00

Key to Grading: Bust

DATE	COIN TYPE/VARIETY/METAL	ABP FINE	AVERAGE FINE
☐ 1926–1945	25 Cents, Wilhelmina—4th Coinage, Obv: Older Head, Silver	—	$4.15
☐ 1948	25 Cents, Wilhelmina, Nickel	—	.42
☐ 1950–1980	25 Cents, Juliana, Nickel	—	.42
☐ 1980	25 Cents, Juliana, Aluminum	—	350.00
☐ 1982 to Date	Juliana, Nickel	—	.42
☐ 1853–1868	1/2 Gulden, Willem III, Silver	—	12.00
☐ 1898	1/2 Gulden, Wilhelmina—2nd Coinage, Silver	—	16.00
☐ 1904–1909	1/2 Gulden, Wilhelmina—2nd Coinage, Silver	—	12.00
☐ 1910–1919	1/2 Gulden, Wilhelmina—3rd Coinage, Obv: Adult Head, Silver	—	5.00
☐ 1921–1930	1/2 Gulden, Wilhelmina—4th Coinage, Obv: Older Head, Silver	—	4.15
☐ 1849–1975	1 Ducat, Trade Coins, Gold	—	145.00
☐ 1851–1866	1 Gulden, Willem III, Silver	—	12.00
☐ 1892–1897	1 Gulden, Wilhelmina—1st Coinage, Obv: Child Head, Rev: Value in Wreath, Silver	—	15.00
☐ 1898–1901	1 Gulden, Wilhelmina—2nd Coinage, Silver	—	25.00
☐ 1904–1909	1 Gulden, Wilhelmina—2nd Coinage, Silver	—	15.00
☐ 1910–1917	1 Gulden, Wilhelmina—3rd Coinage, Obv: Adult Head, Silver	—	20.00

Key to Grading: Bust

DATE	COIN TYPE/VARIETY/METAL	ABP FINE	AVERAGE FINE
☐ 1922–1945	1 Gulden, Wilhelmina—4th Coinage, Obv: Older Head, Silver	—	4.15
☐ 1954–1967	1 Gulden, Juliana, Silver	—	1.20

DATE	COIN TYPE/VARIETY/METAL	ABP FINE	AVERAGE FINE
☐ 1980 to Date	1 Gulden, Nickel	—	$ 1.20
☐ 1989	1 Silver Ducat, Silver Wedding Anniversary, Silver	—	20.00
☐ 1854–1967	2 Ducat, Trade Coins, Gold	—	8000.00
☐ 1849–1874	2½ Gulden, Willem III, Silver	—	20.00
☐ 1898	2½ Gulden, Wilhelmina—2nd Coinage, Silver	—	175.00

Key to Grading: Bust

DATE	COIN TYPE/VARIETY/METAL	ABP FINE	AVERAGE FINE
☐ 1929–1940	2½ Gulden, Wilhelmina—4th Coinage, Obv: Older Head, Silver	—	5.25
☐ 1959–1966	2½ Gulden, Juliana, Silver	—	4.15
☐ 1969–1980	2½ Gulden, Juliana, Nickel	—	4.15
☐ 1980–Date	Juliana, Nickel	—	2.20
☐ 1817–1832	3 Gulden, Willem, Silver	—	325.00

Key to Grading: Bust

DATE	COIN TYPE/VARIETY/METAL	ABP FINE	AVERAGE FINE
☐ 1851	5 Gulden, Willem III, Gold	—	400.00
☐ 1912	5 Gulden, Wilhelmina—3rd Coinage, Obv: Adult Head, Gold	—	55.00
☐ 1987 to Date	5 Gulden, Juliana, Clad	$2.25	4.15

Key to Grading: Bust

DATE	COIN TYPE/VARIETY/METAL	ABP FINE	AVERAGE FINE
☐ 1851	10 Gulden, Willem III, Gold	—	650.00

DATE	COIN TYPE/VARIETY/METAL	ABP FINE	AVERAGE FINE
☐ 1875	10 Gulden, Willem III, Rev: Date at Top, Gold	—	$8.25
☐ 1876–1889	10 Gulden, Willem III, Rev: Date at Bottom, Gold	—	125.00
☐ 1892–1897	10 Gulden, Wilhelmina—1st Coinage, Obv: Child Head, Rev: Value in Wreath, Gold	—	1650.00
☐ 1898	10 Gulden, Wilhelmina—2nd Coinage, Gold	—	1650.00
☐ 1911–1917	10 Gulden, Wilhelmina—3rd Coinage, Obv: Adult Head, Gold	—	80.00
☐ 1925–1933	10 Gulden, Wilhelmina—4th Coinage, Obv: Older Head, Gold	—	80.00
☐ 1850–1853	20 Gulden, Willem III, Gold	—	1200.00
☐ 1982	50 Gulden, Dutch American Friendship, Gold	—	Rare (only 2)
☐ 1982	50 Gulden, Dutch American Friendship, Silver	—	42.00
☐ 1984	50 Gulden, 400th Anniversary of Death of William of Orange, Silver	—	35.00
☐ 1987	50 Gulden, Golden Wedding of Queen Mother, Silver	—	42.00
☐ 1988	50 Gulden, 300th Anniversary of William & Mary, Silver	—	42.00
☐ 1990	50 Gulden, 100 Years of Queens, Silver	—	42.00
☐ 1991	50 Gulden, Silver Wedding Anniversary, Silver	—	35.00

NEW ZEALAND

Various foreign coins including Spanish-American, French, Indian, and British were in use in the early 19th century. In 1859, the copper half penny token was in use, followed by the silver florin in the 1930s. New Zealand's first coinage was issued in 1933 and included silver three pences, six pences, shillings, florins, and half crowns. Decimal coins were used in 1967. The currency today is the dollar.

New Zealand—Type Coinage

Key to Grading: Bust

DATE	COIN TYPE/VARIETY/METAL	ABP FINE	AVERAGE FINE
☐ 1940–1947	½ Penny, George VI, Bronze	—	$ .38
☐ 1949–1952	½ Penny, King George the Sixth, Bronze	—	.38
☐ 1953–1965	½ Penny, Elizabeth II, Bronze	—	.38

Key to Grading: Bust

DATE	COIN TYPE/VARIETY/METAL	ABP FINE	AVERAGE FINE
☐ 1940–1947	1 Penny, George VI, Bronze	—	.38
☐ 1949–1952	1 Penny, King George the Sixth, Bronze	—	.38
☐ 1953–1965	1 Penny, Elizabeth II, Bronze	—	.38

Key to Grading: Tiara

DATE	COIN TYPE/VARIETY/METAL	ABP FINE	AVERAGE FINE
☐ 1967–1988	1 Cent, Decimal Coinage: Silver Fern Leaf, Bronze	—	.38
☐ 1933–1936	3 Pence, George V, Silver	—	.38

Key to Grading: Bust

DATE	COIN TYPE/VARIETY/METAL	ABP FINE	AVERAGE FINE
☐ 1937–1946	3 Pence, George VI, Silver	—	$ .50
☐ 1947	3 Pence, George VI, Cupro-Nickel	—	.32
☐ 1948–1952	3 Pence, King George the Sixth, Cupro-Nickel	—	.50
☐ 1953–1965	3 Pence, Elizabeth II, Cupro-Nickel	—	.32

Key to Grading: Tiara

DATE	COIN TYPE/VARIETY/METAL	ABP FINE	AVERAGE FINE
☐ 1967–1988	2 Cents, Decimal Coinage: Kowhai Leaves, Bronze	—	.38

DATE	COIN TYPE/VARIETY/METAL	ABP FINE	AVERAGE FINE
☐ 1933–1936	6 Pence, George V, Silver	—	1.20
☐ 1937–1946	6 Pence, George VI, Silver	—	1.20
☐ 1947	6 Pence, George VI, Cupro-Nickel	—	1.20
☐ 1948–1952	6 Pence, King George the Sixth, Cupro-Nickel	—	.65
☐ 1953–1965	6 Pence, Elizabeth II, Cupro-Nickel	—	.45

Key to Grading: Bust

DATE	COIN TYPE/VARIETY/METAL	ABP FINE	AVERAGE FINE
□ 1933–1935	1 Shilling, George V, Silver	—	$2.20
□ 1937–1946	1 Shilling, George VI, Silver	—	1.20
□ 1947	1 Shilling, George VI, Cupro-Nickel	—	2.20
□ 1948–1952	1 Shilling, King George the Sixth, Cupro-Nickel	—	1.25
□ 1953–1965	1 Shilling, Elizabeth II, Cupro-Nickel	—	1.20

Key to Grading: Tiara

□ 1967 to Date	5 Cents, Decimal Coinage: Tuatara, Cupro-Nickel	—	.38

Key to Grading: Bust

□ 1933–1936	1 Florin, George V, Silver	—	4.15
□ 1937–1946	1 Florin, George VI, Silver	—	2.20
□ 1947	1 Florin, George VI, Cupro-Nickel	—	2.20
□ 1948–1951	1 Florin, King George the Sixth, Cupro-Nickel	—	2.20
□ 1953–1965	1 Florin, Elizabeth II, Cupro-Nickel	—	.38

Key to Grading: Tiara

DATE	COIN TYPE/VARIETY/METAL	ABP FINE	AVERAGE FINE
☐ 1967 to Date	10 Cents, Decimal Coinage: Maori Mask, Cupro-Nickel	—	$ .38

Key to Grading: Bust

DATE	COIN TYPE/VARIETY/METAL	ABP FINE	AVERAGE FINE
☐ 1933–1935	1/2 Crown, George V, Silver	—	4.15
☐ 1937–1946	1/2 Crown, George VI, Silver	—	4.15
☐ 1940	1/2 Crown, George VI: Centennial of British Settlement, Silver	—	4.15
☐ 1947	1/2 Crown, George VI, Cupro-Nickel	—	.60
☐ 1948–1951	1/2 Crown, King George the Sixth, Cupro-Nickel	—	.55
☐ 1953–1965	1/2 Crown, Elizabeth II, Cupro-Nickel	—	.55

Key to Grading: Tiara

DATE	COIN TYPE/VARIETY/METAL	ABP FINE	AVERAGE FINE
☐ 1967–1989	20 Cents, Decimal Coinage: Kiwi, Cupro-Nickel	—	.55
☐ 1990	20 Cents, Decimal Coinage: 1990 Anniversary Celebrations, Silver	—	10.00
☐ 1990	20 Cents, Decimal Coinage: 1990 Anniversary Celebrations, Cupro-Nickel	—	4.15

DATE	COIN TYPE/VARIETY/METAL	ABP FINE	AVERAGE FINE
☐ 1935	1 Crown, George V: 25th Year of Reign—Treaty of Waitangi, Silver	—	$1200.00
☐ 1949	1 Crown, King George the Sixth: Proposed Royal Visit, Cupro-Nickel	—	2.20

Key to Grading: Hair Lines

☐ 1953	1 Crown, Elizabeth II, Cupro-Nickel	—	2.20

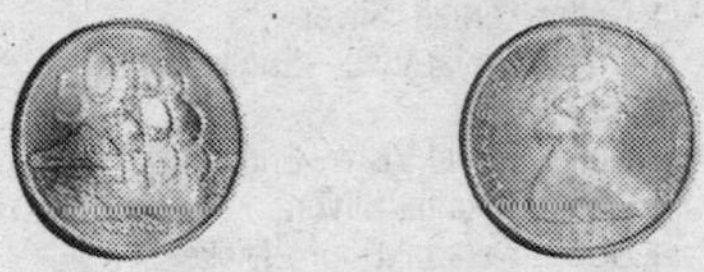

Key to Grading: Tiara

☐ 1967–1985	50 Cents, Decimal Coinage: Endeavour, Cupro-Nickel	—	.55
☐ 1986 to Date	50 Cents, Decimal Coinage: Elizabeth II, Cupro-Nickel	—	.55

Key to Grading: Tiara

☐ 1967–1976	1 Dollar, Decimalization Commemorative, Lettered Edge, Cupro-Nickel	—	1.20
☐ 1969	1 Dollar, Captain Cook—200th Anniversary, Cupro-Nickel	—	.55
☐ 1970	1 Dollar, Cook Islands, Cupro-Nickel	—	4.15
☐ 1970	1 Dollar, Royal Visit—Mount Cook, Cupro-Nickel	—	.75
☐ 1974	1 Dollar, Commonwealth Games, Cupro-Nickel	—	.65

DATE	COIN TYPE/VARIETY/METAL	ABP FINE	AVERAGE FINE
☐ 1974	1 Dollar, Commonwealth Games, Silver	—	$25.00
☐ 1974	1 Dollar, New Zealand Day—Kotuku, Cupro-Nickel	—	2.20
☐ 1977	1 Dollar, Waitangi Day—Treaty House, Cupro-Nickel	—	2.20
☐ 1977	1 Dollar, Waitangi Day—Treaty House, Silver	—	15.00
☐ 1978	1 Dollar, Coronation 25th Anniversary—Parliament, Silver	—	15.00
☐ 1978	1 Dollar, Coronation 25th Anniversary—Parliament, Cupro-Nickel	—	2.20
☐ 1979	1 Dollar, Cupro-Nickel	—	1.20
☐ 1979	1 Dollar, Silver	—	12.00
☐ 1980	1 Dollar, Fantail, Cupro-Nickel	—	1.25
☐ 1980	1 Dollar, Fantail, Silver	—	15.00
☐ 1981	1 Dollar, Royal Visit—English Oak, Cupro-Nickel	—	1.25
☐ 1981	1 Dollar, Royal Visit—English Oak, Silver	—	12.00
☐ 1982	1 Dollar, Takaha, Silver	—	18.00
☐ 1982	1 Dollar, Takaha, Cupro-Nickel	—	1.20
☐ 1983	1 Dollar, 50 Years of Coinage, Silver	—	12.00
☐ 1983	1 Dollar, Royal Visit, Cupro-Nickel	—	2.20
☐ 1983	1 Dollar, Royal Visit, Silver	—	20.00
☐ 1983	1 Dollar, 50 Years of Coinage, Cupro-Nickel	—	2.20
☐ 1984	1 Dollar, Chatham Island Black Robin, Cupro-Nickel	—	2.20
☐ 1984	1 Dollar, Chatham Island Black Robin, Silver	—	20.00
☐ 1985	1 Dollar, Black Stilt, Silver	—	15.00
☐ 1985	1 Dollar, Black Stilt, Cupro-Nickel	—	2.20
☐ 1986	1 Dollar, Royal Visit, Silver	—	18.00
☐ 1986	1 Dollar, Royal Visit, Cupro-Nickel	—	2.20
☐ 1986	1 Dollar, Kakapo, Silver	—	18.00
☐ 1986	1 Dollar, Kakapo, Cupro-Nickel	—	2.20
☐ 1987	1 Dollar, National Parks Centennial, Cupro-Nickel	—	2.20
☐ 1987	1 Dollar, National Parks Centennial, Silver	—	22.00
☐ 1988	1 Dollar, Yellow-eyed Penguin, Cupro-Nickel	—	2.20
☐ 1988	1 Dollar, Yellow-eyed Penguin, Silver	—	45.00
☐ 1989	1 Dollar, XIV Commonwealth Games—Runner, Cupro-Nickel	—	2.20
☐ 1989	1 Dollar, XIV Commonwealth Games—Swimmer, Silver	—	22.00

DATE	COIN TYPE/VARIETY/METAL	ABP FINE	AVERAGE FINE
☐ 1989	1 Dollar, XIV Commonwealth Games—Weightlifter, Silver	—	$18.00
☐ 1989	1 Dollar, XIV Commonwealth Games—Weightlifter, Cupro-Nickel	—	2.20
☐ 1989	1 Dollar, XIV Commonwealth Games—Runner, Silver	—	18.00
☐ 1989	1 Dollar, XIV Commonwealth Games—Swimmer, Cupro-Nickel	—	2.20
☐ 1989	1 Dollar, XIV Commonwealth Games—Gymnast, Silver	—	20.00
☐ 1989	1 Dollar, XIV Commonwealth Games—Gymnast, Cupro-Nickel	—	2.20
☐ 1990	1 Dollar, Kiwi Bird, Silver	—	25.00
☐ 1990	1 Dollar, Anniversary Celebrations, Silver	—	30.00
☐ 1990	1 Dollar, Anniversary Celebrations, Cupro-Nickel	—	2.20
☐ 1990	1 Dollar, Kiwi Bird, Aluminum-Bronze	—	2.20
☐ 1990	2 Dollars, White Heron, Silver	—	28.00

Key to Grading: Crown

DATE	COIN TYPE/VARIETY/METAL	ABP FINE	AVERAGE FINE
☐ 1990	2 Dollars, White Heron, Aluminum-Bronze	—	4.15
☐ 1990	5 Dollars, ANZAC Memorial, Aluminum-Bronze	$25.00	38.00
☐ 1991	5 Dollars, Rugby World Cup, Cupro-Nickel	—	6.00
☐ 1991	5 Dollars, Rugby World Cup, Silver	—	18.00
☐ 1992	5 Dollars, 25th Anniversary of Decimalization, Cupro-Nickel	4.00	7.25
☐ 1992	5 Dollars, 25th Anniversary of Decimalization, Silver	—	22.00
☐ 1990	150 Dollars, Kiwi, Gold	—	375.00

NORWAY

In the 9th century some Anglo-Saxon and Frankish coins were in circulation, but were most likely used as jewelry. Silver pennies were minted in the late 10th century, followed by bracteates and skillings, ducats, and dalers. Anglo-Saxon and German coins were important in the 980s and 990s, but English coins dropped and Danish coins became more important after 1050. The main Norwegian series began around 1047. By the 12th century, the Norwegian penny was a bracteate. The only coins struck in Norway at first were base-silver hvids. Larger silver coins were issued in the 16th century. In 1874 a new decimal system was based on the krone.

Norway—Type Coinage

DATE	COIN TYPE/VARIETY/METAL	ABP FINE	AVERAGE FINE
☐ 1839–1841	1/2 Skilling, Charles XIV, Rev: Lion, Copper	$4.00	$6.25

Key to Grading: Crown

DATE	COIN TYPE/VARIETY/METAL	ABP FINE	AVERAGE FINE
☐ 1863–1872	1/2 Skilling, Charles XV, Rev: Lion, Copper	4.00	7.00
☐ 1819–1837	1 Skilling, Charles XIV, Rev: Lion, Copper	20.00	35.00
☐ 1867–1870	1 Skilling, Charles XV, Rev: Lion, Copper	2.00	4.15

Key to Grading: Crown

DATE	COIN TYPE/VARIETY/METAL	ABP FINE	AVERAGE FINE
☐ 1876–1902	1 Ore, Oscar II, Rev: Lion, Bronze	$4.00	$7.00
☐ 1906–1950	1 Ore, Haakon VII, Monograms, Bronze	—	1.20
☐ 1952–1972	1 Ore, Postwar, Obv: Lion, Rev: Monogram	—	.32
☐ 1822–1834	2 Skillings, Charles XIV, Rev: Lion, Copper	3.00	7.00
☐ 1876–1902	2 Ore, Oscar II, Rev: Lion, Bronze	2.25	4.15

Key to Grading: Crown

DATE	COIN TYPE/VARIETY/METAL	ABP FINE	AVERAGE FINE
☐ 1906–1952	2 Ore, Haakon VII, Monograms, Bronze	—	.80
☐ 1952–1972	2 Ore, Postwar, Obv: Lion, Rev: Monogram, Bronze	—	.32
☐ 1870–1872	2 Skillings, Charles XV, Rev: Lion, Copper	—	4.00
☐ 1868–1872	3 Skillings, Charles XV, Rev: Lion, Silver	—	10.00
☐ 1825–1842	4 Skillings, Charles XIV, Rev: Lion, Silver	—	6.25

Key to Grading: Crown

DATE	COIN TYPE/VARIETY/METAL	ABP FINE	AVERAGE FINE
☐ 1875–1902	5 Ore, Oscar II, Rev: Lion, Bronze	2.00	4.15
☐ 1907–1952	5 Ore, Haakon VII, Monograms, Bronze	—	2.00
☐ 1952–1973	5 Ore, Postwar, Obv: Lion, Rev: Monogram, Bronze	—	.38

Key to Grading: Crown

DATE	COIN TYPE/VARIETY/METAL	ABP FINE	AVERAGE FINE
☐ 1819–1827	8 Skillings, Charles, XIV, Rev: Lion, Silver	—	$30.00
☐ 1845–1856	12 Skillings, Oscar I, Rev: Lion, Silver	—	22.00
☐ 1861–1872	12 Skillings, Charles XV, Rev: Lion, Silver	—	450.00
☐ 1874–1903	10 Ore, Oscar II, Rev: Lion, Silver	—	28.00
☐ 1909–1920	10 Ore, Haakon VII, Monograms Around Hole, Silver	—	7.25

Key to Grading: Crown

DATE	COIN TYPE/VARIETY/METAL	ABP FINE	AVERAGE FINE
☐ 1920–1951	10 Ore, Haakon VII, Monograms Around Hole, Cupro-Nickel	—	.55
☐ 1951–1992	10 Ore, Postwar, Obv: Lion, Rev: Monogram, Cupro-Nickel	—	.55
☐ 1819–1836	24 Skillings, Charles XIV, Rev: Lion, Silver	—	50.00
☐ 1845–1855	24 Skillings, Oscar I, Rev: Lion, Silver	—	20.00
☐ 1861–1872	24 Skillings, Charles XV, Rev: Lion, Silver	—	Scarce
☐ 1876–1904	25 Ore, Oscar II, Rev: Lion, Silver	—	25.00
☐ 1909–1919	25 Ore, Haakon VII, Monograms, Silver	—	14.00

Key to Grading: Crown

DATE	COIN TYPE/VARIETY/METAL	ABP FINE	AVERAGE FINE
□ 1920–1950	25 Ore, Haakon VII, Monograms Around Hole, Cupro-Nickel	—	$ .80
□ 1952–1982	25 Ore, Postwar, Obv: Lion, Rev: Monogram, Cupro-Nickel	—	.28
□ 1819–1844	1/2 Speciedaler, Charles XI, Rev: Lion, Silver	—	100.00
□ 1846–1855	1/2 Speciedaler, Oscar I, Rev: Lion, Silver	—	70.00

Key to Grading: Crown

DATE	COIN TYPE/VARIETY/METAL	ABP FINE	AVERAGE FINE
□ 1861–1872	1/2 Speciedaler, Charles XV, Rev: Lion, Silver	—	Rare
□ 1874–1904	50 Ore, Oscar II, Rev: Lion, Silver	—	26.00
□ 1909–1917	50 Ore, Haakon VII, Monograms, Silver	—	24.00

Key to Grading: Crown

DATE	COIN TYPE/VARIETY/METAL	ABP FINE	AVERAGE FINE
□ 1920–1949	50 Ore, Haakon VII, Monograms Around Hole, Cupro-Nickel	—	.55
□ 1953–1996	50 Ore, Postwar, Obv: Lion, Rev: Monogram, Cupro-Nickel	—	.42

Key to Grading: Bust

DATE	COIN TYPE/VARIETY/METAL	ABP FINE	AVERAGE FINE
☐ 1819–1836	1 Speciedaler, Charles XIV, Rev: Lion, Silver	—	$140.00
☐ 1846–1857	1 Speciedaler, Oscar I, Rev: Lion, Silver	—	140.00
☐ 1861–1872	1 Speciedaler, Charles XV, Rev: Lion, Silver	—	250.00
☐ 1875–1904	Krone, Oscar II, Rev: Lion, Silver	—	50.00
☐ 1908–1917	Krone, Haakon VII, Monograms Around Hole, Silver	—	32.00

Key to Grading: Crown

DATE	COIN TYPE/VARIETY/METAL	ABP FINE	AVERAGE FINE
☐ 1925–1951	Krone, Haakon VII, Monograms Around Hole, Cupro-Nickel	—	.55
☐ 1951–1991	Krone, Postwar, Obv: Lion, Rev: Monogram, Cupro-Nickel	—	.42
☐ 1878–1904	2 Kroner, Oscar II, Rev: Lion, Silver	—	60.00
☐ 1906–1907	2 Kroner, Haakon VII, Rev: St. Olaf Standing, Silver	—	22.00
☐ 1908–1917	2 Kroner, Haakon VII, Rev: Lion & Shields, Silver	—	30.00
☐ 1914	2 Kroner, Haakon VII, Centenary of Constitution, Silver	—	12.00
☐ 1873–1902	10 Kroner, Oscar II, Rev: Lion, Gold	—	225.00
☐ 1910	10 Kroner, Haakon VII, Rev: St. Olaf Standing, Gold	—	150.00
☐ 1873–1902	20 Kroner, Oscar II, Rev: Lion, Gold	—	185.00
☐ 1910	20 Kroner, Haakon VII, Rev: St. Olaf Standing, Gold	—	175.00

PAKISTAN

The first coins were used in the 4th century B.C. and were of silver, followed by copper. The gold stater was in evidence in 130, and the silver dirham in 1028. The silver rupee appeared in 1826. The decimal system was established in 1961. The currency used today is the rupee.

Pakistan—Type Coinage

DATE	COIN TYPE/VARIETY/METAL	ABP FINE	AVERAGE FINE
□ 1961	1 Pice, Bronze	—	$ .38

Key to Grading: Wheat Head

DATE	COIN TYPE/VARIETY/METAL	ABP FINE	AVERAGE FINE
□ 1961–1965	1 Paisa, Bronze	—	.38
□ 1965–1966	1 Paisa, Nickel-Brass	—	.38
□ 1967–1979	1 Paisa, Aluminum	—	.38
□ 1964–1966	2 Paisa, Bronze	—	.38

DATE	COIN TYPE/VARIETY/METAL	ABP FINE	AVERAGE FINE
☐ 1966–1976	2 Paisa, Aluminum	—	$ .38
☐ 1961	5 Pice, Nickel-Brass	—	.38

Key to Grading: Wreath

DATE	COIN TYPE/VARIETY/METAL	ABP FINE	AVERAGE FINE
☐ 1961–1974	5 Paisa, Nickel-Brass	—	.28
☐ 1974–1994	5 Paisa, Aluminum	—	.28
☐ 1950	1 Pie, Bronze	—	.32
☐ 1961	10 Pice, Cupro-Nickel	—	.32
☐ 1961–1974	10 Paisa, Cupro-Nickel	—	.32
☐ 1974–1990	10 Paisa, Aluminum	—	.32
☐ 1948–1952	1 Pice, Holed, Bronze	—	.32
☐ 1953–1959	1 Pice, Nickel-Brass	—	.32
☐ 1963–1967	25 Paisa, Nickel	—	.32
☐ 1967 to Date	25 Paisa, Cupro-Nickel	—	.32
☐ 1976	50 Paisa, Anniversary of Mohammed Ali Jinnah, Cupro-Nickel	—	.32
☐ 1981	50 Paisa, AH1401—1400th Anniversary of Hegira, Cupro-Nickel	—	.32
☐ 1948–1951	1/2 Anna, Crescent, Cupro-Nickel	—	.32
☐ 1953–1958	1/2 Anna, Nickel-Brass	—	.22
☐ 1963–1969	50 Paisa, Nickel	—	.28
☐ 1969 to Date	50 Paisa, Cupro-Nickel	—	.28
☐ 1948–1949	1 Rupee, Crescent to Right, Nickel	—	.75
☐ 1977	1 Rupee, Islamic Summit Conference, Cupro-Nickel	—	.38
☐ 1977	1 Rupee, Centennial of Birth of Allama Mohammad Iqbai, Cupro-Nickel	—	.38
☐ 1979–1988	1 Rupee, Cupro-Nickel	—	.38
☐ 1981	1 Rupee, World Food Day, Cupro-Nickel	—	.38
☐ 1981	1 Rupee, 1400th Hegira Anniversary, Cupro-Nickel	—	.38
☐ 1948–1952	1 Anna, Crescent to Right, Cupro-Nickel	—	.38
☐ 1950	1 Anna, Crescent to Left, Cupro-Nickel	—	4.00
☐ 1953–1958	1 Anna, Cupro-Nickel	—	.38
☐ 1948–1952	2 Annas, Crescent to Right, Cupro-Nickel	—	.38
☐ 1950	2 Annas, Crescent to Left, Cupro-Nickel	—	4.00
☐ 1953–1959	2 Annas, Cupro-Nickel	—	.28
☐ 1948–1951	1/4 Rupee, Crescent to Right, Nickel	$ .20	.32

DATE	COIN TYPE/VARIETY/METAL	ABP FINE	AVERAGE FINE
☐ 1950	1/4 Rupee, Crescent to Left, Nickel	—	$7.00
☐ 1948–1951	1/2 Rupee, Crescent to Right, Nickel	—	.55
☐ 1976	100 Rupees, Conservation Series—Pheasant, Silver	—	48.00
☐ 1976	100 Rupees, Centennial of Birth of Mohammad Ali Jinnah, Silver	—	48.00
☐ 1977	100 Rupees, Centennial of Birth of Allama Mohammad Iqbai, Silver	—	48.00
☐ 1977	100 Rupees, Islamic Summit Conference, Silver	—	36.00
☐ 1976	150 Rupees, Conservation Series—Crocodile, Silver	—	52.00
☐ 1977	500 Rupees, Centennial of Birth Allama Mohammad Iqbai, Gold	—	120.00
☐ 1977	1000 Rupees, Islamic Summit Conference, Gold	—	275.00
☐ 1976	3000 Rupees, Conservation Series—Astor Markhor, Gold	—	600.00

PALESTINE

The following group of coins were produced during Great Britain's rule of Palestine (1922–1948). In 1948, when Palestine became the state of Israel, the coinage was changed significantly to the coins that you will find listed under the ISRAEL section of this book.

Palestine—Type Coinage

Key to Grading: Plant

DATE	COIN TYPE/VARIETY/METAL	ABP FINE	AVERAGE FINE
☐ 1927–1948	Mil, Hebrew-English-Arabic Legends, Rev: Olive Sprig, Bronze	—	$4.15

Key to Grading: Plant

☐ 1927–1947	2 Mils, Hebrew-English-Arabic Legends, Rev: Olive Sprig, Bronze	—	5.25

Key to Grading: Wreath

☐ 1927–1947	5 Mils, Wreath, Cupro-Nickel	—	4.15
☐ 1942–1944	5 Mils, Bronze	—	4.15
☐ 1927–1947	10 Mils, Wreath, Cupro-Nickel	—	5.00

Key to Grading: Wreath

☐ 1942–1943	10 Mils, Bronze	—	8.00
☐ 1927–1941	20 Mils, Holed Wreath, Cupro-Nickel	—	18.00
☐ 1942–1944	20 Mils, Bronze	—	14.00
☐ 1927–1942	50 Mils, Olive Sprig, Silver	—	14.00

Key to Grading: Plant

DATE	COIN TYPE/VARIETY/METAL	ABP FINE	AVERAGE FINE
□ 1927–1942	100 Mils, Olive Sprig, Silver	—	$16.00

PHILIPPINES

The first small, gold coins known as piloncitos were used before the 13th century, followed by cast bronze square-holed coins. Silver dollars were issued in 1827. The silver reales and copper quarto were in use in the 1800s, followed by the silver peso and cupro-nickel piso in the 1900s. The decimal system was established in 1861. Today's currency is the piso.

Philippines—Spanish Colonies Coinage

Key to Grading: Bust

DATE	COIN TYPE/VARIETY/METAL	ABP FINE	AVERAGE FINE
☐ 1864–1868	10 Centimos, Isabel II, Silver	—	$38.00
☐ 1880–1885	10 Centimos, Alfonso XII, Silver	—	32.00
☐ 1864–1868	20 Centimos, Isabel II, Silver	—	32.00
☐ 1880–1885	20 Centimos, Alfonso XII, Silver	—	32.00
☐ 1865–1868	50 Centimos, Isabel II, Silver	—	165.00
☐ 1880–1885	50 Centimos, Alfonso XII, Silver	—	32.00
☐ 1861–1868	1 Peso, Isabel II, Gold	—	50.00
☐ 1897	1 Peso, Alfonso XIII, Silver	—	32.00
☐ 1861–1868	2 Pesos, Isabel II, Gold	—	80.00
☐ 1861–1868	4 Pesos, Isabel II, Gold	—	140.00
☐ 1880–1885	4 Pesos, Alfonso XII, Gold	—	575.00

Philippines—U.S. Territorial Coinage

Key to Grading: Eagle

	ABP	F-12 FINE	EF-40 EX. FINE	MS-60 UNC.	MS-63 UNC.
PHIL 1/2 CENTAVO					
☐ 1903	1.50	2.00	4.25	20.00	38.00
☐ 1903 Proof	35.00	—	—	50.00	100.00
☐ 1904	2.00	4.00	6.00	20.00	35.00
☐ 1904 Proof	40.00	—	—	60.00	120.00
☐ 1905 PF	115.00	—	—	150.00	275.00
☐ 1906 PF	75.00	—	—	120.00	240.00
☐ 1908 PF	75.00	—	—	105.00	225.00

	ABP	F-12 FINE	EF-40 EX. FINE	MS-60 UNC.	MS-63 UNC.
PHIL ONE CENTAVO					
☐ 1903	—	.50	2.50	25.00	45.00
☐ 1903 PF	45.00	—	—	58.00	100.00
☐ 1904	—	1.00	2.00	20.00	30.00
☐ 1904 PF	50.00	—	—	65.00	—
☐ 1905	—	1.00	2.50	35.00	55.00
☐ 1905 PF	100.00	—	—	155.00	—

DATE	ABP	F-12 FINE	EF-40 EX. FINE	MS-60 UNC.	MS-63 UNC.
☐ 1906 PF	80.00	—	—	—	145.00
☐ 1908 PF	75.00	—	—	—	145.00
☐ 1908 S	—	2.50	12.50	30.00	65.00
☐ 1908 S/S Horned S	22.00	28.00	50.00	115.00	240.00
☐ 1908 S/S/S	20.00	30.00	55.00	130.00	250.00
☐ 1909 S	—	12.00	26.00	75.00	140.00
☐ 1910 S	—	4.00	10.00	40.00	80.00
☐ 1911 S	—	2.50	10.00	40.00	80.00
☐ 1911 S over S	20.00	30.00	60.00	95.00	235.00
☐ 1912 S	—	5.00	16.00	100.00	140.00
☐ 1912 S over S	15.00	20.00	45.00	100.00	140.00
☐ 1913 S	—	2.00	10.00	26.00	55.00
☐ 1914 S	—	2.00	10.00	25.00	75.00
☐ 1914 S over S	15.00	25.00	42.00	80.00	150.00
☐ 1915 S	—	25.00	55.00	280.00	500.00
☐ 1916 S	—	6.00	22.00	120.00	220.00
☐ 1916 S over S	18.00	25.00	40.00	140.00	220.00
☐ 1917 S	—	4.00	11.00	45.00	75.00
☐ 1917/6S	45.00	40.00	86.00	380.00	850.00
☐ 1918 S	—	2.00	10.00	42.00	80.00
☐ 1918 Med S	—	10.00	12.00	60.00	120.00
☐ 1918 Large S	—	84.00	480.00	1200.00	3400.00
☐ 1919 S	—	2.00	10.00	50.00	75.00
☐ 1920	—	2.00	15.00	65.00	120.00
☐ 1920 S	12.00	8.00	35.00	120.00	300.00
☐ 1921	—	.75	7.00	40.00	60.00
☐ 1922	—	.50	7.00	35.00	65.00
☐ 1925	—	.50	4.00	22.00	42.00
☐ 1926	—	.50	5.00	22.00	42.00
☐ 1927 M	—	.35	5.00	28.00	45.00
☐ 1928 M	—	.35	5.00	25.00	38.00
☐ 1929 M	—	.35	5.00	28.00	42.00
☐ 1930 M	—	.50	4.00	25.00	42.00
☐ 1930 M/M	7.50	12.00	25.00	110.00	175.00
☐ 1931 M	—	.50	4.00	28.00	42.00
☐ 1932 M	—	.75	4.00	28.00	42.00
☐ 1933 M	—	.25	4.00	28.00	42.00
☐ 1934 M	—	.75	4.00	28.00	42.00
☐ 1936 M	—	.40	4.00	20.00	42.00
☐ 1937 M	—	.40	4.00	18.00	32.00
☐ 1938 M	—	.40	4.00	22.00	30.00
☐ 1939 M	—	.40	4.00	22.00	40.00
☐ 1940 M	—	.40	4.00	16.00	28.00
☐ 1941 M	1.25	.40	4.00	26.00	55.00
☐ 1944 S	—	.40	1.20	5.00	8.00
☐ 1944 S Doubled	2.00	3.50	7.00	25.00	50.00

DATE	ABP	F-12 FINE	EF-40 EX. FINE	MS-60 UNC.	MS-63 UNC.
5 CENTAVOS					
☐ 1903	—	.50	4.00	18.00	40.00
☐ 1903 PF	35.00	—	—	60.00	120.00
☐ 1904	—	.80	7.00	35.00	48.00
☐ 1904 PF	50.00	—	—	65.00	140.00
☐ 1905 PF	100.00	—	—	130.00	240.00
☐ 1906 PF	75.00	—	—	100.00	200.00
☐ 1908 PF	75.00	—	—	110.00	240.00
☐ 1916 S	30.00	40.00	100.00	400.00	675.00
☐ 1917 S	—	6.00	20.00	80.00	220.00
☐ 1918 S	—	2.00	20.00	100.00	235.00
☐ 1918 S Mule	—	150.00	950.00	4200.00	7500.00
☐ 1919 S	—	2.50	18.00	120.00	190.00
☐ 1920	—	3.00	18.00	120.00	190.00
☐ 1921	—	1.50	18.00	120.00	190.00
☐ 1925 M	7.00	5.00	30.00	130.00	180.00
☐ 1926 M	5.00	4.00	16.00	135.00	165.00
☐ 1927 M	5.00	6.00	16.00	135.00	165.00
☐ 1928 M	—	4.00	12.00	95.00	125.00
☐ 1930 M	—	2.00	6.00	75.00	150.00
☐ 1931 M	—	2.00	6.00	75.00	150.00
☐ 1932 M	—	2.00	6.00	60.00	100.00
☐ 1934 M	—	2.00	6.00	75.00	110.00
☐ 1934 Doubled MM	7.00	10.00	15.00	100.00	220.00
☐ 1935 M	—	2.00	5.00	100.00	140.00
☐ 1937 M	—	2.00	4.00	36.00	75.00
☐ 1938 M	—	.50	4.00	32.00	60.00
☐ 1941 M	—	1.00	5.00	32.00	60.00
☐ 1944	—	.40	2.00	3.50	8.00
☐ 1944 S	—	.40	2.00	4.15	7.15
☐ 1945 S	—	.40	2.00	4.15	7.15

DATE	ABP	F-12 FINE	EF-40 EX. FINE	MS-60 UNC.	MS-63 UNC.
10 CENTAVOS					
☐ 1903-S	—	7.50	38.00	160.00	275.00
☐ 1903	—	1.20	6.00	32.00	85.00

DATE	ABP	F-12 FINE	EF-40 EX. FINE	MS-60 UNC.	MS-63 UNC.
☐ 1903 PF	60.00	—	—	85.00	150.00
☐ 1904	—	10.00	40.00	75.00	125.00
☐ 1904 S	—	1.50	9.00	45.00	80.00
☐ 1904	—	—	—	85.00	100.00
☐ 1905 PF	100.00	—	—	150.00	300.00
☐ 1906 PF	80.00	—	—	110.00	240.00
☐ 1907	—	2.00	5.00	80.00	145.00
☐ 1907 S	—	1.20	4.50	80.00	145.00
☐ 1908 PF	100.00	—	—	125.00	200.00
☐ 1908 S	—	1.00	6.00	60.00	100.00
☐ 1909 S	—	14.00	32.00	250.00	380.00
☐ 1911 S	—	1.50	12.00	80.00	160.00
☐ 1912 S	—	2.00	12.00	100.00	200.00
☐ 1912 S/S	20.00	25.00	40.00	210.00	500.00
☐ 1913 S	—	2.00	12.00	100.00	825.00
☐ 1914 S Long Class	10.00	15.00	26.00	235.00	625.00
☐ 1914 S	—	4.00	20.00	185.00	400.00
☐ 1915 S	—	8.00	26.00	300.00	600.00
☐ 1917 S	—	1.00	6.00	32.00	80.00
☐ 1918 S	—	1.00	6.00	32.00	80.00
☐ 1919 S	—	1.00	6.00	32.00	45.00
☐ 1920	—	3.50	8.50	90.00	150.00
☐ 1921	—	.50	4.00	22.00	42.00
☐ 1929 M	—	.50	4.00	22.00	42.00
☐ 1935 M	—	.50	4.00	22.00	42.00
☐ 1937 M	—	.75	4.00	14.00	32.00
☐ 1938 M	—	.50	4.00	14.00	32.00
☐ 1941 M	—	.65	4.00	15.00	32.00
☐ 1944 D	—	.75	1.20	6.00	8.15
☐ 1945 D	—	.75	1.20	6.00	8.15
☐ 1945 D/D	7.00	10.00	20.00	55.00	100.00

TWENTY CENTAVOS

DATE	ABP	F-12 FINE	EF-40 EX. FINE	MS-60 UNC.	MS-63 UNC.
☐ 1903	—	2.00	8.00	42.00	90.00
☐ 1903 S	10.00	8.00	32.00	210.00	365.00
☐ 1903 PF	65.00	—	—	100.00	240.00
☐ 1904	—	15.00	45.00	100.00	240.00
☐ 1904 S	—	2.00	8.00	50.00	100.00
☐ 1904 PF	65.00	—	—	75.00	250.00
☐ 1905 S	—	8.00	38.00	300.00	650.00
☐ 1905 PF	150.00	—	—	300.00	340.00
☐ 1906 PF	135.00	—	—	165.00	340.00
☐ 1907	—	2.00	12.00	35.00	120.00

DATE	ABP	F-12 FINE	EF-40 EX. FINE	MS-60 UNC.	MS-63 UNC.
☐ 1907 S	—	2.00	7.00	35.00	140.00
☐ 1908 S	—	2.00	8.00	34.00	100.00
☐ 1908 PF	125.00	—	—	160.00	325.00
☐ 1909 S	—	8.00	35.00	320.00	615.00
☐ 1910 S	—	8.00	40.00	320.00	615.00
☐ 1911 S	—	8.00	35.00	230.00	460.00
☐ 1912 S	—	5.00	24.00	150.00	460.00
☐ 1913 S	—	3.00	22.00	120.00	250.00
☐ 1914 S	—	2.50	25.00	185.00	485.00
☐ 1915 S	—	4.50	40.00	210.00	550.00
☐ 1916 S	—	4.00	25.00	200.00	400.00
☐ 1917 S	—	2.00	8.00	80.00	120.00
☐ 1918 S	—	1.20	8.00	80.00	125.00
☐ 1919 S	—	2.00	8.00	80.00	160.00
☐ 1920	—	2.00	10.00	90.00	220.00
☐ 1921	—	1.20	7.00	50.00	80.00
☐ 1928/7 Mule	—	4.00	60.00	550.00	1150.00
☐ 1929 Repunch Date	10.00	14.00	45.00	60.00	120.00
☐ 1929 M	—	1.50	5.00	32.00	50.00
☐ 1937 M	—	.85	5.00	20.00	32.00
☐ 1938 M	—	.75	5.00	20.00	38.00
☐ 1941 M	—	1.00	5.00	40.00	75.00
☐ 1944 D	—	.50	1.00	4.00	8.00
☐ 1944 D/S	15.00	20.00	45.00	115.00	210.00
☐ 1945 D	—	1.00	2.00	4.00	7.00

FIFTY CENTAVOS

DATE	ABP	F-12 FINE	EF-40 EX. FINE	MS-60 UNC.	MS-63 UNC.
☐ 1903	—	7.00	16.00	85.00	180.00
☐ 1903 PF	—	—	—	150.00	250.00
☐ 1904	—	35.00	65.00	140.00	225.00
☐ 1904-S	—	15.00	22.00	120.00	220.00
☐ 1904 PF	—	—	—	135.00	225.00
☐ 1905 S	—	26.00	45.00	260.00	475.00
☐ 1905 PF	—	—	—	400.00	615.00
☐ 1906 PF	—	—	—	200.00	400.00
☐ 1907	—	7.00	20.00	150.00	240.00
☐ 1907-S	—	7.00	20.00	150.00	240.00
☐ 1908-S	—	7.00	20.00	150.00	240.00
☐ 1908 PF	—	—	—	260.00	400.00
☐ 1909 S	—	10.00	30.00	260.00	525.00

DATE	ABP	F-12 FINE	EF-40 EX. FINE	MS-60 UNC.	MS-63 UNC.
☐ 1917 S	—	8.00	30.00	175.00	415.00
☐ 1917 S Broken 7	—	15.00	30.00	350.00	600.00
☐ 1918 S	—	4.00	10.00	45.00	150.00
☐ 1918 Inverted S	25.00	35.00	65.00	205.00	350.00
☐ 1919 S	—	4.00	14.00	70.00	150.00
☐ 1920	—	4.00	14.00	70.00	100.00
☐ 1921	—	4.00	6.00	25.00	50.00
☐ 1944 S	—	2.25	4.00	8.00	14.00
☐ 1944 S/S	25.00	35.00	55.00	110.00	200.00
☐ 1945 S	—	2.25	5.00	7.00	14.00
☐ 1945 S/S	35.00	50.00	70.00	140.00	185.00

PESO

DATE	ABP	F-12 FINE	EF-40 EX. FINE	MS-60 UNC.	MS-63 UNC.
☐ 1903	—	15.00	30.00	180.00	375.00
☐ 1903 S	—	10.00	22.00	150.00	340.00
☐ 1903 PF	140.00	—	—	200.00	420.00
☐ 1904	—	60.00	125.00	225.00	400.00
☐ 1904-S	—	12.00	24.00	100.00	340.00
☐ 1904 PF	160.00	—	—	300.00	500.00
☐ 1905-S	—	12.00	35.00	300.00	500.00
☐ 1905-S Straight Serif	—	22.00	75.00	775.00	220.00
☐ 1905 PF	450.00	—	—	775.00	1250.00
☐ 1906 S	—	650.00	2000.00	7000.00	12000.00
☐ 1906 PF	350.00	—	—	430.00	800.00
☐ 1907 S	—	5.00	25.00	85.00	200.00
☐ 1908 S	—	5.00	14.00	80.00	90.00
☐ 1908 S/S	50.00	70.00	100.00	200.00	425.00
☐ 1908 S Double Diz & Inverted MM	75.00	100.00	140.00	475.00	825.00
☐ 1908 PF	325.00	—	—	475.00	825.00
☐ 1909 S	—	4.00	30.00	80.00	175.00
☐ 1909 S/S	25.00	36.00	55.00	150.00	250.00
☐ 1909 S/S/S	55.00	80.00	100.00	200.00	450.00
☐ 1910 S	—	5.00	35.00	150.00	420.00
☐ 1911 S	—	14.00	70.00	1400.00	4500.00
☐ 1912 S	—	14.00	85.00	1500.00	4500.00

COMMEMORATIVE

DATE	ABP	F-12 FINE	EF-40 EX. FINE	MS-60 UNC.	MS-63 UNC.
☐ 1936 50 C	—	12.50	65.00	80.00	140.00
☐ 1936 Murphy Queyer	—	25.00	100.00	150.00	265.00
☐ 1936 Roosevelt Queyer	—	25.00	90.00	150.00	265.00

Philippines—Commonwealth Coinage

Key to Grading: Shield

DATE	COIN TYPE/VARIETY/METAL	ABP FINE	AVERAGE FINE
□ 1937–1944	1 Centavo, Commonwealth, Bronze	—	$ .45
□ 1937–1941	5 Centavos, Commonwealth, Cupro-Nickel	—	.85

Key to Grading: Shield

DATE	COIN TYPE/VARIETY/METAL	ABP FINE	AVERAGE FINE
□ 1944–1945	5 Centavos, Commonwealth, Copper-Nickel-Zinc	—	.45

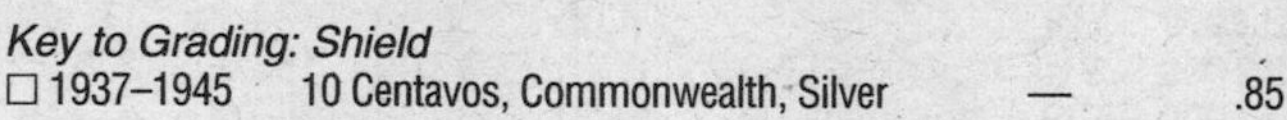

Key to Grading: Shield

DATE	COIN TYPE/VARIETY/METAL	ABP FINE	AVERAGE FINE
□ 1937–1945	10 Centavos, Commonwealth, Silver	—	.85

DATE	COIN TYPE/VARIETY/METAL	ABP FINE	AVERAGE FINE
☐ 1937–1945	20 Centavos, Commonwealth, Silver	—	$2.20
☐ 1936	50 Centavos, Commonwealth Establishment of Commonwealth—Murphy & Quezon, Silver	—	25.00

Key to Grading: Shield

☐ 1944–1945	50 Centavos, Commonwealth, Silver	—	4.15
☐ 1936	1 Peso, Commonwealth, Establishment of Commonwealth—Murphy & Quezon, Silver	—	32.00
☐ 1936	1 Peso, Commonwealth, Establishment of Commonwealth—Roosevelt & Quezon, Silver	—	32.00

Philippines—Republic Coinage

Key to Grading: Shield

☐ 1958–1966	1 Centavo, Republic, Central Bank, Bronze	—	.45

Key to Grading: Shield

☐ 1958–1966	5 Centavos, Republic, Central Bank, Brass	—	.45

Key to Grading: Shield

DATE	COIN TYPE/VARIETY/METAL	ABP FINE	AVERAGE FINE
☐ 1958–1966	10 Centavos, Republic, Central Bank, Nickel-Brass	—	$ .38

Key to Grading: Shield

☐ 1958–1966	25 Centavos, Republic, Central Bank, Nickel-Brass	—	.38

Key to Grading: Shield

☐ 1947	50 Centavos, Republic, MacArthur, Silver	—	2.20

Key to Grading: Shield

☐ 1961	1/2 Peso, Republic, Birth of Rizal Centennial, Silver	—	4.00
☐ 1958–1964	50 Centavos, Republic, Central Bank, Nickel-Brass	—	.38

DATE	COIN TYPE/VARIETY/METAL	ABP FINE	AVERAGE FINE
☐ 1947	1 Peso, Republic, MacArthur, Silver	—	$4.25
☐ 1961	1 Peso, Republic, Birth of Rizal Centennial, Silver	—	5.25
☐ 1963	1 Peso, Republic, Birth of Bonifacio Centennial, Silver	—	6.15
☐ 1964	1 Peso, Republic, Birth of Mabini Centennial, Silver	—	6.15
☐ 1967	1 Peso, Republic, Fall of Bataan & Corregidor—25th Anniversary, Silver	—	5.15

Philippines—Current Coinage

Key to Grading: Shield

☐ 1967–1974	1 Sentimo, Aluminum	—	.38
☐ 1975–1982	1 Sentimo, Aluminum	—	.38
☐ 1983–1990	1 Sentimo, Aluminum	—	.38

Key to Grading: Shield

☐ 1967–1974	5 Sentimos, Brass	—	.38
☐ 1975–1982	5 Sentimos, Brass	—	.38
☐ 1983–1991	5 Sentimos, Orchid, Aluminum	—	.32

Key to Grading: Shield

DATE	COIN TYPE/VARIETY/METAL	ABP FINE	AVERAGE FINE
☐ 1967–1982	10 Sentimos, Orchid, Cupro-Nickel	—	$ .38
☐ 1983–1992	10 Sentimos, Aluminum	—	.38

Key to Grading: Bust

DATE	COIN TYPE/VARIETY/METAL	ABP FINE	AVERAGE FINE
☐ 1975–1982	25 Sentimos, Cupro-Nickel	—	.32
☐ 1983–1992	25 Sentimos, Butterfly, Cupro-Nickel	—	.32

Key to Grading: Bust

DATE	COIN TYPE/VARIETY/METAL	ABP FINE	AVERAGE FINE
☐ 1967–1975	50 Sentimos, Marcelo del Pilar, Cupro-Nickel	—	.38
☐ 1983–1990	50 Sentimos, Eagle, Cupro-Nickel	—	.38
☐ 1992	50 Sentimos, Eagle, Brass	—	.38
☐ 1969	1 Piso, Birth of Aquinaldo—100th Anniversary, Silver	—	7.15
☐ 1970	1 Piso, Papal Visit, Silver	—	7.15

Key to Grading: Busts

DATE	COIN TYPE/VARIETY/METAL	ABP FINE	AVERAGE FINE
☐ 1970	1 Piso, Papal Visit, Nickel	—	.80
☐ 1970	1 Piso, Papal Visit, Gold	—	550.00
☐ 1972–1982	1 Piso, Jose Rizal, Cupro-Nickel	—	.38
☐ 1983–1990	1 Piso, Bull, Cupro-Nickel	—	.38
☐ 1991	1 Piso, Waterfall, Ship, & Flower, Cupro-Nickel	—	.38
☐ 1983–1990	2 Piso, Bonifacio, Cupro-Nickel	—	.38

DATE	COIN TYPE/VARIETY/METAL	ABP FINE	AVERAGE FINE
☐ 1991	2 Piso, Quirino, Cupro-Nickel	—	$ .38
☐ 1991–1994	2 Piso, Bonifacio, Stainless Steel	—	.38
☐ 1975–1982	5 Piso, Ferdinand Marcos, Nickel	—	.40
☐ 1974	25 Piso, Bank Anniversary—25th, Silver	—	6.00
☐ 1975	25 Piso, Aquinaldo, Silver	—	7.15
☐ 1976	25 Piso, FAO Issue, Silver	—	7.15
☐ 1977	25 Piso, Rice Terraces, Silver	—	10.00
☐ 1978	25 Piso, Birth of Quezon— 100th Anniversary, Silver	—	20.00
☐ 1979	25 Piso, UN Conference, Silver	—	20.00
☐ 1980	25 Piso, Birth of MacArthur— 100th Anniversary, Silver	—	25.00
☐ 1981	25 Piso, World Food Day, Silver	—	15.00
☐ 1982	25 Piso, Ferdinand Marcos & Ronald Reagan, Silver	—	40.00
☐ 1986	25 Piso, Washington Visit of Aquino, Silver	—	125.00
☐ 1975	50 Piso, New Society Anniversary, Silver	—	15.00
☐ 1976	50 Piso, International Monetary Fund Meeting, Silver	—	18.00
☐ 1977	50 Piso, Mint Inauguration, Silver	—	16.00
☐ 1978	50 Piso, Birth of Quezon— 100th Anniversary, Silver	—	16.00
☐ 1979	50 Piso, Year of the Child, Silver	—	16.00
☐ 1981	50 Piso, Papal Visit, Silver	—	25.00
☐ 1982	50 Piso, Bataan-Corregidor 40th Anniversary, Silver	—	20.00
☐ 1983	100 Piso, National University 75th Anniversary, Silver	—	15.00
☐ 1991	150 Piso, Southeast Asian Games, Silver	—	38.00
☐ 1987	200 Piso, Wildlife Fund—Buffalo, Silver	—	58.00
☐ 1990	200 Piso, Save the Children, Silver	—	58.00
☐ 1988	500 Piso, People's Revolution, Silver	—	50.00
☐ 1975	1000 Piso, New Society— 3rd Anniversary, Gold	—	150.00
☐ 1976	1500 Piso, International Monetary Fund, Gold	—	340.00
☐ 1977	1500 Piso, New Society— 5th Anniversary, Gold	—	450.00
☐ 1978	1500 Piso, Mint Inauguration, Gold	—	415.00
☐ 1981	1500 Piso, Papal Visit, Gold	—	500.00
☐ 1982	1500 Piso, Bataan-Corregidor 40th Anniversary, Gold	—	450.00
☐ 1977	2500 Piso, New Society— 5th Anniversary, Gold	—	1600.00
☐ 1980	2500 Piso, Birth of MacArthur— 100th Anniversary, Gold	—	275.00

DATE	COIN TYPE/VARIETY/METAL	ABP FINE	AVERAGE FINE
☐ 1986	2500 Piso, Aquino Washington Visit, Gold	—	$750.00
☐ 1992	10000 Piso, People's Power, Gold	—	850.00

PITCAIRN ISLANDS

British and New Zealand currency was initially used. The only coins issued in the name of Pitcairn are commemorative pieces, the silver 50 dollar, and the gold 250 dollar produced in 1988.

Key to Grading: Bust

Pitcairn Islands—Type Coinage

DATE	COIN TYPE/VARIETY/METAL	ABP FINE	AVERAGE FINE
☐ 1988	1 Dollar, Elizabeth II: Drafting of Pitcairn Islands Constitution, Silver	—	55.00 Proof
☐ 1988	1 Dollar, Elizabeth II: Drafting of Pitcairn Islands Constitution, Cupro-Nickel	—	8.00
☐ 1989	1 Dollar, Elizabeth II: Mutiny on the Bounty, Silver	—	55.00 Proof
☐ 1989	1 Dollar, Elizabeth II: Mutiny on the Bounty, Cupro-Nickel	—	8.00
☐ 1990	1 Dollar, Elizabeth II: Burning of the HMAV Bounty, Cupro-Nickel	—	6.00
☐ 1990	1 Dollar, Elizabeth II: Burning of the HMAV Bounty, Silver	—	65.00 Proof
☐ 1988	50 Dollars, Elizabeth II: Drafting of Pitcairn Islands Constitution, Silver	—	175.00 Proof
☐ 1989	50 Dollars, Elizabeth II: Mutiny on the Bounty, Silver	—	175.00 Proof
☐ 1990	50 Dollars, Elizabeth II: Burning of the HMAV Bounty, Silver	—	175.00 Proof
☐ 1988	250 Dollars, Elizabeth II: Drafting of Pitcairn Islands Constitution, Gold	—	440.00 Proof
☐ 1989	250 Dollars, Elizabeth II: Mutiny on the Bounty, Gold	—	440.00 Proof

DATE	COIN TYPE/VARIETY/METAL	ABP FINE	AVERAGE FINE
☐ 1990	250 Dollars, Elizabeth II: Burning of the HMAV Bounty, Gold	—	$650.00 Proof

POLAND

The first coins, silver denars, were used in the late 10th century and into the 12th century. Then came the silver bracteate denar and the silver schilling in the 1400s. The silver taler, gold ducat, and copper boratinki followed in the 1500s and 1600s. The copper polsgrosz and the silver kopek were in use in the 1800s. The first decimal coins were used in 1923. The currency today is the zloty.

Key to Grading: Eagle

Poland—Type Coinage

☐ 1918	Fenig, WWI Military, Iron	—	.80
☐ 1923–1939	1 Grosz, Republic, Bronze	—	.42
☐ 1923	1 Grosz, Republic, Brass	$14.00	20.00
☐ 1939	1 Grosz, WWII Occupation, Zinc	—	.65
☐ 1949	1 Grosz, Republic, Aluminum	—	.65

Key to Grading: Eagle

☐ 1923	2 Grosze, Republic, Brass	—	4.15
☐ 1923–1939	2 Grosze, Republic, Bronze	—	.45
☐ 1949	2 Grosze, Republic, Aluminum	—	.38
☐ 1917–1918	5 Fenigow, WWI Military, Iron	—	.38

Key to Grading: Eagle

DATE	COIN TYPE/VARIETY/METAL	ABP FINE	AVERAGE FINE
☐ 1923	5 Groszy, Republic, Brass	—	$ .55
☐ 1923–1939	5 Groszy, Republic, Bronze	—	.38
☐ 1939	5 Groszy, WWII Occupation, Holed, Zinc	—	.50
☐ 1949	5 Groszy, Republic, Bronze	—	.38
☐ 1917	10 Fenigow, WWI Military, Zinc	$16.00	22.00

Key to Grading: Eagle

DATE	COIN TYPE/VARIETY/METAL	ABP FINE	AVERAGE FINE
☐ 1923	10 Groszy, WWII Occupation, Zinc	—	.38
☐ 1923	10 Groszy, Republic, Nickel	—	.38
☐ 1949	10 Groszy, Republic, Cupro-Nickel	—	.38
☐ 1949	10 Groszy, Republic, Aluminum	—	.38
☐ 1917	20 Fenigow, WWI Military, Zinc	25.00	55.00
☐ 1917–1918	20 Fenigow, WWI Military, Iron	—	1.20

Key to Grading: Eagle

DATE	COIN TYPE/VARIETY/METAL	ABP FINE	AVERAGE FINE
☐ 1923	20 Groszy, Republic, Nickel	—	.45
☐ 1949	20 Groszy, Republic, Cupro-Nickel	—	.38
☐ 1949	20 Groszy, Republic, Aluminum	—	.38

Key to Grading: Eagle

DATE	COIN TYPE/VARIETY/METAL	ABP FINE	AVERAGE FINE
☐ 1923	50 Groszy, Republic, Nickel	—	$ .42
☐ 1938	50 Groszy, WWII Occupation, Iron	—	2.00
☐ 1949	50 Groszy, Republic, Cupro-Nickel	—	.50
☐ 1949	50 Groszy, Republic, Aluminum	—	.50
☐ 1924–1925	1 Zloty, Republic, Silver	—	4.00
☐ 1929	1 Zloty, Republic, Nickel	—	.70
☐ 1949	1 Zloty, Republic, Aluminum	—	.45
☐ 1949	1 Zloty, Republic, Cupro-Nickel	—	1.20
☐ 1924–1925	2 Zlote, Republic, Silver	—	7.00
☐ 1932–1934	2 Zlote, Republic, Silver	—	4.15
☐ 1934–1936	2 Zlote, Republic, Silver	—	4.15
☐ 1936	2 Zlote, Republic, Silver	—	4.15
☐ 1925	5 Zlotych, Republic, Silver	—	150.00
☐ 1920–1932	5 Zlotych, Republic, Silver	—	25.00
☐ 1930	5 Zlotych, Republic, Revolt Against Russians Centennial, Silver	—	20.00
☐ 1932–1934	5 Zlotych, Republic, Silver	—	4.15
☐ 1934	5 Zlotych, Republic, Founding of Rifle Corps 20th Anniversary, Silver	—	6.00
☐ 1934–1938	5 Zlotych, Republic, Silver	—	4.15
☐ 1936	5 Zlotych, Republic, Silver	—	8.00
☐ 1925	10 Zlotych, Republic, Death of Boleslaus I 900th Anniversary, Gold	—	45.00
☐ 1932–1933	10 Zlotych, Republic, Silver	—	4.00
☐ 1933	10 Zlotych, Republic, 250th Anniversary of Relief of Vienna, Silver	—	14.00
☐ 1933	10 Zlotych, Republic, Second Revolt Against Russians 70th Anniversary, Silver	—	14.00
☐ 1934	10 Zlotych, Republic, Founding of Rifle Corps 20th Anniversary, Silver	—	14.00

Key to Grading: Bust

DATE	COIN TYPE/VARIETY/METAL	ABP FINE	AVERAGE FINE
☐ 1934–1939	10 Zlotych, Republic, Silver	—	$4.15
☐ 1925	20 Zlotych, Republic, Death of Boleslaus I 900th Anniversary, Gold	—	125.00

PORTUGAL

The first coins originated in the 2nd century B.C. In 1128 base-silver dinheiros and mealhas were produced, and later the gold morabitino. A range of coins in gold, silver, and base-silver were produced in the 1300s. In the 15th century most coinage was silver leals, with some base-silver reals branco. In the late 15th century the real became the main unit of coinage. In the 1600s systematic dating began appearing on coins. The first decimal coins were used in 1836. The escudo is the currency used today.

Portugal—Type Coinage

Key to Grading: Crown

DATE	COIN TYPE/VARIETY/METAL	ABP FINE	AVERAGE FINE
☐ 1868–1875	III Reis, Luis I, Copper	$2.25	4.15
☐ 1867–1879	5 Reis, Luis I, Copper	4.00	6.00
☐ 1882–1886	5 Reis, Luis I, Bronze	—	.80
☐ 1890–1906	5 Reis, Carlos I, Bronze	—	.35
☐ 1910	5 Reis, Emanuel II, Bronze	—	.40

Key to Grading: Crown

DATE	COIN TYPE/VARIETY/METAL	ABP FINE	AVERAGE FINE
☐ 1867–1877	10 Reis, Luis I, Copper	—	$4.15
☐ 1882–1886	10 Reis, Luis I, Bronze	—	4.15
☐ 1891–1892	10 Reis, Carlos I, Bronze	—	5.00

Key to Grading: Bust

DATE	COIN TYPE/VARIETY/METAL	ABP FINE	AVERAGE FINE
☐ 1867–1874	20 Reis, Luis I, Copper	—	10.00
☐ 1882–1886	20 Reis, Luis I, Bronze	—	2.20
☐ 1891–1892	20 Reis, Carlos I, Bronze	—	4.15
☐ 1862–1889	50 Reis, Luis I, Silver	—	4.15
☐ 1893	50 Reis, Carlos I, Silver	—	6.00
☐ 1900	50 Reis, Carlos I, Cupro-Nickel	—	.75
☐ 1864–1889	100 Reis, Luis I, Silver	—	5.00
☐ 1890–1898	100 Reis, Carlos I, Silver	—	4.15

Key to Grading: Crown

DATE	COIN TYPE/VARIETY/METAL	ABP FINE	AVERAGE FINE
☐ 1900	100 Reis, Carlos I, Cupro-Nickel	—	.60
☐ 1909–1910	100 Reis, Emanuel II, Silver	—	1.75

Key to Grading: Bust

DATE	COIN TYPE/VARIETY/METAL	ABP FINE	AVERAGE FINE
☐ 1862–1865	200 Reis, Luis I, Silver	—	$15.00
☐ 1865–1888	200 Reis, Luis I, Silver	—	35.00
☐ 1891–1903	200 Reis, Carlos I, Silver	—	7.00
☐ 1898	200 Reis, Carlos I, 400th Anniversary: Voyages of Discovery, Silver	—	7.00
☐ 1909	200 Reis, Emanuel II, Silver	—	5.00

Key to Grading: Bust or Crown

DATE	COIN TYPE/VARIETY/METAL	ABP FINE	AVERAGE FINE
☐ 1863–1889	500 Reis, Luis I, Silver	—	6.25
☐ 1891–1908	500 Reis, Carlos I, Silver	—	8.00
☐ 1898	500 Reis, Carlos I, 400th Anniversary: Voyages of Discovery, Silver	—	8.00
☐ 1908–1909	500 Reis, Emanuel II, Silver	—	12.00
☐ 1910	500 Reis, Commemorative, Marquis de Pombal, Silver	—	38.00
☐ 1910	500 Reis, Commemorative, Peninsular War Centennial, Silver	—	42.00

Key to Grading: Bust

DATE	COIN TYPE/VARIETY/METAL	ABP FINE	AVERAGE FINE
☐ 1898	1000 Reis, Carlos I, 400th Anniversary: Voyages of Discovery, Silver	—	16.00

DATE	COIN TYPE/VARIETY/METAL	ABP FINE	AVERAGE FINE
☐ 1899	1000 Reis, Carlos I, Silver	—	$15.00
☐ 1910	1000 Reis, Commemorative, Peninsular War Centennial, Silver	—	42.00
☐ 1864–1866	2000 Reis, Luis I, Rev: Arms in Wreath, Gold	—	75.00
☐ 1868–1888	2000 Reis, Luis I, Rev: Mantled Arms, Gold	—	85.00
☐ 1862–1863	5000 Reis, Luis I, Rev: Arms in Wreath, Gold	—	220.00
☐ 1867–1889	5000 Reis, Luis I, Rev: Mantled Arms, Gold	—	185.00
☐ 1878–1889	10000 Reis, Luis I, Rev: Mantled Arms, Gold	—	325.00

Portugal—Port-Republic Coinage

DATE	COIN TYPE/VARIETY/METAL	ABP FINE	AVERAGE FINE
☐ 1917–1921	1 Centavo, 2nd Coinage, Bronze	—	.42
☐ 1918	2 Centavos, 1st Coinage, World War I Provisional Issue, Iron	$15.00	25.00
☐ 1918–1921	2 Centavos, 2nd Coinage, Bronze	—	.38
☐ 1917–1919	4 Centavos, 2nd Coinage, Cupro-Nickel	—	.38
☐ 1920–1922	5 Centavos, 2nd Coinage, Bronze	—	1.00
☐ 1924–1927	5 Centavos, 3rd Coinage, Bronze	—	.35
☐ 1915	10 Centavos, 1st Coinage, Silver	—	1.00
☐ 1920–1921	10 Centavos, 2nd Coinage, Cupro-Nickel	—	.75
☐ 1924–1940	10 Centavos, 3rd Coinage, Bronze	—	.75
☐ 1942–1969	10 Centavos, 3rd Coinage, Bronze	—	.38
☐ 1969–1979	10 Centavos, 4th Coinage, Aluminum	—	.38
☐ 1913–1916	20 Centavos, 1st Coinage, Silver	—	3.50
☐ 1920–1922	20 Centavos, 2nd Coinage, Cupro-Nickel	—	2.15
☐ 1924–1925	20 Centavos, 3rd Coinage, Bronze	—	.50
☐ 1942–1969	20 Centavos, 3rd Coinage, Bronze	—	.32
☐ 1969–1974	20 Centavos, 4th Coinage, Aluminum	—	.32
☐ 1912–1916	50 Centavos, 1st Coinage, Silver	—	4.00
☐ 1924–1926	50 Centavos, 3rd Coinage, Aluminum-Bronze	—	1.50
☐ 1927–1968	50 Centavos, 3rd Coinage, Copper-Nickel	—	.38
☐ 1969–1979	50 Centavos, 4th Coinage, Bronze	—	.38
☐ 1910	1 Escudo, 1st Coinage, Birth of Republic—October 5th, 1910, Silver	—	15.00

DATE	COIN TYPE/VARIETY/METAL	ABP FINE	AVERAGE FINE
□ 1915–1916	1 Escudo, 1st Coinage, Silver	—	$12.00
□ 1924–1926	1 Escudo, 3rd Coinage, Aluminum-Bronze	—	5.00
□ 1927–1968	1 Escudo, 3rd Coinage, Nickel-Bronze	—	.30
□ 1969–1980	1 Escudo, 4th Coinage, Bronze	—	.32

Key to Grading: Shield

□ 1981–1986	1 Escudo, 5th Coinage, Nickel-Brass	—	.25
□ 1986 to Date	1 Escudo, 6th Coinage, Nickel-Brass	—	.32

Key to Grading: Shield

□ 1932–1951	2½ Escudos, 3rd Coinage, Silver	—	.80

Key to Grading: Boat

□ 1963–1986	2½ Escudos, 4th Coinage, Cupro-Nickel	—	.32
□ 1977	2½ Escudos, 4th Coinage, 100th Anniversary—Death of Alexandro Herculano, Cupro-Nickel	—	.32
□ 1983	2½ Escudos, 4th Coinage, FAO Issue, Cupro-Nickel	—	.28
□ 1983	2½ Escudos, 4th Coinage, World Roller Hockey Championship, Cupro-Nickel	—	.32
□ 1986 to Date	2½ Escudos, 6th Coinage, Nickel-Brass	—	.28

DATE	COIN TYPE/VARIETY/METAL	ABP FINE	AVERAGE FINE
☐ 1932–1951	5 Escudos, 3rd Coinage, Silver	—	$4.15
☐ 1960	5 Escudos, 3rd Coinage, Death of Henry the Navigator—500th Anniversary, Silver	—	2.00
☐ 1963–1986	5 Escudos, Copper-Nickel	—	.30
☐ 1928	10 Escudos, 3rd Coinage, Battle of Ourique 1139, Silver	—	10.00
☐ 1932–1948	10 Escudos, 3rd Coinage, Silver	—	10.00
☐ 1954–1955	10 Escudos, 3rd Coinage, Silver	—	4.15
☐ 1960	10 Escudos, 3rd Coinage, Death of Henry the Navigator—500th Anniversary, Silver	—	5.00
☐ 1971–1974	10 Escudos, 4th Coinage, Cupro-Nickel	—	.28
☐ 1986 to Date	10 Escudos, 6th Coinage, Nickel-Brass	—	.25

Key to Grading: Shield

DATE	COIN TYPE/VARIETY/METAL	ABP FINE	AVERAGE FINE
☐ 1953	20 Escudos, 3rd Coinage, 25 Years of Financial Reform, Silver	—	4.15
☐ 1960	20 Escudos, 3rd Coinage, Death of Henry the Navigator—500th Anniversary, Silver	—	6.00
☐ 1966	20 Escudos, Opening of Salazar Bridge, Silver	—	2.00
☐ 1986 to Date	20 Escudos, Cupro-Nickel	—	.32
☐ 1977–1978	25 Escudos, Cupro-Nickel	—	.32
☐ 1977–1978	25 Escudos, 100th Anniversary—Death of Alexandre Herculano, Cupro-Nickel	—	.42
☐ 1980–1986	Increase Size 28.5 MM	—	.42
☐ 1983	25 Escudos, World Roller Hockey Championship, Cupro-Nickel	—	.42
☐ 1983	25 Escudos, FAO Issue, Cupro-Nickel	—	.42
☐ 1984	25 Escudos, Revolution—100th Anniversary, Cupro-Nickel	—	.38
☐ 1984	25 Escudos, International Year of Disabled Persons, Cupro-Nickel	—	.38
☐ 1985	25 Escudos, Anniversary—Battle of Aljubarrotta, Cupro-Nickel	—	.38
☐ 1985	25 Escudos, Anniversary—Battle of Aljubarrotta, Silver	—	24.00

DATE	COIN TYPE/VARIETY/METAL	ABP FINE	AVERAGE FINE
☐ 1986	25 Escudos, Admission to European Common Market, Silver	—	$75.00
☐ 1986	25 Escudos, Admission to European Common Market, Cupro-Nickel	—	.38
☐ 1968	50 Escudos, Anniversary of Birth of Alvares Cabral, Silver	—	8.00
☐ 1969	50 Escudos, 500th Anniversary—Birth of Vasco de Gama, Silver	—	5.00
☐ 1969	50 Escudos, Centennial—Birth of Marshall Carmone, Silver	—	8.00
☐ 1971	50 Escudos, 125th Anniversary—Bank of Portugal, Silver	—	8.00
☐ 1972	50 Escudos, 400th Anniversary—Heroic Epic "O Lusiadas," Silver	—	8.00
☐ 1986 to Date	50 Escudos, Copper-Nickel	—	.60
☐ 1974	100 Escudos, 1974 Revolution, Silver	—	6.00
☐ 1984	100 Escudos, International Year of Disabled Persons, Cupro-Nickel	—	.80
☐ 1985	100 Escudos, 800th Anniversary—Death of King Henriques, Cupro-Nickel	—	.80
☐ 1985	100 Escudos, 800th Anniversary—Death of King Henriques, Silver	—	20.00
☐ 1985	100 Escudos, 600th Anniversary—Battle of Aljubarrotta, Cupro-Nickel	—	.80
☐ 1985	100 Escudos, 600th Anniversary—Battle of Aljubarrotta, Silver	—	30.00
☐ 1985	100 Escudos, 50th Anniversary—Death of Fernando Pessoa (Poet), Cupro-Nickel	—	.60
☐ 1985	100 Escudos, 50th Anniversary—Death of Fernando Pessoa (Poet), Silver	—	110.00
☐ 1986	100 Escudos, World Cup Soccer—Mexico, Silver	—	22.00
☐ 1986	100 Escudos, World Cup Soccer—Mexico, Cupro-Nickel	—	.75
☐ 1987	100 Escudos, Golden Age of Portuguese Discoveries, Cupro-Nickel	—	.75
☐ 1987	100 Escudos, Amadeo De Souza Caroso, Cupro-Nickel	—	.75
☐ 1987	100 Escudos, Golden Age of Portuguese Discoveries, Silver	—	25.00
☐ 1987	100 Escudos, Amadeo De Souza Caroso, Silver	—	25.00
☐ 1987	100 Escudos, Golden Age of Portuguese Discoveries, Gold	—	650.00

DATE	COIN TYPE/VARIETY/METAL	ABP FINE	AVERAGE FINE
☐ 1988	100 Escudos, Golden Age of Portuguese Discoveries, Platinum	—	$750.00
☐ 1989	100 Escudos, Discovery of Madeira, Palladium	—	525.00
☐ 1989	100 Escudos, Discovery of Madeira, Silver	—	22.00
☐ 1989	100 Escudos, Discovery of Canary Islands, Cupro-Nickel	—	6.00
☐ 1989	100 Escudos, Discovery of Madeira, Gold	—	750.00
☐ 1989	100 Escudos, Discovery of Canary Islands, Gold	—	750.00
☐ 1989 to Date	100 Escudos, Dual Metal	—	.60
☐ 1989	100 Escudos, Discovery of Azores, Gold	—	750.00
☐ 1989	100 Escudos, Discovery of Canary Islands, Silver	—	16.00
☐ 1989	100 Escudos, Discovery of Azores, Silver	—	18.00
☐ 1989	100 Escudos, Discovery of Azores, Cupro-Nickel	—	5.00
☐ 1990	100 Escudos, Celestial Navigation, Cupro-Nickel	—	7.00
☐ 1990	100 Escudos, Camilo Castelo Branco, Cupro-Nickel	—	6.00
☐ 1990	100 Escudos, Celestial Navigation, Gold	—	650.00
☐ 1990	100 Escudos, Celestial Navigation, Silver	—	14.00
☐ 1990	100 Escudos, Camilo Castelo Branco, Silver	—	20.00
☐ 1990	100 Escudos, 350th Anniversary—Portuguese Independence, Cupro-Nickel	—	7.00
☐ 1990	100 Escudos, Celestial Navigation, Platinum	—	1750.00
☐ 1990	100 Escudos, 350th Anniversary—Portuguese Independence, Silver	—	22.00
☐ 1991	200 Escudos, Westward Navigation, Gold	—	650.00
☐ 1991	200 Escudos, Westward Navigation, Silver	—	22.00
☐ 1991 to Date	200 Escudos, Dual Metal	—	.60
☐ 1991	200 Escudos, Columbus & Portugal, Gold	—	600.00
☐ 1991	200 Escudos, Columbus & Portugal, Silver	—	22.00
☐ 1991	200 Escudos, Columbus & Portugal, Palladium	—	350.00
☐ 1992	200 Escudos, New World America—Columbus & Ships, Gold	—	575.00
☐ 1992	200 Escudos, Cabrilho—Map, Silver	—	22.00
☐ 1992	200 Escudos, Portugal's Presidency of European Community, Cupro-Nickel	—	8.00

DATE	COIN TYPE/VARIETY/METAL	ABP FINE	AVERAGE FINE
☐ 1992	200 Escudos, New World America—Columbus & Ships, Silver	—	$22.00
☐ 1992	200 Escudos, Olympics—Runner, Silver	—	22.00
☐ 1992	200 Escudos, Olympics—Runner, Cupro-Nickel	—	6.15
☐ 1992	200 Escudos, Portugal's Presidency of European Community, Silver	—	20.00
☐ 1992	200 Escudos, Cabrilho—Map, Cupro-Nickel	—	7.25
☐ 1992	200 Escudos, New World America—Columbus & Ships, Cupro-Nickel	—	7.25
☐ 1992	200 Escudos, Cabrilho—Map, Platinum	—	1800.00
☐ 1992	200 Escudos, Cabrilho—Map, Gold	—	650.00
☐ 1974	250 Escudos, 1974 Revolution, Silver	—	22.00
☐ 1984	250 Escudos, World Fisheries, Cupro-Nickel	—	25.00
☐ 1984	250 Escudos, World Fisheries, Silver	—	85.00
☐ 1988	250 Escudos, Seoul Olympics—Runners, Cupro-Nickel	—	4.15
☐ 1988	250 Escudos, Seoul Olympics—Runners, Silver	—	18.00
☐ 1989	250 Escudos, 850th Anniversary—Founding of Portugal, Silver	—	32.00
☐ 1989	250 Escudos, 850th Anniversary—Founding of Portugal, Cupro-Nickel	—	8.00
☐ 1983	500 Escudos, XVII European Art Exhibition, Silver	—	50.00
☐ 1983	750 Escudos, XVII European Art Exhibition, Silver	—	15.00
☐ 1980	1000 Escudos, 400th Anniversary—Death of Louis de Camoes, Silver	—	28.00
☐ 1983	1000 Escudos, XVII European Art Exhibition, Silver	—	28.00
☐ 1991	1000 Escudos, Ibero—American Series, Silver	—	60.00

RUSSIA

The first coins were used in the 5th century B.C. and were bronze pieces cast in the shape of dolphins, followed by coin-shaped pieces. In the 4th century, coins were produced in gold, silver, and bronze. Gold staters became popular in 100 A.D., followed by the silver denga in the 15th century, and the silver grossus and silver kopek in the 16th century. The first decimal coins were used in 1704. The currency today is the ruble.

Russia—Type Coinage

Key to Grading: Eagle

DATE	COIN TYPE/VARIETY/METAL	ABP FINE	AVERAGE FINE
☐ 1855–1867	1/4 Kopek, Alexander II, Copper	—	$4.15
☐ 1867–1881	1/4 Kopek, Alexander II, Copper	—	2.50
☐ 1881–1894	1/4 Kopek, Alexander III, Copper	—	4.15
☐ 1894–1916	1/4 Kopek, Nikolai II, Copper	—	2.20

Key to Grading: Eagle

DATE	COIN TYPE/VARIETY/METAL	ABP FINE	AVERAGE FINE
☐ 1855–1858	1/2 Ruble, Czarist Empire, Silver	—	10.00
☐ 1859–1885	1/2 Ruble, Czarist Empire, 2nd Coinage, Silver	—	35.00
☐ 1855–1867	1/2 Kopek, Alexander II, Copper	—	4.15
☐ 1867–1881	1/2 Kopek, Alexander II, Copper	—	4.15
☐ 1881–1894	1/2 Kopek, Alexander III, Copper	—	2.00
☐ 1894–1916	1/2 Kopek, Nikolai II, Copper	—	1.20

Key to Grading: Eagle

DATE	COIN TYPE/VARIETY/METAL	ABP FINE	AVERAGE FINE
☐ 1855–1858	1 Ruble, Czarist Empire, Silver	—	$42.00
☐ 1859	1 Ruble, Nikolai I, Silver	—	70.00
☐ 1859–1885	1 Ruble, Czarist Empire, 2nd Coinage, Silver	—	32.00
☐ 1883	1 Ruble, Alexander III, Silver	—	40.00
☐ 1886–1894	1 Ruble, Alexander III, Silver	—	32.00
☐ 1895–1915	1 Ruble, Nikolai II, Silver	—	20.00
☐ 1896	1 Ruble, Coronation Comm, Silver	—	32.00
☐ 1898	1 Ruble, Alexander II, Silver	—	150.00
☐ 1912	1 Ruble, Alexander III, Silver	—	230.00
☐ 1912	1 Ruble, Napoleon Defeat, Silver	—	—
☐ 1913	1 Ruble, Romanoff Dynasty, Silver	—	24.00
☐ 1914	1 Ruble, Battle of Gangut, Silver	—	400.00
☐ 1855–1867	1 Kopek, Alexander II, Copper	—	6.25

Key to Grading: Eagle

DATE	COIN TYPE/VARIETY/METAL	ABP FINE	AVERAGE FINE
☐ 1867–1916	1 Kopek, Czarist Empire, 2nd Coinage, Copper	—	4.15
☐ 1855–1859	2 Kopeks, Czarist Empire, Copper	—	4.15
☐ 1859–1867	2 Kopeks, Czarist Empire, 2nd Coinage, Copper	—	4.15

Key to Grading: Eagle

DATE	COIN TYPE/VARIETY/METAL	ABP FINE	AVERAGE FINE
☐ 1867–1916	2 Kopeks, Czarist Empire, 2nd Coinage, Copper	—	$ 1.20
☐ 1855–1859	3 Kopek, Czarist Empire, Copper	—	2.00
☐ 1859–1867	3 Kopeks, Czarist Empire, 2nd Coinage, Copper	—	4.15

Key to Grading: Eagle

DATE	COIN TYPE/VARIETY/METAL	ABP FINE	AVERAGE FINE
☐ 1867–1916	3 Kopeks, Czarist Empire, 2nd Coinage, Copper	—	2.20
☐ 1869–1885	3 Rubles, Czarist Empire, 2nd Coinage, Gold	—	200.00
☐ 1855–1858	5 Kopeks, Czarist Empire, Silver	—	4.15
☐ 1855–1859	5 Kopeks, Czarist Empire, Copper	—	4.15
☐ 1859–1867	5 Kopeks, Czarist Empire, 2nd Coinage, Copper	—	4.15
☐ 1859–1866	5 Kopeks, Czarist Empire, 2nd Coinage, Silver	—	4.15
☐ 1867–1916	5 Kopeks, Czarist Empire, 2nd Coinage, Copper	—	5.25
☐ 1867–1915	5 Kopeks, Czarist Empire, 2nd Coinage, Silver	—	5.25
☐ 1855–1858	5 Rubles, Czarist Empire, Gold	—	140.00
☐ 1859–1885	5 Rubles, Czarist Empire, 2nd Coinage, Gold	—	160.00
☐ 1886–1894	5 Rubles, Alexander III, Gold	—	160.00
☐ 1895–1896	5 Rubles, Gold	—	1355.00
☐ 1897–1911	5 Rubles, Reduced Weight Gold	—	60.00
☐ 1897	7½ Rubles, Reduced Weight Gold	—	125.00
☐ 1855–1858	10 Kopeks, Czarist Empire, Silver	—	7.00
☐ 1859–1866	10 Kopeks, Czarist Empire, 2nd Coinage, Silver	—	2.20
☐ 1867–1917	10 Kopeks, Czariest Empire, 2nd Coinage, Silver	—	2.20
☐ 1886–1894	10 Rubles, Alexander III, Gold	—	275.00
☐ 1895–1897	10 Rubles, Gold	—	1650.00
☐ 1898–1911	10 Rubles, Reduced Weight Gold	—	80.00
☐ 1859–1866	15 Kopeks, Czarist Empire 2nd Coinage, Silver	—	5.25

Key to Grading: Eagle

DATE	COIN TYPE/VARIETY/METAL	ABP FINE	AVERAGE FINE
☐ 1867–1917	15 Kopeks, Czarist Empire 2nd Coinage, Silver	—	$2.20
☐ 1897–1897	15 Rubles, Reduced Weight Gold	—	150.00
☐ 1855–1858	20 Kopek, Czarist Empire, Silver	—	5.00
☐ 1859–1866	20 Kopeks, Czarist Empire, 2nd Coinage, Silver	—	4.15
☐ 1867–1917	20 Kopeks, Czarist Empire, 2nd Coinage, Silver	—	2.20

Key to Grading: Eagle

DATE	COIN TYPE/VARIETY/METAL	ABP FINE	AVERAGE FINE
☐ 1855–1858	25 Kopeks, Czarist Empire, Silver	—	6.00
☐ 1859–1885	25 Kopeks, Czarist Empire, 2nd Coinage, Silver	—	18.00
☐ 1886–1894	25 Kopeks, Alexander III, Silver	—	32.00

Key to Grading: Eagle

DATE	COIN TYPE/VARIETY/METAL	ABP FINE	AVERAGE FINE
☐ 1895–1901	25 Kopeks, Nikolai II, Silver	—	12.00
☐ 1876	25 Rubles, Czarist Empire, 2nd Coinage, Gold Proof	—	18,000.00
☐ 1896–1908	25 Rubles, Gold	—	2250.00
☐ 1902	37½ Rubles, Reduced Weight Gold, Gold	—	3500.00

DATE	COIN TYPE/VARIETY/METAL	ABP FINE	AVERAGE FINE
☐ 1886–1894	50 Kopeks, Alexander III, Silver	—	$24.00
☐ 1895–1914	50 Kopeks, Nikolai II, Silver	—	6.15

Russia—Empire Type Coinage

Key to Grading: Eagle

DATE	COIN TYPE/VARIETY/METAL	ABP FINE	AVERAGE FINE
☐ 1803–1810	1 Poluska, Alexander I, 1st Coinage, Copper	$20.00	45.00
☐ 1839–1846	Poluska, Nikolai I, 3rd Coinage, Copper	2.20	5.25
☐ 1849–1855	Poluska, Nikolai I, 4th Coinage, Copper	2.20	5.25
☐ 1855–1861	Poluska, Alexander II, Copper	—	5.25
☐ 1867–1881	Poluska, Alexander II, 2nd Coinage, Copper	2.20	5.25
☐ 1882–1891	Poluska, Alexander III, 2nd Coinage, Copper	3.00	4.15
☐ 1894–1916	Poluska, Nikolai II, 2nd Coinage, Copper	.40	1.50
☐ 1804–1808	1 Denga, Alexander I, 1st Coinage, Copper	40.00	100.00
☐ 1810–1825	1 Denga, Alexander I, 2nd Coinage, Copper	6.00	10.00
☐ 1827–1830	1 Denga, Nicholas I, 1st Coinage, Copper	1.20	4.15
☐ 1839–1848	1 Denga, Nicholas I, 3rd Coinage, Copper	1.60	4.15
☐ 1849–1855	1 Denga, Nicholas I, 4th Coinage, Copper	2.20	4.15
☐ 1855–1861	1 Denga, Alexander II, Copper	2.20	4.15
☐ 1855–1861	1 Denga, Alexander II, 1st Coinage, Copper	2.00	5.00
☐ 1882–1894	1 Denga, Alexander III, Copper	1.20	4.15
☐ 1884–1916	1 Denga, Nikolai II, Copper	1.20	4.15
☐ 1804–1810	1 Kopek, Alexander I, 1st Coinage, Copper	20.00	35.00
☐ 1810–1825	1 Kopek, Alexander I, 2nd Coinage, Copper	1.20	8.00
☐ 1826–1830	1 Kopek, Nicholas I, 1st Coinage, Copper	1.20	6.00
☐ 1830–1839	1 Kopek, Nicholas I, 2nd Coinage, Copper	2.20	5.00
☐ 1839–1847	1 Kopek, Nicholas I, 3rd Coinage, Copper	2.20	5.00
☐ 1849–1856	1 Kopek, Nicholas I, 4th Coinage, Copper	2.20	5.00
☐ 1855–1864	1 Kopek, Alexander II, 1st Coinage, Copper	1.20	4.00
☐ 1867–1881	1 Kopek, Alexander II, 2nd Coinage, Copper	1.20	2.00
☐ 1882–1894	1 Kopek, Alexander III, Copper	.10	.32
☐ 1894–1916	1 Kopek, Nicholas II, Copper	.10	.50
☐ 1802–1810	2 Kopeks, Alexander I, 1st Coinage, Copper	25.00	38.00

DATE	COIN TYPE/VARIETY/METAL	ABP FINE	AVERAGE FINE
☐ 1810–1825	2 Kopeks, Alexander I, 2nd Coinage, Copper	$2.00	$5.00
☐ 1826–1830	2 Kopeks, Nicholas I, 1st Coinage, Copper	5.00	8.00
☐ 1830–1839	2 Kopeks, Nicholas I, 2nd Coinage, Copper	4.00	5.25
☐ 1839–1848	2 Kopeks, Nicholas I, 3rd Coinage, Copper	4.00	5.25
☐ 1849–1855	2 Kopeks, Nicholas I, 4th Coinage, Copper	4.00	6.15
☐ 1855–1865	2 Kopeks, Alexander II, 1st Coinage, Copper	—	6.15
☐ 1882–1894	2 Kopeks, Alexander III, Copper	—	.60
☐ 1894–1916	2 Kopeks, Nicholas II, Copper	—	.75
☐ 1839–1848	3 Kopeks, Nicholas I, 3rd Coinage, Copper	8.00	12.00
☐ 1849–1855	3 Kopeks, Nicholas I, 4th Coinage, Copper	6.00	10.00
☐ 1855–1865	3 Kopeks, Alexander II, 1st Coinage, Copper	6.00	10.00
☐ 1867–1881	3 Kopeks, Alexander II, 2nd Coinage, Copper	—	1.50
☐ 1882–1894	3 Kopeks, Alexander III, Copper	—	2.20
☐ 1894–1916	3 Kopeks, Nicholas II, Copper	—	2.20
☐ 1802–1810	5 Kopeks, Alexander I, 1st Coinage, Copper	8.00	25.00
☐ 1810–1825	5 Kopeks, Alexander I, Silver	—	7.15
☐ 1826–1835	5 Kopeks, Nicholas I, Silver	—	8.00
☐ 1830–1839	5 Kopeks, Nicholas I, 2nd Coinage, Copper	4.00	7.15
☐ 1832–1855	5 Kopeks, Nicholas I, Silver	—	7.15
☐ 1849–1855	5 Kopeks, Nicholas I, 4th Coinage, Copper	5.00	7.15
☐ 1855–1881	5 Kopeks, Alexander II, Silver	—	7.15
☐ 1855–1866	5 Kopeks, Alexander II, 1st Coinage, Copper	2.00	5.00
☐ 1867–1881	5 Kopeks, Alexander II, 2nd Coinage, Copper	2.00	4.00
☐ 1881–1892	5 Kopeks, Alexander III, Silver	—	8.00
☐ 1882–1894	5 Kopeks, Alexander III, Copper	—	2.20
☐ 1894–1916	5 Kopeks, Nicholas II, Copper	30.00	55.00
☐ 1796–1801	10 Kopeks, Paul I, Silver	—	55.00
☐ 1802–1825	10 Kopeks, Alexander I, Silver	—	9.00
☐ 1826–1832	10 Kopeks, Nicholas I, Silver	—	9.00
☐ 1833–1855	10 Kopeks, Nicholas I, Silver	—	10.00
☐ 1855–1881	10 Kopeks, Alexander II, Silver	—	4.15

DATE	COIN TYPE/VARIETY/METAL	ABP FINE	AVERAGE FINE
☐ 1881–1892	10 Kopeks, Alexander III, Silver	—	$2.20
☐ 1860–1881	15 Kopeks, Alexander II, Silver	—	2.20
☐ 1887–1887	15 Kopeks, Alexander III, Silver	—	2.20
☐ 1810–1825	20 Kopeks, Alexander I, Silver	—	8.00
☐ 1833–1855	20 Kopeks, Nicholas I, Silver	—	8.00
☐ 1855–1881	20 Kopeks, Alexander II, Silver	—	4.15
☐ 1881–1892	20 Kopeks, Alexander III, Silver	—	4.15
☐ 1826–1835	25 Kopeks, Nicholas I, Silver	—	12.00
☐ 1855–1881	25 Kopeks, Alexander II, Silver	—	12.00
☐ 1881–1894	25 Kopeks, Alexander III, Silver	—	32.00
☐ 1886–1904	25 Kopeks, Nicholas II, Silver	—	32.00
☐ 1881–1892	50 Kopeks, Alexander III, Silver	—	32.00
☐ 1896–1904	50 Kopeks, Nicholas II, Silver	—	8.00
☐ 1801–1825	1 Ruble, Alexander I, Silver	—	25.00
☐ 1826–1832	1 Ruble, Nicholas I, Silver	—	25.00
☐ 1833–1855	1 Ruble, Nicholas I, Silver	—	28.00
☐ 1855–1881	1 Ruble, Alexander II, Silver	—	28.00
☐ 1881–1894	1 Ruble, Alexander III, Silver	—	30.00
☐ 1894–1916	1 Ruble, Nicholas II, Silver	—	28.00
☐ 1828–1845	3 Rubles, Platinum	—	275.00
☐ 1826–1855	5 Rubles, Gold	—	150.00
☐ 1829–1845	6 Rubles, Platinum	—	1450.00
☐ 1830–1845	12 Rubles, Platinum	—	1450.00

SOUTH AFRICA

The first coins, the silver guilders, were used in 1802. The silver pence, bronze penny, and gold pound were used in the 1800s. The silver florin was used in the 1900s, as were the cupro-nickel shilling, brass cent, and gold krugerrand. The first decimal coins were used in 1961. Today's currency is the rand.

South Africa—Republic Type Coinage

Key to Grading: Bust

DATE	COIN TYPE/VARIETY/METAL	ABP FINE	AVERAGE FINE
☐ 1892–1898	1 Penny, Paul Kruger, Bronze	—	$7.00
☐ 1892–1897	3 Pence, Paul Kruger, Silver	—	5.25

Key to Grading: Bust

DATE	COIN TYPE/VARIETY/METAL	ABP FINE	AVERAGE FINE
☐ 1892–1897	6 Pence, Paul Kruger, Silver	—	5.25

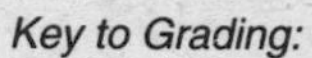

Key to Grading:

DATE	COIN TYPE/VARIETY/METAL	ABP FINE	AVERAGE FINE
☐ 1892–1897	1 Shilling, Paul Kruger, Silver	—	7.00
☐ 1892–1897	2 Shillings, Paul Kruger, Silver	—	12.00

Key to Grading: Bust

DATE	COIN TYPE/VARIETY/METAL	ABP FINE	AVERAGE FINE
☐ 1892–1897	2½ Shillings, Paul Kruger, Silver	—	22.00
☐ 1892	5 Shillings, Paul Kruger, Silver	—	75.00
☐ 1892–1897	½ Pond, Paul Kruger, Gold	—	145.00
☐ 1892–1900	1 Pond, Paul Kruger, Gold	—	160.00
☐ 1902	1 Pond, Veld, Gold	—	625.00

South Africa—Union Type Coinage

DATE	COIN TYPE/VARIETY/METAL	ABP FINE	AVERAGE FINE
□ 1923–1931	1 Farthing, George V, Legend SUID-AFRIKA, Bronze	—	$4.15
□ 1931–1936	1 Farthing, George V, Legend SUID-AFRIKA, Bronze	—	4.15
□ 1937–1947	1 Farthing, George VI, Legend SUID-AFRIKA, Bronze	—	.55
□ 1948–1950	1 Farthing, George VI, Obverse Legend GEORGIUS SEXTUS REX, Bronze	—	.55

Key to Grading: Bust

DATE	COIN TYPE/VARIETY/METAL	ABP FINE	AVERAGE FINE
□ 1951–1952	1 Farthing, George VI, Reverse Legend SUID-AFRIKA—SOUTH AFRICA, Bronze	—	.50
□ 1953–1960	1 Farthing, Elizabeth II, Reverse Legend SUID-AFRIKA—SOUTH AFRICA, Bronze	—	.28
□ 1923–1926	1/2 Penny, George V, Legend SUID-AFRIKA, Bronze	—	8.00
□ 1931–1936	1/2 Penny, George V, Legend SUID-AFRIKA, Bronze	—	2.60
□ 1937–1947	1/2 Penny, George VI, Legend SUID-AFRIKA, Bronze	—	.45
□ 1948–1952	1/2 Penny, George VI, Legend GEORGIUS SEXTUS REX, Bronze	—	.45

Key to Grading: Bust

DATE	COIN TYPE/VARIETY/METAL	ABP FINE	AVERAGE FINE
□ 1953–1960	1/2 Penny, Elizabeth II, Legend Elizabeth II Regina, Bronze	—	.45
□ 1923–1930	1 Penny, George V, Bronze	—	4.00

Key to Grading: Bust

DATE	COIN TYPE/VARIETY/METAL	ABP FINE	AVERAGE FINE
☐ 1931–1936	1 Penny, George V, Legend SUID-AFRIKA, Bronze	—	$1.50
☐ 1937–1947	1 Penny, George VI, Legend SUID-AFRIKA, Bronze	—	.45
☐ 1948–1950	1 Penny, George VI, Legend GEORGIUS SEXTUS REX, Bronze	—	.45
☐ 1951–1952	1 Penny, George VI, Legend SUID-AFRIKA—SOUTH AFRICA, Bronze	—	.45
☐ 1953–1960	1 Penny, Elizabeth II, Legend SUID-AFRIKA—SOUTH AFRICA, Bronze	—	.45
☐ 1923–1930	3 Pence, George V, Legend SUID-AFRIKA, Silver	—	2.00
☐ 1931–1936	3 Pence, George V, Legend SUID-AFRIKA, Silver	—	1.80

Key to Grading: Bust

DATE	COIN TYPE/VARIETY/METAL	ABP FINE	AVERAGE FINE
☐ 1937–1947	3 Pence, George VI, Legend SUID-AFRIKA, Silver	—	1.20
☐ 1948–1950	3 Pence, George VI, Legend, GEORGIUS SEXTUS REX, Silver	—	.60
☐ 1953–1960	3 Pence, Elizabeth II, Silver	—	.80
☐ 1923–1930	6 Pence, George V, Legend SUID-AFRIKA, Silver	—	4.15
☐ 1931–1936	6 Pence, George V, Legend SUID-AFRIKA, Silver	—	4.15
☐ 1937–1947	6 Pence, George VI, Legend SUID-AFRIKA, Silver	—	1.50

Key to Grading: Bust

DATE	COIN TYPE/VARIETY/METAL	ABP FINE	AVERAGE FINE
☐ 1948–1950	6 Pence, George VI, Legend GEORGIUS SEXTUS REX, Silver	—	$1.65
☐ 1951–1952	6 Pence, George VI, Legend SUID-AFRIKA—SOUTH AFRICA, Silver	—	1.65
☐ 1953–1960	6 Pence, Elizabeth II, Silver	—	2.00
☐ 1923–1930	1 Shilling, George V, Legend SUID-AFRIKA, Silver	—	6.00
☐ 1931–1936	1 Shilling, George V, Legend SUID-AFRIKA, Silver	—	4.15

Key to Grading: Bust

DATE	COIN TYPE/VARIETY/METAL	ABP FINE	AVERAGE FINE
☐ 1937–1947	1 Shilling, George VI, Silver	—	4.15
☐ 1948–1952	1 Shilling, George VI, Legend GEORGIUS SEXTUS REX, Silver	—	2.00
☐ 1953–1960	1 Shilling, Elizabeth II, Silver	—	1.50
☐ 1923–1930	1 Florin, George V, Legend SUID-AFRIKA, Silver	—	5.25
☐ 1931–1936	2 Shillings, George V, Legend SUID-AFRIKA, Silver	—	5.25
☐ 1937–1947	2 Shillings, George VI, Legend SUID-AFRIKA, Silver	—	5.25
☐ 1948–1950	2 Shillings, George VI, Legend GEORGIUS SEXTUS REX, Silver	—	10.00
☐ 1951–1952	2 Shillings, George VI, Legend SUID-AFRIKA—SOUTH AFRICA, Silver	—	4.25
☐ 1953–1960	2 Shillings, Elizabeth II, Silver	—	4.25
☐ 1923–1930	2½ Shillings, George V, Silver	—	5.00
☐ 1931–1936	2½ Shillings, George V, Legend SUID-AFRIKA, Silver	—	12.00

DATE	COIN TYPE/VARIETY/METAL	ABP FINE	AVERAGE FINE
□ 1937–1947	2½ Shillings, George VI, Legend SUID-AFRIKA, Silver	—	$5.50
□ 1948–1952	2½ Shillings, George VI, Legend GEORGIUS SEXTUS REX, Silver	—	5.25
□ 1953–1960	2½ Shillings, Elizabeth I, Silver	—	5.25
□ 1947	5 Shillings, Royal Visit Co, Silver	—	5.25

Key to Grading: Bust

DATE	COIN TYPE/VARIETY/METAL	ABP FINE	AVERAGE FINE
□ 1948–1950	5 Shillings, George VI, Silver	—	6.25
□ 1951	5 Shillings, George VI, Legend SUID-AFRIKA—SOUTH AFRICA, Silver	—	6.25
□ 1952	5 Shillings, Capetown Comm, Silver	—	6.25
□ 1953–1959	5 Shillings, Elizabeth II, Silver	—	5.00
□ 1960	5 Shillings, 50th Anniversary, Silver	—	4.50
□ 1923–1926	½ Sovereign, George V, Gold	—	65.00
□ 1952	½ Pound, George VI, Gold	—	90.00
□ 1953–1960	½ Pound, Elizabeth II, Gold	—	175.00

Key to Grading: Bust

DATE	COIN TYPE/VARIETY/METAL	ABP FINE	AVERAGE FINE
□ 1923–1932	1 Sovereign, George V, Gold	—	125.00
□ 1952	1 Pound, George VI, Gold	—	110.00
□ 1953–1960	1 Pound, Elizabeth II, Gold Proof	—	125.00

South Africa—Republic Coinage

Key to Grading: Bust

DATE	COIN TYPE/VARIETY/METAL	ABP FINE	AVERAGE FINE
☐ 1961–1964	1/2 Cent, Brass	—	$ .32
☐ 1970–1976	1/2 Cent, Bronze	—	.32
☐ 1979	1/2 Cent, Bronze PRF	—	1.65
☐ 1982	1/2 Cent, Bronze PRF	—	1.65
☐ 1961–1964	1 Cent, Brass	—	.38
☐ 1965–1969	1 Cent, Bronze	—	.38
☐ 1968	1 Cent, Bronze PRF	—	1.00
☐ 1970–1989	1 Cent, Bronze	—	.20
☐ 1976	1 Cent, Bronze	—	.32
☐ 1979	1 Cent, Bronze	—	.20
☐ 1982	1 Cent, Bronze	—	.32
☐ 1990 to Date	1 Cent, Copper-Steel	—	.32
☐ 1965–1969	2 Cents, Bronze	—	.32
☐ 1968	2 Cents, Bronze	—	.32
☐ 1970–1990	2 Cents, Bronze	—	.20

Key to Grading: Bust

DATE	COIN TYPE/VARIETY/METAL	ABP FINE	AVERAGE FINE
☐ 1961–1964	2 1/2 Cents, Silver	—	2.20
☐ 1961–1964	5 Cents, Silver	—	2.20
☐ 1965–1969	5 Cents, Nickel	—	.28
☐ 1968	5 Cents, Nickel	—	.20
☐ 1970–1989	5 Cents, Nickel	—	.38
☐ 1976	5 Cents, Nickel	—	.38
☐ 1979	5 Cents, Nickel	—	.38
☐ 1982	5 Cents, Nickel	—	.38
☐ 1990 to Date	5 Cents, Copper-Steel	—	.20
☐ 1961–1962	10 Cents, Silver	—	.70

DATE	COIN TYPE/VARIETY/METAL	ABP FINE	AVERAGE FINE
☐ 1965–1969	10 Cents, Nickel	—	$ .28
☐ 1968	10 Cents, Nickel	—	.50
☐ 1970–1989	10 Cents, Nickel	—	.42
☐ 1976	10 Cents, Nickel	—	.42
☐ 1979	10 Cents, Nickel	—	.20
☐ 1982	10 Cents, Nickel	—	.32
☐ 1990–1999	10 Cents, Brass-Steel	—	.28
☐ 1961–1964	20 Cents, Silver	—	1.20
☐ 1965–1969	20 Cents, Nickel	—	.28
☐ 1968	20 Cents, Nickel	—	1.50
☐ 1970–1990	20 Cents, Nickel	—	.38
☐ 1976	20 Cents, Nickel	—	.38
☐ 1979	20 Cents, Nickel	—	.38
☐ 1982–1982	20 Cents, Nickel	—	.38
☐ 1990 to Date	20 Cents, Brass-Steel	—	.38

Key to Grading: Bust

DATE	COIN TYPE/VARIETY/METAL	ABP FINE	AVERAGE FINE
☐ 1961–1964	50 Cents, Silver	—	4.15
☐ 1965–1969	50 Cents, Nickel	—	.50
☐ 1968	50 Cents, Nickel	—	.45
☐ 1970–1990	50 Cents, Nickel	—	.45
☐ 1976	50 Cents, Nickel	—	.45
☐ 1979	50 Cents, Nickel	—	.45
☐ 1982	50 Cents, Nickel	—	.45
☐ 1990 to Date	50 Cents, Brass-Steel	—	.75
☐ 1961–1983	1 Rand, Gold	—	55.00
☐ 1965–1968	1 Rand, Silver	—	4.15

Key to Grading: Coat of Arms

DATE	COIN TYPE/VARIETY/METAL	ABP FINE	AVERAGE FINE
☐ 1970–1989	1 Rand, Silver	—	4.15
☐ 1977–1990	1 Rand, Nickel	—	.70

DATE	COIN TYPE/VARIETY/METAL	ABP FINE	AVERAGE FINE
☐ 1961–1983	2 Rands, Gold	—	$180.00
☐ 1989	2 Rands, Copper-Nickel	—	.75

South Africa—Bullion Coinage

☐ 1980	1/10 Krugerrand, Gold	—	70.00
☐ 1980	1/4 Krugerrand, Gold	—	200.00
☐ 1980	1/2 Krugerrand, Gold	—	375.00
☐ 1967	Krugerrand, Gold	—	750.00

***BV** = These coins are relatively current so their collector value is minimal. Since these coins were minted and sold primarily for their bullion value, their current value is determined by the current "spot" price of the precious metal indicated. For accurate prices, contact your local coin dealer.

SPAIN

The earliest coins from the 4th century B.C. were marked Em. The silver denarius was popular from about 100 B.C. to 45 B.C., with bronze coins and the gold tremissis becoming popular by 600 to 700. Gold coins were popular in the mid-1400s. Decimal coins appeared in 1848, with the peseta being the coin used today.

Spain—Type Coinage

Key to Grading: Bust

☐ 1866–1868	1/2 Centimo, Isabell II, 2nd Decimal Coinage, Bronze	—	7.50
☐ 1866–1868	1 Centimo, Isabell II, 2nd Decimal Coinage, Bronze	—	10.00
☐ 1870	1 Centimo, Bronze	—	.80
☐ 1906	1 Centimo, Alfonso XIII, 4th Coinage, Bronze	—	.80
☐ 1911–1913	1 Centimo, Alfonso XIII, 5th Coinage, Bronze	—	5.25

DATE	COIN TYPE/VARIETY/METAL	ABP FINE	AVERAGE FINE
☐ 1904–1905	2 Centimos, Alfonso XIII, 4th Coinage, Bronze	—	$ .60
☐ 1911–1912	2 Centimos, Alfonso XIII, 5th Coinage, Bronze	—	.55

Key to Grading: Bust

DATE	COIN TYPE/VARIETY/METAL	ABP FINE	AVERAGE FINE
☐ 1866–1868	2 1/2 Centimos, Isabell II, 2nd Decimal Coinage, Bronze	$5.00	8.00
☐ 1868	25 Milesimas, Provisional, Battle of Alcolea Bridge, Bronze	35.00	60.00
☐ 1854–1864	5 Centimos de Real, Isabell, 2nd Decimal Coinage, Copper	8.50	14.00
☐ 1866–1868	5 Centimos, Isabell II, 2nd Decimal Coinage, Bronze	8.50	14.00

Key to Grading: Lion or Bust

DATE	COIN TYPE/VARIETY/METAL	ABP FINE	AVERAGE FINE
☐ 1870	5 Centimos, Bronze	—	4.15
☐ 1875	5 Centimos, Carlos VII, Bronze	—	20.00
☐ 1877–1879	5 Centimos, Alfonso XII, 2nd Coinage, Bronze	—	1.15
☐ 1937	5 Centimos, Republic, 2nd Coinage, Iron	—	.80
☐ 1940–1953	5 Centimos, Nationalist Govt, 1st Coinage, Aluminum	—	.45
☐ 1854–1864	10 Centimos, Isabell II, Decimal Coinage, Copper	—	16.00
☐ 1864–1868	10 Centimos, Isabell II, 2nd Decimal Coinage, Silver	—	28.00

Key to Grading: Lion or Bust

DATE	COIN TYPE/VARIETY/METAL	ABP FINE	AVERAGE FINE
☐ 1870	10 Centimos, Bronze	—	$2.20
☐ 1875	10 Centimos, Carlos VII, Bronze	$12.00	20.00
☐ 1877–1879	10 Centimos, Alfonso XII, 3rd Coinage, Bronze	—	.50
☐ 1940–1953	10 Centimos, Nationalist Govt, 1st Coinage, Aluminum	—	.38
☐ 1959	10 Centimos, Kingdom, Aluminum	—	.38
☐ 1865–1868	20 Centimos, Isabell II, 2nd Decimal Coinage, Silver	—	32.00
☐ 1869–1870	20 Centimos, Obverse Legend: Espana, Silver		140.00
☐ 1949	20 Centimos, Nationalist Govt, 2nd Coinage, Cupro-Nickel	—	.32
☐ 1925	25 Centimos, Alfonso XIII, 6th Coinage, Nickel-Brass	—	.60
☐ 1927	25 Centimos, Alfonso XIII, 6th Coinage, Cupro-Nickel	—	.45
☐ 1933	1 Peseta, Republic, 1st Coinage, Silver	—	4.15
☐ 1934	25 Centimos, Republic, 1st Coinage, Nickel-Bronze	—	.45
☐ 1937	25 Centimos, Nationalist Govt, 1st Coinage, Cupro-Nickel	—	.45
☐ 1938	25 Centimos, Republic, 2nd Coinage, Copper	—	1.20
☐ 1864–1868	40 Centimos, Isabell II, 2nd Decimal Coinage, Silver	—	10.00
☐ 1848–1853	1/2 Real, Isabell II, Copper	—	22.00
☐ 1869–1870	50 Centimos, Obverse Legend: Espana, Silver	—	22.00
☐ 1880–1885	50 Centimos, Alfonso XII, 3rd Coinage, Silver	—	4.00
☐ 1889–1892	50 Centimos, Alfonso XIII, 1st Coinage, Silver	—	12.00
☐ 1894	50 Centimos, Alfonso XIII, 2nd Coinage, Silver	—	5.50

DATE	COIN TYPE/VARIETY/METAL	ABP FINE	AVERAGE FINE
☐ 1896–1900	50 Centimos, Alfonso XIII, 3rd Coinage, Silver	—	$4.15
☐ 1904	50 Centimos, Alfonso XIII, 4th Coinage, Silver	—	2.20
☐ 1910	50 Centimos, Alfonso XIII, 5th Coinage, Silver	—	2.20
☐ 1926	50 Centimos, Alfonso XIII, 6th Coinage, Silver	—	2.20
☐ 1937	50 Centimos, Republic, 2nd Coinage, Copper	—	.75
☐ 1949–1963	50 Centimos, Kingdom, Cupro-Nickel	—	.45
☐ 1966–1975	50 Centimos, Kingdom, Aluminum	—	.45
☐ 1980	50 Centimos, Kingdom, World Cup Soccer Games, Aluminum	—	.32
☐ 1850–1855	1 Real, Isabell II, Arms Without Pillars, Silver	—	8.00
☐ 1857–1864	1 Real, Isabell II, 2nd Decimal Coinage, Silver	—	12.00
☐ 1865–1868	1 Escudo, Isabell II, 3rd Decimal Coinage, Silver	—	20.00
☐ 1869–1870	1 Peseta, Obverse Legend: Espana, Silver	—	12.00
☐ 1869	1 Peseta, Obverse Legend: Gobierno Provisional, Silver	—	4.00
☐ 1876	1 Peseta, Alfonso XII, 2nd Coinage, Silver	—	5.25
☐ 1881–1885	1 Peseta, Alfonso XII, 3rd Coinage, Silver	—	5.25
☐ 1889–1891	1 Peseta, Alfonso XIII, 1st Coinage, Silver	—	16.00
☐ 1893–1894	1 Peseta, Alfonso XIII, 2nd Coinage, Silver	—	12.00
☐ 1896–1902	1 Peseta, Alfonso XIII, 3rd Coinage, Silver	—	4.15
☐ 1903–1905	1 Peseta, Alfonso XIII, 4th Coinage, Silver	—	5.00
☐ 1937	1 Peseta, Republic, 2nd Coinage, Brass	—	1.75
☐ 1944	1 Peseta, Nationalist Govt, 1st Coinage, Aluminum-Bronze	—	4.15
☐ 1947–1975	1 Peseta, Kingdom, Alluminum-Bronze	—	4.15

Key to Grading: Bust

DATE	COIN TYPE/VARIETY/METAL	ABP FINE	AVERAGE FINE
☐ 1947–1963	1 Peseta, Kingdom, 2nd Coinage, Aluminum-Bronze	—	$ .45

Key to Grading: Bust

DATE	COIN TYPE/VARIETY/METAL	ABP FINE	AVERAGE FINE
☐ 1980	1 Peseta, Kingdom, World Cup Soccer Games, Aluminum-Bronze	—	.45
☐ 1982 to Date	1 Peseta, Kingdom, Aluminum	—	.45
☐ 1852–1855	1 Reales, Isabell II, Arms Without Pillars, Silver	—	15.00
☐ 1857–1864	2 Reales, Isabell II, 2nd Decimal Coinage, Silver	—	22.00
☐ 1865–1868	2 Escudos, Isabell II, 3rd Decimal Coinage, Silver	—	28.00
☐ 1865–1868(69)	2 Escudos, Isabell II, 3rd Decimal Coinage, Gold	—	325.00
☐ 1869–1870	2 Pesetas, Provisional, Obverse Legend: Espana, Silver	—	8.00
☐ 1879–1884	2 Pesetas, Alfonso XII, 3rd Coinage, Silver	—	8.00
☐ 1889–1892	2 Pesetas, Alfonso XIII, 1st Coinage, Silver	—	12.00
☐ 1894	2 Pesetas, Alfonso XIII, 2nd Coinage, Silver	—	50.00
☐ 1905	2 Pesetas, Alfonso XIII, 4th Coinage, Silver	—	5.00
☐ 1982–1984	2 Pesetas, Kingdom, Aluminum	—	.45
☐ 1953	$2\frac{1}{2}$ Pesetas, Kingdom, Aluminum-Bronze	—	.45
☐ 1852–1855	4 Reales, Isabell II, Arms Without Pillars, Silver	—	25.00
☐ 1856–1864	4 Reales, Isabell II, 2nd Decimal Coinage, Silver	—	38.00
☐ 1865–1868	4 Escudos, Isabell II, 3rd Decimal Coinage, Gold	—	60.00
☐ 1869–1870	5 Pesetas, Provisional, Obverse Legend: Espana, Silver	—	28.00
☐ 1871	5 Pesetas, Amadeo I, Obverse Legend: Espana, Silver	—	20.00
☐ 1873	5 Pesetas, Republic, Cartagena Mint, Silver	—	32.00

Key to Grading: Bust

DATE	COIN TYPE/VARIETY/METAL	ABP FINE	AVERAGE FINE
☐ 1875–1876	5 Pesetas, Alfonso XII, 1st Coinage, Silver	—	$20.00
☐ 1877–1882	5 Pesetas, Alfonso XII, 2nd Coinage, Silver	—	22.00
☐ 1882–1885	5 Pesetas, Alfonso XII, 3rd Coinage, Silver	—	20.00
☐ 1888–1892	5 Pesetas, Alfonso XIII, 1st Coinage, Silver	—	18.00
☐ 1892–1894	5 Pesetas, Alfonso XIII, 2nd Coinage, Silver	—	18.00
☐ 1896–1899	5 Pesetas, Alfonso XIII, 3rd Coinage, Silver	—	18.00

Key to Grading: Bust

DATE	COIN TYPE/VARIETY/METAL	ABP FINE	AVERAGE FINE
☐ 1949	5 Pesetas, Kingdom, Nickel	$ .50	.80
☐ 1957–1975	5 Pesetas, Kingdom, Cupro-Nickel	—	.25
☐ 1980	5 Pesetas, Kingdom, World Cup Soccer Games, Cupro-Nickel	—	16.00
☐ 1982–1989	5 Pesetas, Kingdom, Cupro-Nickel	—	.38
☐ 1989 to Date	5 Pesetas, Kingdom, Aluminum-Bronze	—	.38
☐ 1851–1856	10 Reales, Isabell II, Arms Flanked by Pillars, Silver	—	42.00
☐ 1857–1864	10 Reales, Isabell II, 2nd Decimal Coinage, Silver	—	120.00
☐ 1865–1868	10 Escudos, Isabell II, 3rd Decimal Coinage, Gold	—	175.00
☐ 1878–1879	10 Pesetas, Alfonso XII, 2nd Coinage, Gold	—	225.00
☐ 1983–1985	10 Pesetas, Kingdom, Cupro-Nickel	—	.40
☐ 1845–1855	20 Reales, Isabell II, Silver	—	85.00
☐ 1850–1855	20 Reales, Isabell II, Arms Flanked by Pillars, Silver	—	65.00

DATE	COIN TYPE/VARIETY/METAL	ABP FINE	AVERAGE FINE
□ 1856–1864	20 Reales, Isabell II, 2nd Decimal Coinage, Silver	—	$65.00
□ 1861–1863	20 Reales, Isabell II, 2nd Decimal Coinage, Gold	—	85.00
□ 1887–1890	20 Pesetas, Alfonso XIII, 1st Coinage, Gold	—	140.00
□ 1892	20 Pesetas, Alfonso XIII, 2nd Coinage, Gold	—	1000.00
□ 1896–1899	20 Pesetas, Alfonso XIII, 3rd Coinage, Gold	—	150.00
□ 1904	20 Pesetas, Alfonso XIII, 4th Coinage, Gold	—	1200.00
□ 1876–1880	25 Pesetas, Alfonso XII, 2nd Coinage, Gold	—	150.00
□ 1881–1885	25 Pesetas, Alfonso XII, 3rd Coinage, Gold	—	240.00

Key to Grading: Bust

DATE	COIN TYPE/VARIETY/METAL	ABP FINE	AVERAGE FINE
□ 1957–1984	25 Pesetas, Kingdom, Cupro-Nickel	—	.38
□ 1980	25 Pesetas, Kingdom, World Cup Soccer Games, Cupro-Nickel	—	.38
□ 1990–1991	25 Pesetas, Kingdom, 1992 Olympics—High Jumper, Nickel-Bronze	—	.38
□ 1990–1991	25 Pesetas, Kingdom, 1992 Olympics—Discus, Nickel-Bronze	—	.38
□ 1992	25 Pesetas, Kingdom, Sevilla Tower, Nickel-Bronze	—	.45
□ 1861–1863	40 Reales, Isabell II, 2nd Decimal Coinage, Gold	—	70.00

Key to Grading: Bust

DATE	COIN TYPE/VARIETY/METAL	ABP FINE	AVERAGE FINE
☐ 1957–1984	50 Pesetas, Kingdom, Cupro-Nickel	—	$ .42
☐ 1980	50 Pesetas, Kingdom, World Cup Soccer Games, Cupro-Nickel	—	.42
☐ 1990	50 Pesetas, Kingdom, Expo 92—Juan Carlos, Cupro-Nickel	—	.42
☐ 1990–1991	50 Pesetas, Kingdom, Expo 92—City View, Cupro-Nickel	—	.42
☐ 1851–1855	100 Reales, Isabell II, Gold	—	320.00
☐ 1856–1862	100 Reales, Isabell II, 2nd Decimal Coinage, Gold	—	175.00
☐ 1897	100 Pesetas, Alfonso XIII, 3rd Coinage, Gold	—	650.00

Key to Grading: Bust

DATE	COIN TYPE/VARIETY/METAL	ABP FINE	AVERAGE FINE
☐ 1966	100 Pesetas, Kingdom, Silver	—	4.15
☐ 1976	100 Pesetas, Kingdom, Cupro-Nickel	—	2.00
☐ 1980	100 Pesetas, Kingdom, World Cup Soccer Games, Cupro-Nickel	—	.75
☐ 1982–1990	100 Pesetas, Kingdom, Aluminum-Bronze	—	1.20
☐ 1989	100 Pesetas, Kingdom, Discovery of America—Mayan Pyramid, Silver	—	5.25
☐ 1990	100 Pesetas, Kingdom, Brother Juniper Serra, Silver	—	8.00
☐ 1991	100 Pesetas, Kingdom, Celestino Mutis, Silver	—	12.00
☐ 1986–1988	200 Pesetas, Kingdom, Celestino Mutis, Cupro-Nickel	—	2.20
☐ 1987	200 Pesetas, Kingdom, Madrid Numismatic Exposition, Cupro-Nickel	$25.00	45.00
☐ 1989	200 Pesetas, Kingdom, Discovery of America—Astrolabe, Silver	—	8.00
☐ 1990	200 Pesetas, Kingdom, Alonso de Frcilla, Silver	—	15.00
☐ 1990	200 Pesetas, Kingdom, Cupro-Nickel	—	4.15
☐ 1991	200 Pesetas, Kingdom, Las Casas, Silver	—	15.00
☐ 1992	200 Pesetas, Kingdom, Madrid—Capitol of European Culture, Copper-Nickel	—	5.25

Key to Grading: Bust

DATE	COIN TYPE/VARIETY/METAL	ABP FINE	AVERAGE FINE
☐ 1987–1990	500 Pesetas, Kingdom, Wedding Anniversary—Juan Carlos & Sofia, Copper-Aluminum-Nickel	—	$2.20
☐ 1989	500 Pesetas, Kingdom, Discovery of America—Juego De Pelota Game, Silver	—	15.00
☐ 1990	500 Pesetas, Kingdom, Juan de la Costa, Silver	—	18.00
☐ 1991	500 Pesetas, Kingdom, Jorge Juan, Silver	—	22.00
☐ 1989	1000 Pesetas, Kingdom, Discovery of America—Capture of Granada, Silver	—	22.00
☐ 1990	1000 Pesetas, Kingdom, Magellanes and Elcano, Silver	—	22.00
☐ 1991	1000 Pesetas, Kingdom, Simon Bolivar & San Martin, Silver	—	22.00
☐ 1989	2000 Pesetas, Kingdom, Discovery of America—Columbus, Silver	—	38.00
☐ 1990	2000 Pesetas, Kingdom, 1992 Olympics—Archer, Silver	—	25.00
☐ 1990	2000 Pesetas, Kingdom, 1992 Olympics—Basketball Players, Silver	—	42.00
☐ 1990	2000 Pesetas, Kingdom, 1992 Olympics—Human Pyramid, Silver	—	25.00
☐ 1990	2000 Pesetas, Kingdom, Hidalgo, Morelos and Juarez, Silver	—	35.00
☐ 1990	2000 Pesetas, Kingdom, 1992 Olympics, Symbols, Silver	—	42.00
☐ 1990	2000 Pesetas, Kingdom, 1992 Olympics, Soccer Player, Silver	—	35.00
☐ 1990	2000 Pesetas, Kingdom, 1992 Olympics, Pelotal Player, Silver	—	42.00
☐ 1990	2000 Pesetas, Kingdom, 1992 Olympics, Greek Runner, Silver	—	42.00
☐ 1990	2000 Pesetas, Kingdom, 1992 Olympics, Ancient Boat, Silver	—	42.00

DATE	COIN TYPE/VARIETY/METAL	ABP FINE	AVERAGE FINE
☐ 1991	2000 Pesetas, Kingdom, Ibero American Series, Silver	—	$82.00
☐ 1991	2000 Pesetas, Kingdom, Olympics—Medieval Rider, Silver	—	68.00
☐ 1991	2000 Pesetas, Kingdom, Olympics—Torch & Flag, Silver	—	68.00
☐ 1991	2000 Pesetas, Kingdom, Olympics—Tennis Player, Silver	—	68.00
☐ 1991	2000 Pesetas, Kingdom, Olympics—Bowling, Silver	—	68.00
☐ 1991	2000 Pesetas, Kingdom, Federman, Quesada and Benalcazar, Silver	—	30.00
☐ 1992	2000 Pesetas, Kingdom, Olympics—Chariot Racing, Silver	—	62.00
☐ 1992	2000 Pesetas, Kingdom, Olympics—Sprinters, Silver	—	62.00
☐ 1992	2000 Pesetas, Kingdom, Olympics—Tug of War, Silver	—	62.00
☐ 1992	2000 Pesetas, Kingdom, Olympics—Wheelchair Basketball, Silver	—	50.00
☐ 1989	5000 Pesetas, Kingdom, Discovery of America—Compass Face, Gold	—	68.00
☐ 1989	5000 Pesetas, Kingdom, Discovery of America—Santa Maria, Silver	—	55.00
☐ 1990	5000 Pesetas, Kingdom, Philip V, Gold	—	70.00
☐ 1990	5000 Pesetas, Kingdom, Cortes, Montezuma, and Marina, Silver	—	68.00
☐ 1991	5000 Pesetas, Kingdom, Pizarro & Atahualpa, Silver	—	100.00
☐ 1991	5000 Pesetas, Kingdom, Fernando VI, Gold	—	140.00
☐ 1989	10,000 Pesetas, Kingdom, Discovery of America—Sphere, Gold	—	140.00
☐ 1990	10,000 Pesetas, Kingdom, Quauchtemoc, Gold	—	140.00
☐ 1990	10,000 Pesetas, Kingdom, Olympics—Field Hockey, Gold	—	140.00
☐ 1990	10,000 Pesetas, Kingdom, Olympics—Gymnast, Gold	—	140.00
☐ 1991	10,000 Pesetas, Kingdom, Regional Autonomy, Silver	—	140.00
☐ 1991	10,000 Pesetas, Kingdom, Discoverers & Liberators, Silver	—	200.00
☐ 1991	10,000 Pesetas, Kingdom, Tupac Amaru II, Gold	—	150.00
☐ 1991	10,000 Pesetas, Kingdom, Spanish Royal Family, Silver	—	180.00

DATE	COIN TYPE/VARIETY/METAL	ABP FINE	AVERAGE FINE
□ 1991	10,000 Pesetas, Kingdom, Olympics—Karate, Gold	—	$240.00
□ 1991	10,000 Pesetas, Kingdom, Olympics—Baseball, Gold	—	240.00
□ 1989	20,000 Pesetas, Kingdom, Discovery of America—Pinzon Brother, Gold	—	170.00
□ 1990	20,000 Pesetas, Kingdom, Tupac Amaru I, Gold		
□ 1990	20,000 Pesetas, Kingdom, Huascar, Gold	—	275.00
□ 1990	20,000 Pesetas, Kingdom, Olympics—Cathedral Tower, Gold	—	250.00
□ 1990	20,000 Pesetas, Kingdom, Olympics—Dome Building, Gold	—	300.00
□ 1990	20,000 Pesetas, Kingdom, Olympics—Ruins, Gold	—	200.00
□ 1990	20,000 Pesetas, Kingdom, Olympics—Montjuic Stadium, Gold	—	275.00
□ 1989	40,000 Pesetas, Kingdom, Discovery of America—Sea Monster Attacking Ship, Gold	—	450.00
□ 1990	40,000 Pesetas, Kingdom, Juan Carlos, Gold	—	575.00
□ 1991	40,000 Pesetas, Kingdom, Imperial Double Eagle, Gold	—	575.00
□ 1989	80,000 Pesetas, Kingdom, Discovery of America—Ferdinand & Isabella, Gold	—	700.00
□ 1990	80,000 Pesetas, Kingdom, Carlos V, Gold	—	750.00
□ 1990	80,000 Pesetas, Kingdom, Olympics—Discus, Gold	—	700.00
□ 1990	80,000 Pesetas, Kingdom, Olympics—Prince Carlos on Horseback, Gold	—	800.00
□ 1991	80,000 Pesetas, Kindgom, Olympics—Women Tossing Man, Gold	—	1200.00
□ 1991	80,000 Pesetas, Kingdom, Carlos III, Gold	—	1000.00
□ 1992	80,000 Pesetas, Olympics—Children Playing, Gold	—	1200.00

SWITZERLAND

The first coins were Celtic issues of gold staters and fractions. The Swiss series began in the 3rd century B.C., and silver coins were issued in the 1st century B.C. In the 6th and 7th centuries, gold tremisses were produced, then silver deniers. In the 13th century, bracteate pfennigs were made. Gold coins were produced in the 1400s. The decimal system was developed in 1798. The currency in use today is the Swiss franc.

Switzerland—Type Coinage

Key to Grading: Bust

DATE	COIN TYPE/VARIETY/METAL	ABP FINE	AVERAGE FINE
□ 1922–1954	5 Francs, William Tell, Rev: Shield, Silver	—	$12.00
□ 1936	5 Francs, Commemorative, Armament Fund, Silver	—	15.00
□ 1939	5 Francs, Commemorative, Zurich Exposition, Silver	—	60.00
□ 1939	5 Francs, Commemorative, Laupen, Silver	—	250.00
□ 1941	5 Francs, Commemorative, Confederation 650th Anniversary, Silver	—	22.00
□ 1944	5 Francs, Commemorative, Battle of St. Jakob 500th Anniversary, Silver	—	22.00

DATE	COIN TYPE/VARIETY/METAL	ABP FINE	AVERAGE FINE
□ 1948	5 Francs, Commemorative, Swiss Confederation Centenary, Silver	—	$6.25
□ 1911–1922	10 Francs, Peasant Girl, Rev: Shield, Gold	—	32.00
□ 1901–1935	20 Francs, Peasant Girl, Rev: Shield, Gold	—	BV

Switzerland—Shooting Festival Coinage

Key to Grading: Figures on Coin

DATE	COIN TYPE/VARIETY/METAL	ABP FINE	AVERAGE FINE
□ 1855	5 Francs, Shooting Festival Solothurn, Silver	—	500.00
□ 1857	5 Francs, Shooting Festival Berne, Silver	—	220.0
□ 1859	5 Francs, Shooting Festival Zurich, Silver	—	65.
□ 1861	5 Francs, Shooting Festival Nidwalden, Silver	—	100
□ 1863	5 Francs, Shooting Festival La Chaux-de-Fonds, Silver	—	10
□ 1865	5 Francs, Shooting Festival Schaffhausen, Silver	—	
□ 1867	5 Francs, Shooting Festival Schwyz, Silver	—	0
□ 1869	5 Francs, Shooting Festival Zug, Silver	—	
□ 1872	5 Francs, Shooting Festival Zurich, Silver	—	.00
□ 1874	5 Francs, Shooting Festival St. Gallen, Silver	—	50.00
□ 1876	5 Francs, Shooting Festival Lausanne, Silver	—	50.00
□ 1879	5 Francs, Shooting Festival Basle, Silver	—	38.00
□ 1881	5 Francs, Shooting Festival Fribourg, Silver	—	38.00
□ 1883	5 Francs, Shooting Festival Lugano, Silver	—	30.00
□ 1885	5 Francs, Shooting Festival Berne, Silver	—	30.00

Switzerland—Helvetian Confederation Coinage

Key to Grading: Bust

DATE	COIN TYPE/VARIETY/METAL	ABP FINE	AVERAGE FINE
□ 1879–1954	5 Rappen, Helvetia Head. Rev: Wreath & Shield, Cupro-Nickel	—	$2.20

Grading: Bust

–1954	10 Rappen, Helvetia Head. Rev: Wreath & Shield, Cupro-Nickel	—	2.20

Key ading: Bust

□ 18 54	20 Rappen, Helvetia Head. Rev: Wreath & Shield, Cupro-Nickel	—	.80
□ 1850 1	1/2 Franc, Helvetia, Silver	—	60.00

Key to Grading: Wreath

DATE	COIN TYPE/VARIETY/METAL	ABP FINE	AVERAGE FINE
□ 1875–1953	1/2 Franc, Helvetia Standing. Rev: Wreath, Silver	—	$20.00
□ 1850–1861	Franc, Helvetia, Silver	—	45.00

Key to Grading: Wreath

DATE	COIN TYPE/VARIETY/METAL	ABP FINE	AVERAGE FINE
□ 1875–1945	Franc, Helvetia Standing. Rev: Wreath, Silver	—	7.00
□ 1850–1863	2 Francs, Helvetia, Silver	—	75.00

Key to Grading: Wreath

DATE	COIN TYPE/VARIETY/METAL	ABP FINE	AVERAGE FINE
□ 1874–1948	2 Francs, Helvetia Standing. Rev: Wreath, Silver	—	7.00
□ 1850–1874	5 Francs, Helvetia, Silver	—	125.00
□ 1888–1916	5 Francs, Helvetia Head. Rev: Wreath & Shield, Silver	—	90.00

SYRIA

The first coins were used in the 5th century B.C. and were Greek issues of silver coinage. The silver tetradrachm was in evidence in 200 B.C., followed by bronze coins in 200 A.D. The copper fals were used in the 600s, followed by the copper dinar, silver dirhem, and silver coins and dirhems in the 12th to 16th centuries. The nickel-brass, cupro-nickel, and aluminum-bronze piastre was used in the 1900s. Decimal coins were used in 1921. The currency today is the pound.

Syria—Syrian Arab Republic

Key to Grading: Eagle

DATE	COIN TYPE/VARIETY/METAL	ABP FINE	AVERAGE FINE
☐ 1962–1973	2½ Piastres, Aluminum-Bronze	—	$ .38
☐ 1962–1965	5 Piastres, Aluminum-Bronze	—	.40

Key to Grading: Eagle

DATE	COIN TYPE/VARIETY/METAL	ABP FINE	AVERAGE FINE
☐ 1971–1979	5 Piastres, FAO Issue, Aluminum-Bronze	—	$ .25
☐ 1962–1974	10 Piastres, Aluminum-Bronze	—	.32
☐ 1976–1979	10 Piastres, FAO Issue, Aluminum-Bronze	—	.32
☐ 1968–1974	25 Piastres, Nickel	—	.45
☐ 1976	25 Piastres, FAO Issue, Nickel	—	.45
☐ 1979	25 Piastres, Cupro-Nickel	—	.45
☐ 1968–1976	50 Piastres, Nickel	—	.55
☐ 1979	50 Piastres, Cupro-Nickel	—	.55
☐ 1968–1978	1 Pound, Nickel	—	.32
☐ 1979	1 Pound, Cupro-Nickel	—	.32
☐ 1991	1 Pound, Stainless Steel	—	.32

Syria—United Arab Republic

DATE	COIN TYPE/VARIETY/METAL	ABP FINE	AVERAGE FINE
☐ 1960	$2^1/_2$ Piastres, Aluminum-Bronze	—	.25
☐ 1960	5 Piastres, Aluminum-Bronze	—	.40
☐ 1960	10 Piastres, Aluminum-Bronze	—	.50
☐ 1958	25 Piastres, Silver	—	1.20
☐ 1958	50 Piastres, Silver	—	4.15
☐ 1959	50 Piastres, Anniversary of Founding of United Arab Republic, Silver	—	4.15

TURKEY

The first coins were used in the late 7th century B.C. and were made of electrum, an alloy of gold and silver. Pure gold and silver coins were produced in 500 B.C. Bronze and copper coins followed through several different periods in Turkey. The decimal system was set up in 1844. A new coinage was initiated in 1934. The currency today is the lira.

Turkey—Type Coinage

Key to Grading: Lettering

DATE	COIN TYPE/VARIETY/METAL	ABP FINE	AVERAGE FINE
☐ 1918–1919	2 Kurus, Mohammed VI, 1st Coinage, Silver	—	$120.00
☐ 1923–1924	100 Para, Republic, Aluminum-Bronze	—	2.25
☐ 1926	100 Para, Republic, Aluminum-Bronze	—	2.25
☐ 1918–1919	5 Kurus, Mohammed VI, 1st Coinage, Silver	—	150.00
☐ 1923–1924	5 Kurus, Republic, Aluminum-Bronze	—	2.25
☐ 1926	5 Kurus, Republic, Aluminum-Bronze	—	2.25
☐ 1918–1919	10 Kurus, Mohammed VI, 1st Coinage, Silver	—	260.00
☐ 1923–1924	10 Kurus, Republic, Aluminum-Bronze	—	4.15
☐ 1926	10 Kurus, Republic, Aluminum-Bronze	—	4.15
☐ 1918–1919	20 Kurus, Mohammed VI, 1st Coinage, Silver	—	100.00
☐ 1918–1919	25 Kurus, Mohammed VI, 1st Coinage, Gold	—	60.00
☐ 1924	25 Kurus, Republic, Nickel	—	4.15
☐ 1926–1928	25 Kurus, Republic, Nickel	—	4.15
☐ 1927–1928	25 Kurus, Republic, Monnaies de Luxe, Gold	—	100.00
☐ 1918–1922	50 Kurus, Mohammed VI, 1st Coinage, Gold	—	175.00
☐ 1926–1928	50 Kurus, Republic, Gold	—	80.00
☐ 1927–1928	50 Kurus, Republic, Monnaies de Luxe, Gold	—	90.00
☐ 1918–1919	100 Kurus, Mohammed VI, 1st Coinage, Gold	—	175.00
☐ 1926–1929	100 Kurus, Republic, Gold	—	175.00
☐ 1927–1928	100 Kurus, Republic, Monnaies de Luxe, Gold	—	140.00
☐ 1918	250 Kurus, Mohammed VI, 1st Coinage, Gold	—	2800.00
☐ 1926–1928	250 Kurus, Republic, Gold	—	350.00
☐ 1927–1928	250 Kurus, Republic, Monnaies de Luxe, Gold	—	BV
☐ 1918–1920	500 Kurus, Mohammed VI, 1st Coinage, Gold	—	1250.00
☐ 1926–1929	500 Kurus, Republic, Gold	—	BV
☐ 1927–1928	500 Kurus, Republic, Monnaies de Luxe, Gold	—	BV

Turkey—Western Date Coinage

DATE	COIN TYPE/VARIETY/METAL	ABP FINE	AVERAGE FINE
☐ 1940–1942	10 Para, Aluminum-Bronze		$2.20
☐ 1948	½ Kurus, Brass	$50.00	80.00

Key to Grading: Wheat

DATE	COIN TYPE/VARIETY/METAL	ABP FINE	AVERAGE FINE
☐ 1935–1937	1 Kurus, President Ataturk, Cupro-Nickel	1.20	2.00
☐ 1938–1944	1 Kurus, President Inonu, Cupro-Nickel	—	.55
☐ 1947–1951	1 Kurus, Brass	—	.32
☐ 1961–1963	1 Kurus, Bronze	—	.32
☐ 1963–1974	1 Kurus, Bronze	—	.32
☐ 1975–1977	1 Kurus, Aluminium	—	.32
☐ 1948–1951	2½ Kurus, Brass	—	.55

Key to Grading: Wreath

DATE	COIN TYPE/VARIETY/METAL	ABP FINE	AVERAGE FINE
☐ 1935–1943	5 Kurus, President Ataturk, Cupro-Nickel	—	.75
☐ 1949–1957	5 Kurus, Brass	—	.32
☐ 1958–1968	5 Kurus, Bronze	—	.28
☐ 1969–1974	5 Kurus, Bronze	—	.32
☐ 1975–1977	5 Kurus, Aluminium	—	.28

Key to Grading: Wreath

DATE	COIN TYPE/VARIETY/METAL	ABP FINE	AVERAGE FINE
☐ 1935–1940	10 Kurus, President Ataturk, Cupro-Nickel	—	2.00
☐ 1949–1956	10 Kurus, Brass	—	.38
☐ 1958–1968	10 Kurus, Bronze	—	.25
☐ 1969–1974	10 Kurus, Bronze	—	.38
☐ 1975–1980	10 Kurus, Aluminium	—	.25

Key to Grading: Wreath

DATE	COIN TYPE/VARIETY/METAL	ABP FINE	AVERAGE FINE
☐ 1935–1937	25 Kurus, President Ataturk, Silver	—	$4.15
☐ 1943	25 Kurus, President Ataturk, Gold Bullion Issue	—	BV
☐ 1943–1949	25 Kurus, President Inonu, Gold	—	BV
☐ 1944–1946	25 Kurus Nickel-Brass	—	.65
☐ 1948–1956	25 Kurus, Brass	—	.45
☐ 1935–1937	50 Kurus, President Ataturk, Silver	—	7.00
☐ 1943–1951	50 Kurus, President Inonu, Gold	—	120.00
☐ 1943	50 Kurus, President Ataturk, Gold	—	150.00
☐ 1947–1948	50 Kurus, Silver	—	4.00
☐ 1934	100 Kurus, President Ataturk, Silver	—	40.00
☐ 1937–1939	1 Lira, President Ataturk, Silver	—	25.00
☐ 1940–1941	1 Lira, President Inonu, Silver	—	15.00
☐ 1947–1948	1 Lira, Silver	—	5.00
☐ 1943–1949	100 Kurus, President Inonu, Gold	—	175.00
☐ 1943–1980	100 Kurus, President Ataturk, Gold	—	165.00
☐ 1943–1980	250 Kurus, President Ataturk, Gold	—	275.00
☐ 1943–1947	250 Kurus, President Inonu, Gold	—	375.00
☐ 1943	500 Kurus, President Ataturk, Gold	—	640.00
☐ 1943–1948	500 Kurus, President Inonu, Gold	—	640.00

UNITED KINGDOM

Britain's first coins in the 1st century B.C. were potin pieces, a combination of tin and bronze, generally called staters. In 55–54 B.C. gold coins were being struck, followed by silver and bronze. In the late 6th century the gold thrymasas or shillings were reduced and replaced by silver pennies, or sceattas. By the 1200s, half pennies, farthings, and groats were produced, and in 1344 the florin, then the noble. The pound, angel, and sovereign existed in the 1500s, then the farthing and guinea in the 1600s. In 1971, the system of pounds, shillings, and pence was abandoned for the decimal system.

THE MODERN ROYAL MINT

Courtesy of the Royal Mint

Today the Royal Mint has become both a business and a Government Department. Since 1975 it has operated as a Government Trading Fund, giving it a degree of commercial freedom but at the same time requiring that income should not only balance expenditure but that there should be an additional return on the capital employed. The Deputy Master, who remains a civil servant like the one thousand or so other members of the staff, presides over a board of directors and acts as chief executive. After ten years under the new system, cumulative sales have exceeded £600 million and the Mint has operated profitably in each of the ten years, achieving an average return on capital which compares favourably with the private sector.

Acting under contract with the Treasury, the Mint continues to be responsible for the production and issue of the United Kingdom coinage. In recent years it has had to cope with the introduction of two new coins, the 20 pence and the pound; the 1/2 penny, on the other hand, has been demonotised and withdrawn, and the Mint is constantly exploring with the help of outside experts the ways in which the coinage might develop in the future. Commemorative coins have become rather more frequent, with particularly successful crown pieces being issued in 1977 for the Queen's Silver Jubilee and in 1981 for the wedding of HRH The Prince of Wales. In 1986 a special two-pound piece was issued for the Commonwealth Games, the first time that a sporting occasion had been commemorated on the United Kingdom coinage. All new designs continue to be submitted to the Royal Mint Advisory Committee which, under the Presidency of HRH The Prince Philip since 1952, now normally meets at Buckingham Palace.

The striking of overseas coins has remained a large and successful feature of Mint output, reflecting a deservedly high reputation for quality and delivery in a business which has become more and more competitive. In most years well over half of total production is exported and in the financial year 1984–85, for instance, the Mint struck coins for no fewer than 67 countries, ranging from Ascension Island to Zambia. Sales staff based in the London office make regular trips overseas, and the Mint cooperates in a consortium with two private mints in Birmingham and the Currency Division of the De La

Rue Company to ensure that as many orders as possible are won for the United Kingdom. As part of its service to overseas customers, the Mint also operates with De Lá Rue a joint company, Royal Mint Services Limited, to provide advice and technical assistance to foreign mints. Results have been such that since the Mint moved to Llantrisant it has twice won the Queen's Award for Export Achievement, first in 1973 and then again in 1977.

An increasingly important aspect of Mint activity has been the sale of proof and uncirculated coins to collectors. Following the outstanding success of the sets of the last £sd coins of 1970 and of the first decimal coins of 1971, proof sets of United Kingdom coins have been struck every year. An expanding range of proof and uncirculated United Kingdom and overseas coins, in gold and silver as well as base metal, is now available by direct mail order from Llantrisant. The regular issue of colourful bulletins and brochures has been a new departure and the Mint has become a frequent exhibitor at shows and conventions, particularly in North America, which has proved a highly receptive market for collectors' coins.

More traditional activities, such as the making of medals and seals, have continued. As at Tower Hill, the production of medals still calls for the hand skills of craftsmen such as silversmiths, but like the rest of the Mint the Medal Department is not immune from pressure. In 1982, for instance, it responded with speed and success to the urgent requirement for medals to be awarded to those taking part in the campaign in the South Atlantic. As well as the normal range of military and civilian decorations, it produces a large variety of prize and commemorative medals for learned societies and private companies. Overseas orders are also received and the Medal Department accordingly makes a contribution to the Mint's export trade.

The modern Royal Mint at Llantrisant houses some of the most advanced coining machinery in the world and it has a larger capacity than any other mint in Western Europe. It is a mint in which the microprocessor and computer are increasingly prominent, yet at the same time there remains a vital role for the inherited skills and craftsmanship which have been built up during an unbroken history of more than 100 years. Clearly it is more than the thread of history which links the present Royal Mint to its Anglo-Saxon predecessor.

MINTING PROCESSES AT LLANTRISANT

The first stage in the coining process is the melting of the constituent metals, usually copper, nickel, zinc, or tin, in the appropriate proportions for the alloy required. At Tower Hill this was essentially a small-scale affair, with the molten metal being poured into vertical moulds, but the new mint has a continuous casting unit in operation twenty-four hours a day. By this system, virgin metals and process scrap are melted in primary electric furnaces and, when examination of a sample by X-ray fluorescence spectrometry has confirmed that the alloy is correct, the molten metal is transferred to holding furnaces. From the holding furnace it is drawn horizontally and continuously in the form of a strip about 200 millimetres wide and 15 millimetres thick, with cutting equipment built into the casting line dividing the strip into manageable 10 metre lengths weighing some 200 kilograms each.

A tandem rolling mill begins the process of reducing the metal to coin thickness. If, as with nickel-brass, intermediate annealing or softening is necessary, the strip is passed slowly through a furnace at a temperature of about 650°C. During the rolling process, for ease of handling, five of the cast lengths are welded together to create a large coil weighing about one tonne. A finishing mill then completes the task, its rolls reversible so that the coil of strip can pass backward and forward until it is reduced to the thickness required. From the finished coils blank discs are punched out in large presses at rates of up to 14,000 blanks a minute and collected in drums. The scrap metal, known for centuries as scissel, is passed back to the furnace for remelting.

The drums of blanks are then transferred from the Melting, Rolling, and Blanking Unit to the Annealing and Pickling Block. Here they are fed from large hoppers into gas-fired annealing furnaces where they are softened by being heated to high temperature, 850°C in the case of cupro-nickel and 750°C for bronze. After cooling they are passed to automatic pickling barrels where stains are removed by a solution of sulphuric acid and, after a final washing in tartaric acid, they are rinsed in water and dried by hot air. Most blanks then go to the marking machines, where they are rolled under pressure down a narrow groove to force the metal inwards in order to thicken the edge of the blank. This then makes it easier to give the coin a raised rim to protect it from wear and to enable coins to be stacked in piles.

The final process is the stamping on the blanks of the obverse and reverse designs and, when required, the milling on the edge. These operations are carried out simultaneously in a coining press, into which the blanks are fed by hopper. With most presses the blank is automatically placed on top of the lower die and is held in position by a restraining collar, which will be plain or milled depending on the type of edge required. The upper die is then squeezed down onto the blank with a force of up to 100 or more tonnes, so that the blank receives the impression of both dies while at the same time the metal is forced outward to take up the shape and pattern of the collar. The rate of striking depends on factors such as the size and design of the coins but with the sophisticated engineering of modern presses 400 coins can often be struck in a minute. A new generation of presses is likely to be faster still, achieving rates of up to 700 coins a minute.

After striking, the coins are automatically ejected from the press and fall into a container for inspection. A statistical sampling technique is used to ensure a rigorous quality control and after passing inspection the coins are counted into bags and check-weighed, the first task on which a robot has been used in the Mint. The bags are then conveyed to a secure area to await dispatch, either overseas or by the road to cash centers in the United Kingdom. Samples of all United Kingdom coins except bronze are taken for submission to the Trial of the Pyx which continues, as it has done for more than seven centuries, to provide an independent check on the accuracy of the coins struck by the Royal Mint.

A separate proof coin section is responsible for the special coins which are struck for sale to collectors. Since the seventeenth century proof coins have represented the perfection of the minter's art, and it is the combination of traditional skills and modern technology which has enabled Royal Mint proofs to reach their current level of excellence. The dies are given a matte finish and then a craftsman, using diamond paste, carefully polishes parts of the surface to produce a pleasing contrast between the frosted features of the design and the mirror background of the field. The blanks, too, are specially polished, either by burnishing or buffing, before being struck in a dust-free atmosphere.

Proofs are struck one at a time on a coining press and receive more than one blow from the dies to ensure that every detail of the designs is faithfully reproduced. The dies are kept clean and are replaced immediately if they show any sign of deterioration. After striking, each coin is carefully removed from the press to prevent damage and once it has satisfied trained inspectors it soon finds its way into the attractive packaging which is a feature of these special issues from the Mint.

DIE-MAKING AT LLANTRISANT

Modern die-making has been transformed by the introduction of the reducing machine. The traditional method whereby engravers cut a matrix or punch by hand, a painstaking process which might easily take three or four weeks, has now been largely superseded by the machine, which produces a master punch in relief from an electrotype copy of an artist's plaster model. The first of these machines to be used in the Mint was acquired by Benedetto Pistrucci in 1819 and a second was officially ordered for William Wyon in 1824; but it was probably not until the turn of the century, when machines were purchased from Janvier of Paris, that the Mint began to make full use of the reducing machine.

The plaster model, prepared either by a private artist or by a member of the Mint's small but highly skilled Engraving Department, is usually between six and ten inches in diameter.

Stages in die-making: the artist at work on his sketch; the preparation of a plaster model; the growing of the electrotype; and an engraver perfecting the steel matrix.

A silicon rubber mould is taken from the model and after one day's curing to make it pliable and flexible the mould is made electrically conductive to enable it to be plated with nickel. After about two hours it is transferred to a copper-plating bath, where it is left for three days to allow a sufficiently thick deposit of copper to back up the nickel on the mould. It is this nickel-faced copper electrotype which is then mounted on the reducing machine.

The machine is essentially a three-dimensional pantograph, so simple in its operation that the Mint craftsmen are still happiest with the old Janvier machines which were transferred from Tower Hill. The details of the electrotype, set firmly in wax and revolving slowly at one end of the machine, are scanned by a tracer at the free end of a rigid bar. The movements of the tracer as it follows the contours of the electrotype are communicated by the bar in reduced amplitude to a rotating cutter at the other end. The cutter, as it moves in and out, accordingly reproduces the details of the design at coin scale onto a block of steel to form a master punch with features in relief as on a coin. A first, or rough, cut takes a day, to be followed by a second cut which takes another day.

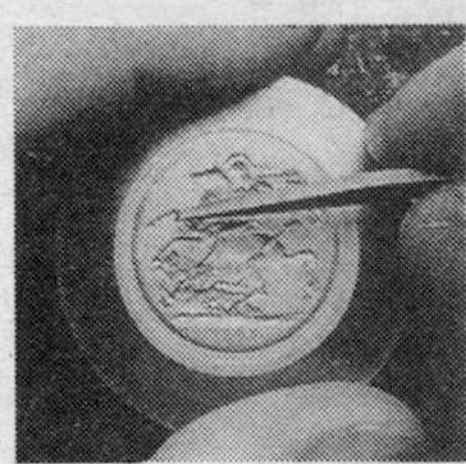

Above, left. An engraver ensures that there are no flaws or blemishes on the matrix.

Above, right. One of the Janvier reducing machines at work.

Minute blemishes and flaws are removed from the reduction punch by hand. It is then hardened so that it can be placed in a hydraulic press and its design transferred under pressure to a piece of soft steel. On this new tool, called a matrix, the design is incuse and it is at this stage that the engraver is able to add by hand the beads, the figures of the date, or any other feature not included on the original model. Once work on the matrix has been completed, it is hardened and then placed in a hydraulic press to produce the working punch. This, like the reduction punch, is in relief, and after turning and shaping it is returned to the engravers for final adjustment and cleaning. It is from this punch that working dies, all absolutely identical, are made for the coining presses.

To protect their surface and prolong their life the dies are chrome plated. Even so the life of an individual die remains a little unpredictable, though most now comfortably exceed 200,000 coins.

United Kingdom—Type Coinage

Key to Grading: Bust

DATE	COIN TYPE/VARIETY/METAL	ABP FINE	AVERAGE FINE
□ 1839–1856	½ Farthing, Victoria, Young Portrait, Copper	$4.25	$7.50
□ 1838–1860	1 Farthing, Victoria, Young Portrait, Copper	4.25	7.50

Key to Grading: Bust

DATE	COIN TYPE/VARIETY/METAL	ABP FINE	AVERAGE FINE
□ 1860–1895	1 Farthing, Victoria, Young Portrait, Bronze	2.00	4.00
□ 1895–1901	1 Farthing, Victoria, Aged Portrait, Bronze	—	2.50
□ 1902–1910	1 Farthing, Edward VII, Bronze	—	2.50
□ 1911–1936	1 Farthing, George V, Bronze	—	2.00

DATE	COIN TYPE/VARIETY/METAL	ABP FINE	AVERAGE FINE
☐ 1937–1948	1 Farthing, George VI, Bronze	—	$ .40
☐ 1949–1952	1 Farthing, George VI, 2nd Coinage, Bronze	—	.45
☐ 1953	1 Farthing, Elizabeth II, Bronze	—	.25
☐ 1954–1956	1 Farthing, Elizabeth II, 2nd Coinage, Bronze	—	.45
☐ 1838–1859	1/2 Penny, Victoria, Young Portrait, Copper	—	4.15

Key to Grading: Bust

DATE	COIN TYPE/VARIETY/METAL	ABP FINE	AVERAGE FINE
☐ 1860–1894	1/2 Penny, Victoria, Young Portrait, Bronze	—	4.00
☐ 1895–1901	1/2 Penny, Victoria, Aged Portrait, Bronze	—	2.20
☐ 1902–1910	1/2 Penny, Edward VII, Bronze	—	2.20
☐ 1911–1927	1/2 Penny, George V, Bronze	—	.60
☐ 1928–1936	1/2 Penny, George V, Bronze	—	.38
☐ 1937–1948	1/2 Penny, George VI, Bronze	—	.38
☐ 1949–1952	1/2 Penny, George VI, 2nd Coinage, Bronze	—	.38
☐ 1953	1/2 Penny, Elizabeth II, Bronze	—	.38
☐ 1954–1967	1/2 Penny, Elizabeth II, 2nd Coinage, Bronze	—	.38
☐ 1902–1910	1 Penny, Edward VII, Bronze	—	2.00

Key to Grading: Bust

DATE	COIN TYPE/VARIETY/METAL	ABP FINE	AVERAGE FINE
☐ 1911–1927	1 Penny, George V, Bronze	—	.90

DATE	COIN TYPE/VARIETY/METAL	ABP FINE	AVERAGE FINE
☐ 1928–1936	1 Penny, George V, Bronze	—	$ .45
☐ 1937–1948	1 Penny, George VI, Bronze	—	.45
☐ 1949–1951	1 Penny, George VI, 2nd Coinage, Bronze	—	4.15
☐ 1953	1 Penny, Elizabeth II, Bronze	—	.80
☐ 1954–1970	1 Penny, Elizabeth II, 2nd Coinage, Bronze	—	.45
☐ 1841–1860	1 Penny, Victoria, Young Portrait, Copper	$4.00	6.00
☐ 1860–1894	1 Penny, Victoria, Young Portrait, Bronze	—	5.00
☐ 1895–1901	1 Penny, Victoria, Aged Portrait, Bronze	—	4.00
☐ 1838–1887	3 Pence, Victoria, Young Portrait, Silver	—	5.25
☐ 1887–1893	3 Pence, Victoria, Golden Jubilee, Silver	—	5.25
☐ 1893–1901	3 Pence, Victoria, Aged Portrait, Silver	—	2.20

Key to Grading: Bust

DATE	COIN TYPE/VARIETY/METAL	ABP FINE	AVERAGE FINE
☐ 1902–1910	3 Pence, Edward VII, Silver	—	2.20
☐ 1911–1926	3 Pence, George V, Silver	—	.80
☐ 1927–1936	3 Pence, George V, Silver	—	.55
☐ 1937–1945	3 Pence, George VI, Silver	—	2.20
☐ 1937–1948	3 Pence, George VI, Nickel-Brass	—	.65
☐ 1949–1952	3 Pence, George VI, 2nd Coinage, Nickel-Brass	—	.80
☐ 1953	3 Pence, Elizabeth II, Nickel-Brass	—	.40
☐ 1954–1970	3 Pence, Elizabeth II, 2nd Coinage, Nickel-Brass	—	.40

Key to Grading: Bust

DATE	COIN TYPE/VARIETY/METAL	ABP FINE	AVERAGE FINE
☐ 1838–1862	4 Pence, Victoria, Young Portrait, Silver	—	6.25
☐ 1838–1887	6 Pence, Victoria, Young Portrait, Silver	—	7.00
☐ 1887	6 Pence, Victoria, Golden Jubilee, Silver	—	4.15

DATE	COIN TYPE/VARIETY/METAL	ABP FINE	AVERAGE FINE

Key to Grading: Bust

DATE	COIN TYPE/VARIETY/METAL	ABP FINE	AVERAGE FINE
☐ 1887–1893	6 Pence, Victoria, Golden Jubilee, Silver	—	$4.25
☐ 1893–1901	6 Pence, Victoria, Aged Portrait, Silver	—	4.25
☐ 1902–1910	6 Pence, Edward VII, Silver	—	4.25
☐ 1911–1927	6 Pence, George V, Silver	—	2.00
☐ 1927–1936	6 Pence, George V, Silver	—	.80
☐ 1937–1946	6 Pence, George VI, Silver	—	.45
☐ 1947–1948	6 Pence, George VI, Cupro-Nickel	—	.38
☐ 1949–1952	6 Pence, George VI, 2nd Coinage, Cupro-Nickel	—	.38
☐ 1953	6 Pence, Elizabeth II, Cupro-Nickel	—	.38

Key to Grading: Bust

DATE	COIN TYPE/VARIETY/METAL	ABP FINE	AVERAGE FINE
☐ 1954–1970	6 Pence, Elizabeth II, 2nd Coinage, Cupro-Nickel	—	.38
☐ 1838–1887	Shilling, Victoria, Young Portrait, Silver	—	6.00

Key to Grading: Bust

DATE	COIN TYPE/VARIETY/METAL	ABP FINE	AVERAGE FINE
☐ 1887–1892	Shilling, Victoria, Golden Jubilee, Silver	—	5.25
☐ 1893–1901	Shilling, Victoria, Aged Portrait, Silver	—	5.25
☐ 1902–1910	Shilling, Edward VII, Silver	—	6.00
☐ 1911–1927	Shilling, George V, Silver	—	4.15
☐ 1927–1936	Shilling, George V, Silver	—	2.20

DATE	COIN TYPE/VARIETY/METAL	ABP FINE	AVERAGE FINE
☐ 1937–1946	Shilling, George VI, Silver	—	$2.20
☐ 1947–1948	Shilling, George VI, Cupro-Nickel	—	.32
☐ 1949–1951	Shilling, George VI, 2nd Coinage, Cupro-Nickel	—	.32
☐ 1953	1 Shilling, Elizabeth II, Cupro-Nickel	—	.32
☐ 1954–1970	1 Shilling, Elizabeth II, 2nd Coinage, Cupro-Nickel	—	.32
☐ 1849	1 Florin, Victoria, Gothic, Silver	—	18.00
☐ 1851–1887	1 Florin, Victoria, Gothic, Silver	—	15.00
☐ 1887–1892	1 Florin, Victoria, Golden Jubilee, Silver	—	7.00

Key to Grading: Bust

DATE	COIN TYPE/VARIETY/METAL	ABP FINE	AVERAGE FINE
☐ 1893–1901	1 Florin, Victoria, Aged Portrait, Silver	—	5.25
☐ 1902–1910	1 Florin, Edward VII, Silver	—	12.00
☐ 1911–1926	1 Florin, George V, Silver	—	5.00
☐ 1927–1936	1 Florin, George V, Silver	—	2.20
☐ 1937–1946	2 Shillings, George VI, Silver	—	2.20
☐ 1947–1948	2 Shillings, George VI, Cupro-Nickel	—	.38
☐ 1949–1951	2 Shillings, George VI, 2nd Coinage, Cupro-Nickel	—	.38
☐ 1953	2 Shillings, Elizabeth II, Cupro-Nickel	—	.38
☐ 1954–1970	2 Shillings, Elizabeth II, 2nd Coinage, Cupro-Nickel	—	.45
☐ 1839–1887	1/2 Crown, Victoria, Young Portrait, Silver	—	15.00
☐ 1887–1892	1/2 Crown, Victoria, Golden Jubilee, Silver	—	12.00

Key to Grading: Bust

DATE	COIN TYPE/VARIETY/METAL	ABP FINE	AVERAGE FINE
☐ 1893–1901	1/2 Crown, Victoria, Aged Portrait, Silver	—	7.25
☐ 1902–1910	1/2 Crown, Edward VII, Silver	—	16.00
☐ 1911–1927	1/2 Crown, George V, Silver	—	6.25
☐ 1927–1936	1/2 Crown, George V, Silver	—	4.15

DATE	COIN TYPE/VARIETY/METAL	ABP FINE	AVERAGE FINE
☐ 1937–1946	1/2 Crown, George VI, Silver	—	$1.75
☐ 1947–1948	1/2 Crown, George VI, Cupro-Nickel	—	.42
☐ 1949–1952	1/2 Crown, George VI, 2nd Coinage, Cupro-Nickel	—	.42
☐ 1953	1/2 Crown, Elizabeth II, Cupro-Nickel	—	.70
☐ 1954–1970	1/2 Crown, Elizabeth II, 2nd Coinage, Cupro-Nickel	—	.55
☐ 1887–1890	2 Florins, Victoria, Golden Jubilee, Silver	—	8.25

Key to Grading: Bust

DATE	COIN TYPE/VARIETY/METAL	ABP FINE	AVERAGE FINE
☐ 1935	1 Crown, George V, Silver Jubilee, Silver	—	7.00
☐ 1839–1847	1 Crown, Victoria, Young Portrait, Silver	—	40.00
☐ 1847–1853	1 Crown, Victoria, Gothic, Silver	—	325.00
☐ 1887–1892	1 Crown, Victoria, Golden Jubilee, Silver	—	15.00
☐ 1893–1901	1 Crown, Victoria, Aged Portrait, Silver	—	25.00
☐ 1902	1 Crown, Edward VII, Silver	—	30.00
☐ 1927–1936	1 Crown, George V, Silver	—	80.00
☐ 1937	1 Crown, George VI, Silver	—	15.00
☐ 1951	5 Shillings, George VI, 2nd Coinage, Cupro-Nickel Proof	—	32.00
☐ 1953	5 Shillings, Elizabeth II, Cupro-Nickel	—	2.00
☐ 1838–1885	1/2 Sovereign, Victoria, Young Portrait, Gold	—	80.00
☐ 1887–1893	1/2 Sovereign, Victoria, Golden Jubilee, Gold	—	80.00
☐ 1893–1901	1/2 Sovereign, Victoria, Aged Portrait, Gold	—	80.00
☐ 1902–1910	1/2 Sovereign, Edward VII, Gold	—	80.00
☐ 1911–1915	1/2 Sovereign, George V, Gold	—	85.00
☐ 1937	1/2 Sovereign, George VI, Gold	Proof	400.00
☐ 1838–1874	1 Sovereign, Victoria, Young Portrait, Gold	—	175.00
☐ 1871–1885	1 Sovereign, Victoria, Young Portrait, Gold	—	175.00
☐ 1887–1892	1 Sovereign, Victoria, Golden Jubilee, Gold	—	175.00
☐ 1893–1901	1 Sovereign, Victoria, Aged Portrait, Gold	—	175.00
☐ 1902–1910	1 Sovereign, Edward VII, Gold	—	225.00
☐ 1911–1925	1 Sovereign, George V, Gold	—	225.00
☐ 1937	1 Sovereign, George VI, Gold	—	1500.00 Proof
☐ 1957–1968	1 Sovereign, Elizabeth II, 2nd Coinage, Gold	—	200.00

DATE	COIN TYPE/VARIETY/METAL	ABP FINE	AVERAGE FINE
☐ 1887	2 Pounds, Victoria, Golden Jubilee, Gold	—	$400.00
☐ 1893	2 Pounds, Victoria, Aged Portrait, Gold	—	450.00
☐ 1902	2 Pounds, Edward VII, Gold	—	400.00
☐ 1911	2 Pounds, George V, Gold	—	2500.00 Proof
☐ 1937	2 Pounds, George VI, Gold Proof	—	1400.00
☐ 1887	5 Pounds, Victoria, Golden Jubilee, Gold	—	800.00
☐ 1893	5 Pounds, Victoria, Aged Portrait, Gold	—	900.00
☐ 1902	5 Pounds, Edward VII, Gold	—	950.00
☐ 1911	5 Pounds, George V, Gold	—	3500.00 Proof
☐ 1937	5 Pounds, George VI, Gold Proof	—	1850.00

United Kingdom—Decimal and Bullion Coinage

Key to Grading: Bust

☐ 1971–1981	1/2 New Penny, Elizabeth II, Bronze	—	.45
☐ 1981–1984	1/2 Penny, Elizabeth II, Bronze	—	.25

Key to Grading: Bust

☐ 1971–1981	1 New Penny, Elizabeth II, Bronze	—	.45
☐ 1981–1992	1 Penny, Elizabeth II, Bronze	—	.25

Key to Grading: Bust

☐ 1993 to Date	1 Penny, Elizabeth II, Copper-plated Steel	—	.45

Key to Grading: Bust

DATE	COIN TYPE/VARIETY/METAL	ABP FINE	AVERAGE FINE
☐ 1971–1981	2 New Pence, Elizabeth II, Bronze	—	$ .28
☐ 1982–1984	2 Pence, Elizabeth II, Bronze	—	.40

Key to Grading: Bust

DATE	COIN TYPE/VARIETY/METAL	ABP FINE	AVERAGE FINE
☐ 1993 to Date	2 Pence, Elizabeth II, Copper-plated Steel	—	.38

Key to Grading: Bust

DATE	COIN TYPE/VARIETY/METAL	ABP FINE	AVERAGE FINE
☐ 1968–1981	5 New Pence, Elizabeth II, Cupro-Nickel	—	.38
☐ 1990 to Date	5 Pence, Elizabeth II, Smaller Planchet, Cupro-Nickel	—	.38
☐ 1982–1990	5 Pence, Elizabeth II, Cupro-Nickel	—	.25
☐ 1990	5 Pence, Elizabeth II, Silver	—	.32

Key to Grading: Bust

DATE	COIN TYPE/VARIETY/METAL	ABP FINE	AVERAGE FINE
☐ 1968–1981	10 New Pence, Elizabeth II, Cupro-Nickel	—	$ .45
☐ 1982–1992	10 Pence, Elizabeth II, Cupro-Nickel	—	.28
☐ 1990–1993	10 Pence, Elizabeth II, Smaller Planchet, Cupro-Nickel	—	.45
☐ 1990	10 Pence, Elizabeth II, Smaller Planchet, Silver	—	.28
☐ 1992 to Date	10 Pence, Elizabeth II, Silver	—	.45

Key to Grading: Bust

DATE	COIN TYPE/VARIETY/METAL	ABP FINE	AVERAGE FINE
☐ 1982 to Date	20 Pence, Elizabeth II, Cupro-Nickel	—	.55
☐ 1972	25 New Pence, Elizabeth II, Royal Silver Wedding Anniversary, Silver	—	32.00 Proof
☐ 1972	25 New Pence, Elizabeth II, Royal Silver Wedding Anniversary, Cupro-Nickel	—	.65
☐ 1977	25 New Pence, Elizabeth II, Silver Jubilee, Cupro-Nickel	—	.80

Key to Grading: Bust

DATE	COIN TYPE/VARIETY/METAL	ABP FINE	AVERAGE FINE
☐ 1977	25 New Pence, Elizabeth II, Silver Jubilee, Silver	—	32.00 Proof
☐ 1980	25 New Pence, Elizabeth II, Queen Mother—80th Birthday, Cupro-Nickel	—	.75
☐ 1980	25 New Pence, Elizabeth II, Queen Mother—80th Birthday, Silver	—	1.25
☐ 1981	1 Crown, Elizabeth II, Wedding of Prince Charles & Lady Diana, Silver	—	1.25
☐ 1981	1 Crown, Elizabeth II, Wedding of Prince Charles & Lady Diana, Cupro-Nickel	—	1.25
☐ 1981	50 New Pence, Elizabeth II, Cupro-Nickel	—	1.25
☐ 1982 to Date	50 Pence, Elizabeth II, Cupro-Nickel	—	2.20

DATE	COIN TYPE/VARIETY/METAL	ABP FINE	AVERAGE FINE
☐ 1973	50 Pence, Elizabeth II, European Economic Community Entry, Cupro-Nickel	—	$2.20
☐ 1992	50 Pence, Elizabeth II, European Council of Ministers—British Presidency, Cupro-Nickel	—	2.20
☐ 1992	50 Pence, Elizabeth II, European Council of Ministers—British Presidency, Silver	—	80.00 Proof
☐ 1992	50 Pence, Elizabeth II, European Council of Ministers—British Presidency, Gold	—	1000.00 Proof
☐ 1983	1 Pound, Elizabeth II, Silver	—	75.00 Proof

Key to Grading: Bust

DATE	COIN TYPE/VARIETY/METAL	ABP FINE	AVERAGE FINE
☐ 1983	1 Pound, Elizabeth II, Nickel-Brass	—	4.15
☐ 1984	1 Pound, Elizabeth II, Scottish Thistle, Silver	—	42.00
☐ 1984	1 Pound, Elizabeth II, Scottish Thistle, Nickel-Brass	—	4.15
☐ 1985	1 Pound, Elizabeth II, Welsh Leek, Nickel-Brass	—	4.15
☐ 1985	1 Pound, Elizabeth II, Welsh Leek, Silver	—	40.00
☐ 1985	1 Pound, Elizabeth II, Blooming Flax, Silver	—	48.00 Proof
☐ 1986	1 Pound, Elizabeth II, Blooming Flax, Nickel-Brass	—	4.15
☐ 1987	1 Pound, Elizabeth II, Oak Tree, Nickel-Brass	—	4.15
☐ 1987	1 Pound, Elizabeth II, Oak Tree, Silver	—	40.00
☐ 1988	1 Pound, Elizabeth II, Silver	—	50.00
☐ 1988	1 Pound, Elizabeth II, Copper-Zinc-Nickel	—	4.15
☐ 1989	1 Pound, Elizabeth II, Scottish Flora, Silver	—	45.00
☐ 1989	1 Pound, Elizabeth II, Scottish Flora, Nickel-Brass	—	4.15
☐ 1990	1 Pound, Elizabeth II, Welsh Leek, Nickel-Brass	—	4.15

DATE	COIN TYPE/VARIETY/METAL	ABP FINE	AVERAGE FINE
☐ 1990	1 Pound, Elizabeth II, Welsh Leek, Silver	—	$45.00
☐ 1993	1 Pound, Elizabeth II, Scottish Flora, Nickel-Brass	—	4.25
☐ 1993	1 Pound, Elizabeth II, Scottish Flora, Silver	—	50.00 Proof
☐ 1986	2 Pounds, Elizabeth II, Commonwealth Games, Silver	—	20.00 Proof
☐ 1986	2 Pounds, Elizabeth II, Commonwealth Games, Gold	—	300.00 Proof
☐ 1986	2 Pounds, Elizabeth II, Commonwealth Games, Nickel-Brass	$4.00	6.25
☐ 1989	2 Pounds, Elizabeth II, Bill of Rights Tercentenary, Nickel-Brass	4.00	6.25
☐ 1989	2 Pounds, Elizabeth II, Bill of Rights Tercentenary, Silver	—	36.00
☐ 1989	2 Pounds, Elizabeth II, Claim of Right Tercentenary, Silver	—	36.00
☐ 1989	2 Pounds, Elizabeth II, Claim of Right Tercentenary, Nickel-Brass	4.00	7.00
☐ 1990	5 Pounds, Elizabeth II, Queen Mother—90th Birthday, Silver	—	55.00
☐ 1990	5 Pounds, Elizabeth II, Queen Mother—90th Birthday, Gold	—	900.00
☐ 1990	5 Pounds, Elizabeth II, Queen Mother—90th Birthday, Cupro-Nickel	10.00	18.00
☐ 1993	5 Pounds, Elizabeth II, Reign—40th Anniversary, Cupro-Nickel	10.00	15.00
☐ 1987–1989	10 Pounds, Gold	—	175.00 Proof
☐ 1990 to Date	10 Pounds, Gold-Silver	—	125.00 Proof
☐ 1987–1989	25 Pounds, Gold	—	300.00 Proof
☐ 1990 to Date	25 Pounds, Gold-Silver	—	425.00 Proof
☐ 1987–1989	50 Pounds, Gold	—	400.00 Proof
☐ 1990 to Date	50 Pounds, Gold-Silver	—	650.00 Proof
☐ 1987–1989	100 Pounds, Gold	—	825.00 Proof
☐ 1990 to Date	100 Pounds, Gold-Silver	—	1400.00 Proof

USSR

USSR—Type Coinage

Key to Grading: Wreath

DATE	COIN TYPE/VARIETY/METAL	ABP FINE	AVERAGE FINE
□ 1921–1922	1 Ruble, 1st Coinage, Legend: PCOCP, Silver	—	$20.00
□ 1924–1925	1 Kopek, 2nd Coinage, Legend: CCCP, Bronze	—	16.00

Key to Grading: Wreath

DATE	COIN TYPE/VARIETY/METAL	ABP FINE	AVERAGE FINE
□ 1924	1 Ruble, 2nd Coinage, Legend: CCCP, Silver	—	10.00
□ 1925–1928	½ Kopek, 2nd Coinage, Legend: CCCP, Bronze	—	4.25
□ 1926–1935	1 Kopek, 3rd Coinage, Legend: CCCP, Aluminum-Bronze	—	.80
□ 1935–1936	1 Kopek, 4th Coinage, Legend: CCCP, Aluminum-Bronze	—	.80
□ 1937–1946	1 Kopek, 5th Coinage, Legend: CCCP, Aluminum-Bronze	—	.50
□ 1948–1956	1 Kopek, 6th Coinage, Legend: CCCP, Aluminum-Bronze	—	.80
□ 1957	1 Kopek, 7th Coinage, Legend: CCCP, Aluminum-Bronze	—	1.75

Key to Grading: Wreath

DATE	COIN TYPE/VARIETY/METAL	ABP FINE	AVERAGE FINE
☐ 1961–1991	1 Kopek, 8th Coinage, Legend: CCCP, Brass	—	$ .32
☐ 1924–1925	2 Kopeks, 2nd Coinage, Legend: CCCP, Bronze	—	14.00
☐ 1926–1935	2 Kopeks, 3rd Coinage, Legend: CCCP, Aluminum-Bronze	—	.65
☐ 1935–1936	2 Kopeks, 4th Coinage, Legend: CCCP, Aluminum-Bronze	—	.65
☐ 1937–1946	2 Kopeks, 5th Coinage, Legend: CCCP, Aluminum-Bronze	—	.65
☐ 1948–1956	2 Kopeks, 6th Coinage, Legend: CCCP, Aluminum-Bronze	—	.55
☐ 1957	2 Kopeks, 7th Coinage, Legend: CCCP, Aluminum-Bronze	—	.65

Key to Grading: Wreath

☐ 1961–1991	2 Kopeks, 8th Coinage, Legend: CCCP, Brass	—	.50
☐ 1924	3 Kopeks, 2nd Coinage, Legend: CCCP, Bronze	—	20.00
☐ 1926–1935	3 Kopeks, 3rd Coinage, Legend: CCCP, Aluminum-Bronze	—	.50
☐ 1935–1936	3 Kopeks, 4th Coinage, Legend: CCCP, Aluminum-Bronze	—	.50
☐ 1937–1946	3 Kopeks, 5th Coinage, Legend: CCCP, Aluminum-Bronze	—	.50
☐ 1948–1957	3 Kopeks, 6th Coinage, Legend: CCCP, Aluminum-Bronze	—	.35

DATE	COIN TYPE/VARIETY/METAL	ABP FINE	AVERAGE FINE
☐ 1957	3 Kopeks, 7th Coinage, Legend: CCCP, Aluminum-Bronze	—	$ .65

Key to Grading: Wreath

DATE	COIN TYPE/VARIETY/METAL	ABP FINE	AVERAGE FINE
☐ 1961–1990	3 Kopeks, 8th Coinage, Legend: CCCP, Brass	—	.45
☐ 1924	5 Kopeks, 2nd Coinage, Legend: CCCP, Bronze		32.00
☐ 1926–1935	5 Kopeks, 3rd Coinage, Legend: CCCP, Aluminum-Bronze	—	2.00
☐ 1935–1936	5 Kopeks, 4th Coinage, Legend: CCCP, Aluminum-Bronze	—	4.00
☐ 1937–1946	5 Kopeks, 5th Coinage, Legend: CCCP, Aluminum-Bronze	—	.80
☐ 1948–1956	5 Kopeks, 6th Coinage, Legend: CCCP, Aluminum-Bronze	—	.80
☐ 1957	5 Kopeks, 7th Coinage, Legend: CCCP, Aluminum-Bronze	—	2.20

Key to Grading: Wreath

DATE	COIN TYPE/VARIETY/METAL	ABP FINE	AVERAGE FINE
☐ 1961–1990	5 Kopeks, 8th Coinage, Legend: CCCP, Aluminum-Bronze	—	.45
☐ 1921–1923	10 Kopeks, 1st Coinage, Legend: PCOCP, Silver	—	4.00
☐ 1923	1 Chervonetz, 1st Coinage Legend: PCOCP, Gold	—	125.00
☐ 1924–1931	10 Kopeks, 2nd Coinage, Legend: CCCP, Silver	—	.75
☐ 1931–1934	10 Kopeks, 3rd Coinage, Legend: CCCP, Cupro-Nickel	—	.70

DATE	COIN TYPE/VARIETY/METAL	ABP FINE	AVERAGE FINE
☐ 1935–1936	10 Kopeks, 4th Coinage, Legend: CCCP, Cupro-Nickel	—	$ .45
☐ 1937–1946	10 Kopeks, 5th Coinage, Legend: CCCP, Cupro-Nickel	—	.80
☐ 1948–1956	10 Kopeks, 6th Coinage, Legend: CCCP, Cupro-Nickel	—	.80
☐ 1957	10 Kopeks, 7th Coinage, Legend: CCCP, Cupro-Nickel	—	.45

Key to Grading: Wreath

DATE	COIN TYPE/VARIETY/METAL	ABP FINE	AVERAGE FINE
☐ 1961–1991	10 Kopeks, 8th Coinage, Legend: CCCP, Cupro-Nickel-Zinc	—	.45
☐ 1975–1980	1 Chervonetz, 1st Coinage Legend: PCOCP, Gold	—	100.00
☐ 1921–1923	15 Kopeks, 1st Coinage, Legend: PCOCP, Silver	—	2.20
☐ 1924–1931	15 Kopeks, 2nd Coinage, Legend: CCCP, Silver	—	2.20
☐ 1931–1934	15 Kopeks, 3rd Coinage, Legend: CCCP, Cupro-Nickel	—	.80
☐ 1935–1936	15 Kopeks, 4th Coinage, Legend: CCCP, Cupro-Nickel	—	.80
☐ 1937–1946	15 Kopeks, 5th Coinage, Legend: CCCP, Cupro-Nickel	—	.65
☐ 1948–1956	15 Kopeks, 6th Coinage, Legend: CCCP, Cupro-Nickel	—	.65

DATE	COIN TYPE/VARIETY/METAL	ABP FINE	AVERAGE FINE
☐ 1957	15 Kopeks, 7th Coinage, Legend: CCCP, Cupro-Nickel	—	.38

Key to Grading: Wreath

DATE	COIN TYPE/VARIETY/METAL	ABP FINE	AVERAGE FINE
☐ 1961–1991	15 Kopeks, 8th Coinage, Legend: CCCP, Cupro-Nickel	—	$ .28
☐ 1921–1923	20 Kopeks, 1st Coinage, Legend: PCOCP, Silver	—	5.00
☐ 1924–1931	20 Kopeks, 2nd Coinage, Legend: CCCP, Silver	—	2.20
☐ 1931–1934	20 Kopeks, 3rd Coinage, Legend: CCCP, Cupro-Nickel	—	.65

Key to Grading: Wreath

DATE	COIN TYPE/VARIETY/METAL	ABP FINE	AVERAGE FINE
☐ 1935–1936	20 Kopeks, 4th Coinage, Legend: CCCP, Cupro-Nickel	—	.55
☐ 1937–1946	20 Kopeks, 5th Coinage, Legend: CCCP, Cupro-Nickel	—	.65
☐ 1948–1956	20 Kopeks, 6th Coinage, Legend: CCCP, Cupro-Nickel	—	.65
☐ 1957	20 Kopeks, 7th Coinage, Legend: CCCP, Cupro-Nickel	—	.65
☐ 1961–1991	20 Kopeks, 8th Coinage, Legend: CCCP, Cupro-Nickel-Zinc	—	.50
☐ 1921–1922	50 Kopeks, 1st Coinage, Legend: PCOCP, Silver	—	6.25
☐ 1961–1991	50 Kopeks, 8th Coinage, Legend: CCCP, Cupro-Nickel-Zinc	—	.50
☐ 1961–1991	Ruble, 8th Coinage, Legend: CCCP, Cupro-Nickel-Zinc	—	.65

VATICAN CITY

The Kingdom of Italy took over the last remaining part of the Papal States in 1870, and the Papacy ceased issuing coinage until 1929. The centesimi and 1 and 2 lire were base metal. The 5 and 10 lire were silver until 1947, when they were changed to aluminum. The gold 100 lire was changed to stainless steel in 1959. Decimal coins were first used in 1929. The currency today is the lira.

Vatican City—Trade Coinage

Key to Grading: Bust

DATE	COIN TYPE/VARIETY/METAL	ABP FINE	AVERAGE FINE
☐ 1929–1938	5 Centesimi, Pius XI, Bronze	—	$2.20
☐ 1933	5 Centesimi, Pius XI, Jubilee, Bronze	—	4.15
☐ 1939–1941	5 Centesimi, Pius XII, Bronze	—	2.20
☐ 1942–1946	5 Centesimi, Pius XII, Aluminum-Bronze	—	18.00

Key to Grading: Bust

DATE	COIN TYPE/VARIETY/METAL	ABP FINE	AVERAGE FINE
☐ 1929–1938	10 Centesimi, Pius XI, Bronze	—	2.20
☐ 1933–1934	10 Centesimi, Pius XI, Jubilee, Bronze	—	4.15
☐ 1939–1941	10 Centesimi, Pius XII, Bronze	—	2.20
☐ 1942–1946	10 Centesimi, Pius XII, Aluminum-Bronze	—	28.00

Key to Grading: Crest or Bust

DATE	COIN TYPE/VARIETY/METAL	ABP FINE	AVERAGE FINE
☐ 1929–1937	20 Centesimi, Pius XI, Nickel	—	$1.75
☐ 1933	20 Centesimi, Pius XI, Jubilee, Nickel	—	4.15
☐ 1939	20 Centesimi, Pius XII, Nickel	—	2.20
☐ 1940–1941	20 Centesimi, Pius XII, Stainless Steel	—	2.20
☐ 1942–1946	20 Centesimi, Pius XII, Stainless Steel	$22.00	34.00

Key to Grading: Crest or Bust

DATE	COIN TYPE/VARIETY/METAL	ABP FINE	AVERAGE FINE
☐ 1929–1937	50 Centesimi, Pius XI, Nickel	—	4.15
☐ 1933	50 Centesimi, Pius XI, Jubilee, Nickel	—	4.15
☐ 1939	50 Centesimi, Pius XII, Nickel	—	2.00
☐ 1940–1941	50 Centesimi, Pius XII, Stainless Steel	—	1.20
☐ 1942–1946	50 Centesimi, Pius XII, Stainless Steel	15.00	26.00
☐ 1929–1937	1 Lira, Pius XI, Nickel	—	1.20
☐ 1933	1 Lira, Pius XI, Jubilee, Nickel	—	4.15
☐ 1939	1 Lira, Pius XII, Nickel	—	2.20
☐ 1940–1941	1 Lira, Pius XII, Stainless Steel	—	4.15

Key to Grading: Crest or Bust

DATE	COIN TYPE/VARIETY/METAL	ABP FINE	AVERAGE FINE
☐ 1942–1946	1 Lira, Pius XII, Stainless Steel	12.00	24.00
☐ 1947–1949	1 Lira, Pius XII, Aluminum	—	2.20
☐ 1950	1 Lira, Pius XII, Holy Year—MCML, Aluminum	—	.80

DATE	COIN TYPE/VARIETY/METAL	ABP FINE	AVERAGE FINE
☐ 1951–1958	1 Lira, Pius XII, Aluminum	—	$ .38
☐ 1959–1962	1 Lira, John XXIII, Aluminum	—	.50
☐ 1962	1 Lira, John XXIII, Ecumenical Council, Aluminum	—	.65
☐ 1929–1937	2 Lire, Pius XI, Nickel	—	2.20
☐ 1933	2 Lire, Pius XI, Jubilee, Nickel	—	4.00
☐ 1939	2 Lire, Pius XII, Nickel	—	2.20

Key to Grading: Crest or Bust

DATE	COIN TYPE/VARIETY/METAL	ABP FINE	AVERAGE FINE
☐ 1940–1941	2 Lire, Pius XII, Stainless Steel	—	.70
☐ 1942–1946	2 Lire, Pius XII, Stainless Steel	—	22.00
☐ 1947–1949	2 Lire, Pius XII, Aluminum	—	2.50
☐ 1950	2 Lire, Pius XII, Holy Year—MCML, Aluminum	—	.80
☐ 1951–1958	2 Lire, Pius XII, Aluminum	—	.40
☐ 1959–1962	2 Lire, John XXIII, Aluminum	—	.90
☐ 1962	2 Lire, John XXIII, Ecumenical Council, Aluminum	—	.90
☐ 1929–1937	5 Lire, Pius XI, Silver	—	2.25
☐ 1933	5 Lire, Pius XI, Jubilee, Silver	—	4.15
☐ 1939	5 Lire, Sede Vacante, Jubilee, Silver	—	45.00

Key to Grading: Crest or Bust

DATE	COIN TYPE/VARIETY/METAL	ABP FINE	AVERAGE FINE
☐ 1939–1941	5 Lire, Pius XII, Silver	—	5.50
☐ 1942–1946	5 Lire, Pius XII, Silver	—	32.00
☐ 1947–1949	5 Lire, Pius XII, Aluminum	—	2.20
☐ 1950	5 Lire, Pius XII, Holy Year—MCML, Aluminum	—	4.15
☐ 1951–1958	5 Lire, Pius XII, Aluminum	—	.50
☐ 1959–1962	5 Lire, John XXIII, Aluminum	—	2.20

DATE	COIN TYPE/VARIETY/METAL	ABP FINE	AVERAGE FINE
☐ 1962	5 Lire, John XXIII, Ecumenical Council, Aluminum	—	$ .40
☐ 1929–1937	10 Lire, Pius XI, Silver	—	6.20
☐ 1933	10 Lire, Pius XI, Jubilee, Silver	—	6.20
☐ 1939	10 Lire, Sede Vacante, Jubilee, Silver	—	6.20
☐ 1939–1941	10 Lire, Pius XII, Silver	—	15.00
☐ 1942–1946	10 Lire, Pius XII, Silver	—	38.00
☐ 1947–1949	10 Lire, Pius XII, Aluminum	—	2.20
☐ 1950	10 Lire, Pius XII, Holy Year—MCML, Aluminum	—	2.20

Key to Grading: Crest or Bust

DATE	COIN TYPE/VARIETY/METAL	ABP FINE	AVERAGE FINE
☐ 1951–1958	10 Lire, Pius XII, Aluminum	—	.50
☐ 1959–1962	10 Lire, John XXIII, Aluminum	—	.80
☐ 1962	10 Lire, John XXIII, Ecumenical Council, Aluminum	—	.80
☐ 1957–1958	20 Lire, Pius XII, Aluminum-Bronze	—	.35
☐ 1959–1962	20 Lire, John XXIII, Aluminum-Bronze	—	.50
☐ 1962	20 Lire, John XXIII, Ecumenical Council, Aluminum-Bronze	—	.50
☐ 1955–1958	50 Lire, Pius XII, Stainless Steel	—	1.20
☐ 1959–1962	50 Lire, John XXIII, Stainless Steel	—	.75
☐ 1929–1937	100 Lire, Pius XI, Gold	—	135.00
☐ 1933	100 Lire, Pius XI, Jubilee, Gold	—	125.00
☐ 1939–1941	100 Lire, Pius XII, Gold	—	125.00

Key to Grading: Crest or Bust

DATE	COIN TYPE/VARIETY/METAL	ABP FINE	AVERAGE FINE
☐ 1942–1949	100 Lire, Pius XII, Gold	—	120.00
☐ 1950	100 Lire, Pius XII, Holy Year—MCML, Gold	—	120.00

DATE	COIN TYPE/VARIETY/METAL	ABP FINE	AVERAGE FINE
☐ 1951–1958	100 Lire, Pius XII, Gold	—	$125.00
☐ 1955–1958	100 Lire, Pius XII, Stainless Steel	—	.45
☐ 1959–1962	100 Lire, John XXIII, Stainless Steel	—	.45
☐ 1959	100 Lire, John XXIII, Gold	—	125.00
☐ 1962	100 Lire, John XXIII, Ecumenical Council, Stainless Steel	—	.45
☐ 1958	500 Lire, Sede Vacante, Silver	—	2.85

Key to Grading: Crest or Bust

DATE	COIN TYPE/VARIETY/METAL	ABP FINE	AVERAGE FINE
☐ 1958	500 Lire, Pius XII, Silver	—	4.00
☐ 1959–1962	500 Lire, John XXIII, Silver	—	4.25
☐ 1962	500 Lire, John XXIII, Ecumenical Council, Silver	—	4.25
☐ 1963	500 Lire, Sede Vacante, Silver	—	4.50

VENEZUELA

The first coins were used in 1802 and were mostly Spanish coins. Between 1808 and 1813, coins were issued in Maracaibo. In 1817, the copper real was issued, followed by the centavo, bolivares, and copper-clad steel centimos. The first decimal coins were used in 1843. The currency today is the bolivar.

Venezuela—Type Coinage

DATE	COIN TYPE/VARIETY/METAL	ABP FINE	AVERAGE FINE
☐ 1843–1852	1/4 Centavo, Liberty Head, Copper	$8.00	$14.00

Key to Grading: Bust

DATE	COIN TYPE/VARIETY/METAL	ABP FINE	AVERAGE FINE
☐ 1843–1852	1/2 Centavo, Liberty Head, Copper	8.00	14.00

Key to Grading: Bust

DATE	COIN TYPE/VARIETY/METAL	ABP FINE	AVERAGE FINE
☐ 1843–1863	1 Centavo, Liberty Head, Copper	8.00	14.00
☐ 1858	1 Real, Liberty Head, Silver	—	155.00
☐ 1858	2 Reales, Liberty Head, Silver	—	240.00

Key to Grading: Bust

DATE	COIN TYPE/VARIETY/METAL	ABP FINE	AVERAGE FINE
☐ 1858	5 Reales, Liberty Head, Silver	—	225.00

VIETNAM

The first coins were used in 970 and were cast, round, bronze coins with a square hole. Zinc coins were used in the 19th century, as were the silver ounce bar coin and the silver dollar. The first decimal coins were used circa 1830. The currency today is the dong.

Vietnam—Type Coinage

Key to Grading: Bust

DATE	COIN TYPE/VARIETY/METAL	ABP FINE	AVERAGE FINE
☐ 1958	1 Xu, Aluminum	—	$ .90
☐ 1958	2 Xu, Aluminum	—	.90
☐ 1958	5 Xu, Aluminum	—	1.20
☐ 1953	10 Su, Aluminum	—	.45
☐ 1945	20 Xu, Aluminum	—	45.00
☐ 1953	20 Su, Aluminum	—	.45
☐ 1946	5 Hao, Aluminum	—	4.15
☐ 1953	50 Su, Aluminum	—	2.20
☐ 1960	50 Su, Aluminum	—	.45
☐ 1963	50 Xu, Cupro-Nickel	—	.45

Key to Grading: Bust

DATE	COIN TYPE/VARIETY/METAL	ABP FINE	AVERAGE FINE
☐ 1946	1 Dong, Aluminum	$25.00	40.00
☐ 1960	1 Dong, Cupro-Nickel	—	.45
☐ 1946	2 Dong, Bronze	8.00	12.00

HOUSE OF COLLECTIBLES SERIES

Title	ISBN	Price	Author
The Official® Price Guides to			
Antique Jewelry, 7th ed.	9780609809136	$27.95	Kaplan
Clocks	9780609809730	$19.95	Korz
Collecting Books, 6th ed.	9780375722936	$21.95	Tedford/Goudey
Collector Knives, 15th ed.	9780375722806	$21.95	Price
Disney Collectibles, 2nd ed.	9780375722622	$27.95	Hake
Dolls	9780375720369	$20.00	Van Patten
Glassware, 4th ed.	9780375721823	$24.95	Pickvet
Pop Culture Memorabilia	9780375722820	$34.95	Hake
Hislop's International Fine Art, 2nd ed.	9780375722141	$24.95	Hislop
Mickey Mouse Collectibles	9780375723070	$12.95	Hake
Mint Errors, 7th ed.	9780375722158	$21.95	Herbert
Overstreet Comic Book Companion, 10th ed.	9780375722813	$9.99	Overstreet
Overstreet Comic Book Grading Guide, 3rd ed.	9780375721069	$24.95	Overstreet
Overstreet Comic Books, 39th ed.	9780375723117	$29.95	Overstreet
Overstreet Indian Arrowheads, 10th ed.	9780375722462	$26.00	Overstreet
Records, 18th ed.	9780375722363	$26.95	Osborne
Star Wars Memorabilia	9780375720758	$17.95	Beckett
The Official® Guides to			
Coin Collector's Survival Manual, 6th ed.	9780375723056	$22.95	Travers
One-Minute Coin Expert, 6th ed.	9780375720406	$14.95	Travers
Scott Travers' Top 88 Coins to Buy and Sell	9780375722219	$13.95	Travers
The Official® Beckett Sports Cards Price Guides			
Baseball Cards 2009, 29th ed.	9780375723131	$8.99	Beckett
Basketball Cards 2009, 18th ed.	9781400007158	$8.99	Beckett
Football Cards 2009, 28th ed.	9780375722981	$8.99	Beckett
The Official® Blackbook Price Guides to			
U.S. Coins 2010, 48th ed.	9780375723186	$8.99	Hudgeons
U.S. Paper Money 2010, 42nd ed.	9780375723216	$8.99	Hudgeons
U.S. Postage Stamps 2010, 32nd ed.	9780375723247	$8.99	Hudgeons
World Coins 2010, 13th ed.	9780375723155	$8.99	Hudgeons